PETER THOMPSON

THE BATTLE FOR SINGAPORE

The True Story of Britain's
Greatest Military Disaster

PORTRAIT

VISIT OUR WEBSITE AT: www.portraitbooks.com

Copyright © 2005 by Peter Thompson

First published in 2005 by **Portrait**
an imprint of Piatkus Books Limited
5 Windmill Street
London W1T 2JA
e-mail: info@piatkus.co.uk

Reprinted 2006

The moral right of the author has been asserted

A catalogue record for this book is available from the British Library

ISBN 0 7499 5068 4 HB
ISBN 0 7499 5085 4 PB

This book has been printed on paper manufactured with respect for the environment using wood from managed sustainable resources

Edited by Penny Phillips
Text design by Paul Saunders
Illustrations by Rodney Paull

Typeset by Phoenix Photosetting, Chatham, Kent
Printed and bound in Great Britain by
MPG Books Ltd, Bodmin, Cornwall

For Russell Savage and Bill Drower

'God was ridiculed. Civilisation was buried and the dignity of mankind trampled. Everywhere tears flowed. Everywhere blood splattered. And everywhere terror reigned.'

PAN SHOU, writing about the Japanese occupation
in the *Nanyang Journal*, Singapore, 1984

Contents

Acknowledgements

The Fall of Singapore on 15 February 1942 is a military and civil disaster of enduring fascination and seemingly unshakable myth. I am indebted to the many people who have shared their memories of the pre-war years, the outbreak of the Pacific War, the siege of Singapore and the Japanese occupation.

I am extremely grateful to the following for granting me interviews: Frank Baker, Mervyn Blyth, Len Butler, Francis Chan, Bernard Clifton, Beryl Stevenson Daley, Frank Davies, Dr Jim Dixon, Bill Drower, Maisie Duncan, Genevieve Evans, Tony Ferrier, Sir Leslie Froggatt, Paul Gemmell, Barbara Glanville, Dr Bob Goodwin, Maureen Gower, Harry Hesp, Dr William Horsfall, Alan Lewis, Clive Lyon, John McGrory, Jennifer Martin, Alastair Morrison, Jim O'Rourke, Cliff Olsen, Olga Page, Terpie Pattara, Charles Peall, Alexander Pimson, Dr Rowley Richards, Barton Richardson, Alan Ryall, Fred Ryall, the Reverend Ray Rossiter, Russell Savage, George Shelly, Sheridan Stumm, Harry Schulman, Major-General David Thomson and John Wyett.

My special thanks go to John Broe for permission to quote from his father Vince Broe's unpublished diary covering every one of his 1,277 days in captivity; to Sir Leslie Froggatt for permission to quote from his father's memoirs, *Nothing Lasts for Ever: Singapore Swan Song – and After*; to Joan Bulley and Frederick Jones of the Association of British Internees Far East Region; to Alan Ryall, Fred Hesp and Fred Ryall of the Far East Prisoners of War Association; to Carole Cooper and Keith Andrews of the Children of Far East Prisoners of War Association; to Rod Mackenzie, Archivist of the Argyll & Sutherland Highlanders Museum; to Dr Rowley Richards and Ron Ferguson of the 8th Division AIF Association; to Bob Batty of the Returned and Services League of Australia; to Paul Gemmell of the 2/18th Battalion AIF Association; to James Keady of the 2/20th Battalion AIF Association; to Roger Perry of the Royal New South Wales Regiment incorporating the 2/19th Battalion AIF Association; to Fred Hodel of the 2/26th Battalion AIF

Association and the Ex-Prisoners of War Association of Australia; and to Annie Choy of Raffles Hotel and Simon Gow of the Changi Museum. I must also include Joan Bright Astley, Charles Edwards, George Housego, Phillip Knightley, Madeline Lyon, Elliott McMaster, Robert Macklin, Sue Mitchell, Stanley O'Grady, John Parker, Les Read, Lieutenant-Colonel Tang Tong Seng, Patricia Savage, Colin Spence, Wong Hwai Fey and George Wee.

I am grateful to the staff at the National Archives of Singapore, the Curators of the Changi Museum and the Kranji War Cemetery, and the Librarian of the Tanglin Club (Singapore); the National Archives (formerly the Public Record Office), the Reading Room at the Imperial War Museum (London), the London Library and the Librarian of the Reform Club (London); the Mitchell Library and State Library of New South Wales (Sydney); the Oxley Library and State Library of Queensland (Brisbane); and the Research Centre of the Australian War Memorial (Canberra).

Among those who allowed me access to their private collections, Clive Lyon and Major Bill Bentsen (US Army retired) deserve special mention. Those who authorised me to use photographs, letters and diaries include Ruth Brown, Mel Bruce, Len Butler, Frank Davies, Bill Drower, Maisie Duncan, Tony Ferrier, Barbara Glanville, Olga Page, Terpie Pattara, Russell Savage, Harry Schulman and Mrs Joan Wyett.

Peter Thompson
London, February 2005

The Malay Peninsula and Singapore Island

Part One

The Countdown

CHAPTER 1

Blood on the Sun

THERE WAS NO BREEZE. The swaying *punkah*s of Raffles Hotel had stopped moving. The north-east monsoon had come to an end, and under a pewter sky the stifling heat shimmered on the baked tarmac of Beach Road and danced all the way down to the dead calm sea. All that day European men, women and children who had been too stubborn, too disbelieving or too unlucky to evacuate the stricken colony had filed into the hotel, where their names were taken down in a register at the behest of Hirohito's triumphant army.[1]

The hotel's ballroom had been converted into a hospital ward for the wounded; the card tables – where, usually, bridge was practically compulsory – were covered with surgical dressings. All trappings of colonial life had disappeared in a matter of hours: even the bar, home of the Singapore sling, was shut. All stocks of liquor had been destroyed on government orders (although one British officer, thinking it sacrilegious to waste Napoleon brandy, had made off with several bottles). Somebody had also removed the sign on the hotel's clock tower. It had been a vainglorious touch anyway. It read, 'They can't stop our clock'.[2]

The final edition of the *Straits Times*, a single sheet dated 14 February 1942, admitted that the previous day – Black Friday, 13 February – 'was probably Singapore's worst day since fighting began', but it still carried the slogan beneath its masthead: '"*Singapore Must Stand; It SHALL Stand*" – *His Excellency the Governor*'. The slogan was still there in the *Sunday Times* on 15 February, above a report claiming that Allied troops 'are disputing every attempt by the Japanese to advance further towards the heart of Singapore town'.

Such bravado was typical of Sir Shenton Thomas, a cocky, rotund, red-faced former schoolmaster, who had refused to countenance the idea that British rule in Singapore might actually be over. To make his point, Thomas had taken over the implacably hostile *Straits Times*, which had advocated that Prime Minister Winston Churchill's emissary Duff Cooper be appointed Dictator of Singapore for the duration of the crisis.

Gambler though he was, Duff Cooper had no stomach for this particular fight. He had left Singapore with his glamorous film-star wife Lady Diana Cooper on 13 January 1942, soon after General Sir Archibald Wavell had been appointed Supreme Commander of ABDACOM, the cumbersome new combined American, British, Dutch and Australian Command. Despite pleas from Wavell for him to remain, Duff Cooper had insisted that his powers had come to an end, and departed with what he describes as 'an uncomfortable feeling that I was running away'.[3]

Had he stayed on as Military Governor, a tremendous amount could have been accomplished during the desperate days of January to prepare the island for the final assault and then, once the blow had fallen, to rally the troops and the population into mounting a fierce, last-ditch resistance. As things were, it had been left to Shenton Thomas, with his ailing wife Daisy at his side, to hold the fort. To keep up appearances, the Governor refused to leave Government House and insisted that male guests should wear a collar and tie at lunch and dinner, even though bombs were blowing huge divots in his pristine lawns and the servants were being cut down by shrapnel.

Only a few days before the end he told *The Times* correspondent Ian Morrison that he was confident Singapore could withstand a long siege; there was enough food, water and medical supplies, and plenty of soldiers. These were stirring times, he said, and Singapore had an opportunity to write an epic in imperial history. It could, he thought, become another Malta, another Tobruk; there was no place on earth he would rather be.[4]

On the night of 8 February, Japanese forces had swarmed across the inky black ribbon of water separating mainland Malaya from Singapore Island and, finding gaps between the little fortified clusters among the mangrove swamps, rivers and inlets on the north-west coast, had fallen upon the Australian defenders of the 22nd Brigade AIF. The moon had not yet risen; the darkness was broken only by muzzle flash, flare light and the incandescence of a burning barge.

In that world of shadow and firelight, the Japanese had succeeded in enveloping the sorely isolated defenders, many of them raw teenaged recruits who had never fired a rifle before, and then breaking through the hastily reformed defensive line time after time to claim their prize. The conquest of Malaya and Singapore had taken just 70 days.

In the grand ballroom at Raffles Hotel, scene of great revelry where huge overhead electric fans dispensed cooling air to the celebrants as they danced to the Dan Hopkins Orchestra and sang 'There'll Always Be an England', the wounded could do nothing but pray for deliverance. Other Europeans gathered in the Palm Court and tried to come to terms with the disaster that had befallen them, talking in hushed tones in the unnatural silence. More than the Governor's bomb-damaged palace, in its great 100-acre park overlooking the colonial district, and more than the High Command post at Fort Canning, Raffles Hotel was the defining symbol of British rule in Asia. The shining white neo-Renaissance building, with its line of coconut palms along Beach Road, its motor garage, its capacious bar and billiard room, its luxurious suites and its famous clientele, represented the white man's superiority over the humble Asian.

Perhaps unwittingly, a photographer had captured precisely this image in a photograph of the hotel's imposing façade which had been used as a Christmas card in 1938. Progressing along Beach Road in front of the hotel, a tiny Oriental is seen hauling a huge, canopied rickshaw containing a large passenger and an even larger trunk. Few Europeans in the East at that time thought it odd that human beings were used as beasts of burden. Indeed, one Singapore club displayed a sign outside its doors saying, 'No dogs or Chinese'. Joseph Conrad had warned of the inevitable outcome of such an attitude, describing the East as the place 'where a stealthy Nemesis lies in wait, pursues, overtakes so many of the conquering race, who are proud of their wisdom, of their knowledge, of their strength'.[5]

The privileged position occupied by the British – ever since Raffles had stepped ashore 'to secure to the British flag the maritime superiority of the Eastern Seas' – owed everything to their country's predominance as a naval power. But Shenton Thomas and his almost exclusively white staff in the Colonial Service and the Malayan Civil Service knew that their position was accepted by the multiracial population only for as long as they could offer the protection of Britain's armed forces, most notably from the marauding Japanese armies whose restless quest for new territories had become the focal point of Asian *realpolitik* in the preceding decade.

But Britain's only fleet was fully occupied fighting the Germans and the Italians in Europe, and the concept of a two-hemisphere Empire defended by a one-hemisphere Navy, which had sounded feasible to Admiralty strategists strolling around the duck pond in St James's Park, was beginning to look like a very lame duck indeed. Singapore was an impregnable fortress, they said, adopting the same tone of voice that had declared the *Titanic* 'unsinkable'.

It was at Raffles Hotel that Martha Gellhorn, Ernest Hemingway's wife and a correspondent for *Collier's* magazine, had ruffled colonial feathers during a visit to Singapore to examine the state of British defences against a possible Japanese attack. Gellhorn threw a party at Raffles, where she scandalised polite society (and outraged the powers-that-be in Government House and Fort Canning) by saying 'Balls!' to a highly placed civil servant who informed her that the colony would never be invaded.[6]

Ladies did not utter words like 'balls' in 1941 – but that was only the first of her heresies. Gellhorn concluded from her investigations that Singapore was virtually defenceless, while believing itself to be unassailable. She marvelled at the tea dances in the Raffles ballroom and at the way everyone told her that all was well despite evidence to the contrary. Her article in *Collier's* magazine bristled with indignation about the snobberies of British colonial life, but it also sounded a sober warning about the colony's lack of preparedness. Like everything else that offended Singapore society, it went unheeded.[7]

General Wavell, who had taken over as Commander-in-Chief India, shared Gellhorn's views as far as the public's attitude was concerned. He visited Singapore a few months later and noted, 'My impressions were that the whole atmosphere in Singapore was completely unwarlike, that they did not expect a Japanese attack and were very far from being keyed up to a war pitch.'[8]

The reason for this insouciance was the vast Singapore Naval Base, which had been built at Sembawang on the north-east corner of the island after years of debate in Whitehall. The base had finally been opened in 1938, a £60 million insurance policy for Britain's eastern colonies and dominions from Hong Kong and Malaya to Australia and New Zealand. The batteries of Changi Fire Command on the east coast and the Faber Fire Command overlooking Keppel Harbour could sink any ship afloat, while squadrons of bombers, hidden in faraway airfields carved out of the steaming Malayan jungles, testified to the British Government's determination to defend its Far Eastern bastion.

The Times had published a special supplement to mark the opening of the Naval Base by Sir Shenton Thomas on 14 February 1938.[9] Resplendent in his vice-regal uniform, he had chugged into the 1,000-foot-long King George VI graving dock in the 800-ton steam-driven yacht *Sea Belle II* after cutting a ceremonial ribbon stretched across the entrance. The Naval Base also boasted a floating dock which had been towed all the way from England at vast expense. It was said that 60,000 men could stand on the bottom of this seaworthy wonder (although there seemed no good reason for them to do so). Yet despite the fanfare, the Naval Base was still not operational; work would continue for a further four years on its forts and workshops, its storerooms and generating plant, its radio station, its township, swimming pool and 17 football fields.

Even then it would lack many basic facilities which had been pruned from the blueprint by Winston Churchill as Chancellor of the Exchequer in Baldwin's Government from 1924 to 1929. The former First Lord of the Admiralty had reasoned that as the distance between Singapore and Tokyo was the same as that from Southampton to New York – some 3,000 miles – the chances of the Japanese mounting a surprise attack against the base were negligible and, in the event of a hostile move in Singapore's direction, there would be ample time to make good any deficiencies.[10]

The one thing Singapore Naval Base lacked from the very beginning was a British battle fleet. No Eastern Fleet had been available at the time it was opened, nor would one be available in the future under the financial strictures of the age. Indeed, the most impressive naval force at the opening ceremony had been a squadron of three American cruisers, which happened to be passing on a goodwill visit.

The central plank of the Singapore Strategy, which had brought the base into existence after Admiral Lord Jellicoe had nominated the island the key strategic point in the Far East in 1919, had been embodied in the reassuring phrase 'Main Fleet to Singapore'. This required the British Navy to steam through the Suez Canal and cross the Indian Ocean if Singapore ever came under attack. In the meantime, the Royal Air Force would protect the Naval Base, while the Army's job was to protect the airfields.

It was a cockeyed strategy, and by the time the Japanese launched their assault in the Pacific in December 1941, the 'Main Fleet to Singapore' concept had been quietly jettisoned. Unfortunately, the Air Force had fallen woefully short of the minimum strength of first-line aircraft required to halt an invasion, while the Army was so undermanned it could not even protect the airfields. Churchill's strategic priorities at that time had been to defeat Rommel in the Western Desert and to sustain Stalin's forces against the German Panzers, rather than to defend Britain's possessions in South East Asia; the token naval force he had committed to the East – the modern battleship *Prince of Wales*, the old battle-cruiser *Repulse* and four antiquated destroyers – was unbalanced without an aircraft carrier or any air cover, and had lasted less than two hours in combat against Japan's twin-engine naval bombers in the South China Sea.

After that catastrophe, the Naval Base had been a useless impediment, a white elephant. There were now no Royal Navy ships there at all and, following the loss of the vast supplies of Malayan rubber and tin which were shipped from Keppel Harbour, the entire *raison d'être* for the defence of Singapore Island had evaporated like raindrops in the equatorial heat.

The Naval Base had been quietly abandoned in the last days of January 1942. Rear Admiral Ernest J. 'Jackie' Spooner, the Naval Commander-in-Chief, ordered the entire European naval and civilian dockyard staff to quit the base and fall back on Singapore City, from where they were shipped off to Ceylon. The Official Historian General Stanley Woodburn Kirby, author of *The War Against Japan*, admits, 'The hurried evacuation of the Base left an unfortunate impression in the minds of many soldiers who did not know that the Admiral, although perhaps precipitately, was acting under instructions.'[11]

Most incomprehensible of all was that Churchill, despite warnings from his Chiefs of Staff, had not realised that Singapore was as good as lost until, on 19 January, he received a cable from General Wavell spelling out the parlous state of the island's defences. Churchill was suddenly confronted with, in his words, 'the hideous spectacle of the almost naked island and of the wearied, if not exhausted, troops retreating upon it'.[12] 'I warn you,' he told the Chiefs of Staff, 'this will be one of the greatest scandals that could possibly be exposed.'[13]

By a curious coincidence, the souvenir issue of *The Times* of 3 March 1938 had named the officer who would be set up as the principal scapegoat for the disaster at Singapore when it recorded the appointment of Colonel A. E. Percival, DSO, OBE, MC, hero of the Great War and one of the most brilliant staff officers of his generation, as Brigadier on the General Staff, Aldershot. Percival, who had watched the creation of the Naval Base as Chief of Staff to the General Officer Commanding Malaya in 1936–38, had been sent back to Singapore in May 1941 as GOC and as such shouldered the primary responsibility for defending the base.

On Boxing Day, as his army retreated down the Malay Peninsula, Percival had been challenged about the lack of fixed defences in Johore, where the decisive battle for Malaya would be fought, and on the north shore of Singapore Island, which would become a killing ground should the Japanese prove victorious in that battle. Percival's Chief Engineer, Brigadier Ivan Simson, called on his commanding officer and sought permission to undertake the work but was told, in 10 words that would become Singapore's epitaph, 'Defences are bad for morale – for both troops and civilians.'[14]

It was an extraordinary answer and it would seem hardly credible that

Percival could have given it, had he not repeated the same words to Wavell the following month, after they had made a tour of the north shore just before the axe fell. The Supreme Commander insisted that the work should be carried out but he failed to get his point across with sufficient vigour to galvanise Percival into action.

Lieutenant James A. Richardson had spent his working life as a geologist in the Malayan rainforests and mountains and, after volunteering for military service, had ended up in the Intelligence Corps on Singapore Island. He says, 'The gravity of the situation could not be ignored. Wally [Pollock] and I made a survey of the northern part of the island a week before the Japs crossed the Straits. There was virtually nothing defensive. One or two of Singapore Fortress's 15-inch guns were eventually swivelled round to fire north, not south, and salvoes of armour-piercing shells were fired into Johore Bahru. I doubt that they did much to influence the inevitable débâcle.'[15]

At the height of the Blitz, Churchill had declared, 'The sound of the cannon gives me a tremendous feeling,' but he would not have enjoyed the reduction of Singapore. Len Butler, a 15-year-old sailor who had survived the sinking of the *Empress of Asia*, was working at Singapore General Hospital. 'We'd been out in an ambulance picking up the wounded and we had seen that the city was being bombed to pieces,' he says. 'Japanese planes were coming over in lots of 27 and the front plane would fire his machine guns and the whole lot would release their bombs and devastate an area of a square mile. Singapore was a densely populated city and the death rate was incredible. People weren't being killed only by shrapnel. Shards of glass and splinters of wood were going through them; bits of concrete and tiles from roofs were flying around. All manner of things kill people when a bomb falls.'[16]

Unlike little Malta which had defied the German blitz for 20 months, Singapore had no rocky ramparts and its highest hill, Bukit Timah, was a mere 600 feet above sea level. The million people who had crowded into Singapore City on the southern shores of the island, many of them terrified refugees driven out of the mainland, had almost no protection. Proper bomb shelters had not been constructed because Shenton Thomas shared Percival's belief that morale would be damaged by overt signs of war. The public had to make do with sandbagged trenches and filthy drains.

The death toll was rising almost hourly, but rigid military censorship suppressed the truth in the local media. For the preceding two weeks, army censors had even enforced a ban on the word 'siege'. 'Siege', newsmen were told, was 'bad for morale'.

The forces at General Percival's disposal for the defence of Singapore Island amounted to 85,000 men. In reality, his army was far smaller than that – and not all that effective. At least 15,000 were baseline non-combatants and medical staff; many thousands of others, harried from the air and cut off by the Japanese, had lost their rifles during the retreat down the peninsula. Many were raw recruits who had spilled on to the docks just in time to take part in the drama's tragic last act. Thousands more lay wounded or sick in hospital.

The Japanese commander of the 25th Imperial Japanese Army, General Tomoyuki Yamashita, a tough and uncompromising martinet, had three crack Japanese divisions – the 5th, the 18th and the Imperial Guards – many of them, like himself, veterans of the war in China and all of them cock-a-hoop after a succession of victories on the Malay peninsula. It was a formidable striking force of 30,000 troops, backed by a further 35,000 troops and impressed labourers manning supply lines down the Malay peninsula, but Percival, owing to faulty intelligence estimates, thought he faced an immediate threat from at least five divisions totalling 100,000 troops. This misjudgement was crucial because it had coloured the placement of his forces to face the Japanese assault on Singapore Island. He spread them thinly all around the island's perimeter to meet every eventuality, instead of concentrating a large force at two inland switchlines – strong points – to counterattack once the Japanese had shown their hand. Yamashita also had an overwhelming advantage in that his infantry were supported by an armoured force of around 200 tanks and a similar number of warplanes. Percival had no tanks, few anti-tank guns and just one squadron of fighters, which would shortly depart for Sumatra.

Nevertheless, when General Wavell arrived for his last visit to Singapore on 10 February, he instructed Percival to hold the island at all costs, following an order from Winston Churchill that there should be no surrender. 'There must at this stage be no thought of saving the troops or sparing the population,' Churchill cabled. 'The battle must be fought to the bitter end at all costs. Commanders and senior officers should die with their troops. The honour of the British Empire and of the British Army is at stake.'

That same day Lieutenant Richardson visited the Battle Box, Malaya Command's air-conditioned, bomb-proof concrete bunker sunk deep into the hill behind Fort Canning. He scribbled a note in his diary: 'Order of the Day from General Wavell: "It would be a disgrace if our large Forces were finally defeated by a much smaller Nip force. We must therefore fight to the very last etc. etc. . . ." No good! The end of this show was fore-ordained even before it started.'

In the evening, Wavell visited Sir Shenton and Lady Thomas at Government House. 'He sat in our living room,' Thomas noted in his diary, 'thumping his knees with his fists and saying, "It shouldn't have happened," over and over again.' Lady Thomas, who was ill with dysentery, declined Wavell's offer to accompany him to Java, and he left shortly after midnight.[17]

Stanley Prout, a marine engineer from Devon who had fought with the Royal Navy in World War I, had joined the Local Defence Force. He was digging trenches outside the Convent of the Holy Infant Jesus in Victoria Street. His two daughters, Olga and Maisie, were boarders at the convent but had been evacuated to the mainland after the Japanese bombed the island. 'He went into the convent to see if we had reappeared,' his daughter Maisie Duncan says. 'The Mother Superior told him that we were still up-country and that we were cut off. They both knew Singapore was doomed. Mother Superior gave him a cup of tea and a biscuit, and said, "I have no idea when we will see them again but I promise you I will do my best to look after them after Singapore falls." Dad said he would try to escape to Australia.'[18]

One of the refugees sheltering in the convent was a former pupil, Terpie Pattara, 19-year-old daughter of a wealthy Greek merchant who had named his five daughters after Greek goddesses. While her mother and three of her sisters had been evacuated in one of the last ships to leave the colony, Terpie – short for Terpsichore, the muse of dance – had stayed behind in Singapore in the hope of marrying her fiancé, a Polish schoolteacher. 'Our house had been bombed and we had lost everything,' she says. 'My mother and three of my sisters had set sail on Friday 13 February hoping to reach Australia. My youngest sister and I were in the chapel praying, "Do not bomb us," and there were bombs falling all around us.'

By now, Governor Thomas had accepted the fact that his bailiwick was in serious trouble and had moved from Government House to the Singapore Club in Fullerton Building. Realising the end was near, he ordered a total prohibition on all liquor throughout the island, to prevent a recurrence of the atrocities perpetrated by drink- and drug-crazed Japanese troops in Nanking and Hong Kong. Thousands of bottles of the finest spirits, wines and liqueurs and thousands of gallons of beer and *sake* were smashed or their contents poured down drains.[19] At the Tanglin Club and the Singapore Cricket Club, members drank as much as they could and then set about destroying the remainder.

On Sunday 15 February, Lance-Bombardier Alan Toze, of Virginia Water, Surrey, was drinking a bottle of beer on the balcony of the Supreme Court Building overlooking the Padang, the sports ground with the hallowed Australian turf of the Singapore Cricket Club at one end, the tennis courts and bowling greens of the Singapore Recreation Club at the other. 'Fort Canning lay between us and the enemy, the Union Jack hanging from the yard of its tall flagstaff obscured by the smoke of battle,' Toze wrote in his diary. '[Shells] would come our side of the fortress hill so frequently that after a while I ceased to duck and cover my ears but watched to see where the dust and debris spouted up. There were fires everywhere; the Senoko Dump on the north of the island formed a huge grimy cloudbank and dozens of others masked the sky until it was impossible to distinguish between smoke and clouds.

'Our guns in their "backs to the wall" position along the seafront road-side roared and leaped as they sent their shells at an incredible rate – the air trembled with the almost constant whistling rush of steel just skimming the roof. At intervals there was a rush to cover as high-level bombers drummed through the smoke pall to unload around us, starting even more fires, holding quite steadily in their formation through a hail of AA fire of all calibres. Dive-bombers crackled their way over the rooftops, spraying indiscriminately with tracer bullets. A few bullets spattered on to the wide balcony just as I legged it behind a column and a ricochet whanged against the bronze scales in the hand of Justice in the bas-relief panel over my head.'[20]

Retiring to a comfortable leather chair in Courtroom No. 3, Toze, a battery surveyor with the 122nd Field Regiment, Royal Artillery, drank his beer while listening to the 'hellish echoes rolling in from the doomed city'. He picked up the Bible and read a few pages of Revelation. Then, suddenly, at 8.30 p.m., the guns stopped firing, and silence descended.

While Singapore adjusted to this eerie sensation after weeks of incessant noise, the Bishop of Singapore, the Right Reverend Leonard Wilson, held a service in St Andrew's Cathedral. In common with the Singapore Club, the Cricket Club, Raffles Hotel, the Goodwood Park Hotel, the General Post Office and many other places, this great Gothic building provided shelter for both civilian and military wounded. The pews had been removed and the nave was packed with bodies, some on camp-beds but most on blankets on the brown flagstones. Overhead electric fans fought a losing battle against the heat and the stench of suppurating wounds. Several hundred civilians, mostly Asians, had crowded into the choir stalls for the service.

While an army major played the organ, Bishop Wilson led the singing of the first hymn, 'Praise, my soul, the King of heaven'.

Three blocks away Brother Vincent, a 23-year-old Canadian, had evacuated a group of students from Bukit Timah village to St Joseph's Institution. The three-storey schoolhouse, bounded by Bras Basah Road and Queen Street, was also crowded with wounded soldiers. Shelling and bombing had continued practically non-stop for the last four days. 'We couldn't sleep, we had no appetite,' Brother Vincent says. 'There was nothing we could do except to hope it would come to an end. Everyone welcomed the decision to end the war, rather than fight to the last soldier and still have to surrender.'

Singapore, the Gibraltar of the Orient and cornerstone of an empire upon which the sun never set, had gone down in a blaze of ignominy when General Percival capitulated to the Imperial Japanese Army at 6.10 p.m. on 15 February 1942, Chinese New Year's Day. It was an irreparable blow to British prestige. Churchill, who had succeeded in converting the evacuation of Dunkirk into a British victory of sorts, could do nothing except admit that the fall of Singapore had been a massive defeat. After the war, he described it as 'the worst disaster and largest capitulation in British military history'.

Photographs of the surrender party arriving at the Ford Motor Factory in Bukit Timah ('Hill of Tin') had been disseminated around the world by the Japanese propagandists of the Denai News Agency. Major Cyril Wild, who was carrying the white flag, flung it into a ditch in disgust when he saw the cameras and realised their purpose. Japanese newsmen then photographed the corpulent figure of the victorious General Yamashita as he faced a tense, reed-thin Arthur Percival across the conference table in the factory's canteen. In one photograph, the British commanding officer stands beside the table supporting himself on his extended arms, fists clenched. He is white-faced, drawn and exhausted; it is the portrait of a broken reed.

Back in Singapore City, rumours abounded. Gradually, word got around that it was all over. 'There were soldiers in the streets, soldiers in the park, soldiers all over the place,' says Brother Vincent.[21] 'They didn't know where to go or what to do. I saw a soldier shooting at the engine of a jeep. [They were] destroying their cars, destroying their weapons.'

Major Tony Ferrier, then a 22-year-old company commander with the 5th Battalion, Royal Norfolk Regiment, recalls, 'All around I could see the oil tanks burning and great palls of smoke. The whole island seemed to be in complete desolation and I could hear firing going on all around. When I got back to my company, I had to tell my platoon commanders the bad news. I had had very little sleep for a fortnight, but for the past three days I had had virtually only catnaps because I had been in action continuously, and I felt extremely emotional that we had to lay down our arms and surrender. It was a very emotional moment and I was almost in tears at the very thought of it. But those were the orders and they had to be obeyed.'

Russell Savage, a gunner with the 2/10th Field Regiment, AIF, says, 'I couldn't believe we were surrendering. We were still a good fighting unit, so why had the fighting stopped? Rumours were coming in that troopships were arriving with reinforcements and that Hurricanes had been landed in crates and were being assembled. We didn't know there was no chance of assembling anything.'[22]

Len Butler knew that further resistance was pointless. 'We couldn't have carried on,' he says. 'We had no water, no food. When people say 30,000 Japanese beat 60,000 British troops – they did. The Government in the UK abandoned us. Their main priority was the desert and keeping the oil and the Suez Canal. The Naval Base wasn't worth much and they had Trinco-malee in Ceylon and Bombay in India, and Durban and Simonstown in Africa. They didn't need Singapore.'

The British defeat shocked Elizabeth Choy, a 31-year-old Chinese teacher at St Andrew's School who had been nursing the wounded. 'We were so dumbfounded we didn't know what to do,' she says. 'But we felt very, very sorry for the Britishers. A lot of them were our friends and our church people and our colleagues in teaching. Everybody was stunned.'[23]

There was one notable absentee: Major-General Gordon Bennett, the fiery, ginger-haired Australian commander, had disappeared. Shortly after the guns had fallen silent on Sunday, Bennett and two staff officers, Major Charles Moses and Lieutenant Gordon Walker, had slipped away in the General's motor car from Tanglin Barracks, the 8th Division's headquarters a few miles to the east of the colonial district. Bennett had been planning his escape ever since the Allied forces had retreated to Singapore Island and blown up the Causeway on 31 January. 'They won't get me,' he had vowed.

Inside Tanglin Barracks, Major John Wyett, a member of Bennett's staff, realised that his commanding officer had indeed run away. He went to the General's quarters to make sure nothing sensitive had been left behind. The first thing Wyett found was a cache of rare whisky, bottled in Scotland especially for Bennett's friend the Sultan of Johore. He smashed the bottles – but not before pouring himself a couple of *stengahs*.[24] In his autobiography, Bennett makes a great fuss about how he had burned his papers before departing so as to leave nothing of use to the enemy,[25] but Wyett found photographs of Bennett and the Sultan's much younger Romanian wife, Marcella, some of which he described as compromising; they were in an envelope marked 'Not for Australia'. Heedless of his erstwhile friend's safety (or the Sultana's reputation), Bennett had carelessly left them behind for the Japanese to find. Wyett made the photographs into a pile and set fire to them.

Accepting the blame was a rarity for anyone who actually bore any responsibility for the Singapore catastrophe but Leslie Froggatt, an English marine engineer, felt very bad indeed. He put his feelings into words that resonate down the years: 'I betrayed my Malay gardener. He cut my hedges, watered my flowers, cut and rolled my tennis lawn, and brushed up the leaves that blew down from the trees. I betrayed my round fat amah, who liked me, and amused me with her funny ways. I betrayed my Hokkien cook, who had a wife and four lovely children, whom he kept beautifully dressed at all times on the money he earned from me.

'I betrayed "Old Faithful", our No. 2 Boy, who knew no word of English or Malay and padded round the house silently in bare feet, always working cheerfully. I betrayed the caddie who carried my bag, searched for my ball, and always backed my game with a sporting bet. I betrayed all the helpless little babies with their almond eyes and soft black shining heads. From the college student to the Tamil coolie who swept the street, I betrayed them all.'[26]

The unanswered question was: how had it happened?

Chapter 2

Good Times

IN THE 1930S WHEN the Sultans, the rubber planters and the tin-mining magnates were making fortunes again after the Great Slump, Malaya was referred to locally as the Land of Tidapathy. It was a word coined from the Malay phrase *t'ida apa*, meaning 'it doesn't matter'. In those languid days before the outbreak of World War II, the expatriate community needed some stoical peg on which to hang the indolence engendered by extremes of heat and thirst. 'Tidapathy' fitted the bill nicely; it was the Spanish *mañana* with an Oriental twist.[1]

All that changed in September 1939 when Britain declared war on Germany after Hitler had torn up Chamberlain's 'piece of paper' and sent the Wehrmacht storming into Poland. Suddenly, Malaya mattered a great deal to a desperate Britain and a rearming America; suddenly, there was a chance for the Land of Tidapathy to help the Mother Country's war effort and, at the same time, make a tidy profit.

Mainland Malaya had more than three million acres under cultivation to *Hevea brasiliensis*, the Brazilian rubber tree, while half the world's tin was gouged out of the great mines halfway down the mountainous spine of the 400-mile-long peninsula. In an endless procession, railway wagons shuttled along the antiquated single-line railway from the Kinta Valley to Singapore Island, where they dumped their cargoes into the holds of tramp steamers lining the docks at Keppel Harbour, on the southern edge of Singapore City.

The only proviso that the British made in the wartime boom was that nothing should be done to make the natives restless. It was decided that the best way of maintaining the status quo was for the European population – a mere 31,000 people, scattered from the Thai border to the southern shores of Singapore – to carry on as normal. Any rumblings of nationalism or discontent among the 5.5 million Chinese, Indians, Malays and Tamils could then be quickly detected and quietly stilled.

No one advocated this policy more assiduously than Sir Shenton Thomas. He was attending evensong at St Andrew's Cathedral when the

BBC broadcast news of the outbreak of the war in Europe on Sunday 3 September 1939. It did not unduly concern him. As the *Straits Times* editorial put it the following day, 'At this distance from the scene of battle, with our defences perfected and Japanese participation in the struggle on the side of Germany an extremely remote possibility, Malaya has little to fear.'[2]

The Colonial Office ordered Shenton Thomas to keep the dollars flowing into Britain's overextended Treasury, and he was happy to oblige. In a broadcast on 5 September, he urged British men to stay at their posts in Malaya and not return home to enlist in the armed forces. The economy prospered as never before. 'This is not a temporary boom,' one Australian businessman reported to his government. 'Singapore seems to have emerged from being merely a progressive city and is now the hub of the Orient.'[3]

The novelist J. G. Farrell described Britain's hold on the colony as the 'the Singapore Grip' – 'the grip of our Western culture and economy on the Far East'[4]. No one was holding on more tightly than Shenton Thomas. He had turned 60 in 1939 and should have retired, but he had been asked to stay on – even though he was considered in some quarters to be 'too old and out-of-date'.[5] In January 1940, he wrote to the Colonial Office, 'I conceive it to be our duty to give absolute priority to the claims of industry.' And he had succeeded: Malaya's dollar earnings had jumped from $98 million in the first year of the war to $135 million in 1940–41. Malaya, in the words of the Governor, had become the 'dollar arsenal of the Empire'.

Shenton Thomas had arrived in Singapore in November 1934 to replace Sir Cecil Clementi. The eldest son of a Cambridgeshire vicar of Welsh descent, he had been born on 10 October 1879 and christened Thomas Shenton Whitelegge Thomas. With four brothers and one sister, he was raised in a Georgian rectory straight out of Trollope: there was croquet on the lawn and servants to do the menial chores – but very little money for anything except the essentials of life.

After studying at St John's, Leatherhead, where he excelled at cricket, young Shenton won a scholarship to Queens' College, Cambridge, where he read classics. He then completed a seven-year stint as a schoolmaster in a Yorkshire prep school, before deciding in 1909 to seek fresh pastures in the Colonial Service. Having taken a year off to travel the world, he joined the Colonial Service and progressed up the Secretariat ladder in Kenya, Uganda, Nigeria and the Gold Coast, until in 1929 he was appointed Governor of Nyasaland (Malawi). In 1932, he returned to the Gold Coast as Governor and two years later was offered the prestigious post of Governor of the Straits Settlements, the four territories that jointly constituted a single crown colony.

Arriving in Penang with his wife Daisy on the P&O liner SS *Ranpura*, Thomas was greeted by a 17-gun salute from a Royal Navy warship, while the ship's company lined the decks and a reception committee of military and civilian dignitaries waited on the quayside. The Governor spent only a few hours in Britain's oldest possession in Malaya before crossing the channel to Prai in Province Wellesley and boarding the night mail express to Singapore.

Singapore, an integral part of the Crown Colony since 1867, was tucked into the toe of the Malay peninsula, just 85 miles above the equator. The island measured 25 miles by 15 miles, and was linked to Malaya by a causeway across the Straits of Johore. To the south, the Straits of Malacca separated it from Sumatra, Java and the multitude of other islands that formed the Dutch East Indies (later Indonesia).

The founding of modern Singapore had come about after Thomas Stamford Raffles, Lieutenant-Governor of Bencoolen, Sumatra, realised that unless Britain broke Holland's monopoly of the spice trade she would become a second-rate power in the East Indies. In 1818, Raffles petitioned the Governor-General of India, Lord Hastings, to authorise a fortified British trading post at the southern tip of the Malay peninsula which would go some way towards correcting that imbalance. It would also provide a secure stopping point for traders taking the shortest sea route between India and China.

With Hastings's blessing, Raffles set off from Bencoolen to find a suitable anchorage. He examined a group of islands to the west of Singapore but found them unsuitable. Sailing eastwards, he reached Singapore Island and realised he had stumbled on the perfect location. On 29 January 1819 Raffles stepped ashore on the northern bank of the Singapore River accompanied by Colonel William Farquhar, former Resident of Malacca and a fluent Malay speaker. The two colonial administrators discovered that Singapura – 'lion gate' in Sanskrit – was little more than a village, its tiny population scattered among swampland and tiger-infested jungle. But the island lay on the main trade route between India and China, and had an excellent deepwater harbour and plentiful supplies of drinking water and timber. It had not been occupied by the Dutch and was ruled by a Malay chief or Temenggong, Abdul Rahman. 'Singapore is everything we desire,' Raffles later wrote; 'it will soon rise in importance.'

On 30 January Farquhar spoke to Abdul Rahman and discovered that he was willing to help Raffles set up a trading post for the East India Company. A provisional treaty was signed that day. The Dutch, however, protested at Raffles's incursion into 'their' territory and declared the agreement illegal. Indeed, Singapore belonged to Abdul Rahman's overlord, the Sultan of Johore, who was backed by the Dutch. But Raffles learned that when the old Sultan had died, his elder son and heir, Tunku (Prince) Hussein, had been away in Pahang getting married, and his younger half-brother, Tunku Abdul Rahman, had claimed the throne with the support of the Bugis chiefs from Celebes and the Dutch.

With very little authority but a great deal of bravado, Raffles held a ceremony at the Padang on Singapore Island on 6 February 1819 to recognise Tunku Hussein as the rightful Sultan of Johore. His Highness the Sultan Hussein Mohammed Shah and the Temenggong then signed a new treaty allowing Raffles to build a British settlement on Singapore in return for pensions of $5,000 and $3,000 a year respectively. The British flag was hoisted on a flagpole and gunshots rang out, a simple ceremony marking the founding of modern Singapore. Raffles wrote to his employer, 'You may take my word for it, this is by far the most important station in the East; and, as far as naval superiority and commercial interests are concerned, of much higher value than whole continents of territory.'[6]

The territorial dispute with the Dutch was finally resolved with the signing of the Treaty of London five years later, in March 1824. According to the treaty, the British acquired Malacca, Penang and Singapore, while the Dutch were given undisputed control of Java and Sumatra. Then in August 1824 a Treaty of Friendship and Alliance was signed with the Sultan and the Temenggong, which handed over governance of the island to the British. As a free port at the foot of the Straits of Malacca, Singapore's rise was meteoric. With a steady flow of Malays, Chinese and Indians seeking work with European merchants, by the time the first census was held in 1824 the population had reached 10,683, including 3,317 Chinese, 756 Indians, 4,580 Malays and 74 Europeans. By 1911, it was 311,303.

After the East India Company was abolished in 1858, Singapore was placed under the direct control of the new Government of India, which knew nothing about its character or special problems. This arrangement led to protests at Westminster, and in 1867 responsibility for administering all British holdings in Malaya was transferred to the Colonial Office. Two forts, Fort Canning and Fort Fullerton, had been built on Singapore Island to protect the citizens from attack by Malay pirates and other insurgents (and to protect the administrators from its own citizens should the need arise).

The harbour was named after Sir Henry Keppel (1809–1904), the British admiral who had fought against piracy in the 1840s.

Singapore was invariably compared with the Isle of Wight because of its similar diamond shape, but there were other similarities which Shenton Thomas would have found pleasing. With its landscaped gardens, pillared terraces and elegant staterooms, Government House compared favourably with Osborne House, Queen Victoria's grand Italian villa overlooking the Solent, while the Singapore Yacht Club in Trafalgar Street at Tanjong Pagar was pure Cowes.

Raffles had returned to his duties at Bencoolen in 1819, leaving Major Farquhar as Singapore's first Resident to clear the jungle and start work on building the town. Three years later Raffles was back in the new colony and, after surveying the work already completed, drew up a detailed plan for its development.[7] 'Our object is not territory but trade,' he wrote to a friend, 'a great commercial emporium, and a *fulcrum*, whence we may extend our influence politically as circumstances may hereafter require.'

Raffles stamped a British colonial character on Singapore City by levelling one of the hills south of the Singapore River to form a new commercial district, Raffles Place. He then subdivided the city into *kampongs*, or villages, according to race, with the area west of the river's mouth being given to Chinese immigrants as far inland as Cantonment Road. To the east, Kampong Glam between Rochor River and the sea was reserved for the homes and businesses of Arab and Malay merchants, while Indians predominated in Kampong Kapor and Serangoon Road. Europeans, meanwhile, congregated mainly to the north-east of the colonial district or in the spacious western garden suburbs.

As Singapore took shape, there were many reminders of the Mother Country. Here was Parliament House, where the Legislative Council deliberated, and there the Victoria Memorial Theatre, where the works of the Bard were celebrated. Raffles himself, cast in bronze, stood on a plinth in Empress Place. Nearby, the Singapore River was spanned by an iron bridge that had been cast in Glasgow and shipped to the East piece by piece. The British jurist Sir Roland Braddell described the colony in his 1935 book *The Lights of Singapore* as 'so very George V ... if you are English, you get the impression of a kind of tropical cross between Manchester and Liverpool'. In Raffles Place and its main artery Battery Road, shoppers made a beeline for Kelly & Walsh's bookshop or the General Post Office in Fullerton Building, the neo-classical monstrosity built on the site of the old Fort

Fullerton, or Maynard's the chemists, or Robinson's, the big new air-conditioned department store, or Whiteaway Laidlaw.

The north bank became the setting for Parliament House, the Museum and the Library at the base of Fort Canning Hill, home of the British Army. The city green was the historic Padang, where Europeans played cricket, tennis and bowls. The new Supreme Court and the Municipal Building were sited on its eastern flank, adjacent to St Andrew's Cathedral. A block away on Beach Road the four enterprising Sarkies brothers had opened Raffles Hotel in 1887. Joseph Conrad and Rudyard Kipling were among the early guests; Charlie Chaplin, Noël Coward and Maurice Chevalier had signed the visitors' book and promised to return, while Somerset Maugham composed some of his work under the frangipani trees.

Maugham was now, however, *persona non grata*. When Captain Bill Drower asked for a copy of one of his books at the Singapore Library, he was tartly informed that Maugham was not considered suitable reading for Singaporeans. 'Willie' Maugham had committed the gross solecism of including dialogue from various socialites and planters.

One of the regular couples on the Raffles dance floor were Richard and Dorothy Lowery. Singapore offered unrivalled opportunities for young British professional men like Lowery, who had arrived in 1938 to take up a position with the Singapore Harbour Trust. Born in Newcastle upon Tyne in January 1910 and educated at Heaton Technical School, Rutherford Technical College and Durham University, he had trained as a naval architect with a Tyneside shipbuilder before being appointed assistant general manager of the Singapore Harbour Trust – the colony's biggest employer, who operated the wharves, five graving docks and a floating dock.

Dorothy, a tailor's daughter, excelled at Scottish and English traditional dancing and her stunning, home-made ballgowns became one of the features of the Raffles smart set. 'Dancing was how they met and dated,' their son Peter Lowery says. 'They loved Raffles and dancing – they were quite good and won several competitions.'

One of the city's most successful merchants was Zacharia Pattara. He and his wife Anthoula had come to Singapore from Athens as a newly married couple during World War I. After travelling widely in the East and learning several languages, Zacharia had opened a store in High Street adjacent to Parliament House. 'He sold clothes, hats and shoes and also his own brands of coffee called Camel and Volcano,' Terpie Pattara says. 'The Sultan of Johore used to come in every Friday to buy some Volcano coffee.'

Zacharia and his wife were naturalised, so that both they and all their five daughters were British subjects. The first two girls were twins and were named Ino (goddess of the sea) and Clio (muse of history) after characters in Greek mythology. Thetis (mother of Achilles), Terpsichore (muse of dance) and Thalia (muse of comedy) followed until the Pattaras' big house in St Michael's Road, a pleasant residential street at Serangoon, was filled with girlish chatter and music. Two of the girls learned the piano and several took up painting and dancing. Zacharia was a good provider and he doted on his five little Greek goddesses. All of them were enrolled at the Victoria Street convent. 'We travelled to and from school with Father each day in a chauffeur-driven car,' Terpie recalls. 'We were dropped off at school and then Father would go to his shop and in the evening we would collect him.'

Terpie grew into a beautiful young woman, with the same dark curly hair and soulful brown eyes as her four sisters. When she was 18 she fell in love with Wencelaus Bernard 'Benny' Szynkiewicz, a Polish teacher who taught languages and maths at a small private school. His father, a general in the Polish Army, had been killed by the Russians during the dismemberment of Poland in 1940. Despite the tragic news from Europe, the young couple became engaged and started to plan a life together.

A couple of miles south of the Pattaras' house, the five Bruce children lived in their grandmother's sprawling, split-level house in Glasgow Road, Payuh Lebar. Two flame-of-the-forest trees stood either side of the wrought-iron gates, and a long driveway led past rows of orchids to a turning circle in front of the house, with a garage and separate chauffeur's quarters on one side. Coconut palms swayed at the back.

Barbara Glanville (née Bruce) says, 'There were four brothers – Syd, Mel, Bryan and Errol. I came in the middle and I must admit I was thoroughly spoiled.' Her father, Herbert Ernest Bruce, had joined the Royal Marines as a boy soldier in his native Scotland and served as a bugler in Ireland during the Troubles. After joining the Colonial Service in Singapore, he met Gwendolyn Anchant, whose father had been a professor of mathematics at the Sorbonne. 'Her name was Gwendolyn but everyone called her Gwyneth,' Barbara says. 'The Anchants were an old French family and my mother was chaperoned everywhere she went. My grandmother came from Ceylon and was very strict. Her family, the Labroys, owned and trained racehorses in Singapore, Kuala Lumpur and Ipoh. My parents had one of those old-fashioned courtships – Granny used to sit in the front seat of the car and keep her eye on the mirror while they sat in the back.'

Herbert Bruce had risen to become Chief Inspector of Vehicles and was responsible for issuing licences for every type of conveyance from yellow cabs to rickshaws. 'We used to get a taxi to take us to school and home again,' his son Mel remembers. 'Grandpa had died but we were a big family, with three live-in servants. On Saturdays Hassan, the chauffeur, would drive us to the Cathay cinema for the 11 a.m. show with our amah Sai Mui to look after us, then take us to Raffles Hotel for tiffin with our parents.' Once a year, the Bruce children were driven across the Causeway to the Sultan of Johore's Moorish-style palace at Johore Bahru, where a huge marquee had been set up in the gardens to entertain the children of the Colonial Secretariat.

The boys attended St Andrew's School in Stamford Road, where one of their teachers was Elizabeth Choy, a graceful and talented young woman who had been born Yong Su-Moi into a Chinese Lutheran family in Sabah, British North Borneo. At the Anglican mission school at Sandakan, Chinese pupils were invited to select a Western first name. Su-Moi chose Elizabeth. She had come to Singapore in 1929 aged 19 and been educated at the Convent of the Holy Infant Jesus, where she gained her Senior Cambridge Certificate. Elizabeth loved children and in her holidays made clothes for orphans at the convent and helped handicapped children. In August 1941, she married a Straits-born Chinese businessman, Choy Khun Heng. 'She was a fantastic person,' says Mel Bruce, 'and we were all pleased when we heard she had got married.'

No one was happier with his lot than Stanley Prout, who had been appointed senior marine engineer of the Straits Steamship Company, a subsidiary of the Blue Funnel Line. Since 1890 its sturdy little ships, mostly christened after Malay place-names such as Kelantan, Klang and Kedah, had operated a coastal service out of Singapore. The pride of the fleet was the *Kedah*, a 2,000-ton, twin-screw turbine vessel which travelled at an average speed of 18 knots, sailing from Singapore at 11.30 a.m. every Thursday and arriving at Georgetown, Penang, at 8.30 a.m. the next day.[8]

Stanley Prout's appointment entailed moving his young family from Georgetown to Singapore. Prout had met a local Penang girl, Alice Vaz, when her father, Captain Peter Vaz, invited him to his home. A man of robust Portuguese ancestry from Goa, Captain Vaz had settled in Penang in 1876 after marrying a Eurasian girl. The couple had 12 children, seven of them daughters, and Vaz was in the habit of inviting eligible ship's officers and engineers to meet them, with a view to possible courtship and marriage.

One of the high points of such evenings was Alice's singing to her sister

May's piano accompaniment. Says Alice's daughter Olga Page, 'My father fell in love with her voice and then he fell in love with her.'[9] Stanley Prout made sure he received further invitations to the Vaz household in Arratoon Road, and soon realised he had found the woman he wanted to marry. He was devastated to learn that she was already engaged to another man, a Welsh civil servant who was also her singing instructor. Stanley, however, pressed his suit until Alice, a sailor's daughter, returned the Welshman's ring and went off with a sailor of her own.

Stanley hailed from Tedburn St Mary, a cluster of stone cottages deep in the Devon countryside north-west of Exeter. Though Stanley was a Freemason, he and Alice were married in a Catholic church in Penang by a French priest, Father Adrian Devals. The Prouts had three children: a son, John, born in 1925, and two daughters, Olga (1928) and Maisie (1931). All were baptised by Father Devals in the Catholic faith. Stanley told his daughter Maisie, 'Whenever he came aboard my ship, we'd spend the evenings after dinner in my cabin sipping brandy and smoking cigars. We'd touch on every topic under the sun – except religion!'

In Singapore, the family moved into a house close to the beach at Katang. The children were enrolled at the Victoria Street convent and the boy at nearby St Joseph's. Life seemed idyllic in those balmy pre-war days: money was plentiful, there were servants to do the cooking and housework, and the house rang with the sound of children's laughter and Alice's singing. There were ice-cream treats at the Polar Café on North Bridge Road and the family monopolised the local Roxy Cinema to such an extent that the manager would reserve a box for them whether they showed up or not.

There was one serious threat to the Prout family's happiness, however: Alice suffered badly from asthma. Although Stanley took her to England to consult Harley Street specialists, nothing could be done to cure her. After one severe attack in 1938 Alice was taken to hospital, where she contracted pneumonia and died.

As a widower, the most difficult time for Stanley Prout was when he was away at sea. Olga, who was 10 at the time, says, 'My father used to do the weekly run up to Penang and back, so we were looked after by our servants. We got a bit wild. We used to be picked up from school in our Hillman car. We would get in the car and climb through the sunroof and make a lot of noise. We did this until two of the nuns saw us and ordered us to get back inside the car. The Mother Superior, the Reverend Mother St James, sent for my Dad and said, "If you want your children to grow up as ladies and gentlemen, you had better make them boarders." That was in 1939. We became boarders. Our amah was a very loyal Chinese and every Saturday she would come and see us in the convent and bring us an orange and a bar of chocolate each.'

Helmut Newton, the German photographer, pitched up in Singapore in 1938 after escaping from Nazi Germany. He was 19 years old, Jewish, and grateful to have been accepted into 'a little bit of England at the tip of the Malay peninsula. It was like winning the lottery,' he wrote in his autobiography.[10] Newton was put on the society beat of the *Straits Times*, pukka mouthpiece of the ruling class. Let loose among the colony's flower-hatted dowagers at Government House tea parties, he created something of a legend by failing to produce a single publishable photograph. After two weeks, he was sacked.

As someone in the basement of Singapore society, the penniless photographer was in a good position to study the way Britain treated her subject peoples. He concluded that Chinese and Tamil coolies were 'worse off than slaves'. For a $1-a-day pittance, they loaded and unloaded the ships on the wharves in blistering heat all day and were then penned up for the night in airless godowns, where they cooked their rice and slept on mats.

Newton was overpowered by Singapore's smell, an aroma of spices mixed with bad sanitation, drying fish and *belacan*, the fermented shrimp paste that is an essential ingredient of Malay cooking. 'There are smells so violently esoteric that they must exhale from the corruption of what is very rich and fecund,' wrote the novelist H. M. Tomlinson. 'A newcomer has a suspicion that he has wandered off the beaten track; he has slipped into another dimension.'[11]

The new dimension was a place of infinite wonder. Street stalls in the heaving markets sold live snakes, turtles, bird's nests, shark fins and monkey soup, while the *click-click-click* of mah-jong tiles emanated from the gaudily painted shop-houses. For all ailments, there were foul-smelling potions brewed from bark, leaves and entrails, or the East's most celebrated cure-all, the ubiquitous Tiger Balm. The Cold Storage at the end of Orchard Road provided for every culinary need: fresh meat, oysters and strawberries from Sydney, pheasants and apples from England, butter from New Zealand, turnips from Sumatra, potatoes and oranges from Palestine, tomatoes from Java, and Edam cheese and chocolates from Holland, while bread and rolls were freshly baked on the premises.

Alcohol was duty-free and cheap: $1 would buy a whisky and a bottle of beer. Fifty cents purchased 10 dances with one of the beautiful Chinese taxi girls in the great dragon-walled barn of the Great World amusement centre.

The curious Westerner could wander about in complete safety, watching Chinese plays in the noisy, tinny theatres, or gaping at the *ronggeng* dancers, or thrilling to the exploits of the jugglers and the high-wire acrobats.

Sir Shenton Thomas presided over Singapore's administrative life from his office at Government House, a white stone building constructed on a low hill by convict labour from India in 1869. For an annual salary of £5,500 (plus liberal expenses), Thomas was Governor and Commander-in-Chief of the Crown Colony, consisting of Penang and the adjacent Province Wellesley, Singapore Island, Christmas Island and the Cocos and Keeling Islands in the Indian Ocean, plus Malacca Settlement and Labuan Island off the coast of north-west Borneo, 700 miles from Singapore.

He was also High Commissioner of the four Federated Malay States of Perak, Selangor, Negri Sembilan and Pahang, with their federal capital at Kuala Lumpur, and the five Unfederated Malay States of Johore, Trengganu, Kedah, Kelantan and Perlis. The 10th state was that of the oil-rich Sultan of Brunei on the north-west coast of Borneo. Finally, Shenton Thomas was Agent for British North Borneo and Sarawak, two vast areas covering more than 80,000 square miles with a total population exceeding half a million.

Thomas had been hand-picked by the Colonial Office to take over these daunting responsibilities following the recall of his predecessor, Sir Cecil Clementi, a dyed-in-the-wool imperialist. Clementi had ignored the leaders of the Chinese community on important issues and had ridden roughshod over public opinion. Thomas, an extrovert who thought he got along with people well, was the complete opposite. He knew the drill from his 24 years in Africa and worked hard to heal the breach between the Chinese community and the King's representative – at least during office hours.

Government House was soon ringing to the sounds of state dinner parties which, in the words of one aide-de-camp, were 'always lavish'. Guests, including visiting dignitaries and a sprinkling of Bright Young Things, would assemble for cocktails in the ground-floor reception room, falling silent when Shenton Thomas and Lady Thomas descended the grand staircase. Dinner was served by Indian bearers in long scarlet-and-gold tunics who, observing strict protocol, always served the Governor first. No one thought it unusual that there were few Chinese or Indian guests, and that the Malay contingent was confined to the Sultans. Even under Shenton Thomas, the indigenous people were rarely entertained at Government House.

Leslie Froggatt, a marine engineer and naval architect with Straits Steamship, saw more of Thomas than many of his countrymen. He considered the Governor 'a very mild sort of person – [he] could make witty speeches and we had a certain affection for him'.[12] To his underlings in the Malayan Civil Service, he was 'Tom-Tom', a clever pun on his name (Thomas Thomas) and the fact that he had spent much of his life within hearing distance of African drums. Indeed, he liked to say that the only type of warfare he understood was the tribal kind.

Thomas's most pressing concern in 1940 was to keep the dollars rolling in. He made it clear to the military that, in his view, the presence of large numbers of troops was more likely to attract hostilities than to repel them. He was dismissive of concerns that the Japanese might invade, stating, 'Who but a fool thinks Japan wants Singapore!'[13]

Despite the Governor's concerns that Singapore was becoming an armed camp, defence forces were actually thin on the ground. The garrison responsible for protecting Singapore and the whole of the Malay peninsula, as well as Penang, Sarawak and Borneo, consisted of just nine infantry battalions totalling 10,000 troops. These included the 2nd Gordon Highlanders, 2nd Loyal North Lancashires, 1st Manchesters (later turned into a machine-gun battalion), 2/17th Dogras and 1st Malays. The RAF, the glamorous new service whose aircraft had revolutionised warfare, was also poorly represented. It could put 90 'first-line aircraft' into the air, but these included two squadrons of obsolescent, fabric-covered Vildebeeste biplanes known as 'the Flying Coffins'. There were no fighters.

Japan's withdrawal from the League of Nations in April 1933 had prompted the British Cabinet to step up its plans to improve the defence of the Naval Base, which was still in the process of construction. The only RAF airfield on Singapore Island at the time was at Seletar, and the only airfields on the mainland were at Alor Star and Port Swettenham on the west-coast air route from Calcutta to Singapore. Work began on a new airfield at Kluang in the centre of Johore, which showed a curious bias in favour of creature comforts. One officer noted, 'No one seemed quite clear as to why part of the $6 million construction cost hadn't been diverted to providing all-weather concrete strips on the 'drome runways but plenty had been spent on the officers' mess.'[14]

Additional airfields also took shape on Singapore Island at Tengah and Sembawang, and at Kota Bahru, Gong Kedah, Machang and Kuantan on Malaya's east coast, which had hitherto been left undeveloped to present an invading enemy with an 'impassable' jungle barrier.[15] All of the new Malayan airfields were vulnerable to attack by a force landing on the sandy beaches dotted along the east coast, yet the Air Force had insisted on these sites – despite objections from the Army whose job was to protect them. The RAF's argument was that the airfields at Gong Kedah and Machang were needed to give its aircraft extra range for reconnaissance over Indochina. The War Office announced that the Army had insufficient manpower to guard them and suggested that the Air Force would have to do it themselves. This was the origin of a serious rift between the two services.

Since World War I, British policy for the defence of Singapore and her Eastern dominions had been based on the 'Main Fleet to Singapore' strategy under which the Royal Navy's fleet would sail from home waters if Singapore was threatened and arrive there in a maximum of 70 days. It was assumed that the enemy would mount a seaborne attack on the colony's southern shores, rather than land troops on the east-coast beaches and then tackle the supposedly impregnable jungle.

This theory was challenged by General Officer Commanding Malaya, Major-General (Sir) William Dobbie, who set up an exercise to land troops on the east coast during the north-east monsoon of 1936–37. Dobbie proved not only that it was possible to make a successful landing at that time of the year, but that the heavy cloud cover actually protected the invading forces from air reconnaissance and attack. Dobbie wrote to the War Office, 'It is an attack from the northward that I regard as the greatest potential danger to the fortress. Such attack could be carried out during the period of the north-east monsoon. The jungle is not in most places impassable by infantry.'[16]

Dobbie never doubted for a moment that Britain's potential enemy was Japan. There were only 3,000 Japanese in Malaya but their effectiveness in intelligence-gathering and fifth-column activities was out of all proportion to their numbers. Dobbie learned that Japanese espionage was channelled through the Japanese Consulate-General in Singapore, while Japanese companies such as the Nissan group furthered the country's political objectives through the Japanese Chamber of Commerce and the Japanese Commercial Museum.

Japanese fishermen charted rivers and coastlines; *mama-sans* in Japanese-run brothels passed on gossip from clients; Japanese photographers snapped military installations and personnel (the official photographer at Singapore Naval Base was later identified as Colonel Nakajima of Japanese Intelligence); Japanese journalists at the Eastern News Agency and the English-language *Singapore Herald* collated files of anti-British data; even the humble Japanese barber, bowing and hissing, was likely to have an intelligence role. Leslie Froggatt noted that the Japanese dealt 'mostly in teeth and photographs, haircuts and *sukiyaki*' but their main export to the home islands was information. Every useful nugget was passed to Japan's military planners and added to the overall strategic picture of Malaya and Singapore.

General Dobbie was determined to end this blatant abuse of British hospitality and was instrumental in having Lieutenant-Colonel Francis Hayley Bell, an old China hand with expert knowledge of the East, appointed as MI5's Defence Security Officer in Singapore in 1936.[17] Hayley Bell recruited a small team from the British Army and set about tracking down enemy agents. One of his men was a Gordon Highlander, Captain Ivan Lyon, whose tenacious character was shown in the large tiger tattooed on his chest. Ivan, born in August 1915 and educated at Harrow, Churchill's old school, was the son of Brigadier General Francis Lyon of the Royal Field Artillery. His family was a collateral branch of the Strathmores, one of Scotland's most illustrious dynasties, and shared a common Strathmore ancestor with King George VI's consort, Queen Elizabeth, the former Lady Elizabeth Bowes-Lyon, in David Lyon of Baky and Cossins.[18]

Bell's counter-espionage team penetrated the Japanese spy ring and learned that in the event of war the Japanese would land an invasion force in Thailand and northern Malaya and move rapidly south down the coastal plain. This was an unpopular view with the Governor, who clung to the belief that the monsoon and the impenetrable jungle would rule out any such eventuality. But the man on the spot, John Dalley, head of the police force in the eastern Malay state of Trengganu, had informed Ivan Lyon that these natural defences could easily be surmounted by a determined foe such as the Japanese, and had the revolutionary idea of recruiting Chinese – mainly Communists – as jungle fighters to be pitted against them in the event of war.

Hayley Bell's activities had elicited strong protests from Shenton Thomas and the British Minister in Bangkok, Sir Josiah 'Bing' Crosby, but his next act demonstrated just how vulnerable Singapore was to an enemy attack. At his direction, Ivan Lyon and a small force posing as saboteurs staged a mock commando raid on the colony's vital installations. The commandos simulated an attack on the Naval Base which would have disabled both the graving dock and the floating dock. They 'set fire' to the RAF's fuel dump, 'sank' a fleet of flying boats moored off RAF Headquarters, 'destroyed' the switchboard at the civil telephone exchange and 'bombed' the main power station, all without being detected. The operation caused outrage at Government House and Fort Canning, and complaints were made to the War Office, culminating in the termination of Hayley Bell's services just at a time when they were most needed.

Ivan Lyon, meanwhile, had fallen in love with a beautiful French girl, Gabrielle Bouvier, the 19-year-old blue-eyed daughter of the governor of the prison island Poulo Condore. Lyon contrived to meet her by sailing his yacht *Vinette* to the prison and paying a call on her father, Commandant Georges Bouvier. At first Gabrielle was wary of Ivan's intentions – and there was also the question of his huge tiger tattoo. 'My mother loathed it,' says their son Clive Lyon. But over the next few months the ardent young suitor gradually overcame Gabrielle's resistance; they were married in Saigon on 27 July 1939.[19]

General Dobbie, whose military background was in engineering, decided – with the enthusiastic support of his Chief of Staff, Colonel Arthur Percival – to build a line of fixed defences across southern Johore that would make it impossible for an invading army to range their artillery against the Naval Base. He also planned to construct a network of fixed defences on the north coast of Singapore Island to protect the immediate approaches to the base across the Straits of Johore. But if the army commander expected the Governor's support for these measures, he was to be disappointed. Indeed, Dobbie admitted that he 'never approached the civil administration without meeting complete indifference or active opposition'. His plan for the Kota Tinggi line, so-called because it ran along a river and through a town of that name, was no exception. Thomas refused to co-operate. As he was leaving Singapore, Percival had a vivid recollection of Dobbie saying to him, 'That man will break my heart.'[20]

The General was made of stern stuff, however, and he wrote to the War Office, 'I consider it imperative that such essential defences as can be created in peace must be done now. For this purpose I estimate £250,000 is required for immediate expenditure on work which will take at least 12 months to complete and which must be put in hand without delay.'[21] The Whitehall mandarins deemed this excessive and slashed Dobbie's budget from £250,000 to £60,000, but it was still enough to start work on a jungle clearance scheme and the building of a belt of machine-gun pillboxes across southern Johore.

The military situation improved considerably in August 1939 when the 12th Indian Infantry Brigade Group, commanded by Brigadier A. C. M. Paris, arrived from India. This brigade consisted of the 2nd Battalion of the Argyll and Sutherland Highlanders, the 5/2nd Punjab Regiment and the 4/19th Hyderabad Regiment. The Argylls were known as 'the Old 93rd' after the 93rd Sutherland Highlanders who had distinguished themselves against the Russians at Balaclava. *The Times* war correspondent William Henry Russell, who witnessed their steadfastness in the face of a cavalry charge, described the Highlanders as 'the thin red streak tipped with a line of steel', soon condensed into 'the Thin Red Line'.[22]

The Argylls shared Gillman Barracks on Singapore Island with some old friends, the 2nd Battalion of the Loyal North Lancashire Regiment, while a new home was being built for them at Tyersall Park near the Botanic Gardens. At the end of September they became involved with the Kota Tinggi line when the 12th Brigade was placed in charge of a 25-mile strip from Endau to Mersing on the eastern Johore coastline.

The Argylls had their doubts about the wisdom of defending a line of concrete pillboxes in jungle and rubber country. It was felt that the defenders could be outflanked and their supply lines cut, leaving them stranded behind enemy lines. General Dobbie, however, had retired as GOC after reaching the compulsory retirement age and his scheme was quickly abandoned, even though only £23,000 of the £60,000 budget had been spent.

The pillboxes that had been constructed rapidly disappeared beneath a tangle of jungle vines and were soon forgotten. Just as the so-called 'phoney war' – the *drôle de guerre* – had begun in Europe, Singapore embarked on a two-year period of mismanagement which would seal her fate.

CHAPTER 3

Bad Times

THE DRIVING FORCE BEHIND the Argyll and Sutherland Highlanders was
Major Ian Stewart, the battalion's second-in-command. 'He was a very
slender man and in their pocky humour they called him "Busty" and would
have followed him anywhere,' one of his officers, Captain Kenneth I.
McLeod, says.[1] Stewart realised that Malaya Command had no idea of how
to fight an enemy in the Malayan countryside. While the jungles presented
difficulties of movement, the vast rubber plantations provided good fields
of fire and the system of well-made roads was ideal for armoured and
motorised transport.

There were no instruction manuals relating to such diverse and contra-
dictory conditions, and the only manual on tank warfare was sitting unread
in a cupboard at Fort Canning. This failure to come to grips with the
problem of defending Malaya stemmed from the fact that, according to one
well-placed source, 'the higher command was torn by internal squabbling
about what was to happen, and about who was responsible for doing what'.[2]

Most of the Argylls were young city men from the industrial heartlands
of Scotland who had never set foot in the dense, tangled rainforest known
as jungle. Stewart, in collaboration with Brigadier Archie Paris, decided that
his battalion would undertake a rigorous programme of bush warfare
training, irrespective of the climatic extremes. Word soon flashed around
the officers' mess at Fort Canning and the watering holes of Raffles Hotel
and the Tanglin Club that Stewart was roughing it with his men in swamps
and jungles. 'He was regarded as completely barking,' says Major-General
David Thomson, the regiment's former colonel, or 'father', 'but he was a
quite outstanding man. He was one of those completely unique and individual officers. He was not of a mould but very much his own man.'[3]

While fortress troops were square-bashing and carrying out standard
regimental drills, Stewart was developing a new type of fighting. When
Brigadier Hugh Ellis raised the Tank Corps in France in World War I, his
staff captain was Ian Stewart – a fact that had eluded the strait-laced minds

at Malaya Command. General Thomson says, 'Here was a man whose name was written into history as the colonel of flat-footed infantry but who actually had a wider background in all-arms warfare than anybody else.'

The Argylls had been issued with 10 Bren-gun carriers soon after their arrival in Malaya and later took delivery of four Lanchester armoured cars and three Marmon-Herringtons. The carriers were awkward, unstable vehicles, but each was armed with a Bren gun, a .303 Vickers machine gun and a .45 Thompson machine gun. The armoured cars had seen better days, but also had useful firepower. Built between 1925 and 1930, the Lanchesters were equipped with two Vickers machine guns and a .5 anti-tank machine gun, while the Marmons each had a Vickers machine gun and a .55 Boys anti-tank rifle.

With his knowledge of tank warfare, Stewart created fast-moving, highly mobile 'Tiger Patrols', which could encircle enemy troops and drive them up against a roadblock, where the gunners in the armoured cars would cut them to pieces. The key to these aggressive tactics was to 'hold the road in depth' to frustrate enemy outflanking movements and drive the attackers back into the jungle or make them stand and fight.

The more sedentary troops of Singapore Fortress looked askance at these unorthodox activities. They nicknamed the Argylls 'the jungle beasts' and speculated that Ian Stewart must be suffering from a touch of the sun. However, when Lieutenant-Colonel Hector Greenfield returned to Britain on 20 February 1940, Stewart was promoted to command the regiment.

Ian MacAlister Stewart had been born in India on 17 October 1895, the son of a polo-playing medical officer in the Poona Horse. Educated at Cheltenham and Sandhurst, he passed out in December 1913 as the youngest officer in the British Army. As an 18-year-old platoon commander, he was the first British officer to land on French soil in World War I when he led an Argyll charge wielding a claymore 'like his Jacobite ancestors'. He had fallen to the ground, apparently wounded, only to rise explaining that he had tripped over his scabbard. Stewart was awarded the Military Cross in 1915 and a Bar in 1917, and twice received a Mention in Dispatches.[4]

Kenneth McLeod was 6 foot 3 inches tall, sparsely built and a tremendous golfer. He says that Stewart's aim in Malaya was to build an outstanding fighting force 'and reverse the foolish tactics employed by some officers and units in the First World War. Stewart had learned their faults by going over the top and fighting shoulder to shoulder with the troops. He saw how useless some officers were and how they caused many avoidable deaths. He thought an officer's job was to train his men to kill the enemy but in so doing to ensure that they received as few casualties as possible themselves.

'He was strong-willed and a great tactician but he was always prepared to discuss situations and listen to other options if any. He was not inclined to suffer fools gladly. When officers came out from the UK to bring the battalion to fighting strength, he would reject those that he did not think were sufficiently athletic and would find them jobs in other units. He was a great mixer with the men and got to know them and, through this, acquired their confidence. He ensured that his officers picked the best to be leaders as NCOs for the jobs they would have to undertake in facing the enemy. He had to train his men extremely hard, which was not always appreciated, but when it came to fronting the enemy they acknowledged the fact that all the rigorous jungle training had held them to good account. Ian Stewart became the battalion icon.'

Stewart's popularity with his men was not reciprocated at Fort Canning after he disproved one of Malaya Command's pet theories – that the Kranji River in the north-west corner of Singapore Island was unfordable to troops. 'Ian Stewart took one look at it and decided it was a worthless obstacle,' says Captain David Wilson, second-in-command of one of the rifle companies. 'But Malaya Command did not agree; none of them had even dipped their big toes in it. So one day we staged a battalion exercise, and got the whole lot across the horrid muddy affair.'[5]

There was further friction when Stewart challenged the concept that Singapore could hold out for months until the fleet arrived. He had seen the Japanese in action in Shanghai and pointed out that Malaya Command had no idea what tactics they might employ. He was prevented from embellishing his comments by a brigadier who told him 'to shut up and sit down', adding for good measure that everyone regarded his ideas as dangerous fanaticism'.[6]

Desperately rearming to withstand an expected German onslaught across the Channel in the summer of 1940, Britain was stuck with the Singapore Strategy in the Far East. The 'period before relief' was extended from 70 to 180 days and authority was given for reserves of food and munitions to be built up accordingly. These matters were considered by the Singapore Defence Committee, which consisted of the three service chiefs and representatives of the civil administration, sitting under the chairmanship of the Governor. At General Dobbie's suggestion, the Defence Secretary for the past year had been a senior civil servant, C. A. Vlieland.

Charles Archibald Vlieland, an Oxford-educated man, had joined the

Malayan Civil Service in 1914 at the age of 24. Rising through the ranks of the Secretariat, he had acquired an incomparable knowledge of the country and its problems. He had also acquired a nickname, 'Starchy Archie' – a dig at his rather superior manner and his habit of wearing a dinner jacket every night.

Vlieland had travelled widely in Malaya, hunting game in forests and shooting over open countryside and around the coasts. He also had his own network of planters, miners, prospectors, foresters and game rangers reporting to him on any suspicious Japanese activities in their areas. From this intelligence, Vlieland learned that the Japanese had a habit of investing personnel at key strategic points, notably in the mining districts of Trengganu and Kelantan and along a line stretching across Johore from Kota Tinggi to rubber plantations at Batu Pahat on the west coast. He concluded after studying the military situation that Japan was likely to attack these areas and that it was imperative for Britain to defend the whole of the Malay peninsula rather than just Singapore Island; anything less than total commitment would mean forfeiting Malaya's mineral wealth and losing the Naval Base into the bargain.

According to Vlieland, he had been given 'practically a free hand to pursue my aims'[7] but he found himself on a collision course with Dobbie's replacement, Major-General (Sir) Lionel Bond, who had taken over on 1 August 1939. Bond objected to a civilian's having a big say in defence matters and, although he was an engineer like Dobbie, he had no intention of following his predecessor's policy of having fixed defences in Johore and on the north coast of Singapore. At their first meeting, Bond curtly informed Vlieland that his orders were to defend Singapore Island and did not permit him to concern himself with the peninsula.[8]

If this were so, Vlieland retorted, then the War Office had exceeded its powers by determining the defence policy of Malaya without reference to the Government. He was adamant that the Army should participate in his policy of extended defence and refused to alter his view. Even if the Japanese seized the Naval Base, Vlieland pointed out, they would not be able to use it if Britain still held the Malay peninsula.

Vlieland was on friendly terms with the Royal Air Force commander, Air Vice-Marshal John Babington, who saw things with monochromatic clarity. As far as he was concerned, the Army's primary function was to protect his forward airfields. When the Governor sided with Vlieland and Babington, Bond found himself outmanoeuvred and outvoted – but it made no difference: the Defence Committee had no executive powers to enforce its recommendations, all of which Bond cheerfully ignored.

Babington, one of Britain's first air force heroes, was known as a man with a stubborn streak. As a pilot, he had flown through heavy flak in November 1914 to bomb the Zeppelin airship sheds and factory at Friedrichshafen, leaving them a blazing ruin.[9] From the outset, it was daggers drawn between Babington and Bond; the outbreak of World War II, which might have been expected to unite them in a common cause, did nothing to ameliorate the situation.

One of the main points under discussion on the Defence Committee – renamed the War Committee after September 1939 – was Operation Matador, Britain's plan for a pre-emptive strike against a Japanese invading force in Thailand. British strategists had known for years that it was essential to prevent the enemy from forming beachheads at the two most suitable landing places in southern Thailand: Singora and Patani on the Kra Isthmus. Operation Matador was designed to destroy the Japanese as they were going ashore at those points, but it required a co-operative effort between the Army and the Air Force. In the present climate of inter-service hostility, this was unlikely to be forthcoming. Relations between General Bond and Air Vice-Marshal Babington were so dire that it was no longer safe for Singapore's hostesses to invite them to the same party. Vlieland says he found the whole thing 'more than tiresome.'[10]

Governor Thomas, meanwhile, was fighting a losing battle to protect Malaya from European war fever. One of his bugbears was the *Malaya Tribune*, an English-language newspaper owned by the Mayor of Singapore, Dr S. Q. Wong, holder of a Doctorate of Law from Harvard University and a millionaire several times over. He enjoyed annoying the *Straits Times* and had primed his editor Edwin 'Jimmy' Glover and his news editor George Hammonds to fight for the rights of the underdog against the colonial establishment. The Governor was particularly incensed by the paper's 'Buy a Bomber for Britain' campaign, which urged readers to contribute to a fund for that purpose. Shenton Thomas thought that buying bombers was a matter for the authorities and no place for a meddling newspaper.

After the Governor had made his opinions known, Jimmy Glover, a quick-witted Yorkshireman, published a story that ridiculed him for opposing the scheme. The article was illustrated by a cartoon showing the Governor snatching up dollars that were meant to feed a sickly donkey, representing Britain, and throwing them away. The headline was 'Doubting Thomas'. Retribution was swift. Shenton Thomas discovered that the author of the story was Lorraine Stumm, a former Fleet Street journalist who was married to Flight Lieutenant Harley Stumm, an Australian-born

RAF officer based at Seletar. He ordered her to leave the colony within 24 hours for 'scandalous reporting'.

The Governor's diktat threw the young couple into a panic. Harley, a barrister in civilian life, examined the legal position and concluded that the Governor had absolute powers to expel anyone from the Crown Colony if he so wished. Lorraine, however, still had one card up her sleeve. She asked Jimmy Glover to arrange a meeting between her and the Governor. Thomas agreed to meet her but warned that nothing she could say would make him change his mind; indeed, he was looking forward to bawling her out.

At Government House, Lorraine was ushered into a reception room in which a cheery fire blazed in the grate – an odd sight, she thought, in steamy Singapore. This room was air-conditioned; it appeared that the Governor was trying to simulate English climatic conditions. As soon as he walked in, however, the atmosphere turned frosty.

'Was it my style of reporting that you objected to?' Lorraine asked him.

'Yes indeed it was,' the Governor replied.

'Well, sir,' she said, 'you possibly know that I worked in London. Your brother Cecil Thomas was my editor on the *Daily Mirror* and he and his staff taught me to write that way.'

Thomas was nonplussed. The last thing he wanted was for it to become common knowledge in Singapore that his brother worked for a Fleet Street tabloid. He thought for a moment, then strode to the other end of the room. 'Very well,' he said. 'This is a private matter between you and me. You may stay.'

Harley and Lorraine lived in a rented flat on the waterfront at Kallang, with a 'cook boy' to do the household chores. These were happy times for them but, she says, 'I was regarded with suspicion by some of the heads of the forces, particularly RAF Command.' The powers-that-be were concerned that she might expose in the *Tribune* the Air Force's state of unpreparedness. Harley had approached Air Vice-Marshal Babington to complain that he and the other pilots were not getting enough flying time, but they found little sympathy. Babington huffed that the ground staff couldn't be expected to give up their siesta hour to get the planes into the air; furthermore, there were too few ground staff to service them after they had been flown. Lorraine was furious at Babington's short-sightedness but she did not write the story, knowing it would rebound on her husband.

The Air Force commander had reported to the Air Ministry in March 1940 that if the Army was unable to prevent Japanese landings, then the defence of Malaya, Thailand and Borneo would have to be left to the RAF and the Navy. As it could not safely be assumed that naval forces would be available for the Far East, such defence would inevitably fall to the Air Force. Babington added he had no doubts that 'if the Japanese gained a foothold in Malaya, the fate of Singapore would be scaled'.[11]

Not to be outdone, the following month General Bond submitted a new appreciation, in which he appeared to change his mind about forward defence. He said he considered that the northern frontier with Thailand might have to be held by a considerable force for several months provided he had an army in the order of 40 battalions, or four divisions, with three machine-gun battalions and two tank regiments. As it would be impossible for Britain to provide a force of such magnitude, he argued that the RAF 'could and should be made absolutely responsible, if not for the detection and destruction of a Japanese expedition before it landed, at least for ensuring that no base can be maintained and no lines of communication can be operated within striking distance of our airfields'. Provided this was done, Bond said, the army requirement could be reduced to a more attainable 25 battalions with supporting arms, including three anti-tank batteries and one company of armoured cars or tanks.

These matters remained unresolved when Sir Shenton and Lady Thomas set off in April 1940 to take their leave in London. It was decided before he departed that the defence situation and the urgent need for reinforcements would be discussed by the Governor at the highest levels in Whitehall. Thomas was owed three months' leave (although owing to travel difficulties both ways he was in fact away from Singapore for a total of eight months). In his absence, the Colonial Secretary, Stanley Jones, would take over the Governor's responsibilities, including his chairmanship of the War Committee. On the day he sailed to England, Thomas told Archie Vlieland, 'Remember, Vlieland, I rely on you to hold the fort while I am away and not to let Bond get away with it. Jones knows very little about the defence side, and you'll have to keep him straight.'[12]

Jones, however, upset the balance of power by siding with General Bond. 'Jones had it all his own way, not only to the exasperation of the AOC (Air Officer Commanding) and myself, but to the bewilderment and perturbation of the general public in Malaya,' Vlieland wrote. 'Most people thought I was responsible for, or at least party to, many of the strange things which were happening.' This included the building of defences along the *southern* coast of Singapore to repel a seaborne invasion, while nothing was done on the island's exposed northern shore or in the Malay States.

One of the newcomers to Singapore was Bernard Clifton, son of a former Chief Inspector of the Straits Settlements. Bernie had been born in Penang in April 1924 to Inspector Thomas Frederick Clifton and his wife Elsie. 'My father and his brother both went into the Straits Settlements Police Force in 1919,' he says. 'Recruits joined up in Singapore and did their exams and then they were distributed all over the five colonies in Malaya. Each colony had its own police stations [which had] nothing to do with the Federated or Non-Federated States.

'Then in 1940 he was offered the job of Government Censor – they wanted someone with experience to vet all the incoming mail from informers and so forth after the outbreak of the war. I went to St Andrew's School, where the principal was an Australian, Mr Adams.[13] I finished my education at Pitmans College in Tank Road and got a job at Wakefields, the oil people.'

Another new arrival in 1940 was Brother Vincent, a teacher at the noviciate training centre off Bukit Timah Road north of Singapore City. Born Vincent Barbe to Catholic parents in a French farming community on the outskirts of Montreal, on New Year's Day 1919, he had trained as a teacher in Montreal and joined the Brothers of St Gabriel, before completing his education at King's College, London University.

Brother Vincent had been in Singapore for only a few weeks when Germany launched her attack on the Low Countries and France in May 1940. Two of the order's French brothers were called up by the French Army for service in Indochina, and Brother Vincent was transferred to Singapore to replace one of them at Holy Infants English School, Serangoon. Four months later, Japanese troops occupied northern Indochina – with the connivance of France's Vichy regime – to end the reinforcement of Chiang Kai-shek's army via the route from Haiphong to Chungking, and to move its forces within striking distance of Thailand and Malaya.[14]

One of the French brothers returned to Singapore with the news that the Japanese had occupied the whole of Indochina. They had soldiers, tanks, guns, an air force and a fleet and, he warned, 'anything can happen from now on'. But the warning was not taken seriously among his colleagues, who believed that the Japanese were too far away and wouldn't dare to challenge British supremacy. 'We took it as a joke,' Brother Vincent says.

Meanwhile, the brawling on the War Committee had attracted the ire of Vice-Admiral Sir Geoffrey Layton, Commander-in-Chief China Fleet, who had moved to Singapore from Hong Kong and established his headquarters at the Naval Base. Layton was a gruff, 57-year-old, bullet-headed seadog whose salty language belied a deep belief in the Anglican faith. He cabled the Admiralty about the dissension between Bond and Babington, and the First Sea Lord, Admiral Sir Dudley Pound, raised the matter at a Chiefs of Staff meeting in late June.

On the available evidence the Chiefs of Staff concluded that the feud 'was due more to the lack of resources than to questions of principle'. It was time to appoint a Commander-in-Chief Far East who would be senior to both Bond and Babington.[15] This decision coincided with another, in August, that the fleet could no longer be sent to the Far East because of commitments in the Mediterranean, the Atlantic and home waters. As it would be up to the RAF to repel invaders in Malaya, it was agreed that the post of Commander-in-Chief Far East should go to an airman, the veteran Air Chief Marshal Sir Robert Brooke-Popham. The revised Singapore Strategy embraced the defence of the whole of Malaya, as Vlieland had advocated, and the Army's role was spelled out as: (a) the close defence of the Naval Base and airfields; (b) internal security; and (c) to deal with any enemy land force that might succeed in gaining a foothold despite the action of the Air Force.

In October, Admiral Layton presided over a Defence Conference at Singapore to discuss the vital issue of reinforcements. The local commanders estimated that the minimum number of aircraft required to defend Malaya and Burma was 582. The conference's report was sent to London, where it was handed over to be assessed by the joint planning staff – who were still deliberating on their findings when the avuncular figure of Sir Robert Brooke-Popham arrived in Singapore to knock some sense into the recalcitrant Vlieland, Babington and Bond.

Brooke-Popham had retired from the Air Force in 1937 and become Governor of Kenya, a post he held until he was appointed Commander-in-Chief Far East. According to his orders, he was responsible 'for the operational control and direction of training of British land and air forces in Malaya, Burma and Hong Kong, and for the co-ordination of plans for the defence of these territories'. He was also 'in charge of British air forces in Ceylon and reconnaissance squadrons in the Indian Ocean and Bay of Bengal'. However, he had no control over Admiral Layton or his naval forces.

Brooke-Popham's brief would have tested a man in the prime of life, but he was 62 years old and had not worn particularly well. When General Headquarters Far East opened at Singapore on 18 November 1940, he proved incapable of adapting to the operational and equatorial climates and found himself snoozing through many crucial meetings. Known to his staff as 'Brookham', he had been born Henry Robert Moore Brooke in 1878 and had added the 'Popham' by Royal Warrant in 1904 in honour of an admired relative. Educated at Haileybury and Sandhurst, he joined the Oxfordshire Light Infantry in 1898, then fought in the Boer War and was promoted to captain in 1904. Attached to the Air Battalion during manoeuvres of 1911, he learned to fly and gained British flying certificate No. 108 in July 1911.

Brooke-Popham transferred from the Oxfordshire Light Infantry to the Royal Flying Corps the following year and remained in the RFC throughout World War I, rising from squadron commander to Deputy Quartermaster General. After the war, he became a key figure in the formation of the Royal Air Force as the first Commandant of both the RAF Staff College and the Imperial Defence College. He held a number of other impressive positions, including Air Officer Commanding, British Forces in Iraq (1928–30), Air Officer Commanding in Chief, Air Defence of Great Britain (1933–35) and Principal Air Aide de Camp to King George V (1933–37).

Having been alerted to the schism on the War Committee, Brooke-Popham stayed awake for his first meeting with Vlieland and the others, and was appalled by what he witnessed. He wrote despairingly to Churchill's Chief of Staff, General Hastings 'Pug' Ismay, 'that not only do they have no Agenda but that no Minutes are kept; individuals merely make notes on scraps of paper'.[16]

Brooke-Popham went on the offensive soon after Shenton Thomas returned from leave in December. In London, the Governor had been grilled by the War Cabinet Sub-committee about the goings-on in Singapore. It had been made clear to him that both land and air reinforcements were in short supply and that all this bickering would have to cease. 'Starchy Archie' sensed trouble when Thomas avoided him for a week after his return and his calls to Government House went unanswered. At a meeting of the War Committee on 13 December, he discovered that the Governor had performed a complete volte-face. When Vlieland took up his usual position at the conference table at the Governor's right hand, Thomas cut him dead and said to Brooke-Popham, 'I think you have something to bring up, Sir Robert?' This was Brooke-Popham's cue to launch a full-blooded assault on Starchy Archie.

'The C-in-C Land and Air then made a savage attack on me,' he says. 'It was, in effect, more of an attack on Sir Shenton's previous regime than on myself. No one else said a word. Bond and Layton nodded their approval and my friend the AOC could not rally to my support in defiance of his Air

Chief Marshal. Sir Shenton Thomas remained silent with head bowed.' Vlieland realised he had lost the argument. 'It stank of midnight oil and careful briefing by Bond and Layton, since it referred to matters before Brooke-Popham's arrival in Singapore. I was accused of persistent refusal to take the army line.'[17] Vlieland resigned the following day, and left the colony soon afterwards.[18]

Meanwhile in London, the joint planners, having dissected the Defence Conference's report, replied, in January 1941, 'Both the Defence Conference and the commanders themselves appear to take too pessimistic a view and to overestimate the Japanese. Thus, even in their final estimate, when they propose a first-line of 566 aircraft [actually raised to 582 at the conference] to meet the Japanese total of 600 to 700, some 500 of which are carrier-borne, they allege that they will still be "heavily outnumbered" and may have to scale up their estimate if Japanese forces increase. This appears to be entirely divorced from reality. The Japanese have never fought against a first-class Power in the air and we have no reason to believe that their operations would be any more effective than those of the Italians.' The joint planners concluded that a first-line of 336 aircraft 'should give us a reasonable degree of security'.[19]

At the time of Brooke-Popham's arrival in Singapore, the RAF had just 88 aircraft, of which only 24 Blenheim bombers and 24 Hudsons could be counted as modern. The 24 Vildebeeste torpedo bombers were straight out of the pages of Biggles books, and a squadron of 12 Wirraways from the Royal Australian Air Force could be used only for 'general purpose' duties. The remaining four aircraft were slow-moving flying boats.

Nevertheless, new RAF airfields popped up like mushrooms on the east coast of Malaya and at Tengah and Sembawang on Singapore Island. The Army had not been consulted about the location of any of these airfields, yet it was expected to deploy troops to protect them all. According to Sir Lewis Heath, commander of the III Indian Corps, the plan forced upon Bond 'a ridiculous degree of dispersion'.[20]

However, the Army received a substantial injection of new blood on the strength of General Bond's submissions. Two additional brigades – the 6th and 8th Indian Infantry of the 11th Indian Division, commanded by Major-General David Murray-Lyon – arrived from India, while two British battalions, the 2nd East Surreys and the 1st Seaforth Highlanders, were shipped in from Shanghai following the British evacuation of China. Major-General Frank Keith Simmons, commanding officer in Shanghai, became GOC Singapore Fortress in charge of the island's fixed defences.

Churchill, however, wrote to the Chiefs of Staff on 13 January 1941, 'I do not remember to have given my approval to these large diversions of force. On the contrary, if my minutes are collected they will be seen to have an opposite tendency. The political situation in the Far East does not seem to require, and the strength of our Air Force by no means warrants, the maintenance of such large forces in the Far East at this time.'[21]

The Chiefs of Staff placated their volatile leader with the news that it was planned to send only two squadrons of outmoded Brewster Buffalo fighters from the United States to Singapore which, at that time, had no fighter aircraft at all. Australia had been asking awkward questions about Far East defence, and the War Office's greatest concern was that the Australian Government, under pressure from the Labour Opposition, would refuse to supply any more troops to the Middle East battlefields until it was satisfied that the island was adequately defended.

The Australian Prime Minister was the Liberal Party leader (Sir) Robert Menzies, one of Churchill's most ardent admirers. When Churchill replaced Chamberlain in May 1940, Menzies arranged a place for himself in the British War Cabinet. He was appalled to discover that Churchill had little interest in the Far East or the Japanese threat. The two men clashed heatedly on the subject and Menzies's admiration of his hero turned to mistrust. Despite misgivings about Churchill's attitude, Australia agreed to send a division of its own troops to Malaya.

Menzies was still in London when Brooke-Popham flew down to Australia in February 1941 to pacify the Australian War Cabinet and its leading members, the new Prime Minister Arthur Fadden and the Labour Party Leader John Curtin. The Australians weren't too sure what to make of their elderly visitor. He was a large, balding, unkempt man with a reddish moustache, a high-pitched voice and a giggling laugh. He lacked knowledge of all aspects of modern warfare, yet believed that the Japanese were so inferior to the British in their fighting qualities that Britain could hold her own against them, even with inadequate resources.[22]

With a flourish, Brooke-Popham told the Australians that 67 Brewster Buffalo aircraft would be committed to the defence of Singapore. They would be flown by British pilots who were 'considerably superior' to their Japanese counterparts.[23] Furthermore, he maintained that Singapore could defend itself for six months, even nine months, giving a British battle fleet ample time to arrive and protect the island from Japanese invasion. Churchill had instructed him on his departure from London to 'hold Singapore until capital ships could be sent' and, he added, Churchill had promised, 'We will not let Singapore fall.' For good measure, he also threw in the canard that a landward attack down the Malay peninsula was unlikely to occur because of the impenetrable terrain.

This was dangerous nonsense, yet there is no indication in the minutes of the Australian War Cabinet meeting on 14 February 1941 that Fadden, Curtin or anyone else challenged Brooke-Popham's statements. No one pointed out that the Buffalo – also known as the Flying Beer Barrel because of its rotund shape – was an outdated aircraft which was taking no part in the European war because it had been superseded by faster, more efficient fighters. No one mentioned that the 'Main Fleet to Singapore' strategy had already been abandoned, or that the myth about Malaya's 'impenetrable terrain' had been successfully exploded as long ago as 1937.

Brooke-Popham's views on the Japanese were based on nothing more substantial than his own brief observations on the Hong Kong border and a deeply ingrained racial prejudice.[24] 'I had a good close-up, across the barbed wire, of various sub-human specimens dressed in dirty grey uniform, which [sic] I was informed were Japanese soldiers,' he wrote in one letter to the War Office. 'If these represent the average of the Japanese army, the problem of their food and accommodation would be simple, but I cannot believe they would form an intelligent fighting force.'[25]

The Australians, however, came to respect Brooke-Popham's opinions and his apparent concern for their well-being. He returned to Singapore well satisfied with his mission. He advised London that Australia had recommitted herself to the idea of imperial defence and would continue to provide troops for service in the Middle East. In a letter to General Ismay, Brooke-Popham related that he had not been impressed with the calibre of Australian politicians, although he had quite liked the Opposition Leader, John Curtin.[26]

Brooke-Popham's dismissal of Japan's capabilities reflected an attitude common among RAF and Royal Navy officers, who believed that the Japanese were poor aviators and shipbuilders, 'slow thinking, badly trained and unable to cope with crises. Ignorance and racial prejudice seem to have been the main causes of such inaccurate assessments.'[27] The captain of the HMS *Tamar* concluded after observing the Japanese Navy in Hong Kong for two months that Japanese naval officers were 'wooden-headed automatons'. He added that 'the bogie of their superiority in battle has vanished and it appears improbable that they can rank as a first-class fighting power until they have learned how to properly educate their people'. The captain was apparently unaware that one of the legacies of the

Meiji Restoration was that Japan enjoyed one of the highest literacy rates in the world.[28]

Brooke-Popham's main appeal to the Chiefs of Staff was his willingness to toe the Whitehall line. 'It was pointed out to me that the requirements of Home Defence, the Battle of the Atlantic and the Middle East must take precedence over those of the Far East,' he says. Later, he would be told that Russia must come first and, at another time, it was Iraq and Iran. He had no illusions about his lowly place in the War Office's pecking order for pilots and aircraft. 'It was obviously our duty to be content with the essential minimum,' he said, 'to consider what we could do without rather than what we would like to have, and to make the fullest use of local resources. But we always regarded the strength of 336 aeroplanes as an irreducible minimum.'

The Commander-in-Chief Far East was well aware that he could not muster even half that number, yet he travelled several times to Malaya, Burma and Hong Kong and made two trips to Australia, three to Manila and five to the Dutch East Indies to convince the local commanders and administrators that their security was in safe hands. He increased his staff from seven to 15, but found that overwork and the enervating Malay climate took a heavy toll on his men. 'The most serious case was that of my Chief of Staff, Major-General [Dicky] Dewing, who went to hospital on 8 April and remained there until he started for England in May,' he says. 'General Playfair arrived to take his place on 21 June, but for a period of some ten and a half weeks I was without a Chief of Staff.'[29]

The loss of Dewing was a serious blow to the hard-working officers of the Far East Combined Intelligence Bureau, which continually warned GHQ about Japan's military build-up. The bureau, located in large concrete buildings at the Naval Base under the control of the Admiralty, consisted of branches of naval, army and air force intelligence. Its director of military intelligence, Colonel Gordon E. Grimsdale, wrote to his friend, General Ismay, 'I have always felt that one of the worst bits of bad luck was when Dicky Dewing had to be invalided home. He had an appallingly difficult job and a very patchy staff to help him. Yet he had the whole thing so well taped that if he had been able to carry on I am perfectly certain his presence would have made an immense difference. Directly he went the rest of GHQ staff never believed us and always called us "alarmist".'[30]

Brooke-Popham's view was that the organisation was 'somewhat unbalanced in that attention was mostly concentrated on Naval intelligence'. As the Japanese Army would be transported to Malaya's shores in ships, this seemed a sensible preoccupation.

The first contingent of the Australian Imperial Force – a total of 5,850 men – arrived in Singapore on 18 February 1941. 'The *Queen Mary* was still being converted into a troopship and there were rocking horses in the children's nursery and we had a first-class lounge,' remembers Russell Savage, then a 20-year-old gunner. Sir Shenton Thomas, General Bond and a crowd of army and navy officers greeted the Australian troops when the *Queen Mary* moored at the Naval Dock. 'There was a strike on when we got to Singapore and the skipper berthed her up against a solid concrete wharf without the assistance of tugs,' Savage says. Some of the Australians, spotting an opportunity for a bit of horseplay, tossed coins to the distinguished reception committee. Thomas was not offended. After looking over the troops, he declared them 'splendidly fit'.

The Australian force comprised the headquarters and services of the 8th Division under Major-General Gordon Bennett, with the 22nd Australian Infantry Brigade Group. While the other ranks were taken off to Singapore Railway Station to entrain for the long, hot journey to their camps at Malacca and Port Dickson, some Australian officers were driven to Raffles Hotel for a drink and then taken on a sightseeing tour through Singapore's crowded markets and wide boulevards, to the New World amusement park. John Wyett says, 'We were horrified to see the city ablaze with life and everything going on as usual. The whole atmosphere was that Singapore could not fall – it was impossible.'[31]

The Governor invited Gordon Bennett and 25 AIF officers to dinner at Government House, and a party of eight stayed there for a few days in vice-regal splendour. Entertainment included two dances, under the glittering candelabra of the ballroom, each attended by more than 700 guests. 'The orders from England were that all brassware must be blackened on uniforms; no polished brassware to be seen,' John Wyett remembers. 'The units in Singapore took absolutely no notice of this. There they were in all their splendid regalia, holding a dance with bands playing. We felt like poor cousins amid all this splendour.'

Russell Savage recalls, 'It was still the old empire – Raffles and the pukkas – and coming from Brisbane it was a bit of a culture shock.' Savage was a member of 20th Battery, 2/10th Field Artillery Regiment, an all-Queensland unit. He was a good-looking young man, a shade under six feet tall, with even features and a dimpled chin. After studying at Brisbane Boys College and Scots College, Savage joined the Militia to learn gunnery, and in 1940 enlisted in the AIF for overseas service. 'A lot of chaps joined up for the excitement, but we had some loyalty to the Empire and the Crown,' he says.

'I had no dependants and thought it was up to the single fellows to join up. We took over a school in Malacca and trained with 18-pounders and World War I howitzers.'

Savage found barrack life monotonous, but things livened up when he discovered gambling. 'There was always an illegal game in the canteen on pay night,' he says. 'I knew nothing about gambling and neither did my friend, Alan McNevin, but one night one of the Crown and Anchor tables went broke and couldn't pay the punters, so we put up the money and took it over ourselves.'[32] Savage and McNevin were smart enough to realise that they wouldn't last long in this cut-throat world, so they hired Harry Nesbitt, an experienced gambler, to run the table for them. The money started rolling in. 'I never did guard duty,' Savage says. 'I paid someone to do it for me. I went to the Malacca Rest House to wine and dine in the evenings. I had more money than I'd ever seen.'[33]

Sir Robert Brooke-Popham's secretary was a young army wife, Beryl Stevenson, whose husband was a lieutenant in the Manchester Regiment. Born Beryl Speirs at Tumut, New South Wales, in January 1916, she had bought Wagga Commercial College in 1931 at the remarkably young age of 15 – too young even to sign cheques – and served as principal until 1939 when she sailed for London. 'I was studying at Pitmans College in London when war broke out,' she says. 'I was a high-speed shorthand writer and I had gone to Britain to get the qualifications I should have had when I bought the college.'[34] She landed a job as minute secretary to Lord Lloyd, chairman of the British Council and later Colonial Secretary under Churchill. Beryl took courses in first aid, learned to drive an ambulance and worked as a nurse at Oldchurch Hospital, Romford.

In August 1940 Beryl accepted a job to escort 477 British children who were being evacuated to Australia. On board ship she met John Drysdale Stevenson, who was returning to his regiment in Singapore, and the couple enjoyed a shipboard romance. They were married by the captain – but were then separated when the ship berthed at Singapore. Beryl continued on to Sydney with the refugees, and resigned herself to spending a lonely war without her husband. But 'Steve', as he was called, wrote to her in early 1941 to say that he was being sent on an officers' training course at Poona, in India, and she could join him there.

'We had a wonderful seven or eight weeks in Poona, and then Steve was booked on a ship to go back from Madras to Singapore,' she says. 'The captain agreed to take me as well. Our cargo was raw onions in the lower hold and raw Indian recruits on the decks. On the captain's small deck there was the postmaster-general of Kuala Lumpur and his wife, and two brigadier generals from Fort Canning. There was no room for this handful of passengers even to walk about, so we played bridge all the way across the Bay of Bengal. Whenever one of the brigadiers played with me, he won, so he got the impression I had a brain.

'When I got to Singapore, I had to report to the police, and it was made plain to me that there was a plane leaving for Sydney on the third day and I had to be on it. On the morning of the second day, the brigadier rang me from Fort Canning and said, "Put on your best bib and tucker. I'm taking you out to the Naval Base to introduce you to the Commander-in-Chief. He needs a secretary." So I started to work for Air Chief Marshal Sir Robert Brooke-Popham, the man who mucked things up. He was a fairly ordinary sort of Britisher and I worked for him at the Naval Base. It was May 1941 and I had both a job and the right to stay in Singapore.'

Brooke-Popham had not only displaced Archie Vlieland from the Defence Committee but had also seen off General Bond and Air Vice-Marshal Babington. The new Air Officer Commanding was Air Vice-Marshal Conway Walter Heath Pulford, a rangy, jug-eared airman who had been awarded the Air Force Cross in 1926 for leading four RAF Fairey IIIDs in a record-breaking flight from Cairo to Cape Town.

One of the first things Pulford noticed was the enmity between British and Australian branches of his service. Squadron Leader William J. Harper, an RAF officer and veteran of the Battle of Britain, arrived at RAAF Station Sembawang on 4 October 1941. After an interview with Pulford, he took command of No. 453 RAAF Squadron, which was equipped with Brewster Buffaloes. The squadron's emblem was a beady-eyed kookaburra and its motto: *Ready to Strike*. Apart from a handful of flight commanders, the officers were young Australians who had recently graduated from pilot training school.

'I was amazed to notice among many of the Australian personnel on the station the prevalent dislike that some of them bore for the English,' he says. 'Englishmen were spoken of as "Pommies" with an air of contempt. I did not pay a great deal of attention to this, but it was this that grew into the strong dislike for RAF administration later in the war. It should be noted in turn that RAF personnel elsewhere ostracised the Australians.'[35]

It was a fact that the only fighting taking place in Singapore was between British and Australian servicemen. The most famous altercation was 'the Battle of the Union Jack Club' between Australian soldiers and the fiery Scots of the Argyll and Sutherland Highlanders. It started when an

Australian made a remark to one of the Argylls that was considered offensive, and the Scot poured beer over his head. Many soldiers on both sides were injured in the ensuing ruckus. Later, an Australian soldier was killed in a brawl in what became known as 'the Battle of Lavender Street'.[36]

Russell Savage says, 'The powers-that-be decided that the best way to deal with the problem [of fighting] was to transfer some Australians into British units and vice versa.' He was one of 40 gunners who were integrated into a British artillery regiment. With the wealth he had accumulated from gambling, he was able to employ an Indian batman who 'would not only clean my boots a few times a day but would shave me before I got up in the morning'. Savage discovered that British soldiers did not share the same 'terms of endearment' as his Australian countrymen. 'I was flattened when I jokingly called a Brit a "silly bugger",' he remembers. 'I couldn't fight and didn't come off too well.

'We were used to carrying billycans, tea and a few supplies in the ammunition limbers of our guns. We'd boil up, sit round and have a smoke – but it didn't go down well with the Brits. Officers who had come up through the ranks were difficult about it, whereas officers who had graduated from military college dismissed it as Australian eccentricity. We noticed that officers from the ranks were not as popular as those who were brought up to believe they were born to rule.

'All of us were almost looking forward to mixing it with the Japanese. We thought of them as funny little men from a country famous for its two-bob watches and cheap junk. We were told that they were almost blind without thick glasses, were frightened of the dark and useless in the jungle. Their equipment was no thicker than tinplate and their bullets could not penetrate even that, while their pilots passed out if they flew above 10,000 feet. This was the sort of disinformation we were fed. Britain, America and Australia totally underestimated the Japanese fighting machine. We were right up near the Thai border when we were suddenly rushed back to rejoin the 2/10th in Johore. It was apparent that something serious was about to happen.'

Few people in Singapore knew the Japanese better than William Mortimer 'Bill' Drower, a captain in British Intelligence who arrived in the colony in August 1941. Drower had been born in June 1915 in Southampton, where his grandfather was a parson. 'His little rectory was bombed out of existence in October 1940,' he says. His father was Sir Edwin Drower, Britain's legal counsel in Baghdad, while his mother, Ethel Stafana, was the author of such seminal works as *The Mandaeans of Iraq and Iran*, *Folk Tales of Iraq* and *Peacock Angel*.

Bill Drower had an Irish governess who beat him so badly that at the age of eight he was handed over to the tender mercies of the English public school system. 'I was sent to Clifton in 1924 and stayed there until 1933 when I was 17,' he says. 'I got an exhibition in history for Exeter College [Oxford University] and came out with a bad degree in 1936, having wasted time. I was lucky to get a job at the Japanese Embassy in London.'

CHAPTER 4

Asian Sphinx

THE NEW JAPANESE AMBASSADOR at the Court of St James's in 1936 was Shigeru Yoshida. Born in Tokyo in 1878 into a samurai family from Tosa – one of the four provinces that led the Meiji Restoration – Yoshida was the man who would become Japan's Prime Minister and lead her post-war reconstruction. 'Yoshida admired Churchill and affected a large cigar,' says Bill Drower, who became his secretary. 'He was quite small but he was very tough. He was an intelligent man and he was nice to me from the beginning.

'My jobs were fascinating for a youngster fresh out of university. I started the day giving him an analysis of press comment, then I would suggest the wording of letters to people like angry archbishops. I would also use his seat in the Distinguished Strangers' Gallery at the House of Commons to listen to the debates – for example, I gave him a rundown on Eden's resignation as Foreign Secretary. I learned to speak a little Japanese and I learned a bit about the Japanese political system.'[1]

Through the indoctrination of her people and the suppression of democratic ideals, Japan had become a totalitarian state. To the outside world, she was the Sphinx of Asia, a feudal riddle wrapped in a modern enigma; a country where business magnates in top hats and frock-coats mingled with peasants in costumes as old as antiquity.[2]

As one of Japan's most important representatives abroad, Yoshida vigorously supported the expansion of Japan in Asia. 'He was quite happy that they should exploit China, especially in commercial things and in providing jobs for the Japanese,' Bill Drower says. 'But he wasn't extreme enough for the Japanese Navy. They were ultra-right wing and had it in for him. One of them was a fanatical admiral who wrote to him saying he was far too friendly with the *Ei/Beis* (the British and the Americans) and that he should be more patriotic. Then he announced he was coming to see him at the embassy in Portman Square. Yoshida knew the navy clique could have him assassinated, but he was not going to be intimidated. The Admiral banged on the embassy door and demanded to see the Ambassador. Yoshida came down the grand staircase, walked straight past him and said, "I'm not at home."'

Yoshida survived as Ambassador until 1939 when he was recalled to Tokyo, where the advocates of the New Order had seized control. 'The navy clique wanted to have him shot,' Drower says, 'but instead he was placed under house arrest.'

The spokesman for the New Order was the garrulous pro-Nazi Foreign Minister Yosuke Matsuoka, a law graduate of the University of Oregon. 'The era of democracy is finished and the democratic system bankrupt,' he informed an American reporter for the *New York Herald Tribune*. 'Fascism will develop in Japan through the people's will. It will come out of love for the Emperor.'³

When British diplomats admonished Japan for taking the path of ultra-nationalism, the Japanese pointed out that the British Empire was hardly a democratic institution and that millions of its Asian subjects were disenfranchised and impoverished. The same applied to the Asian subjects of the French, the Dutch and the Americans. It was Japan's sacred duty, they said, to liberate her Asian brothers and sisters and bestow upon them the bene fits of Japanese civilisation. The concept of a Greater East Asia Co-prosperity Sphere, based on the pan-Asian ideal of universal brotherhood (*hakko ichi'u* – the eight corners of the world under one roof), had been propagated abroad since the summer of 1940 under the slogan 'Asia for Asians'. The Japanese, a resolute and resilient people, firmly believed it was their destiny to rule the world.

Westerners tended to scoff at such braggadocio. Indeed, Japan's image in the West was based largely on the Gilbert and Sullivan operetta *The Mikado*, with its catchy tunes, comical Lord High Executioner and giggling, pale-faced geisha girls. They saw only the clockwork toys, 'two-bob watches and cheap junk' churned out by Japanese factories for the bottom end of the market, and had no conception of the capabilities of the *zaibatsu*, the indus-trialists who controlled the great combines such as Mitsubishi and Mitsui. No one paid much attention when, to a Hollywood-style fanfare, a bevy of showgirls unveiled Nissan's first luxury car – the Datsun Model 70 – which showed that Japan possessed all the means of mass production enjoyed by the leading industrial nations and that she was ready to challenge them in the world's markets.

The Japanese had become adept at borrowing Western innovations and philosophies and imbuing them with 'Japanese spirit' to make them integral parts of Japanese culture. The naturalist Charles Darwin and the evolutionary philosopher Herbert Spencer were two Western scientists who found favour with Japan's militarists. Darwin had established the idea of survival of the fittest through natural selection, while Spencer preached Social Darwinism in which the principles of natural selection, when applied to society, concluded that the only way nations could advance and progress was by engaging in periodic wars in which only the fittest would survive. This philosophy appealed immensely to Japan's leaders in their quest for markets against aggressive Western competitors. The big difference was that whereas Westerners believed they had descended from apes, the Japanese believed they had descended from gods.

Isolated in their remote and mystical archipelago, the Japanese people had been forced at the barrel of a gun to make contact with the West when Commodore Matthew C. Perry's four Black Ships hove to off Nagasaki in 1853. The young Emperor Mutsuhito (1852–1912), known posthumously as Meiji ('the Great') and grandfather of Hirohito, ascended the Chrysan-themum Throne as a 15-year-old in 1867. Under the guiding hand of a group of young reformers from south-western Japan, he reclaimed the kingdom from the Tokugawa shoguns who had ruled Japan since 1603. Although deprived of power under the shogunate for 700 years, the monarchy stretched back to the first emperor Jimmu, who had reigned from 660BC to 585BC. *The Times* commented in 1921, 'The Imperial Line of Japan is by far the oldest reigning dynasty in the world. Compared with it, the Hapsburgs and Romanoffs, even the Maison de France, are creations of yesterday.'[4]

Mutsuhito's supporters were determined to modernise their country in order to compete with the rapacious foreigner. They sent fact-finding missions to the West to bring back the latest technological and cultural ideas. A great store of knowledge was obtained, but their initiatives would have failed had they not overcome the major impediment in switching from a feudal society to a modern economy: the samurai, the only class in Japan permitted to bear arms. To surmount the samurai's influence, Mutsuhito's advisers reintroduced emperor worship, or what the Japanese called *kami no michi*, 'the way of the gods'. Shinto was proclaimed the state religion. It preached that the Emperor was a deity, a descendant of the Sun Goddess Amaterasu Omikami whose tears had formed the sacred home islands. He was declared 'sacred and inviolable' in the new Meiji Constitution.

The next step was to enlist the samurai's support for a militant new philosophy embodied in the slogan 'Enrich the country, strengthen the army'. Universal conscription was introduced in 1873, and the Army General Staff was created in 1878 to mobilise Japan's martial capabilities in the national interest. Her factories were industrialised and her armed forces revitalised. Militarily, she looked to the British Navy for a maritime model, while Prussian officers were brought in to train the Imperial Japanese Army.

In 1894 Japan sent an expeditionary force to Korea, a Chinese vassal state, after China intervened to quell a rebellion against the Korean Throne. Armed with the latest Western weapons, Japan inflicted a series of humiliating defeats on China's army and navy. In the Treaty of Shimonoseki of April 1895, Japan seized the Chinese island of Formosa (now Taiwan) and, on Korea's western flank, the Chinese Liaotung Peninsula of southern Manchuria, including China's pride and joy, the fortified, warm-water harbour of Port Arthur on the Yellow Sea. The Japanese also demanded a £35 million indemnity for the damage inflicted on their armed forces during the war.[5]

But Japan's triumph was short-lived. Posing as China's protectors, France, Germany and Russia forced the Japanese to relinquish most of their gains on the mainland, including all territory in Manchuria. Through military pressure and the bribery of corrupt Manchu officials, Russia then acquired leasehold rights in the Liaotung Peninsula and placed its Eastern Fleet at Port Arthur. By 1898, she had expanded in Manchuria and was encroaching into northern Korea. The Meiji Emperor, who ruled on behalf of the country's newly emergent oligarchies, saw it as his duty to re-establish a foothold in China and reclaim Manchuria.

When the Boxer Uprising of 1900 threatened to annihilate all 'foreign devils' in China, Japanese troops joined the international rescue force which captured Beijing and ended the 55-day Siege of the Legations. In the Boxer Protocol of the following year, Japan gained the right with Western nations to station troops permanently in some Chinese cities, including Beijing and Shanghai, to protect Japanese diplomats and nationals.

Britain had stood aside from the so-called Triple Intervention of 1895 and was rewarded with an Anglo-Japanese treaty in 1902 under which Britain was committed to intervening on Japan's side in the event of war between Japan and Russia if a third power joined in on Russia's side. Britain knew this would give Japan a free hand to come to blows with Russia, Britain's main opponent in China, without being concerned about interference from France or Germany.

Two years later, the Japanese crushed the Tsar's Imperial Russian Army and sank two of his navies in the Russo-Japanese War. The Japanese opened hostilities by striking unexpectedly against the Russian fleet at Port Arthur. Then Admiral Togo destroyed the Tsar's Second Pacific Fleet which had steamed halfway around the world from the Baltic. Togo was tipped off by the British about the fleet's progress, and on 28 May 1905 Japanese warships intercepted the Russians in the Tsushima Straits between Korea and Japan and won a resounding victory in what became known as 'the Trafalgar of the East'.

Although she was clearly winning the war, Japan's resources were almost exhausted; she had lost 110,000 troops and was heavily in debt to foreign banks. Reluctantly, she agreed to a peace settlement brokered by the American President, Teddy Roosevelt, under which she took over Russia's lease-hold of the Liaotung Peninsula and a 700-mile-long section of the Trans-Siberian railway in southern Manchuria. It was the first time a modern European power had been humbled by an Asian nation. More significantly, Japan was back in Manchuria.

It became apparent during the Russo-Japanese War, in which weapons of mass destruction were used for the first time, that Japanese soldiers had been brutally trained to withstand extremes of cold and hardship. Recruits, mostly from the impoverished peasantry, were subjected to a callous regime which destroyed their individuality and made them part of a fanatical, well-disciplined unit. Beatings (*bentatsu*) were an inbuilt part of the military system. Senior officers struck junior officers with fists or bamboo poles for minor misdemeanours, while junior officers laid into other ranks at the slightest excuse, the blows increasing in ferocity on the way down the line. 'The common soldier had no human rights and was subject to incessant oppression, brutality and cruelty from his superiors. The gloom and grimness of this tradition of Japanese militarism were symbolised in the deliberate drabness of the Japanese uniform.'[6]

The Japanese soldier was the Emperor's blunt instrument in achieving Japan's political ends, but it became apparent to Westerners that it was the oligarchs and his elder statesmen – the *genro* – who were pulling the strings. For despite his heroic mien in paintings and photographs, the Emperor cut rather a pathetic figure. *The Times* correspondent G. E. Morrison, who was introduced to Mutsuhito in Tokyo in 1909, described him as 'a man of about ordinary height in the most ill-fitting uniform ever seen, with white kid gloves'. He had a 'tremulous, bleary, pimply face sodden it seemed to me with alcohol. He was very nervous, stepped one step forward and shook me by the hand.' Morrison exited backwards, 'feeling somewhat ashamed to render so much homage to bibulous Royalty'.[7]

During Mutsuhito's lifetime the Anglo-Japanese Alliance was revised and renewed in 1905 and again in 1911 and, under his successor, Japan was a

British ally during World War I. She stopped short of sending troops to the Western Front, but her navy escorted Anzac troopships to Europe and her army, accompanied by 1,500 British soldiers, occupied Tsingtao, the German concession in the Shantung province of China. Two months later Japan secretly tried to enforce her notorious 21 Demands on China, 'giving a clear warning that she intended to dominate China and thus the Far East both politically and commercially'.[8]

At Versailles, Japan's delegation was well received among the victorious nations, while the fledgling Chinese Republic, which had provided more than 300,000 coolies to dig trenches on the Western Front, had great hopes that the Peace Conference would accept President Woodrow Wilson's 14 Points to enshrine the principles 'of justice to all peoples and their right to live on equal terms of liberty and safety with one another, whether they be strong or weak'. That, they believed, meant an end to the agreements imposed by Japan in the wake of the 21 Demands.

Woodrow Wilson, however, wanted to deal first with his beloved League of Nations, and that involved a Japanese proposal for a clause ensuring racial equality in international affairs. 'Now is the time,' said the Japanese delegation leader, Prince Saionji, 'to confront international racial discrimination.' The Japanese, like the Chinese, had been vilified on purely racial grounds ever since the West had forced its attentions upon them. In the resulting compromise, Japan was handed Tsingtao, as well as being given a mandate over the former German colonies of the Marianas and the Caroline and Marshall Islands in the Pacific Ocean. The clause on racial discrimination was quietly dropped.[9]

The Sphinx analogy was made by the Australian Prime Minister Billy Hughes following the Imperial Conference which started in London in June 1921.[10] Hughes had violently opposed the anti-racism clause at Versailles, saying that 'sooner than agree to it I would walk into the Seine – or the Folies Bergère – with my clothes off', but he pressed Britain at the Imperial Conference to renew the Anglo-Japanese Alliance, a plea that went unheeded.[11] Back in Australia, Hughes warned his countrymen about the danger of Japan's life-or-death struggle to find markets for her expanding economy. He told Parliament, 'This is the problem of the Pacific – the modern riddle of the Sphinx, for which we must find an answer.'[12]

Japan was a nation of nearly 70 million people, 'crowded together on the margin of subsistence', Hughes said. 'She wants both room for her increasing millions of population and markets for her manufactured goods. And she wants these very badly indeed. America and Australia say to her millions, "Ye cannot enter in." Japan, then, is faced with the great problem which has bred wars since time began. For when the tribes and nations of the past outgrew the resources of their own territory they moved on and on, hacking their way to the fertile pastures of their neighbours.'

Despite the mystical aura attached to the home islands, the Japanese inhabited a cramped, inhospitable country subjected to frequent typhoons and earthquakes. As in Hitler's Germany, the desire for *Lebensraum*, or 'living space', became the driving political force. The difficulty was that the Japanese Navy and the Army General Staff could not agree on which direction this expansion should take. The Navy advocated a southward advance (*nanshin*), while the Army favoured a northern push (*hokushin*) through Manchuria and Mongolia. The Navy's argument was that essential supplies of oil, rubber, tin and iron ore were available in the South Pacific and South East Asia. As Japan had emerged from World War I as the world's third-largest sea power, behind America and Britain, she now had the means to go after them.

This attitude hardened when the Anglo-Japanese Alliance, the mainstay of relations between the two nations and a source of great pride to the Japanese, was unceremoniously scrapped at the end of 1921, during the Washington Conference to limit naval tonnages. Australia and New Zealand both saw the treaty as a guarantee of stability in the Pacific and protested against its abrogation. America and Canada, however, argued that Britain could have only one foreign ally in the Pacific, and that the alliance was preventing her from forging closer links with the US. The Japanese regarded the treaty's abandonment as a national insult. It had been discarded, according to former Japanese Foreign Minister Viscount Ishii, 'like an old pair of sandals'.

The US, supported by Britain, then attempted to limit Japan's naval expansion by urging the five principal naval powers to agree to the following limits on naval strength in ships of the larger classes: USA 525,000 tons; Britain and her Dominions 525,000; Japan, 315,000; France and Italy, each 175,000. Thus Britain and America envisaged that Japan's capital ship tonnage would be restricted to 60 per cent of their own. For every five RN and five USN battleships, the IJN would get three, while France and Italy would be entitled to just 1.75.

The Washington Conference represented the turning point in the Pacific, the moment when Britain chose the Anglo-Saxon option of siding with America at the expense of her Asian ally. While Japan protested about the new alignment, it actually placed her at an advantage: all of her naval forces were concentrated in the Pacific, whereas British and American ships were scattered at various bases worldwide. In the Pacific, Japan actually enjoyed a battleship superiority of 5:3:2 over Britain and the US. At Japan's insistence, the Western powers had also agreed not to build any further naval bases in the western Pacific.

The alliance had been terminated just a few months after Hirohito returned from a European tour during which King George V had lauded the Japanese as Britain's 'loyal and gallant' allies. Japanese respect for British technology was reflected in the Imperial Japanese Navy, which had been modelled on the Royal Navy in every respect, from its gleaming battleships down to the buttons on its naval cadets' uniforms. Indeed, the *Katori* in which the Prince had travelled to England had been built at the Vickers shipyard, Barrow-in-Furness.[13] While the Crown Prince was away, his father's health declined so seriously that he was appointed Regent. Hirohito had already acted as the Emperor's deputy on many occasions, even opening the Imperial Diet and delivering the Speech from the Throne. The regency opened his eyes to many of the problems of state and laid him open to extremists who opposed the democratic aspirations of Japanese statesmen. Universal suffrage had been introduced and, to the fury of the armed forces, the Cabinet had even given up Japan's Shantung concession as a gesture of international goodwill and co-operation.

Hirohito had been born on 29 April 1901 in the Aoyama Palace, Tokyo. His father, Imperial Crown Prince Yoshihito, was the son of one of the Meiji Emperor's concubines and had contracted cerebral meningitis as a baby. Despite his passion for modern things, Mutsuhito insisted that his stricken infant son be treated with traditional herbal medicines, rather than Western-style drugs. Yoshihito suffered irreversible brain damage and, although he had periods of good health, was an invalid for most of his life. He managed to get married, however, and father four sons. Following Yoshihito's death on Christmas Day 1926, Hirohito ascended the throne, as Japan's 124th Emperor.

His rule was called Showa, or Enlightened Peace. He believed that the success of his reign was inextricably entwined with Japan's quest for new territories. Like his grandfather the Meiji Emperor he looked to China, a bounteous country of 400 million people, for territorial exploitation, thus setting the course for Japan's participation in World War II. 'The world is now in a process of evolution,' he wrote in his Rescript. 'A new chapter is being opened in the history of human civilisation. This nation's settled policy always stands for progress and improvement.'

Owing to Yoshihito's illness, the cult of emperor worship had fallen into decline during his reign, and Hirohito and his courtiers launched a campaign to indoctrinate the masses in a new form of subservience to the throne, with strong military overtones. The Meiji Emperor's military glories were extolled to the new generation and the Showa monarchy was venerated as a revival of the Meiji era. Emperor Hirohito, dressed in military uniform and riding one of his imperial greys, was shown in newsreels at the head of his strutting armed forces.

Nationalism gained momentum when the Japanese economy collapsed in the Great Depression. The earnings of industrial and rural workers plummeted by as much as two-thirds, and the price of raw silk – one of the main sources of agricultural income – fell by 65 per cent. Rice riots broke out in the provinces. One by one the tenets of constitutional democracy which had been established in the Taisho era were rescinded, while the Japanese Navy cleverly circumvented the limits imposed by the Washington Naval Treaty by cutting back on the construction of battleships, the great leviathans of the deep, and building instead heavy cruisers and aircraft carriers, the warships of the future.

In September 1931, a handful of officers in the Kwantung Army, operating without the approval of the Japanese Cabinet, blew up a 31-inch section of Japanese-owned South Manchurian Railway line at Mukden, the city that had been the scene of a great Japanese victory against the Russians.[14] 'The Manchurian Incident' was blamed on Chinese saboteurs and provided the Army General Staff with a pretext for the occupation of the three rich Manchurian provinces, which, the following year, were converted into a Japanese possession named Manchukuo under the puppet rule of the last Manchu emperor, Henry Pu-Yi.

The Chinese Nationalist leader Chiang Kai-shek made no serious attempt to condemn the invasion which, he believed, would destroy his enemies, the Chinese Communists under Mao Tse-tung.

At the League of Nations in Geneva, Japan claimed that she was merely protecting her interests in northern China. This was not a war but an 'incident', and their Chinese adversaries were not soldiers but 'bandits'. Those captured in battle were denied the status of prisoners of war; many were massacred, tortured, or drafted into Japanese labour camps. The Japanese people were informed that the Manchurian campaign was being undertaken in order to 'punish the people of China for their refusal to acknowledge the superiority and leadership of the Japanese race and to co-operate with them'.[15]

When the Lytton Commission censored Japan over her actions in China in 1933, her chief delegate, Matsuoka, walked out of the League of Nations' chamber. The following year Japan tore up the naval agreements and laid down the keels for two Yamato class battleships, the most powerful warships ever built.

In July 1937 Japanese and Chinese troops exchanged gunfire at the Marco Polo Bridge over the Yunting River near Beijing. Unlike Muckden, the incident was unpremeditated, but it gave the Japanese General Staff an excuse to attack Chiang's Kuomintang forces in Beijing, Nanking and Shanghai. Wave after wave of Japanese bombers dropped incendiary bombs on Shanghai, and a Japanese fighter pilot contemptuously machine-gunned the limousine of the British Ambassador, Sir Hughe Knatchbull-Hugessen. He was badly wounded but survived. The Chinese, it was explained by Japanese propagandists, were being not conquered but 'liberated', and Britain was advised to get out of the way.

The worst atrocity occurred in the nationalist capital of Nanking when troops under Lieutenant-General Iwane Matsui, commander-in-chief of the central China area, massacred an estimated 250,000 people in December 1937. 'The slaughter of civilians is appalling,' reported an eye-witness, Dr Robert Wilson of the International Red Cross. 'Rape and brutality [are] almost beyond belief.'[16]

The Japanese referred to the Chinese as *chancorro*, a sub-human species who could be mistreated at will. Although Nanking was the most hideous – and best documented – of Japanese war crimes in China, there were hundreds of other instances of rape and murder. Chinese men were routinely used for bayonet practice, and medical experiments were conducted on healthy Chinese. Hirohito sanctioned the use of tear gas in China, even though it was banned under the Versailles peace treaty signed by the Japanese. He also authorised 'special chemical warfare units' to be sent to China.[17] Poison gas was used on hundreds of occasions against Chinese soldiers, while rats contaminated with plague at Unit 731, Japan's infamous biological warfare research unit, were dropped by planes in 'infected-rat air raids'.[18]

Through these unspeakable methods, the Japanese Army had by the start of 1938 overrun five provinces in northern China. As the year progressed, Japan turned her attentions to the south, in May landing troops at Amoy, 300 miles north-east of Hong Kong, and in October seizing Canton on the south coast and Hankow on the Yangtse.

By 1939, the Japanese population of Manchukuo exceeded 800,000, ranging from farmers and engineers to carpetbaggers and prostitutes. Chinese citizens were arrested and executed on the flimsiest of charges, while Japanese drug pushers ran a lucrative trade in opium, heroin and morphine among the Chinese population. Meanwhile, Manchurian timber, coal and iron ore fed Japan's vastly expanded production lines.[19] The rapid expansion, however, hit an unexpected obstacle the following year: 'The development of Manchukuo has proceeded at such a pace that it has over-reached itself and the effect of the European war has been disastrous,' A. G. Hard, Australia's Commercial Secretary, reported in June 1941. 'It will be many years before this country recovers. It seems the Japanese already there are determined to make as much money as possible in the shortest possible time and then return to their homeland.'[20]

The acquisition of new territories had done nothing to allay the fanatical rivalry between the Japanese Army and Navy, who were at loggerheads over strategy. The Army insisted that it should complete the subjugation of China before undertaking any moves to the south, while the Navy under Admiral Yamamoto was anxious to extend Japan's influence down to the Malay Barrier, the great arc of islands from Sumatra to Timor which included the Dutch oilfields. An Australian visitor to Japan reported to Australian Naval Intelligence, after talking to several young IJN officers over a few drinks, that they considered Singapore to be a great base, but that 'it is vulnerable from the north, by land, and also that it is useless without a fleet ... In general, the Japanese are all convinced that they have a "mission" to improve the world.'[21]

At Yamamoto's insistence, the Navy's Air Force was built up to the formidable strength of 1,750 fighters, torpedo bombers and bombers. Blooded in the war against China, Japanese pilots were equipped with fast, light and easily manoeuvrable Mitsubishi A6M Zero fighters, named after their 00 fuselage markings,[22] or the big Mitsubishi G4M 'Betty' bombers, or the slightly slower Type 96 'Nell'. The Zero was powerfully armed with two 7.7mm guns and two 20mm cannon, and had a maximum speed of 345 mph and a range, with detachable fuel tanks, of 1,500 miles, making it the most dangerous fighter of its time.[23] The Navy also possessed Long Lance oxygen-fuelled torpedoes, the most advanced in the world, while its gunnery could outrange any opponent and its navigators and pilots were trained in night fighting. Despite all of these known attributes, in the Western media the stereotype of the Japanese as 'little buck-toothed monkeys' still prevailed.

Japan's political system was so constructed that the Cabinet's responsibility was to the Emperor rather than to Parliament. The Government had no control over the armed forces, who provided the Army and Navy Ministers from its officer corps. The armed forces could compel any Cabinet to resign simply by withdrawing its representatives and refusing to nominate replacements. All important policy decisions were taken in the presence of the Emperor to give them the stamp of infallibility. Ministers and not the Emperor, however, were held responsible for the outcome of these policies.

The Japanese public, meanwhile, had been carefully conditioned for war. A three-year National Spiritual Mobilisation movement had been launched by the Government in October 1937 under which symbolic economies were encouraged, such as the 'rising-sun lunchbox' (*hinomaru bento*), a pickled red plum on a bed of white rice reproducing the pattern of the national flag (*Hinomaru*). When those three years were up, the Government announced the New Order movement to reorganise domestic society into more tightly controllable segments.

As in Nazi Germany, Japanese propaganda harped on the theme of racial purity. The Yamato (Japanese) race, it was claimed, was 98 per cent pure. Far from practising equality in Japanese society, the Yamato treated other subjects as lesser beings. The indigenous, light-skinned people of northern Hokkeido were persecuted, while the *eta* – Japan's untouchables – were treated as slaves.[24] The *eta* were confined to tasks surrounding death, such as the handling of dead bodies or butchering and tanning, all taboo under Shinto. This made them 'unclean' in Yamato eyes and they were segregated from the bulk of the population. When they encountered members of other castes, the *eta* were expected to display overt signs of subservience. Koreans, Formosans, Okinawans and other members of Japan's empire were regarded as colonials and also treated as inferiors.

Monitoring all levels of society for signs of dissent were the Kempeitai, the military police force founded by the Meiji Council of State in 1881 to deal with acts of indiscipline in the Japanese Army. Under Hirohito, the Kempeitai was granted a licence of life and death over all Japanese citizens, soldiers and civilians alike. Ordinary people were supposed to prostrate themselves in the street if a member of the Kempeitai approached and to remain prostrate until he had passed.

The Kempeitai worked hand in glove with the Tokubetsu Koto Keisatsu, or Tokko, the Special Higher Police better known as the Thought Police, who scoured Japanese society for evidence of liberal thinking. In one three-year period, 59,013 people were arrested for possessing 'dangerous thoughts'. Churchill wrote in 1937, 'I have often written about Germany re-arming. Let us gaze for a moment at Japan. Here again is a nation imbued with dreams of war and conquest, where every voice of moderation is silenced by death.'

While Japan regarded Britain and America as her future enemies, it was Soviet Russia that presented the main threat to her territorial ambitions in northern China. In April 1939, the 23rd Division of the Kwantung Army crossed the Manchukuo frontier into Outer Mongolia, with the apparent intention of defending its northern borders but actually with orders to occupy the heights of Nomonhan, a disputed sector on the Manchukuo-Korean-Mongolian frontier. This incursion forced Stalin – already wary of Japan after she had joined Germany in an Anti-Comintern Pact in 1936 – to dispatch a massive force under Lieutenant-General Georgi Zhukov to eastern Siberia to expel the invaders.

In the Battle of Khalkin-Gol, known by the Japanese as 'the Nomonhan Incident', tanks from opposing armies clashed on the battlefield for the first time. Zhukov's 500 T32 tanks – forerunners of the classic T34 which later destroyed Hitler's Panzers and Panthers – pulverised the Japanese tankettes and wreaked havoc among Japanese troops with their 76mm cannon. The Soviet commander also used 550 front-line aircraft, 20 cavalry squadrons and 35 infantry battalions, outnumbering the Japanese forces by three to two.

Zhukov's masterstroke was to convince the Japanese that he was mounting a defensive campaign and would not attack them. Japanese commanders intercepted false orders broadcast by Zhukov to his commanders in easily breakable codes. The Kwantung Army fell for the deception and sent many of its officers away on leave. They were absent when, on 20 August 1939, Zhukov unleashed the world's first blitzkrieg, a terrifying combination of armour, artillery, air power and infantry. Japanese losses totalled as many as 50,000 men killed and wounded.[25]

It was a salutary lesson and a timely one for the Japanese Army, which realised that Russia under Stalin was a much tougher proposition than it had been under the Tsar. But there was an even greater shock in store for the Japanese military establishment. Within days of the defeat at Khalkin-Gol, Germany signed the Russo-German Non-aggression Pact in Moscow. The treaty guaranteed Russia immunity from a German invasion in the West, while offering Hitler a free hand to invade Poland.

Japan was horrified. At a stroke, the threat to her northern flank by Russia forced the abandonment of all plans for southern expansion. Huge numbers of troops were mobilised on the Eastern Front; a Soviet attack was expected at any moment. But Stalin, while taking a large bite out of Poland himself, stayed his hand in the East. It wasn't until France fell in June the following year and a German invasion of the British Isles looked increasingly likely that Japan revived her plans for the southward advance.

On 1 August 1940 at the behest of Hirohito, the new Premier, Prince Fumimaro Konoe, declared a 'New Order in Greater East Asia'. Konoe, a member of the Great Asia Association, had articulated this doctrine in a speech to Parliament as early as 1935. 'We must be prepared to devise new principles of international peace based on our own standpoint, on our own wisdom,' he said. 'We must then boldly and candidly challenge the whole world with the righteousness of our principles.' The limited goal of 'East Asia' had now been extended to 'Greater East Asia', which Britain interpreted to mean all of South East Asia.

Prince Konoe had held the Prime Ministership from June 1937 to January 1939 and was thought of in the West as a moderate, partly because he was known to have a liking for English poetry. However, he quickly became a tool of the militarists. The driving force behind the New Order was the philosophy of *hakko ichi'u* which sprang from the three central beliefs that had dominated Japanese life since the Meiji Restoration: that Japan was the centre of the world, ruled by the *Tenno*, or Emperor, a divine being who derived his divinity through ancestral descent from Amaterasu Omikami; that the *kami* (or pantheon of Japanese gods) had Japan under their special protection and thus the people and soil of *Dai Nippon* (Mighty Japan) and all its institutions were superior to all others; and that all of these attributes were fundamental to the *Kodoshugisha* (the Imperial Way) which gave Japan a divine mission to bring all nations under one rule.[26] The Yamato people would become head of the human family under the *Tenno* and oversee all other nations with a patrician benevolence.[27]

The task of propagating the New Order was placed in the hands of two hawks, Foreign Minister Yosuke Matsuoka and War Minister General Hideki Tojo, former head of the Kempeitai military secret police in Manchuria. Both agitated for Japan to sign the Tripartite Pact, a military alliance with Germany and Italy which would advance Japan's international aims but place her in conflict with Britain and, indirectly, the United States. Conservative forces in the Imperial Navy under the Navy Minister Vice-Admiral Zengo Yoshida opposed the alliance, warning that Japan would have essential war materials for only one year if imports from British possessions and the US were stopped. 'Only a fierce but reckless tiger will rush into hostilities with a war potential sufficient for but a year,' he said.[28]

Noting Japan's hesitancy, Hitler sneered at her people as 'lacquered half-monkeys'.[29] The staunchly pro-German Matsuoka and the army clique paid no heed to the doubters, and when Yoshida suffered a nervous breakdown his objections were swept aside. Churchill later declared, 'Nations, like individuals, commit irrational acts and there were forces at work in Japan, violent, murderous, fanatical and explosive forces which no one could measure.'

On 27 September 1940 the Tripartite Pact came into being in Berlin; under it Japan recognised the leadership of Hitler and Mussolini in 'the New Order in Europe', while Germany and Italy recognised Japan's dominance in 'Greater East Asia'. The pact's main aim was to encourage the United States to maintain its isolationist stance and not intervene in East Asia or Europe, either as a combatant or as a supporter of any of the signatories' enemies.

British Intelligence was well aware of Japan's military planning through its signals intelligence (Sigint) derived from intercepts of Japanese telegraphic messages. Commander Eric Nave, a prickly member of the Royal Australian Navy's cryptographic unit, and Hugh Foss, a red-bearded Scot, were the two principal figures involved in breaking Japanese naval codes and ciphers in the pre-war years.

The Japanese written language was based on *kanji* – pictorial characters originally borrowed from the Chinese – and about 70 phonetic symbols called *kana*. To adapt the Morse code, a system of transliteration known as *romanji* was developed in which the *kana* syllables were spelt out in Roman letters. Luckily, Nave's Royal Navy operators intercepted a practice message in which the Japanese operator had obligingly run through the entire Japanese Morse code symbol by symbol. Then, when Hirohito's father died at the end of 1926, the official report of his death and the succession of his son to the Chrysanthemum Throne were relayed word for word to every Japanese diplomatic, naval and military outpost around the world. It was a simple task to follow it through the various codes, breaking each in turn. However, in 1939 Japan adopted a totally new coding system, including the main Japanese Navy code, JN25, which first appeared in June of that year. Bletchley Park had broken it within weeks.

Japan's own intelligence efforts were extremely thorough. She had used spies effectively against China in 1895 and Russia in 1904–05, while her naval operators had intercepted Russian fleet signals in the same war. During its Siberian intervention in the early 1920s, the Imperial Japanese Army had formed Special Service Organisations (*tokumu kikan*) to gather intelligence on Soviet guerrillas and to carry out sabotage and subversion (*boryaku*). The Japanese Foreign Ministry had its own political intelligence agency, which relied on journalists and businessmen, as well as military and naval attachés in diplomatic posts.

Through these sources, the vulnerability of the Singapore Naval Base was well known to the Japanese. In December 1940, they received documentary proof of the woeful state of Britain's forces in Asia when the German naval attaché in Tokyo handed over copies of secret British reports seized from the Blue Funnel cargo liner *Automedon*. The ship had been intercepted on 11 November, 300 miles off the Sumatran coast, by the German raider *Atlantis*. The *Atlantis* struck so quickly, shelling the bridge and killing the captain and six officers, that there had been no opportunity for anyone to destroy a bag containing highly secret documents before it was seized by an armed boarding party.

The documents were addressed to Sir Robert Brooke-Popham and included a copy of the minutes of the War Cabinet meeting of 15 August 1940. These summarised Britain's strategic policy in the Far East, including details on the defence of Malaya and the Dutch East Indies. They also revealed that Hong Kong and Borneo were indefensible, while Britain would not be able to provide adequate reinforcements to save Singapore in the event of a Japanese invasion. Furthermore, the Japanese were intrigued to learn that Britain would not go to war if they attacked Thailand or took over all of Indochina.

Japan had already occupied northern Indochina at the 'invitation' of the Vichy French authorities, despite a warning from the US State Department that such a move would not be tolerated. To show he wasn't bluffing, President Franklin D. Roosevelt slapped a partial ban on the export of American oil and scrap iron to Japan. One of the voices raised most loudly in favour of Japanese expansionism was that of Yosuke Matsuoka, who had grown up in the United States and experienced anti-Japanese discrimination from the age of 13.

Much to America's chagrin, Matsuoka scored an important diplomatic coup when Thailand, seeing an opportunity to regain territory lost to the French in Laos and Cambodia, made overtures to Japan through her Prime Minister, Major-General Luang Pibulsongkram, to intercede on her behalf with the Vichy regime.[30] Matsuoka agreed, and much of north-western Cambodia was duly handed back to Thailand. The price of Japanese mediation was that Thailand accepted the New Order and agreed not make pacts with countries that could be considered hostile to Japan. The American envoy reported that the Thai leaders 'in order to acquire their mess of pottage from the prostrate French in Indochina have gone along and deliberately put their heads into the Japanese noose'.[31]

The Navy assured Prince Konoe that not only was it safe to take over the rest of Indochina, but it was a necessary strategic move to secure southern bases to prevent an American blockade of the sacred home islands. Matsuoka, however, knew that Japan could not afford to make any further southward moves until the Russian bear had been muzzled. To resolve the Soviet threat, he negotiated the Soviet-Japanese Neutrality Pact, signed in Moscow on 13 April 1941. This secured Japan's northern flank and enabled her to proceed with her takeover of Indochina. Stalin was so impressed with Matsuoka that he saw him off at Moscow railway station and gave him a comradely bear hug.[32]

It was at this point that the War Office appointed a new GOC Malaya, who was tailor-made to provide a calming influence in Singapore following the unsettling occupancy of the fractious General Bond.

CHAPTER 5

Quiet Commander

WHEN LIEUTENANT-GENERAL ARTHUR E. PERCIVAL lowered his long thin legs on to the tarmac at Kallang airport on 16 May 1941 to take charge of British defences in Singapore, the war in Europe had been raging for 19 months. 'I realised that there was the double danger,' he said, 'either of being left in an inactive command for some years if war did not break out in the East or, if it did, of finding myself involved in a pretty sticky business with the inadequate forces which are usually to be found in the distant parts of our Empire in the early stages of war.'[1]

Percival had no idea that the Japanese would attack Malaya in 205 days' time, but he had no doubts that the clock was ticking. The British Army, unlike the Royal Navy and Royal Air Force, appreciated the skills of their counterparts in the Imperial Japanese Forces. As far back as 1924, Major A. C. Alford of the Royal Artillery had written that 'the Japanese Army is the most powerful fighting force in the world today'.[2] Of most immediate concern to the conscientious new General Officer Commanding Malaya was the fact that he was running late. He had been due to leave England by air in April, but because his flying boat developed engine trouble he had not taken off until five weeks after the date of his appointment. The flight from London had then taken 14 days, with refuelling stops at Gibraltar, Malta, Alexandria, Basra, Karachi and Rangoon, where he had transferred to an RAF bomber for the final legs to Alor Star and then down to Singapore.

It was a long, hot, tedious flight, and Percival had borne the discomfort with stoical silence. He had spent his waiting time in London at the War Office discussing the Far East situation with his mentor, the Chief of the Imperial General Staff Sir John Dill, and swotting up on the latest intelligence reports from Malaya and Singapore. One of the documents in the General Staff's archives was a 1937 report by Major G. T. Wards, an assistant military attaché who had seen the Japanese Army in action in Shanghai. He reported that it was 'a formidable force, well able to cope with any opposition likely to be met with at the present time in the Far East'. He concluded that Japan was hostile towards Britain and that she had decided to eliminate all foreign nations from Asia.[3]

Percival was well over six feet tall, angular and sparely built but immensely fit, with a good eye for shooting and great cricket and tennis skills. He had a clipped moustache and two protruding front teeth which inevitably led to cracks about buck-toothed rabbits. He came from solid, respectable, middle-class Protestant stock, having been born on Boxing Day 1887 at Aspenden, Hertfordshire, where his father worked as agent for the highly profitable Hamels Park estate. He was given the forenames Arthur Ernest.[4]

After attending Bengeo, a local private school, young Arthur went off to join his much brighter elder brother at Rugby in 1902. He studied Greek and Latin but, in the words of one of his masters, was 'not a good classic'. Throughout his time at Rugby he had the misfortune to be compared unfavourably with his brother, and he would probably have developed a sense of inferiority had he not excelled in non-academic areas, notably as a member of the school's Rifle Corps and as a fine cross-country runner, batsman and tennis player.

There was a direct route to Sandhurst through the school's Army Class, but Percival did not take it. On leaving Rugby in 1906 he joined the iron-ore merchants Naylor, Benzon & Company in the City of London. His military career started when he was 26: on the first day of World War I he resigned from his office job and enlisted in the Army. Without setting foot in Sandhurst, he was sent to France in 1915 as a lieutenant with the 7th Bedfordshire Regiment, saw action on the Somme and was awarded the Military Cross, a Distinguished Service Order, the Croix de Guerre, a Brevet Majority and two Mentions in Dispatches.

After commanding a platoon, he took charge of a battalion in 1917 with the temporary rank of lieutenant-colonel and then, for a brief period in 1918, was put in charge of a brigade. His biographers say he forged strong bonds with the fighting soldiers under his command in all of these positions and was widely respected by both officers and other ranks. He was, it seemed, destined for great things.[5] His arrival at the Staff College at Camberley, however, was delayed by two further campaigns. In 1919 he served as second-in-command of the 46th Royal Fusiliers fighting Bolshevik forces in northern Russia – where he earned a Bar to his DSO and another Mention in Dispatches. After two months' leave on his return to England, he joined the 1st Battalion of the Essex Regiment at Kinsale, County Cork, as a company commander.

The battalion had been ordered to enforce a policy of search and arrest of IRA leaders at the height of the Troubles. Percival was put in charge of the riverside market town of Bandon, where he discovered that his troops were half-trained recruits and that the local Royal Irish Constabulary, whom he was supposed to protect, were suffering from a crisis of morale following a series of violent IRA seizures of weapons and explosives.

As Secretary of State for War, Churchill's solution to the Irish problem was to enlist 8,000 ex-soldiers to reinforce the RIC, leading to the formation of the notorious Black and Tans and later the even more extreme Auxiliary Division. Percival thought them 'generally a very fine lot of men', and as one unit was based only a few yards from Bandon Barracks, he must have been aware of their thuggish activities.[6]

Following the assassination of an RIC sergeant at church in July 1920, Percival arrested Tom Hales and Patrick Harte on suspicion of murder. His reputation soared among his Essex colleagues and the British public when Hales was discovered to be commander of the IRA West Cork Brigade and Harte the brigade's quartermaster. The *Daily Mail* exulted in the fact that the capture 'has robbed Sinn Feiners of West Cork of two strong leaders and striking personalities'. It also admitted that 'both men were injured while being taken'.

Although there was no evidence connecting the two men to the sergeant's murder, they were beaten by members of the Essex Battalion on the way to the barracks. Harte never recovered from a blow to the head with a rifle butt and he died some years later in a mental hospital. Tom Hales named Percival as the 'Chief Architect of the dastardly performance'. In his biography of IRA leader Michael Collins, Tim Pat Coogan wrote, 'On capturing Hales and Harte [Percival] first ordered that they be stripped and beaten. After this he had them dressed, bound with leather straps and caused a charge of guncotton to be placed on their backs. The detonators failed to go off and the prisoners were made to run while being prodded with bayonets. They were then thrown into a lorry and on the way to Bandon Barracks were again beaten with rifle butts, Harte receiving a particularly severe blow to the temple from which he apparently never recovered.' After more beatings at the barracks at the hands of an Intelligence Officer named as Captain Kelly, an Irishman, Hales was taken upstairs to a room where there were six officers, including Kelly and Percival. He was then allegedly beaten with canes and had his fingernails ripped out with pliers until he passed out.[7]

Commenting on these allegations, Percival's biographer Major-General

Clifford Kinvig says, 'In the sense that he was responsible for their capture, this is certainly true. As to any subsequent brutality, it is most unlikely that Percival was involved, even indirectly. Given the very clear General Staff HQ Ireland instructions on the treatment of prisoners during interrogation, mere expediency on the part of an experienced officer such as Percival, aside from his own strong principles, would have ruled it out.' General Kinvig later described the allegations as 'entirely unsubstantiated'.[8]

Percival had created so much trouble for the IRA that Tom Barry, a former bombardier in the British Army and commander of the 'flying column' of the IRA's West Cork Brigade, resolved to assassinate him. The first attempt failed when Percival did not follow his usual routine of leaving Bandon Barracks for dinner at a regular hour. The Sinn Fein High Command then offered a reward of £1,000 for his capture dead or alive, but that came to nought.

In the New Year's Honours list, Percival was awarded the OBE for gallantry in counter-insurgency operations against the IRA. He was also promoted to Intelligence Officer of the Essex Battalion with the rank of major. When Barry was arrested by the Essexes shortly afterwards, he was examined by Major Percival. 'The cruelty of his set face was accentuated by the two buck-teeth which showed like small fangs at either side of his bitter mouth,' he wrote. Percival, however, let Barry slip through his fingers. He merely listened to an account of the prisoner's interrogation, stared into his eyes, removed his hat, stared at him once more, then ordered him to be released.[9]

Michael Collins sent a hit squad to London to murder Percival while he was on holiday in March 1921. On 16 March the assassins waited for him at Liverpool Street Station after a tip-off, but fled minutes before his arrival when they learned from one of their informants that Scotland Yard was on the way to arrest them. Back in County Cork, Percival led a raid which killed one of the gunmen, Tadhg O'Sullivan.

The Essex Regiment, known in Bandon as 'Percival's Crowd', then moved to safer climes at Carrickfergus in the heart of loyalist Ulster. In 1922 Percival formed an attachment with a local Irish girl, Margaret Elizabeth MacGregor Greer, of Tallylagan Manor, County Tyrone. Known as Betty to her family, she was to become his wife, although in his methodical way it took him several years to summon up the courage to propose.

Percival was already 36 when he reached Camberley in 1923 after the intervention of the War Minister, Winston Churchill, who was familiar with his exploits in Russia and Ireland. He had met Churchill and the Prime

Minister, David Lloyd George, at Inverness Town Hall in September 1921 to give an expert witness account of the Troubles at the time the Government was engaging in truce negotiations with the Irish.[10]

Percival found the Staff College enormously to his liking. The college commandant, General Edmund 'Tiny' Ironside, who had commanded the British forces against the Soviets in northern Russia and already knew Percival from that campaign, described him as 'an officer of exceptional ability and intelligence' and marked him down as one of eight outstanding students for accelerated promotion.[11] His sporting prowess also made him popular with his younger contemporaries when he whacked a half-century in his first cricket match.

After graduation, Percival spent three years with the Nigeria Regiment at Kaduna, West Africa; during his home leave in 1927 he and Betty were married. Returning to Britain, Percival spent a year as a student at the Royal Naval College, Greenwich, and was then appointed an instructor at Camberley, where General Dill was now commandant. Dill had no doubts about Percival's capabilities, writing in a confidential report in 1932 that his protégé had 'an outstanding ability, wide military knowledge, good judgment and is a very quick and accurate worker'. Dill thought it prudent to append a note about Percival's appearance: 'He has not altogether an impressive presence and one may therefore fail, at first meeting him, to appreciate his sterling worth.'

To ensure that Percival's abilities were not overlooked, Dill personally took charge of his career. After two years as commander of the 2nd Cheshire Regiment, Percival was sent to the Imperial Defence College in 1935 on his patron's recommendation. Dill had then moved from Camberley to become Director of Military Operations and Intelligence at the War Office, where he was instrumental in securing Percival's promotion to full colonel and his appointment to a post that would have a direct bearing on the rest of his life: General Staff Officer 1st Grade (GSO1), Malaya Command.

Percival's ambition was to serve with troops in Britain rather than take up another staff job in the tropics, but he agreed to the posting on condition that he serve for two years instead of the usual three. Percival was now a father as well as a husband. While he had been at Greenwich, Betty had given birth to a daughter, Dorinda Margery, and their second child, a son named James, was born in Singapore. Percival returned to England in 1938 and was appointed Brigadier General Staff (BGS) Aldershot, to serve under Dill who was then GOC at the home of the British Army.

After the outbreak of World War II, Dill became commander of I Corps and appointed Percival his BGS. He was with the British Expeditionary Force in France but was brought back to England in February 1940 to command the 43rd Wessex Division. He had been in this post for only a matter of weeks when Dill was made Vice-Chief of the Imperial General Staff. One of his first actions was to summon Percival to join him at the War Office.

After Dunkirk, Percival took command of the 44th Territorial Division and was engaged in anti-invasion work with this division when he received a War Office telegram promoting him to temporary lieutenant-general and appointing him General Officer Commanding Malaya. The next step up from a division would normally have been command of a corps containing several divisions, but Dill had seen to it that he had been given command of an entire army.[12] He settled his wife and family in Hertfordshire and set off for the East, where one of his most urgent tasks was to train the thousands of green young Indian troops who had arrived in Singapore after only the most elementary instruction.

Percival soon discovered that the commander of III Indian Corps, Lieutenant-General Sir Lewis Heath, objected to taking orders from him. Heath was two years older than Percival and had previously outranked him. Their respective commands, Headquarters India and the War Office, appeared to have given no thought to whether their two appointees would get along together.

Lewis Macclesfield 'Piggy' Heath had been born in Poona on 23 November 1885 and educated at Wellington. Going up the stairs after Chapel one evening a boy had slapped him on the bottom and said, 'You fat little piggy.' That became a nickname that followed him to Sandhurst and stuck to him throughout his service. In fact, Heath had slimmed down over the years and was a handsome man, with attractive laughter lines around his eyes and an engaging smile, but he had a withered left arm after being wounded during an attack on the Dujailah Redoubt, Mesopotamia, on 8 March 1916 while serving with the 59th Scinde Rifles. In 1939 he was raised to the rank of major-general and at the outbreak of war was given command of the new 5th Indian Division, which quickly distinguished itself in the Siege of Keren in the Battle for Eritrea.

Two years later Heath was promoted to lieutenant-general to command III Indian Corps in Malaya. He had recently married a much younger woman, an Auckland nursing sister named Katherine Lonergan. There was friction from the beginning between Heath and Percival, and the latter, lacking the confrontational style to establish his authority, allowed the problem to fester. It became apparent to other commanders that Heath, being the stronger character, overawed Percival.[13] The one bright spot was that Percival had struck up a friendship with the Air Officer Commanding, Conway Pulford. Like Percival, Pulford had left his family back in England, and he accepted an invitation to share the GOC's official quarters, Flagstaff House.

Financial strictures which had bedevilled the building of the Naval Base during the 1920s and '30s now inhibited the build-up of Malaya's defensive forces. Treasury bureaucrats, operating through the War Office, dead-batted every request submitted by Percival for assistance, including pleas for a realistic rise in the daily rate paid to local labourers to work on fixed defences. The going rate for a labourer in Singapore was $1.10 a day plus rations, but the War Office expected Percival to offer less than half that – a miserly 45 cents without rations. The result was that the labourers refused to work for the Army until the rate was raised. Moreover, the War Office machine cranked out its decisions so slowly that Percival's planning was continually disrupted by long delays. It was the same story with equipment. Anticipating that the Japanese would include tanks in their invasion force, he asked twice for a tank regiment to be sent to Singapore, but none arrived.

Since his previous tour, Percival had undergone a change of heart on the question of fixed defences, and his difficulties in obtaining labour to build them seem to have hardened his attitude. Brigadier Ivan Simson of Scottish Command had been sent to Malaya as Chief Engineer a few weeks earlier. He was profoundly shocked to discover that all senior commanders were indifferent to expanding and modernising Singapore's defences. Many of them had fought in World War I, yet they seemed to have forgotten 'the tremendous stopping power of barbed wire covered by fire from trenches and pillboxes'.[14]

Simson believed this 'anti-defence complex' emanated from a fallacious belief that fixed defences were an obstacle to winning a war and that 'attack was the best form of defence'. It had been noted towards the end of World War I that troops became reluctant to attack across open ground once they had become accustomed to the safety of trenches and well-defended posi-tions. But the situation in Malaya was quite different: Singapore was supposed to be a fortress, and fortresses needed all-round defences in order to survive an attack by a better equipped and better trained army.[15]

A further complication arose for Percival when Oriental Mission, the eastern branch of the Special Operations Executive launched in Europe by Hugh Dalton's Ministry of Economic Warfare, opened an office at

Singapore in May 1941. Commanded by Valentine St John Killery, SOE operatives were tasked with committing acts of sabotage and subversion and disseminating black propaganda in enemy and enemy-controlled countries. '[Killery] and his staff were keen and capable, but they had no experience and very little knowledge of how to set about their work,' Brooke-Popham says in his Dispatch. 'There was a curious reluctance on the part of many people to have anything to do with these activities, or to help on the work.'

Considering the opposition lined up against him – much of it from Brooke-Popham himself – it was a wonder that Killery achieved anything at all. He set up No. 101 Special Training School in a spacious two-storey bungalow at Tanjong Balai, at the mouth of the Jurong River on Singapore Island, to train guerrilla fighters to form 'stay-behind' parties to work behind enemy lines if and when the Japanese invasion took place. The school was run by Lieutenant-Colonel Jim Gavin, an officer in the Royal Engineers, and his second-in-command Captain Freddie Spencer Chapman. Lieutenant-Colonel Alan Warren of the Royal Marines acted as liaison officer with GHQ Far East.

Spencer Chapman, a Seaforth Highlander who had once taught the future Duke of Edinburgh at Gordonstoun, says that a detailed plan for stay-behind parties, including Chinese, Malays and Indians, was put to Shenton Thomas for approval in August 1941 but was rejected. A variety of reasons was trotted out: the scheme would be too great a drain on European manpower; Europeans would be easily spotted in occupied territory; the morale of the Asian population would be damaged by 'defeatist talk' that the enemy might hold part of Malaya. 'In 1941 the High Command in Malaya were not in the least interested in guerrilla warfare in any of its forms,' Spencer Chapman says. 'The idea of stay-behind parties consisting of Europeans and Asiatics seemed an extravagant and impracticable notion; the defence of Malaya was considered to be a purely military undertaking and to be already well under control "through the proper channels".'[16]

Killery had neglected to inform Percival of his plans, and when the GOC accidentally found out about the school's existence he complained to Brooke-Popham. 'I discussed with the GOC the question of left-behind parties in Malaya,' Brooke-Popham wrote to Killery. 'As a result of this conversation, I have decided not to proceed with this project.'

A further opportunity was missed when Lai Te, the secretary of the Communist Party of Malaya who provided a useful intelligence service to Singapore Special Branch, approached his controller to suggest that

Communist volunteers should be trained by the British Army. They could be formed into special defence units and come under the direct orders of General Percival. When the proposal was placed before the Governor, he rejected it out of hand. In no circumstances would he agree to arm a bunch of Communist subversives.[17]

Roosevelt, who mistrusted British imperialism, was adamant that British troops should not launch a forestalling action against Japan in Thailand. To circumvent that problem, Killery decided to stage a *coup d'état* in Thailand which would depose the pro-Japanese Prime Minister. Killery's intention was to replace the General with a pro-British figurehead who would invite British forces into Thailand and thus frustrate Japanese plans for an invasion of that country. On 30 July he cabled his plan to SOE, London, adding that he realised 'the obvious danger of Japanese military action to protect existing regime during disorder of *coup d'état*'.[18]

The British Minister 'Bing' Crosby was outraged when Killery outlined the plan to him. He protested to the Foreign Office about the 'reckless and irresponsible amateurs serving under Killery' and the plan was abandoned.[19] Percival's verdict on Oriental Mission in his Dispatch was hardly flattering: 'It suffered from an excess of secrecy and from a lack of knowledge on the part of the gentlemen advising as to how to set about the work. Thus valuable time was lost. Later, however, some very useful work was done by this organisation.'

Meanwhile, Singapore maintained its appearance of unruffled calm. Lorraine Stumm gave birth to a daughter, Sheridan, at Singapore General Hospital on 22 June 1941, the day Hitler launched Operation Barbarossa against Russia. Harley, who had been promoted to flight lieutenant, visited the hospital just in time to hand his baby daughter to her mother. The couple moved to Amber Mansions next to the Cathay Building in Orchard Road, and as soon as Lorraine had hired an amah to help with the baby she was able to return work at the *Tribune*.

The invasion of Russia provided Japan with an unexpected opportunity to strike in Indochina but Foreign Minister Matsuoka immediately reversed his support for the southward advance in favour of an attack against his erstwhile ally, Russia. His reversal angered Prince Konoe, who ditched him as Foreign Minister. At the end of July, 40,000 Japanese troops landed unopposed in southern Indochina – and Japan had acquired a naval base within 750 miles of Singapore.

In retaliation, President Roosevelt froze all Japanese funds in the US, which prevented her from buying any American products. Such severe economic sanctions, when supported by Britain and Holland, cut off nearly all Japan's supplies of raw materials including, crucially, oil. Hirohito and Japan's militarist clique were faced with the stark choice between abandoning their territorial ambitions in Asia, or going to war and capturing the oilfields of the Dutch East Indies and the rich rubber, tin, iron ore, manganese and bauxite resources of Malaya.

Any chance that Percival and Pulford had of receiving the necessary arms and warplanes to defend Malaya had evaporated with the invasion of Russia. Churchill immediately embraced Stalin, a man for whom he had previously felt only revulsion, as his ally in the fight against 'Nazidom' and ordered British tanks and planes to be shipped to the northern Russian ports of Archangel and Murmansk to reinforce the Red Army. The first convoy departed on 21 August, with 48 operational Hurricanes on board an aircraft carrier, while more Hurricanes were stacked in crates on the decks of freighters. Hundreds of tanks followed shortly afterwards and a monthly shipment of 250 tanks and 200 planes was promised until June 1942, even though the Russians already had 39 armoured divisions, three more than their German adversaries.

Ismay admitted that 'it was equipment that we most grievously needed for ourselves – tanks, aircraft, anti-tank guns, anti-aircraft guns. We were giving away our life's blood.'[20] He could have added that Churchill's blinkered view was also throwing away Britain's chances of retaining her eastern Empire. Ismay was aware of the threat, noting that 'we would be unable to do very much to strengthen our position in the Far East'.

Churchill's second priority was to supply more tanks and planes to power Auchinleck's offensive against Rommel in the Middle East as a prelude to the invasion of Sicily to knock Italy out of the war. In view of the Prime Minister's single-minded determination to destroy Germany before considering the Japanese threat, Percival had little chance of getting his reinforcements. Brooke-Popham complained to Ismay, 'I wish I could see more clearly how to adapt Vildebeestes to attain the object of sinking Japanese troopships if they're escorted by cruisers and covered by fighters off carriers.'[21]

Towards the end of August Bill Drower moved into a little pavilion in the garden of a large boarding house in Orchard Road. After leaving the Japanese Embassy, he had joined the Territorials as a gunner. 'When Chamberlain declared war, I was in the Royal Horse Artillery, except we had no horses and no artillery. I was a plain gunner until 1940 when there was a boxing competition and I had a rather fine scrap with a miner. The colonel said, "Take his name," and I was on the way to being sent to officers' training camp at Aldershot.'

Drower had developed into an impressive figure, 6 foot 3 inches tall with clear blue eyes, curly hair, an Errol Flynn moustache and a broad, smiling mouth set in a firm jaw. After graduation, he joined British Intelligence which was looking for linguists. He had good German and some knowledge of Japanese. 'They were looking for officers who spoke Japanese to go to Singapore,' he says. 'I got the posting, but I knew very little Japanese and had to work like hell on the boat.'

Drower was based at Fort Canning – 'a fairly dull place: not even a canteen' – while a Combined Operations Room for the Army and Air Force was being built in a long, narrow hut in Sime Road adjacent to the Singapore Golf Club. 'I did the rounds of the battalions and met people, including Brooke-Popham, whom my parents had known when he was based at the Habbaniyah airfield in Iraq,' Drower recalls. 'I was only a lowly captain and he gave me the minimum courtesy. I invited some of the local people to my new home for a cocktail party. It was held in the garden beneath several large trees full of fruit-bats who bestowed profusely unwelcome gifts on them.'

The most important social event that month was Lady McElwaine's fair at the residence of the Chief Justice, while Raffles Hotel held an Old-Fashioned Night at which women dressed up as Edwardian showgirls and the men came as Burlington Berties. But it was not all merrymaking. English women worked alongside Eurasian and Asian women in the Passive Defence Services, in First Aid and Home Nursing and in the Medical and Transport Auxiliary. Leslie Froggatt says, 'All our women friends flung themselves into lessons on blood, bones and bandages.' European men joined the Air Raids Precautions service and the Auxiliary Fire Brigade, or enlisted in the Straits Settlements Volunteer Force as officers and NCOs in charge of Asian recruits guarding key installations, such as bridges and power stations.[22]

Froggatt's son, Leslie Jnr, was surprised at the atmosphere in the colony when he arrived for a visit with the merchant marine. 'My parents went to Singapore when I was 14 and I was left in England,' he says. 'I stayed there until the war broke out, working for Shell. Two of us put our applications to join up into the same pillar box and my friend was accepted but I was told to wait. I joined the Merchant Navy and my ship stopped off in Singapore. It was a bit unreal, having come from England. Life hadn't changed very much and it seemed rather strange. They were having charity balls to raise money for food parcels to send to the UK.'[23]

Churchill had not forgotten the Far East entirely. He sent Duff Cooper, the 51-year-old former Minister of Information, on a tour of investigation to Singapore to ascertain how Britain's military, civil and political administrations in the region might be co-ordinated to help the war effort. Cooper, who had resigned from Chamberlain's Cabinet over Munich, was given the title of Chancellor of the Duchy of Lancaster, and Cabinet rank. With his wife Lady Diana Cooper, one of the most striking society beauties of the age, he touched down in Singapore on 11 September 1941 after travelling via the United States, where he had informed the Washington press corps that it would be suicidal for the Japanese to enter the war, adding 'but the Japanese are, as a people, addicted to suicide'.[24]

Lady Diana was the daughter of the Duchess of Rutland and the 'palely handsome, intensely romantic' *bon vivant* Harry Cust.[25] She had made her stage début as the Madonna in the immensely successful play *The Miracle* and, billed under her maiden name Diana Manners, had starred in several films including *The Glorious Adventure* (1922) and *The Virgin Queen* (1923). She had retired from show business to run a pig farm in Bognor but was delighted to be back in the spotlight. 'Commander-in-Chief Brooke-Popham on the jetty,' she noted, 'and the whole set-up entirely to my liking – liveries of ostentatious gold and white and scarlet on Malay and Indian servants, ADCs. Movie-men, gaping coolies. God's acres being mown by the fingers and thumbs of natives advancing on all fours in a serried row and plucking the growing grass-blades.'

The Coopers spent their first week in Singapore as guests of Shenton Thomas at Government House – 'cool as a fishnet', according to Lady Diana, 'no doors or windows closed'. Thomas was furious over Duff Cooper's appointment but successfully hid his displeasure. His main concern was that Duff Cooper would expose the failings of the Malayan Civil Service. Duff Cooper's son John Julius Norwich, on the other hand, described his father as 'a romantic, passionate, dramatic man' and said his mission in Singapore was 'to knock the heads of the three Services together'.[26]

The new arrivals moved into the 'Duff Coopery' in Jervois Road, two houses with adjoining gardens, which served as both residence and offices. With a staff of six dancing attendance, Duff Cooper travelled around his new constituency on a tour of inspection and compiled information for a report on the current state of Britain's Far Eastern possessions. 'The future is so uncertain and so dependent on the little yellow gentlemen who, in my opinion, have not yet made up their own minds on what to do next,' he wrote to a friend.[27]

In October, Brooke-Popham headed back to Melbourne to brief the new Australian Prime Minister, John Curtin, who had taken over from Arthur Fadden. Addressing the War Council, Brooke-Popham said that Malaya was going from strength to strength, with the arrival of another Australian brigade and one from India. A further anti-tank regiment and anti-aircraft units were on the way from England. The strength of the Air Force was improving and there were now five fighter squadrons equipped with Brewster Buffaloes 'which are superior to the Japanese and well suited for the work in Malaya'.

Curtin had heard all this before. What had happened, he asked, to the 336 aircraft required for the defence of Burma, Malaya and Borneo that had been promised by the Chiefs of Staff? Brooke-Popham replied that there were about 180 aircraft in hand, including seven Catalina flying boats based on Ceylon for surveillance in the Indian Ocean. Curtin was unimpressed. The vital reinforcements that had been promised were still outstanding, he said, and supply 'had not been as effective as might have been hoped'. He was not unmindful of the demands on the United Kingdom to meet Russian requirements but considered that the urgent needs of the Far East should be represented strongly to the UK authorities. Brooke-Popham replied that he had made all possible representations short of resigning but he felt that the Chiefs of Staff were not neglecting the Far East and that probably they had made a fair allocation from the resources available.[28]

Brooke-Popham noted a grittier, less subservient attitude among the Labour Prime Minister and his ministers. In a letter to Sir Arthur Street at the Air Ministry in London, he stressed the importance of making Australia 'feel that we, in England, look upon them as definitely part of one Empire and we must do everything we can to keep them in the Empire and not run any risk of their slipping out of it'.[29]

When Brooke-Popham returned to Singapore, Duff Cooper invited him to a conference with the Governor, Admiral Layton, the ambassadors to China and Thailand, and Sir Earle Page, who was on his way to London as the Australian envoy to the British War Cabinet. Astonishingly, Percival and Pulford were excluded, even though Cooper had already ascertained that Brooke-Popham – whom he called 'Old Pop-off' – was a spent force.

The conference unanimously agreed that the only deterrent to Japanese aggression in South East Asia would be the presence of a British battle fleet based at Singapore. As no fleet was available, the Government should be urged to send one or two battleships to Singapore for propaganda purposes. The conference also noted that with Japan concentrating her forces in

Manchuria and with the north-east monsoon about to break on Malaya's east coast, no Japanese invasion of Malaya was likely in the foreseeable future.

Duff Cooper's report to Churchill, dated 29 October, echoed Brooke-Popham's optimism and consequently failed to ring any alarm bells in Downing Street. He contented himself with some rather anodyne comments – the system under which two Commanders in Chief, one for the Far East and one for China, lived side by side in the Naval Base was 'unsound' and had led in practice to 'considerable inconvenience' – and pointed out that 'there was one GOC Malaya and an AOC Far East at the other end of the island'. His conclusion was inept: 'The impression that I personally formed from such inquiries as I made into the state of the defences of Malaya and Burma led me to the conclusion that the former was somewhat over insured at the expense of the latter.'

But if Cooper held back, Sir Earle Page did not. Once in London, he tackled the War Cabinet about the alarming deficiencies he had observed in Singapore's defences, notably that the Air Force was still nearly 200 planes short of its recommended minimum strength. Sir Alexander Cadogan winced at Page's diatribe: '... [he] goes on in an endless, cockney monotone. I asked [Eden], who was sitting next to him, whether he couldn't find a handle or something that would switch off the talk.'[30] Yet again, Churchill stated that Britain accepted 'supreme responsibility' for Australia's defence and would abandon the Middle East if Australia became threatened. He cabled Curtin, 'Japan will not run into war with the ABCD powers unless or until Russia is decisively broken. Perhaps even then they will wait for the promised invasion of the British Isles in the spring. Russian resistance is still strong especially in front of Moscow and winter is now near.'[31]

The Chiefs of Staff had urged Churchill as early as August to replace Brooke-Popham with a younger man, after receiving a complaint from the Governor of Burma, Sir Reginald Dorman-Smith. But it was only when Duff Cooper informed the Prime Minister that the Commander-in-Chief was 'damned near gaga' that he acted. On 5 November Churchill cabled Brooke-Popham, 'It has been decided, in view of developments in the Far East, that the duties of C-in-C Far East should be entrusted to an Army Officer with up-to-date experience.'[32]

The Australians, who had come to trust Brooke-Popham, protested vociferously at his removal. Curtin telephoned Duff Cooper in Singapore to demand an explanation. Cooper professed ignorance, so Churchill got the blame. Australia had not been consulted about the move, despite the fact that she was supplying large numbers of troops and airmen for the defence of Singapore. In London, High Commissioner Stanley Bruce expressed his dissatisfaction to the British Government. Churchill furiously denounced Curtin's Government, claiming that it was 'out to make the most trouble and give the least help'.[33]

Brooke-Popham's replacement was to be Major-General Sir Henry Pownall, formerly Chief of Staff of the British Expeditionary Force in France and currently Vice-Chief of the Imperial General Staff. However, Brooke-Popham remained *in situ* during the critical weeks of November and December while the Chiefs of Staff debated the powers of his successor and Churchill attempted to calm the political storm, instructing Duff Cooper to explain to Curtin why he had felt that Brooke-Popham should be replaced.[34] It must have been reassuring for Brooke-Popham when Wavell, Commander-in-Chief India and very much 'an Army Officer with up-to-date experience', wrote to him on 13 November, 'Personally I should be most doubtful if the Japs ever tried to make an attack on Malaya, and I am sure they will get [it] in the neck if they do.'[35]

As November rolled into December, Diana Cooper lamented to a friend about the lack of earthly diversions available to her husband in Singapore: 'He is such a one for pleasure. Old English ones, girls, champagne, bridge, clubs, weekends, libraries and a spot of sport. None of them here.'[36] Duff Cooper paid a visit to Gordon Bennett at his headquarters, where his 'pansy hat – wide-brimmed straw with a multi-coloured scarf around it' – incited sniggers. The nearest Australian troops were 80 miles away 'so that I had not time to visit them', Duff Cooper said.[37]

Meanwhile, the three little Prout children were coming to terms with the death of their mother. The girls were boarders at the Convent of the Holy Infant Jesus in Victoria Street, and a place had been found for John at St Patrick's, Katong. The Victoria Street convent had been founded in 1840 by a French order, the Sisters of the Seine. 'We had first boarders, second boarders and orphans,' says Olga Page. 'First boarders had to pay fees, second boarders paid if they could afford it and orphans paid nothing: they had been abandoned. The nuns brought them up until they were old enough to get married.' Unwanted babies were left at the convent's side entrance on Bras Basah Road. It was called the Gate of Hope.

Stanley Prout started seeing a family friend, Charmaine Hurley, the mother of three young children, and moved into an apartment with her at Tiong Bahru. In 1940, he retired from the Straits Steamship Company and moved north to take up a position at Pacific Tin Mines outside Kuala Lumpur.

Olga and Maisie missed their father but they saw quite a lot of his friend, the former Georgetown parish priest Father Devals, who had been consecrated as Catholic Bishop of Singapore. The Bishop lived in a fine residence in Victoria Street next door to the Cathedral of the Good Shepherd. 'He was a frequent visitor to our convent,' Maisie Duncan remembers. 'He was tall, with a very erect figure and a friendly smile. He had a long, salt-and-pepper moustache like Jimmy Edwards and he would twirl the ends of it while he was talking. He was very popular.'[38]

Olga remembers her first sight of Australian soldiers in Singapore. 'The convent had a holiday bungalow at Katong Beach for weekends and I saw my first Australian when we were looking out of the windows there,' she says. 'We saw this detachment of troops going past in slouch hats while the nuns were bathing. They were in barracks not far from the Katong Beach Convent and they used to march past on the beach. The nuns had certain times for bathing and we were not allowed to see them in their bathing togs, even though they were covered by chemises. We were locked up in the dormitory upstairs so we couldn't see them bathing.

'The troops marched past and saw this group of European women with their bathing caps bobbing up and down and they began singing, "*Mademoiselle from Armentières, never been kissed in 40 years*". We could hear them singing so we opened the shutters. We could see these lads passing by and we knew they weren't British troops because British troops were much better behaved and these men were also wearing slouch hats. We began to wave and shout back at them. There was one nun on duty and she ordered us to close the windows and behave like young ladies.'[39]

In Tokyo, Tojo replaced Prince Konoe as Prime Minister on 17 October and the course for war was set. Eight Liaison Conferences were held at the Imperial Palace between 23 October and 1 November 1941 to discuss the southward advance. Hirohito did not attend these meetings but was present at the Imperial Conferences that followed each session. Breaking with the tradition of his grandfather, he asked many questions and posed numerous scenarios, until his Cabinet and the armed forces had arrived at a consensus – that Japan could win a war against the Western democracies if she acted quickly and unexpectedly.

It was decided that Japan's negotiators, Ambassador Kichisaburo Nomura and Special Envoy Saburo Kurusu, would continue their talks with the American Secretary of State Cordell Hull in Washington until midnight on 30 November and, if by then there was no settlement, she would wage war against America, Britain and Holland at the beginning of December.

The Emperor helped his constitutional draftsmen to compose the wording of the Imperial War Rescript: 'We, by the grace of Heaven, Emperor of Japan, seated on the throne of a line unbroken for ages eternal, enjoin upon you, our loyal and brave subjects: We hereby declare war on the United States of America and the British Empire ...'

Hirohito was not only sovereign head of the Imperial Japanese Empire (*genshu*) but supreme commander of her armed forces (*daigensui*). As commander-in-chief, he sanctioned all of the key elements in the High Command's plan of attack, including Yamamoto's strike on the American Pacific Fleet at Pearl Harbor. Giving the lie to the notion that his military title was merely an honorific, he moved military headquarters into the Imperial Palace and, as the time for action drew near, insisted on being kept informed of every important diplomatic and military move.

Yamamota, the key commander in the southward advance, was a great gambler who enjoyed poker, bridge and mah-jong. He was fond of saying that he had joined the Navy so that he 'could return Commander Perry's visit'.[40] At his disposal were 11 battleships and 10 aircraft carriers, with an air corps of 1,500 skilled pilots. But having seen America's industrial might at first hand as naval attaché in Washington, Yamamoto was pessimistic about Japan's chances of winning a protracted war. 'If I am told to fight regardless of consequences, I shall run wild for the first six months or a year,' he said, 'but I have utterly no confidence for the second and third year.' Hirohito thought six months or a year would be long enough to ensure victory. All-powerful yet unworldly, the Emperor believed that Germany would defeat Britain and that the US, lacking the will to tackle a massive Japanese defensive arc across the Pacific, would sue for peace.

Hirohito's decision to make war placed a huge burden on the shoulders of his armed forces, but the Japanese High Command believed that the fanatical faith of their young soldiers, sailors and airmen in their Emperor's infallibility would ensure victory. Everything depended on the element of surprise. Tricks to gain advantage over an opponent were highly regarded in the ancient warrior code of *bushido*. Under Tojo, however, the code had been diverted from its original mystical purpose. Young soldiers going into battle were now urged to fight fearlessly 'so as not to shame the spirits of the departed'. The accent was shifted from the chivalry of the *Bushi* warriors of old, with their veneration of age and respect for women, to personal sacrifice.[41]

Article 2 of the Imperial Army Military Training Regulations stated, 'The duty of the military is to sacrifice their lives for the Emperor's country. It is a tradition inherited from the time of the old samurai. A samurai's loyalty to his country has been considered even more important than the worth of his own life.'[42] The samurai's belief in righteousness, courage, humanity, propriety and sincerity was corrupted into a form of blind obedience. The Japanese soldier was encouraged to believe that he should die in battle rather than live with the shame of surrender.

Japanese soldiers were indoctrinated with the belief that they were on a divine mission from Hirohito to liberate their Asian brothers and sisters from white tyranny. According to a political pamphlet handed to Japanese soldiers on their way to war, the colonial powers' greatest fear was that, with the help of Japan, 'the peoples of Asia will work together for independence. The aim of the present war is the realisation, first in the Far East, of His Majesty's august will and ideal that the peoples of the world should each be granted possession of their rightful homelands. To this end, the countries of the Far East must plan a great coalition of East Asia. Through the combined strength of such a coalition we shall liberate East Asia from white invasion and oppression.'

The Japanese High Command appointed Lieutenant-General Tomoyuki Yamashita as the head of the 25th Army which would lead the country's southern expansion. Yamashita was a brawny, growling bear of a man with a low centre of gravity and a swaggering gait. Born in the village of Osugi Muraon on the island of Shikoku in 1885, he was the son of a country doctor who, noting that his sturdy son had little aptitude for book learning, encouraged him to take up a military career.

Young Tomoyuki did well at the Military Academy in Hiroshima and graduated with honours at the Staff College. In 1916, he married the daughter of a general and travelled widely as military attaché in Switzerland, Germany and Austria. It was inevitable that he would become involved in Japanese military politics. By 1926 he was a major-general and a leading member of the Imperial Way (*Kodoha*) faction of the Army, which saw the Emperor as the living embodiment of Japan past and present and rejected Western democracy and all forms of liberalism.

However, it was the Control faction (*Toseiha*) of General Tojo that gained dominance over the Imperial Way in the Japanese Army. *Toseiha* was less concerned with internal reconstruction and more interested in the creation of a 'defence state', under military control, which would conquer China for economic gain. Yamashita found himself in conflict with Tojo, a former friend, after 1,500 young *Kodoha* officers of the 1st and 3rd Regiments of the Imperial Guards Division mutinied on 26 February 1936 and seized a section of Tokyo near the Imperial Palace.

General Watanabe, the Inspector-General of Military Education, was assassinated along with politicians noted for their opposition to the military. The highest-ranking victim was the Finance Minister, who had imposed limits on military spending. He was trapped in his house, shot repeatedly and slashed with swords. As the killers departed, one of them apologised to the Minister's servants 'for the annoyance I have caused'.[43]

The insurrection collapsed after three days when Hirohito said he would personally command troops to quell it. Without the Emperor's support, the mutineers were doomed. As a former commander of the 3rd Regiment, Yamashita was suspected of having organised the coup. This was not the case, but he fell from grace when he urged the young insurgents to commit *seppuku* – ritual suicide by disembowelment – and then petitioned the Emperor to send an imperial representative to witness their deaths. Furious that Yamashita had invoked his divine name without permission, Hirohito ordered the rebels back to barracks – where the ringleaders were executed.

On the Emperor's orders, Yamashita was banished to Korea in command of a brigade, but he was too intelligent and too effective a commander to remain in obscurity for long. At the time of the German invasion of Russia, Yamashita was back in Tokyo, where he urged his superiors to prepare for war against Russia. The Japanese mobilised their army in Manchukuo and, at Tojo's insistence, Yamashita was appointed commanding officer of the Manchukuo Defence Army.

Three days after Japan had decided to go to war pending the outcome of the Washington talks, Yamashita was hauled out of Manchuria and flown to Saigon to take command of the 25th Army. Planning and training for the invasion of Malaya and the capture of Singapore had been taking place in secret under the Commander of the Southern Army, Count Terauchi, a member of Tojo's Control faction. The strategy for the assault on Malaya had been masterminded by the 25th Army's chief operational planner, Colonel Masanobu Tsuji, another member of the Control faction.

Tojo had seen to it that his rival would be surrounded by enemies as he made his way down the Malay peninsula. Yamashita was soon confiding to his diary about Tsuji: 'This man is egotistical and wily. He is a sly dog and unworthy to serve the country. He is a manipulator to be carefully watched.'

CHAPTER 6

Angry Australian

Pᴿᴇᴄᴏᴄɪᴏᴜꜱ ᴀꜱ ᴀ ʏᴏᴜɴɢ ꜱᴏʟᴅɪᴇʀ and irascible as an old one, Henry Gordon Bennett had been born on 16 April 1887 at Balwyn, a suburb on the outer limits of late Victorian Melbourne. As a major in the Gallipoli campaign, he was one of the leaders of the advance to Pine Ridge on 25 April 1915 – the original Anzac Day – but he was wounded while directing fire at Turkish positions. He was evacuated to a hospital ship but absented himself and returned to the front, a reckless act which brought him a great deal of kudos.

With the British forces making little headway, Bennett gained a reputation for leadership and courage under fire, but his superiors also noted that he was quick to anger and incapable of taking criticism. Furthermore, he was involved in an apparently insoluble feud with another officer, Thomas Blamey. The trouble had started in 1912 when a prankster pushed Blamey into a horse trough during an army course. Blamey accused Bennett, who claimed he had been mistaken for another young officer. Then in November 1916 Bennett's superior officer in France, General Birdwood, approved 14 days' leave for him to go to England to marry his Melbourne sweetheart, Bessie Buchanan. 'While Birdwood was away, Blamey intercepted my leave pass and reduced it to 10 days' leave,' Bennett says. Despite this apparently mean act, the wedding went ahead at the Scottish National Church, Chelsea, and the newlyweds had time for a short honeymoon before Bennett had to report back to the front.

At the age of 29 he was promoted to temporary brigadier and given command of the 3rd Brigade AIF. His reputation as a brilliant front-line commander was confirmed in actions at Bullecourt, the Menin Road, Passchendaele and on the Hindenburg Line. But his fractious personality and penchant for acting without orders provoked Major-General Sir William Glasgow to observe, 'Bennett is a pest!' C. E. W. Bean, the official Australian historian of World War I, noted that Bennett was 'always jealous and critical of his superior officers and the men of his own rank. [He was] always a fighting leader of his men, but always quarrelling with the men beside him.'

Bennett left the Army in 1919 with an intense loathing for the Staff Corps, the regular officers who had made the Australian Army their career. According to Bennett, they 'lack the common touch and do not seem to recognise that they are here to serve the men as well as to demand service from them'. His particular *bête noire* was Thomas Blamey, a Cornish butcher's son who would go on to command the Australian forces in World War II, a position coveted by Bennett more than anything else.

Between the wars Bennett moved to Sydney, where he became a successful businessman. He made time to command the Militia's 9th Infantry Brigade from 1921 to 1926 and was promoted to major-general on 1 August 1930 while in command of the 2nd Division. Bennett was proud to be a member of the Militia – later named the Citizens Military Forces – and his dislike of career officers intensified during two decades of peace. He also developed a dislike for politicians who had crippled Australia's armed forces with savage cuts in defence expenditure.

In late 1937, Bennett wrote a series of articles for the Sydney *Sun* in which he criticised the country's defence policy, singling out the attitude of regular officers as one of the main problems. He argued that senior Militia officers were being passed over for the command of divisions in favour of officers of the Permanent Staff Corps, who were trained mainly in staff work and were unfit to command a division in war. His articles caused uproar in the services and the final instalment of the series was withheld following official complaints to the editor. Bennett was censured by the Military Board.

On the outbreak of World War II Bennett was junior only to Sir Brudenell White and Sir William Glasgow in the Australian Army, and expected to be called to lead the 2nd Australian Imperial Force when it was ordered overseas to support British troops in the Middle East. He was devastated when Major-General Sir Thomas Blamey, his arch rival from World War I, was appointed to command the 6th Division and thence the AIF in the Middle East. Bennett complained that he had been ignored on account of his outspoken criticisms, but in fact the reason he had been passed over was that it was thought he would be incapable of working with British officers. Bennett's suspicions that he was being ostracised were confirmed when he failed to gain command of any one of the three new AIF divisions – the 7th, 8th and 9th – as they were formed. He might never have served abroad again had it not been for General White's death in a plane crash at Canberra in 1940. The 8th Division commander, Major-General Sir

Vernon Sturdee, on being appointed Chief of the General Staff, nominated Bennett as his replacement to command the 8th Division.

When he flew to Singapore in February 1941, Bennett had not forgotten the humiliation he had suffered at the hands of the Military Board. He had turned into a gruff, short-tempered and distrustful man, always on the lookout for 'whisperers' – conspirators – among his staff. John Wyett says, 'Bennett couldn't trust anybody. He was a very suspicious man and a trifle touched. He also believed in astrology.'[1]

John William Cardwell Wyett, born in July 1908, had received extensive military training both in the Naval Reserve and in the Militia. By profession he was a qualified pharmacist; he had also received a science degree from the University of Tasmania. He put these skills to good use as an employee of Cadbury's in Hobart, but when he tried to enlist in the AIF he was turned down because making chocolate was a reserved occupation. It was only by pulling strings with a friendly brigadier that he managed to join the AIF.

After studying his hot-tempered commander's mental state, Wyett came to the conclusion that while Bennett was not mentally ill, 'he was mentally taken up wholeheartedly with himself and his own ideas and how bad everybody else was, but there wasn't anything wrong with his brain or brain power'. Bennett had no liking for Malaya, which he considered a sideshow while the real war was taking place in the Middle East – where, in addition, his rival Blamey was making a name for himself. 'He was absolutely set on taking over command of the whole of the Australian Army,' Wyett says, 'so his opinion of those who did was very low indeed.'

Bennett's first arguments in Malaya were with the commander of the 22nd Brigade, the doughty Brigadier Harold B. Taylor, a World War I veteran whose heroism under fire had earned him the Military Cross and Bar. Taylor had served with Bennett in the Militia between the wars and, knowing his peculiarities, realised there would be some bumpy times ahead. Nevertheless, he knuckled down to the job of training his brigade to fight in the Malay climate. Fighting in close country meant there were no fields of fire from static defence positions. Troops had to be mobile and able to find their way without reference to the usual tactical features such as hills or distinctive trees. The all-important manoeuvre was to encircle the enemy and drive him on to pre-prepared roadblocks where he could be cut down by small-arms fire.

Major Charles 'Andy' Anderson, the tough South African-born second-in-command of the 2/19th Battalion, put his men through gruelling routines to build up their stamina. Thirty hand-picked Diggers were ordered to undertake a 30-mile march from 6 a.m. to 6 p.m. in full battle kit. Only four finished the route – but these four were tough enough to go to a dance that night. The men made long marches through the jungle, using compasses for directions, sometimes subsisting on a rice diet. Particular attention was paid to bayonet practice, with the men charging over a breast-works screaming battle cries and attacking sandbags.[2]

On 28 February the Deputy Chief of the Australian General Staff, Major-General John Northcott, arrived in Singapore to attend a staff conference. He told General Bennett the disconcerting news that his two other brigades – the 23rd and the 27th – would not be coming to Malaya. The 23rd Brigade was being moved to the Northern Territory, whence two of its battalions would be sent to Timor and one to Ambon in the Dutch East Indies if war broke out. Meanwhile, the 27th Brigade would probably go to Alice Springs in the centre of the outback. Northcott informed Bennett that he must arrange with Percival to take responsibility for a particular area in Malaya, or return to Australia to take command of the larger part of the 8th Division.

Bennett regarded the prospect of returning to Australia with abhorrence. He decided that in order to remain in Malaya he had to build up his power base through an expanded divisional headquarters. He wrote in his diary, 'I asked that a complete Div HQ be formed here or alternatively my Div HQ be sent from Australia and that I be authorised to form a complete Base HQ. [Northcott] said he would recommend it to Military Board.'

Brigadier Taylor was soon inundated with orders from Bennett's headquarters. On 3 March *he* noted in *his* diary, 'Finding it extremely difficult to get things done on account of Div insisting that everything goes through them. If this is insisted upon in action I am afraid there will be a grave risk of a debacle as far as the Bde is concerned because Div have not the staff to handle [it] and don't realise it. This I shall not allow even if it means a break with Div Comdr and my return to Aust.'[3]

Taylor raised the matter with Bennett but found him unyielding. The bad feeling between the two men exploded into the open when Malaya Command held an exercise to simulate war conditions. The 22nd Brigade was ordered to move from its base in the Seremban-Port Dickson area by road and rail, via Kluang, to Mersing on the east coast. Brigadier Taylor, however, received confusing instructions from divisional headquarters about the timing of the brigade's move, and when he sought clarification from Bennett there was a clash. 'It looks as if the Div Comdr has made up his mind to command the Bde Gp in the field when it moves,' Taylor noted in his diary. 'He should be in Singapore, not here.'

After a heated exchange between the two men, Bennett recorded, 'Had words with Taylor. He resents receiving orders and does his best to thwart me. He stated that he was well equipped mentally for his job, that I knew nothing and that the last war was [a] useless experience.' Bennett had cabled Melbourne requesting a second infantry brigade, a machine-gun battalion, a pioneer battalion and other unit, but learned from General Sturdee that his requests had been turned down.

From long personal experience, Taylor should have known the depth of Bennett's insecurities and sidestepped a confrontation, but when the interference continued he decided to have it out with his commanding officer. 'I again opened up the subject of the Bde Gp, pointing out that I wanted it for training purposes only and that unless this training was done I (meaning the Bde) was facing disaster. I was told that unless I altered my attitude I was facing disaster (meaning Aust for me). He then said that he considered that I was attempting to get control of the AIF in Malaya. Personal motives are apparently the only ones he recognises.'

There was more trouble when a move by the 2/19th Battalion had to be postponed after a mix-up over exactly where the troops were supposed to be heading. According to Bennett, Taylor 'upset the show by a wrong map-reading'. Taylor, however, claimed that Bennett's headquarters had not passed on the code for deciphering map references, thus making it impossible for him to carry out the order.

After the brigade returned to Port Dickson, Bennett asked his Chief Signals Officer, Lieutenant-Colonel Jim Thyer, to advise Taylor to co-operate in future; he also wrote a letter to Taylor expressing the same wish. Interpreting this as an overture for peace, Taylor drove to Kuala Lumpur to see Bennett. The truce lasted until after dinner when they had what Taylor described as a 'ding dong go'. Bennett claimed that Taylor was still 'endeavouring to control [the] show – far from respectful – inclined to bluff'.

However, the evening ended with the two men shaking hands, and Taylor recorded that he hoped a permanent understanding had been reached. But Bennett had no intention of interfering less or of lessening the pressure on Taylor. When the Brigadier issued orders that the brigade was to undertake night training and neglected to inform divisional headquarters, Bennett wrote to Taylor and his unit commanders making it clear that in future such orders were to come from *him*.

There was no improvement when Colonel Harry Rourke, Bennett's Chief of Staff, and Colonel Ray Broadbent, senior administrative officer, arrived in Malaya to join Bennett's headquarters. Having discussed the

Taylor problem with them, Bennett wrote in his diary, 'Both agree that I have been over-tolerant and see no alternative to suspending Taylor. Have decided to do so on grounds that he is temperamentally unfitted for comd. I have given Rourke permission to see Taylor to let him know what is coming. If Taylor adopts a repentant attitude, then I may reconsider my attitude. Rourke leaves today and will return this evening.'

Over lunch at Seremban, Rourke informed Taylor that he was going to be sent back to Australia. The letter of dismissal had already been written; Bennett was holding it back only long enough for Rourke to speak to Taylor. Throughout his difficulties with Bennett, Taylor had remained reasonably calm – but this news shook him to the core. With his military career at stake, he decided to go to Kuala Lumpur to see Bennett.

The meeting gave Bennett great satisfaction. 'Taylor very humble and assured full support etc.,' he wrote. 'Regretted his recent action. Stood firm and said I must be quite satisfied this time and could take no more risks. He gave every assurance. Told him I would hold over my letter to Melbourne till after Easter and would then see him to confirm his attitude. I still doubt if he can alter a temperament that it has taken many years to develop.'

Taylor had one trump card up his sleeve. Bennett's reputation for prickliness was well known, and he was mindful of the damage Taylor could cause him back in Melbourne. 'I don't think he is game to send [the letter] – not on my account but on [that of] the effect on his career,' Taylor wrote. 'He knows that I could cause a riot if I wished to and this would wreck him also.' His assumption was correct. After Easter, Bennett visited 22nd Brigade headquarters and told his brigadier that he did not intend to take the matter further. Taylor then 'asked that I forget everything and start afresh. I agreed.' Taylor found his commander 'very nice' and accepted an invitation to join him for a weekend at Fraser's Hill, the up-country station where officers took their leave.

Meanwhile, the troops of the 22nd Brigade had been mastering the strange conditions. After three months in Malaya, one 'Jacky Roo' reported in the 2/19th Battalion's magazine, 'We sweated and toiled and swore in the jungle and the hilly rubber country. Bivouacs meant sleeping under mosquito nets and wondering whether one would roll over into a King Cobra in the night. Leeches, scorpions, snakes, mosquitoes – we suffered them all. We saw red when well-meaning folk wanted to know if we were having a nice holiday. We found the equatorial heat exhausting but we got used to it.'[4]

The troops also became familiar with the pleasures of weekend leave in

Kuala Lumpur, where they discovered the wonders of the chit system. Members of the 2/19th Battalion signed hundreds of chits for services rendered in the names of their officers, including the commanding officer, Lieutenant-Colonel Duncan Maxwell. The Happy Entertainment Centre figured prominently, as well as cafés, tailors and souvenir shops. There was no chance of catching the culprits, so Maxwell paid off the debts out of battalion funds. Advertisements were then placed in local newspapers warning all businesses that Australian soldiers were no longer to be given credit.[5]

Despite the ructions at the top, the 22nd Brigade had been moulded into a formidable fighting force. The Australians practised snapshooting from the hip to sharpen reflexes on jungle paths and lived in the jungle for days on end, making shelters, beds and rafts from bamboo. Each battalion also sent out companies on a 30-mile circuit that took them through rubber plantations and jungle, where they were set upon by roving platoons. The three battalions then took part in exercises to improve rapid movement by transport and the use of flying columns to seize important localities ahead of the main force.[6]

Meanwhile, word had reached Melbourne about the embarrassing situation in Malaya. The Chief of the General Staff, General Sturdee, sent Brigadier C. A. 'Boots' Callaghan, the 8th Division's artillery commander, to Malaya at the end of June to investigate the trouble between Bennett and Taylor. Taylor responded with a frank recital of events since their arrival, and Harry Rourke also passed on his impressions of Bennett's command. Sturdee, meanwhile, asked Blamey to consider Bennett as a substitute for General Sir Iven Mackay as commander of the Australian Home Forces. Bennett was 'very senior' – that is, too old for his present command – and, he added, 'an energetic junior commander' would fit in better with Malaya Command.

Bennett learned of his impending dismissal, but he had no time to plan a new offensive before the arrival of the 27th Brigade Group brought a lull in hostilities. Three Australian infantry battalions – the 2/26th, 2/29th and 2/30th – along with the 2/15th Field Regiment and other units arrived in Singapore on 15 August. Believing their movements to be top secret, the troops were alarmed to see a huge banner bearing the words *Welcome to the AIF* slung across a city street on their way to camp. 'That's Lavender Street,' a young English private informed them. It took the Australians a week to discover that Lavender Street was the city's most notorious red-light district.[7]

The 27th Brigade had arrived minus its commanding officer because of ill health. Bennett took the opportunity to appoint one of his favourites, Duncan Maxwell, to the post. Maxwell was a doctor in civilian life and, at 6 foot 3 inches, towered over Bennett, but he deferred to his commanding officer in a manner that the latter found most satisfactory. Bennett also felt a sense of triumph when Harry Rourke – now regarded as another 'whisperer' – was posted back to Australia. 'All's well that ends well,' he chortled to his diary. Jim Thyer was appointed Chief of Staff, but he too was soon at the sharp end of his commander's pen: 'Thyer's comments on my appreciation of the Johore situation reveal his complete ignorance of tactics. He misses the point and advocates unsound theories. He should not comment if he wishes to save his reputation.' Bennett's paranoia was on the rise. He saw conspiracies everywhere and was determined to curb the 'whispering gallery' among his staff officers who he was convinced were plotting against him.

Lieutenant-General (Sir) Sydney Rowell visited Malaya and concluded that Bennett was 'somewhat out of balance'. John Wyett says, 'It's a historic fact that Rowell went to Malaya to check up on Bennett. They tried very hard to get Canberra to do something about it. It was a bit difficult for them but it was too late anyway.'

General Sturdee followed up Rowell's visit with one of his own during which he raised the question of Bennett's health with the division's senior medical officer, Colonel Alf Derham. In a letter dated 26 August, Derham wrote to Sturdee, 'After our conversation this morning, I felt that unintentionally I had not been quite fair to you in my reply to your question about the health of Maj. General Gordon Bennett. What I told you was accurate, in that, from what knowledge I have of his medical condition, he is in reasonably good health for his age. He has been suffering from indigestion since he came to Malaya, and has been treated for this. When he last consulted me I advised him to get the opinion of Lt-Col Cotter Harvey, Senior Physician 10 AGH, who would probably make certain investigations – test meal, X-ray etc. This General Bennett promised to do some weeks ago, but when I spoke to him again about a week ago, he told me that his indigestion had been completely relieved since he changed the Chinese cook in his mess. It is unlikely that I will be able to get him to see a hospital physician unless his symptoms return.

'Although he does not seem to be ill, and says he has gained rather than lost weight, he is not robust even for his age, gets overtired easily, and seems to feel the effects of strain unduly. It is my opinion as a medical officer that he is too old for active service in the field and that he would not stand the strain of operations for more than a few days or weeks at most. As you well know, this applies to many senior officers in the AIF. Although this note is marked "Confidential", it is my official opinion, and I am prepared to accept responsibility for it in every way.'

Sturdee now had the ammunition he needed to remove Bennett from Malaya on health grounds, but before taking that step he asked General Percival whether he was satisfied with Bennett's performance – knowing that any adverse comment from Percival would end Bennett's military career. However, Percival declined to get involved in AIF politics.

At the end of August Percival granted Gordon Bennett's request that the 8th Division be released from Command Reserve and given a definite area of responsibility. He ordered the Australians to take over the defence of Malacca and Johore, even though he later commented, 'The Australian units were composed of excellent material but suffered from a lack of leaders with a knowledge of modern warfare.'[8] Leaving Bennett in charge of the AIF was one of Percival's biggest mistakes – a fact he acknowledged in his Dispatch.

The 22nd Brigade replaced the 12th Indian Brigade in the Mersing-Endau area, the most favourable spot on the east coast for an amphibious landing. The 27th Brigade was deployed from Singapore to north-west Johore, where it would be available to support the 22nd Brigade. If the Japanese launched a successful attack on Johore's east coast, they would be within easy striking distance of Singapore Island. Such a move would cut the peninsula from east to west and isolate III Indian Corps in north-west Malaya. 'There were two narrow roads that led back to Singapore, one on the west coast and one on the east coast,' recalls Lieutenant Bob Goodwin, a retired doctor and former Australian artillery officer. 'They were the only points of entry to the island. Both were narrow roads, with thick jungle on either side. There wasn't a lot of room for manoeuvring the big heavy vehicles pulling our guns, but we were glad to be given an operational role after all the training we'd done in Malacca.'

Bennett established his headquarters at Johore Bahru. Donning his smartest uniform, he presented himself at the Sultan of Johore's green-tiled palace at Bukit Serene. Sultan Ibrahim was a rotund, much-married *bon viveur*, who wore military uniform as commander-in-chief of his own battalion. For the distinguished Australian soldier he rolled out the red carpet.

CHAPTER 7

Slippery Sultan

His Royal Highness Sultan Sir Ibrahim ibn Sultan Abu Bakar of Johore was the most politically perceptive of the Malay rulers. Born in 1873, he inherited the sultanate at the age of 22. His father, Sultan Abu Bakar, the first maharaja, had shrewdly encouraged British, Chinese and Japanese investment in Johore as part of a strategy to build his state into the wealthiest and most independent in Malaya. As a sign of fealty to the British Crown, however, he kept life-size portraits of Queen Victoria and other members of the Royal Family in his palace. He was also the only non-European member of the exclusive Tanglin Club.

Ibrahim was a large, athletic man with the features of his Scandinavian grandfather and his Malay and Bugis ancestors. As a younger man he had excelled at cricket and tennis, ridden well and hunted big game, and had also been gifted with his father's astute political brain. He enjoyed playing one nation off against another, while retaining his own civil service and military forces.

Independence was important, and the Sultan could become very prickly indeed if he felt the dignity of his royal house had been slighted. One European was expelled from the state for singing 'For He's a Jolly Good Fellow' during the playing of the Johore national anthem.¹ Nor was he shy about upsetting Britain's vice-regal representative. In 1924, Sir Laurence Guillemard had to postpone the opening of the road section of the Causeway when Ibrahim refused to attend. In common with the other Sultans, he had received a numbered invitation, placing him around number 65 in importance. Before the ceremony could proceed, fresh invitations had to be sent out, in the correct Jawi script and addressed individually to members of the Sultanate.

Ibrahim had a fondness for high living and was drawn to the bright lights of London and Paris. He had an income in England of £40,000 a year, which he lavished on dancing girls, particularly a former Gaiety Girl named Nellie whom he apparently married. Ian Morrison's father, G. E. Morrison,

95

lunched with him in London in early 1906 soon after he had bought £30,000 worth of jewels for Nellie and given her the lease of a mansion at 34 Park Lane. Morrison noted that the Johore Advisory Board had resigned in desperation over the Sultan's largesse.

On his return trip to China, Morrison stopped off in Singapore and took the train to Johore to visit the Regent, 'a fine old Malay', who was ruling the state in the Sultan's prolonged absence. Acting as an unofficial envoy for the British Government, Morrison explained that the Colonial Office viewed with disfavour the Sultan's relationship with Nellie, 'his lavishing jewels on her and his flaunting her before the public'. They also frowned on his gift of 25,000 acres of valuable rubber land in Johore to Sir Frank Swettenham, the then Governor of the Straits Settlements and High Commissioner of the Federated Malay States, as 'little better than a bid for favour'. In short, his conduct was considered unworthy of a great ruler and he was strongly advised to return to Johore.[2]

Ibrahim took Morrison's advice and went home. In 1930 he married Mrs Helen Wilson, a widowed governess, and insisted that she be recognised as Sultana. In 1934 he visited Tokyo on a goodwill visit and was showered with imperial honours for having advanced Japanese financial interests in Johore. Politically, however, he remained faithful to Britain, and the following year on King George V's Silver Jubilee he donated £500,000 towards the defence of Singapore, £400,000 of which was used to finance the installation of two of the three 15-inch guns guarding the Straits of Johore.

His marriage to Helen Wilson having ended in divorce, Ibrahim developed a liaison with a cabaret dancer named Lydia Hill. The British regime looked askance at Miss Hill and used its influence to prevent the Sultan from marrying her. She returned to England in 1938 – but the Sultan refused to abandon her. He followed her to London, where staff at the German Embassy took pains to sympathise with his treatment at the hands of the 'racist' British. During a trip to Germany to receive treatment for gout in 1939, he was introduced to Hitler, a meeting that led to the French arresting him on suspicion of spying and induced Shenton Thomas to ask the Colonial Office to block his return to Johore.

Ibrahim remained in London, where he donated £250,000 to the British war effort to prove his loyalty to the Crown. His relationship with Miss Hill continued – but then ended tragically when she was killed in the Blitz. Soon after her death, he was sheltering from the Luftwaffe in the Grosvenor House Hotel when he bumped into Marcella Mendl, a Romanian émigrée from whom he had earlier purchased a Red Cross flag. After a brief romance, they were married in November 1940 and returned together to Johore to a 21-gun salute.

Singapore Special Branch kept a close watch on the Sultan for any signs of subversive behaviour. Its investigators claimed that prominent Malays – including friends of the Sultan and high-ranking officers of the Johore Military Force – were entertained at sumptuous Japanese parties. 'The expense of these entertainments was provided by local Japanese firms, but they were instructed to debit the amounts to "special account" of their Head Offices in Japan,' their report stated. 'As a result of this policy, there occurred in May 1941 a series of visits to the Japanese Consulate in Singapore by certain JMF officers who enjoyed the Sultan's confidence, as well by the Sultan's personal ADC.'[3] Suspicions about the Sultan's loyalty were revived when he welcomed Lady Diana Cooper to Singapore with the gift of a parrot that spoke only Japanese.

Gordon Bennett heard the rumours but chose to ignore them. 'Even the Sultan of Johore, who has often been accused of being anti-British, showed practical sympathy for our cause,' he wrote. 'He invested freely in British war loans and gave freely to war charities. During the period when I was in charge of our troops in Johore, I was brought into close, almost daily, contact with him. His friendliness to the Australian troops was outstanding. He placed his private polo field at their disposal for football, and even gave the teams refreshment whenever they played, which was two or three times a week. He accepted my suggestion for an interchange of officers between the AIF and his Johore Regiment. There were eight Australian officers in this regiment during the period of the fighting. From these and many other actions of the Sultan of Johore, I became firmly convinced of his loyal support to our side.'[4]

The Sultan plied Bennett with drink and cigars. He made sure that cases of his own brand of Scotch were delivered to his quarters. 'The Sultan and [Bennett] were quite good friends,' John Wyett says. 'He seemed to be even friendlier with the Sultana. She was very pleasant, youngish and easy to talk to. I think it was a bit more than that with him. They were flirting with each other – the Sultan didn't seem to mind.'

To protect the Sultan's state and bar the road to Singapore, Bennett planned to hold the beaches at Mersing with two battalions of the 22nd Brigade, while the third battalion stayed in reserve inland at Jemaluang. One company would be posted further north at Endau to give early warning of any Japanese landing. Brigadier Taylor informed his unit commanders at a conference on 30 August that the defence plan was based on a system of platoons, each one self-contained and able to fire in all directions. The platoons would be distributed in depth and would support one another, while the areas between them would be covered by mortar and artillery fire.

The gunners were members of the 2/10th Field Regiment. 'We had solicitors, kangaroo shooters, graziers, even a politician – it was a volunteer unit from all walks of life,' Bob Goodwin says. 'There were three batteries and each battery had two troops, with four guns per troop – a total of 24 guns. These were moved by Marmon-Herrington trucks attached to an ammunition limber, with the gun on a towbar behind the limber. The 18-pounders and howitzers had been replaced with 25-pounders which we calibrated by shooting out to sea and correcting the sights. Accurate shooting depended on an accurate survey with theodolites and directors, and the initial firing was done from maps which had to be pretty accurate. We plotted our positions on a board, then the target would be identified and the observation officer would be in a position to see where the shells landed.'[5]

Russell Savage remembers, 'The night the new 25-pounders turned up, Tokyo Rose announced that we should look after them because the Japanese Army would soon be coming down to take them away from us. We were eagerly waiting. The war was about to start and it got the adrenalin flowing. We thought we were better than the Japanese. You had doubts, of course, but mostly about how you would perform as an individual. There were very few disappointed people when the war came.'

Brigadier Taylor was a doctor of science, majoring in chemistry. He converted the existing makeshift defences at Mersing into a sophisticated system of fortified positions surrounded by mines, barbed wire and booby-traps. A series of platforms was constructed in the shallow waters on which drums of petrol were placed. These would be burst by explosives and turn the water into an inferno. To guarantee that the petrol blazed fiercely, containers of Condy's crystals would be tipped sideways so that a phial of glycerine inside them poured over the contents. This mixture would ignite spontaneously and burn with a fierce blue flame under any conditions.

Bush tracks were hacked out of the dense vegetation to be used if the main road became impassable. 'We can expect the Japanese to be bold,' Brigadier Taylor told his men. 'They greatly admire German methods and will develop the maximum strength in the minimum of time. Japanese infantry can maintain themselves for several days without transport in difficult terrain.'

General Bennett visited Mersing to survey the progress. Russell Savage says, 'He was a smallish fellow, very outspoken, very definite. He stood on the back of a truck and talked to us. We thought, "At last we've got someone who knows what they're doing." Bennett's attitude was that to win a war you had to kill more of the other side than they killed of you and there wasn't much point being polite about it.' The troops had just finished building a prisoner-of-war camp behind their lines to hold large numbers of captured Japanese soldiers. Bennett told them, 'You're probably wondering why you're building a POW camp. The reason is that you're going to be cut off for at least three weeks once the fighting starts – completely isolated. The Japanese will infiltrate between your positions on the beaches, and when they're captured you will need somewhere to keep them.'

Meanwhile, the Sultan was playing host to Mrs Mary Thomson and her three children, Michael, Annette and Brenda. Mary, who was expecting her fourth child, lived with her husband Cyril in Swatow, one of the smaller treaty ports on mainland China. 'We're very much a China family,' says her son, General David Thomson. 'All four of my grandparents left Aberdeen in the middle of the 19th century and settled in China. Both my parents were born in Shanghai. My father was in the linen business, and Swatow was the centre of China's linen trade, halfway up the coast between Hong Kong and Shanghai.'⁶

The little treaty port had been occupied by the Japanese since the start of the Sino-Japanese War in 1937. For four years Cyril and Mary Thomson had watched them tighten their grip on China; they were appalled at the treatment of defenceless Chinese civilians. 'My parents were pretty much used to having the Japanese around, but when my father took his leave in Hong Kong in 1941 he realised that things were much more serious than he had suspected, and that a war involving the Brits was about to break out. He decided that if he was ever to do business again in the Far East then he would have to stay put – he couldn't disappear and then come back and pretend that nothing had happened.

'So he stayed in Hong Kong, working for the Government as deputy food controller, and my mother went on to Singapore with the children.' Thanks to the Sultan's Secretary, a family friend, the Thomsons were invited to stay at the palace. 'My mother felt she had gone far enough, but the Secretary told her in early November that she mustn't stay in Malaya, that war was coming and that when the Japanese attacked, they would attack there and right across the Pacific. He put my mother on a boat for Australia and she reached Perth on 20 November. I was born there in January 1942. My mother's experience contradicts the idea that civilians had their heads in the sand and didn't know what was going on. Otherwise, she would have been captured – as was my father and many of my parents' friends in Hong Kong and Singapore.'

Meanwhile, Lorraine Stumm was making her mark at the *Tribune*, interviewing generals, society leaders and the Sultan of Johore's new Romanian wife. 'Life revolved around the grand dinners at Raffles, visits to the Swimming Club, tennis and cards at the Tanglin Club and holidays in the cooler weather "up-country", for whites only,' she says. 'No Asians were allowed in these hallowed places, which was disgraceful especially considering it was their country.'[7]

The best reporter on the *Tribune* was Leslie Hoffman, who was classified as Eurasian. Lorraine was upset to discover that Hoffman, one of the most brilliant journalists of his time, was paid only half her salary. The rights of the underdog apparently did not extend to the *Tribune*'s newsroom.[8] Another friend was Mabel Wong, an elegant young Chinese woman and daughter of her proprietor. 'She was such a Singapore asset that she was one of the few Chinese women to grace the ballroom of Raffles Hotel with parties of friends, evening after evening,' Lorraine says. 'This was a time when people of "other races" were not particularly welcome at Raffles.'

Sheridan Stumm recalls, 'My mother was quite egalitarian and she used to say it was dreadful that people were kept out of the Tanglin Club because of their race. She felt terrible about it, but there was also a strong element of snobbery in Singapore and she would have complained if the riff-raff had been let in.'[9]

On 30 October Gordon Bennett celebrated his elevation from General Officer Commanding 8th Australian Division to GOC Australian Imperial Force, Malaya. He was in a cocky mood when his old adversary General Blamey arrived at Singapore on 6 November on his way from the Middle East to Australia to confer with the War Cabinet. But Bennett's ebullience evaporated when Blamey informed him that he wanted the 8th Division to be transferred from Malaya to the Western Desert, a posting that would nullify all Bennett's efforts in Malaya and place him under Blamey's command. The Military Board confirmed this intention and suggested that Bennett visit the Middle East to familiarise himself with the command. Taylor gleefully recorded, 'GOC is going to Middle East – may be forerunner of a move.'

Bennett left Malaya by air on 18 November. After two weeks' touring of Australian positions in the Western Desert, he wrote scathingly that the

Allied offensive against Rommel 'lacked drive, punch and co-ordination', that the 'elephantine' headquarters of the army in Egypt 'had grown usually at the expense of the number of men available to fight'; and that 'too many officers were so far removed from the battles that were being fought that they lost touch with reality. Departments became water-tight and out of touch with other departments. Perfect co-operation was extremely difficult.'[10]

Lady Brooke-Popham arrived in Singapore from Kenya on 24 November to be reunited with her husband. As wife of the country's former Governor, she had been using her influence to find homes for children evacuated from British cities. During November Brooke-Popham received reports of a strong concentration of Japanese sea, land and air forces in southern Indochina and the South China Sea. The Chiefs of Staff warned him that negotiations between Japan and the US in Washington might collapse at any moment, precipitating a Japanese attack on Thailand, the Dutch East Indies or the Philippines.

Percival knew his men were not ready to fight. His troops, especially those in northern Malaya, were relatively untrained and 'throughout the Army there was a serious lack of experienced leaders, the effect of which was accentuated by the inexperience of the troops'. Moreover, there simply weren't enough combat troops to cover all of the airfields and beaches. In early December, Percival's force — excluding engineers, drivers, signallers and ancillary units, local volunteers and Indian and Malayan State forces — consisted of 31 infantry battalions, giving him an infantry strength of about 3½ divisions. There were seven field regiments (five of 24 guns; two of 16 guns), 1 mountain regiment (24 guns), 2 anti-tank regiments (one of 48 guns; one of 36 guns) and 2 anti-tank batteries (one of eight Breda guns; one of six 2-pounders). The total strength of regular and volunteer forces was nearly 88,600, of whom 19,600 were British, 15,200 Australian and the greater number Asian (Indian 37,000 and locally enlisted 16,800).

This was 17 infantry battalions, four light anti-aircraft regiments and two tank regiments short of the agreed requirement for defending Malaya and protecting the Naval Base. Percival had no tanks, few armoured cars, insufficient anti-tank rifles and a serious shortage of mobile anti-aircraft weapons. The main defence work in hand throughout his area of command was a single anti-tank line at Jitra in north-west Kedah and beach obstacles on the south side of Singapore Island, which already had the protection of the fortress cannon. Brigadier Simson, the Chief Engineer, had undertaken an extensive tour of Singapore Island and the Malay peninsula, noting possible defensible points in the northern Malay states, in southern Johore and particularly on the north shore of Singapore Island. He had put forward his suggestions to Percival and his BGS, Brigadier K. S. Torrance, at a meeting in Singapore in October.

Simson informed them that there was no shortage of labour or materials, as large quantities of stores and equipment – including sandbags, pickets and the latest types of barbed wire, including high-tensile steel anti-tank Dannert wire – had been shipped to Singapore and placed up-country in 1938–39 on the grounds that shipping for such purposes would be in short supply once the war had started.

As an indication of how the Japanese might strike at Malaya, Simson referred to the Russo-Japanese War of 1904–5. Japan had attacked Port Arthur without warning, and half the Russian naval fleet in the Yellow Sea had been put out of action. Japanese troops had followed up with amphibious landings and laid siege to the Russian forces at Port Arthur which, having been prepared, had held out for five months. Percival listened attentively while Simson outlined his five-point plan:

1. Anti-tank and machine-gun positions would be placed in depth across roads and railways at as many natural defiles down the Malay peninsula as possible to prevent deep tank penetration, as had occurred in France in 1940. Demolition plans would be drawn up in advance for all major bridges and mine chambers built into these structures. Since the Japanese had used tanks in China, Simson expected them to be used in Malaya.

2. Flanks around the main positions could be canalised for ambushes, while others were blocked by anti-personnel mines. Additional protection would be given by barbed wire, trip wires, booby-traps and suchlike, all aimed at inflicting casualties and causing delay.

3. A complete ring of permanent and field defences would be constructed round Johore Bahru to keep the Naval Base out of shell range. Simson's reconnaissance had uncovered General Dobbie's line of machine-gun pillboxes in the jungle near Kota Tinggi. This line would be extended and developed, with flanks on the sea and in the Johore Straits.

4. For the north shore of Singapore Island covering the waters and opposite shores of the Johore Straits, Simson proposed defences in depth consisting of mutually supporting wired trenches, switchlines, pillboxes and various underwater obstacles, mines, petrol fire traps, anchored but floating barbed wire, and methods of illuminating the water at night.

Up-country rivers could be defended in the same way. The idea was that the water surface and shoreline should always be the main killing ground.

5. Chinese and Malay volunteers should be organised into guerrilla bands to operate behind enemy lines, while the members of indigenous tribes should be recruited as guides and to give warning of enemy movement through the jungle.

Percival and Torrance questioned Simson closely about some of the details. 'I had great hopes that some defences at least would now be ordered,' Simson said, 'but finally General Percival decided to take no action at all. He would give me no reason.'

In Washington on 26 November the American Secretary of State Cordell Hull handed Ambassador Nomura America's terms for lifting the oil and scrap-iron embargo against Japan and ending the freeze on Japanese assets. These were that Japan would withdraw her troops from China and Indochina, that she would give no support to any Chinese regime other than that of Chiang Kai-shek, that she would cancel the Tripartite Pact with the Axis Powers and that she would conclude a non-aggression pact with America, Britain, China, Holland, the Soviet Union and Thailand.

The Hull Note sent shock waves through Tokyo. In exchange for an end to America's stifling economic blockade, Japan was asked to wipe out everything she had fought for since 1931. The view in the Army, the Navy and the Foreign Office was that acceptance would relegate Japan to the second division of powers. At an Imperial Conference on 1 December, the decision was taken to wage war against the United States, Britain and Holland. All preparations had been made. The Japanese would strike in the first week of December. Hirohito gave his approval.[11]

President Roosevelt had no doubts that a Japanese strike in the southwest Pacific was imminent. Warnings were issued to Britain and Australia. On 29 November, Secretary for War Henry Stimson and General Miles, head of US Army Intelligence, told the Australian Minister in Washington, Richard Casey, that the Japanese had withdrawn troops from central China and embarked them for a southern destination. A naval task force was being built up on Formosa and on Hainan Island, consisting of three or four battleships – 'this is possible but not certain' – three aircraft carriers, 11 heavy and five light cruisers, 47 destroyers, 16 submarines and attendant auxiliary craft.

There were at least 7,000 Japanese troops, substantial numbers of aircraft and large quantities of military equipment in southern Indochina, as well as 50,000 troops on Hainan Island. The US Intelligence report concluded, 'It appears evident that the Japanese have completed plans for further aggressive moves in South-east Asia. This force is now en route southward to an as yet undetermined rendezvous.'

Casey said that Army Intelligence was 'of the opinion that the initial move will be made against Thailand from the sea and overland through southern China. It is further believed that the Japanese are uncertain of the reaction of the ABD Powers to this move and therefore have organised in sufficient strength to cope with any opposition they might initially encounter from those Powers in the South China Sea.' The United States Navy had sent precautionary war-warning telegrams to the Commanders of the United States Pacific and Asiatic fleets. Simson's War Department had dispatched similar warnings.

General Percival was inspecting his meagre forces in Sarawak that day – 29 November – when he heard on the radio news that all troops had been ordered to report to their units. This was swiftly followed by an order from Brooke-Popham for him to return to Singapore. Not having the use of his own aircraft, the GOC Malaya was obliged to hitch a lift in a destroyer. Arriving on 1 December, he learned that America's negotiations with Japan in Washington were on the brink of collapse and that Japan's southward thrust might occur at any time. Percival put the whole of Malaya Command on the second degree of readiness and ordered the Volunteer Force to be mobilised. He also asked the RAF to intensify their reconnaissance over the South China Sea.

In London that day, General Alan Brooke replaced Percival's mentor General Dill as Chief of the Imperial General Staff. 'I had discussed the possibility of Japan entering the war with Dill,' Brooke wrote in his diary. 'He had told me frankly that he had done practically nothing to meet this threat. He said that we were already so weak on all fronts that it was impossible to denude them any further to meet a possible threat.' Brooke stated that Britain's position in the Far East was, therefore, 'lamentably dangerous'.[12]

There could have been no more timely arrival than that of Britain's newest battleship, HMS *Prince of Wales*, with the veteran battle-cruiser HMS *Repulse* and four destroyers. They steamed into Keppel Harbour under the great guns on Blakang Mati Island on 2 December to take up station at Singapore. *Prince of Wales* was commanded by Admiral Sir Tom Phillips, who had spent the previous two years in a desk job as Vice-Chief of Naval Staff. Only five feet two inches tall, Phillips was known to lower ranks as 'Tom Thumb', but he was one of the smartest men in the Navy and seemed to know it. Churchill called him 'the Cocksparrow'.

Phillips had enjoyed a meteoric rise up the Admiralty's greasy pole. For a golden period he was a popular weekend guest at Chequers, where his powers of analysis and razor-sharp wit stimulated many an after-dinner discussion. However, he had made the mistake of criticising some of Churchill's catastrophic diversion of troops and supplies from North Africa to Greece in April 1941 and had henceforth been dropped from the charmed circle. His appointment as Acting Admiral in charge of the Far Eastern Fleet, jumping him up two places, followed shortly afterwards – to get him away from Churchill, it was whispered.

The 53-year-old Phillips was an excellent skipper of small boats and had served as Commodore, then Rear Admiral, Destroyers, Home Fleet for 13 months, but he had no experience at all of an air attack on a task force at sea and dismissed as poppycock the idea that aircraft posed a serious threat to a properly armed battleship. He was so entrenched in his opinions, so sure of his infallibility, that another admiral, Somerville, referred to him as 'the Pocket Napoleon'.[13]

Once the Far Eastern Fleet reached Colombo, Phillips had flown ahead to Singapore, arriving on 30 November, to consult with Brooke-Popham. On his arrival Phillips automatically replaced Admiral Geoffrey Layton as the Navy's senior commander. Layton, a Liverpudlian who had joined the Royal Navy as a cadet in 1899, was far from happy at being superseded. When he had taken over as Commander-in-Chief China Fleet in 1940, he had been given to understand that his force would be strengthened if war broke out with Japan and that he would remain in command. However, he had been informed by the Admiralty that the proposed Eastern Fleet would have its own Commander-in-Chief and, once the fleet reached Singapore, the appointment of C-in-C China Station would be abolished.

Layton had been appalled when he heard that the post of Commander-in-Chief Eastern Fleet had gone to Tom Phillips. It was his style to express his points of view with such force that he was known to his contemporaries as 'Windy'. He restrained himself with difficulty over Phillips, who was not only junior and less experienced than him, but whom he regarded as an unsound flag officer who had once been responsible for a collision at sea. 'It's the biggest blow I've had in my life,' he fumed. 'In time of war I've always said that one must do what one is told and not bellyache. So there it is. But – Tom Phillips!'[14]

The whole of Singapore turned out to welcome *Prince of Wales* as she entered Keppel Harbour. With her ship's complement lined up on deck in dazzling white and the band playing stirring anthems, it seemed as though King George VI had spared his greatest Christmas present for his Far Eastern subjects. The next day the headlines hailed *Prince of Wales* as 'HMS *Unsinkable*', the glamour ship of the Royal Navy that was going to save Singapore from the Japanese aggressor. *Repulse*, the old campaigner, hardly rated a mention.

Phillips knew by now that he was going to have to make do without air support from the aircraft carrier HMS *Indomitable*. The carrier had hit a reef in fog off Kingston Harbour, Jamaica, and had limped to a naval ship-yard at Norfolk, Virginia, for repairs. On board were the 45 aircraft – including nine Hurricane fighters – that were intended as air cover for Phillips's miniature task force.

After showing the flag to the population of Singapore City, *Prince of Wales* steamed around the island and proceeded up the eastern channel to the Naval Base, where the top brass and civil dignitaries had gathered in the garden of Admiral Layton's residence. General Percival and his friend Air Vice-Marshal Pulford, Sir Robert Brooke-Popham, the Duff Coopers and the Shenton Thomases were all present as *Prince of Wales*, *Repulse* and four destroyers anchored at the Naval Base. Lady Diana Cooper described the little fleet as 'a lovely sight but on the petty side'.

Admiral Phillips invited everyone to cocktails in his flagship. Percival had met Tom Phillips during his time at the War Office, while he remembered the captains of both ships, Jack Leach of *Prince of Wales* and Bill Tennant of *Repulse*, from his days at the Greenwich Staff College. Leach and Tennant were good friends and both popular with their men. At 47, Leach was a tall, broad-shouldered man who still excelled at sports. Tennant, six years older, had been beachmaster at Dunkirk and one of the last men to be evacuated from France.

Now that the Fleet had arrived, the *Malaya Tribune* assured its readers that there was nothing to worry about. 'The Japanese are caught in a trap of their own making,' it stated. 'Neither by land nor sea nor in the air do they have even a glimmer of a chance of victory.' The article was illustrated by a cartoon of a short-sighted, buck-toothed, half-witted Japanese soldier.

Richard Smith, a 19-year-old rating in *Repulse*, said the crew had been fed a similar line by their officers on the journey out. 'Everybody was told that the Japanese fleet was absolutely useless and that it was just a lot of rice paper and string,' he says. 'We would go up there and knock them about and cause havoc – it would be a walkover and we would enjoy ourselves. This was the whole mentality when we were lying in the harbour with all the lights on. Everybody was ashore wining and dining and all the colonials we saw were making merry and having a wonderful time. The Fleet had arrived and Japan would not now enter the war.'[15]

The following morning Admiral Phillips decided to send *Repulse* to Darwin to allay Australian fears about security and to have *Prince of Wales*'s boilers cleaned out. That evening the commander of the Naval Base, Admiral E. J. 'Jackie' Spooner, and his wife Megan threw a party at their residence, Admiral's House, in honour of *Prince of Wales*. 'Everybody was cheerful and confident,' Duff Cooper noted and then, quoting Byron on the Duchess of Richmond's ball on the eve of Waterloo, he added, 'There was a sound of revelry by night'.[16]

On 5 December, Phillips boarded a Catalina flying boat and set off across the South China Sea to discuss the possibilities of joint naval operations with the commander of America's Asiatic Fleet, Admiral Thomas C. Hart. The two men met at Cavite Naval Base, near Manila, and spoke for most of that afternoon. 'I had pictured a big, husky, personable, magnetic sort,' Hart wrote in his diary. 'He's a bare 5' 2" and decidedly the intellectual type.'

Hart introduced Phillips to America's most decorated soldier, General Douglas MacArthur, who had been spending his retirement as a highly paid military adviser to the Philippines President, Manuel Quezon, when he was recalled to active service in the US Army. MacArthur had been made Supreme Commander of United States Army Forces in the Far East on 26 July 1941. He informed Washington that the Philippines could be held against a Japanese attack for up to six months. Personally he doubted there would be an invasion – not while he was around anyway. According to Hart, MacArthur gave Phillips 'his usual wordy spiel' about Japan's lack of willingness to fight.

In the Middle East, Gordon Bennett noted in his diary on 3 December, 'Indochina has been well prepared [by the Japanese] as a springboard from which to make the dive into Thailand, Malaya and Netherlands East Indies. I fear that the move may start before my return, so I have decided to push off at once.'

He would be too late.

Part Two

The Invasion

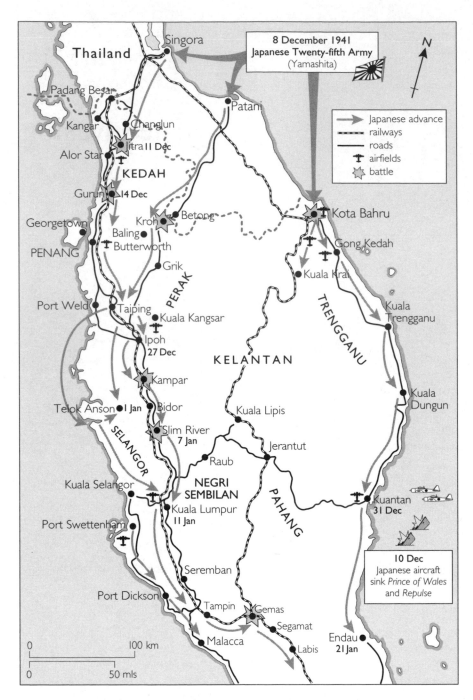

The Japanese invasion of Thailand and Malaya, December 1941

CHAPTER 8

Matador Farce

AT 12.12 P.M. ON Saturday 6 December 1941 a Lockheed Hudson bomber of No. 1 Royal Australian Air Force Squadron, based at Kota Bahru and at the limit of its patrolling range, spotted a Japanese cruiser and three 10,000-ton transports south of Cape Cambodia at the tip of Indochina, steaming north-west towards the Gulf of Thailand. Thirty-four minutes later, Flight Lieutenant John C. Ramshaw and his aircrew were looking down at a much bigger Japanese convoy of 18 transports, with a heavy escort of cruisers and destroyers, also heading west but some distance south of the first one. Ramshaw flew up and down the convoy at less than 1,000 feet. The Japanese warships did not open fire but launched a seaplane; the 27-year-old airman ducked into the clouds to avoid trouble, while his radio operator signalled news of the two convoys back to Kota Bahru.

The north-east monsoon was at its most turbulent and, according to the official report, 'tropical downpours periodically made unaided navigation and accurate ship recognition matters of considerable difficulty', but it was evident to the Australian airmen that the convoys constituted an invasion force and one that was well within steaming range of Kota Bahru.' The information could not have come at a more advantageous time for Far East Command and its 63-year-old Commander-in-Chief, Sir Robert Brooke-Popham. Two and a half hours later, a second patrolling Hudson from the same squadron, flown by Flight Lieutenant Jimmy Emerton, also located the main convoy and confirmed Ramshaw's sighting.

Unbeknown to the two Australian pilots, the transports contained 26,640 soldiers of General Yamashita's 25th Army. The main convoy had assembled at Hainan Island, 250 miles south of Hong Kong, where the soldiers had been practising amphibious landings. As dawn had broken on 4 December, the ships cleared Samah Harbour and headed into the open sea. Scanning the skies from the deck of *Ryujo Maru*, Yamashita noted that the sun and the moon were both visible to the naked eye – a good omen for his campaign. He wrote a poem that day to mark the occasion.

Yamashita's convoy was due to rendezvous in the Gulf of Thailand with two other convoys, one launched from Cape St Jacques, 40 miles south-east of Saigon, and one from Phu Quoc Island, off the south-west coast of Indochina. The fleet would then split up for six different destinations: Singora and Patani on the Kra Isthmus in southern Thailand, three smaller ports in northern Thailand and Kota Bahru in north-east Malaya. Singora and Patani were to act as springboards for the invasion of Malaya, while occupation of the three minor Thai ports would enable Japanese forces to cross into Burma and capture Victoria Point airfield, a vital link on Britain's air reinforcement route from India to Singapore. The six separate missions had to be synchronised to prevent warning of Japan's sneak attacks being passed across the Pacific to the biggest prize of all, the American Pacific Fleet at Pearl Harbor.

In the first phase of Japan's thrust to capture the Asian possessions of Britain, the United States and Holland, the Southern Army was to invade Malaya, northern Sumatra, the Philippines, British Borneo, Hong Kong, Guam and Wake Island. Rabaul, Ambon, Timor and southern Sumatra would be taken in the second phase, and Java and central Burma in the third. Admiral Isoroku Yamamoto, Commander-in-Chief of the Combined Fleet, held his First Fleet in reserve and ordered the Second Fleet to deliver the 25th Army to Malaya, while the Third Fleet would take the 14th Army to the Philippines. The Fourth Fleet, still undetected and comprising six aircraft carriers, two battleships and two heavy cruisers, would attack Pearl Harbor and then take the 144th Infantry Regiment to Guam, Wake Island and Rabaul.[2]

The spearhead of the 25th Army was Lieutenant-General Takuro Matsui's 5th Division, which would land at Singora and Patani, while Takumi Force, a detachment of Lieutenant-General Renya Mutaguchi's 18th Division, would go ashore at Kota Bahru. The third division of Yamashita's force, the Imperial Guards, would capture Bangkok and then make its way south to link up with Yamashita in Malaya at a later date. The task of capturing Victoria Point and occupying southern Thailand went to Uno Force, a regiment of 55th Division, which had been given to Yamashita for the operation.

The 5th Division had been recruited in the Hiroshima district and consisted of many hard-core veterans of the China campaign. It had served continuously in China from 1937 to 1941, earning a fearsome reputation for ruthlessness among Chinese civilians. From November 1937, it operated in the Nanking area; it had taken part in the infamous Rape of Nanking.[3]

The 18th Division, recruited in the Kurume district, had appeared in the Hangchow Bay and Nanking areas in September 1937 and remained there until it participated in the taking of Canton in a joint operation with the 5th and Imperial Guards Divisions in October 1938. It then advanced into Kiangsi and captured Nanning with the 5th Division and Imperial Guards. It was stationed in the Canton area again from February 1940 to August 1941 when it moved to Indochina.

The regiments of the Imperial Guards Division were the most recognisable in the Japanese Army. They had superior physiques and a distinctive cap badge, a five-pointed yellow star inside a wreath. The division had been embodied for the express purpose of protecting the Emperor. It was recruited from all districts of Japan in order to fulfil the highest physical standards in the Japanese Army. The Guards were stationed in Tokyo until September 1939 when the 1st Guards Brigade was sent to South China, and thence to northern Indochina, before returning to Tokyo in April 1941. Meanwhile, in June 1941 the 2nd Guards Brigade, after serving in Shanghai and South China, moved to Hainan Island, where it was reinforced and reorganised into a three-regiment field division and trained especially for the Malayan campaign. From Hainan Island, the division was sent to southern Indochina in July 1941 under the terms of the Vichy-Japanese Agreement.

These were the troops that Yamashita would throw into battle against British and Thai forces. They were backed up by an armoured division of more than 230 light and medium tanks. Less well known was that the 25th Army included 'suicide squads' of Formosans and Koreans whose job was to take the edge off the enemy's defences. In the air, Yamashita commanded the 3rd Air Division of 354 first-line aircraft based in Indochina, including many of the latest type of Zero fighter. In addition, the 22nd Air Flotilla, consisting of the Genzan and Mihoro Air Corps stationed in and around Saigon, was supporting the invasion with 180 aircraft of its own. This made a formidable air force of 534 modern aircraft, compared with the 158 inadequate or obsolescent machines that Air Vice-Marshal Pulford could put into the air.[4]

For the first part of its journey around Indochina, Vice-Admiral Jisaburo Ozawa, naval commander of Malaya Force in his flagship *Chokai*, kept the Second Fleet close to the coast to avoid detection from the air and, once he sailed into open water on 4 December, luck was on his side – heavy rain and thick clouds cloaked the Japanese ships from aerial observation. General Percival's headquarters had ordered air reconnaissance of the area to commence that day from Kota Bahru to Cape Cambodia, then southwest to the Anamba Islands and westwards to Kuantan, but bad weather had closed Kota Bahru airfield and No. 1 Squadron was grounded. However, Kuantan airfield, 150 miles to the south, was still operational and No. 8 Squadron RAAF was able to carry out its surveillance duties, although nothing suspicious was spotted. The same limitations applied the following day, but the rain eased on 6 December and the two Hudsons took off from the slippery grass runway at Kota Bahru with the intention of flying all the way to Cambodia Point.

The positive sightings of the convoys by these two planes sent a frisson of excitement through Air Headquarters, Singapore. All the rumours and bits and pieces of intelligence gathered over recent months contributed to the inescapable conclusion that a Japanese invasion was in progress. That same day the Combined Intelligence Bureau, at the nerve centre of the entire British fighting organisation in the Far East, was alerted to the departure of these convoys from harbour and the actual points of attack. Thai border guards were also reported to be building barricades near the Malay frontier across roads leading to Singora and Patani.[5]

The RAAF's news about the convoys was passed to Sir Robert Brooke-Popham at General Headquarters Far East at 2 p.m. on 6 December. In the absence of Tom Phillips it was up to Brooke-Popham to decide whether to order Operation Matador to meet the Japanese threat head-on in southern Thailand, or to instruct the troops to occupy a line of fixed defences at Jitra, a small village at a road junction in northern Kedah 18 miles south of the Thai frontier.

Knowing his days in Singapore were numbered, Brooke-Popham was not about to blot his copybook by starting a war with Japan. He did not consider the two sightings to be sufficient evidence that the Japanese ships were going to attack Thailand and ordered further reconnaissance planes to shadow the Japanese ships overnight. Brooke-Popham then alerted the commander of America's Asiatic Fleet, Admiral Hart, who was in conference with Admiral Phillips in Manila. While Phillips boarded his Catalina to return to Singapore, Brooke-Popham waited to see whether the Japanese ships maintained their aggressive course or whether it was a bluff to force Britain's hand.

Throughout 1941 the Foreign Office had been emphatic in its insistence that no aggressive move should be made against Thailand that might provoke a militant reaction from pro-Japanese elements in Thailand or from Japan itself. Churchill wished to make it clear to Roosevelt that if hostilities broke out in South East Asia it would not be of his making. Nevertheless, elaborate preparations had been made for a British thrust into Thailand should the necessity arise. Maps had been printed, Thai currency bought and pamphlets drafted to explain to the Thai population the reasons behind the occupation of their country. British officers, dressed in civilian clothing and posing as tourists, slipped into Thailand to carry out reconnaissance of the target areas. They encountered Japanese officers on similar missions and often stayed at the same hotel – the German-run Zoo Hotel at Haad Yai. Both sides studiously ignored each other, while taking careful note. One Japanese spy was amused to see a British 'tourist' hurriedly change step when he got out of step with his companion.[6]

Brooke-Popham had initially been forbidden to order Matador without the permission of the War Cabinet, which would convey its approval through the Chiefs of Staff in a telegraphic cable, the fastest method of reaching the Far East.[7] Churchill had been sweating on a pledge of American support in South East Asia but Roosevelt kept him waiting. The breakthrough came when FDR told the British Ambassador in the US, Lord Halifax, at a meeting in Washington on 1 December that Britain could rely on American backing in the event of a war with Japan. Halifax reported to Churchill that if Japan attacked a British possession 'we could certainly count on their support, though it might take a short time – he spoke of a few days – to get things into political shape here'.[8] Thus when Brooke-Popham sought authority from the Chiefs of Staff the following day to launch Matador on his own initiative, permission was granted on 5 December in a cable addressed to him and Admiral Phillips. There were strings attached, however. The Commanders-in-Chief were informed that America's assurance of armed support was 'conditional on the Japanese attacking British territory, or the Netherlands East Indies, or on Matador being undertaken either to forestall a Japanese landing on the Kra Isthmus or as a reply to a violation of any other part of Siamese territory'.[9]

After reading the telegram, Brooke-Popham's Chief of Staff, General Playfair, remarked drily, 'They've made you personally responsible for declaring war on Japan.' This was the last thing Brooke-Popham wanted to hear, but he informed Percival on 5 December that Matador could now be put into effect without reference to London 'if I had information that a Japanese expedition was advancing with the apparent intention of landing on the Kra Isthmus, or if the Japanese violated any other part of Thailand'. He added in his Dispatch, 'A few days earlier it had been impressed on me that carrying out Matador if the Japanese intended to make a landing in southern Siam would almost certainly mean war with Japan, and in view of this I considered it my duty to be scrupulously careful in acting on the telegram of the 5th December.'

On the other side of the International Dateline in Washington DC, the following exchange took place on 5 December at a Cabinet meeting in the White House:

Frank Knox, Secretary of the Navy: 'We have very secret information that mustn't go outside this room that the Japanese fleet is out. They're out of the harbour. They're out at sea.'

President Roosevelt: 'The question is, in the mind of the Navy and in my mind, whether the fleet is going south.'

Several Cabinet Ministers: 'Singapore?'

President Roosevelt: 'Probably. That's the presumed objective if they go south.'

Frank Knox: 'Every indication is that they are going south.'[10]

Roosevelt sent an eleventh-hour appeal to Hirohito saying that the concentration of large Japanese forces in Indochina had created 'a reasonable doubt of its defensive character' and that the peoples of the Philippines, the Dutch East Indies, Malaya and Thailand could not sit indefinitely 'on a keg of dynamite'. He and the Emperor had 'a sacred duty to restore traditional amity and prevent further death and destruction in the world'. By the time this message had been translated into Japanese, encoded and transmitted to Tokyo, it was too late to have any effect.[11]

On the morning of 6 December, Percival had taken a scheduled flight to Kuala Lumpur to iron out some of the difficulties in Operation Matador with General Sir Lewis Heath. The commander of III Indian Corps vigorously opposed Matador, believing it to be a half-cocked idea and potentially dangerous. It would place his troops in limbo until a decision was made about whether they would be charging into Thailand to confront the Japanese on the beaches or would man the partly prepared Jitra Line.

Percival received news of the Japanese convoys by telephone from Singapore at III Corps headquarters at 3 p.m. 'At 1515 hours I ordered the Commander III Indian Corps to assume the first degree of readiness,' Percival says, 'and, anticipating that Operation Matador might be ordered, to instruct the Commander 11 Indian Division to be ready to move at short notice.' He also contacted the Federated Malay States Railway to arrange for trains to be waiting at prearranged points to pick up Indian troops for the cross-border expedition.

Matador had been modified in 1941 when it was accepted that, owing to a shortage of troops, it would be impossible to occupy both Singora and Patani. Under the revised scheme, the main force, the 11th Indian Division commanded by Major-General David Murray-Lyon and based in northern Kedah, would head for Singora, 130 miles north of the Malayan border by road and rail, while a separate force – consisting of the 3/16th Punjab Regiment, the 5/14th Punjab Regiment from the Penang garrison, one company of sappers and miners, one field ambulance and a light battery of the Federated Malay States Volunteer Force (MSVF) – would drive along the Patani road from the border town of Kroh, but only as far as a position known as the Ledge, 35 miles on the Thai side of the frontier. At this point, the road had been cut into the sheer side of a hill and could easily be blocked by demolition. Thus the Japanese would be resisted at Singora but allowed to land at Patani and then halted at Kroh as soon as they attempted to cross into Malaya. The Singora operation was known as Matador, and the Patani-Kroh operation was labelled Krohcol.

In Malaya, there were numerous beaches suitable for amphibious landings on the east coast but the four most likely were Kota Bahru, defended by the 8th Indian Brigade; Kuantan, defended by other units of the 9th Indian Division; and Endau and Mersing, defended by the 8th Australian Division. For the greater part of the year the seas were comparatively calm, but during the north-east monsoon from December to February storm-tossed waves crashed on to the sandy shores, making conditions extremely hazardous for seaborne troops. However, Dobbie's 1937 study had ascertained that landings would be possible even during the monsoon, although the invaders might have to suspend operations for two or three days at a time when the storms were at their height.

The fixed defences at Jitra were not due to be completed until February 1942 and the location left much to be desired. It had been chosen because it was the best on offer to protect the airfields at Alor Star, Sungei Patani and Butterworth. On the left flank, a stretch of low country, intersected by small canals and ditches, ran west to sea. The main defences were concentrated astride two main roads using a chain of pillboxes combined with natural obstacles. Plans were made to flood an area adjacent to the north–south railway line, which seemed to be the most probable line of enemy advance. An anti-tank ditch was being dug across the main road by a cumbersome mechanical digger, but the ditch's effectiveness would be lost once the Japanese took possession of the trunk road from Singora. Ivan Simson had suggested setting up roadblocks to prevent such an eventuality, but nobody appeared to be listening to him.

Percival returned to Singapore from his meeting with Heath at 6.30 p.m. on 6 December expecting to find that Brooke-Popham had activated Matador. He was disconcerted to discover that the Commander-in-Chief was still making up his mind. A less cautious man would have accepted that all the evidence pointed to a Japanese invasion of Thailand, but taking risks was not in Brooke-Popham's character. He demanded absolute confirmation that an invasion was in the offing and, in the meantime, as Percival, Heath and their staffs anxiously checked their watches, the chances of saving Malaya dwindled with every passing hour.

At the Naval Base, Brooke-Popham took his concerns about the convoys' destination to Admiral Layton and Rear Admiral Arthur Palliser, Chief of Staff of the absent Admiral Phillips. After consultation with the Navy, he concluded that the convoys had probably turned north-west and were making for the shelter of Kao Rong Bay on the west coast of Indochina, which would take them further away from Singora than when first sighted. Believing that this diversion would give him some breathing space, even if Singora was the fleet's ultimate destination, he informed Percival that he would not make a decision on Matador until he had more definite information.

Percival had always deferred to Brooke-Popham on the grounds of seniority, but this was the moment when the GOC should have insisted on a decision as far as Operation Krohcol was concerned. It would have made all the difference to the defence of the Jitra Line if the Ledge position had been occupied in advance of a Japanese landing at Patani. But Percival, correct, punctilious and loyal, was not the man to insist on anything from a superior officer.

Percival's lack of mobility around his command and the absence of efficient communications had already had an adverse effect on his preparations. The fragmented nature of Brooke-Popham's command now started to influence events. The Army and Air Force had moved into the Combined Operations Room in Sime Road, while the Administrative Branch of Malaya Command remained at Fort Canning, partly because its accommodation at Sime Road was not complete and partly so that it could remain in close contact with government departments in the city. The Navy and Brooke-Popham remained firmly ensconced at the Naval Base, half an hour's drive away on the northern side of the island.

Percival and the other commanders darted backwards and forwards between these various locations for meetings. That night, Percival made a final call on Shenton Thomas at Government House to report that the code word 'Raffles' had been given to activate the first degree of readiness in all troops under his command. He then retired to bed at Flagstaff House.

Meanwhile, there had been a flurry of diplomatic activity to clarify British and American obligations towards the tiny Asian kingdom whose security was now threatened. President Roosevelt suggested that the British Government should tell the Thais it had no intention of invading their country but were anxious to see her sovereignty and independence preserved. On 4 December, Sir Josiah Crosby informed the Foreign Office of his growing impatience at the 'unwillingness of either London or Washington to give Thailand a clear-cut promise of military support in the event of a Japanese invasion'. Crosby further reported that the Thai Foreign Minister had 'pressed me very urgently indeed this morning for an immediate declaration from us to Japan that she would find herself at war with us if she attacked Thailand'. The following day Crosby cabled that he had received an urgent appeal from the Thai Prime Minister, Major-General Pibulsongkram, who expected a Japanese attack 'within the next few days' and begged 'most earnestly for [an] immediate public statement by His Majesty's Government that Japan will find herself at war with us if she attacks Thailand'. Lord Cranborne thought it prudent that the details of Operation Matador should be conveyed to Crosby 'for his most secret and personal information'. Cranborne told the Ambassador, 'It is important that if and when the operation is carried out it should not meet with Thai resistance.'[12]

Crosby was startled to learn that British troops might soon be pouring over the Thai border and on 7 December he sent an impassioned plea to Brooke-Popham not to violate Thai sovereignty. Pro-Japanese members of the Thai Government had suggested that British troops would cross the border into Thailand if Japan landed troops at Kota Bahru and, as Britain would then be the aggressor, Thailand could legitimately declare war on her. It was not until later that day that the Thai Prime Minister received a message from Churchill telling him something he already knew: 'There is a possibility of imminent Japanese invasion of your country,' Churchill cabled. 'If you are attacked, defend yourself. The preservation of the full independence and sovereignty of Thailand is a British interest and we shall regard an attack on you as an attack on ourselves.'[13]

Meanwhile, the Japanese invasion fleet was having a run of good luck. Air reconnaissance had failed to locate it again in the afternoon of 6 December and the first Catalina sent out during the night was also unsuccessful. However, a second Catalina took off from Singapore at first light on the 7th with orders to search the west coast of Indochina to test the theory that the convoys had concentrated at the anchorage in Kao Rong Bay. This aircraft located the main convoy 80 miles south of Cape Cambodia sailing westward towards Thailand. As soon as he saw the flying boat, Ozawa ordered his air cover to destroy it. The Catalina, capable of only 135 mph, was shot down by fighters before it could make radio contact with its base.

Three Hudson aircraft sent out on the morning of the 7th failed to find the Japanese owing to poor visibility, which forced two of them to abandon the search. Further Hudson flights were made, but only single merchant vessels were sighted in the Gulf of Thailand, at 1.45 p.m. and 3.45 p.m. that day. Thirty vital hours had passed since the first sightings when, on Sunday evening, positive reports came in from Air Headquarters at Kota Bahru: at 5.50 p.m. one of the Hudson reconnaissance aircraft had sighted a merchant vessel and a cruiser off the Thai coast. The cruiser had opened fire on the Hudson but had missed. At 6.48 p.m. four Japanese vessels, perhaps destroyers, had been seen 70 miles off Singora, steaming south towards Patani and Kota Bahru.

The criteria for launching Operation Matador had now been met, but it was too late to put it into action. The enemy convoy, if it was bound for Singora, would reach its destination about midnight on 7–8 December, whereas it was unlikely that the leading British troops could arrive there before 2 a.m. on 8 December – even then provided that they encountered no opposition from Thai troops on the way.

Percival judged that an encounter battle between the Japanese and his small force would make the enterprise 'very risky, especially as the enemy force was expected to include tanks'. The GOC informed Brooke-Popham at a conference at Sime Road on the evening of 7 December that he 'considered Operation Matador in the existing circumstances to be unsound'. He conferred by telephone with Heath and then drove to the Naval Base with Brooke-Popham who, infuriatingly, was still undecided. Brooke-Popham wrote in his Dispatch, 'If the report of the Catalina flying boat having been shot down by Japanese aircraft on the morning of 7 December, 1941, is correct, then this was the first act of war in the Malaya area between Japan and the British Empire. If not, then the first act was the firing on the Hudson reconnaissance aircraft by a Japanese ship on the evening of the 7 December.'

At the time, however, he did nothing. Brooke-Popham and Percival adjourned to the War Room in the Dockyard Offices at the Naval Base at 9 p.m. At 10.30 p.m. Tom Phillips, who had arrived back from Manila, joined them. Within the hour a decision had been reached. Percival instructed General Heath by phone at 11.20 p.m. that Matador was not to be activated that night but he was to be ready to put it into effect at dawn on 8 December if so ordered.

Heath could hardly believe his ears. Brooke-Popham's prevarication had placed him in an invidious position. His men would have to stand-to in pouring rain all night awaiting an order – which might or might not come in the morning – to move into Thailand. The delay would cause serious dislocation in arrangements for their move to Jitra if Matador was called off and give them less time to complete their defences once they got there.

There was only one telephone line between Kota Bahru and Singapore; at 12.30 a.m. on 8 December an excited voice conveyed the news that gunfire had been seen off Kota Bahru.[14] Brooke-Popham roused Percival from his bed at Flagstaff House, and at 1.15 a.m. Percival woke up Governor Thomas with the news that Japanese troops had landed at Kota Bahru. Thomas said, 'Well, I suppose you'll shove the little men off.'[15]

Thomas rang the Colonial Secretary, Stanley Jones, and the Inspector-General of the Straits Settlements Police, A. H. Dickinson, instructing them that all male Japanese in Singapore should be rounded up and interned. Then he dressed and took coffee with Lady Thomas on the large first-floor balcony of Government House, where he pondered the possible consequences of the events taking place 400 miles to the north. He did not have to wait long for further developments. The phone rang and he was summoned to attend a conference called by Admiral Phillips in the War Room at the Naval Base at 2.30 a.m.

Phillips had used his time on the flight back from Manila to decide what to do with his ships. While the Army and the Air Force were constrained by matters of diplomacy, there was nothing to stop him taking his small fleet to sea and heading for the northern Malayan coast. He reasoned that if an invasion was taking place and he could intervene successfully, it would probably not start again. Phillips intended to put this plan into action, but first he wanted to test the reaction of the other commanders. On the way to the Naval Base, Governor Thomas had picked up two government officials and he arrived to find Phillips, four naval officers, Sir Robert Brooke-Popham and Air Vice-Marshal Pulford at the conference table. General Percival had returned to Singapore but was represented by two members of his staff.

No official minutes were kept of the meeting but a young naval officer, Lieutenant-Commander J. W. McClelland, who was stationed in the signals cubby-hole at one end of the room, surreptitiously kept notes.[16] According to McClelland's account, Phillips opened the meeting by saying that he did not think the Japanese would deploy capital ships or aircraft carriers in Malayan waters as long as the United States Fleet remained undefeated. His main danger, he thought, was from Japanese submarines and, after that, attacks by aircraft. He dismissed high-level bombing as being unlikely to achieve any significant results in the face of his anti-aircraft armaments – unless he was extremely unlucky.

Dive-bombing was likely to cause damaging hits but should not cripple either of his two capital ships; in any case he understood that the Japanese naval dive-bombers operated only from carriers and he had already said that he did not expect to encounter one. As the torpedo was the weapon to which heavy ships were especially vulnerable, the principal danger from aircraft came from the torpedo bomber, as had been amply demonstrated in the destruction of the German pocket battleship *Bismarck*. But in the thick cloud prevalent during the monsoon season it would be difficult to execute simultaneous attacks, while the torpedo bomber itself would be vulnerable to attack by fighters during its approach. Protection by shore-based fighters was thus essential, as the loss of the carrier *Indomitable* had left him devoid of fighter protection. Phillips concluded that if the factor governing the situation was the preservation of his ships, there was no doubt at all that he should retire westward and await reinforcements. He then sat down. McClelland says that Shenton Thomas broke the silence that followed. He said that he knew nothing about warfare, except of the tribal kind, but it had come as a complete surprise to him to learn that the arrival of the battleships was only a bluff, and furthermore that the Japanese might be about to call it. If they did, would this not change the circumstances completely? Shouldn't they ask the Government in London what they wished the Admiral to do? After all, the Japanese would surely be as aware of the shortcomings of the British force as the Admiral himself, and would make every effort to exploit them.

Brooke-Popham then spoke. He disagreed with Thomas and said it was useless to ask for fresh orders. He did not expect a Japanese seaborne attack during the north-east monsoon and still hoped that the occupation of Thailand was the Japanese objective. He finished with a familiar little homily: 'Once he is in a fight, the only way to get a Jap out of it is to kill him!'

In response to Phillips, Conway Pulford emphasised the limitations of his aircraft and the lack of training of his fighter pilots in a fighter-protection role at sea, stressing particularly the difficulties they would run into when out of sight of land. However, within these limitations he would support the Admiral's plan, whatever it might be. Pulford then left the meeting. Shenton Thomas said the provision of fighter protection during any operation was obviously a vital factor in attempting to ensure the safety of the battleships. In his opinion the ships should not be employed on any offensive task unless fighter protection could be guaranteed and he wished that Pulford had not left so he could hear him say so too.

Turning to Brooke-Popham, the Governor said that he could no doubt give the necessary assurances. The Commander-in-Chief remained silent – perhaps, McClelland thought, he realised his aircraft were still on the ground when they should have been attacking Japanese transports at Kota Bahru. Indeed, Brooke-Popham had vital matters on his mind. He was trying to resolve his problem of whether an attack on Kota Bahru fulfilled the Matador criteria, even if the Japanese had not attacked Thailand. While disparaging Shenton Thomas's suggestion, he had in fact cabled London for an answer to this question and was awaiting a reply, even though one of the conditions of America's supplying aid was a Japanese attack on British territory. In the meantime, he said to Phillips, 'Do you know, Admiral, I am beginning to believe that if the Japanese intend to attack, your intervention is the only thing that can prevent the invasion succeeding.'

Suddenly, the meeting was interrupted when 'Air Raid Warning Red' was declared, indicating an imminent attack on the Naval Base. As it was too late to get to the base shelters, the distinguished group in the War Room got down on the floor and crawled under the conference table.[17] At 3.30 a.m. radar stations at Changi and Mersing had reported unidentified aircraft heading for Singapore. Around the same time Fighter Control Operations Room in Singapore had alerted all service establishments that unidentified aircraft were approaching from the north-east. An hour later at 4.30 a.m., twin-engine Japanese bombers raided the Singapore area after flying 700 miles from Indochina.[18]

No air-raid alarm had been sounded and Singapore was not blacked out. It was only when the bombs started exploding that people were alerted to the fact that war had broken out in the Pacific and that they were one of the first targets. The ARP headquarters were manned but the head warden had gone to see a late-night movie and had taken the key to the alarm switch with him.[19] The city's lights blazed throughout the raid; many of them were gas lamps that could be extinguished only by a man (usually on a bicycle) with a long pole. Even if a blackout had been in force, it was a bright moonlit night and the Japanese pilots would have had no difficulty in locating their targets. Most of the bombs fell on Tengah and Seletar airfields and military facilities around Keppel Harbour, but several also hit Raffles Place and Chinatown, where 61 people were killed and 133 injured.

The RAF's official report states, 'Radar detected the approaching raid at a distance of 130–140 miles from Singapore (giving more than 30 minutes' warning). Its approach was promulgated from the Fighter Control Operations Room. Unfortunately the staff of this room was unable to obtain any response from the HQs of the Civil ARP organisation, with the result that the civil population received no effective warning, nor was the Civil Air Defence Scheme put into effective action until it was too late.'[20]

The diary of Sergeant Ron J. Buntain, an Australian crew chief servicing No. 453 Squadron's Buffaloes at Sembawang airfield, reads, 'Monday, 8 Dec 1941 – Was awakened by siren at Naval Base at 0345 hours. Air raid warning yellow was given over amplifier system. 453 Squadron told to report to hangar immediately, while on the way to hangar we saw a formation of bombers which had been picked up in the searchlight beams. All told 17 bombers. Anti-aircraft guns went into action. Saw flashes of tracer bullets bursting around the kites [aircraft]. Bombs began to fall. The first indication that they were the Japs ...'

Terpie Pattara's house was close to Seletar airfield. 'The first bombing took place on 8 December – the Feast of our Lady – and I was asleep in bed,' she says. 'We heard the bombs but there were no sirens. They went off afterwards.'[21] Duff Cooper had been woken at 3 a.m. by his private secretary, Martin Russell, with news of the Japanese landing at Kota Bahru and was nodding off to sleep again when he heard 'the familiar sound of falling bombs, followed by explosions, followed by guns and finally by air-raid warnings'.

Ian Morrison, deputy director of the Far Eastern Bureau of the Ministry of Information, remembers that he and his wife Maria were awakened by sirens in their flat on top of the Cathay Building. From the balcony, he saw searchlights probing the skies to pinpoint enemy aircraft, then he heard the drone of the bombers and the sound of explosions from the docks and the city centre. Anti-aircraft guns blazed away into the night sky without any noticeable effect. The street lights shone brightly throughout the attack.

Planter's daughter Elizabeth Kennaway had the bizarre experience of watching the bombs falling against a Hollywood backdrop. 'We could look over the town and see the lights of the cinema going round and round: *The Road to Rio* with Dorothy Lamour, Bob Hope and Bing Crosby.'[22]

Maisie and Olga Prout were asleep at the Victoria Street convent. 'I heard planes fly overhead early in the morning,' Olga says. 'We'd heard planes before but this was a large squadron. Then suddenly bombs exploded and shook the old wooden dormitory. There were no sirens. We all jumped out of bed and looked out from the balcony and we could see plumes of smoke coming from Chinatown. All the lights were on – there was no blackout. We had had a few air-raid practices but we didn't have any shelters so the nuns hurried us downstairs and packed us into the concrete corridors on the first floor. We were all very excited and we asked the nuns, "Is this the war?" and they said, "Yes, this is it." Then we heard a siren but it was too late.'[23]

The morning after the bombing, the Mother Superior, the Reverend Mother St James, discussed with Bishop Devals the probability that Singapore would be the focus of the main Japanese attack. They decided it would be wise to send the boarders up-country to a convent at Seremban, 40 miles south of Kuala Lumpur. 'We were so sure the British forces would mop up the Japanese in no time,' Maisie says. 'We thought they wouldn't get much further. According to British propaganda, the Japanese were all bow-legged and squinty-eyed and they all had very bad teeth. They would be no match for our troops, so they would be annihilated before they reached Kuala Lumpur. It was quite safe to send us up there.' The sisters' brother John was sent to stay with his Aunt Frances and Uncle Bertie Contes in Penang after his boarding school at Katong was taken over as a military barracks.

Brother Vincent was asleep when the first bombs exploded in the harbour. He heard the wail of sirens and the sound of anti-aircraft guns firing and saw the Japanese planes caught in the searchlights. 'The British had said in a communiqué that the Japanese could hardly fly their aircraft,' he remembers, 'but when we saw them up there, we knew that they knew their business. There was a lot of danger.'

In Orchard Road, Bill Drower heard the bombs exploding and thought, 'That's it – we're at war.' He heard no sirens. At the boarding house, the *jaga* – nightwatchman – hurriedly turned on all the lights so that everyone could see what was happening. Drower turned them off, whereupon the *jaga* promptly flooded the place with light again. 'This happened three times until another guest and I sat on his head,' he says.

When the 'all clear' was sounded at the Naval Base, Sir Shenton Thomas, Sir Robert Brooke-Popham, Admiral Phillips and the others clambered out from under the table and their meeting was deemed to have ended. Phillips signalled his intentions to the Admiralty at 6 a.m. on 8 December and London sent back its 'proof of receipt' by 9.30 a.m. Singapore time. The signal itself is missing from official records but Phillips told McClelland,

'I've drafted a fairly long urgent signal to send to the Admiralty to tell them I'm taking Force Z out this evening to try to scotch the Japanese round Kota Bahru. I rate the chances of getting there no higher than 50–50 but I'm sure it's the only way in which to halt the invasion and if it can be halted, they should find it impossible to start it again. Surprise is absolutely essential but it is just possible in this thick monsoon weather, given even an average amount of luck. But, if we are spotted, which is bound to happen sooner or later, we shall be attacked.'

At the Cathay Building, Ian Morrison dashed downstairs to his office where his boss, Robert 'Rob' Scott, told him that the Japanese had attempted to land troops at Kota Bahru and that British bombers were attacking the Japanese ships. Sir Robert Brooke-Popham had been up all night with his staff dealing with the emergency.

At Amber Mansions, Lorraine Stumm was wakened by her amah when the anti-aircraft guns started firing. Grabbing her baby Sheridan, Lorraine dashed downstairs and sheltered with other residents under the building's concrete staircase. A bomb exploded in the next street and the building shook. When daylight broke, Lorraine went to Raffles Place and saw the bodies of 16 Chinese civilians lined up on the pavement outside Robinson's. The department store had suffered a direct hit which had destroyed its new air-conditioned restaurant, shattered its plate-glass windows and deposited expensive luggage and gifts on to the footpath.

Later that day Lorraine was astonished to receive a cable from Ken Hord, news editor of the *Daily Mirror*, offering her a job. It read, 'Delighted to know you are safe. Can you become our accredited war correspondent and start filing stories immediately?' Ian Morrison received a similar cable from *The Times*, the newspaper his father had served with distinction for 20 years.

The bombs that had been dropped on the Seletar and Tengah airfields had caused little damage. Three Buffalo pilots of No. 453 Squadron RAAF, Flight Lieutenants Timothy A. Vigors, Richard D. Vanderfield and Bert A. Grace, had been ready to take off at Sembawang to intercept the Japanese bombers but had been forbidden to do so. Vigors, a 20-year-old Irishman educated at Eton and RAF College, Cranwell, had fought in the Battle of Britain. Despite his youth, he was temporarily in command of the squadron in the absence of Squadron Leader Harper, who had gone to Australia to recruit more pilots.

Vigors had shot down a Messerschmitt 109 on his second sortie,[24] while Vanderfield and Grace, both from Sydney, had seen combat in

Britain and the Middle East. All were eager to go into action against the Japanese; when Vigors suggested they might chance their luck and take off anyway, he was sternly informed that they would be charged with disobeying orders if they did. In the circumstances, the three young airmen could do nothing except watch the bombers drone across the moonlit sky. One explanation for the decision was that their Buffaloes might have been mistaken for Japanese aircraft and shot down by anti-aircraft fire. Another reason, widely published, was that they were not trained in night flying, even though all three were experienced airmen and Vigors had the distinction of having shot down a Heinkel 111 bomber in a solo night sortie over England. There were suspicions that the ban related to the bad feeling between the Australian squadron and the RAF's fighter controllers.

In London, Churchill told the House of Commons that the Japanese High Command – 'a curious form; not the Imperial Japanese Government' – had declared war on Great Britain and the United States. He described the bombing of Singapore, Kota Bahru and Hong Kong as 'wanton acts of unprovoked aggression, committed in flagrant violation of international law'.[25] Churchill told MPs that Japan's 'insane ambition and insatiable appetite' had triggered the state of war. 'We can only feel that Hitler's madness has infected the Japanese mind,' he said.

Sir Henry Pownall, Vice-Chief of the Imperial General Staff, wrote in his diary that Churchill 'didn't believe that the Japs would come into the war – not yet at any rate. For once his long range vision was at fault, and badly. I only hope we shall not pay dearly for the mistake.'[26]

The most perplexing aspect of this bewildering night was why Brooke-Popham had not released the 11th Division from its Matador commitment and ordered Krohcol to advance into Thailand after receiving news of the landings at Kota Bahru and the air raid on Singapore. When one of Percival's staff telephoned GHQ Far East on the morning of 8 December, he was told the Commander-in-Chief was awaiting the results of the latest air reconnaissance over Singora and Patani before deciding which course of action to take. Air reconnaissance at dawn showed that enemy forces had indeed landed at Singora and Patani, that a number of ships were lying off the Thai coast and that Japanese planes were using Singora airfield.

At 8 a.m. Brooke-Popham received a cable from London granting him authority to move British troops into Thailand if the Japanese had landed at Kota Bahru but had not attacked Thailand itself. He now had no reason for any further delay in activating Krohcol, yet at 8.20 a.m. GHQ Far East told Malaya Command that Operation Matador had been approved by the Chiefs of Staff in London but added, 'Do not act.'

Instead of questioning the absurdity of this instruction, Percival quietly informed Heath at his Kuala Lumpur headquarters at 9.30 a.m. that the Japanese were already at Singora and Patani and authorised him to send a mobile force – not Krohcol – across the Thai border to 'harass and delay the Japanese advance' while Brooke-Popham made up his mind about Matador and Krohcol. The message finally cancelling Matador was sent from GHQ to Percival's headquarters shortly before 10 a.m., but at that hour Percival was in the chamber of the Legislative Council reporting on the outbreak of war. When Heath rang the Combined Operations Room for clarification, he was fobbed off by Brigadier Torrance with the answer that Percival was at the Legislative Council and could not be interrupted. Percival's Dispatch says that the order to execute Krohcol was finally passed on to Heath 'at about 1100 hours'.

Heath was furious about the mix-up. 'I find it impossible to excuse General Percival for permitting Air Chief Marshal Sir Robert Brooke-Popham not to arrive at a decision on 7 December when everything pointed to the certainty of Japan initiating the war in Malaya,' he wrote after the war. To make matters even more difficult for the 11th Division, the vital message 'Matador off, man Jitra' was not received by General Murray-Lyon in northern Malaya until 1.30 p.m. on the 8th, despite Percival's telephone call to Heath more than two hours earlier.

It was all woefully muddled and the only beneficiaries were the Japanese. The switch from storming into Thailand in an offensive operation to manning the partly completed, waterlogged defensive line at Jitra had a damaging psychological effect on the 11th Division troops, who had been drenched after standing-to all night in pouring rain. The main culprit for the Matador farce was undoubtedly Sir Robert Brooke-Popham, who had given the Japanese a 10-hour start at Singora and Patani. He had been terrified that the Japanese were bluffing, yet he was incapable of cancelling the operation of his own volition, or of ordering Krohcol even though he had been given the green light from London. But Percival was also at fault for not insisting that the Ledge should be occupied as early as the 7th, irrespective of whether Matador was launched or not.[27]

The Japanese landings came as no surprise to British intercept operators working at the Kranji listening post in Singapore. They had been monitoring Japanese naval signals so thoroughly for the previous two months that they knew the names of every ship in the Japanese invasion fleet that had massed in the Gulf of Thailand. A further message from the Japanese Ambassador in Bangkok to Tokyo revealed one of the ships' destinations as Kota Bahru. All of the information had been passed to GHQ Far East in plenty of time.

Britain's primary source of high-grade intelligence in 1941 came from intercepts of the Japanese naval code JN25. Decrypts of these Morse code messages were available to the Prime Minister and his military hierarchy. It has been suggested elsewhere in Brooke-Popham's defence that he knew from reading these decrypts the precise details of the Japanese convoys and their targets but he could take no action until this information had been corroborated from other sources, to prevent the Japanese from learning that their codes had been broken. Brooke-Popham, however, already had his corroboration in the RAAF's visual sightings of the convoys on 6 December. Moreover, the Japanese knew they had been spotted and would have thought the British were acting on that evidence. Indeed, Admiral Ozawa, the foremost tactician in the Imperial Japanese Navy, had been expecting a pre-emptive air strike against his task force for that very reason and was surprised it never materialised.[28]

The only bit of luck on the opening day of hostilities was that the Japanese bombers had missed the biggest prizes of all – *Prince of Wales* and the *Repulse*. Britain's pin-up battleship and the veteran cruiser were anchored at the Naval Base, sitting ducks for air attack. Richard Poole, then a young officer in *Repulse*, recalls, 'On the morning of the 8th, air-raid warnings were given and the city's lights went on everywhere. We rushed up to our Repel Aircraft positions and there was a complete hush all over the ship with just the odd command from the captains of the guns and the noise of shells being unloaded from the ready-use lockers and thumping on the deck.

'The next thing we saw searchlights fingering about the sky and revealing 10 or 12 aircraft, very high and flying dead over the top of us. We all opened up, spectacularly, masses of flame from the muzzles of the guns of *Prince of Wales*. They flew on; no bombs were dropped on us but they had already dropped them on Singapore.

'Then there was a broadcast by the commander to say that the Japanese Navy had attacked Pearl Harbor and as of that moment we were at war with Japan. Next day, the captain went to several meetings and then at midday gave orders to prepare to go to sea. At 5 o'clock that night *Prince of Wales* left her berth and passed us and we all fell in astern. Everyone was very keyed up and excited.'

In the Combined Operations Room at Sime Road, Bill Drower asked one of the RAF officers how many planes were available to fight the enemy. He replied, 'Maybe 60 – and some of them won't fly.'

CHAPTER 9

First Blood

KOTA BAHRU, FIVE MILES up the Kelantan River from the rain-swept coast of north-east Malaya, was a busy little place with a cinema, restaurants, an arts and crafts shop and a jail. In December 1941 the township was bursting with troops from the 8th Brigade of Major-General A.E. 'Bustling Bill' Barstow's 9th Indian Division.[1] A visitor who dined in the officers' mess on Thursday 4 December says, 'As I remember, nobody expected war just then. They had a lot of mines laid along the beaches and we heard a good few go off, set off either by dogs or by coconuts dropping on them!'

Seventy minutes before Japan's sneak attack on Pearl Harbor, troops from General Yamashita's 25th Army poured ashore on the beaches at Kota Bahru, yet nothing was done to warn the Americans in Manila, where Admiral Phillips had so recently discussed Japanese intentions with General MacArthur and Admiral Hart.

The Imperial Japanese Navy knew all about the arrival of *Prince of Wales* and *Repulse* in Singapore from aerial surveillance, broadcasts on Radio Singapore, reports in the local press and their own agents. Ten submarines had been deployed off eastern Malaya to intercept the British capital ships or any other British naval craft heading for the Japanese landing zones. But there was no sign of the Royal Navy, and Admiral Ozawa decided to go ahead with the landing at Kota Bahru.

The Royal Air Force Station, Kota Bahru, the most vital link in the Kelantan air power chain, was situated a mile and a half inland from the beachfront, where the commander of the 8th Brigade, Brigadier Berthold W. 'Billy' Key, had dispersed the 3/17th Dogra Regiment. In common with Percival's other troop placements throughout northern Malaya, the men were charged with protecting the airbase rather than defending the town. The Dogras manned a triple line of pillboxes and Dannert wire entanglements on Badang and Sabak beaches to the north-east of Kota Bahru airfield, with machine-gun emplacements, large numbers of anti-personnel and anti-tank mines, and with artillery dug in at key points. But the defences were not as effective as they seemed: the beaches were slightly south of the estuary of the Kelantan River and although there was a boom across the river mouth, a navigable creek ran down to the sea between Badang and Sabak beaches. There were also gaps of up to 1,000 yards between each of the Dogras' pillboxes, and visibility between them and the beach was blotted out for hours at a time by torrential rain.

Further south, Brigadier Key placed the 2/10th Baluchistan Regiment on a long stretch of beach to defend the airfields at Machang and Gong Kedah. Some pillboxes in the Baluchis' area weren't even real structures but wooden dummies, erected to fool Japanese reconnaissance aircraft. Furthermore, the two forward Baluchi battalions were responsible for a front of more than 30 miles, with the average company front exceeding 8,000 yards.

At 11.45 p.m. on Sunday 7 December the Dogras reported three enemy transports anchoring in heavy seas off their section of coast. Soon afterwards, as the first fully loaded landing craft were lowered into the water, British 18-pounders opened fire. Japanese warships escorting the transports but standing further offshore replied with a bombardment aimed at the beach defences. The Japanese striking force was Major-General Hiroshi Takumi's detachment, comprising the 56th Infantry Regiment of the 18th Division, one battery of mountain guns, two quick-firing guns, one battery of anti-aircraft guns, one company of engineers, one section of signallers, one section of medical and sanitation personnel and one field hospital. The force totalled 5,300 men, mostly of tough peasant stock from Japan's harsh Kyushu region.

The Kota Bahru landing had been synchronised to coincide with the air raid on Pearl Harbor but it took place 70 minutes earlier when, at 12.25 a.m. on 8 December, the leading Japanese troops swarmed ashore at the junction of Badang and Sabak beaches in the teeth of savage machine-gun fire from the Dogras. Visibility was poor and the lights of Kota Bahru township were not visible from the sea. General Heath's belief is that the Japanese were guided to their landing place by a fifth columnist. 'We spotted that there were lights being shown,' he says. 'They were apparently being operated by a Chinese smuggler whom we had tried to get arrested months previously but there was insufficient evidence.'[2]

Many in the first wave of Japanese troops were killed or wounded and the remainder burrowed into the wet sand to avoid the fusillade. Some used their steel helmets as entrenching tools to gouge out the sand in front of them, enabling them to crawl forward to the first line of barbed-wire entanglements, where exploding landmines annihilated the front ranks, but then other Japanese climbed over their bodies and severed the wire. At the first pillbox, a Japanese soldier threw his body over a loophole, whereupon a group of soldiers rushed the position with hand grenades and bayonets to attack the occupants. Some of the landing craft slipped unseen into the creek between Bandang and Sabak beaches, and Japanese shock troops jumped out and attacked the Dogras from the rear. By 1 a.m., after heavy hand-to-hand fighting, the enemy had succeeded in capturing all of the pillboxes in this section of beachfront.[3]

Brigadier Key's headquarters telephoned the operations room at Kota Bahru airfield to request an attack on the enemy transports. Wing Commander R. H. 'Curly' Davis, the controller, informed Air Headquarters, Singapore, that Japanese ships were shelling the shore and he intended to call out the station. Brooke-Popham, however, had issued an order to the Air Officer Commanding that no offensive action was to be taken even if the Japanese convoys were found. Davis was ordered to send up a reconnaissance aircraft to photograph the Japanese ships with the help of flares. Davis allegedly replied, 'No. I'm giving the order now that we're going out to bomb the landing fleet.'[4] Brooke-Popham's order was rescinded when Pulford pointed out to the Commander-in-Chief that Malaya was actually being invaded.

Kota Bahru was home to No. 1 Squadron RAAF, whose flight crews had already been alerted to the emergency by the sound of gunfire. Flight Lieutenant Oscar Diamond remembers, 'The CO, Curly Davis, said, "Everybody out – this is not a drill. We've got a war on our hands." I didn't worry too much about it because I thought, "Well, that's what we're here for, that's what we've trained for."' Of the 13 Hudsons in No. 1 Squadron, three were in a state of disrepair awaiting spare parts which had been ordered but had not been delivered, but six aircraft were bombed-up and the remaining four were soon made ready. Nevertheless, two waves of enemy troops had landed on the beaches before the first Hudson, piloted by Flight Lieutenant John Lockwood, took off at 2.08 a.m. armed with four 250-pound bombs.[5]

The 22-year-old pilot from Geelong, Victoria, was barely airborne when he saw three Japanese transports – later identified as *Awagisan Maru*, *Ayatosan Maru* and *Sakura Maru* – in the waters beneath him less than two miles offshore. In clearing weather under a rising moon, he dived down to 50 feet and released two bombs at masthead height. Both missed their target and his attack drew heavy anti-aircraft fire from all directions, forcing him to bank sharply. But he flew in again to attack the same ship and dropped his two remaining bombs from a similar height.

John Ramshaw, who had followed Lockwood into the attack, confirmed that these bombs scored direct hits on the vessel amidships. This was *Awagisan Maru*, containing tanks, artillery, troops and Major-General Takumi himself. Oscar Diamond launched his attack a few minutes later. 'The aerodrome was waterlogged, but we managed to get off all right and the first thing I saw was a ship unloading troops and I do believe they had small tanks,' he says. 'We attacked it straight away [in] two runs at masthead height. I dropped a couple of bombs on the first run that straddled it, but on the second run we seemed to have hit it right in the middle with two bombs and there was a terrific explosion. At the same time, my aircraft got badly damaged from flak or bomb shrapnel, and one engine cut out.'

The Hudson had two Browning .303-inch machine guns in the nose and two in the rear turret, while the muzzles of two other guns poked through openings cut in the perspex of the side windows. As the Hudson veered away, the gunners raked the vessel's decks, hitting a number of Japanese troops. Diamond got his first whiff of cordite when the rear gunner started firing. He remembers, 'I smelled it and I thought, "Jeepers, are we on fire?" I started to call him, "Is there a fire there?" He said, "No, no, we're not on fire."'

Awagisan Maru burst into flames and had to be abandoned. The Hudsons also claimed six hits on a second transport, *Ayatosan Maru*, which was set on fire but was later salvaged. Japanese soldiers wearing lifejackets and holding their rifles aloft leaped over the sides and scrambled into landing craft or swam to the shore. Two bombs exploded in the centre of a group of 10 barges close to the beach and several capsized; others were repeatedly strafed. Anti-aircraft fire was heavy and accurate and two Hudsons were shot down, while most of the others were riddled with bullet holes. The first plane to be lost was Flight Lieutenant Ramshaw's, which was shot down on his second sortie. It crashed into the sea and Ramshaw and two of his crew, Sergeant Garet S. White and Sergeant Jeffrey C. Coldrey, were killed. The sole survivor, 24-year-old Flying Officer Donald A. Dowie, of Adelaide, was picked up by a Japanese ship, earning him the dubious distinction of becoming the first Australian prisoner of war in Japanese hands.

Oscar Diamond limped back to Kota Bahru, where his aircraft was declared a write-off. 'The fitters later showed me some shrapnel they'd taken out of the oil tank and they said the aircraft looked like a sieve,' he says. Debriefing of the RAAF crews who returned to base estimated the

Japanese task force at six warships – probably three cruisers and three destroyers – three transports and a landing-barge carrier.

The morning of 8 December dawned clear and bright, but out to sea the cloud ceiling was down to 500 feet. During the night, all Europeans at Kota Bahru township had been driven to the railhead at Kuala Krai for the 150-mile train ride to Kuala Lipis. At 5 a.m. Curly Davis ordered a break in the attack on the Japanese landing craft to give his Hudsons time to refuel and rearm. The aircrews estimated that as well as sinking one transport and damaging another they had sunk or overturned at least 24 barges. At 7.10 a.m. John Lockwood made a reconnaissance out to sea and reported that all the enemy ships had retired, except the transport which was blazing fiercely. This was confirmed soon afterwards when a number of British formations, among them No. 36 Squadron's Vildebeestes from Gong Kedah and No. 62 Squadron's Blenheims from Alor Star, arrived at Kota Bahru to discover that the Japanese troopships and their naval escorts had left the area. The Blenheims proceeded to the neighbourhood of Patani, where they encountered a force of Zero fighters, and although Japanese ships were sighted and bombed, the attack 'was probably ineffective'.[6]

Soon after 9 a.m. the Japanese replied when navy Zeros and army Type 97 fighters attacked Kota Bahru airfield. Diving from 7,000 feet to almost treetop height, the enemy pilots attacked the airfield's anti-aircraft defences, displaying great aeronautic skills. The raids continued at intervals throughout the day, with the pilots switching their attentions to ground crew and the surviving Hudsons but causing few casualties and little damage.

At 10.30 a.m. Brigadier Key ordered the 2/12th Frontier Force Regiment (less two companies) to counterattack the enemy on the beaches from the south and the 1/13th Frontier Force Rifles to strike from the north. General Percival placed the 4/19th Hyderabads, who were in reserve in Negri Sembilan, under the command of III Indian Corps and they began the long rail journey to Kota Bahru. Around midday, brigade headquarters, acting on inaccurate information, reported that three enemy transports were disembarking troops at the mouth of the Kelantan River. Four Hudsons and three Vildebeestes were scrambled to attack but although several armoured patrol boats were seen and attacked, there was no sign of a fresh enemy landing. Two of the Hudsons were damaged by fire from the enemy boats, leaving only five serviceable aircraft on the station.[7]

Throughout the morning, 150 aircraft of the 7th Japanese Air Brigade, 65 of them long-range fighters and all flying initially from southern Indochina, made heavy attacks on the seven major airfields in northern

Malaya – Alor Star, Sungei Patani, Butterworth, Penang, Kota Bahru, Gong Kedah and Machang – often catching British aircraft returning from their own sorties or refuelling in preparation for further ones.[8] 'The performance of the Japanese aircraft of all types and the accuracy of their high-level bombing had come as an unpleasant surprise,' Percival says. 'Our own air force had already been seriously weakened.'

Pulford had started the day with 110 operational aircraft in northern Malaya but ended it with just 50, 40 planes having been destroyed and 20 seriously damaged. He was forced to order his remaining aircraft to fly to safer airfields in the south. The Japanese had won air superiority on the first day of the Pacific War and were never in danger of losing it, despite desperate pleas to London for replacement aircraft and last-minute attempts to fill the gap with a seaborne cargo of 51 crated Hurricanes.

One of General Heath's complaints was that 'the Air Force promised us that they could dispose of 40 per cent of any ships coming this way or towards south Thailand. [But] the ships apparently were coming in too close for torpedo-carrying aircraft, it being only seven fathoms deep.'[9]

The most damaging Japanese air raids were against Alor Star and Sungei Patani. At Alor Star, 27 twin-engine Type 97 bombers attacked the airfield 20 minutes after the return of No. 62 Squadron from its raid on Patani. Using 150-pound bombs, partly high-explosive and partly incendiary, the Japanese attacked from a height of around 15,000 feet, catching the British aircraft while refuelling. Ten Blenheim bombers were put out of action, four being completely destroyed. The fuel dump and airport buildings were set on fire and, as the water supply was put out of action, the fires could not be extinguished until repairs had been carried out. Seven men were killed. Alor Star was defended by four 3-inch 20-hundredweight guns which failed to bring down any enemy aircraft. At Sungei Patani, most airport buildings were shattered by bombing and the airfield had to be evacuated.

General Heath says, '[It was] amazing the quickness with which the Japanese Air Force got going. Their success was due to two things: (a) the belly-tanks which their Air Force carried: we knew they had these from their attacks in China. When they met our Air Force they pressed a button, released their belly-tanks and then became more than a match for our Buffaloes; and (b) the remarkable accuracy of their high-level bombing: quite remarkable that they could pick off just what they wished. During an attack on Alor Star aerodrome they hit the operations room, petrol dump and wireless station. These bombing attacks were from high altitudes of

15,000 feet and more.'[10]

It was too late to do anything about the Japanese troops in the Singora and Patani areas, where most of the Japanese 5th Division had gone ashore in the early hours against token resistance from the Thai Army. The most serious casualty was said to be an officer who sprained his ankle.[11] Yamashita was among the first to land at Singora. Several officers accompanied the Japanese Consul to the local police station, where they were fired on. Leaving their cars, they crawled to the gate, shouting, 'The Japanese Army has come to save you.' Further north, Uno Force landed on the narrow neck of the Kra Isthmus and took the airfield at Victoria Point across the Burmese border without difficulty. The enemy quickly moved 60 aircraft to Singora airfield and 80 to 100 to Don Muang airfield, Bangkok.

Brooke-Popham's contribution to the British war effort was to release an Order of the Day, over which he had sweated for many hours prior to the opening of hostilities. Translated into several languages and widely distributed to the civilian population, it perpetuated the myth that all would be well. It read, in part, 'We are ready. We have had plenty of warning and our preparations are made and tested ... Our defences are strong and our weapons efficient ... We see before us a Japan drained for years by the exhausting claims of her wanton onslaught on China ...'

Meanwhile, Brigadier Key's counterattack against the Japanese at Kota Bahru had broken down in dense, waterlogged country in the Kelatan estuary. At 4 p.m. on 8 December a rumour spread like wildfire around Kota Bahru airfield that Japanese troops had broken through and reached the airfield's perimeter. The rumour gathered strength when stray bullets from the fighting near the beach whizzed across the runways. Instructions were issued by an unauthorised person – never identified – to put the airfield denial scheme into operation. The station buildings, including the operations room, were set ablaze, and air crew bundled emergency rations and spare parts into the five airworthy Hudsons – one of them held together with wire – and hastily took off.

Brigadier Key and Wing Commander C. H. Noble, the station commander, hastily checked the airfield themselves and discovered that the rumour was false, but it was too late to stay the evacuation. Hearing that the airfield was under attack by ground forces, Pulford had ordered all serviceable aircraft to be flown down the coast to Kuantan and the airfield to be closed down. Once the Hudsons had disappeared over the treetops, the ground staff set off in borrowed trucks for the railhead at Kuala Krai. Key says, 'To the best of my knowledge the aerodrome was not penetrated by the

Japanese until approximately midnight.' However, Oscar Diamond says he went to his hut to retrieve a radio set and photographs of his family and witnessed hand-to-hand fighting between Indian and Japanese troops. '[The Japanese] were right on the airfield and actually fighting in our quarters,' he remembers. No. 1 Squadron's report, vetted by Davis, states that considerable enemy ground fire had seriously interfered with movement on the airfield during the day.

Huge stocks of bombs and large supplies of petrol were abandoned at Kota Bahru and the runways had not been cratered. There was little Key could do about the bombs and the runways, but he called in the 73rd Field Battery who fired at point-blank range into the petrol tanks. According to the Official Historian, 'The hurried evacuation of the airfield at Kota Bahru was premature and not warranted by the ground situation.'[12] No offensive or reconnaissance aircraft were now available at Kota Bahru, and the Battle of Kelantan was as good as lost.

By 7 p.m. that day, Japanese ships returned to Sabang beach with reinforcements and the enemy started to infiltrate between the beach posts. Brigadier Key telephoned 9th Division headquarters, where he found Barstow, his divisional commander, in consultation with General Heath. Hearing that the position was untenable, they gave Key permission to withdraw from the beachfront; he decided to take up a position covering Kota Bahru town. Torrential rain had started again, field telephone lines had been cut and communications reduced to liaison officers moving among the various units. Some of the orders went astray, so that some members of the 1/13th Frontier Force Rifles were left sitting in their trenches, while other troops became hopelessly lost in the dark.

Heath and Barstow thought that a more decisive break would be preferable and wanted to move Key's brigade to Kuala Lipis, meaning a withdrawal of more than 150 miles to a point midway between east and west Malaya. There was no road between Kuala Krai and Kuala Lipis, and the only means of escape was along a single railway line which crossed many rivers and ravines in mountainous country. Barstow argued that there was a good chance of losing the brigade if it remained on the east coast, whereas at Kuala Lipis it could easily move west to counter the main Japanese threat to the 11th Division. Bill Barstow had been at Staff College with Percival and the two men were on good terms. The GOC, however, refused to sanction the move. It was only the second day of the campaign and he was furious that his corps commander and one of his divisional commanders were proposing to surrender most of Kelantan to the

Japanese. Relations between Heath and Percival, already strained, became even more difficult.

No. 62 Squadron RAF, which had moved from Alor Star to Butterworth at dawn on 9 December, was ordered to bomb Singora at 5 p.m., but the airfield was attacked by Japanese aircraft just as the Blenheims were taking off and many were badly damaged. Only one Blenheim, piloted by Squadron Leader Arthur Scarf, cleared the airfield along with a few Buffalo fighters. Twenty-eight-year-old Scarf, known to his family and aircrew as 'Pongo',[13] circled overhead for a time and, having witnessed the devastation of the planes on the ground, flew alone to Singora, where he bombed the airfield despite heavy anti-aircraft fire and the attentions of enemy fighters. Although badly wounded in the back and left arm, he flew his plane back to Malaya while conducting a running fight with the enemy. Realising he would not make it as far as Butterworth, he remained conscious long enough to crash-land with the help of his navigator, Flight Sergeant Paddy Calder, in a rice-field near Alor Star. Scarf's crew escaped unhurt and the heroic pilot was rushed to Alor Star hospital, where his wife Sallie was a nursing sister.

She says, 'On 9 December 1941, during the afternoon, I was off duty when Pat Boxall, another Nursing Sister at Alor Star Hospital, came over to tell me an English casualty was being brought in. I was very shocked when I found the patient was my late husband Pongo who had by some miracle managed to land his plane in a paddy-field nearby to the aerodrome and hospital, his two sergeants being unscathed. Dr Peach who brought him in had administered some medication and Pongo was cheerfully saying, "Don't worry," but he was severely wounded in his left arm and back. He was quietly settled in a twin-bedded ward and a saline drip was put up. As soon as the doctor saw him he ordered at least two pints of blood. As I was found compatible, two pints were taken. Pat Boxall went with him to the [operating] theatre. Pongo was still cheerful and said, "Don't worry, keep smiling, chin up!" Pat returned soon afterwards to tell me he just slipped away whilst under anaesthesia. I couldn't believe it and went along to the theatre to verify the tragic news.'[14] Arthur Stewart King Scarf was awarded a posthumous Victoria Cross.[15]

General Headquarters cabled London that, at the current rate of attrition, it was unlikely that the Air Force would last more than two or three weeks. To Percival, it was clear 'that the success of the enemy's attack on our northern aerodromes would considerably handicap our own air action and that this in turn would unfavourably prejudice our fortunes in the fighting on land'. Dutch air reinforcements arrived in Singapore Island, consisting of three squadrons of Glenn Martin bombers totalling 22 aircraft, and one squadron of nine Buffalo fighters. However, none of the air crews had had any training in night flying, and squadron by squadron the bombers were sent back to the Dutch East Indies to complete training.

Japanese landing operations at Singora and Patani had been delayed by rough seas, but the numbers steadily grew until there were 13,500 troops at Singora and 7,550 at Patani. The total number of troops in these two Thai ports and at Kota Bahru was 25,640, of whom 17,230 were combat troops. The Thai Minister for Foreign Affairs informed 'Bing' Crosby that his government had signed, under duress, an agreement with Japan allowing Japanese troops to cross the Thai border to attack Malaya or Burma.

Kota Bahru town was captured at 2 p.m. on 9 December. The Japanese had lost 320 men killed and 538 wounded, as well as losing the burned-out *Awagisan Maru* and the damaged *Ayatosan Maru*. The 8th Indian Brigade's casualties were listed as 68 killed, 360 wounded and 37 missing.

In Singapore on 10 December, Duff Cooper was appointed Resident Minister for Far Eastern Affairs and, in accordance with instructions from Westminster, the War Committee was upgraded to the Far East War Council, with Cooper as chairman. The council members were Sir Shenton Thomas, Sir Robert Brooke-Popham, Admiral Phillips, General Percival, Air Vice-Marshal Pulford and V. G. Bowden, the Australian Trade Commissioner. Major-General Gordon Bennett was invited to attend the council's meetings if he so wished.

Cooper's terms of reference were to give the Commanders-in-Chief political guidance and to relieve them of extraneous responsibilities so they could give their full attention to the campaign. He was also given the power to settle emergency matters on the spot when there was no time to refer them to London and to authorise expenditure in the same circumstances.

But if Cooper thought he might be able to play a key role in fighting the Japanese he was to be sadly disappointed. Shelton Thomas and Brooke-Popham were both implacably opposed to what they perceived to be 'political interference' in service matters. They made it plain at the first meeting of the War Council that they would oppose Cooper at every turn. Brooke-Popham informed him that he would report only to the Chiefs of Staff, while Thomas announced that the Colonial Office remained his sole lord and master.

Bowden, who had served with the British Army in France in World War I and was a former President of the Anzac Society, had represented Australia in China and Japan for 25 years and quickly became a vocal member of the War Council. He cabled Canberra that the Chief of the Special Branch, Mervyn Wynne, had told him that the situation was 'slipping hourly' and that martial law was urgently needed. Wynne despaired of impressing the Administration with the seriousness of the situation, and criticised the Governor for his preoccupation with red tape and his unwillingness to deal with the crisis. 'Indications are that Singapore will shortly be in [a] virtual state of siege,' Bowden reported, 'and I feel appropriate control measures should be introduced immediately while facilities for organisation are still intact.'[16]

When Duff Cooper asked Brooke-Popham for a list of military require-ments, the C-in-C replied that he had already sent one to the Chiefs of Staff who had turned his request down. Cooper offered to bring the matter to Churchill's attention, but Brooke-Popham informed him that he could not 'be guilty of disloyalty to the Chiefs of Staff'.[17] Angrily, Cooper told Brooke-Popham that 'if he thought loyalty to the Chiefs of Staff was of greater importance than winning the war I could not agree with him, and that if he really believed that the supply of certain weapons was essential there were no methods which he should not adopt to secure those weapons'.[18]

As the disasters of December became known in London, the unfortu-nate Commander-in-Chief suffered the indignity of being described by Lord Addison in the House of Lords as 'a nincompoop'.[19] The editors of *Time* magazine cast a sceptical eye on Singapore and published some trenchant observations in an article headlined 'World at Stake?' It read:

'Be prepared,' warned the London *Daily Herald*, 'to learn from some military spokesman or semi-official syrup dispenser that the situation in the Far East is scarcely relevant to the general trend of the war. Be prepared for the revival of soothing phrases about "keeping a sense of perspective".

'Be prepared for reminders that, my dear fellow, the real enemy is Germany, and for suggestions that the war with Japan is little more than an exciting sideshow.' These were typical of the angry, worried words which flew in the capital of the British Empire last week when it was learned that Singapore, farthest-flung fortress of the Empire, was in grave danger. But the warning was amiss.

The Government dispensed no syrup. It appointed Alfred Duff Cooper, onetime Secretary of State for War, onetime First Lord of the Admiralty, onetime Minister of Information, who has been in Singapore for 15 weeks, to be Resident Minister for Far Eastern Affairs. He will have Cabinet rank, will be equal, if not superior, to Commander-in-Chief Air Chief Marshal Sir Robert Brooke-Popham.

This was reassuring to the British people, who were a little shaken on Sir Robert. He had given them an exaggerated sense of complacency about Singapore by saying, in the course of 1941:

- 'The whole of the East Indies and the Far East are in a high state of preparedness for any eventuality.'
- 'We are in a position to handle any war situation that may arise.'
- 'As long as we are awake and Japan sees it, I think the situation will remain as it is.'
- 'We have had plenty of warning and our preparations are made and tested.'

By contrast, Minister Duff Cooper's first statement was neither sweet nor soothing: 'Let us not blind ourselves to the gravity of the situation or the seriousness of the task that awaits us. Let us frankly admit that so far the Japanese have been extremely successful.'

In his worst nightmare, Brooke-Popham could not have envisaged the carnage that his hesitancy would inflict on the 11th Indian Division and the RAF. His air reconnaissance showed that the Japanese were already operating large numbers of aircraft from airfields in southern Thailand. On Singora aerodrome alone there were 100 planes with comparatively little anti-aircraft gun protection – a marvellous target for RAF bombers had it possessed a half-decent striking force. Without enlisting Duff Cooper's assistance or invoking his name, Brooke-Popham again cabled the Chiefs of Staff calling for urgent reinforcements, especially of long-range bombers and night fighters.

Pulford's air force in the whole of Malaya and Singapore had been reduced to 100 aircraft, including those of dubious serviceability, and it was decided that bombing could be carried out only at night because of the enemy's fighter superiority. The primary tasks of British fighters would be the defence of the Naval Base and the protection of convoys bringing land and air reinforcements to the island. It was made clear to the Army that its troops could not expect any support from the Air Force. 'I accepted this situation,' Percival says. Since the Army had disposed its forces to protect the airfields, this caused a great deal of bad feeling among the troops.

According to the Official Historian, it had been clear since August 1941 that the RAF would be too weak to carry out its defensive task, yet Percival had unwisely committed virtually half his infantry force to the defence of northern airfields. Instead, he should have concentrated his battalions in depth at defended localities on the western arterial route to Singapore, which was certain to be the Japanese line of advance. These positions, and the key maritime base of Penang, should have been strongly held and supported by mobile infantry forces. The northern airfields, only lightly defended, could have had demolitions prepared ready to crater the runways once they were no longer required.[20]

Percival's biographer Clifford Kinvig argued that Percival had no reason to believe in August that the Japanese would attack in December but he had every reason to hope that by the time they did the RAF strength would have been built up. This could have happened quite speedily via the air-reinforcement route. There was, he said, no inkling in Brooke-Popham's correspondence with the Air Ministry that he was dissatisfied with the quality of his fighters. He genuinely seems to have believed that the Buffalo was superior to Japanese fighters and well suited to Malay conditions. There was thus every reason for Percival to protect the northern airfields at which two-thirds of Pulford's aircraft might need to be concentrated. Moreover, Shenton Thomas would never have accepted that Percival should leave the northern states of Perlis, Kelantan and Kedah unprotected from the Japanese.[21]

The fact remains that Percival could easily have moved more troops north as and when Pulford informed him that air reinforcements were on the way. As it was, Pulford received very few reinforcements before the war started, and none at all from India or Burma after the fall of Victoria Point on 8 December.

As 10 December dawned in Singapore, Percival's dilemma lay in how to prevent further withdrawals in northern Malaya from threatening the Naval Base. General Heath was on his way to Singapore to discuss the situation with him. Neither man had any way of knowing that the need for a Naval Base was about to disappear beneath the waves off the Malayan coast.

CHAPTER 10

Battleship Disaster

THE GREAT CAPITAL SHIPS *Prince of Wales* and *Repulse*, with the destroyers *Electra*, *Express*, *Tenedos* and *Vampire* on anti-submarine duties, slipped out of the Naval Base at 5.30 p.m. on the first day of the Pacific War, heading north through the South China Sea to intercept Japanese troopships off Kota Bahru, Patani and Singora. Shortly before sailing, Admiral Tom Phillips had designated the miniature fleet Force Z. As it passed the boom at the entrance to the Straits of Johore, a visual signal from Phillips's Chief of Staff, Rear Admiral Arthur Palliser, was flashed from Changi signal station: 'Regret fighter protection impossible.'[1]

Phillips shrugged. 'Well, we must get on without it,' he said. He had hoped for fighter protection when he reached the danger zone off Kota Bahru or Singora in two days' time on 10 December, but with the Army desperately fighting against the Japanese in northern Malaya, it would be shameful if the Navy held back. Palliser also warned Phillips that 'Japanese have large bomber forces based southern Indochina and possibly also in Thailand ... Kota Bahru aerodrome has been evacuated and we seem to be losing grip on other northern aerodromes due to enemy action.'

Phillips ignored both warnings. Honour and the operational imperative dictated that he confront the enemy despite the risks of air attack. He seemed to be in luck: weather conditions on 9 December were favourable for evasion, with frequent rainstorms and low cloud concealing the whereabouts of the fleet. In the afternoon, however, Force Z was spotted by a Japanese submarine and, when the skies cleared between 5 p.m. and 6.30, by three Japanese seaplanes. The Japanese knew the exact location of Phillips's fleet and scrambled a huge striking force to sink it. Richard Poole, who was in *Repulse*, says, 'The full implications did not really dawn on the more junior officers and ship's company, and subsequently the Admiral made another signal saying that since we had been spotted by enemy air reconnaissance, he was going to continue on course until after dark and then reverse course and head back to Singapore.'

In the early hours, however, Phillips received a signal from Singapore that there had been an enemy landing at Kuantan, on the east coast of Malaya, which was directly on his course back to Singapore. He decided that since his ships weren't going to be where the Japanese expected them to be, he should at least go in and have a look. The unconfirmed report about a landing had been received at midnight from Admiral Palliser at the Naval Base. He had passed it on to Phillips without any means of checking its veracity.

Force Z reached the Kuantan area at 8 a.m. on 10 December and the destroyer *Express* was sent in to investigate. She reported that the harbour was in a state of 'complete peace'. Phillips must have been disappointed, but he remembered that on the way to Kuantan he had passed a small ship and a number of barges or junks. He decided to go back and investigate them before returning to Singapore.[2] He was still pottering about east of Kuantan at 10.15 a.m. when a Japanese reconnaissance plane spotted his ships and contacted the 85 Japanese bombers – 34 high-level bombers and 51 torpedo bombers from the Naval Air Arm based near Saigon – that had been searching for Force Z further south. They had been returning to base when they were alerted to its new location and, through a sudden break in the clouds, spotted the British ships.

Ten minutes earlier, Phillips had received a signal from HMS *Tenedos*, which was limping back to Singapore with engine trouble, indicating that she was being attacked by Japanese bombers. He could have radioed Singapore Air Base for fighter protection, which was available just 76 minutes' flying time away, but he maintained radio silence and engaged in cumbersome fleet manoeuvres by flag. The destroyer, however, sent a message to Singapore that she was being attacked and requested air cover for the incoming ships. This message was never received.

The Japanese bombers attacked at 11.00 a.m., 45 minutes after Phillips first knew he was being shadowed by a spotter plane. The bombers had no fighter protection, and their compact formation and unswerving approach made them ideal targets for the British gunners manning the ships' 5.25-inch cannons, Oerlikons and Bofors, and the multiple pom-poms, known as 'Chicago pianos'. It was 11.13 before the aircraft were in range and the gunners given the order to fire.

'*Prince of Wales* opened up with her 5.25 high-angle guns and we could see the shell-bursts all around the formation, but this did not deter them at all and we had the impression this was as good as anything we had seen,' Richard Poole in *Repulse* remembers. 'When you are in that sort of situation, with an enormous number of guns firing, there is the most tremendous racket, the whole ship is shaking and great clouds of yellow cordite smoke are coming back at you. It is terribly exciting and impressive and [there is] a great deal to think about. The bombers passed right over us and we then heard the scream of the bombs and one momentarily shuts one's eyes, wondering what the hell's going to happen – is this going to be my last moment, so to speak.

'Two bombs hit my ship, one of them 30 feet from where I was standing at the time. I went over to look into the hole, and smoke and steam were coming up from it as the senior engineer officer moved in with the fire and repair parties. The message came up that this bomb had killed quite a large number of marines under the armoured deck. It had gone right through and exploded inside. The one close to my area had fractured a steam pipe but the damage was under control. We were steaming at about 26 knots and everyone was concentrating on where and when there would be a target for one's own guns. On the horizon, I saw another formation of bombers dropping down to sea level and it seemed to us that it must be a torpedo attack. It was difficult to assess which ship they were going for, but as they came in they released their torpedoes immediately at a range beyond anything we had expected.

'In that very first attack, one torpedo hit *Prince of Wales* and I have a vivid memory of her just keeling over as she was hit and an enormous column of dirty, grey water shot up close to her stern. Very shortly after that, we saw aircraft coming in for us and we prepared to open fire. Tactics for torpedo bomber attacks were to fire a fixed barrage with shells fused to explode at the range, and the idea was to put up a screen through which they had to fly. But it was soon evident that they had dropped their torpedoes outside the range of our barrage and could then evade our fire.

'Once again, there was this hideous din of battle and the ship was turning, manoeuvring very well to avoid the torpedoes, and I think five or six individual attacks were made on *Repulse* and each time Captain Tennant avoided them. Finally, we were caught and, from my position, I could see the torpedo in the water coming towards us. It's quite a frightening thing to see this enormous thing with 1,000lb of TNT in the head coming straight at you and you know it's going to hit you. It hit the ship abreast the mainmast and there was a tremendous shuddering explosion and the mainmast, all 150 feet of it, sort of whipped and the ship staggered but she picked up and carried on. I think most of us who saw this on the upper deck had a very good idea that we could not stand much more of this. Unbeknown to us, *Prince of Wales* was already hit and crippled.'

John Gaynor, a gunnery rating in *Prince of Wales*, saw *Repulse* under fire. 'The reason we had time to look around was that the torpedoes had already hit us in the screws,' he says. 'The propellers were like a car's fan belt: when they turned they drove the motors that supplied the electricity for the entire ship. *PoW*, being modern, was all electric; there was nothing hydraulic, no messy mechanics. So when the electricity went, everything ceased. We couldn't control a gun electronically and all the concentration of this modern technology was thrown out of sync. We were hit by two torpedoes in the bows and one in the stern and, give the Japanese pilots their due, they were pressing home their attack in wonderful aircraft.

'By then, *PoW* began to take a list to port, which meant the starboard side was coming up out of the water and, as with all battleships, she had a 12-inch armoured belt where shells were liable to strike, but below that was the vulnerable underbelly that showed when the ship listed. So the Japanese pilots went around again and now they came in on the exposed portion of the ship and in came the torpedoes, because she could no longer fire back at them. One minute she was looking as if she was going over to port, then she rocked back to starboard. I looked over and saw the torpedoes, the wreckage and people hanging all over the place, lots of bodies floating around. It was carnage. This was the time for the survivors, of which I was going to be one ...'[3]

Captain Tennant saw that *Prince of Wales* was in trouble and went to offer assistance despite his own damage. Richard Poole says, 'He turned back when he saw *PoW* flying the nautical signal for being not under control, which was two black balls. He signalled to the Admiral, "Can we help?" and received no reply at all and it was at that time that another wave of bombers came over, and then another wave followed, randomly in fours, sixes and ones. They were being very clever: getting the ship to turn one way, while another aircraft came in from the other side and fired.

'*Repulse* was hit three times in fairly rapid succession – making five hits altogether – and suddenly I realised that our guns wouldn't elevate enough. It then dawned on me that it wouldn't elevate because it was already at full elevation, because the ship had a tremendous heel to the port side. At that point, the gunnery officer was shouting over the back of the bridge relaying the order to abandon ship. It had been broadcast as well but no one had heard it because of the noise. The Captain realised the ship was going to sink and that if 1,300 men were going to get away they had to go now. He gave the order only just in time.'

Richard Poole scrambled on to the deck, which was slippery with the blood of men who had been killed by cannon fire. *Repulse* was still making five or six knots, yet he found himself walking more or less vertically on the ship's side. 'I wasn't quite sure what I was going to do,' he says. 'There were a lot of people jumping off. I had time to think of a very famous picture of a German World War I battleship lying on her side with the ship's company walking down the side and jumping into the sea. And I thought, "Here we are, doing the very same thing." I was also very aware of the propellers still going round. I finally took a gigantic jump into the water and swam as hard as I could to get clear of the suction. Then I got into a panic and took my clothes off, which was a stupid thing to do because I got horribly sunburned. I swam away and turned to look back in time to see the bows of the ship rear out of the water and see it shining in the sun and slide away down below. I started to swim slowly that way, encouraging people to follow me. Some people were hanging on to bits of wreckage. In the distance, I saw one of the destroyers coming towards us ...'

Richard Smith says *Repulse* had always been 'a very lucky ship, a very happy ship, but she was nothing like so heavily armed as *Prince of Wales* and, as regards anti-aircraft guns, she was very nearly naked. Sending us out there was absolute folly, a terrible thing to do. It was like sending a lamb to the slaughter.'

Meanwhile, *Express* had managed to get alongside *Prince of Wales* and take off a large number of the ship's company, but she had to pull away for her own safety when the giant battleship began to turn turtle prior to sinking. John Gaynor clambered on to the ship's foredeck and released Carley life-rafts, and anything else that would float, into the water. 'To my amazement, the deck on which I was standing had assumed alarming proportions and I was now looking down into the water. To my right, the ship was beginning to tower up above me. We were going down but one could not instantly recognise that fact. Remembering tales I'd heard about ships sucking people with them when they go, I thought, "It's about time I left."

'I was forever climbing upwards and suddenly found myself on the bottom of the ship as it rolled over. I sat between the two great twin keels and I looked towards the stern, where I could see four enormous propellers still idly turning. As I looked down, I saw that the water was gradually coming up towards me like the tide coming in, so I slid down on my behind and bang, bang, bang over the bottom of the ship and into the water. When I came up, it was like swimming in black custard and it burned your eyes and mouth. I looked around and there were heaps of wreckage but it was just like a bed sheet with lumps underneath it, and these lumps were bits of debris, pieces of ship and bodies.

'As I was striking out towards a raft, one of these lumps suddenly lifted itself up and tried to grab me. It was a fellow who said, "Help me, I can't swim." Here am I, in the China Sea, faced with the dilemma of someone who looks like a Kentucky minstrel telling me he can't swim. I said to him, "Right, here you are, mate, you hang on to this and then follow me." I pushed him over something that was floating. It was impossible to keep track of him.

'I had been in the water near enough two hours when a boat came along and they hauled me in and then we went among all this debris to see if we could see anybody else. On board the destroyer, there were so many survivors that they were stacking those who had been killed like firewood, five one way, five another. I will always remember gazing into the eyes of a fellow who was a messmate of mine. He was dead but didn't seem to have a mark on him and I almost felt like saying, "What are you doing there?"'

Repulse had gone down at 12.30 p.m. and *Prince of Wales* 50 minutes later. In the words of one survivor, the Royal Navy's glamour ship was like 'a mortally wounded tiger trying to beat off the *coup de grace*'. Tom Phillips did not attempt to leave the bridge and went down with his flagship. So did the *Prince of Wales* captain, Jack Leach, and most of the officers on the captain's bridge.[4]

Had the Singapore fighter planes – the Buffaloes of No. 453 Squadron – arrived on the scene at the height of battle, they could well have made a fight of it, but it is highly unlikely they could have saved either ship. Having been alerted by a radio message from Captain Tennant at 12.04 p.m., they arrived overhead just in time to see *Prince of Wales* go down. Remarkably, 1,285 out of the ship's company of 1,618 were rescued. The crew of *Repulse* was far less fortunate, with only 796 out of 1,306 surviving.

Flight Lieutenant Tim Vigors says that as he flew around the scene of the disaster, every one of the hundreds of men clinging to bits of wreckage and battling to stay alive in the filthy oily waters 'waved and put his thumb up as I flew over him. After an hour, lack of petrol forced me to leave but during that hour I had seen many men in dire danger waving, cheering and joking as if they were holidaymakers at Brighton waving at a low-flying aircraft. It shook me for here was something above human nature. I take off my hat to them, for in them I saw the spirit that wins wars.'

Richard Poole says, 'After an hour in the water, I arrived at *Electra*. They had rope ladders and scrambling nets over the side and people were lining the rails, pulling us up. The upper deck was boiling hot, covered in bodies, oil fuel and gun crews and at that moment we received another alarm of enemy aircraft. However, we weren't attacked and we then backed up towards the main body of survivors until we picked up all those we could find, before setting off very gingerly for Singapore. The destroyer was absolutely crammed. There was not a space anywhere with an extra 500 on board. We just sat down, and sometime in the early hours of the morning we got back to the Naval Base. All the officers went to *Exeter* which had just arrived to join Force Z. They laid on a buffet meal and lots of whisky, rather like a peacetime cocktail party. We ate and talked until about three in the morning when we were taken to the officers' club, where they laid out mattresses all over the floor and we had a shower and solvent to get the oil off.'

Alexander Pimson was a 17-year-old boy sailor in *Exeter*. 'The survivors were brought alongside us in the destroyers,' he says. 'We provided them with rum and whatever else we had but we didn't have enough spare clothes to go round. I had a mate in *Prince of Wales*, Eric Harrop, and wondered what had happened to him. We had been brought up in Dukinfield, Cheshire, and I didn't know whether he had survived. He came on board *Exeter* at one o'clock in the morning and told the master-at-arms he was my brother. Instead of being in my hammock, I was asleep in the mess with a cushion rolled up for a pillow. I was shaken awake by the master-at-arms. He said, "Your brother is here to see you." It was so good to see him – we'd known each other since we were five years old.'[5]

In his report to the Admiralty, Captain Tennant, the senior surviving officer in both ships, paid tribute to 'the magnificent spirit of my officers and ship's company throughout their ordeal. Cases occurred of men having to be ordered to leave their guns to save themselves as the ship was actually turning over.'

The task of informing London of the disaster fell to Arthur Palliser. His cable reached the Admiralty at 8.27 a.m. on 10 December, and a few minutes later the First Sea Lord Sir Dudley Pound telephoned the Prime Minister, who was going through his ministerial boxes in bed. 'His voice sounded odd. He gave a sort of cough and gulp, and at first I could not hear quite clearly. "Prime Minister, I have to report to you that *Prince of Wales* and the *Repulse* have both been sunk by the Japanese – we think by aircraft. Tom

Raffles Hotel as it appeared in the hotel's 1938 Christmas card during the heyday of Britain's Oriental Raj. In the foreground, a Chinese hauls a huge canopied rickshaw along Beach Road.

British soldiers relax in the informal atmosphere of a services club in Singapore prior to the outbreak of hostilities in December 1941.

ABOVE LEFT Gunner Russell Savage, 2/10th Field Regiment, AIF.
ABOVE CENTRE Captain Bill Drower, British Intelligence.
ABOVE RIGHT Major Harry Schulman, Royal Norfolk Regiment.

LEFT Lance-Corporal Frank Davies, Royal Ordnance Corps.

BELOW Mrs Alice Prout and her children John, Maisie and Olga.

LEFT Stanley Prout in his World War I naval uniform.

Mrs Anthoula Pattara and her five little goddesses (from left) twins Ino and Clio, Thetie, Terpie and Thalia.

Major Tony Ferrier, Royal Norfolk Regiment.

Terpie Pattara, Singapore 1941.

Sir Robert Brooke-Popham, Duff Cooper, Sir Earle Page (Australia's representative), Sir Archibald Clark Kerr (British Minister in Shanghai), Sir Shenton Thomas and Sir Geoffrey Layton at General Headquarters, Singapore, 30 October 1941.

Reporter Lorraine Stumm, Singapore 1940.

Elizabeth Choy, Chinese heroine of the Japanese Occupation.

LEFT Major John Wyett, 8th Division AIF, during a post-war visit to Singapore.

Sir Robert Brooke-Popham and General
Archibald Wavell, Singapore 1941.

ABOVE General Arthur Percival (left) receives a
cold-eyed stare from General Gordon Bennett.

Scapegoat: General Percival
in his outmoded Wolseley
helmet.

Ill-fated Admiral Sir Tom Phillips of Z Force (right) and his Chief of Staff, Rear Admiral Arthur Palliser, December 1941.

BELOW The orderly evacuation of the stricken HMS *Prince of Wales*, 10 December 1941. The photograph was taken by Lieutenant Commander Cartwright from the rescuing destroyer HMS *Express*.

Buffalo fighters – the Flying Beer Barrels – had no chance against superior Japanese Zeroes.

Members of the
Manchester Regiment
build defences on
Singapore's southern
shore, November 1941.

ABOVE Gunners of the 4th Anti-Tank Regiment AIF open fire on Japanese tanks in the Battle of Johore, January 1942.

Japanese soldiers rode pushbikes down the Malay peninsular.

Victor: General Tomoyuki Yamashita, the Tiger of Malaya.

Phillips is drowned." "Are you sure it's true?" "There is no doubt at all." So I put the telephone down. I was thankful to be alone. In all the war I never received a more direct shock.'

There were now no British or American capital ships in the Indian Ocean or the Pacific except the American craft that had survived Pearl Harbor, which were returning to Californian ports. 'Over all this vast expanse of waters Japan was supreme,' Churchill wrote, 'and we everywhere were weak and naked.'6

After disseminating the news to his colleagues at the Admiralty, Pound walked around the pond in St James's Park for three-quarters of an hour to compose himself. Tom Phillips had been one of his greatest friends and he expressed his grief in a letter to Lady Phillips. 'His death is one of the tragedies of the war – much more so, infinitely more so, than the loss of those two ships,' he wrote. 'In time we can replace the ships – we can never get another Tom.'7

The loss of face was enormous. Japan's prestige soared around the world when the news was broadcast, and the ease with which both ships had been sunk bolstered a belief in Japan's 'invincibility'. In Berlin, Hitler was cock-a-hoop when he broke the news to his generals. He then made the catastrophic mistake of declaring war on the United States.

Churchill addressed the House of Commons on the afternoon of 10 December: 'I have bad news for the House, which I think I should pass on to them at the earliest possible moment. A report has been received from Singapore that His Majesty's Ship *Prince of Wales* and His Majesty's Ship *Repulse* have been sunk while carrying out operations against a Japanese attack on Malaya.' The Prime Minister followed up with a statement on the war in the Far East the following day: 'In my whole experience I do not remember any naval blow so heavy or so painful as the sinking of *Prince of Wales* and *Repulse* on Monday last. Admiral Phillips was undertaking a thoroughly sound, well-considered offensive operation, not indeed free from risk, but not any different in principle from many similar operations we have repeatedly carried out in the North Sea and in the Mediterranean. It may well be that we shall have to suffer considerable punishment ... We have a very hard period to go through.'

Questioned as to whether the Navy had adequate aircraft protection, Churchill replied, 'I cannot say that our Air Force anywhere is as strong as I would like to see it ... I understand it was not possible for shore-based aircraft to give the support to the ships that had been hoped for because of the attack which had been made on their aerodromes.'8

Sir Dudley Pound said he could see no reason why Phillips should not have asked for fighter cover once Force Z had been spotted, 'but he may well have been influenced by the fact that he was 400 miles from the established enemy aerodromes, that the Army was fighting hard in Malaya and wanted all the Air it could get, and that, not knowing the time of the attack, all he could ask for was a standing patrol and what they could have sent him would really have been little good'. He added, 'I do not know why but both the House of Commons and the public seem to think that the sinking of an important ship is a crime, whilst nobody takes any notice of the loss of 30 or 40 bombers in one night due to inaccurate meteorological reports, or to the many failures of the Army.'[9]

On his return to Singapore, Captain Tennant had been met by a distressed Air Vice-Marshal Pulford. 'My God,' he said, 'I hope you don't blame me for this. I had no idea where you were.' Both Pulford and Rear Admiral Jackie Spooner later blamed Sir Shenton Thomas for the absence of aircraft protection provided for Force Z. They were adamant that as soon as Thomas knew of the possibility that fighter aircraft might be diverted from the air defence of Singapore to provide air cover for Force Z, he had protested most vehemently against their use for this purpose.[10]

Thomas flatly denied the accusation: 'I had no knowledge of the matter at all and in my opinion this was right. It did not fall within my province.'[11] That might have been so – but it had not prevented him from meddling in numerous other military matters.

Lady Thomas was so upset when she heard the news of the disaster that she dashed into the private quarters of her husband's male secretary seeking confirmation. She found the young man *in flagrante delicto* with a married woman. 'How could you be so base at the very time when the *Repulse* and the *Prince of Wales* have been sunk,' she scolded.

'I'm very sorry, Lady Thomas,' replied the young Lothario, 'but I don't see what that has to do with my private life.'[12]

Duff Cooper and Brooke-Popham agreed that the Resident Minister's first task should be to break the news of the disaster to the citizens of Singapore in a radio broadcast. At 8.30 that evening, Cooper reassured the population that Malaya now stood only where she had stood a month ago. 'We were not safe then; we are not safe now,' he said. 'But in these great days, safety seems hardly honourable and danger is glorious.'

Brother Vincent had no doubts about the seriousness of the loss of the two capital ships: 'Our hearts sank with them,' he says. In the Combined Operations Room at Sime Road, Brigadier Torrance ordered Bill Drower to 'take those poor old ships down'. The young officer pulled out some drawing pins and removed all trace of *Prince of Wales* and *Repulse* from the operational wall charts.

Meanwhile, Lieutenant Alan Lewis of the 1st Cambridgeshire Battalion had reached Cape Town with the 18th British Division in the troopship USS *West Point*, believing he was on his way to join General Auchinleck's forces in the Middle East. After weeks on an American ship, Lewis and a friend were thirsting for a cup of English tea. As soon as they were given leave, they jumped into a taxi and asked to be taken to the best teashop in town. As Lewis sat down, the waiter pushed the afternoon paper in front of him. The headline read, '*Prince of Wales* and *Repulse* lost'. Lewis turned to his companion. 'That's where we're going,' he said, 'Singapore.'

CHAPTER 11

Retreat from Jitra

GENERAL YAMASHITA HAD moved fast on 8 December to capitalise on the unopposed landings of his forces in Singora and Patani, which had given him a chance to consolidate his bridgehead in southern Thailand and strike south in 'the great sacred war' against Britain. Desperate to heal the rift with his Emperor, he had set himself a deadline for taking Singapore: 11 February 1942. This was *Kigensetsu*, Japan's National Day, commemorating the coronation of Hirohito's mythical ancestor, the first emperor, Jimmu, in 660BC. Victory, Yamashita hoped, would restore him to favour in the Imperial eyes.

The first phase of his offensive was to drive south across the north-west Malay border and crush all opposition in Perlis and northern Kedah, using the tactics of *kirimomi sakusen* (a driving charge). This entailed a headlong blitzkrieg by his armoured division and swift encirclement by his fast-moving, lightly equipped troops. Takumi Detachment, meanwhile, would deal with British forces from the 9th Indian Division on the east coast after landing reinforcements at Kota Bahru. Yamashita intended to occupy Kuala Lumpur by 14–15 January 1942 in order to reach the Straits of Johore by 31 January.

The Japanese soldier had great affinity with the tank – *sensha* in Japanese (*sen* – battle, *sha* – wagon) – and commanders used it as a spearhead to infantry operations whenever possible. Japan had built several hundred tanks in the early 1930s, placing it fourth behind the Soviet Union, France and Germany as a tank-building nation. By the time war against China began in 1937, the IJA had an armoured force of 1,060 tracked and wheeled armoured vehicles. The Japanese adopted the French system of spreading their tanks in small units throughout their army in support of infantry. These units were effective against the Chinese, who had no tanks of their own and no proper anti-tank weapons.

The Type 97 CHI-HA medium tank taken to Malaya had one 57mm gun (120 rounds) and two 7.7mm machine guns, one in the rear of the turret and one in the bow (2,350 rounds). This was a considerable step up in firepower from its predecessors and had resulted from the rout of the Japanese Army at Nomonhan in 1939. There was a two-man turret which enabled the commander to control the tank while a gunner fired the main armament. The tank was propelled by a Mitsubishi 12-cylinder air-cooled diesel engine and could cruise at a speed of 24 mph for 130 miles.[1]

On 8 December, elements of General Matsui's 5th Division set off down the only two roads running south from Singora and Patani with the aim of breaking through to the Perak River. Two regiments of the 9th Japanese Infantry Brigade – the 11th and the 41st – supported by a tank battalion and a battalion of field artillery, took the Singora–Alor Star road to attack the British forces in the Jitra Line, while the 42nd Japanese Infantry Regiment, with two companies of light tanks and a battery of field artillery, left Patani for the border town of Kroh to cut the 11th Indian Division's lines of communication north of the Perak River.

Krohcol's task was to prevent this Japanese force from reaching the coast and blocking the trunk road east of Butterworth airfield, which would strand the division in its Jitra redoubt. To succeed in its objective, Krohcol had to win the race to the Ledge, the easily defensible six-mile stretch of road cut into the hillside above the Patani River. Murray-Lyon's special force got off to a bad start after the 5/14th Punjabis and a mountain battery failed to arrive at Kroh from their base in Penang on 8 December owing to an organisational blunder. Lieutenant-Colonel Henry Moorhead's battalion, the 3/16th Punjabis, was obliged to begin the advance into Thailand without them. Running hours late to meet the advancing Japanese, Krohcol embussed in lorries driven by the hardy veterans of the 2/3rd Australian Reserve Motor Transport Company and crossed the frontier into Thailand at 3 p.m. on 8 December. The Thais had taken Churchill's advice to defend their country – not against the Japanese but against the British, and Moorhead's men received a hostile reception from 300 armed Thai policemen manning roadblocks.

The 11th Division's first casualty of the Malayan Campaign was a sepoy who was shot dead as he tried to pass through the customs barrier. Thai resistance delayed the Punjabis until the following afternoon and they did not reach the town of Betong, only five miles inside the frontier, until the evening of the 9th. During the night the troops were subjected to sniper fire from the Thais, but at dawn resistance ceased and they drove to within six miles of the Ledge without further opposition.

The young Indian soldiers continued warily on foot, but after only a mile the advance guard came under fire from the Japanese 42nd Regiment, which had beaten them to the Ledge. The Japanese commander then threw his two companies of light tanks into action – a terrifying experience for Krohcol's young Indian members who had never seen a tank before.

In Singapore, Percival issued a special order of the day urging his troops to do their patriotic duty. 'In this hour of trial the General Officer Commanding calls upon all ranks Malaya Command for a determined and sustained effort to safeguard Malaya and the adjoining British territories,' he said. 'The eyes of the Empire are upon us. Our whole position in the Far East is at stake. The struggle may be long and grim but let us all resolve to stand fast come what may and to prove ourselves worthy of the great trust which has been placed upon us.'

Appeals on behalf of the Empire were wasted on the Indian troops of Krohcol who were fighting for their lives and suffering heavy casualties. Two Punjabi companies were cut off from the battalion, and although one company rejoined later that morning, most of the men in the second were never seen again. Fearing he could lose his whole battalion, Moorhead requested permission from Murray-Lyon at divisional headquarters at Sungei Patani to withdraw his battalion to Kroh. Permission was granted, and Moorhead planned to withdraw the following morning through the 5/14th Battalion which had caught up with the battle. He set 9 a.m. on 12 December as the pull-out hour, but during the night the Japanese enveloped the Punjabis' flanks, surrounded C Company and killed all but 10 men, including the company's two British officers. Moorhead was lucky to escape in one of the carrier platoon's four remaining vehicles. When he reached the 5/14th Punjabis, he admitted that he might have 'hung on for too long'.

Meanwhile, the mobile force requested by Percival to 'harass and delay' the Japanese advance had crossed the Thai border at the same time as Krohcol. Named 'Laycol' after Brigadier William Lay, commander of the 6th Brigade, this was a mechanised force consisting of the carrier platoon of the 1/8th Punjabis, a section of the 273rd Anti-Tank Battery and some artillery pieces. Having advanced 10 miles into Thailand from north Kedah, Laycol had halted at dusk on the 9th on the Singora–Jitra road, where it encoun-tered a column of enemy tanks, headlights blazing, and a convoy of 30 motor vehicles. The British force opened fire and brought the column to a halt, whereupon large numbers of Japanese infantry immediately jumped from their trucks and started an enveloping movement. Laycol pulled back to the frontier, destroying road bridges, and rejoined the 11th Division at Jitra. To the west, in the tiny state of Perlis, an armoured train had been sent from Padang Besar across the Thai frontier containing a platoon of the 2/16th Punjab and some engineers. It destroyed a railway bridge on the line to Singora and then retreated back to Perlis without encountering any Japanese.

In the words of the first company commander to make contact with the Japanese, 'They were absolutely first-class – we completely surprised their lorry columns on the road, but they tumbled quickly out of their lorries and immediately commenced an enveloping movement with incredible speed. They combined these head-on thrusts down the roads, spearheaded by tanks, with mobility and subterfuge, to which the British and Indian soldier had no answer – and indeed for a time simply could not comprehend.'

The 11th Division had spent so much time waiting for Brooke-Popham to make up his mind about Operation Matador that the Jitra Line resembled a building site, and not a very impressive one at that. It was still raining when the troops of the 6th and 15th Indian Infantry Brigades started digging, wiring and bailing out flooded trenches. The downpour would continue for the next few days, dampening the men's morale and affecting the explosive charges used in demolitions. 'I had always impressed on General Murray-Lyon that I never thought that Matador would ever come off,' Sir Lewis Heath says. 'But they were all impressed with the spirit of Matador – it meant a forward movement and they were looking forward to it.'[2]

One reason Murray-Lyon had favoured Matador was that he did not rate his chances of holding the hotchpotch of wooded hills, rice-fields and marshlands that constituted the Jitra Line. Two roads led into Jitra from the north, the Singora road and, further west, the Perlis road. Murray-Lyon might have been expected to concentrate his forces in depth along these approaches. Instead he spread them thinly over a 12-mile-wide strip running from Jitra to the sea. The 15th Brigade, on the right, was responsible for Jitra itself, plus a three-mile swathe of jungle, swamp, rice-fields and rubber plantations. The 6th Brigade, on the left, was given the rest of the swampland draining towards the coast, with most of its units defending little islands of vegetation surrounded by flooded fields. Platoons were out of touch with one another and with company headquarters.

Of the 15th's two forward battalions, the 2/9th Jats extended from the hills on the right flank to a point exclusive of the Singora road. On their left were the 1st Leicesters, whose front included both the Singora and the Perlis roads. West of the latter they linked up with the 2nd East Surreys, the right battalion of the 6th Brigade, whose position included a wooded salient forward of a canal. On their left the 2/16th Punjabis were responsible for the whole front from the railway to the sea.[3]

The difficulties Murray-Lyon was up against in preparing his units for battle were exemplified in the divisional reconnaissance regiment, the 3rd Indian Cavalry, which had only recently handed over its horses and had arrived in Malaya without any armoured vehicles. It consisted of three squadrons of men, many of them poorly trained recruits and few of whom could actually drive the unit's one armoured car and various trucks. Percival commented that it was 'totally unfit for its role'.

To give the 6th and 15th Brigades time to finish their defensive preparations, Murray-Lyon sent the 1/14th Punjabis of the 15th Brigade north of Jitra to hold the Japanese at Changlun until 12 December. It was at this moment that the RAF chose to abandon Alor Star after heavy bombing on the morning of 9 December. Alor Star was the capital of Kedah, and its airfield was the main one entrusted to the protection of the 11th Division and for which its men were about to lay down their lives. Its squadrons, along with those at Sungei Patani, had already been withdrawn by Air Vice-Marshal Pulford to prevent their being destroyed on the ground, thus removing the last chance of close air support for the beleaguered troops. No communiqué had been issued informing the Army that Alor Star was being evacuated; the first Murray-Lyon and his commanders knew about it was when troops reported that airport buildings were being ripped apart by explosions and that the fuel dumps were on fire. It was discovered that ground staff had implemented a scorched-earth policy – despite the fact that the Army were relying on many of the stores at the airport. Morale among the troops, already low as a result of the Matador farce, sank to new depths.[4]

The first impact of the Japanese onslaught on Jitra was felt early on the 10th when Colonel Saeki's armoured reconnaissance detachment ran into the Punjabis' forward elements astride the Singora road. After sustaining casualties, the Punjabis fell back, demolishing bridges and causeways as they went, and rejoined their battalion near the Changlun crossroads, 12 miles north of Jitra. Fighting continued throughout the day and the commander of the 15th Brigade, Brigadier K. A. Garrett, requested reinforcements to hold the enemy at bay. The three Gurkha battalions of the 28th Brigade had been kept in reserve, and Murray-Lyon sent one of them – the 2/1st Gurkha Rifles – to take over an outpost at Asun, a few miles north of Jitra on the Singora road.

At 8 a.m. on 11 December the Japanese, heedless of casualties, made a head-on attack on 1/14th Punjabis in the Changlun position but were driven back. By midday, however, a Japanese attack from the right flank had penetrated into the middle of the position and the commander decided to withdraw, calculating that he would be able to reach the Asun outpost before enemy tanks could negotiate damaged bridges. At 2.30 p.m., however, he was ordered by Murray-Lyon to occupy Nangka, a position 1½ miles in front of Asun, with a view to imposing a further delay on the enemy.

At 4.30 p.m. the Punjabis were moving to their new position when 12 medium Japanese tanks, having crossed the hastily repaired bridges, suddenly came roaring out of the mist with machine guns blazing. Followed by other light tanks and truckloads of infantry, the leading tanks crashed through the battalion's rearguard and drove right through the column, overrunning the 2nd Anti-Tank Battery whose guns were attached to their carriers. The Punjabis lost two Breda anti-tank guns.

'The tanks advanced through the column inflicting casualties and causing much confusion and approached the bridge in front of the Asun outpost position,' Percival says. 'The demolition exploder failed but the leading tank was knocked out by anti-tank rifle fire and blocked the road. The blitz was temporarily stopped but at considerable cost in men and material. Some 200 men of the 1/14th Punjab Regiment, who had been cut off, rejoined the following day, but the battalion was temporarily rendered ineffective.'

By 6.30 p.m. the Japanese had cleared away the wrecked tank on the bridge; their armour then smashed into the 2/1st Gurkhas at Asun with the same devastating effect as at Nangka. The Gurkha commander decided to withdraw, but communications had been cut and only 20 survivors of the forward companies ever rejoined the battalion. More than 500 men, seven anti-tank guns and four mountain guns were lost.

Further vital weapons had to be abandoned when a bridge on the Perlis road further west was blown up prematurely while both the covering and outpost troops of 6th Brigade were withdrawing within the main Jitra position. All transport, guns and carriers of the column, together with seven anti-tank and four mountain guns, were lost. Furthermore, the withdrawal of all British forces from Perlis provoked the Sultan of Perlis to protest most strongly to Shenton Thomas that the British had broken its treaty obligations by leaving him defenceless in the face of the Japanese advance.

Percival says, 'Withdrawals are admitted to be among the most difficult operations of war even for seasoned troops, and the above incidents serve to illustrate the great difficulty of conducting them successfully with inexperienced troops. They had a profound influence on the Battle of Jitra. At the same time I am of the opinion that some of the trouble might have been avoided had the commanders reacted more swiftly to the problems created by the appearance of tanks on the battlefield.'

The anti-tank ditch at Jitra was still incomplete, and the ditch-digging machine was hard at work when the Japanese fell upon the 2/9th Jats shortly after midnight on 11–12 December. In driving rain, Japanese tanks roared down the unblocked Singora road, closely followed by motorised infantry. The tanks penetrated deep into both the Jats' position and the neigh-bouring 1st Leicesters. During three hours of intense fighting, the Leicesters held the Japanese in their sector, but the enemy were able to advance through a 2,000-yard gap of swamp and undergrowth which separated the two battalions.[5]

With Brigadier Garrett cut off to the north of Jitra, Brigadier W. St J. Carpendale, commander of the 28th Brigade, had taken charge of the 15th Brigade at Murray-Lyon's request. Believing the Japanese breakthrough to be more serious than it was, Carpendale called on Brigadier Lay, commanding the 6th Brigade, to send him reinforcements, without first checking with Murray-Lyon. During the night Lay committed one and a half battalions of his Punjabi troops to the battle in the 15th Brigade's sector, thus using up his entire brigade reserve. The reinforcements enabled Carpendale to prevent a wholesale Japanese advance, but he lacked the power to mount a counterattack.

At 8.30 a.m. on the 12th Murray-Lyon decided it was impossible to hold the Jitra Line any longer. His reserve force was already committed and he had no fresh troops to meet any renewed attack. Krohcol was also being forced to withdraw towards Kroh, and once they had passed that point the Japanese would be able to swing in behind him. Murray-Lyon contacted Heath's headquarters in Kuala Lumpur for permission to withdraw his divi-sion to Gurun, 30 miles to the south, and possibly later to the Krian River. Heath was at that time on a train bound for Singapore to confer with Percival over his rejection of Bill Barstow's plea for his 9th Division to with-draw from the east coast to Kuala Lipis. Murray-Lyon's message was tele-phoned direct to the Combined Operations Room at Sime Road, where Percival was taken aback to receive a request from the second of Heath's divisional commanders for another long withdrawal.

Such a retreat had not even been considered in pre-war discussions and would prejudice Percival's chances of denying the airfields at Alor Star, Sungei Patani and Butterfield to the enemy, even though these no longer contained any British planes and ground staff had been evacuated from both Alor Star and Sungei Patani. 'I felt that such a withdrawal would have a most demoralising effect on both the troops and on the civil population,' he says. Percival referred the problem to the War Council, which was sitting at the time. It confirmed Percival's view that withdrawal was out of the question, and the GOC instructed Murray-Lyon that the battle was to be fought out on the Jitra Line. 'At that time the Jats were, in point of fact, the only battalion which had incurred serious losses,' he says, 'although two battalions had, as already recorded, been rendered ineffective on the previous day.' This might have been so, but Percival's inability to handle a tactical matter himself, or to take the word of the commander on the ground about the seriousness of the situation, augured badly for the future.[6]

Murray-Lyon contained the enemy in heavy fighting throughout the morning of 12 December, with the help of British artillery batteries which inflicted losses on Colonel Saeki's force. But at midday Japanese reinforcements in the shape of the 2nd Battalion of the 41st Infantry Brigade reached the battlefield and attacked the Jats' forward left company. After two hours of fierce fighting, the Jat commander made telephone contact with battalion headquarters to report that his men were almost out of ammunition and that many weapons were clogged with mud.

'The men cannot fire, sir.'

'I can't give you permission to withdraw.'

'Okay, sir, we will fight it out with grenades and bayonets. The men are splendid. I reckon we have got about five minutes left.'

'Good luck.'[7]

In the afternoon, a big gap had appeared in the Jitra Line between the Jats and the Leicesters, and the trunk road south of Jitra – the division's exit route – had come under close-range fire from enemy artillery. Acknowledging that Krohcol had failed to protect his right flank and fearing that Japanese tanks would destroy his division the following day, Murray-Lyon again sought permission to withdraw. The request was telephoned at 7.30 p.m. to Percival, who was still in conference with Heath at Sime Road. This time permission was granted, but the commander was reminded that 'your task is to fight for the security of north Kedah. Estimated that you are only opposed by one Japanese division at most. Consider best solution may be to hold up advance enemy tanks on good obstacle and dispose your forces to obtain considerable depth on both roads and to obtain scope for your superior artillery.'

This was elementary military procedure, but first Murray-Lyon had to extricate his division from its hazardous position and then find the suggested 'good obstacle'. Moving a division and its ancillary forces and artillery with all their goods and chattels was a huge undertaking at the best of times; carrying it out in the middle of the night in driving rain and with poor communications was well-nigh impossible. Murray-Lyon's orders for the pull-out were issued at 9 p.m. With units mixed up as a result of the day's fighting, there were long delays in the orders getting through – and in some cases they did not reach units at all. Troops stumbled about in the dark, losing much of their equipment. The only road south to Gurun was jammed with scores of trucks, guns and gun carriers, so some troops struck out across country, not even sure of their bearings in the blinding rain. Others reached the coast and took boats, hoping to rejoin the division further south. Those who had not received their orders were still in their original positions the following morning.

The withdrawal turned into a rout. Contact with the enemy was finally broken at 4.30 a.m. but later that morning the damage became all too clear. The 15th Brigade had been reduced from 2,400 men to 600 and was temporarily unfit for duty. The 6th Brigade, although still a fighting formation, had also suffered seriously. In the 28th Brigade, the 2/1st Gurkha Rifles, except for one company, had been almost wiped out. The other two Gurkha battalions had suffered 100 casualties between them. One thousand troops had been taken prisoner. The haemorrhaging of equipment had been catastrophic, with guns and vehicles being either caught on the wrong side of demolished bridges or inextricably bogged down in the mud. 'We were defeated and no doubt about it,' Heath says, 'and we were defeated because we had not taken proper precautions when we knew that the enemy had tanks.' The General opined that his troops should have dropped back with all their vehicles and made sure the bridges were blown up. At the time, however, driving rain had not only made conditions chaotic but dampened many of the explosives which had consequently failed to ignite.[8]

According to Percival, 'It is unlikely that the Japanese employed more than one division during the Battle of Jitra. Their success was won primarily by bold and skilful infantry tactics and by the use of tanks. They employed no artillery heavier than the infantry gun and in this action they made little use of aircraft in support of ground forces. They exploited the moral value of noise behind the defences. They also appear to have had an organised "fifth column" plan which had at least a partial success by spreading false rumours.'

Percival's estimate of the Japanese strength was highly inflated. The main body of the 5th Division had not been employed at any stage of the battle. An advance guard equivalent to two battalions, supported by a company of tanks, had driven the 11th Division from its prepared defensive position in 36 hours. The Official Historian attributed the division's dismal performance to the fact that its troops had not been in a fit condition to meet a first-class enemy on equal terms. This was mainly due to trained men's being constantly recalled to India to raise new units and to the inadequate standard of their replacements. Moreover, the speed of movement of Japanese units, their ability to overcome obstacles and their bold use of tanks had come as a complete surprise to the 11th Division's commanders. 'Against partly trained troops, without armour or air support, ill-provided with anti-tank weapons and already off their balance as a result of the period of indecision, the sudden Japanese onslaught proved decisive.'[9]

No one in the 11th Division was more exhausted than General Murray-Lyon. '[He] was magnificent and showed no sign of the tremendous strain he was undergoing,' Colonel A. M. L. Harrison, his Chief of Staff, writes. 'All that the world saw was a calm and confident leader. And then suddenly at a conference he fell down in a faint from sheer lack of sleep. But he was up on his feet again as soon as he had hit the ground and insisted on carrying on.'[10]

Over on the east coast in Kalantan, Percival had finally agreed that the 8th Indian Brigade should be moved out of harm's way. After holding the Japanese until 16 December, troops along with their guns, equipment and stores were shifted south by truck to Kuala Krai, where they boarded the train for Kuala Lipis. The railhead at Kuala Krai was evacuated three days later and the huge railway bridges blown up. By 22 December the 8th Brigade had reformed in the Kuala Lipis-Jerantut area in central Malaya.

The 11th Indian Division also needed to be rested and reorganised before being called on to fight again, but no reinforcements were available. Instead, the exhausted Indian and British troops regrouped at Gurun, a road junction where the rice-fields of the western plains merged with the rolling, thickly wooded rubber country of south Kedah. With the jungle-clad slopes of Kedah Peak barring the route to the coast, Percival rated Gurun as perhaps the best natural defensive position in Malaya, but although it had been reconnoitred, the large labour force that had been ordered to work on fixed defences had failed to appear and the troops were devastated to discover that no work had been done on their positions.

As at Jitra, the men tackled the backbreaking task themselves, with the 28th Brigade digging in on the right and the 6th Brigade on the left, while the weak 15th Brigade was held in reserve. Japanese fighter planes now had airports close to the fighting, and even when Allied troops sheltered in rubber plantations the Japanese pilots knew they were somewhere beneath the canopy and bombed and strafed regardless. Nothing seemed capable of stemming the Japanese advance down the west-coast trunk road. With an Arisaka rifle slung over his shoulder, a ration of fish and rice-balls in his pack and rubber-soled boots on his feet, the Japanese infantryman mounted a bicycle and peddled furiously southward, while artillery and tanks followed along the bituminised roads, mending blown-up bridges as they went.

Colonel Harrison says, 'Infiltration was simplified by the wearing of Malay or Chinese dress by many of the Japanese. Their infiltration was extremely brave and they were expert stalkers; no doubt they were specially selected men and given specialist training. Their use of crackers had a demoralising effect on young and exhausted troops. They also used mortars lavishly and though the destructive force of their bombs was small, the noise they made was almost equal to that of a 4.5 shell.'

Churchill, meanwhile, was crossing the Atlantic in HMS *Duke of York*, sister battleship of the tragic *Prince of Wales*, to consolidate his 'marriage' to Roosevelt in the Grand Alliance. He intended to seduce the President into agreeing to defeat Germany first before avenging himself against Japan in the Pacific – a tall order, considering the fury of the American public at Japan's treachery.

In response to Duff Cooper's plea for reinforcements, Churchill cabled from the high seas that the 18th Division, now rounding the Cape of Good Hope, was being diverted from Egypt to the Far East, as well as four fighter squadrons and a quantity of anti-aircraft and anti-tank guns. Regarding bombers, Churchill said, 'Libyan battle goes well but till we have a definite decision I cannot withdraw anything from there.' However, arrangements were being made 'to transfer four to six Bomber Squadrons to your theatre at earliest possible moment thereafter'.[11]

Even at this early stage, Churchill held out little hope of holding Malaya. In a note to the Chiefs of Staff, he warned, 'Beware lest troops required for ultimate defence Singapore Island and fortress are used up or cut off in Malay peninsula. Nothing compares in importance with the fortress. Are you sure we shall have enough troops for the prolonged defence?'[12] No one among that eminent body picked up Churchill on his use of the word 'fortress'; no one pointed out that far from being a fortress, Singapore was indefensible to an attack from the mainland; no one told him that there were not enough troops to repel a Japanese landing.

CHAPTER 12

Disgrace at Penang

Pᴇɴᴀɴɢ Iꜱʟᴀɴᴅ, the Pearl of the Orient, had been officially described as a fortress since 1936, but the clinical manner in which the Japanese put it to the sword should have alerted Churchill to the dangers facing Singapore. From the outset of the Malayan Campaign, General Yamashita realised that he must capture the little tropical island at the top of the Malacca Straits, or face the prospect that it would become a 'dagger in our flank' – a spring-board from which the British could launch air and sea attacks on the 25th Imperial Japanese Army.[1]

It was indeed General Percival's intention to hold 'Fortress Penang'. Georgetown had a superb harbour, and was the terminal of two underwater cables connecting Malaya with Ceylon and India on the telegraphic route to the United Kingdom. His pre-war instructions to General Heath had been that if the 11th Division was driven south it would fall back on the axis of Malaya's main road and rail arteries, reinforcing the Penang garrison with up to two additional infantry battalions, plus supporting troops. That plan was now in tatters. The garrison's most able units were already fighting on the mainland and there was no possibility of sending two additional battalions.

Enemy aircraft had bombed Penang airfield every day since 8 December, using mainly fragmentation and anti-personnel bombs to kill ground staff without damaging the runways. The only defence that the tiny garrison could offer was small-arms fire. There were two antiquated 6-inch cannons to repel seaborne invaders but no anti-aircraft defences, because the guns and searchlights, although ordered from the UK, had not yet arrived. It was official policy that the Naval Base, RAF airfields, Singapore Harbour and Kuala Lumpur had priority for ack-ack guns. Penang had only a civilian airport, so it came well down the list despite its vital harbour.[2] The island's only fighter protection had been provided for just 24 hours by five Brewster Buffaloes operating from Butterworth on the mainland directly opposite Georgetown. This airport had also been the target of intense Japanese bombing and strafing, and thousands of the island's citizens had packed the capital's seafront to watch the spectacle across the two-mile-wide Kra channel.

On 11 December, when 41 bombers escorted by fighters approached Georgetown in V formation, thousands of people poured into the streets to see the latest attack and, it was hoped, witness a dogfight between British planes and the enemy. Suddenly, as bombs started falling along Bishop Street, the people realised to their horror that they were to be the target of the latest sortie. One eyewitness described the bombers as being 'leisurely and unopposed, as if at practice'. There had been no air-raid warning and there were no shelters. Caught in the open and with no time to run, many people were cut down where they stood.

Twenty minutes later there was a second attack when some of the enemy planes swooped in low and machine-gunned civilians. Then many more returned and strafed the town, which was now burning fiercely. Tattered copies of Sir Robert Brooke-Popham's proclamation flapped in the wind: '... *We are ready ... We have had plenty of warning and our preparations are made and tested ... Our defences are strong and our weapons efficient ...*' More than 2,000 men, women and children, mainly Asians, were killed or wounded in the air raid on 'Black Thursday'. Many of the victims were trapped in the teeming bazaars and blazing shops of the Chowrasta market in Penang Road.

There were further air raids on Georgetown in the next two days, and the casualty figures rose to 5,000. On the 12th, the Japanese targeted the harbour's dock installations and nearby fishing villages, machine-gunning ferryboats and launches and causing heavy casualties among crews and fishermen. On the 13th, eight Buffaloes of No. 453 Fighter Squadron were flown up from Singapore to Butterworth and Ipoh, central Malaya, to engage the enemy over Penang. The 'Buffs' shot down five unescorted Japanese bombers when they attacked later that day. One of the pilots was Tim Vigors, who was credited with three kills. In one dogfight, his petrol tank exploded and he was forced to bale out over the island. As he descended, an enemy pilot made several attempts to kill him, but every time he opened fire Vigors, although suffering burns to his hands and arms, collapsed the canopy of his chute and dropped out of range. He was wounded in the thigh, but managed to land in a clearing on Penang Hill and was taken to hospital.[3]

On the 14th, the British fighters disrupted three separate attempts to bomb Penang, and after a further failed attempt on the 15th the air raids petered out. But the damage inflicted on civilian morale and the island's municipal services was irreparable. Mutilated bodies lay putrefying in the streets, and looters were at work in deserted shops and houses. Law and order had broken down after the local *mata-mata* (police) had fled into the country.[4] Many Sikh policemen were killed when the main police station in Penang Road received a direct hit. The ornate Queen Victoria clock tower had been knocked sideways and more than 1,000 houses destroyed.

Half the town was ablaze and the main fire station in Beach Street had virtually been demolished. Water mains were broken – but fortunately a torrential downpour doused many of the fires in the late afternoon. Thousands of citizens fled to the hills in the centre of the island to avoid further carnage. Rats scurried among the bodies in the streets, increasing the threat of pestilence.

Soldiers, including members of the 2/3rd Australian Reserve Motor Transport Company, had been brought across from the mainland to assist the civil administration in digging trenches and burying the dead. Fifty naval ratings from *Prince of Wales* and *Repulse* arrived from Singapore to help local volunteers operate the ferry service after their crews disappeared. Among the bravest and most disciplined workers were Straits Chinese who acted as ARP wardens throughout the air raids. They transported 850 wounded to first-aid posts and the hospital, where surgeons worked at five operating tables to save lives. Every physician on the island reported for duty, and volunteer surgeons and doctors were flown in from Kuala Lumpur and Singapore.[5]

The Straits Steamship Company appealed to the naval authorities for permission to withdraw its ships south for safety. This appeal was refused; seven of its steamships remained in the harbour.

On 12 December, the Fortress Commander Brigadier C. A. Lyon – a Boer War veteran, known as 'Tiger' Lyon – and the civil administrator, the Resident Counsellor Leslie Forbes, ordered the evacuation of all European Service families, all civilian European women and children, and patients of the military hospital. 'This decision was taken as a normal measure to evacuate *bouches inutiles* (useless mouths),' Percival says, but that was not the real reason. Japanese propaganda, disseminated through leaflets and radio broadcasts, had informed the island's Asian population that Japan was 'waging war solely against the "White Devils"', and urged them to 'burn up the whites in a blaze of victory'.

Brigadier Lyon surmised that there would be violent recriminations against Europeans when the Japanese landed, whereas non-European inhabitants might expect more cordial treatment. The Chinese, however, were not optimistic about their chances. Penang had contributed millions of dollars through the China Relief Fund to Chiang Kai-shek's Kuomintang forces on the Chinese mainland, and many of the island's Straits Chinese wished to leave Penang and join relatives in Singapore.[6]

After discussing the situation with Percival, Shenton Thomas sent a telegram to Leslie Forbes endorsing the evacuation of the *bouches inutiles*, but with instructions that 'European males should not, repeat not, be encouraged to leave, and to all who stay of whatever race I send my sincere thanks for their courage and determination and my sympathy in this time of trial'. Thomas wrote in his diary that night, 'I asked whether we were going to defend the place or leave it. Percival replied that we shall defend to the last, to the best of our ability. Decided that I should advise European women and children to leave *and other Europeans who wanted to*.'[7]

At 9 p.m. on 13 December General Heath and his entourage set off north from Kuala Lumpur by rail, in two special saloon cars, to set up an advance headquarters nearer the fighting in Kedah. Packed with members of the commander's staff, clerks, servants and a number of Military Police, the train travelled through the night and arrived at Bukit Mertajam in Province Wellesley at 5.30 a.m. The great Muda River was in spate when Heath drove over it on his way to visit Murray-Lyon at 11th Division head-quarters at Harvard Estate, four miles north of Sungei Patani.

Heath found a very confused situation. The 11th Division was expecting an attack at Gurun, but the enemy's whereabouts were not known and many conflicting reports were being received. Heath then asked to be driven to Butterworth, where he walked on to the quay to gaze across the straits at Penang. Slow columns of smoke curled up from burning buildings, and Penang Hill looked like an erupting volcano. Heath drove back to his head-quarters at Bukit Mertajam with a heavy heart.

That afternoon, the enemy attacked Gurun down the trunk road in their usual manner, with tanks followed by truckloads of infantry and supported this time by fighter aircraft. This attack was beaten off, but in the evening Heath telephoned Percival to say that the 11th Division should be with-drawn further south across the great expanse of the Perak River, with a brief intermediate stand on the Muda near Sungei Patani to allow time for Penang to be evacuated. During the night the enemy penetrated deep into the Gurun position and at 7 a.m. on the 15th attacked the headquarters of the 6th Brigade, killing all of the officers except the commander, Brigadier Lay, who had just left the building. With most of its men tired and dispirited, the 11th Division was in no condition to offer effective resistance to the marauding Japanese, and it was a defeated army that pulled out of Gurun and fell back the 17 miles to the Muda.

The first evacuations from Penang had taken place on the night of the 13–14 December, when 650 members of the European community were given one hour's notice to assemble in the great domed lobby of the Eastern and Oriental Hotel in Farquhar Street, where they were divided into groups, transported to the harbour and embarked in an array of vessels. Most were taken across the straits to Prai in the railway ferry *Violet* and put on board a train for Singapore; others were landed further south at Port Swettenham, while one ship sailed all the way to Singapore. On orders from General Percival the evacuations were carried out secretly and in great haste to prevent word from spreading to Asian citizens that the British were abandoning them to the Japanese.

Percival says in his Dispatch, 'Lack of transport would have made it quite out of the question to evacuate large numbers of Asians.' Considering that 24 self-propelled vessels, several dozen junks, private yachts and a collection of sampans, barges and rafts – all later found to be capable of ferrying Japanese soldiers – were left bobbing at anchor in Penang harbour, this was one of Percival's more disingenuous statements. He added, 'Moreover, it was undesirable at that stage to increase the population of Singapore.' Yet that did not prevent him from urging the War Council to consider the great value that all European personnel, civil and military, could make to the war effort if they were repatriated to Singapore.

Shenton Thomas broadcast an appeal for volunteers to provide temporary shelter for the trainload of Penang evacuees expected to cross the Causeway early on 15 December. He went to Singapore Railway Station himself to greet the refugees. Many Chinese families who had gathered at the station expecting to find relatives on the train were shocked to discover that only Europeans had been evacuated.

Many of the European women with small children had no luggage and little money and had to rely on the kindness of strangers for food and lodgings. Other mothers who had hoped to stay in Singapore and then take their children home to England were allegedly locked into railway carriages and fed refreshments through the windows. At 10 a.m. on 15 December after sending a pre-worded telegram to their husbands – 'Leaving now for unknown destination' – they were embarked on the SS *Nellore* for Batavia and thence to Australia.[8]

Shenton Thomas sent another telegram to Leslie Forbes instructing him that 'preference should be given to those who are essential to the war effort without racial discrimination'. This led to a further argument in the War Council when Duff Cooper and Admiral Layton demanded 'that every effort should be made to evacuate white women and children in view of the bestiality and brutality of the Japanese'. The Governor, however, stuck to his guns and the phrase 'no racial discrimination' was retained.

The last of the *bouches inutiles* had just departed Penang when the Municipal Commissioners of Georgetown informed Brigadier Lyon that outbreaks of cholera and typhoid were likely owing to the fouling of the water catchment area and the collapse of the sanitary system. Percival referred the Penang crisis to the War Council, where Admiral Layton confirmed that the port was no longer of any value to the Navy. The council decided that holding Penang depended entirely on the outcome of the Battle of Kedah, and that unless the Japanese could be halted in their tracks the island must be abandoned by the military.

Percival cabled Heath, 'Importance of covering Penang is increased by fact that bulk of remaining cables to UK and India pass through that island. Considered that ability to hold Penang depends upon result of Kedah battle. You are at liberty therefore to use any part of the garrison of Penang that can be made available to take part in Kedah operations, particularly Independent Company. Should it become impossible to cover Penang from mainland, policy will be to evacuate Penang removing by sea the garrison and such essential stores as possible and destroying remainder. Preliminary arrangements should be made as necessary but to avoid causing alarm it is of utmost importance that such arrangements should be kept secret. Resident Counsellor Penang is being given similar instructions.'

With ground staff fleeing from Butterworth airfield, Heath had little chance of covering Penang for much longer. Yamashita had already moved his headquarters to Alor Star, where he and his senior staff officers held a celebratory dinner in the officers' mess. On the 15th the battered commander of III Indian Corps, who had been fighting Britain's enemies for the past two years from Ethiopia to the equator, ordered the evacuation of the small Penang garrison. These troops were taken off the island with several hundred European men in four small coastal vessels on the night of 16–17 December. Europeans who had been told to report to Railway Pier at 5 p.m. with only a suitcase arrived to discover that mining officials were loading their cars on board the ferries and occupying valuable space with golf bags and other sporting items. The night was right for drama, with lightning cracking around the hills and a sudden Sumatra – a violent electrical storm – soaking the evacuees jostling one another on the wharves. The Europeans had been sworn to secrecy, but word had leaked out and many Asians turned up to join the exodus. Everybody scrambled for shelter when the air-raid siren sounded and Japanese planes droned overhead – but visibility was poor and the enemy departed without dropping any bombs.

The Asians were forced to remain behind on the pier while hundreds of European evacuees crowded on to the ferries which then set sail for the mainland. The ferry *Kulim*, heading for Port Swettenham, broke down with engine failure and after all passengers and crew had been transferred to a Royal Navy minesweeper, she was sunk by shell fire. The first shot blew a hole in Brigadier Lyon's motor car which was lashed to the deck, causing a great cheer to rise from the spectators.[9]

A handful of Europeans remained in Penang of their own free will, while Asians serving in the Volunteer Force were given the choice of being evacuated or throwing away their uniforms and staying with their families. The great majority – 500 men – opted to stay. John Prout, aged just 16, who had been evacuated from Singapore a few weeks earlier, was, as the son of an Englishman, in considerable peril in Penang. Bravely, he decided to stay with his Eurasian relatives.

The staff of the *Malayan Gazette* signed off on 16 December with a poignant editorial: 'People in Penang are still stunned by the sudden invasion of the Japanese and are still shocked by the desertion of the British. Has Britain really deserted us? Is this the last day of Penang? Will the morrow bring alien troops to our shores?' General Heath says he was right to order the evacuation. 'Georgetown was ablaze and [the Japanese] continued to attack it even after we had evacuated it,' he says. 'Everything was brought to a standstill at Penang: Harbour Board, Municipal Services, Police and it certainly was no mistake ordering the evacuation.'[10]

The demolition squads entrusted with denying anything of value to the enemy achieved only partial success in the time available. Although the Prai power station was blown up and most of the ammunition and fuel supplies destroyed, many seaworthy craft, including the Straits Steamship Company's seven vessels, were left in the harbour. The squads smashed the valves of the Penang Broadcasting Station but failed to destroy the transmitter. The smelting works was left largely intact, handing the Japanese 1,299 tons of refined tin ingots, plus another 1,700 tons of ore in the furnaces of the Eastern Smelting Company. Shenton Thomas had instructed F. D. Bisseker, the company's chairman and a member of the Legislative Council, to repatriate these huge stocks of tin to Singapore, but Bisseker had replied that he did not even have enough labourers to throw them into the sea. He complained that 'there seemed to be some at the head of affairs who had no conception of what it meant to be at war'.

Millions of dollars in the vaults of Penang banks also fell into the hands of the Japanese. Only one bank manager – N. De P. Fussey of the Hong Kong & Shanghai – managed to save his depositors' cash when he threw bags containing $10 million into the back of his car and made it safely to Singapore.

The preferential treatment of Europeans in the evacuation of Penang soured relations between the British *tuans* and many of their Asian subjects. One author, Bryan C. Cooper, claims that 'there were other launches and trains running for several days and these carried passengers free of charge if they were unable to afford the fare. Every Eurasian and Asian who reportedly wished to leave Penang Island had an opportunity of doing so, and large numbers did avail themselves of this. Although broadcasts from Singapore made the non-European community in Penang quickly aware of the evacuation, they did not rush to the pier.'[11]

According to the Official Historian, 'There was however insufficient shipping to evacuate large numbers of Asians, nor was it considered desirable to add to the large population of Singapore. It was also thought that their welfare and conditions generally would probably be better if they remained in their homes on the island.'[12] It is difficult to see how this applied to Straits Chinese who would be at considerable risk in enemy hands.

Duff Cooper was never forgiven for a diplomatic *faux pas* in a broadcast to the people of Singapore. 'It has been necessary to evacuate many of the civilian population,' he said. 'We can only be thankful so many people have been safely removed.' Chinese and Indian communities knew he was referring to European evacuees and reacted angrily.[13] Stanley Jones, the Colonial Secretary, and A. B. Jordan, the Secretary of Chinese Affairs, volunteered to go to Penang to show the flag, but the island had been cut off by the Japanese. It had been left to Leslie Forbes to leave a letter for General Yamashita requesting humane treatment for all of Penang's citizens. Forbes had also ordered the release from the Penang jail of Japanese internees, one of whom was sent to enemy headquarters at Sungei Patani to advise General Yamashita that the British had left the island. Mr M. Saravanamuttu, the Indian editor of the *Straits Echo*, lowered the Union Flag at Fort Cornwallis. Two companies of Japanese troops from the Kobayashi Battalion of the 5th Division arrived in Georgetown at 4 p.m. on the 19th and captured the island without a shot being fired. Penang Radio was soon back on the air: 'Hello, Singapore. This is Penang calling. How do you like our bombing?'[14]

The Kobayashi Battalion had come direct from Shanghai and had not been subjected to Yamashita's strict discipline over the preceding weeks. The Japanese commander had warned his troops that incidents of rape and pillage would be treated as capital offences. When three soldiers raped women in Georgetown and began looting shops, Yamashita had them court-martialled and executed. Their commanding officer, Lieutenant-Colonel Kobayashi, was placed under close arrest on the battlefield for 30 days – much to the chagrin of his friend Colonel Tsuji.

By the morning of 16 December, the weakened 11th Division was south of the swamplands around the Muda River and had passed into Province Wellesley, heading for Perak. The following day Heath ordered that all European women and children should be evacuated from that state to avoid the fighting. Word of the order reached Stanley Jones, who complained to Shenton Thomas that this was a further breach of the civil government's policy of no racial discrimination. Thomas issued a statement that Heath's order was unauthorised and drafted a series of measures which he described later that day to the War Council. Duff Cooper wrote to Churchill that Thomas proposed that '... no evacuation was to be permitted, that trains travelling south were forbidden to carry passengers who appeared to be evacuees, that first-class carriages were to be taken off the trains in order to prevent Europeans from travelling, that motor cars travelling south were to be turned back, that petrol should not be supplied to private individuals and that they should not be allowed to telephone long distance ... He announced that he had taken these steps with an air of triumph, expecting to be congratulated on having been so quick off the mark. What, however, terrified me most of all was that no member of the Council including General Percival, General Heath's immediately [sic] superior officer, said a word or raised an eyebrow – until I suggested that it was the first time in the history of the British Empire when it had been our policy to evacuate the troops first and to leave the women and children to the tender mercies of a particularly cruel Asiatic foe.'

The War Council quickly overturned Thomas's draft order and relations between the Governor and the Resident Minister slumped to a new low.[15] Thomas, however, was not to be denied. He circumvented the War Council's objections by sending a telegram to the station master at Kuala Lumpur saying that no more people were permitted to come to Singapore and that all civilian passengers should be turned off the trains at KL. This order affected the many Asian civilians who were heading south from Perak after being displaced by the military. Christopher Dawson, who had replaced 'Starchy Archie' Vlieland as Secretary of Defence, told the War Council that the abandonment of the local population by the Europeans would have a catastrophic effect on both Asian morale and British prestige. Duff Cooper snapped back that he 'considered this view was profoundly wrong. The future of Malaya was infinitely small compared with winning the war. Our task was to defeat the enemy. People did not run away in Penang to save their skins; they came back in order to be of more use to their country in the war effort.'[16]

The most immediate threat to the 11th Division was from Japanese forces heading west from Kroh, either down the well-metalled road to the village of Titi Karangan, or along a narrow, hilly track to Grik, where a sealed road ran further south to Kuala Kangsar on the banks of the Perak River. Murray-Lyon was concerned that the Japanese could cut in on his rear along either route.[17] A, B and D Companies of the Argyll and Sutherland Highlanders from Brigadier Archie Paris's reserve 12th Brigade were urgently summoned from Ipoh to occupy positions near Baling on the main road from Kroh. C Company and several Lanchester armoured cars headed for Grik just in case the Japanese managed to come down the mountain track, even though it was thought to be impassable to trucks and tanks.

Once these deployments had been made, Brigadier Paris realised that the main danger to his own brigade was from the 5th Japanese Division heading south from Jitra, which could easily come up behind his troops who were blocking both the routes from Kroh. To counter this threat, he ordered the 5/2nd Punjab Battalion, commanded by Lieutenant-Colonel C. C. Deakin, to hold the bridge over the Muda at Batu Pekaka, slightly north of Titi Karangan, and he moved the Argylls down the Kroh road to Titi Karangan itself. He had acted just in time: on 16 December Japanese masquerading as Malays in sarongs, T-shirts and straw hats swung inland from the Jitra road and tried to rush the Punjabis at the bridge. The attempt failed and the bridge was destroyed when the Punjabis withdrew.

The Japanese were not delayed for long, however. At 10 a.m. the following day they headed towards Titi Karangan, where the Argylls were waiting in ambush half a mile north of the village. This was to be the first contact between the Japanese and the immortal Thin Red Line of the 93rd. Lieutenant-Colonel Ian Stewart had trained his battalion in the same fix-and-encircle jungle tactics as the enemy and great things were expected of them. A Company, with its mortar and machine-gun sections camouflaged, planned to fix the Japanese frontally astride the road which ran towards them through a jungle-covered defile. B Company, similarly armed and hidden in the rubber of the Karangan Estate 700 yards to the east, would then cut the Japanese to pieces when they tried their enveloping move. Two armoured cars would liaise between the units and provide extra firepower from their twin Vickers machine guns. D Company was placed west of the flooded Karangan River, a tributary of the Muda, to defend the road into Titi Karangan. When the time came to pull out, all three rifle companies would have to leg it to reach their transport situated four miles south of the village.

Three weeks prior to the Japanese attack on Malaya, Stewart had been dismissed by Malaya Command as a crank. Yet he had anticipated this day during the endless hours he had spent with his men wading knee-deep through mud up Kranji Creek or sweltering in semi-darkness beneath the jungle canopy. He would never ask them to do something he could not do himself, he said, and today, resplendent in his red-and-white checked Glengarry cap, he had set up his headquarters with an unobstructed view of the most probable Japanese line of attack. Stewart had been ordered to hold Titi Karangan until midday, but he had not been warned that the Japanese were disguised as Malays, and when a group of men in native dress emerged from the jungle on to the road, the Argylls hesitated, thinking they might be Tamil rubber-tappers.

Their doubts were dispelled when the group opened fire and quickly disappeared back into the jungle. One battalion then attacked A Company head-on, while a second battalion moved into the rubber, as expected, to develop an outflanking movement. The Argylls' ambush had failed but the Japanese had walked right into B Company's rifle, mortar and machine-gun fire and suffered heavy losses. One of the dead – who was shot through a rubber tree by an Argyll with a Boys anti-tank rifle[18] – was a European in a peaked cap. Although the man was never positively identified, he was suspected of being a German member of the French Foreign Legion in Indochina who had thrown in his lot with the Japanese.[19]

The enemy attacked again at 10.45 a.m. with long-range mortar fire which proved highly accurate, causing several casualties. Stewart, who had moved his headquarters into A Company's section of the road as the battle developed, knew that his men were outnumbered and that it was only a matter of time before the Japanese mounted a much deeper envelopment to cut them off. He chose to attack, with A and B Companies taking the fight to the Japanese at bayonet point. The bugler had played the Regimental Call and was about to sound the Advance when a dispatch rider dashed up to Stewart and handed him an order from brigade headquarters giving him permission to withdraw 'at his discretion'.

Stewart stopped the bugler in mid-blast and told him to play Stand Fast instead. He then ordered the Argylls to withdraw. The last units passed through Titi Karangan at 11.55 a.m. with the Japanese in hot pursuit. Just in front of the village, 15 Japanese failed to see one of the Lanchesters, concealed beneath freshly cut branches, and were cut down by its machine guns. A similar fate befell another group of Japanese, who emerged from the jungle a mile past the village only to encounter a rearguard of Lanchesters and Bren gun carriers which raked them with fire until the battalion was clear.

Ian Stewart says, 'Had the battalion been asked to delay another quarter of an hour, its counterattack would have had to go in ... By that time too the wide Jap encircling move would have got established across the road behind, and what had been a most successful action would within a few moments have turned into a disastrous defeat.'[20]

With the Japanese momentarily halted at Titi Karangan, the 12th Brigade could safely cross the Krian, whereupon it joined the 11th Division under Murray-Lyon's command and followed the road as far as Selama. The spotlight then switched to the secondary route from Kroh to Grik, where the Argyll's C Company had been attacked by the Japanese 42nd Infantry Regiment on 16 December and sustained a large number of casualties. Although the Argylls were backed up by their armoured cars, they were clearly outnumbered and had fallen back to Sumpitan, a few miles from their Argyll comrades at Selama.

Further south, Heath's train passed through Taiping to Ipoh, the capital of Selangor lying in a semicircle of limestone cliffs. When he had established his new advance headquarters, Percival travelled up from Singapore to discuss the crisis with him. From the fighting so far, Percival had concluded that his troops were up against one Japanese division on the west-coast trunk road, one on the Patani–Kroh–Grik road and another on the east coast, compared with his two Indian brigades in the east and the equivalent of a division in the west. One option was to replace the exhausted 11th Indian Division with the fresh 8th Australian Division in Johore, but he still needed to maintain a strong presence in Johore, particularly to defend Mersing from a possible Japanese landing. He also he knew he would face stiff opposition from Gordon Bennett if he tried to break up the Australian brigades and send Australian units to join the 11th Division. He decided to leave his dispositions as they were.

Percival and Heath held a long conference on 19 December in Ipoh, and after spending the night in Heath's saloon car, the GOC returned to Singapore on the 20th. During their discussions Percival authorised Heath to withdraw the 11th Division over the Perak River and to arrange for a reconnaissance on the Slim River in south Perak. He also ordered the amalgamation of the 6th and 15th Indian Infantry Brigades into the 6/15th Indian Infantry Brigade, with the East Surreys and Leicesters forming one unit known as the British Battalion and the 2/9th Jat Regiment and the 1/8th Punjab Regiment forming the Jat/Punjab Battalion. Heath was instructed to consider the question of the division's leadership because Percival felt 'that an officer with the widest possible experience of bush warfare was required'.[21]

While Percival was in Ipoh, Duff Cooper had chaired a conference of British, American, Dutch, Australian and New Zealand representatives, which reported to the Chiefs of Staff that the armed forces urgently needed large numbers of fighters and bombers, another brigade group in addition to the 18th Division, reinforcements for the 9th and 11th Divisions, three light and two heavy anti-aircraft regiments, an anti-tank regiment, 50 light tanks and a supply of small arms and ammunition. Duff Cooper also entrusted a personal letter to Churchill into the care of Captain Tennant of the *Repulse* who was flying back to London. The letter contained savage criticisms of Shenton Thomas and Brooke-Popham – but Churchill would not receive it until 6 January when it was forwarded to him in the US. In the meantime, Cooper wired criticisms of Percival's handling of Singapore's defence. This cable was passed to General Brooke, the new Chief of the Imperial General Staff, who discussed the question with the War Minister, David Margesson, but no decision was reached and an opportunity to order Percival, through Brooke-Popham, to address the criticisms was missed.[22]

Although he was due to be relieved, Brooke-Popham still had nominal control of the Army and Air Force and had moved his headquarters from the Naval Base to new accommodation at Sime Road close to the Combined Operations Room. As accredited war correspondent for the *Daily Mirror*, Lorraine Stumm was able to observe the Commander-in-Chief's deteriorating condition. At one press conference he fumed, 'Those cads the Japs are disguising themselves as Malays and there's nothing we can do to stop them'.[23]

After his return to Singapore, Percival expanded his thoughts in an instruction to all units describing the tactics to be used against the Japanese: (i) enemy outflanking and infiltration tactics must not lead to withdrawals which should take place only on order of higher authority; (ii) immediate counterattacks should be exploited – these should, whenever possible, be planned beforehand and, owing to the necessity for speed, should usually be carried out by small bodies of a company on the initiative of local commanders; (iii) it was suggested that the defences should consist of a holding group dug in astride the main communications, with striking forces forward on the flanks which should attack as soon as the enemy made contact with the holding groups; (iv) the spreading of rumours must be suppressed; (v) the enemy *could not be defeated by the troops' sitting in prepared positions and letting him walk round them.*[24] The imperative was to play him at his own game and attack on every occasion. The efficiency, cunning and alertness of the individual were of primary importance.

Meanwhile, General Heath and his staff were scouring the countryside along the Perak River in search of a suitable place for the 11th Division to make a stand behind a natural obstacle. On 20 December he reconnoitred the country north-west of Ipoh and crossed the river to visit Kuala Kangsar, where he held a conference with Murray-Lyon in the library of the Malay College, the boys' school regarded as the 'Eton of the East'. The country he had seen so far was mostly rubber and jungle, with no natural defences, and he told Murray-Lyon it looked unpromising. He decided to let the Japanese cross the Perak River unopposed and to stop them further south, even though this would mean conceding more territory.

On 22 December Heath arrived at Kampar, a tin-mining town 23 miles south of Ipoh on the road to Kuala Lumpur. The surrounding district had been cleared and was pockmarked with mining excavations, while the high ground provided a good field of fire for artillery. The dominant feature was Bujang Melaka, a 4,000-foot-high limestone crag covered in thick jungle. The mountain divided the Kampar position into two halves which were completely isolated from each other but, despite this disadvantage, Heath decided that it was the best natural barrier he had seen and ordered it to be reconnoitred.

However, he had reached the conclusion that he could not hold the enemy for long at Kampar or any other point in central Malaya. When he got back to Ipoh, he found that Brigadier Simson had arrived to discuss anti-tank defences with him. Heath listened to Simson's plans for pre-prepared positions and then gave him a message for Percival. It was impossible, he said, for his troops to fight all day, then retreat and dig in again without the prospect of rest or relief. He said he hoped the GOC would arrange to have successive lines of defence constructed by the time his troops had reached Johore.

Simson wrote down the message and read it back to Heath, who made some minor amendments. Simson then asked him to sign it, but Heath declined. He would not explain why, but the reason was clear: it was one thing for Simson to report verbally to Percival what he had seen and heard, but quite another matter for the commander of III Indian Corps to put such 'defeatist' observations in writing over his own signature.

Simson had been astonished on his arrival at Heath's headquarters to see his two rail carriages sitting in an exposed siding at Ipoh Railway Station. They were the only rolling stock in the yard and clearly visible from the air. At Simson's urging, Heath gave orders for the carriages to be moved the following morning to a branch line overhung by trees. Just as the carriages were being shifted, Japanese bombers attacked and both cars were damaged. Fortunately, no one was hurt.

Meanwhile, C Company of the Argyll and Sutherland Highlanders had fought the Japanese down 150 miles of the Grik road to its junction with the trunk road. With the support of the 1st Independent Company and the 5/2nd Punjabis, the Scots had stood and fought at Sumpitan, Lenggong and Kota Tampan. 'We had the services of the 2/3rd Australian Reserve MT Company who had taken over from our truck drivers,' Kenny McLeod remembers. 'They were always at the waiting points ready to take our troops. Every now and again, they would grab a rifle and have a shot at the enemy. They were great chaps.'[25]

Brigadier Paris also had the services of the 12th Brigade's third battalion, the 4/19th Hyderabads, which had arrived back from Kelantan. He placed them east of the Perak River to cover the 11th Division's crossing. On the night of 22 December the remainder of the 12th Brigade Group withdrew across the Perak, covered by troops of the 28th Brigade Group. By the night of 23 December all troops were safely east of the river and the bridges were destroyed.

As the Japanese 5th Division started massing on the banks, the Imperial Guards Division made its appearance in Malaya in the Taiping/Port Weld area to the north. General Murray-Lyon moved his headquarters to Ipoh, while Heath's advance HQ shifted 24 miles south to the Mines Office at Tapah on the road to Kuala Lumpur. All this chopping and changing had a destabilising effect on Heath's staff, but the shake-up announced on 23 December rattled III Corps to its foundations: David Murray-Lyon was dismissed as commander of the 11th Division.

He was replaced by Major-General Paris, who was thought to have the requisite 'bush warfare experience' after two and a half years in Malaya. Paris, however, was a British service officer; Heath had wanted an Indian Army officer to command the Indian division. His preference was for Brigadier Key, commander of the 8th Indian Brigade, who had shown exceptional skill in handling the Japanese attack in Kelantan. As Paris was senior to Key, Percival had ruled in his favour.[26] All of the division's infantry brigade commanders were in hospital, so Lieutenant-Colonel Moorhead was promoted to command the combined 6/15th Brigade, while Lieutenant-Colonel Stewart was appointed to the 12th Brigade and Lieutenant-Colonel W.R. Selby to the 28th Brigade.

The news of his dismissal reached Murray-Lyon on Christmas Eve. With tremendous panache, he thanked his commanders and staff for their efforts, wished them a Merry Christmas and departed. It was a good time to be leaving Malaya. Bowden, the savvy Australian representative on the War Council, warned his government that the deterioration of air defences was assuming 'landslide proportions' and was likely to cause a collapse in the whole defence system. He concluded, 'As things stand at present, [the] fall of Singapore is to my mind only a matter of weeks.'[27]

On Christmas Day Colonel Harrison looked back on the disasters of the previous 17 days: 'Fatigue had stretched the men's minds to the limit and the moral ascendancy which the Japanese had achieved in these few weeks included a "psychic" side. The troops were beginning to attribute almost supernatural powers to the Japanese. They were absolutely at the end of their tether – fought to a standstill. The Japanese tanks had played a great part in this. The material effect of their fire had been small. It was the moral effect of having no adequate counter and above all of knowing that we had no tanks in Malaya at all (just as we had no Navy and no Air Force) which shook the exhausted men.'[28]

Gordon Bennett entertained the Sultan of Johore and his wife to Christmas dinner. According to Bennett, 'The Sultan over and over again expressed his determination that he would stand or fall by the Australians in the fight against the Japanese.' On 27 December the five Bruce children attended the children's Christmas party at Government House. Mel Bruce says, 'The Governor assured us that Japan would not consider invading Singapore and that we were quite safe.'

CHAPTER 13

Defeat at Slim River

SIR HENRY POWNALL arrived in Singapore on 23 December to relieve Air Chief Marshal Sir Robert Brooke-Popham as Commander-in-Chief Far East. Pownall, who had once been a pupil of Brooke-Popham's at the Imperial Defence College, was due to take command on 27 December, and so had a few days to study his former instructor informally. 'It is of course time B-Popham left; he is pretty tired and is quite out of business from dinnertime onwards,' Pownall confided to his diary.[1]

The new C-in-C wasted no time in familiarising himself with the battle-fields of the Western Front on which the fighting spirit of the 11th Division had been broken time and again on the Japanese anvil. On Christmas Day there was a lull while the Japanese 5th Division was crossing the swollen Perak River; Pownall chose that day to tour the 11th Division's new positions, starting with a visit to III Corps's advance headquarters 50 miles south at Tapah.

After discussing the tactical situation with Heath, Pownall headed further north to see the Kampar site for himself. As a former gunner, he was particularly interested in the gun placements and their fields of fire, which offered the gunners an excellent opportunity to inflict serious damage on the enemy. He found that the 22nd Mountain Regiment had set up its head-quarters in one of the Sultan of Perak's palaces, a mausoleum of a place stuffed with ghastly Victorian bric-à-brac, while the 15th Brigade's HQ was a bungalow owned by a French citizen who had thoughtfully bequeathed his cellar of fine French wines to the mess.

Pownall returned to Tapah for afternoon tea and then headed back to Singapore. 'The 11th Division have had a pretty good shaking up,' he wrote. 'They were thrown on to the wrong leg and took some time – indeed too long – to recover. Heath is, I think, all right. He has aged a lot since I knew him in India. He's not "full of fire" but he does know what is to be done to pull the troops around.'

Pownall's directive as Commander-in-Chief differed from Brooke-

Popham's in that he had no operational control over the Army and Air Force, but he would not in any case stay in the job long enough to make any impression. He was, however, a keen observer of his fellow officers. As Field Marshal Gort's Chief of Staff, he had come in contact with Percival in France in 1940. His experience of Percival in Malaya did not impress him; on the contrary, Pownall told his diary that Percival was 'an uninspiring leader and rather gloomy'. He added, 'I hope it won't mean that I have to relieve Percival, pro tem, until someone tougher than he can come from elsewhere. But it might so happen.'[2]

Boxing Day was Arthur Percival's 54th birthday, but the only let-up in his 18-hour working day was that he decided to turn in a little earlier than usual, at 11.30 p.m. He was heading for his bed when the doorbell rang at Flagstaff House: it was Ivan Simson, who insisted on speaking to him. The Chief Engineer had travelled south from Ipoh through two air raids – having to change cars after one vehicle was destroyed by a Japanese bomb – to reach Singapore that night. In a state of some desperation, Simson read out General Heath's message about the need for fixed defences to provide safe harbour for the III Indian Corps on the route south to Johore. Simson had 6,500 engineers under his command, and there was still time for them to make a big difference to the fighting on the mainland if Percival would give the green light. He refused.[3]

Simson hammered away for two and a half hours, repeating all of his arguments of October about the desirability of building fixed defences in Johore for the exhausted Indian troops to fight behind, and adding that time was also running out to secure the north shore of Singapore should it become necessary to retreat on to the island. Percival would not be swayed. 'I strongly urged him to reconsider this decision as it appeared to me to go directly against all the military thinking, teaching and experience of the history of fortresses; and said that in none of our several previous discussions on the subject had he ever given me a reason why he was against defence works. I reminded him too that I have been sent to Malaya for the express purpose of creating such works which had been considered necessary by the War Office and that a fortress without defences was a contradiction in terms. General Percival gave me an explanation. He said, "Defences are bad for morale – for both troops and civilians."'

Simson was thunderstruck. Quite unaware of Percival's instruction that the enemy could not be defeated by the troops' 'sitting in prepared positions', he continued to argue for Heath's place of safety in Johore, but Percival remained unyielding until, Simson admits, 'the argument became

dangerous for both of us'. The one concession Percival made was to authorise Simson to raise the matter of north-shore defences with Major-General
Keith Simmons, the Commander of Singapore Fortress. If Keith Simmons
accepted Simson's proposals for Singapore, Percival said, he would raise no
objection. Simson already knew that Keith Simmons agreed with Percival,
but it was the best he could do in the circumstances and he reeled away from
Flagstaff House at 2 a.m. wondering what quirk of training or experience
had produced such an obvious blind spot in such a senior military mind.

It seems Percival believed that if the 11th Division learned there were
fixed defences in Johore and on the north shore of Singapore, they would
continue retreating until they had reached them. By 'bad for morale', the
GOC actually meant that fixed defences prevented troops from carrying out
his injunction to Heath: 'We must play him at his own game and attack on
every occasion.' Brooke-Popham rarely uttered a word of criticism about
his GOC, but he commented in his Dispatch that 'steps should have been
taken before war broke out to strengthen the defences on the northern and
north-western sides of Singapore Island'.

Later that morning Simson was disappointed again when Major-
General Keith Simmons repeated almost word for word Percival's explanation about defences being bad for the morale of troops and civilians. It was
impossible to see how the construction of fixed defences in central Malaya
or on Singapore's scantily populated north shore could damage civilian
morale. The inconsistency in the Percival/Keith Simmons stance was that
Singapore's south coast bristled with fixed defences, which were in full view
of the vast majority of the island's population. Indeed, shortly after his
conversation with Simson, Keith Simmons ordered tubular scaffolding
poles to be installed on the beaches of the south coast as a further deterrent
to landing craft. Ivan Simson thought this was 'gilding the lily' when the
poles would have been more valuable on the north shore.[4]

Percival was under immense strain and his behaviour was becoming
inconsistent. Five days after his quarrel with Simson, he informed Heath
and Bennett that he had arranged with the Director of Public Works to
form works groups in selected areas under state engineers who would
report to them for orders. 'The object of this was to prepare a series of
obstacles, especially anti-tank obstacles, in great depth on the probable line
of the enemy's advance,' Percival says in his Dispatch. 'The idea was that the
officers of the Public Works Department should be given outline instructions and be left to carry out the work themselves with civil labour.' For
reasons known only to himself, Percival did not inform Simson of this

decision – but in any case his order to the Public Works Department achieved very little. Working independently, however, Simson's staff deposited hundreds of cylindrical concrete bollards at key points in Johore which could be linked by chains or steel cables to act as effective anti-tank obstacles. In the absence of any instructions from the commanders, his men had to choose the dumping sites themselves.

Percival also performed a volte-face with regard to guerrilla operations when he suddenly swung behind John Dalley's idea of training a force of Chinese Communists to fight the Japanese. 'Arrangements were to be made for land raiding parties and for "left behind" parties to harass the enemy's communications,' he says. Shenton Thomas held a meeting with Chinese leaders which formalised the creation of the Dalforce Irregulars. Recruits would be put through an intensive two-week course in weapons and explosives at the hastily revived 101 Special Training School, and then smuggled into jungle hideouts on the mainland. Ivan Lyon and John Dalley worked with other SOE operatives, notably Englishmen John Davis and Richard Broome, shuttling between Singapore and Johore to set up secret supply dumps and to assist the newly graduated Chinese guerrillas in slipping past the advancing Japanese.

With the Japanese strung out along the banks of the Perak River, Percival seized the chance to take offensive action. 'I now foresaw that if the Japanese advanced into Perak, their communications would become very vulnerable to raids from the sea coast,' he says. 'I therefore arranged for a small force of about 50 picked Australians to be organised for seaborne raids on the enemy's communications, using Port Swettenham as a base.' The force was known as Rose Force, and the idea had been put to Percival on 17 December by an Argylls officer, Major Angus Rose, who was one of his GSO2s at Malaya Command.[5]

Rose wanted to land an entire battalion behind the 5th Japanese Division to sabotage their supply lines, but Percival would authorise only a raid west of the Perak by two Australian platoons, with Rose acting as an observer for Malaya Command. Rose Force set off from Port Swettenham on Boxing Day in two naval motor launches, part of the Perak Flotilla which Percival had created. The intention was to sail both launches up the Trong River, north of Ipoh, but when the engine of one of the craft refused to start, Lieutenant Ralph Sanderson's platoon was ordered to carry on alone.

Sanderson and his men landed at 9 a.m. on 27 December near a road outside the village of Trong, and shortly afterwards ambushed five Japanese vehicles – a car, three trucks and a utility – on the main south-coast road.

The car was hit by a grenade and ran off the road, whereupon Sanderson emptied his tommy-gun into it, killing the passengers. The two leading lorries toppled over an embankment and their occupants were also shot. The soldiers in the remaining lorry and the utility hid behind a culvert but were killed by grenades. The platoon then pulled out, returning to Port Swettenham on the 29th. Sanderson's platoon was the first group of Australian infantry to see action against the Japanese in the Malayan Campaign.

Captain Freddie Spencer Chapman and two companions slipped through Japanese lines at the Perak River, intending to meet Rose Force at a prearranged point and guide it to suitable targets, but the rendezvous failed after they had difficulty crossing the flooded river and, once across, they had to hide out from large numbers of advancing Japanese. He saw '... hundreds and hundreds of them, pouring eastwards towards the Perak River. The majority were on bicycles in parties of 40 or 50, riding three or four abreast and talking and laughing just as if they were going to a football match. Indeed, some of them were actually wearing football jerseys. They seemed to have no standard uniform or equipment and were travelling as light as they possibly could. Some wore green, others grey, khaki, or even dirty white. The majority had trousers hanging loose or enclosed in high boots or puttees. Some had tight breeches, and others shorts and rubber boots or gym shoes.' Spencer Chapman added that in marked contrast British and Indian troops 'were at this time equipped like Christmas trees with heavy boots, web equipment, packs, haversacks, water-bottles, blankets, ground-sheets, and even great-coats and respirators, so that they could hardly walk, much less fight'.[6]

Percival thought that with a little more persistence, even greater results might perhaps have been obtained, but any chance of repeating the Rose Force exercise disappeared when five fast Eureka coastal vessels – which the Army had purchased from America and handed over to the Navy – were attacked by aircraft on their way north to Port Swettenham and were either sunk or driven ashore.

While the 11th Division moved through Ipoh to take up its new positions at Kampar, the 12th Brigade fought a delaying action against the Imperial Guards 10 miles north of Ipoh at Chemor, on 26 and 27 December, with the 5/2nd Punjabis inflicting heavy casualties on the enemy but suffering serious losses themselves. Among the last to quit their posts in Ipoh were Chinese and Eurasian female telephonists who connected military calls through the manual telephone exchange right up to the last minute, despite constant bombing and the imminent threat of capture. The 12th Brigade pulled back on the night of the 27th to Gopeng, on the trunk road to Kampar, where at 10 a.m. on 29 December they were attacked by advance units of the Imperial Guards. The brigade retreated again under aerial bombardment towards Dipang, just north of Kampar. That afternoon eight Japanese tanks caught the Argylls on the road without anti-tank support and, although the battalion's armoured cars and carriers tried to cover their retreat, serious damage was done to both the men and their vehicles. The Argylls were forced back on to the 5/2nd Punjabis, where anti-tank gunners brought the leading tank to a halt three-quarters of a mile north of Dipang. General Paris contacted Ian Stewart at his Dipang headquarters and ordered the brigade, which had suffered severely, to withdraw through the Kampar position and go into reserve at Bidor between Kampar and Slim River.

Despite this reverse, it was evident that Paris had injected a new spirit into the 11th Division. Colonel Harrison wrote, 'His confident, cheerful temperament was infectious; his tactical and administrative foresight had spared the troops the weariness which results from rushed orders and administrative chaos. His strategical appreciations, now and subsequently, were almost invariably accurate. Percival and Heath went up to visit 11 Div HQ on the 30th and were most impressed with Paris's clear grasp of the situation and his calm and confident manner.'[7]

Having enjoyed an unopposed crossing over the Perak, the Japanese were now advancing in strength on Kampar, with thousands of troops on bicycles leading the way. Brigadier Paris placed the 6/15th Indian Brigade Group, revitalised after a three-day break and supported by the 88th Field Regiment and the 273rd Anti-Tank Battery, in the main position covering the township on a front four miles wide. Its eastern flank reached jungle-clad Bujang Melaka, with extended fields of fire across mining country to the north, west and south, while the mountainside provided artillery observers with a grandstand view of the whole district. The trunk road ran around the western base of the mountain and through the town and was thus covered by the 6/15th. However, as Heath had seen, the vast bulk of the mountain split the position into two halves; Paris placed the 28th Brigade at Sahum at the top of a loop road which branched off the trunk road, skirted the eastern side of the mountain and rejoined it below Kampar. He dispatched one battalion back to the Tapah area to protect Heath's HQ.

On New Year's Eve the Japanese attacked the two Gurkha battalions at Sahum but were repulsed. The Gurkhas, armed mainly with *kukris*, proved superior to the Japanese in savage hand-to-hand encounters and, supported by the 155th Field Regiment, inflicted heavy losses on the enemy. At 7 a.m. on New Year's Day 1942 the enemy switched their attack to the main Kampar position and, after a heavy bombardment, the 41st Infantry Regiment, backed by tanks and artillery, attacked the British Battalion to the east of the trunk road. 'The garrisons of the defended localities held on grimly and localities lost were immediately recaptured by counterattack,' Percival says. 'At the end of the day all positions were intact.' However, the enemy had secured a foothold on one of the ridges of Bujang Melaka on the extreme right of the position and the following day attacked the East Surreys and Leicesters with renewed ferocity. The Englishmen fought valiantly under the inspired leadership of Lieutenant-Colonel C. E. Morrison and held their position against a superior force. Late in the afternoon the Sikh Company of the Jat/Punjab Battalion, led by Captain Graham and accompanied by the blood-curdling Sikh war cry of '*Sat Siri Akal*', successfully drove the enemy out of another vital position. Only 30 members of the company survived.

As the Japanese had abandoned their attack against the Gurkhas at Sahum, Paris left one Gurkha battalion in place and withdrew the other two further south to contest any enveloping movement of the main Kampar position. Indeed, the main danger to the 11th Division developed in the estuary of the Perak River on the coast south of Kampar. On 1 January, the Japanese sailed a tug towing barges carrying the 4th Guards Regiment into the mouth of the river, while a large group of craft holding the 5th Division's 11th Infantry Regiment appeared nine miles south at the mouth of the Bernam River. Either the boats had been found in Penang harbour, or they were collapsible motor launches which had been used in the landing at Singora and transported south by road. The two rivers were linked by a road which led to the village of Telok Anson, 20 miles inland, where the 1st Independent Company had been stationed to guard the rear of the Kampar position.

When news of the landings reached Paris, he sent the 12th Brigade from Bidor to confront the enemy. The Argylls and Hyderabads were covering the Telok Anson area when the Guards sailed up the Perak River and landed there on 2 January. Fierce fighting broke out in the village between the Japanese and the 1st Independent Company, which was withdrawn through the Argylls, who then bore the brunt of the attack. By nightfall, the 12th Brigade had been forced to concede ground and there was a danger that the 6/15th Brigade would be attacked from the rear. Paris had no choice except to abandon Kampar. All three brigades – the 15th, 28th and 12th – success-fully disengaged and withdrew to the Slim River area.

Considering its current rate of withdrawal, there was every likelihood that the 11th Division would reach Johore in a few days' time. This prospect concerned General Gordon Bennett, who regarded the state as his personal fiefdom. In a diary entry dated 31 December, Bennett wrote, 'The 11th Indian Division, finding itself outflanked by the enemy and being unable to with-stand frontal attacks, withdrew from the Kampar positions, the intention being to fall back by stages to the Slim River. The 9th Indian Division is withdrawing from Kota Bahru and Kuantan to avoid being left high and dry in the event of further withdrawals. General Percival is a very worried man. He is trying hard to stop the retreat but, being burdened by tired and weak unit commanders, and being without adequate reserves to replace his exhausted troops, his task is difficult if not impossible.'[8]

Percival, however, did not support this view; for once, he was quite bullish. 'The Battle of Kampar, where our troops fought extremely well, showed that trained British troops are at least the equal of the best Japanese troops,' he says. 'The infantry were splendidly supported by the artillery, the 88 Field Regiment on the Kampar front doing some particularly good work.' Percival was further heartened when the 45th Indian Brigade, the first of the promised reinforcements, reached Singapore. One brigade group of the 18th British Division was due in mid-January and the rest of the divi-sion, the 44th Indian Infantry Brigade, the 2/4th Australian Machine Gun Battalion, and Australian and Indian reinforcements, as well as 51 Hurricane fighters in crates, would arrive later in the month or early in February.

Bowden's gloomy prognosis that Singapore would probably fall within a matter of weeks had reached Churchill and Roosevelt on Christmas Eve when Richard Casey, Australia's Minister in Washington, called at the White House. Churchill had just persuaded the President – by dangling before him the possibility of an Allied invasion of Europe as early as 1943 – to concentrate American efforts on the war in Europe, and this was the last thing he wanted to hear. He had suffered a mild heart attack and was carrying on under great difficulty. But he roused himself to cable John Curtin that Britain intended to defend Singapore with the 'utmost tenacity', adding a proposal that Australia might withdraw one division from the Middle East and send it to India or Singapore. He said that he did not share the Australian view 'that there is the danger of early reduction of Singapore Fortress. You have been told of the air support which is already on the way ... we have instructed C-in-C Middle East to concert a plan for sending

fighters and tanks to Singapore immediately the situation in Libya permits
... you may count on my doing everything possible to strengthen the whole
front from Rangoon to Port Darwin.'

But Churchill's promises were starting to wear thin with the Australians.
Sir Earle Page raised the question at a meeting of the Defence Committee in
London. According to Sir Alan Brooke, Page had 'the mentality of a green-
grocer' and 'wasted a lot of our time'.[9] Curtin cabled both Churchill and
Roosevelt that the present plans for reinforcement were utterly inadequate
and that he would 'gladly accept United States command in Pacific'. The
following day he published a signed article in the *Melbourne Herald* in
which he told the Australian people, 'We look for a solid and impregnable
barrier of democracies against the three Axis Powers and we refuse to accept
the dictum that the Pacific struggle must be treated as a subordinate
segment of the general conflict ... The Australian Government, therefore,
regards the Pacific struggle as primarily one in which the United States and
Australia must have the fullest say in the direction of the democracies'
fighting plan. Without any inhibitions of any kind, I make it quite clear that
Australia looks to America, free of any pangs as to our traditional links or
kinship with the United Kingdom. We know the problems that the United
Kingdom faces ... But we know, too, that Australia can go [under] and
Britain can still hold on. We are, therefore, determined that Australia shall
not go, and shall exert all our energies towards the shaping of a plan, with
the United States as its keystone, which will give to our country some confidence of being able to hold out until the tide of battle swings against the
enemy.'

Although the article had been pre-planned, its timing was unfortunate
for Anglo-Australian relations. Churchill was 'deeply shocked' by Curtin's
'insulting speech' and, according to Richard Casey's wife, Maie, the President thought it disloyal.[10] Churchill later wrote that Curtin's sentiments
'produced the worst impression both in high American circles and in
Canada'.[11] Curtin was unrepentant. 'The truth is that Britain never thought
Japan would fight and made no preparations to meet that eventuality,' he
said.[12]

Meanwhile, Gordon Bennett's egomania had reached a new pitch. He
demanded that Percival grant him operational control of III Indian Corps
if it fell back to Johore. Percival rejected the proposal, but agreed that III
Corps would be responsible for defence of the west coast and the AIF for the
east coast. The main line of resistance would stretch from Mersing in the
east to Muar in the west.

Both Percival and Bennett attended a conference in the Sultan of Johore's rest-house at Segamat, in northern Johore, on 5 January. General Heath, three brigadiers of III Corps and Brigadier Horatio Duncan, commander of the newly arrived 45th Indian Brigade, were also present. The news was all grim: the enemy were making landings at Kuala Selangor and Port Swettenham on the west coast 70 miles behind the 11th Division in southern Perak. The 73rd Battery of the 5th Field Regiment had scored two hits on a 1,500-ton steamer and sunk three launches in repulsing one enemy landing at Kuala Selangor, but the Japanese had persisted. In Kalantan, the 9th Division was falling back to Jerantut in central Malaya, having been driven from its position at Kuantan. Heath had been forced to relinquish Kuantan airfield or risk the loss of Brigadier George Painter's 22nd Indian Brigade. General Barstow had ordered Painter to withdraw to Jerantut on 3 January, but at 7.30 p.m. that night the enemy caught up with the rearguard of the 2nd Frontier Force Regiment as it was preparing to leave the airfield. Fierce fighting broke out in the dark; Lieutenant-Colonel Arthur Cumming, commander of the 2nd FFR, was wounded when he led the resistance. He was helped into a Bren-gun carrier and, firing a tommy-gun, drove around the battlefield rallying his men. He desisted only when he was wounded a second time and collapsed from loss of blood. He was awarded the Victoria Cross.

In view of the reverses on both fronts, Percival decided that III Corps would execute a phased withdrawal to northern Johore, where the final stand on the mainland would be made. Kuala Lumpur would be abandoned, but it was essential to protect the airfields there and at Port Swettenham until 14 January to ensure that the next convoy, carrying the 54th Brigade, reached Singapore safely. The GOC accepted that it would be impossible to defend the three small states of Selangor, Negri Sembilan and Malacca owing to their dense road networks, which would enable the Japanese to bypass roadblocks and outflank fortifications. As Percival headed back to Singapore, he must have felt that in the circumstances he had done the best he could. Within 48 hours, however, the events at Slim River would make a mockery of his plans.

At dawn on 4 January Brigadier Ian Stewart's 12th Brigade stopped at Trolak, a village on the narrow, winding road which followed the railway line through jungle cuttings into rich rubber country on the border of Perak and Selangor. The three Gurkha battalions of 28th Brigade, commanded by Brigadier W. R. Selby, were bivouacked a few miles further south, near Slim River village. Despite his confident demeanour, General

Paris must have been desperately worried as he set up his headquarters, at Tanjong Malim on the trunk road 23 miles south of Trolak village, with the battered 6/15th Brigade deployed around him. None of his battalions could now muster more than three poorly armed companies or more than two anti-tank rifles. The 5/2nd Punjabis had lost 250 men since 8 December, the Argylls 13 officers and 200 men, and the 4/19th Hyderabads a similar number.

Lieutenant-Colonel Deakin, commander of the 5/2nd Punjabis, wrote in his diary, 'The battalion was dead tired; most of all, the commanders whose responsibilities prevented them from snatching even a little fitful sleep. The battalion had withdrawn 176 miles in three weeks and had only three days' rest. It had suffered 250 casualties of which a high proportion had been killed. The spirit of the men was low and the battalion had lost 50 per cent of its fighting efficiency.'[13] The Argylls, however, were immensely heartened when 100 replacements arrived in the middle of the night to join them. They consisted of veterans who had recovered from wounds, some experienced men who had been taken by Percival to act as orderlies at Malaya Command, and 40 new recruits.

The Trolak sector of the Slim River position extended for three miles forward from Trolak village and was divided into three battalion sub-sectors. The rear sub-sector, covering the village in depth, was held by the Argylls under their new commander, Lieutenant-Colonel L. B. 'Robbie' Robertson, formerly Duff Cooper's ADC. The terrain in the two forward sub-sectors, held by the 4/19th Hyderabads and the 5/2nd Punjabis, consisted of thick jungle through which the road and railway ran in narrow parallel corridors 400 yards apart. This jungle was impassable for armour, and it was also poor country for artillery support. Paris reinforced the 12th Brigade with an additional infantry battalion and a squadron of mechanised cavalry. Both the 12th and the 28th Brigades were supported by a regiment of field artillery and one troop of an anti-tank battery. Paris decided to hold the rest of the divisional anti-tank guns back at Tanjong Malim in case the forward positions were overrun.

To block the southern road against tanks, the troops used Simson's supply of concrete cylinders. Owing to the constant presence of enemy aircraft, which flew up and down the road bombing and machine-gunning through the canopy all day, work on the defences had to be done under cover of darkness. The 12th Brigade had only 24 anti-tank mines out of a divisional reserve of 1,400 and very few anti-tank guns, with the result that its roadblocks lacked Simson's vital requirement that they have adequate cover by anti-tank guns. The enemy attacked down the railway corridor on the afternoon of 5 January, an attack that was beaten off by the two Indian battalions, with heavy Japanese losses. The troops were strafed by Japanese fighters throughout the next day, but the enemy continued to be held back along the railway line.

However, on the night of the 7th, the Japanese attacked down the trunk road with tanks and succeeded in clearing the poorly defended roadblocks. At 3.30 a.m., with shafts of moonlight penetrating thick storm clouds, 15 tanks followed by infantry charged through the Hyderabads. On reaching the Punjabis in the second sub-sector, the leading tank struck an anti-tank mine, and some 30 tanks piled up behind it in close formation. The attack was held up for two hours during which seven tanks were destroyed by anti-tank guns and petrol bombs. The Indian soldiers then withdrew towards Trolak, and after Japanese troops had cleared the road of obstacles the tanks continued their advance, closely followed by infantry. Telephone lines between the forward positions and the Argylls had been cut; the first warning the Scottish battalion received that the Japanese had broken through was when the retreating Indians began to stream through their line.

Owing to poor communications, in all that time no news of the tank menace had reached Selby's 28th Brigade at Slim River, only a few miles further south. In fact, the two commanders, Stewart of the 12th and Selby of the 28th, had committed a fatal tactical error by placing their headquarters on a hill outside Slim village; this put them out of touch with events on the road. Two battalions of Gurkhas were overrun by the tanks while marching along the road to occupy their positions. One battalion was badly mauled and the other annihilated. Stewart's reserve battalion, the 5/14th Punjabis, was similarly surprised and two of its companies destroyed. It was not until the tanks had reached a point two miles south of Slim village and 15 miles from their starting point that they were stopped, by a 4.5-inch howitzer of the 155th Field Regiment. Lieutenant-Colonel Augustus Murdoch, the regiment's commander, was killed in this engagement.

Enemy tanks were now in control of the Slim River road bridge, and all of the 11th Division's wheeled transport was trapped on the far side. The enemy infantry had followed up quickly and there was considerable fighting during the day in the forward areas. In the afternoon, brigade commanders issued orders for a withdrawal down the railway line to Paris's headquarters at Tanjong Malim, 17 miles to the south. Of the 5,000 men in the 12th and 28th Brigades prior to the battle, only 1,173 officers and men were left standing, the remainder having been either killed or wounded. In the words of the Official Historian, 'The action at Slim River was a major disaster. It resulted in the early abandonment of Central Malaya and gravely prejudiced reinforcing Formations, then on their way to Singapore, to arm and prepare for battle ... The immediate causes of the disaster were the failure to make full use of the anti-tank weapons available ... No attempt was made to employ [the field regiment of artillery] in an anti-tank role.'[14]

Percival says in his Dispatch, 'Our losses from this battle were very heavy. The three battalions of the 12th Brigade mustered only the equivalent of about a company each. One battalion of the 28th Brigade had been obliterated, while the remaining two had a total strength of less than one battalion. In the artillery, the engineers and the administrative units, the losses were on the same scale. A large number of guns and wheeled vehicles had been lost. It would be easy, but unprofitable, to attribute the defeat at the Slim River Battle to the inadequacy of the anti-tank defences, the failure to blow the bridges or to a variety of other causes. The real cause lay in the utter weariness of the troops, both officers and men. They had been fighting and moving by day and by night for a month, and few of them had had any proper rest or relief.

'In the exhausting and enervating climatic and topographical conditions of Malaya this is far too long. The enemy's troops also no doubt suffered from the local conditions which were no more natural to them than to the majority of ours. But the enemy, with the initiative conferred by the offensive and by the freedom of the sea and air and with the ability to concentrate the whole of their forces against portions of ours in detail, could always relieve their tired troops or ease the pace whenever they found it necessary. Without reserves we were able to do neither.'

Percival's narrative fails to mention the central point: that the troops of the 11th Division had no safe or secure place to fight behind, or in which to recuperate from their travails, *precisely because he had forbidden Ivan Simson to build one for them.* Eleven days had elapsed since Simson had intruded upon Percival's sleep and virtually begged for permission to construct fixed defences to aid Heath's retreating army. With 6,500 engineers at his disposal, Simson could have built in those 11 days a series of sophisticated redoubts that no armoured column could have penetrated. Percival's secret order to the Public Works Department to carry out such work as Heath or Paris might require had proved lamentably ineffective.

Percival's biographer General Kinvig attributed the blame for the destruction of the 11th Division at Slim River to General Paris and Brigadier

Stewart. Both commanders had long experience in Malaya, he said, and there had been an opportunity for the Trolak area to be fully reconnoitred, for anti-tank obstacles, mines and artillery to be deployed, and for the position to be defended in depth. 'There was at least a reasonable prospect of a successful delaying action being fought,' he says. 'However, basic mistakes by these local commanders in the deployment of units, guns and defences played an important part in the débâcle, as did the speed and resourcefulness of the Japanese.'

Stewart accepted his share of the blame. 'I am rightly criticised for the location of Brigade Headquarters, and for not using the Field Artillery in an anti-tank role,' he wrote to the Official Historian. 'It is no excuse, but I had never taken part in an exercise embodying a co-ordinated anti-tank defence or this type of attack. The use of tanks on a road at night [was] a surprise.'15

However, General David Thomson says, 'One of the things that Ian Stewart knew from the start was that the Japanese would drive down the road and then stick to the road. Their forays into the jungle were very limited indeed; they would go off the road to outflank the opposition but they didn't do long outflanking jungle marches. On both the coasts, they did a certain amount of boat-hopping, but Stewart knew they would concentrate on the road. War imposes untold additional physical and mental strains – especially on men who by age or their lack of physical robustness were well past their peak. The result is to impair judgement and decision-making, and disaster so often swiftly follows. By the time of Slim River, they were all exhausted, Ian Stewart no less than the others.'16

One of the casualties of Slim River was Archie Paris, commander of the 11th Division, who was demoted at General Heath's insistence. The post went to Heath's first nominee, Brigadier Key. Paris returned to the 12th Brigade, displacing Ian Stewart who rejoined his beloved Argylls as commanding officer. Henry Moorhead stepped down voluntarily as commander of the 6/15th Brigade and returned to the 3/16th Punjab Battalion. His place at the head of the 6/15th Brigade was taken by Brigadier B. S. Challen.

The 11th Indian Division had temporarily ceased to exist as an effective fighting formation and passed into reserve to rest and recuperate. There was now practically nothing between the victorious Japanese and Kuala Lumpur. To stay on schedule, Yamashita had a week to get there. It was at this point in the campaign that General Archibald Wavell, a poet-warrior like his Japanese opponent, arrived in Singapore to stop him.

CHAPTER 14

Enter the Chief

GENERAL WAVELL, Commander-in-Chief India, was enjoying a day's pig-sticking at Meerut on 30 December 1941, when a telegram arrived from Churchill appointing him Supreme Commander South West Pacific. Wavell's heart must have sunk. 'You are the only man who has the experience of handling so many different theatres at once,' he read, 'and you know we shall back you up and see you have fair play.' As if to sympathise, Churchill added, 'Everyone knows how dark and difficult the situation is.'[1]

Churchill later reflected that he knew it was almost certain that Wavell 'would have to bear a load of defeat in a scene of confusion,'[2] but at the time Wavell – known to his staff as 'the Chief' – accepted his new posting with a joke: 'I have heard about being handed the baby but this is twins.' As the enormity of the task sank in, Wavell increased the number of babies at different times from twins to triplets to quadruplets.[3] Wavell's appointment meant that he outranked Sir Henry Pownall, Commander-in-Chief Far East, so, after only three days in the post, Pownall stepped down and prepared to become Wavell's Chief of Staff.

Wavell had fought in the Boer War and had lost his left eye in World War I. He once described 'the actualities of war' as tiredness, hunger, fear, lack of sleep, weather, inaccurate information and 'the time factor on troops in battle'.[4] He despised the Japanese Army and had never believed that Japan would dare to challenge Britain in Asia. Four weeks after the Japanese invaded Malaya, however, the new Supreme Commander landed in Singapore in a Catalina flying boat, on the overnight flight from Ceylon, to discover that British and Indian troops fighting the Japanese in Malaya were being overwhelmed by the 'actualities of war'.

Wavell's appointment had emerged from Churchill's Arcadia talks with President Roosevelt in Washington at Christmas. While Roosevelt agreed with Churchill that Hitler must be defeated first before they could devote their attentions to Japan, he insisted that a new command should be put in place in the south-west Pacific to unify all American, British Empire and Dutch forces.

Churchill was travelling from Washington to Ottawa by rail on 28 December when he cabled John Curtin to explain that Wavell 'would receive his orders from an appropriate joint body who will be responsible to me as the Minister of Defence and to the President of the United States'. This body turned out to be the Combined Chiefs of Staff, drawn from the military hierarchies of Britain and the US.[5] Despite ABDACOM's imposing multi-national provenance, neither the Dutch nor the Australians had any say in its higher direction. Richard Casey informed Canberra that General George Marshall, the US Chief of Staff, had been 'the moving spirit' behind the proposal for a unified command and had suggested Wavell as Supreme Commander, with US General George H. Brett, the charismatic commander of America's small force in Australia, as his deputy. 'Marshall regards urgent achievement of unified command as a vital first step,' Casey said. 'He realises that the present plan may not be perfect but it is a plan on which he believes the several Governments and many fighting services involved ought to be able to agree.'[6]

John Curtin discovered to his chagrin that ABDACOM's area of responsibility would exclude Australia, even though Australian soldiers, sailors and airmen were at the forefront of the unified command. Nor would the US Pacific Fleet protect Australia's eastern seaboard from Japanese attack. Curtin complained to Churchill that his country was being offered as a sacrifice to the Japanese who would be tempted to avoid 'the main Allied concentration of force in the south-west Pacific' and head south to attack a weakly defended Australia.[7]

Churchill replied tetchily, 'Night and day I am labouring here to make the best arrangements possible in your interests and for your safety, having regard to other theatres and other dangers which have to be met from our limited resources. It is only a little while ago that you were most strongly urging the highest state of equipment for the Australian Army in the Middle East.' Churchill denied that Britain and the US were assembling a 'main Allied concentration of force' under Wavell and added that Australia had been excluded from his command because it was outside the fighting zone.[8]

According to his doctor Lord Moran, Churchill was in a 'belligerent mood' over Curtin's cable. He accepted that the Prime Minister's views were not necessarily those of all Australians, but he commented in a fit of pique that 'Australians came from bad stock'.[9] More to the point, Australia was reaping the whirlwind for having invested so parsimoniously in its own defence in the years between the wars. Australian historian Robert O'Neill concluded that it was 'scarcely to Australia's credit that it had preferred to take British reassurances at face value and to do so little of its own volition to exploit the defensive worth of the long approaches to its own shore'.[10]

After his visit to Ottawa, Churchill headed for the sun. He spent five days at Pompano, a little resort near Miami, where he received a daily courier service of papers and telegrams from the British Embassy in Washington. On 6 January he received Duff Cooper's letter of 18 December which had been forwarded from 10 Downing Street. After 10 days of war, Cooper had written, 'Sir Robert Brooke-Popham is a very much older man than his years warrant and sometimes seems on the verge of nervous collapse. I fear also that knowledge of his own failing powers renders him jealous of any encroachment on his sphere of influence. He has looked upon me with suspicion ever since my arrival, disliked my recent appointment [as Resident Minister] and fought hard against the creation of the War Council.

'The Governor, Sir Shenton Thomas, is one of those people who find it impossible to adjust their minds to war conditions. He is also the mouth-piece of the last person he speaks to. When I informed him of my appointment he professed himself delighted, welcomed the idea of a War Council, and was most helpful at the first meeting which we held the same afternoon. That evening he dined with Sir Robert Brooke-Popham and at the meeting the next morning he supported the latter's attitude in contesting the need for a War Council and produced stronger arguments against it than Sir Robert Brooke-Popham could produce himself.'

Thomas, Cooper continued, was 'much influenced by his Colonial Secretary, a sinister figure called Stanley Jones who is universally detested in the Colony, where he is accused of having been defeatist since the beginning of the war'. General Percival was 'a nice, good man who began life as a schoolmaster [*sic*]. I am sometimes tempted to wish he had remained one. He is a good soldier, too – calm, clear-headed and even clever. But he is not a leader, he cannot take a large view; it is all a field day at Aldershot to him. He knows the rules so well and follows them so closely and is always waiting for the umpire's whistle to cease fire and hopes that when that moment comes his military dispositions will be such as to receive approval.'

Churchill did not spend long pondering Duff Cooper's missive. He had already removed Brooke-Popham from Singapore, but although he must have considered recalling Shenton Thomas and Percival, he decided to gamble on Wavell's being able to overcome the difficulties that had so clearly defeated his Resident Minister. Churchill cabled Duff Cooper that same day, 'The increasingly large arrangements which have been developing from our discussions here and Wavell's appointment as Supreme Commander-in-Chief South West Pacific Ocean necessarily bring your mission to an end. You should at your convenience by whatever is the safest and most suitable route come home. If possible without undue risk you should confer with Wavell at his headquarters in Java and tell him what you think and know. Pray let me know your plan. HM Government are entirely satisfied with the way in which you have discharged your difficult and at the time dangerous task and I look forward to our future work together in a world situation which with all its trouble has changed decisively for the better.'

Shenton Thomas was not above sending his own confidential reports to the Colonial Office. He wrote to Lord Moyne, Secretary of State for the Colonies, 'The news of DC's appointment to the Far East had been received with little enthusiasm ... We felt we were being landed with a failure. We remembered Sir Stafford Cripps' description of him as a "petulant little pipsqueak". At one of the first meetings there was a heated argument as to the powers of the [War] Council, heated on DC's part. He seemed to think we were to run the war which was not Brooke-Popham's interpretation of the Prime Minister's telegram laying down the terms of reference. I agreed with Brooke-Popham. He had his orders from the Chiefs of Staff and I had mine from the Secretary of State. No man can serve two masters. Eventually DC told Brooke-Popham that he was the worst example of the old school tie he had ever come across. This was to the C-in-C, Far East, in the presence of junior officers and myself. Brooke-Popham behaved splendidly and merely said that the remark was not fair.'[11]

Churchill's suggestion that Duff Cooper possibly visit Wavell at his headquarters in Java was a little premature. Wavell was still in India. 'The war couldn't really start in Java until the office got there, as it were,' Beryl Stevenson says. Having weathered the storms breaking around Brooke-Popham's head, Beryl had left Singapore in the SS *Anking* with another secretary, Elspeth Evans, who was also married to an officer in the Manchester Regiment. 'I had Brooke-Popham's GHQ records in my possession,' Beryl says, 'and we went to Java, where the new headquarters was being set up. When we arrived in Batavia, it was all pretty haphazard and a bit chaotic. We were put up in fancy hotels for a few days before being transported to Lembang [a resort near the capital, Bandung, in the Javanese uplands]. Once headquarters was set up, Wavell arrived and I worked for his Chief of Staff, Henry Pownall.'

Wavell left Delhi at 7 a.m. on 5 January in his personal DC2 for Madras and then Ceylon, where he switched to a Catalina for the overnight flight to Singapore. General Pownall was waiting on the quayside when he landed. It was 7 January 1942 – the morning of the Slim River débâcle – and Wavell spent the day at GHQ Far East with Pownall and Arthur Percival. In the evening, he and Pownall dined with the Duff Coopers. Cooper explained that he had just received notice that Wavell's appointment had terminated his mission as Resident Minister and he was going home.

Hours later, Cooper was roused from his slumbers in the Coopery by a message from Pownall, containing the draft of a telegram that Wavell intended to send to the Prime Minister. It said, 'I would ask you to cancel orders to Duff Cooper for return and to leave him for time being in present position in which he has done much to improve defence situation in Singapore from civilian point of view and in which his resolution in present crisis is most valuable.' Cooper promptly told Wavell that he could not remain in his present position 'because I had no position at all. Having no position, I had no authority.'[12] Wavell did not send his telegram. He knew that Churchill could easily have reinstated Cooper, but that Cooper, despite his semantics, did not wish to stay. No wonder Cooper felt he was running away. Curiously for someone with no position, he continued to preside over the War Council.[13] 'I think my father hated Singapore,' says John Julius Norwich. 'By the time he got there, it was far too late.'[14]

Percival dismissed Cooper with few words of regret. 'During the whole of the four months he was in Singapore Duff Cooper hardly ever visited Malaya Command Headquarters,' he says. 'He dined with me once at Flagstaff House but I was never asked either to his house or his office, either in peace or war. He had no grasp whatever of the Army machine and allowed himself to be influenced by people who for years had been critical of the Government of Malaya. The result was confusion.'[15] Sir Shenton Thomas was elated that his adversary had been given his marching orders. He summed up Cooper in his diary as 'a rotten judge of men, arrogant, obstinate and vain'.[16] Lady Diana, the Governor claimed, 'has not appeared in public since the war began, and we gather has complete jitters'. Lady Diana had gone down with an attack of dengue fever and on her recovery had spent most of her time indoors ciphering and deciphering telegrams for her husband.

Singapore's fate was now in the hands of General Wavell, but Lady Diana had little faith in his ability to turn the tide. 'The impression he gives,' she wrote, 'is not brightened by his being very deaf and by having one wall-eye dropping and sightless.'[17] The day before he left Singapore, Cooper sent Wavell a copy of an explosive letter dated 12 January. Addressed to the Prime Minister and Lord Moyne, it aimed a Parthian shot at his old enemy, Shenton Thomas. 'Before leaving Singapore,' Cooper wrote, 'I think it right to tell you that I believe that certain changes in the local administration are of the first importance. A breakdown on the civil side may well paralyse the fighting services. There exists a widespread and profound lack of confidence in the administration. I believe that the simplest solution would be to declare a state of siege and appoint a Military Governor for the duration of emergency.'[18]

Churchill was now in favour of getting rid of Thomas, but Lord Moyne[19] demurred and passed the buck to Wavell, saying, 'I believe you are the best judge of whether in present situation change of Governor would assist you in defence of Malaya.' Instead of grasping the opportunity, Wavell decided that Thomas was 'a good figurehead' and let him remain. A scapegoat was required, however, and the axe fell on the scheming Stanley Jones, who was sacked as Colonial Secretary. Thomas bitterly resented the dismissal of his acolyte and expressed his feelings to anyone who would listen. He was given Duff Cooper's job as chairman of the Far East War Council. That ineffectual body had been renamed War Council, Singapore and, as Hong Kong had fallen on Christmas Day and it could do nothing to help Burma, its scope was limited to the area under Malaya Command.

Bowden was thoroughly dissatisfied with the lack of positive action. He told his superiors in Australia that Duff Cooper was an able man but not a dominant one, and he had not provided the War Council with the strong leadership it required. Brooke-Popham had shown 'an extraordinary diffidence of manner for a man in his position' and was 'definitely too old for such a post in wartime', whereas his replacement, General Pownall, had become the outstanding figure on the Council. Percival appeared to be an able soldier but lacked a strong personality, while Air Vice-Marshal Pulford was 'very worried and greatly overworked'. When it came to Shenton Thomas, Bowden noted the Governor's infuriating penchant for producing reasons for not doing things, rather than getting on with them.

The Malayan Civil Service, meanwhile, was criticised for sticking to the old bureaucratic maxim that action ran the risk of creating problems while there was safety in doing nothing.[20] By leaving Thomas in place – indeed, promoting him to the chairmanship – Wavell had made his first error of judgement.

Wavell, who had acquired the nickname 'Podgy' at Winchester, had become a national hero during the dark days of 1940–41 when he won a series of brilliant victories over Mussolini's Italian armies in Cyrenaica, North Africa. But he had subsequently suffered a succession of defeats, against the Germans during the invasion of Greece and the loss of Crete and finally against General Rommel in the Western Desert. After the failure of Operation Battleaxe to stem the Panzer tide in July 1941, Churchill relieved Wavell of his command in the Middle East. 'At home we had the feeling that Wavell was a tired man,' he said. 'It might well be that we had ridden the willing horse to a standstill.'[21] He was swapped with General (Sir) Claude Auchinleck, Commander-in-Chief India. 'Wavell,' Churchill thought rather unkindly, 'would enjoy sitting under the pagoda tree.'[22]

In September that same year, however, Wavell found himself sitting in the Special Information Room in the War Cabinet Offices. The centre was located next to the Minister of Defence's office and was run by Joan Bright, who saw quite a bit of Churchill and his advisers. After riffling through various 'Top Secret' reports on the war, Wavell invited Joan to lunch with him at the Senior United Service Club, where he ate his meal in silence. The attractive young secretary must have been wondering why he had invited her to accompany him when, on the walk back to the office through St James's Park, he suddenly asked in his croaky voice, 'Why does Winston dislike me, Joan?' It was an astonishing question to put to a stranger, and Joan replied that she had no idea. But the war hero and the secretary became close over the next few weeks; she admired his military record and he desperately needed a confidante. 'It was a tragedy that Churchill had lost confidence in Wavell but more of a tragedy that Wavell was so inarticulate,' she says. 'His failure to be articulate was unfortunate in a man who could express himself so ably and smoothly on paper.'

When Wavell arrived in India he put those talents to good use in letters to Joan Bright.[23] Just before the Japanese attacked Malaya, Wavell wrote to her, '1941 has on the whole been a better year than we had a right to expect with our backwardness of preparation   I hope that whatever happens the PM's position will remain untouched, his courage and drive and leadership are indispensable. A very great man, if he had a better balanced judgement and chose men with his head rather than his heart he would be almost superhuman, and how unpleasant people approaching the superhuman are!

'Man is a greedy, stupid, short-sighted animal, however he is governed, and as a writer rather aptly remarked in the last war: "I see no reason why the human race, so inefficient in time of peace, should suddenly become efficient in time of war"... If we devoted all our attention to war for 8 or 10 years, God forbid that we ever should, I think we should on the whole make a better job of it than the Germans ... Only two things really matter, as a poet said just before getting killed in the last war –

The beauty of this green earth
And the gallantry of man.

'Courage and kindliness are the only two qualities that excuse human existence. A people like the Egyptians are kindly but not brave, so we despise and rather bully them. The Germans are brave but not kindly so we hate them and fight them. Can we claim as a nation to be both brave and kindly?'[24]

This seemed a strange mindset for a man who had commanded troops in battle against the Nazis and was about to tackle the Japanese. The answer to the question he had posed to Joan Bright was that Churchill found it impossible to like Wavell.[25] They had first met in London in August 1940 before Wavell's victories at Bardia, Tobruk and Benghazi had made him a household name. Instead of having the chance to meet his Prime Minister man to man, Wavell was asked to attend a full-blown meeting of the War Cabinet and the Chiefs of Staff. John Connell wrote, 'One who was present has described as "disastrous" the way in which the emotional temperature dropped in the face of Wavell's taciturnity.' Wavell himself 'did not think Winston quite knew what to make of me and whether I was fit to command or not'. Churchill had wanted a virtuoso performance from his Commander-in-Chief Middle East on his plans to beat the Italians in North Africa and made no secret of his own disappointment. In understanding a man, Churchill needed to hear something about his childhood and upbringing. He had no key to Wavell's character. There was no key, hence no communication.

Lieutenant-General Sir John Cowley says that as a staff officer in North Africa he had woken Wavell one night to tell him that the Australians had captured Sidi Barrani. Wavell sat down and composed a personal note to Churchill. Cowley says, 'I was sitting four feet from the Commander-in-Chief for half an hour and he never said anything, not even "Good night" or "Thank you very much". Not a word. A strangely silent man.'

Wavell flew out of Singapore in an Australian Hudson on his way north at 4.30 a.m. on 8 January 1942, landing at Kuala Lumpur in time for breakfast with General Heath. 'Podgy' Wavell already knew 'Piggy' Heath from his Eritrean days as commanding officer of the 5th Indian Division, but it was a solemn reunion. Heath was having some difficulty establishing exactly what had happened to the 11th Division at Slim River over the previous 24 hours. Wavell's ADC Alexander 'Sandy' Reid Scott wrote in his diary for that day, 'At HQ III Corps we hear things are in a bad way for the 11th Division. After a bad breakfast Heath takes us to HQ 11th Division – Major-General Paris who I gather is good. They have little information which I can't understand as their communications with their two leading brigades come straight back along the only road. So the Chief, Heath and I continue north up the road ...'[26] Wavell and Heath travelled the 35 miles to the forward headquarters of the 12th and 28th Brigades, where the commanding officers, Brigadiers Stewart and Selby, described the rout of the 11th Division at the hands of the Japanese. 'I have never seen two men look so tired,' Reid Scott wrote.

Back in Singapore that night, Wavell cabled the Chiefs of Staff that the 12th and 28th Brigades had been 'overrun by Japanese tanks and infantry and at present consist of about 400 very tired men each, in 12th Infantry Brigade less than 200 are armed. Sixteen 25-pounder guns and seven anti-tank guns were lost yesterday. Also saw Commander of amalgamated 6th and 15th Brigades which are watching left flank on coast. Units under his command are at more reasonable strength but they are very tired and morale of most units doubtful. Much the same applies to units left in 9th Division on eastern flank which has now only five battalions. In fact, in judgement of their Commanders formations and units of 9th and 11th Divisions with very few exceptions are no longer fit to withstand attack.

'My own judgement from what I heard and saw would confirm this opinion. These divisions have now been fighting for over month without rest and retreating continuously under most trying conditions. Retreat does not bring out best qualities of Indian troops and men are utterly weary and completely bewildered by Japanese rapid encircling tactics, by enemy air bombing (though this has luckily been only intermittent) and by lack of our own air support. Divisional and brigade Commanders I saw were calm but very tired ... After seeing Percival and Gordon Bennett will tomorrow send plan to meet what has become somewhat critical situation in Malaya.'

Wavell confirmed Percival's view that a decisive battle should be fought on the north-west frontier of Johore using the Australians and the 45th Indian Brigade as the main Allied forces. This would provide time for the 9th and 11th Divisions to rest and reorganise, and for the arrival of the 18th British Division, comprising fresh Territorial units from East Anglia.

Wavell discussed his plans with Bennett at Johore Bahru on 9 January. He was impressed with the Australian's *toujours l'attaque* philosophy and his contention that the Japanese had yet to encounter any real opposition in their southward drive down the Malay peninsula. Nor was Bennett shy in expressing his views about the qualities of Indian soldiers, the lack of fighting spirit in the Indian Army and the 'retreat complex' of General Lewis Heath and his commanders. It would never happen in the AIF, he said. Meanwhile, he bombarded Australian reporters and politicians with headline-grabbing statements such as 'One Australian is worth 10 Japanese,' and 'I have never met men with a higher morale. They are as happy as sandboys at the thought of being able to get at our new enemy, the yellow Huns of the East . . .' Like many officers in the Australian camp, John Wyett found Bennett's crassness unacceptable. 'We used to feel ashamed of him,' he says.[27]

In the Middle East, Wavell had used the 6th Australian Division in the capture of Bardia, Tobruk and Benghazi and was a great fan of the division's fighting qualities – although he had unfortunately sent it to its doom in Greece and Crete. He decided on the spur of the moment that Bennett, as the more openly aggressive commander, should play the leading role in the Battle of Johore. 'Wavell was a nice fellow,' John Wyett says. 'I felt very sorry for him, because he had the wrong end of the stick right through the Middle East and then he was given Malaya. We were all assembled and he came in and took his cap off, threw it up in the air and it went in a great arc and landed on a little card table. I thought, "You must be pretty sure of yourself to do that in front of a lot of blokes like ourselves."

'It was a bit of a gimmick but done with a purpose to make himself *au fait* with people, and it worked very well in many respects because a lot of people were very dubious about this new high-ranking bloke coming in on top of all the ones who were already there. He said, "Sit down gentlemen. You know during the course of my military career I've quite often been in a situation where I've been left carrying the baby. This is the first time in my whole career where I've been handed triplets."

'They had landed him with the Far East, and God knows what he was supposed to do with it – from India down to Java. Last-minute panic, I'd call it. The High Command handled the whole operation in the East very poorly; that's not to say there weren't some good blokes among them – there were – but when you have one side pulling against another, orders coming from Britain and elsewhere, they didn't know where they were and nobody seemed to be strong enough to say, "Go to hell, this is what we're going to do." Wavell had only just arrived and he didn't know the situation very well. He had a very bad trot and, of course, Churchill had said to him, "I've got to have something to show the public." But Wavell was only in a position to hand him one disaster after another.'[28]

After discussing the situation with Bennett, Wavell summoned Percival and presented him with a *fait accompli*: an entirely new dispersal for the defence of Johore, which was the direct opposite of Percival's plan that the AIF would take care of the east coast while Heath's III Corps defended the west coast. Wavell had decided that the 8th Division, less the 22nd Brigade, would move immediately to the north-west frontier of Johore and prepare to defend the line Muar–Mount Ophir–Segamat. The 22nd Brigade would rejoin the division as soon as it could be replaced on the east coast of Johore by troops from Singapore. The 9th Indian Division and the 45th Indian Brigade would come under Bennett's command as 'Westforce'. Meanwhile, Heath's III Corps would withdraw into Johore, pass through Westforce and take up positions further south along a line running from Mersing in the east, through Kluang in central Johore, to the town of Batu Pahat on the west coast.

Wavell decided that the Japanese encircling tactics could easily be countered and he had every faith in Bennett's ability to do it. 'Gordon Bennett has studied theatre and trained his division in appropriate tactics,' he cabled London. 'He will conduct very active defence and will I hope be able to delay enemy till collection of reserves enables us to deliver counter-stroke which will not be before middle of February.'[29] Everything depended on holding the Japanese in northern Johore until reinforcements could be mustered on Singapore Island for Wavell's counterattack.

Percival realised he had lost the Supreme Commander's confidence at the very beginning of their relationship, but he still attempted to get his own way. He wrote in his Dispatch, 'After visiting Headquarters III Indian Corps and troops of the 11th Indian Division on 8 January General Wavell left Singapore for Java. The Far East Combined Intelligence Bureau accompanied him, except for a few officers who were left to strengthen the intelligence branches of the service staffs at Singapore.' Wavell, however, was still in Singapore on the 9th – he did not leave for Java until the 10th – and, according to Bennett, when it became clear that Percival was reluctant to replace the 22nd Australian Brigade with troops from Singapore, Wavell 'instructed him that he must do everything possible to strengthen the western side of Johore which was immediately threatened'.

Bennett's version of the meeting in his Segamat headquarters was that Wavell ordered Percival to give him the 22nd Brigade as well as the 27th Brigade, the 45th Indian Brigade and the 9th Indian Division. The orders issued by the GOC Malaya the following day at another conference at Segamat, however, stipulated that Bennett's Westforce would consist of the AIF less the 22nd Brigade; the 9th Indian Division; the 45th Indian Brigade Group; the 2nd Battalion of the Loyal North Lancashire Regiment less one company; an Indian Pioneer Battalion; and additional artillery, engineer and administrative units.

Heath's III Corps would encompass the 11th Indian Division plus corps troops, Taylor's 22nd Brigade Group and a battalion from Singapore Fortress (the 2/17th Dogras). 'To the best of my belief these orders were in accordance with the instructions received from the Supreme Commander, South-west Pacific,' Percival says. 'He has since stated that he directed that the Australian Brigade Group in the Mersing area should be moved as soon as possible to join the remainder of the AIF. I have no record or recollection of such instructions, though it was my intention, if opportunity offered at a later date, to relieve this brigade group by a newly arrived formation.' Percival added, 'The Supreme Commander, South-west Pacific has also stated that he directed that the 9th Indian Division should be employed in the southern portion (i.e. the Muar Sector) of the position to be occupied. I have equally no record or recollection of this instruction.'

Wavell's intentions were made patently clear in a cable to the Chiefs of Staff on 9 January: 'After discussion with Percival and Gordon-Bennett [sic] have laid down following general plan for defence of Malaya: 8 Australian Division less one Brigade Group in Mersing Area to move forthwith to north-west frontier of Johore, and prepare to fight decisive battle on general line Segamat-Mount Ophir-mouth of Muar River. Brigade Group in Mersing area to be moved to above general line as soon as it can be relieved by troops from Singapore Island. This cannot be completed before arrival 53rd Infantry Brigade.' Wavell added that he had urged Percival to reunite the two AIF brigades at once, but Percival had demurred on the grounds that a replacement was needed before the Mersing group could be moved because of the danger of a Japanese landing on the east coast. Nor would Percival move many troops from Singapore Island because he was terrified that the Japanese would stage a *coup de main* by landing a seaborne force on the island's south coast. Wavell later concluded, 'I have always regretted since that I did not insist on the move without replacement.'

Colonel Jim Thyer, who was with Bennett when he received his orders from Percival to command Westforce, says Percival contended that if Johore was lost, the battle for Singapore was lost. 'General Bennett had now been given the responsibility of resisting the main Japanese thrust, a task which he relished, but it was at a cost of temporarily losing his 22nd Brigade at Mersing. It proved a most unfortunate decision, both in principle and in the light of subsequent tactical failures.'

General Pownall was aware of Wavell's doubt about the capabilities of both Heath and Percival, and wrote in his diary that the Supreme Commander was 'not at all happy about Percival, who has the knowledge but not the personality to carry through a tough fight'.

After their conference on the 10th, Percival and the top brass recon-noitred the positions to be occupied. Percival gave particular attention to an Australian plan to stage an ambush on the road west of Gemas. John Curtin cabled Churchill in the US, 'It is observed that the 8th Australian Division is to be given the task of fighting the decisive battle. The Government has no doubt that it will acquit itself in accordance with the highest traditions of the AIF. However, I urge on you that nothing be left undone to reinforce Malaya to the greatest degree possible in accordance with my earlier repre-sentations and your intentions. I am particularly concerned in regard to the air strength as a repetition of the Greek and Crete campaigns would evoke a violent public reaction.'[30]

Meanwhile, the great 150-mile exodus of the 11th Division through Selangor, Negri Sembilan and Malacca to Johore began on the morning of 10 January, when a convoy comprising every conceivable type of vehicle headed south. It was one of the cruel ironies of the campaign that the 11th Division's emblem was an 11-spoked wheel. There were truckloads of exhausted Indian and British troops, commandeered Rolls Royces and tiny Austin 7s, 11 steamrollers, two fire-engines, enormous jungle-clearing trac-tors, Red Cross ambulances and ordnance vans, while dispatch riders on motor bikes darted in and out of the traffic.[31]

At railway crossings, troop-trains whistled south containing thousands of troops, many of them sick and wounded. Among the firemen shovelling coal into the boilers were stokers from *Prince of Wales* and the *Repulse*. Malays, Chinese and Tamils watched in silence as the great procession snaked through their *kampong*s, signalling the end of British rule in Malaya. The most amazing feature of the withdrawal was the absence of the Japanese Air Force. The weather was cloudy during those two desperate days but, even so, there seemed no reason except perhaps good luck

Ian Morrison spent the morning of the 11th in Kuala Lumpur, where he discovered dismaying scenes of chaos. Most of the British forces had already headed south, but there was still a small rearguard 15 miles to the north, and in the city itself demolition squads were blowing up the few remaining bridges. Percival's hopes of retaining control of Kuala Lumpur and Port Swettenham airfields until 14 January had evaporated. In the absence of British policemen, law and order had broken down and looters were busy stripping the big foreign department stores of all their goods.

The streets were knee-deep in boxes and cardboard cartons and paper which the looters had discarded after seizing the contents. One man had a Singer sewing-machine over his shoulder; another had tied a long roll of linoleum to the back of his bicycle. Radios, rolls of cloth, tins of preserved foods, furniture, telephones, carpets, golf-clubs – every conceivable object was being carted away. Morrison saw one man loading up an ox-cart with products from Whiteaway Laidlaw's store.

Morrison visited the Residency and found it deserted, the Union Flag nowhere to be seen. A half-finished whisky-and-soda stood on a small table in the drawing-room; on a desk upstairs lay dispatches addressed to the Governor which had been typed out but were unsigned. In the offices on the ground floor, the staff appeared to have downed pens in the middle of whatever they were doing and made off. A lorry, still in good order, was parked at the side of the building. Glass cases filled with beautiful silver ornaments and daggers of superb native workmanship adorned the hall. The official portraits of the King and Queen smiled down from the walls. But the thing that incensed Morrison most was that in the office of the Government Survey Department he found thousands of maps, abandoned to the Japanese.

On the outskirts of the doomed city, huge columns of black smoke billowed over the countryside as all stocks of rubber were burned. Morrison visited one rubber estate where sacks of rice were being distributed to Indian and Chinese labourers. Each labourer would have enough rice to keep him for at least two months. In the processing plant, all the machinery had been smashed up. One old Chinese seemed utterly bewildered after being ordered to take a sledge-hammer to the engine that had provided power for the plant for the past 20 years.

It seemed self-evident to Morrison that while the destruction of vital road and railway bridges, factories and power stations and other public amenities would hinder the Japanese, the scorched-earth policy was bound to alienate the local population, who could see their very livelihoods being methodically ripped apart by their former masters. This was the low point of British rule in Malaya. If it were to have any chance of recovery, Percival would have to hold Johore.

Forty miles south of Kuala Lumpur, Olga and Maisie Prout were in their convent in Birch Road, Seremban, when the Japanese arrived in the middle of the night. The girls had heard on Radio Malaya that Allied troops were preparing to engage the enemy on the outskirts of Kuala Lumpur, but it was another of those little official lies circulated to put some gloss on an embarrassing defeat. That night the convent was shaken by bombs; the nuns moved the 200 boarders from the upstairs dormitories to downstairs classrooms. From the windows, the girls saw soldiers on push-bikes pedalling past on their way south. As a precaution, they were told to go to bed in their day clothes so they would not be caught in their pyjamas if the Japanese came during the night.

At 2 a.m., a squad of Japanese soldiers climbed over the front fence and in small bands searched the convent. They had heard that English women were hiding there and also that the convent was home to 'girls no one wants' – the orphans. 'They call them the suicide squad because they come first and they're allowed to do whatever they like for three days,' Olga says. 'We were lying on the floor of the classrooms when they came in and we were told to be careful and not look at them because if they saw any white faces they might shoot us. They walked up and down shining a torch on all the girls and we pretended to be asleep.'

Maisie remembers, 'We had one Indian man looking after us and they put a gun to his head and said, "Japan YES?" And he had to say, "Yes! Yes!" Then they asked him whether we had any Englishwomen and he said, "No, none." So they left the school and went across to the orphanage, looking for children they could take as comfort girls, but the nuns barred their way and said, "Cannot take – holy place." The nuns then all knelt around in a prayer circle with their rosary beads. There were crucifixes around the place and the Japanese might have been a bit superstitious. They brought out their little cooking stoves and had breakfast for a couple of hours. We were still on the floor and the nuns were still praying when they suddenly all got up and left.'

In the morning the Mother Superior, the Reverend Mother St Pauline, went with Brother Joseph, principal of St Paul's, the boys' school, to see the new Japanese Governor who had taken up residence across the *padang* in the King George V School. The Governor spoke only Japanese but his aide-de-camp had excellent English. 'St Pauline didn't know anything about Japanese culture, but she hit on the right reason to stop them – she said it would be very *shameful* if it was known that the Japanese had defiled a holy place,' Olga says. 'The Governor agreed and gave the Reverend Mother a banner to hang on the main gate of the convent. It said that nobody below the rank of officer could come in without permission and if they did they would be beheaded.'

Fifty miles further south at Gemas, General Bennett gave his orders for the planned ambush. Brigadier Maxwell's 27th Brigade would block the trunk road, while men from the 2/30th Battalion would wait in ambush several miles further north. One company would cover a bridge across the Gemencheh River, 10 miles north of Gemas, where the bulk of the battalion would be hiding. Bennett had chosen the position in talks with Lieutenant-Colonel 'Black Jack' Galleghan, commanding officer of the 2/30th.

The weakness of the plan was that the forward company was too far away from the main body of the battalion and could be cut off if the Japanese practised their usual enveloping tactics. Both Percival and Major-General Barstow of the 9th Indian Division had commented on this flaw when they inspected the position. John Wyett thought it was 'an absolutely crazy plan' for the same reason, and told Jim Thyer so.[32] But Bennett was adamant that after the bridge had been blown, the fast-flowing river would prevent the Japanese from threatening his troops. Barstow's division was placed behind the 27th Brigade, while Brigadier Lay's 8th Brigade and Brigadier Painter's 22nd Brigade covered other roads in the area. Barstow was senior officer on the Segamat front; it was noted that he fostered an excellent spirit of co-operation between British, Australian and Indian troops.

As there was only a ferry crossing over the broad river at Muar, all motor transport of the retreating 11th Division had to pass through Segamat; the defending troops stood in silence as the pathetic convoy crawled slowly past them. The right flank of Westforce was supported by four field-artillery regiments (less one battery), and one anti-tank battery. Bennett allotted the left flank on the coast to Brigadier Duncan's 45th Indian Brigade, supported by 200 gunners of the 65th Battery of the Australian 2/15th Field Regiment. Duncan's task was to cover the coast road south of the Muar River, to guard against possible seaborne incursions and to patrol inland as far as Lenga, a distance of 25 miles.[33]

'At this time General Bennett was obsessed with the invincibility of his own troops while he had a correspondingly low opinion of the fighting value of the Indian troops,' General Percival says. 'Wherever possible, there-fore, he used his own troops to support and protect the flanks of the Indian troops.' The only reason that Bennett had disposed the 45th Indian Brigade on his left flank, knowing that they had just arrived and were still green, was that he had discounted the possibility of the enemy's posing a serious threat in that area. He was convinced that the Japanese would advance down the trunk road to Gemas, a strategic point in rubber country at the junction of the rail lines from Kota Bahru in the east and Kuala Lumpur in the west. He expected the three Japanese forces from the west coast, Kota Bahru and Kuantan to converge at this point. There would be no withdrawal, he told General Barstow, and he impressed upon Maxwell and Duncan the danger of creating fixed defensive positions, urging them to maintain mobile units for counterattack.

Churchill cabled Curtin from the US, 'I have great confidence that your troops will acquit themselves in the highest fashion in the impending battles. So far the Japanese have only had two white battalions and a few gunners against them, the rest being Indian soldiers. Everything is being done to reinforce Singapore and the hinterland. Two convoys bearing the 45th Indian Brigade Group and its transports have got through, and a very critical convoy containing the leading brigade of the British 18th Division is timed to arrive on 13 January. I am naturally anxious about these 4,500 men going through the Straits of Sunda in a single ship. I hope, however, that they will arrive in time to take their stand with their Australian brothers.'[34]

After visiting Bennett at Segamat, Wavell was optimistic. He cabled the Chiefs of Staff that 'Gordon-Bennett [*sic*] and Australians are in good heart and will handle enemy roughly, I am sure'. It seemed that Bennett's judgement was sound when a message was flashed from the 2/30th Battalion to Bennett's headquarters at 8 p.m. on 12 January informing him that Japanese patrols had been sighted west of Gemas. The enemy was about to fall into the trap. Gordon Bennett consulted the zodiac. After a lifetime of controversy, his hour of destiny had finally arrived.[35]

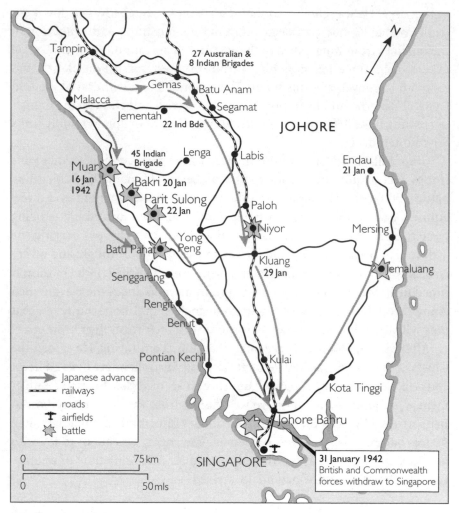

The Battle of Johore, January 1942

CHAPTER 15

Battle of Johore

RICHARD ANTHONY PLOWDEN FERRIER, known as Tony, was a soldier to the hilt. His father had fought in the trenches in World War I, and his grandfather on his mother's side was Major-General George Ward Chichele Plowden, a leading figure in the Indian Army who had fought in the siege of Delhi during the Indian mutiny of 1857 and had later taken part in the relief of Lucknow. 'The Plowdens were a great Indian family since Clive's day – Indian Civil Service, Indian Army, Indian politics,' Tony Ferrier says. 'The family seat is Plowden Hall in Shropshire, where they have lived since the 12th century.'[1]

Another distinguished relative was General Sir Trevor Chichele Plowden, whose beautiful daughter Pamela had attracted the eye of Winston Churchill when he was stationed in Hyderabad with the British Army. They were informally engaged, but Pamela's father refused to give his consent and she went on to marry Victor, Earl of Lytton, the son of the Viceroy of India. She and Churchill remained firm friends, however. On 19 July 1942 he sent her a letter of condolence after her second son had been killed in action. 'My heart bleeds for you,' he wrote; 'both your gallant and splendid sons have given their lives [but] heroes have not given their lives without a purpose being fulfilled.'

Tony Ferrier was born in Norfolk on 13 January 1920; after prep school at Lowestoft and five years at Radley he went to the Royal Military College, Sandhurst, from where he graduated in 1939. Second Lieutenant Ferrier joined the Royal Norfolk Regiment and was sent to the regiment's 1st Battalion in India. He was in Bangalore until May 1940, when nine British battalions in India were embarked for England with the intention of their being sent to France to join the British Expeditionary Force, 'but Dunkirk happened while we were on our way and we returned to England in June 1940'.

Captain Ferrier was posted to one of the regiment's Territorial battalions – the 5th Norfolks – and on 29 October 1941 he sailed from the Clyde with the 53rd Brigade Group of the 18th Division in the liner *Duchess of Atholl*, bound for the Middle East via Canada, the Caribbean and South Africa. At Halifax, Nova Scotia, the brigade's three battalions – the 5th and 6th Norfolks and the 2nd Battalion of the Cambridgeshire Regiment – were transferred from the *Duchess* to the American transport *Mount Vernon*, which reached Cape Town under American naval escort in mid-December. There, the troops heard about the outbreak of the Pacific War and the loss of *Prince of Wales* and the *Repulse*. Instead of sailing up the African coast to the Suez Canal and the Middle East battlefields, *Mount Vernon* headed east for Singapore.

'I don't think we were best pleased,' Ferrier says. 'After all, when you've trained to fight one particular type of warfare against Europeans, the idea of suddenly being slung into a jungle battle against the Japanese whom one knew really nothing about definitely had an effect on morale. We wondered what it was all about and what the future held for us.' The immediate future was fairly grim because the British soldiers in the *Mount Vernon* were informed that 'very large formations of Japanese bombers were looking for us but fortunately the weather was extremely bad – it was raining and misty, and they never found us'.[2]

The *Mount Vernon* reached Singapore on 13 January – Ferrier's 22nd birthday – in the middle of an air raid, but rain and mist providentially obscured the ship. Commanded by Brigadier C. L. B. 'Bulger' Duke, the 53rd Brigade trooped ashore at the Naval Base in a downpour early that afternoon. General Percival welcomed the first units of the 18th Division in person; the Norfolks were then driven to Woodlands Camp, a comfortable, hutted establishment near the Causeway. The Cambridgeshires were less fortunate: their camp was a makeshift arrangement on Bukit Timah racecourse, which consisted largely of mud and pools of water. The men were told in a lecture by a member of Malaya Command that the enemy employed tanks and artillery to blast through fixed defences, or moved men behind those defences in outflanking movements. They either infiltrated through the jungle in a left hook, or carried them by sea to the right for a landing on the coast. According to Tony Ferrier, the Japanese were presented as 'a lot of gangsters and we didn't have much to worry about if we took 'em on at their own game. Although we hadn't been in action at that time, we were told we were as good as they were, provided we carried out our tactics and remained mobile.'

Meanwhile, Gordon Bennett's Westforce was about to encounter the enemy in north-west Johore for the first time. The site chosen for the 2/30th

Battalion's ambush at Gemas was a stretch of road running through thick bush to a bridge 30 feet long spanning the Gemencheh River, normally little more than a creek but now a rushing torrent. Lots were drawn among the battalion's four companies to decide which one would carry out the ambush. Captain John Duffy of B Company won the honour. Duffy led his men into position, covering 700 yards of road immediately east of the Gemencheh River and three miles in front of the main battalion position. Platoons were concealed in thick jungle bordering the road at 60-yard intervals, with 10 Platoon astride the road behind 12 Platoon in the forward position, and 11 Platoon at the rear. This stretch of road had a cutting 40 yards long and 15 feet high, which provided 12 Platoon with an excellent elevated vantage point from which to see the advancing Japanese. The leading platoon was 170 yards clear of the bridge, which had been mined by the 2/12th Field Company.

Communication between Duffy's headquarters and Black Jack Galleghan's battalion headquarters was via a telephone line running for four miles along the side of the road. At a given signal, the 2/15th Field Regiment would open up with an artillery barrage, which would smash the Japanese forces congregating at the broken bridge.

Colonel J. W. Wright, the gunners' commanding officer, wrote in his diary, 'The crux was that only one system of communication was allowed by Lt-Col Galleghan: that was by line telephony. He vetoed having a dispatch rider at a listening post some short distance away who could have brought back the news. The Infantry CO would allow no vehicle movement in the area. Also wireless was definitely out because detectors might give them away. But what was there to hide once the bridge had been blown?'[3] Galleghan saw the Gemas ambush as purely an infantry operation and regarded the presence of the gunners as a nuisance. He had been curt with Lieutenant Bill Peck of the 4th Anti-Tank Regiment when he reported for duty with two anti-tank guns.

'Let's get this straight, Peck,' Galleghan said. 'You've been ordered to report with two guns under the command of the 2/30th Battalion.'

Peck replied, 'No, sir, I'm sorry, but my orders were *in support of* and *not under the command of.*'

There was no time to waste in argument, so Galleghan permitted Peck to site his two guns on the trunk road some distance from the ambush site. He placed one gun in front of the other, facing a cutting 200 yards away. There was a bend in the cutting, and Japanese tanks heading south would have committed themselves to rounding it before they saw the anti-tank guns.

Bennett was gung-ho about the ambush's potential results, describing it as 'an ambitious plot, requiring good judgement on the part of the leaders and grim fighting quality on the part of the men. I feel we have both.'

It was still raining when the final column of the III Indian Corps rear-guard – 40 vehicles in all – crossed the Gemencheh Bridge at 10 a.m. on 14 January. Galleghan signalled the code word 'Switch', which meant that the withdrawal of III Corps was complete and control of the battle area had been transferred from General Heath to General Bennett.[4] At 4.02 p.m. the first Japanese appeared on the bridge. The attackers had hoped to see large numbers of tanks and motor transport but, instead, hundreds of Japanese soldiers *cycled* into view. The cyclists, the advance guard of the Mukaide Detachment, started to cross the bridge five abreast in columns 100 to 150 strong. Captain Duffy allowed many to go past the ambush area while he waited for the tanks and motor transport to arrive.

At this crucial point Duffy discovered that his telephone line had been severed by some of the Japanese he had allowed to pass. He was unable to contact either the artillery or his battalion headquarters to alert them that the Japanese had arrived at the bridge and that some were cycling towards them. With several hundred more cyclists approaching the bridge, Duffy decided to act. There were about 50 Japanese on the bridge when the deto-nation order was given. One of the ambush party later wrote, 'With a roar like the crack of doom, the bridge and the Japanese on it soared skywards on a dense column of smoke and fragments. This was the signal for hellfire to break out. From each side of the road for a length of half a mile, the Aussies poured into the congested, panic-stricken ranks of the Japanese cyclists a devastating fire with machine guns, sub-machine guns and rifles; while our men leisurely removed pins from Mills grenades and rolled them over the lip of the defile to further rend the enemy ranks with their ear-splitting bursts. The order was given to retire. The job was done.'[5]

No body count was carried out, but the Australians estimated the number of dead, dying or wounded at around 800. This was the moment that the artillery bombardment should have inflicted heavy punishment on the Japanese congregated beyond the bridge – but the guns remained silent. 'In artillery terms,' Colonel Wright wrote in his diary, 'we ought to have been in a splendid position to carry out our role. We were able to get local survey data of each mile post on the road, thus shooting should be accurate.' Duffy ordered his men to withdraw from the scene of the ambush and rejoin the battalion. However, sections of the company were cut off by groups of Japanese who, having passed through the ambush at the head of the column, had turned around when they heard the explosion. Many of B Company were effectively behind enemy lines and had to fight their way out in hand-to-hand combat.

Despite Bennett's predictions, the Japanese repaired the bridge within six hours, and truckloads of reinforcements were soon pouring towards the 2/30th's main position at Gemas. Galleghan finally gave permission to the gunners of the 2/15th Field Regiment to open fire on enemy targets. One troop of 25-pounders was placed well forward of the main position and fired into the Japanese over open sights, inflicting serious casualties.[6]

At 10 a.m. on 15 January the first Japanese armoured vehicles rumbled into view around the bend at the spot where Bill Peck had placed his two anti-tank guns. The gun commanders were Lance-Sergeant Kenneth Harrison and Lance-Sergeant Charlie Parsons. They and their crews had been trained on French artillery weapons of World War I vintage; this was the first time they had actually fired a British two-pounder anti-tank gun.

The first vehicle to approach the gunners was an armoured carrier, which was struck by the Australians' first shell – a high-explosive round which set it on fire. Harrison says, 'Japs began pouring out but as they were running in all directions our second shell crashed home and the carrier rose in the air and toppled on its side.'[7] By this time, a large tank had pulled up behind the blazing carrier and started firing at the gunners. This tank presented a difficult target as only the turret was exposed, so Harrison asked Gunner Jock Taylor, the gun loader, to change to armour-piercing shells and instructed Gunner Joe Bull to fire right through the burned-out carrier. After six or seven shots had crashed through the hull of the derelict, the Australian gunners saw the tank suddenly burst into flames and had a momentary glimpse of the turret flying open.

Two other tanks then ranged up on either side of the derelict and opened fire. As the duel between the tanks and the gunners continued, several members of the Australian gun crews were killed or wounded. The Australians had only four shells left when Harrison 'slammed another shell into the breech, tapped Joe [Bull] on the shoulder and then stood peering hopefully at the inferno up the road. There was a *whoomp* and a flash from the cutting and something screamed by like an express train. This was followed by a deafening roar as Joe fired back at where a red flash had momentarily appeared amid the drifting pall of smoke.' The accuracy of Joe Bull's shot convinced the Japanese tank commanders that the risk of continuing the contest was too high; they retreated, leaving the Australians in possession of the field.

The gunners' heads were ringing from the reverberations of the gunfire – but suddenly their ears caught another sound. Over to the gunners' right where they had watched the contest in awestruck silence, a group of Australian infantrymen were waving their rifles in the air and cheering the gunners' bravery and marksmanship.[8]

Attack and counterattack went on throughout the day, in the course of which a total of eight or nine tanks were destroyed. Around midday, John Duffy's ambush company reached the battalion's lines in exhausted groups. In two days of fighting, the Australians had lost one officer and 16 other ranks killed, nine other ranks missing and 55 wounded. Gordon Bennett claimed that the battle 'accounted for over a thousand enemy dead', a wild exaggeration.[9] Galleghan was awarded the DSO, while Duffy received the Military Cross.[10] Percival wrote, 'This ambush was actually laid on my instructions. I always felt that it was the way to fight the Japanese – but you have to have fresh troops to do it, and that we seldom had.'

The history of the 2/30th Battalion disputes Percival's version, saying, 'Undoubtedly the first to appreciate [the ambush] possibilities in the jungle some few miles west of Gemas was Maj.-Gen. Gordon Bennett.' Galleghan had spoken to him at Segamat on the morning of the 10th about a company ambush forward of the main battalion position and he had enthusiastically concurred. The final dispositions were decided on 12 January at a meeting attended by Bennett, Galleghan and Brigadier Maxwell, commander of the 27th Brigade. Maxwell, however, said that it was he who had found the ambush position at Gemas and suggested where Galleghan put his companies. He had done so because Bennett 'studiously avoided such detail'.

Despite everything, Gemas had still been the most successful operation of the campaign, and with a little more expertise on the part of the commanders it would have been extremely damaging to the enemy. But it had failed to halt the Japanese. The Battle of Muar, on which the outcome of the Battle of Johore would depend, was about to begin. Bill Barstow visited Bennett on the evening of 15 January and strongly urged him to prepare lines of retreat, but Bennett was adamant. 'I told him there would be no retreat,' he says.[11]

Meanwhile, Churchill was back in Washington after visiting Florida. All his strategic planning was based on the belief that even if the British lost the mainland of Malaya, Singapore would be able to mount a resistance of at least two months against a full-scale Japanese attack.[12] Just as Churchill was preparing to return to England, Wavell placed doubts in his mind, with a cable from ABDA headquarters in Java: 'Battle for Singapore will be close-run thing and we shall need luck in getting in convoys safely and up to time.' Seeking clarification, Churchill asked Wavell on 14 January, 'What are the defences and obstructions on the landward side? Are you sure you can dominate with Fortress cannon any attempt to plant siege batteries?'[13]

Churchill regarded the situation as so serious that instead of returning to England in the *Duke of York* he undertook a hazardous 20-hour transatlantic flight in a Boeing flying boat, so as to reach London as soon as possible. After 'a merry dinner', the Prime Minister took the controls briefly as the huge, two-storey, 30-ton machine ploughed through the night. By the time it arrived at Plymouth on 17 January, the situation in Malaya had changed dramatically.

With four brigades at his disposal, General Bennett was so convinced that the Japanese would attack down the trunk road from Gemas to Segamat and Labis and thence to Yong Peng that he had placed three of them – the 27th Australian Brigade, the 8th Indian Brigade and the 22nd Indian Brigade – in the Segamat area, with the 45th Indian Brigade on the west coast at Muar. Brigadier Duncan had been instructed to deploy his battalions in the following order: the 7/6th Rajputana Rifles on a front of nine miles to the left of Muar, and the 4/9th Jats along a 15-mile river frontage to the right of the town. There were no bridges across the Muar and it was unfordable, yet Bennett ordered that each battalion must place two companies north of the river to ambush the Japanese. He did not seem to realise that without an exit route they would prove easy prey for enemy patrols. The third battalion, the 5/18th Royal Garhwal Rifles, went into reserve at the crossroads near Bakri, a village eight miles east of Muar.

Percival noted that Bennett's dispositions were eerily similar to Murray-Lyon's at Jitra but refrained from comment. Bennett was so sure he had read Japanese intentions correctly that he had supplied the 45th Brigade with only one artillery battery – the 65th Battery of the 2/15th Australian Field Regiment – instead of the usual three. Under the direction of Major W. W. Julius, the gunners set up their 25-pounders behind the Indians' trenches and facing the river. They were alarmed to discover that the young soldiers had no idea how to handle their rifles and were receiving last-minute tuition from their British officers.[14]

The Battle of Muar began on the morning of 15 January when the 4th Guards Regiment virtually annihilated the Indians in both forward companies of the Rajputana Rifles on the north side of the river. Field telephone lines across the 500-yard-wide stream had been cut; the first Brigadier Duncan knew of the attack was when enemy troops appeared unopposed on the waterfront opposite the town. They were engaged from the southern shore by the 65th Battery and forced to withdraw, but later that day boats were spotted off the mouth of the river and Japanese infantry started landing on the coast between Muar and Batu Pahat 30 miles to the south.

At 2 a.m. on 16 January the 5th Guards Regiment crossed the Muar a few miles upstream and set up a roadblock east of the town. Sharp fighting took place in this area all through the morning. At 1 p.m. a collection of landing craft appeared off Muar, some of which were sunk by artillery fire. By nightfall, all troops of the 45th Brigade south of the river had been driven from the town and were concentrated at the crossroads in the Bakri area. The enemy were crossing the Muar in force – and if they could cut the trunk road at Yong Peng, 50 miles away, the whole of Westforce would be stranded around Segamat. Brigadier Duncan signalled Bennett's headquarters that he was marshalling his forces for a counterattack to recapture the town.

'This withdrawal of the 45th Indian Brigade is most serious,' Bennett noted in his diary. 'By allowing the enemy to across the Muar River, the side door is thrown open for a wide flanking movement to Yong Peng. Westforce has the bulk of its force 56 miles ahead of Yong Peng and there is nothing between Yong Peng and Singapore Island.'[15] He added, without any hint of self-censure for having placed the Indians in mortal danger, 'It is now quite evident that the 45th Indian Brigade is insufficiently trained for the present difficult task.'

Percival considered the battle so important that he travelled up from Singapore each day, after attending the morning session of the War Council, to direct it with Bennett. Captain Bill Drower accompanied him as aide-de-camp on one of these long round trips and attested that the sheer physical strain day after day would have been enough to exhaust any man. 'Things were going badly and getting worse,' he says. Percival's biographer Brigadier John Smyth says that the full extent of Percival's fortitude 'can begin to be understood when one remembers the anxiety which he was undergoing all the time about the outcome of the operations and the constant necessity to look cheerful and confident at every conference and on every visit'.[16]

According to Ray Broadbent, Percival used to 'suggest' things to Bennett; he did not give him orders. Bennett always opposed ideas and the result was chaotic. Percival was far too diffident and there was no real co-operation between the two senior commanders. At the same time, Heath and Bennett were antagonistic towards each other, Black Jack Galleghan told the Official Historians, yet both believed in quickly concentrating their forces in Johore rather than prolonging resistance in northern Malaya. Had they pulled together they might have persuaded Percival to act more quickly. Galleghan added that Bennett did not go forward during the campaign. He worked on a four-inches-to-the-mile map – too small to indicate important geographic features – while his Chief of Staff Jim Thyer was too compliant: Bennett needed someone who would stand up to him occasionally.[17]

Percival placed the 53rd Brigade under General Heath and ordered it to move 60 miles north of Singapore to Ayer Hitam on the road to Yong Peng to protect Westforce's lines of communication. 'We were loath to order an immediate withdrawal from Segamat, which we thought would be damaging to morale, and decided to strengthen the Yong Peng–Muar front by every means at our disposal,' he says.

Bennett reacted slowly to the threat to his left flank. Early on the 17th he sent the 2/29th Battalion, less one company, from the Segamat front to Bakri. He instructed Lieutenant-Colonel J. C. Robertson, the battalion commander, to counterattack towards Muar, taking a troop of the 4th Anti-Tank Regiment with him. Robertson was informed by divisional headquarters that a small party of Japanese had crossed the Muar River and were attacking the 45th Indian Brigade. Still refusing to believe that Muar had been strongly attacked, Bennett estimated the enemy force at about 200 strong.

Considering the enormity of the risk in the Muar salient, Bennett's response fell far short of requirements. Kenneth Harrison, of the 4th Anti-Tank Regiment, was informed that a small Japanese force 'was making a nuisance of themselves by sniping at traffic. Still, I remember wondering a little when I noticed that a ten-mile strip along the Muar coast was shown on the map as Japanese-controlled. It seemed an awful lot of territory for 200 men.'[18]

The Australian task force reached the outskirts of Muar that evening, just as units of the 45th Indian Brigade were pulling out of the town. The 2/29th rushed forward to plug the gap, taking two anti-tank guns with them, but retreating vehicles blocked the narrow road. Indian drivers were racing their engines in low gear, blowing their horns and shouting at each other, so impeding progress towards the front line. 'Our big three-ton truck towing the gun was caught right in the middle of it all,' Harrison says. 'We eventually got there but not before we had knocked down a police-station notice board and rammed an armoured car.'[19]

During the night the Imperial Guards landed at least 5,000 men in addition to 12 tanks and a number of guns at Muar. The Australians were forced back into a rubber plantation outside the town. Like 'Black Jack' Galleghan at Gemas, Colonel Robertson did not believe his battalion needed anti-tank guns. He told the commander of the anti-tank troop, Lieutenant Bill McCure, 'I have orders from the General that I should be accompanied by a troop of anti-tank guns, but as far as I am concerned, you're not wanted. I don't want you to interfere with us in any way. I don't expect the Japanese to use tanks, so for my part you can go home.'[20]

Fortunately for the men of the 2/29th, McCure ignored the senior officer. After conducting his own reconnaissance, he deployed one gun forward on a bend in the road from Muar to Bakri, with a second gun covering it from a cutting 400 yards further back. 'The colonel had made it quite clear to me that he didn't want our guns anywhere near his troops,' Bill McCure says. 'I defied that order. [But] I didn't expect any tanks and I knew the colonel, who would have been better informed than I, didn't expect any either.'

The Australians formed a hollow square at the Bakri crossroads, where heavy fighting broke out during the night. The Guards succeeded in penetrating the square, and 'each side of the perimeter turned inwards and fired furiously at the intruders, while in the centre of the holocaust men fought bitter hand-to-hand battles in the blackness'.[21] In the dark, some Australians were shot by their own men. The enemy were repulsed, however, and at first light on 18 January the Japanese commander sent in his armour.

As the first tank rounded the bend on the road from Muar, it was side-on to the foremost anti-tank gun. Lance-Sergeant Clarrie Thornton gave the order to fire. 'We hit it and moved quickly on to the second tank,' he says. 'We got direct hits on both tanks, but we were firing armour-piercing shells and they seemed to go straight through them.' He called for high-explosive rounds, and McCure and his batman Titch Morley brought them forward from the ammunition truck. McCure says, 'Each time I dumped a container at their gun, I gave Clarrie a slap on the shoulder and urged him on. He was doing a great job and his crew seemed to be crazily enjoying the action, completely ignoring the danger of the battle raging on around them. There was no time to be afraid.'

Thornton was shot in the hip but continued to fire directly at each tank in turn until he had scored hits on all nine tanks in the convoy, destroying six with high-explosive shells. The first two tanks had rolled on towards the second gun in the cutting, where Sergeant Charlie Parsons destroyed them with high-explosive shells. Members of the Madras Sappers climbed on to three of the smouldering hulks, opened their hatches and dropped explosive charges inside to kill any surviving crew.

Percival reported this action in curiously dispassionate terms in his

Dispatch: 'Early on the morning of 18 January the 45th Indian Infantry Brigade, with the 2/29th Australian Battalion attached, was strongly attacked by the enemy in its perimeter position west of Bakri. Nine enemy tanks were destroyed by the Australian anti-tank guns and tank-hunting platoons.'

Percival had no doubts about the threat to Westforce from the west, and he ordered Bennett to send the 2/19th Australian Battalion from Jemaluang to assist the 2/29th Battalion at Muar, while the 5th Norfolks – the 53th Brigade's reserve battalion – were ordered to join the remaining two Australian battalions on the east coast. Tony Ferrier led an advance party to reconnoitre the Australian position at Jemaluang. 'The very great majority of our soldiers had been recruited from Norfolk and they had never been out of England before,' he says. 'I, at least, had the advantage of having served in India for a year, but the terrain was all very new to us. We drove through miles and miles of tarmac road with rubber plantations on each side.

'When we got to Mersing it was rather more open country, with quite long fields of fire over broken ground and a certain amount of cover. We recced the positions and met our opposite numbers in the AIF, and then our battalion arrived 24 hours later and took over from the 2/19th. Their defensive position had been extremely well prepared.'

Captain Bob Hamond, commanding officer of the Norfolks' A Company, was travelling in a car which broke down in a *kampong* 15 miles short of Jemaluang. While his vehicle was being fixed, Hamond sent his men ahead and then noticed a lot of pigeons flying around the village, 'so I got out my 12-bore and shot a couple'. The shots not only killed the pigeons but stampeded half a dozen Australian troops who were resting in one of the village houses. Thinking the enemy had arrived, they rushed out with tommy-guns and rifles at the ready. 'They stared at me for a moment and then burst out laughing at the "green Pommy officer" who was indulging in field sports in the front line,' Hamond says.[22]

The rest of the 53rd Brigade had reached Ayer Hitam at midday on 17 January. General Key dispatched the 6th Norfolks to hold Bukit Pelandok, a vulnerable defile on Muar Force's exit route from Bakri via the town of Parit Sulong. The enemy had succeeded in cutting the road between the 2/29th Battalion at Bakri and brigade headquarters in a planter's bungalow one mile to the east. While the 2/29th was fighting for its life on the morning of 18 January, the 2/19th Battalion crossed the bridge over the Simpang Kiri at Parit Sulong. Lieutenant-Colonel 'Andy' Anderson, who had taken over from Duncan Maxwell as commander of the 2/19th Battalion, met the guide from the 45th Brigade – Major Tingghi Maxwell of the FMSVF, a Malay planter and Duncan's brother.

According to the 2/19th's history, Maxwell reported that the situation was uncertain. Two of the Indian battalions, the Rajputs and the Garhwalis, were too badly damaged to fight; all of the senior officers and most of their junior officers and NCOs had been killed. The fate of the third battalion, the Jats, was unknown: they had been out of touch for 36 hours but were believed to be still intact. Meanwhile, the 2/29th was still in action, having taken up a defensive position one and a half miles west of Bakri, after beating off enemy attacks and destroying 11 tanks.[23]

Anderson went forward with his reconnaissance party to meet Brigadier Duncan. At 9.30 a.m. he arrived at brigade headquarters, where Duncan confirmed the details of his brigade's perilous position. All contact with the 4/9th Jats had been lost, but they were thought to be about eight miles north of Bakri village and had not been in action. The 65th Battery had deployed one troop at Bakri and the other at brigade headquarters; both were engaged in harassing fire. Colonel Robertson arrived during this conference and reported that his men were well dug in 1,200 yards west of Bakri. It was decided that the 2/19th should move from Parit Sulong and link up with the 2/29th at Bakri, thus providing a safe perimeter for the Indian troops whom, Brigadier Duncan explained, had been recruited only three months earlier and were largely immature young men aged 17–18.

Colonel Robertson was returning to his battalion, riding pillion with his dispatch rider, when he was hit by enemy fire. He was knocked off the bike and fell heavily on to the road. He was rescued by a Bren-gun carrier which brought him back to the battalion lines. Bill McCure happened to be standing nearby when Robertson went past on a stretcher. He told the gunner that his persistence in defying orders had prevented the wholesale slaughter of his battalion. 'I'm so sorry,' he said. A few minutes later he was dead.

On the afternoon of the 18th, British Intelligence reported that the Japanese force on the west coast consisted of two divisions, with the Imperial Guards in the Muar area and the 5th Division on the main road. The full extent of the threat to Westforce's left flank suddenly became apparent to Gordon Bennett. Despite his assertion to Barstow that there would be no withdrawal, he knew that unless he pulled Westforce out of Segamat, his main force would be destroyed.

That evening Bennett stormed into a meeting of his commanders at their advance headquarters 'talking wildly about the lack of fighting spirit, the incompetence of senior British commanders and their withdrawal complex. After about 20 minutes of this tirade he suddenly stopped, glared around at the puzzled faces and abruptly left the room, departing as quickly as he had come. No withdrawal plans had been discussed.'[24] The whole thing had been a performance by Bennett to make it appear that the withdrawal had been forced upon him, rather than being at his own instigation.

Percival says in his Dispatch that the request for an immediate withdrawal behind the Segamat River had emanated from Bennett on the evening of 18 January 'as a preparatory step to a further withdrawal should such become necessary'. In the same conversation, Bennett agreed to Percival's proposal that the whole of the Muar front should be placed temporarily under General Heath. 'My reasons for this were that I thought it difficult for the Commander Westforce with his small staff to give the close attention to the Muar front which the dangerous situation there demanded, as well as controlling the operations on the Segamat front some 70 miles distant,' Percival says. 'It would obviously be necessary to build up a supporting front west of Yong Peng in order to keep open communications both with the Muar and Segamat forces. This could only be done by troops at that time under command of III Indian Corps.'

Bennett admits in his book, 'I rang up General Percival who realised the position and who readily approved of a withdrawal to a more secure position behind the Segamat River. I rushed forward to contact General Barstow and Brigadier Maxwell to arrange details. Both were out, so I dealt with their staffs.' In fact, Bennett's only contribution was his aforementioned tirade. The withdrawal plans were drawn up by members of his staff in collaboration with General Barstow's G1, Brigadier J. B. Coates.

Westforce's withdrawal was effected on the evening of 19 January, over the one narrow bridge across the Segamat River. The bridge spanned a deep gorge and had the Japanese bombed it Westforce would have been trapped. There were delays in getting through the town because all the shops along the main street were on fire. Brigadier Eric W. Goodman, CRA of the 9th Indian Division, was at the bridge with General Barstow. He noted, 'Some bright fellow (an Australian I believe) had set fire to some houses in the town which lit up the bridge and would have made it a good target for an aeroplane if any had come over, which fortunately they didn't.'[25] The fire had been started by one of Bennett's favourite officers, Major Charles Moses, to destroy a large stock of bagged rice in some warehouses, but the blaze had spread and destroyed shops and houses. The rice was barely scorched.

General Heath, meanwhile, had spent the morning of the 18th with Brigadier Harold Taylor of the 22nd Australian Brigade at Mersing creating a new formation to be called 'Eastforce'. It would consist of Taylor's two remaining battalions – 2/18th and 2/20th – as well as the 5th Norfolks and all other troops in the Mersing area. From 6 a.m. the following day, its task would be to protect the Jemaluang–Kota Tinggi road in southern Johore from Japanese forces coming down the east coast. Lieutenant-Colonel E. C. Prattley, commander of the 5th Norfolks, sent out a patrol under Forbes Wallace, a Malay-speaking scout, to see whether Japanese troops had infiltrated as far south as Mersing. While they were away, however, the situation around Muar had deteriorated so seriously that Prattley was ordered to take the 5th Norfolks west to Batu Pahat to join III Indian Corps.

Tony Ferrier remembers, 'On the way to Batu Pahat we stopped for the night and sent out patrols to locate the Japanese, and two of our men were killed. The next day we ran into the enemy when they set up a roadblock of fallen trees and we had to get out of our lorries and go into the bush. One slight disadvantage was that our soldiers found it difficult to distinguish between Chinese, Japanese and Malays and, to make it more difficult, the Japanese put on Malay clothes. We were also completely unacclimatised and not fighting fit after three months at sea. It was a very frustrating action because we were being fired upon and sustaining casualties but we couldn't see the enemy.

'There were snipers tied to the tops of trees in rubber plantations and there was not much light. They seemed to be using very high-velocity bullets which made much more of a crack than our own weapons. We did have the odd success – a couple of the Japanese snipers were shot when we realised fire was coming from the treetops and we sprayed them with machine-gun bullets. It was quite extraordinary: they looked more like some kind of an animal they were so covered in camouflage and bunting, with their faces darkened.

'Then we heard that another battalion in our brigade, the 6th Norfolks, had been ambushed [in the Bukit Pelandok defile] and had sustained quite a number of casualties. Brother officers we knew had been killed or wounded. We proceeded towards Batu Pahat, and when we stopped for the second night the Japanese attacked us again. Two or three officers were killed, including one in my company.'

On the morning of 19 January heavy fighting developed in the Bakri area when an enemy force attacked the 45th Brigade's carriers on a timbered ridge 500 yards from the Australian troops at the crossroads. Brigadier

Duncan withdrew the carriers and ordered Colonel Anderson to send the 2/19th's A Company to drive the Japanese off the ridge. Anderson instructed one platoon to make a frontal attack, while a second platoon worked its way along the ridge to hit the enemy's right flank. Meanwhile, B Company set off to encircle the Japanese and attack them from the rear.

The élite Guards had not expected a three-pronged assault from aggressive, jungle-trained Australians and, according to Lieutenant P. R. Reynolds of B Company, they 'literally ran round in circles'. Unlike at Gemas, the Australians had time to count the enemy dead – a total of 140, including several who fought on after being wounded. The Guards did not forgive the Australians for the loss of their comrades, and a terrible price would later be exacted for every death. In the action, the Australians lost ten killed and 14 wounded. Reynolds was hit by shrapnel when one of the prostrate Japanese pulled the pin on a grenade before he could shoot him dead.

Around midday, the battle turned in favour of the Japanese when the right forward battalion of the 45th Brigade, the 4/9th Jats, was ambushed while rejoining the main force and suffered heavily. Then a dive-bomber soared over the crest of a hill and, following a line of staff cars that led up to the bungalow where brigade headquarters was holding a meeting, dropped a torpedo through its roof. Nearly everyone in the room was killed; Brigadier Duncan was badly concussed. Among the mortally wounded was Major Julius of the 65th Battery.[26]

At the request of the brigade major, Colonel Anderson took temporary control of Muar Force, which now consisted of the two Australian battalions plus attached gunners and the remnants of the 45th Indian Brigade. Anderson was 44 years old and had fought with the King's African Rifles in East Africa in World War I. After leading game-hunting safaris in Africa, he had married an Australian girl and emigrated to Australia in 1934. He was ruggedly well built and had maintained his fitness by working on his own grazing property in New South Wales. He wore spectacles, which gave him a misleading academic air. In battle, he was unflappable and totally fearless. He carried two hand grenades in his binoculars case, explaining that in the Malayan terrain they were more useful than field glasses.[27]

Tony Ferrier says, 'I had met Charles Anderson at Jemaluang and was very impressed with him. We could hear a tremendous battle going on to the north of us and learned that it was the Battle of Muar. The thing that really shook us all was to see lorry-loads of Indian troops completely flaked out. One imagined they had been fighting for several days or weeks with very little sleep. When they reached their stopping places, we could seem them being lifted out of these vehicles. They were absolutely all in. They had obviously had a tremendously hard time.'

With Japanese troops pouring in from all sides and food and water in short supply, Bakri had become a death-trap. Anderson decided to take Muar Force along a road snaking through rubber plantations and over a flooded causeway to Parit Sulong. If they could cross the bridge a mile past the town, the road would take them to Yong Peng. During their months of hard training, Anderson had drummed into his junior officers and men the absolute necessity of gaining the upper hand when meeting the enemy unexpectedly at close quarters – especially in hand-to-hand combat with the bayonet. 'There's a lot of talk that the fanatical fighting of the Japanese makes them unbeatable,' he said, 'but they can be pushed around and made to move in the wrong direction like any other troops. Handle them roughly.'

Anderson reorganised the 45th Brigade into one Australian battalion of five companies, and merged the remnants of the three original Indian battalions into one. Muar Force set off at dawn on the 20th, with three Australian companies at the head of the column and one at the rear, with the Indians in between. One Australian company was in reserve. As the column moved slowly down the road, with a convoy of 50 trucks and other vehicles carrying the wounded and the Marmon-Herrington gun tractors hauling the few remaining 25-pounders, Japanese planes roamed up and down, machine-gunning at will. They could have wiped out Muar Force with bombs, but they wanted to preserve the vehicles for their own use.

At 8 a.m. the column encountered the first in a series of roadblocks, guarded by a machine gun, which opened fire. Rather than taking evasive action through the swamp and jungle on either side of the road, Anderson confronted the Japanese head-on. With the bespectacled commander leading the charge himself, the Australian companies attacked the enemy with mortars, rifles, bayonets and axes, killing a number of them and putting the rest to flight – but at a cost to themselves of 15 dead and 20 wounded. The roadblock was made from rubber trees, which they shattered with axes.

Having been brainwashed about 'bandy little four-eyed Japs', the Australians were astonished at the fine physiques of the Japanese dead – 'not a pair of spectacles among the lot'.[28] Noting the wreath-and-star insignia, one Australian said, 'Imperial Guards.'

In the two hours it took to dispose of the roadblock, the Japanese from Bakri caught up with the column's rearguard. They seized several trucks and attacked one of the Indian companies. Brigadier Duncan was killed while bravely leading a counterattack to retrieve the vehicles.

Contact with the enemy was then broken and the column resumed its tortuous progress, but it ran into three more roadblocks, which could be cleared only by a concerted attack using every available heavy weapon. The first roadblock consisted of three trucks sited round a slight bend. A 25-pounder was pushed, muzzle first, around the bend and three rounds were fired at 75 yards' range: the trucks were actually blown off the road. The column was not clear of the final roadblock until late afternoon, and would have to keep going through the night to negotiate the flooded causeway into Parit Sulong. A line of Australian infantrymen standing knee-deep in water silently guided the column along the causeway in the dark, using the red glow of cigarettes cupped in their hands as markers.[29]

Once Westforce had been withdrawn from Segamat, Percival placed Gordon Bennett in command of all troops in the Muar area, which now included the 11th Indian Division. Bennett ordered General Key to clear the Bakri–Parit Sulong road to allow safe passage to Muar Force, but owing to an operational blunder the 53rd Brigade's commander, Brigadier Duke, did not receive his orders. Then Duke complained that his men were not fit enough to undertake the task on their own, so the 2nd Loyals were sent to strengthen them – but they became lost in a swamp after a causeway was prematurely blown and returned to their original position. The final straw was Duke's insistence that his artillery should test the range of their guns before his men set off. The attack was cancelled; Anderson was left to fight on alone.

It was not until midnight on 20 January that the head of his beleaguered column reached the rubber estates two miles short of Parit Sulong. At 6 a.m. two dispatch riders were sent to the arched bridge on the far side of town to check its occupancy; they returned to report that it was in enemy hands. Throughout the 21st, four bayonet charges failed to force a passage over the bridge, while the long, unprotected column, stretching back through the township, provided easy pickings for Japanese planes and artillery. That night Anderson formed a perimeter in one of the rubber estates bordering the main road. The Japanese from Bakri had caught up with the column again and attacked in force with mortars and bayonets, but they failed to break the line. Enemy tanks were called in, and a shot from the leading tank's cannon set fire to the ammunition limber of one of the gun carriages, which blazed fiercely at the edge of the plantation. The tank then clanked into the firelight, closely followed by a second. A lone gunner, Jack Menzies, manned the 65th Battery's one remaining 25-pounder and fired a shell over open sights from a range of no more than 50 yards. The first tank disintegrated; Menzies then reloaded and knocked out the second tank. The rest of the enemy's armour turned tail and disappeared into the night.[30]

Anderson had intermittent contact with Westforce through a field radio – with failing batteries – and he sent a message on the night of 21 January urgently requesting food, ammunition and morphia to be dropped into the town. As all of Muar Force's cipher books had been destroyed, the message had to be sent *en clair*, so the Japanese would have been alerted to the request. To disguise the fact that the drop was to be made at dawn, Jim Thyer replied to Anderson, 'Look up at Sparrowfart.'

The Official History of the RAAF says two obsolete Albacores from Singapore flew under cover of darkness and, guided by a flare, dropped food and morphia. 'That was the most that the air force could do for those gallant troops. Though pathetically little for their needs, it was typical of Anderson and his men that they were deeply grateful: the supplies, they reported, had been dropped very accurately. But no effective air attack in support of his column could be mounted.'[31] Gunner Russell Braddon tells a different story. He saw one plane – 'the oldest biplane in the world still capable of becoming airborne' – drop food and medical supplies among the Japanese on the bridge, while the pilot deposited a bomb inside the Muar Force perimeter, killing several Australians.[32]

The depleted 45th Brigade had now held up the Imperial Guards Division for a week and saved Westforce from encirclement. However, at 9 a.m. on the 22nd, following one final failed attack, Anderson decided that his position was hopeless and reluctantly gave the order for all vehicles and heavy weapons to be destroyed. All those who could walk would slip past the Japanese and make their way through the jungle to Yong Peng, while the wounded would be left behind in the care of volunteers. After a hazardous overland trek, Anderson and 100 of his men were the last of 550 Australians and 400 Indians to reach safety. Only four of the valiant anti-tank gunners survived. Percival says, 'I regret to have to record that the wounded who were left behind were, almost without exception, massacred by the Japanese.'

There were two survivors among the 135 prisoners, both Australians: 18-year-old AIF private Jimmy Wharton and Lieutenant Ben Hackney. Jimmy had been tied up with the other casualties, machine-gunned and bayoneted, but although he and a mate were seriously wounded they were still alive. Jimmy whispered urgently, 'Don't move, don't move,' but the boy writhed in agony and groaned. The Japanese noticed him, pushed Jimmy off him into a deep storm-water drain and riddled his friend with machine-gun bullets.

Jimmy Wharton spent hours hidden among the reeds in the water, from where he saw the prisoners machine-gunned, bayoneted, drenched with petrol and set alight. He heard the screams, pleas and curses of those still alive when they smelled the petrol and realised what their fate was going to be. He also witnessed trucks being driven back and forth over the bodies to destroy evidence of the massacre. Then he heard the Japanese 'singing and exhilarated' as they marched out of Parit Sulong. For almost a week Jimmy wandered through the jungle with a wound that went right through his chest but miraculously had not penetrated the lungs. Then he was captured by a Japanese patrol and taken to Pudu Jail in Kuala Lumpur, where he was looked after by other prisoners.

Ben Hackney's left leg had been shattered by a mortar shell during the fighting. He had been bayoneted *eight times* by the Japanese at Parit Sulong, but he had successfully feigned death and remained mute even when one of the Japanese soldiers had roughly dragged his boots off his feet. In fact, Hackney stayed conscious throughout his agonising ordeal and observed the arrival of a short, stocky Japanese commander whom the Japanese soldiers treated 'almost as a god'. Covered in bayonet wounds to his legs and body and with his broken left leg bent at a hideous angle, Hackney was also found by a Japanese patrol and taken to Pudu. He swore to himself that he would find a way of punishing the men responsible for the massacre.

Thanks to the two Australian battalions and their gunners, between 16 and 22 January the Japanese had lost a company of tanks and the equivalent of one battalion of the Imperial Guards. General Yamashita was now running behind his self-imposed schedule. He was livid. He complained to his diary that Nishimura, commander of the Imperial Guards Division, and Matsui, commander of the 5th Division, had refused to obey orders and had delayed the advance. There had been hostility between Yamashita and Nishimura from the moment the divisional commander had arrived in Malaya from Bangkok. Yamashita regarded him as arrogant and aloof, and distrusted both him and his Chief of Staff, the even more big-headed Major-General Imaye, a former lecturer at Tokyo War College.

Brigadier Goodman, who had been at Segamat, wrote in his diary, 'The Australians, who had promised much through their commander Gordon Bennett, delivered little and in fact compared very unfavourably with other troops, British and Indian. In fairness to them I do not think that GB represented their opinion and he was not popular with many of them. He appeared to be a politician and soldier, not a good combination, especially if the soldier side is weak.'

While there was ample justification for Goodman's criticism of Bennett, the idea that the 2/19th and 2/29th Battalions had 'delivered little' was a travesty of the truth, but at the time of writing Goodman was in ignorance of these actions. The performance of the Australians in rescuing survivors of the 45th Brigade from the Muar death-trap and delaying an entire Japanese division for a week was exemplary. No one begrudged Colonel Andy Anderson his Victoria Cross. 'Charles Anderson was an outstanding man with a ton of guts,' says Russell Savage.

After the Battle of Muar, the 45th Indian Infantry Brigade had ceased to exist. Those killed included the brigade commander, Brigadier Duncan, every battalion commander and second-in-command and two of the three adjutants. Percival said that Duncan 'had set a magnificent example of courage and fortitude and can in no way be held responsible for the disaster which overtook his untrained brigade'. He added, 'This brigade had never been fit for employment in a theatre of war. It was not that there was anything wrong with the raw material but simply that it was raw. It was the price of our unpreparedness for war and over-rapid expansion.' Percival later criticised Gordon Bennett for placing the 45th in a suicidal position. If he had placed them south of the river, 'instead of wasting four companies north of it, he would have had quite a good chance of stopping the enemy crossings'.[33]

Wavell thought the heavy fighting on the Muar front showed 'what determined resistance your troops are making against odds. You have not much ground behind you and this resistance is necessary and well timed. I have no doubt that troops have inflicted severe casualties on the enemy. Well done.' But the Battle of Johore had not been a cause for congratulation. It had ended not in victory but in bitter defeat. The Naval Base was now useless and Singapore was threatened as never before.

Having discovered from a liaison officer that Percival had no scheme for a withdrawal to the island or for its defence, Wavell had cabled him on 19 January, 'You must think out problem of how to withdraw from mainland should withdrawal become necessary and how to prolong resistance on island ... Will it be any use holding troops on southern beaches if attack is coming from north? Let me have your plans as soon as possible. Your preparations must of course be kept *entirely secret*. Battle is to be fought out in Johore till reinforcements arrive and troops must not be allowed to look over [their] shoulders. Under cover of selecting positions for garrison of island to prevent infiltration of small parties you can work out scheme for large force and undertake some preparation such as obstacles or clearances but make it clear to everyone that battle is to be fought out in Johore without thought of retreat.'[34]

The same day Wavell drew Churchill's attention to the weakness of the defences of Singapore Island against attack from the north and expressed his doubt whether it could hold out for long if Johore were lost. 'Until quite recently all plans were based on repulsing seaborne attacks on [Singapore] island and holding land attack in Johore or farther north, and little or nothing was done to construct defences on north side of island to prevent crossing of Johore Straits, though arrangements had been made to blow up the Causeway,' Wavell said. 'The fortress cannon of heaviest nature have all-round traverse, but their flat trajectory makes them unsuitable for counter-battery work. Could certainly not guarantee to dominate enemy siege batteries with them.'

Churchill's worst fears were suddenly realised. He addressed a furious minute to the Chiefs of Staff Committee: 'I must confess to being staggered by Wavell's telegram. It never occurred to me for a moment that the gorge of the fortress of Singapore, with its splendid moat half a mile to a mile wide, was not entirely fortified against an attack from the northward. What is the use of having an island for a fortress if it is not to be made into a citadel? To construct a line of detached works, with searchlights and cross-fire combined with immense wiring and obstruction of the swamp areas, and to provide the proper ammunition to enable the fortress guns to dominate enemy batteries planted in Johore, was an elementary peace-time provision which it is incredible did not exist in a fortress which has been 20 years building. If this was so, how much more should the necessary field works have been constructed during the two and a half years of the present war? How is it that not one of you pointed this out to me at any time when these matters have been under discussion? More especially should this have been done because in my various minutes extending over the last two years I have repeatedly shown that I relied upon this defence of Singapore Island against a formal siege, and have never relied upon the Kra Isthmus plan.'

Churchill added that having no fixed defences or forts to protect the island's rear was not to be excused on any grounds. Such 'neglect' meant that the Singapore fortress had been placed 'at the mercy of 10,000 men breaking across the Straits in small boats'. He concluded, 'I warn you this will be one of the greatest scandals that could possibly be exposed.' Yet, he insisted, there was still time to redress the island's deficiencies. In a personal message to Wavell on the night of 19 January, Churchill said, 'I want to make it absolutely clear I expect every inch of ground to be defended, every scrap of material or defences to be blown to pieces to prevent capture by the enemy and no question of surrender to be entertained until after protracted fighting among the ruins of Singapore City.'[35]

Churchill also replied to Curtin's criticisms about the lack of reinforcements for the Far East. 'I have not been responsible for the neglect of our defences and the policy of appeasement which preceded the outbreak of war,' he said. 'I had been for 11 years out of office and had given ceaseless warnings for six years before the war began. On the other hand I accept the fullest responsibility for the main priorities and general distribution of our resources since I became Prime Minister in May 1940. The eastward flow of reinforcements and aircraft from this island has been maintained from that date forward to the utmost limit of our shipping capacity and our means of moving aircraft and tanks. I deem the Middle East a more urgent theatre than the now-christened ABDA area. We had also to keep our promises to Russia of munitions deliveries ... We must not be dismayed or get into recrimination but remain united in true comradeship. Do not doubt my loyalty to Australia and New Zealand. I cannot offer any guarantees for the future and I am sure that great ordeals lie before us, but I feel hopeful as never before that we shall emerge safely and also gloriously from the dark valley.'[36]

Wavell, meanwhile, replied to Churchill that he held out little hope of a prolonged defence. Churchill read this cable when he woke up on 21 January. He had just learned that large numbers of Japanese had crossed the Thai border and launched a full-scale attack on Burma. 'Officer whom I had sent to Singapore for plans of defence of island has now returned,' Wavell said. 'Schemes are now being prepared for defence of northern part of island. Number of troops required to hold island effectively probably are as great as or greater than number required to defend Johore. I have ordered Percival to fight out the battle in Johore, but to work out plans to prolong resistance on island as long as possible should he lose Johore battle. I must warn you however that I doubt whether island can be held for long once Johore is lost. The fortress guns are sited for use against ships, and have mostly ammunition for that purpose only; many can only fire seawards.[37] Part of garrison has already been sent into Johore, and many troops remaining are doubtful value. I am sorry to give you depressing picture, but I do not want you to have false picture of the island fortress. Singapore defences were constructed entirely to meet seaward attack. I still hope Johore may be held till next convoy arrives.'[38]

Churchill rattled off a long memorandum in time for the Chiefs of Staff Committee meeting at 11.30 a.m. that day: 'In view of this very bad telegram from General Wavell, we must reconsider the whole position at a Defence Committee meeting tonight. We have already committed exactly the error which I feared ... Forces which might have made a solid front in Johore, or at any rate along the Singapore waterfront, have been broken up piecemeal. No defensive line has been constructed on the landward side. No defence has been made by the Navy to the enemy's turning movements on the west coast of the peninsula. General Wavell has expressed the opinion that it will take more troops to defend Singapore Island than to win the battle in Johore.

'The battle in Johore is almost certainly lost. His message gives little hope for prolonged defence. It is evident that such defence would be only at the cost of all the reinforcements now on the way. If General Wavell is doubtful whether more than a few weeks' delay can be obtained, the question arises whether we should not at once blow the docks and batteries and workshops to pieces and concentrate everything on the defence of Burma and keeping open the Burma Road.

'(2) It appears to me that this question should be squarely faced now and put bluntly to General Wavell. What is the value of Singapore [to the enemy] above the many harbours in the South-west Pacific if all naval and military demolitions are thoroughly carried out? On the other hand, the loss of Burma would be very grievous. It would cut us off from the Chinese, whose troops have been the most successful of those yet engaged against the Japanese. We may, by muddling things and hesitating to take an ugly decision, lose both Singapore and the Burma Road. Obviously the decision depends upon how long the defence of Singapore Island can be maintained. If it is only for a few weeks, it is certainly not worth losing all our reinforcements and aircraft.

'(3) Moreover, one must consider that the fall of Singapore, accompanied as it will be by the fall of Corregidor, will be a tremendous shock to India, which only the arrival of powerful forces and successful action on the Burma front can sustain. Pray let all this be considered this morning.'

The Chiefs of Staff prevaricated. The Defence Committee was undecided. Churchill did not press his view. The only thing that seemed incontestable to all parties was that the responsibility somehow rested with the man on the spot, General Wavell. Sir Earle Page was not privy to the deliberations of the

Chiefs of Staff, nor was he a member of the Defence Committee, but he was inadvertently shown a copy of Churchill's explosive memorandum. Page immediately telegraphed the contents to Canberra. That was not all: Bowden reported from Singapore on 23 January that Percival had formed a special staff under Keith Simmons 'to make final preparations for defence of Singapore Island'. Keith Simmons, Bowden said, had revealed to him 'that all fixed defences Singapore Island are directed seawards. None are directed towards mainland.' After the War Council meeting that day, Bowden had asked Rear Admiral Spooner at what stage he would demolish the Naval Base. Spooner answered that he would have to begin as soon as the Japanese reached the Straits of Johore. Bowden had replied, 'My deduction from that is that Singapore will not be held, for with the Naval Base and all natural resources of Malaya gone, Singapore will have nothing more than sentimental value.' Spooner had concurred, but Percival, who was within earshot, 'said nothing'. Bowden continued that 'only the Governor naturally maintained that Singapore would be held and said he would cable the Imperial Government for their confirmation of this intention. From remarks of the General Officer Commanding Malaya at the War Council it appears likely that Singapore Island will be in a state of siege within a week.'[39]

The following day Churchill received an angry cable in Curtin's name, expressing Australia's horror at Churchill's memorandum. 'Page has reported that the Defence Committee has been considering the evacuation of Malaya and Singapore,' it said. 'After all the assurances we have been given the evacuation of Singapore would be regarded here and elsewhere as an inexcusable betrayal. We understood that it was to be made impregnable, and in any event it was capable of holding out for a prolonged period until the arrival of the main fleet. Even in an emergency, diversion of reinforcements should be to the Dutch East Indies and not Burma. Anything else would be deeply resented, and might force the Dutch East Indies to make a separate peace. On the faith of the proposed flow of reinforcements, we have acted and carried out our part of the bargain. We expect you not to frustrate the whole purpose by evacuation.'[40]

In fact, it was not Curtin who had sent the cable. The Prime Minister was suffering from exhaustion and had left Melbourne on 21 January for a holiday in Western Australia. During his absence, the Deputy Prime Minister, Frank Forde, had presided over the War Cabinet meeting at Victoria Barracks. The telegram had been dispatched under Curtin's name, but the inflammatory phrase 'inexcusable betrayal' had nothing to do with him; it been inserted by Dr Bert Evatt, his fiery Minister for External Affairs.

Following his exertions in North America, Churchill was in a gloomy frame of mind. He was not only exhausted but also depressed and suffering from a bad cold. Talk of 'inexcusable betrayal' wounded him deeply. He complained bitterly to Anthony Eden about the Australian Government's intransigent attitude. But the clamour from Down Under added weight to his fear of a propaganda backlash in the US over what would be perceived as a British scuttle from Singapore, and he reluctantly decided that Britain must be seen to be making a fight of it. In the end, he did nothing to stop the bulk of the 18th Division and 51 crated Hurricane fighters from reaching Singapore. Meanwhile, Wavell flew into the island on 20 January to check on Percival's preparations for the siege. The Chief discovered that despite his instructions the GOC had taken little action to defend the vulnerable north shore from a Japanese attack. Barring a miracle, Singapore was as good as lost.

CHAPTER 16

Over the Causeway

UNLIKE THE VAST majority of his comrades in the 5th Norfolks, Captain Harry Schulman was at home in the jungle. After graduating in forestry from Cambridge, he had worked on a tea-growing estate in north-east Assam, where he joined the Indian Army's Territorials. The army trained him in weapons and riot control, and also gave him two horses for playing polo and for patrolling the outer line of the frontier with a detachment of Gurkhas. 'There was tea on one side of the line and drugs on the other,' he says. 'Assam was very jungly in those days and I used to go into the jungle to shoot on my leave. I would hire an elephant and take two Gurkhas and go up into the foothills of the Himalayas and live off the country. We shot tigers and leopards if they upset our plantations, but I used to fish rather than shoot – I didn't like shooting things.'

After five years in India, he returned to England at the end of 1936 and took up farming in the quieter pastures of Abbey Farm at North Creake, Norfolk. 'The war was imminent in 1938 and there were three of us on the farm,' he says. 'We pointed to one man who was the least warlike of the three of us and said he could stay and look after the farm while we joined up. I joined the 5th Norfolks.'

At the outbreak of war Harry Schulman transferred to No. 1 Commando, which trained in a requisitioned football ground at Southampton. 'I was a founding member of the commandos,' he says. 'We went back to France after Dunkirk to the St-Valéry area to see if we could find anyone of the 51st Division. We didn't succeed. Churchill then sent a commando expedition to capture an airfield in Guernsey but it was a terrible failure. I came back to Cornwall, where I heard that the Norfolk Regiment was going abroad, so I wrote to the commanding officer that the commandos weren't looking after my life as I liked and I would like to come back. It was out of the fat into the fire.'

Captain Schulman was second-in-command of A Company when the Norfolks took their place on the battlefield, but found himself commanding

B Company as an acting major after Captain S.C.H. Boardman was shot dead by a sniper while trying to outflank a Japanese roadblock on the way to Batu Pahat. The rubber-growing port, a favourite resting place for travellers, had become the key point in the defence of Johore following the fall of Muar. It was situated on the south bank of a river crossed by a ferry and provided access to three roads, one to Yong Peng, one to Ayer Hitam and one to the village of Senggarang on the coast further south.

General Percival was determined to hold the Imperial Guards and the Japanese 5th Division north of the line Batu Pahat–Kluang–Mersing. He risked losing the whole of Johore if the Japanese broke through his defensive arc; it would be his last throw of the dice on the Malay peninsula. General Nishimura, the Guards commander, having routed the British forces between Muar and Bakri, saw an opportunity to isolate Batu Pahat and wipe out the garrison. He ordered the Guards Reconnaissance Battalion to attack the town from the north-east, while the 4th Guards Regiment moved overland to join the 1/4th Guards Battalion, which had been landed by sea near Senggarang.

As the enemy tightened its stranglehold on Batu Pahat, Brigadier Challen, commander of the 15th Indian Brigade, had been instructed by Generals Heath and Key during a visit to his headquarters on 21 January to hold the town at all costs. Heath saw Batu Pahat as another Tobruk, a major stumbling block to the Japanese advance down the trunk road to Singapore. He issued orders for the town to be stocked with 10 days' supplies and for the 5th Norfolks to join the garrison of the British Battalion, the 2nd Cambridgeshires, a company of the 2nd Malay Battalion and one battery of the 155th Field Regiment.

Working round to the south-east of the town on 22 January, the 5th Guards Regiment cut the Ayer Hitam road and succeeded in ambushing the Cambridgeshires' B Echelon which was bringing in fresh supplies. A number of vehicles were destroyed in the action; the quartermaster was wounded but managed to escape with two of his trucks. It took a joint operation by the 5th Norfolks from Ayer Hitam and the British Battalion from Batu Pahat to clear the roadblock.

Over on the coastal road, the Japanese attacked the artillery positions five miles south of Batu Pahat, killing the commander and seizing its 25-pounders. Units from the British Battalion and the 2nd Cambridgeshires mounted a counterattack and rescued all of the guns except one. On the 23rd, the Ayer Hitam road was again blocked and the 5th Norfolks started to make a long detour to reach the beleaguered town along the coastal road via Benut, Rengit and Senggarang. As the enemy had also seized the Yong Peng road after crossing the river some miles outside the defence perimeter, this was the only road that remained open.

Brigadier Challen's greatest fear was that Batu Pahat would become a death-trap like Bakri and he was eager to evacuate the garrison before it became completely surrounded. When he lost radio contact with Westforce headquarters, he decided to withdraw his troops down the coastal road to Senggarang to meet up with the Norfolks, who were approaching from that direction. Soon after nightfall on the 23rd, the troops broke off action and slipped out of the town. They formed up on the coastal road and began to march south, with their last surviving armoured cars in the lead. Once radio communications were restored, Challen reported his action to General Key, who expressed concern that such a withdrawal would give the enemy access to Westforce's left flank through Batu Pahat. He instructed Challen to re-occupy the town.

The new orders were greeted with little enthusiasm by the troops, who felt their previous positions would now be in enemy hands. Fortunately, the Japanese had had no time to do anything more than conceal themselves in some of the houses when Challen's men re-entered Batu Pahat later that night. At 7 a.m. on the 24th, the 5th Norfolks reached the outskirts to find street fighting in progress, with a Cambridgeshire company actively involved in the centre of town. The Norfolks were ordered to take two enemy-occupied hills overlooking the exits to the Ayer Hitam and coastal roads, but owing to an oversight no ammunition lorries had been included in the Norfolks' convoy and their artillery could offer very little support to the attacking troops. By nightfall, the Norfolks were still short of their objectives.[1]

'One of the companies of the Cambridgeshire Regiment had been sent to capture the town and got very badly mauled,' Harry Schulman says. 'They were withdrawing after one of their Bren-gun carriers received a direct hit from a mortar shell, killing and wounding not only the men in the carrier but many members of a platoon advancing alongside the carrier. But the Cambridgeshires had turned the Japanese out and I was sent into Batu Pahat with orders to hold it.'[2]

On the morning of the 25th, Nishimura made a sustained effort to retake the town from the north-east after sending in truckloads of reinforcements. Meanwhile, Challen had received a reconnaissance report from an officer of the 2nd Malay Battalion who had penetrated the Japanese line disguised as a coolie. He reported that an enemy battalion was hidden in a rubber plantation north of Senggarang and would shortly cut the coastal road. Challen again sought permission to withdraw before it was too late, but he was told that a decision could not be made until General Percival had discussed the matter at Westforce headquarters that afternoon.

Harry Schulman realised that the Japanese had only to come round the Norfolks' flanks and tackle them from the rear and they would be completely cut off. 'The Japanese didn't attack on a frontal basis,' he said. 'They infiltrated round and through the forward companies – they were the ones who did the most fighting.' Percival's conference began at 3.15 p.m. Learning of the dire threat to the 15th Brigade, he ordered it to withdraw down the coastal road and link up with the 53rd Brigade which would move north from Benut to Senggarang.

Batu Pahat Force pulled out during the night of 25–26 January under cover of a bombardment by the gunboat *Dragonfly*. 'We reached Senggarang at dawn to find that the Japanese had occupied the bridge and buildings at the southern end of the village and had already blocked the road south,' Schulman says. 'The Cambridgeshires cleared the buildings and the bridge and then tackled the roadblocks.' The road was built on an embankment, with thickly wooded swamps on either side. According to regimental historian David Langton, three attacks were launched from dawn on the 26th, with cooks, drivers, signallers and batmen joining forces with the infantry. The opening of the road was a matter of urgency, as the brigade was still carrying its accumulated casualties from the last four days' fighting, but every attack was repulsed by Japanese light and heavy automatic weapons. Up to their knees in mud and water, the men struggled to reach the roadblocks and suffered further heavy casualties from concealed weapons. While the battle was in progress, the guns in the village itself were constantly attacked by Japanese aircraft and threatened by infiltration parties closing in on the houses armed with machine guns and mortars. Behind the Post Office, members of the 168th Field Ambulance worked under continual fire.

General Key visited Brigadier Duke's 53rd Brigade at Benut and, hearing of Challen's predicament and remembering Duke's failure to assist Muar Force, he ordered Duke to send a relief column up to Senggarang. This force, consisting of artillery, armoured cars, carriers and a detachment of infantry, left Benut at 12.30 p.m. on the 26th. It was led by Major C. F. W. Banham in a carrier driven by a young Punjabi NCO. North of Rengit the column ran into a roadblock; every vehicle was destroyed except for Banham's carrier, which broke through the block and carried on towards

Senggarang. The Punjabi driver crashed through or avoided a succession of further roadblocks until he reached the last one. Challen's troops saw the carrier appear on top of the roadblock, balance precariously for a few moments and then topple to safety.[3]

Brigadier Challen was about to launch a full-scale attempt to break through to the south, but he abandoned this plan when Banham reported that there were no fewer than six roadblocks and ambushes on the road between Senggarang and Benut. Realising he had no chance of making it, Challen gave orders for all guns to be spiked and the transport destroyed, and for the men to break out through the jungle and link up with the nearest British forces at Rengit or Benut.

Harry Schulman says, 'I was in charge of the rearguard and my job was to blow the bridge, but Brigadier Challen came through my company and gave the order, "Every man for himself!" By the time I got to the bridge, it had been blown up and there must have been 80 to 90 of our vehicles on the wrong side of it. I was told to destroy them, which was impossible. We could still walk over the bridge, so I sent my company ahead. From Senggarang to Singapore was 70 miles as the crow flies, and the Japanese were closing in from both the north and the south. We had a choice of going through the jungle on the eastern side or going down to the sea along the river on the western side.'

Challen accompanied the group heading west. They halted at the river during the night of the 26th–27th and the Brigadier went in search of a crossing point. He was seized by a Japanese patrol but the others managed to escape, whereupon Lieutenant-Colonel C. E. Morrison of the British Battalion took command and led the men to the coast. 'I had visions of getting down to a sandy beach but instead we found ourselves in a village surrounded by mangrove swamps,' Schulman says. 'There were well over 1,000 men in that village. We had a wireless set that worked and we contacted our headquarters and Singapore sent up two Yangtse riverboats (*Dragonfly* and *Scorpion*) to take us off. I was evacuated by sea. We swam out through the mangrove swamps to board them. We didn't lose any men there but we lost everything else – I arrived back in Singapore with just my trousers on.'

One hundred badly wounded men in ambulances were abandoned to the Japanese in Senggarang. Captain J. A. Mark and Captain Robbie Welch, both of the Royal Army Medical Corps, and Padre Noel Duckworth of the 2nd Cambridgeshires volunteered to stay behind with them. Padre Duckworth had been cox of the Cambridge Eight in the early 1930s. When the

Japanese arrived in Senggarang, he was astonished to be addressed by an Imperial Guards officer with the words, 'You are Duckworth, aren't you?' The officer informed him, 'I met you at Henley.' Unlike their unfortunate comrades at Parit Sulong, none of the men was harmed; all were later taken to Kuala Lumpur and incarcerated in Pudu Jail.[4]

Captain Forbes Wallace, the Malay Police scout with the 5th Norfolks, had accompanied Schulman to Senggarang but was then placed in charge of the party of 1,000 troops who would strike inland through the jungle to Benut. He began his 25-mile trek to Benut with Colonel Prattley and 1,200 men on the evening of 26 January, keeping five miles north of the road in order to avoid the Japanese clustered around the roadblocks. As the 5th Guards Regiment was advancing across their line of retreat through jungle and rubber, it was miraculous that the Allied party did not bump into them. 'It was heavy going getting off the road and up the slippery paths alongside the river,' Wallace says. 'I had to keep encouraging everyone to press on without pause as I knew undue delay would be fatal for our chances of evading the enemy's net.'[5]

Wallace had served in Johore for ten months in 1934 but knew little of the topography north of Johore Bahru and had to rely on an army map of the area. After several hours' march with only short rests, the column was exhausted when it reached a stream 25 yards wide. Luckily, it was only four feet deep and non-swimmers were able to keep their toes on the bottom and struggle across.

Three hours later Wallace decided everybody should get some sleep, even for a couple of hours, as they would be walking all through the following day. At 11 p.m. they collapsed in the mud and slept where they fell. Starting off again at dawn, they reached an agricultural area of rice-fields and pineapple and coconut plantations. The local Malays were helpful and said they had seen no signs of the enemy. They climbed coconut trees and threw down coconuts for the troops, as well as drawing water from their wells.

Wallace discovered that the Benut River was far wider and deeper than he had expected. Leaving the main body behind, he found a canoe and crossed over with Major Charles Wood, one of the company commanders. Luck was on their side when they met Siow Ah Kiu, the Chinese police clerk from Port Dickson whose father lived in the village. He was delighted to see Wallace and immediately set about collecting dozens of small boats and canoes to ferry the troops across. Charles Wood remained behind to organise the ferry operations, while Wallace set off on a borrowed bicycle to reach Benut two miles away, hoping that units of the 53rd Brigade would still be there. He took a young Chinese on the carrier to act as guide. 'The number of times we fell off on the slippery and muddy paths is nobody's business,' he says. At Benut, he was greatly relieved to find Brigadier Duke and all his staff in the local village school. After hearing Wallace's report, Duke ordered him to return to the *kampong* and guide the column down to the main road as quickly as possible. There was not a moment to lose: Japanese patrols were within five to ten miles of the village.

Wallace cycled back to the column, where Wood informed him that Siow Ah Kiu had produced enough boats to get all the men across the river. He had also supplied hot coffee, laced with Chinese brandy, for the walking wounded. Shortly after midnight the remnants of Batu Pahat Force reached Benut. Lorries then ferried them 20 miles further south, where the 5th Norfolk's 2nd Echelon was waiting with hot stew and strong tea and rum.

Siow Ah Kiu would not take a penny in payment for his services. He also gave tremendous assistance to a later party of Argyll and Sutherland Highlanders who had been cut off further north. When the Japanese arrived in his village, one of his neighbours informed them about his pro-British activities and he was summarily beheaded.

At 7.45 a.m. on 26 January – Australia Day – a Hudson bomber flown by the redoubtable Oscar Diamond spotted a Japanese convoy 20 miles north-east of Endau. The convoy, consisting of four cruisers, one aircraft carrier, six destroyers, two transports and 13 smaller craft, was carrying the 96th Airfield Regiment and stores to supply the airfields at Kahang and Kluang once they were captured. Diamond's radio signals to Air Headquarters Singapore were jammed by the Japanese, and the Hudson was attacked by three enemy fighters. Diamond's two gunners fought them off and the plane made it back to Singapore, where he reported the convoy. By then, it was 9.20 a.m. – 90 vital minutes had been lost.

Air Vice-Marshal Pulford, at his wits' end, decided to attack the convoy with the Vildebeeste torpedo bombers of No. 36 and 100 Squadrons, despite the fact that the vintage biplanes travelled at only 100 mph and were at their most vulnerable in daylight, and that their crews were dog-tired after gruelling night-time operations in central Johore. Pulford, however, was determined to hit the Japanese as hard as he could. He estimated that the convoy would have reached shallow water by the time it could be attacked, so the Vildebeestes were rearmed with bombs instead of torpedoes.[6]

By early afternoon, Pulford had assembled a force of 12 Vildebeestes and nine Hudsons, escorted by 23 Buffaloes and Hurricanes. Looking more like exhibits at an air show than a front-line striking force, they headed north as dark skies closed around them. The Vildebeestes chugged up the Endau estuary through a bank of cloud and emerged over the target area at 3 p.m. The black hulks of the two Japanese transports – *Kanbera Maru* and the larger *Kansai Maru* – lay a couple of miles offshore. The Vildebeestes went straight into the attack, scoring direct hits on both ships and a nearby cruiser, while troops in barges and on the beaches were bombed and strafed.

However, the Japanese gunners opened fire on the slow-moving bombers at the same time as enemy fighters swooped down from on high. Flight Lieutenant Mowbray Garden, the Buffalo leader, says, 'Quite soon the air was full of broken and crashing Vildebeestes and parachutes, while what seemed to me to be an enormous force of Zeros was descending on us from the sun in one long line-astern formation.'[7]

Five of the Vildebeestes were shot down, but at 5.30 p.m. nine more Vildebeestes and three Albacores, escorted by 12 fighters, arrived over the target. The cloud had disappeared, making it easier for the air crews to see enemy ships – but also removing their protective cover from attacking fighters and anti-aircraft gunners. A further five Vildebeestes, two Albacores and a fighter were lost in this attack, which caused little damage to the convoy. The Vildebeeste and Albacore air crew who took part in the two raids totalled 72, of whom 27 were killed, seven wounded and two made prisoner.

Russell Savage saw the planes fly overhead into battle. 'The Air Force had rounded up every plane that could take to the air to try and repel the landing at Endau,' he remembers. 'There were Hudsons, Vildebeestes, Buffaloes. We thought, "Well, we're on the offensive again with this mighty Air Force." Our chaps flew the Vildebeestes over the treetops so slow and so low that the Zeros had trouble getting down to them. Then they would go up to take on the Zeros – they were either game or mad. After an hour, we saw about four planes limp home.'

On General Heath's orders, the 22nd Brigade had withdrawn 10 miles south from its strongly prepared positions in Mersing to the Jemaluang crossroads. Here, Brigadier Taylor approved a plan from Lieutenant-Colonel Arthur Varley of the 2/18th Battalion for an ambush on the night of the 26th in the rubber plantations on the Chinese-owned Nithsdale and Joo Lye estates. The Japanese bombed Mersing heavily during the day, but did not prevent the 2/20th and the 2/18th Battalions from assuming their ambush positions. They formed a large V astride the Mersing–Jemaluang Road into which the enemy was expected to advance, whereupon the 20th and 60th Batteries of the 2/10th Field Regiment would lay down a creeping barrage, separating the leading Japanese from the main force estimated at 1,000.

During the evening, groups of Japanese passed through the area firing random shots and letting off crackers in an attempt to draw fire, but the Australians maintained silence. The gunners had made a careful survey of the area and worked out the co-ordinates for just such an action. Lieutenant Bob Goodwin recalls, 'The Japanese made contact with the company holding the flank east of the road at 2.20 a.m. and heavy fighting broke out in that area. The enemy were pushed into compact groups, which made them better targets for our guns. We opened fire at 3.30 a.m. and did a great deal of damage.'

As the Japanese swarmed forward, Private Colin Spence of the 18th Battalion was slashed down the back by a Japanese officer with a sword after he had ducked behind a tree to avoid a grenade. Spence fired from his hip, as he had been trained to do, and as the Japanese went down he bayoneted him through the back of the neck.

Bob Goodwin says, 'We had prepared a creeping barrage which advanced 100 yards every two minutes and went right through the area and then started again. It had all been worked out on paper and the infantry knew exactly what we were doing with our guns. They came behind the barrage with machine guns, mortars and bayonets and killed a whole battalion of Japanese. We didn't cease firing until 8.30 a.m.'[8]

The Australians lost 98 officers and men killed or missing in the ambush. Vern Swenke had been mortally wounded in the stomach and had no chance of evacuation. He asked to be propped against a tree with extra clips for his Bren gun so he could cut down as many Japanese as possible while waiting to die. After the Nithsdale Estate ambush, the Japanese were forced to retire to Mersing, and later admitted that their advance had been delayed for three days.[9]

In Singapore, General Percival received a signal from Wavell on 27 January giving him discretion to withdraw to Singapore Island if he considered it advisable. On that day, the impact of the dispersal of the Batu Pahat Force and the opening to the enemy of the west-coast road became apparent to the GOC. He knew that the remaining troops on that road would not be strong enough to stop the enemy's advance for long, and no reserves were available. The bulk of the 18th British Division on which he had gambled so much had still not arrived. 'I felt that any further delay might result in the loss of the whole of our forces on the mainland,' he says.

'I therefore decided to authorise a withdrawal to Singapore Island, even though this meant failure to achieve our object of protecting the Naval Base.'

Megan Spooner wrote in her diary, 'Jack [Admiral Spooner] feels that Percival has lost his grip – if he ever had it! He is charming and easy but has no drive.'[10]

In the House of Commons, Winston Churchill prepared MPs and the British people for the worst with some unpalatable facts prior to a vote of confidence in his ministry. 'We have had a great deal of bad news lately from the Far East and I think it highly probable, for reasons which I shall presently explain, that we shall have a great deal more,' he said. 'Wrapped up in this bad news will be many tales of blunders and shortcomings, both in foresight and action. No one will pretend for a moment that disasters like these occur without there having been faults and shortcomings. I see all this rolling towards us like the waves in a storm ...'[11]

Churchill had barely sat down when disaster overtook the 9th Indian Division after a railway bridge over a stream near Layang Layang – a village between Kluang and Johore Bahru – was blown prematurely. As a result of faulty map references and muddled orders from Malaya Command, the 8th and 22nd Indian Brigades found themselves on either side of the bridge. Brigadier Lay, commanding the 8th Brigade, failed to occupy a vital ridge just south of the bridge, as he had been instructed, and enemy troops slipped through the gap during the night and occupied the village.

Shortly after dawn, the divisional commander, Major-General Bill Barstow, went forward to see his commanders. He was accompanied by Colonel W. A. Trott, an Australian on his divisional staff, and the AIF's Lancashire born liaison officer, Charles Moses.

When they reached 8th Brigade's headquarters, according to Trott, Brigadier Lay told Barstow, 'We blew that bridge accidentally last night.'

'Well,' Barstow snapped, 'what is the position?'

'There is a good deal of fire coming from the right flank.'

'Hell take you, man,' Barstow stormed. 'Get a battalion on to that high ground.'

Barstow, Trott and Moses then went up the railway line in a trolley car to see Brigadier Painter, commanding 22nd Brigade. At the 8th Brigade's forward position, Barstow was warned that the Japanese were up ahead, but he clambered over the broken bridge and walked along a high railway embankment towards the village.

'General Barstow walked very fast,' Trott says. 'He and Moses got nearly

100 yards ahead of me. Suddenly, I saw a fellow step out of the side of the cutting [and] hold up his hand. I shouted out. [The Japanese] opened fire with troops in ditches near the cutting. I was walking along the left of the embankment, slid down the side and moved up to see if I could get in touch with the other two. Automatic machine-gun fire opened up. I got under the embankment, could see nobody and brought a good deal of fire down. So I got through the *lalang* [coarse grass] into the jungle. I had hardly got into the jungle when I heard a noise and saw Moses. I inquired from Moses and he said the General went over the right-hand side of the embankment. We worked over to the other side of the embankment but fire came down again. We decided we would have to try and get back.'

Moses said he and the General were about 150 yards forward of the demolished bridge in front of the 8th Brigade's position when they were fired on by the Japanese. He saw Barstow easing himself down the right-hand side of the embankment. They were still under fire. Moses moved to the left-hand side, where he met up with Trott. Avoiding a Japanese patrol, they waded across the stream and made their way back to the 8th Brigade's lines.[12]

Hearing that the Japanese were on the attack, Brigadier Lay ignored the misfortune that had apparently befallen his commanding officer and decided to withdraw from the area. 'If you think Lay's reaction would have been to draw his sword and rush in, you're quite wrong,' Trott says. 'Lay was useless. He was washed up.' Bustling Bill Barstow's body was found by the Japanese at the foot of the embankment.[13]

Percival was unaware of the tragedy when he held a conference with Bennett and Heath in the Sultan of Johore's hunting lodge to discuss evacuation of the mainland. Wavell had stipulated the night of 31 January–1 February for the withdrawal but, according to Bennett, Percival said, 'All right, let us make it 30–31 January.' On the spur of the moment, he had altered the date.[14] After the conference, Bennett did not return immediately to divisional headquarters but took the opportunity to say goodbye to his friends the Sultan of Johore and his wife at the Sultan's palace. One week earlier Sir Ibrahim had sent the Sultana to Singapore to be evacuated with the rest of the European women, but he had missed her so much that he had pleaded with her to return.

Bennett spent the remainder of the 28th at the palace. He discussed the possibility of escape if the situation on the island deteriorated to the point where he might be in danger of being captured. The Sultan did not want his palace shelled or bombed once British troops had withdrawn to Singapore

Island and the Causeway had been demolished. Bennett promised to do everything in his power to ensure that the palace was not damaged. The Sultan, ordering his staff to close up the palace, then moved to one of his residences some distance inland. Bennett told reporters that Sir Ibrahim was 'extremely depressed and thoroughly fed up with the British and everyone else'.[15]

When Bennett returned to his headquarters, he learned that General Barstow was missing in action, believed killed. Several days earlier Barstow had come to him and asked for 'two good Australian commanders' to take command of his brigades because Brigadiers Painter and Lay had let him down 'on every possible occasion'. Bennett suggested Maxwell and Galleghan, but there had been no time to raise the matter with Percival before Barstow disappeared.[16]

Meanwhile, Brigadier Painter, in an effort to rejoin the 9th Division, had moved the 22nd Brigade off the railway line and taken to the jungle west of Layang Layang. With the 5/11th Sikhs in the vanguard driving off Japanese patrols, the column followed a track marked on Painter's map, but came to a dead end at the edge of a swamp. Throughout the daylight hours, a platoon of Garhwalis used their *kukris* to hack a way south on a compass bearing, while stretcher-bearers carried the brigade's wounded with great difficulty in single file through the gaps.

In pitch dark, the long, straggling column ground to a halt on the narrow path. Captain Denis Russell-Roberts, a British officer with the 5/11th Sikhs, says, 'Men dropped where they were in a huddled heap and propped themselves up in a sitting position, one against the other, their senses too numb even to feel the leeches and ants on their skin.'[17] There was no hope of supplies, and Painter had no alternative but to push forward in the morning. Many units became separated and hopelessly lost, the vast majority falling into Japanese hands. 'The final withdrawal [to the island] was postponed as long as possible in an effort to recover this brigade but without success,' Percival says, 'Arrangements were made to ferry them across the Straits from a point east of Johore Bahru.' Only about 100 were saved in this way, including Denis Russell-Roberts.

Aircraftsman Fred Ryall, a 25-year-old Londoner, had been based at Kluang airport when the Japanese swarmed into Johore. 'We beat a hasty retreat down to Singapore,' he says. 'Ships were arriving with troops and I found out later they were known to the Japanese as "Churchill *presento*" – gifts from Churchill.'[18]

On 22 January, the 44th Indian Infantry Brigade, commanded by

Brigadier G. C. Ballantine, had arrived with 7,000 raw and untrained re-inforcements. Two days later, 1,900 young Australians turned up in no better shape than the Indians. They were accompanied, however, by the West Australians of the 2/4th Australian Machine Gun Battalion, which would add much-needed punch to the Australian defences in the forth-coming siege.

On 29 January, the bulk of the 18th British Division, commanded by Major-General M. B. 'Becky' Beckwith-Smith and consisting mainly of the 54th and 55th Brigade Groups, trooped ashore from the American trans-ports *Wakefield* and *West Point* and three British ships, *Duchess of Bedford*, *Empress of Japan* and *Empire Star*. The same convoy included a light tank squadron from India – the only tanks to reach Malaya during the campaign. They had been collected from training establishments and were not only obsolescent but dilapidated and had to be taken into workshops for repair.

Apart from the 22nd Indian Brigade, which was cut off and out of contact, the withdrawal of the remaining British forces from the mainland began after dark on 30 January. Bennett says he discovered that three forces were due to converge on the Causeway by different roads but no timetable had been prepared. He pictured them all arriving at the same time and the Japanese creating havoc. On his protesting to General Heath, he says, the two of them sat down together and worked out a timetable. In fact, Bennett drove to Singapore that evening, leaving the reorganisation in the hands of his hard-pressed staff. The Japanese, however, were taken by surprise by the speed of the withdrawal. There was no sign of their air force, even though it was a moonlit night and enemy fighters would have created mayhem among the long, slow-moving columns of retreating troops.

Having seen too many bridges blown up prematurely with troops and transport cut off, John Wyett had become uneasy about the planned demo-lition of the Causeway and went to investigate. Passing the main demolition site a little to the north of the centre, he walked as far as the bascule bridge at the Johore end. This bridge, which could be raised to allow boats to pass through, had been mined by a sapper detachment from Fortress Command. Wyett was amazed to learn from the sergeant in charge that the bridge was due to be blown at midnight. It was then already well after 11 p.m. and Wyett calculated that the head of the Australian column was still two hours or more away. 'I explained this situation to the sergeant and told him it could be five or six hours yet before the last troops were across, so he would have to hold the demolition until then,' Wyett says.

The sergeant rejected this information and announced that the bridge would be blown at midnight regardless. Wyett tried to reason with him, pointing out that army regulations stated explicitly that the man on the spot was allowed the discretion to change an order if the situation warranted it.

'Orders are orders,' the man replied, 'and I am going to carry them out.'

'All right, I'll give you an order if that's what you want,' Wyett snapped. 'You will not attempt to carry out this demolition until I say so.'

The sergeant replied that he was not taking orders from any so-and-so Australian.

Wyett then drew his revolver and said, 'If you will not take orders from me, perhaps you will from this.' The sergeant stared dumbfounded at the revolver and then at Wyett. 'If you make any attempt to blow that bridge before I say so,' the Australian told him, 'I am going to blow your bloody head off.'

The sergeant could see that Wyett meant business and, after considering his position for a moment, shrugged and slouched off. Wyett went across the short bridge to the Johore side of the Causeway and there, on a flat grassy patch, were the Argylls, all 250 of them, the proud remnants of a whole battalion that had been in action almost continually since the Japanese first invaded Malaya. Wyett explained his confrontation on the Causeway to Ian Stewart. 'Good show,' Stewart said. 'Keep me informed, won't you; we are going to be the last across.'

After the last of the Australian troops had filed on to the Causeway at dawn, Wyett rejoined Stewart and the Argylls. He hoped that the abandoned 22nd Indian Brigade would appear, but there was no sign of them; they were never seen again. Then the Argylls fell in and, led by their two remaining regimental pipers, moved off to the skirl of the pipes playing 'Hielan' Laddie'. When they reached the other side, Wyett turned to Stewart and said, 'Now, sir, will you tell me why you did it?'

Stewart smiled and, placing a hand on his shoulder, said 'You know, Wyett, the trouble with you Australians is that you have no sense of history. When the story of the Argylls is written you will find that they go down in history as the last unit to cross the Causeway – piped across by their pipers.'

In the morning, Bowden cabled Australia with the news: '*All British forces withdrawn from peninsula to Singapore Island last night following which Johore Causeway was blown up.*'[19]

Singapore was on its own.

Part Three

The Siege

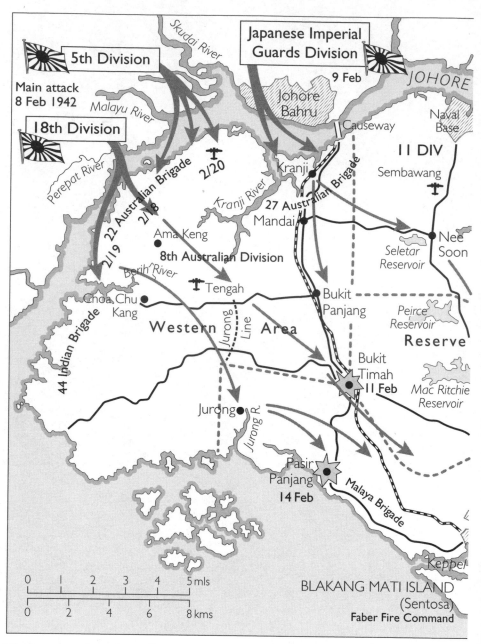

The Japanese invasion of Singapore Island, February 1942

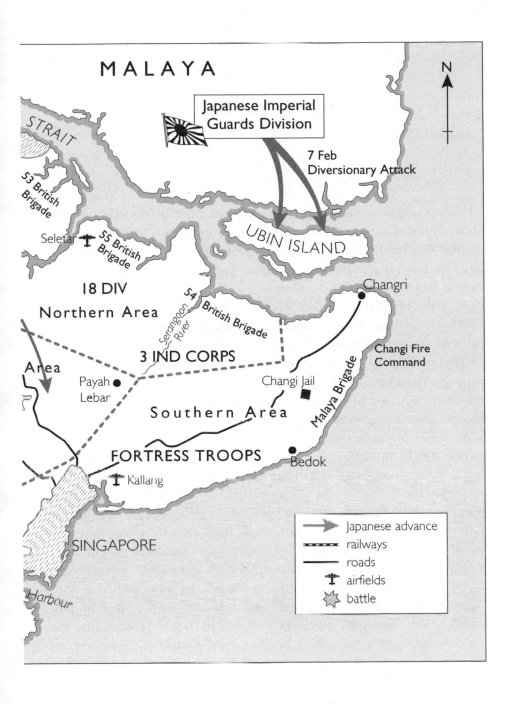

MALAYA

N

Japanese Imperial
Guards Division

7 Feb
Diversionary Attack

STRAIT

53 British
Brigade

Seletar ✚ 55 British
Brigade

UBIN ISLAND

18 DIV
Northern Area

54 British Brigade

Serangoon River

Changri

3 IND CORPS

Changi Fire
Command

Area

Payah
Lebar

Changi Jail

Malaya Brigade

Southern Area

FORTRESS TROOPS

Bedok

✚ Kallang

SINGAPORE

Harbour

	Japanese advance
	railways
	roads
✚	airfields
✶	battle

CHAPTER 17

Phoney Fortress

ON BEACH ROAD frangipani trees had been blasted to pieces and the plumed crowns of the coconut palms hung limply down. In the past week, familiar landmarks and much decorative foliage had been destroyed by Japanese bombing. Many of the elegant European-owned bungalows of Tanglin had been devastated and, as well as the airfields and the docks, the Padang, the Municipal Building, Chinatown and Government House had all taken their share of punishment. In Empress Place, one of the faces of the clock on the Victoria Memorial Theatre had been blown out.

Next to the latest war news, however, the *Straits Times* still carried front-page advertisements for the nightly dinner dance at Raffles Hotel. Even as the enemy stormed south through Johore, the gentlemen of the Oriental Raj and their womenfolk congregated at Raffles. The ballroom was now shrouded in blackout curtains but the orchestra still played from 8 p.m. until midnight. Bookings were required to ensure a table[1] and the manager, Guido Cevini, needed a full staff to cope with the demand. While secretly preparing for the worst, the Singapore *bon ton* followed the Governor's injunction of 'business as usual' and danced the nights away. Denis Russell-Roberts, who visited Raffles with his wife Ruth after his escape from the mainland, says, 'It seemed quite fantastic that this should be happening at Singapore's largest hotel within days of invasion and possible extinction.'[2]

By day, however, the Raffles ballroom was one of the assembly points for the growing stream of Europeans leaving Singapore. Lorraine Stumm found herself there with her daughter Sheridan in mid-January after she was advised to quit the colony by Sheridan's godfathers, Rear Admiral Thomas Drew and John Galvin, a colourful character who had acted as adviser to Duff Cooper. Later that day, mother and child boarded a Qantas flying boat at Kallang bound for Java and thence for Australia. 'My god-fathers were both well placed and knew that things were grim,' Sherry Stumm says. 'John Galvin was a rather mysterious character who spent a lot of time talking to my father. I think he was a member of MI6.'[3]

The exodus of Europeans grew after Churchill's gloomy prognostications in the House of Commons on 27 January were relayed to Singapore by the BBC. His forthright admission of impending doom persuaded a number of European men that it was time to evacuate their families in the big troopships that were preparing to sail to Ceylon virtually empty. Four hundred British women and children were booked on *Wakefield* and 1,276 evacuees – including civilians, naval officers and their families, dockyard workers, a 16-man RAF contingent and 225 naval ratings – on *West Point*. *Wakefield* was refuelling at Keppel Harbour on 30 January prior to embarking her passengers when two formations of Japanese bombers loomed overhead and bombed the docks. One bomb struck *Wakefield*'s B deck and penetrated through to C deck, where it exploded in the sick bay. The blast killed five crew members and wounded nine. The captain hastily completed refuelling, embarked his passengers and set sail along with *West Point*, heading due west under cruiser escort through the Banka Straits and on to Batavia, where more refugees were embarked for Ceylon.

Europeans who remained behind in the stricken colony retained their customary sang-froid. Captain Tony Ferrier perceived a reluctance to face up to reality when he was sent ahead to make preparations for the evacuation of the 5th Norfolk Battalion to the island. 'I got back to Singapore and was told I could do what I liked for 24 hours,' he says. 'I hadn't seen anything of Singapore City and so went off with a brother officer for lunch. We came into this restaurant and, having been in action less than 24 hours earlier, we were rather dishevelled and dirty.

'We got some curious looks from the other diners. They seemed to be carrying on as though nothing was happening – women nicely dressed, men in suits. The picture one got was that they didn't realise that there was a war on even though there was fighting taking place less than 25 miles away. It really was quite shaking to see the little interest in the war. I felt like saying, "Go and get cracking – don't sit here eating with the Japs just up the road."'

This impression was misleading. Leslie Froggatt Snr saw the apparent nonchalance as 'the brave face that Singapore tried to put on in spite of the growing sense of bewilderment, confusion and utter chaos'. He recalled, 'The nastiest jibe of all was made by a visiting journalist who charged us publicly with "swilling" while our Rome burned.'[4] On the contrary, most able-bodied European men, including members of the colonial administration, had been called up into the Volunteers and many European women were working as nurses. Others were simply biding their time awaiting permission from the Governor to leave for Australia, India or Ceylon.

Meanwhile, they danced at Raffles or packed any cinema that hadn't been requisitioned as a food store. At the Alhambra, Ronald Coleman starred in *My Life with Caroline* – 'FRISKY as a French farce! ZESTY as a stolen kiss! A laughing lesson in romance!' For many people, the cinema was the only place where they could get a couple of hours' respite from the bombs and forget their anxieties over the escalating crisis.

Herbert Bruce had been fighting with the Volunteers on the mainland and had injured his leg. When he returned to Singapore, he realised that his young family was in mortal danger from the Japanese bombardment of the north-east suburbs. His son Mel remembers, 'Our Gran's house was a bit too close to the RAF base at Seletar, so Dad bought us a bungalow in Simon Road, Upper Serangoon, and the whole family moved there. Our school, St Andrew's, had been partially bombed and we were kept at home. One day a Catalina flying boat flew low over our house with flames and smoke pouring from its fuselage. The pilot headed for a large clearing away from the houses but he never made it. The plane nosedived into the ground and was engulfed in flames.'

The task of protecting the citizenry from shelling and bombing had fallen to Ivan Simson. He had been appointed Director-General of Civil Defence by Duff Cooper at a meeting of the War Council on New Year's Eve. His deputy was F. D. Bisseker, whose main assignment was to solve the colony's chronic manpower shortage. Bisseker was one of the sternest critics of the Malayan Civil Service, and Stanley Jones, the Colonial Secretary, placed every possible obstruction in his way. It was obvious to Simson that Jones was settling old scores when requests for staff and accommodation were met with 'unnecessarily rude non-co-operation'. Simson discovered that from the Governor downwards, no civil servant would help Bisseker, or anybody who was associated with him. At his own expense, Bisseker rented and furnished an office as Civil Defence headquarters and quietly got on with his work.[5]

The Official Historian says that considering Singapore was already under bombardment at the time of Simson's appointment, it was largely due to his efforts and to the devotion of his staff that the civil defence services functioned as well as they did.[6] The situation was desperate. Rohan Rivett, a young Australian reporter at the Malayan Broadcasting Corporation, wrote in his diary, 'Bombs, bombs, everywhere, bombs whistling down diagonally with an unmistakable scream, bombs bursting on streets, on shops, on houses, on military targets – 80 major raids in 24 days in this fair town.'[7] As the death toll steadily climbed, few Singaporeans would have shared Churchill's eloquent view that 'Existence is never so sweet as when it is at hazard.'[8]

Rescue, fire-fighting and demolition teams were increased in mid-January when the Japanese began low-level carpet bombing because of the absence of fighters and effective anti-aircraft fire. The bombers arrived 27 at a time, or in multiples of 27, in triple-arrow formation and, at a given signal, unloaded their bombs at all once. To handle the destruction, two Chinese liaison officers, Lim Bo Seng and his brother, worked with members of the Chinese Mobilisation Council to organise a daily workforce of 12,000 labourers. They carried out vital work, particularly filling in bomb craters on airfield runways.[9]

Once Shenton Thomas had dropped his opposition to arming Chinese volunteers, Tan Kah Kee, chairman of the China Relief Fund, and his advisers had arranged for guerrilla experts to be sent down to Singapore from China to assist Spencer Chapman and Alan Warren in training the eager young recruits at SOE's 101 Special Training School. John Dalley was appointed commanding officer with the rank of lieutenant-colonel. Most of the volunteers were members of the Kuomintang and the Communist Party of Malaya, which had temporarily buried the hatchet to present a united front against the Japanese. Their nickname was 'Dalley's Desperadoes'.

One of SOE's priorities was to assist the safe passage of Europeans and pro-British Chinese and Indians who would have to leave Singapore if the situation deteriorated any further. Captain Ivan Lyon set up supply bases along an escape route from Singapore to the Indragiri River in Sumatra. Clive Lyon says, 'The idea was that people fleeing Singapore would be met at the mouth of the Indragiri and be ferried 150 miles upriver. When they reached Rengat, they would be conducted through the mountains to the west-coast port of Padang. There they would take their chances about getting to India or Ceylon. My father was responsible for saving the lives of many hundreds of people.'[10] Lyon also worked with John Davis and Richard Broome in placing small parties of Chinese guerrillas in different parts of Malaya to commit acts of sabotage behind Japanese lines after they had completed their trainings.

Meanwhile, the Norfolks arrived back in Singapore after their exhausting withdrawal from Batu Pahat on 28 January, three days in advance of the deadline for the retreat of all British forces from the mainland. They were taken to Bidadari Camp, north-east of the city. Tony Ferrier was sent to the north shore to carry out a reconnaissance of the area to be occupied by his battalion. 'We were to take up a position on the east of the Naval Base,' he recalls. 'We had one company in the base and we were covering a front two or three miles wide eastwards in the mangrove swamps on the edge of the Johore Straits. The base had been abandoned by the Navy and was in a bit of a mess.'

Back in 1938, *The Times* had described the inauguration of the base as 'perhaps the most significant day in the history of British influence in the Far East'. When the Army moved in four years later, it was one of the worst. The modern barrack blocks used by Asian workers were deserted and the labour force of 12,000 had been scattered far and wide, never to be regathered for vital defence work. Papers had been strewn everywhere in the administration buildings and there were signs of systematic looting. The great crane which could lift an entire gun turret out of a warship was just standing there, still in good working order; ships' boilers, building materials, spare parts for seaplanes and shelves of radio equipment were still neatly stacked in workshops and storerooms. The giant floating dock which had been towed all the way from England had been scuttled, but its superstructure remained visible above the water.

So rapid had been the evacuation that half-eaten meals lay rotting on the tables, while the godowns were packed with enough food to feed an army for several months. In the ordnance stores, 180,000 tons of ammunition – ranging from 15-inch armour-piercing shells to .303 bullets – lined the shelves.[11] It had taken the Army seven days using a fleet of 120 trucks to salvage the most valuable supplies and store them elsewhere on the island. Ian Morrison described the sights at the Naval Base as 'my most tragic memory of the whole Malayan campaign'.[12]

General Gordon Bennett says that the destruction of the Naval Base had a seriously damaging psychological effect on his troops when they returned to Singapore Island. 'There was a feeling that all was lost and from now on we were achieving nothing,' he says. 'To say that one was depressed was to put it very mildly. No positive note was struck and no imagination displayed.'[13]

Percival had lost 19,123 men during the Malayan Campaign, mainly as prisoners to the Japanese, but he had 85,000 men on Singapore Island. That number looks far less impressive when it is taken into account that 15,000 were non-combatants such as medical staff, supply units, transport companies, pay clerks, cooks and a dozen other categories, while several thousand wounded were in hospitals or recuperating elsewhere. Churchill estimated that of the total figure 'probably 70,000 were armed'.[14]

Percival's army comprised 38 infantry battalions – 17 Indian, 13 British, six Australian and two Malay – plus three machine-gun battalions – two British and one Australian – and nine artillery regiments, three anti-tank regiments and 152 anti-aircraft guns. Even before the campaign began, Indian battalions had been stripped of many of their experienced, Urdu-speaking British officers and NCOs in a shake-up of the Indian Army to provide Britain with more Indian divisions in the Middle East. Many of their replacements had been killed in the Malayan Campaign, while thousands of the new recruits were youths of 17 or 18 years of age who had little idea about how to fire their rifles and had never set eyes on a tank until being confronted with one bearing down on them with machine guns blazing. Seven of the British battalions were under-strength, and six had been in Singapore for less than two weeks after a three-month voyage from Britain which had rendered them rubber-legged, physically unfit and mentally unprepared for active service.

Five of the Australian battalions had been seeded with 1,900 reinforcements who had been whisked off to Singapore after barely two weeks' training in Australia. General Kirby lamented in *The War Against Japan*, 'The decision to select these untrained Australian reinforcements for Malaya was unfortunate.' One of the scandals of the fall of Singapore was that thousands of well-trained Australian reinforcements had been available in Middle East base camps, and could have been sent to Singapore in their place.[15]

Food supplies for three months and thousands of tons of ammunition had been stockpiled in dumps and depots at Bukit Timah and Changi, or were stored in the godowns at Keppel Harbour, or in air-conditioned cinemas; 17 million gallons of water a day were available from the island's reservoirs now that the pipeline from the mainland had been severed. The armoury, however, had almost run out of weapons. It was estimated that III Indian Corps had lost 30,000 rifles, 1,500 light machine guns, 70 per cent of its anti-tank rifles and 1,000 15-cwt trucks during its retreat down the Malay peninsula. Ammunition for the artillery pieces that would engage the Japanese gunners in counter-battery work were also in short supply. Percival imposed a limit of 12 rounds a day on 25-pounders, 25 rounds on 18-pounders and 29 rounds on 4.5-inch howitzers. These rounds were non-transferable from gun to gun and non-accumulative from day to day.

To place his forces, Percival divided the island into four zones:

Northern Area, including Seletar and the Naval Base, defended by III Indian Corps (the 11th Indian Division strengthened by the 8th Indian

Brigade from the disbanded 9th Indian Division, and the 18th British Division);

Western Area, including the Kranji River and Tengah airfield, defended by the 8th Australian Division, consisting of the 22nd and 27th Brigades, each of three battalions; its south-west sector was held by the newly arrived 44th Indian Brigade supported by two batteries from the 2/10th Field Regiment and the 2/15th Regiment;

Southern Area, covering Singapore City and the southern beaches, defended by two Malay battalions and the Straits Settlements Volunteer Force; and

Reserve Area, including the reservoirs, defended by the command reserve, the 12th Indian Brigade.

Percival's troop dispersions reflected his belief that the Japanese would attack to the east of the Causeway. This was where the Naval Base was located and, throughout the Malayan Campaign, his orders had been to defend it to the end. As he said in his Dispatch, 'the object of the defence was not to hold Singapore Island, but to protect the Naval Base'. How one could be achieved without the other was clear only to the GOC. It seemed to be ingrained in his mind that the base would be the main focus of the Japanese attack, even though it had been abandoned by the Royal Navy, its fuel tanks were ablaze and all of its working parts were being systematically destroyed by army demolition experts. Irrespective of the fate of Singapore, Arthur Percival would be able to record for posterity that he had carried out his orders.

General Wavell had told Percival during his visit to Singapore on 20 January that in his opinion the Japanese would attack the north-*west* side of the island where the straits were at their narrowest. His reasoning was simple: the Japanese had attacked all the way down the west coast of the Malay peninsula and were unlikely to vary their winning strategy by moving their entire invasion force across Johore from west to east in order to cross the straits at a wider spot than was available in the west. Such a move did not made sense to anyone except Percival.

'I had instructed General Percival to place the fresh 18th Division on the front most likely to be attacked and the 8th Australian Division in the next most dangerous sector, keeping the Indian troops as far as possible in reserve for reinforcement and counterattack,' Wavell says. 'He estimated that the Japanese were most likely to attack in the north-east of the island

and placed the 18th Division there. He put the Australians in the north-west.'[16]

Having interferred with Percival's placements in the Battle of Johore with disastrous consequences, Wavell did not insist that the troops should be switched around, with the numerically stronger and fresher 18th Division defending the most likely point of contact. Compared with the 8th Division's six weakened battalions, three field artillery batteries and three anti-tank batteries, the 18th Division under the command of Major-General Beckwith-Smith consisted, at full strength, of the following:

53rd Infantry Brigade (Brigadier C. L. Duke): Headquarters, the 5th and 6th Battalions of the Royal Norfolk Regiment, and the 2nd Battalion of the Cambridgeshire Regiment.

54th Infantry Brigade (Brigadier E. H. W. Backhouse): Headquarters, the 4th Battalion of the Royal Norfolk Regiment and the 4th and 5th Battalions of the Royal Suffolk Regiment.

55th Infantry Brigade (Brigadier T. H. Massy-Beresford): Headquarters, the 1st Battalion of the 5th Sherwood Foresters, the 5th Battalion of the Bedfordshire and Hertfordshire Regiment and the 1st Cambridgeshire Regiment.

Divisional troops: the 9th Battalion of the Northumberland Fusiliers and the 18th Division Reconnaissance Corps (the 5th Battalion of the Loyal Regiment).

Four regiments of Royal Artillery.

Two anti-tank regiments.

Four companies of Royal Engineers.

Percival placed these brigades side by side on the north east shore, with the 53rd Brigade nearest the Causeway, then the 55th Brigade and finally the 54th Brigade furthest east. Two switchlines had been nominated to protect the centre of the island if the enemy landed in the east and west. The eastern line, known as the Serangoon Line, was sited between Kallang airport and Payah Lebar village. The western line was just south of Tengah airfield between the headwaters of the Kranji and Jurong rivers, the former flowing north to the Straits of Johore and the latter south to the sea.

Brigadier Simson had inspected embarkation sites on the Johore side of the straits and concluded that the most favourable facilities for any Japanese embarkation of troops were opposite this area. Like Wavell, he was convinced that the enemy would launch their main attack in the west. It was obvious to him that they would cross the straits at the narrowest point in order to expose their troops to fire for the shortest possible time.

The whole of the north shore, both east and west, was wide open. 'The preparation of field defences and obstacles, though representing a good deal of local effort, bore no relation to the mortal needs which now arose,' Churchill says. 'There were no permanent defences on the front about to be attacked.'[17] Tony Ferrier's men got to work to build up beach defences. 'On my right there was a mangrove swamp, slushy and wet, forming a natural defensive position,' he remembers. 'There were no troops in that area as it was considered the Japanese wouldn't land there. We had no defensive works at all and had to put up barbed wire and beach lights. We started working by day but that immediately brought down mortar and shell fire from across the straits, so we then had to work by night and try to sleep by day.

'We were in this position for a week, preparing it as best we could with the limited resources we had, which amounted to putting Dannert wire along the beaches and installing land mines and beach lights. The idea was that when the Japanese came across and attacked us by night – and we knew they would; it was just a matter of time – we would put these lights on and see where to fire at them.'[18]

Percival's explanation for the lack of preparation is given in his Dispatch as follows: 'Prior to the outbreak of hostilities with Japan no defences had been constructed on the northern or western shore of Singapore Island. This has been imputed in some quarters to a lack of foresight on the part of successive General Officers Commanding. It has however perhaps not been fully realised that the object of the defence was not to hold Singapore Island, but to protect the Naval Base. To do this it was necessary at least to prevent the enemy bringing that base under observed fire and also, as far as possible, to keep the enemy out of close bombing range.

'Not long after the commencement of the Malayan Campaign it became apparent that we might be driven back to Johore, or even to Singapore Island. On 23 December therefore I issued orders to the Commander Singapore Fortress to arrange for a reconnaissance of the northern area of Singapore Island to select positions for the defence of possible landing places.[19] Early in January 1942 orders were given that the preparation of the defences of the northern part of Singapore Island was to be undertaken at once as an urgent measure. Labour difficulties however then interfered. All the troops in Singapore Island had their allotted tasks in manning the defences, and the few military labour companies which existed were fully employed. Civil labour, from the beginning of January 1942 onwards, failed to an increasing extent as the bombing became heavier.

'I gave first priority to this labour for work on the aerodromes and new airstrips. The Air Force seldom got enough and there was none available for our defence works. In fact I had to make available men from the Reinforcement camps for work on the aerodromes. Nevertheless, a great deal of work was done. The defences were planned in skeleton as it was not known what the strength of the garrison would be. Sites for the forward defended localities and for reserves were selected. Artillery observation posts and gun positions were reconnoitred and selected. Locations of formation headquarters were fixed and communications arranged.'

Percival then claims, 'Machine-gun positions were constructed, oil obstacles and depth charges were placed in creeks which appeared to be likely landing places. All available spare searchlights and Lyon lights were collected and made available. Anti-tank obstacles were constructed and made available.' This was not so. These defensive stores had been not installed but dumped on the north-west shore on the orders of the Deputy Chief Engineer who, in the absence of orders from Percival or Malaya Command, had taken the initiative himself. The stores consisted of coils of barbed wire including anti-tank high-tensile Dannert wire, pickets, booby-traps, drums of petrol and other incendiaries to fire the water surface, and anti-tank cylinders and chains. 'Owing to the far better embarkation facilities for the enemy west of Johore Bahru, the defence stores were dumped on the island west of the Causeway, inclusive,' Brigadier Simson says. 'General Wavell later came to the same conclusion independently that this would be the more likely point of attack. However, late in January, HQ Malaya Command ordered all this material to be moved east of the Causeway.'[20]

Percival's orders to formation commanders on 23 January for the defence of the island began with the gloomy observation that the northern and western shores were too intersected with creeks and mangroves to make any ordinary form of beach defence possible. Instead, his general plan was that small defended localities should be established in each area to cover obvious approaches such as rivers, creeks, roads and tracks. These localities would be supported by mobile reserves in suitable assembly areas, from which they could operate against infiltrating parties of the enemy. The essential requirement of these assembly positions was to be concealment from air and ground observation. Percival nominated the Fortress Commander, Keith Simmons, to be the officer responsible for 'developing' the defence plan in collaboration with Brigadier Paris and commanders from III Indian Corps and the AIF.

'Singapore was not a fortress in the old sense of the word,' he says. 'It comprised a large defended and inhabited area, with a maximum length of about 35 miles and a maximum width of about 15 miles, which included the large and densely populated town of Singapore. The area had strong anti-ship defences, reasonably strong anti-aircraft defences but weak infantry defences and no tanks at all. The coasts facing the Straits of Johore were, when war broke out, completely undefended. From time to time exaggerated statements had appeared in the press as to the strength of the Singapore defences. It is probable that, as a result of these statements, the public believed the defences were stronger than they really were. It is certain that the troops retiring from the mainland, many of whom had never seen Singapore before, were disappointed not to find the immensely strong defences which they had pictured.'

Thus ran Percival's post-war account. At the time, he estimated that he had one week's grace while the Japanese marshalled their forces in Johore, yet he planned for a three-month siege. He did not appreciate that the Japanese, having charged down the length of the peninsula in 55 days, would not allow themselves to be detained by a narrow strip of water. He did not understand that Yamashita – in common with every other Japanese commander involved in the Pacific campaigns – was working to a rigid timetable. He did not know that Yamashita intended to present Singapore to his Emperor as a gift on 11 February, Japan's National Day.

Percival's failings as the commander of an army had become evident during the campaign, but the quality he lacked above all others was luck, an essential ingredient, according to Napoleon (and Churchill), in any successful commander. Percival had no luck at all but it would have required some form of divine intervention to make any difference to the outcome of the siege of Singapore. John Wyett says, 'He was a mild-mannered, relatively useless fellow. I quite liked him as an individual but he was utterly unable to cope with the situation he'd been placed in. That's not saying much against him – it would take a very strong man to do much better than he did in that particular circumstance. He had other high-ranking officers to consult with but he didn't know which way to turn. He should have ignored the Governor and the civilians and done the sensible thing, but he wasn't mentally strong enough to take over and get things cracking. Orders were coming from London on what he should do – it was an utterly ridiculous situation.'

Gordon Bennett, meanwhile, expounded his *toujours l'attaque* philosophy to all and sundry as he travelled around the island. 'Our duty now is to recapture Malaya at the earliest possible opportunity,' he told himself in his diary on 31 January. 'We owe it to the natives! We owe it to ourselves!' The following morning, however, Percival informed Singaporeans in a broadcast from the Malaya Broadcasting Corporation studios at Caldecott Hill, 'Our task is to hold this fortress until help can come, as assuredly it will come; this we are determined to do. Any of the enemy who sets foot in our fortress must be dealt with immediately. The enemy within our gates must be ruthlessly weeded out. There must be no more loose talk or rumour-mongering. Our duty is clear. With firm resolve and fixed determination we shall win through.'

Percival also addressed a packed press conference to assure the sceptics of the fourth estate that he intended to hold Singapore. He appealed for co-operation between the military and civilian elements; the one could not fight properly without the help of the other. 'Much of what the General said was sensible,' Ian Morrison says. 'But never have I heard a message put across with less conviction, less force.' After he finished speaking, Percival took questions from the floor but answered in such a desultory manner that normally garrulous journalists lapsed into silence. 'I felt that the General not only did not know how to deal with a group of pressmen,' Morrison says, 'but he did not know how to deal with any group of men.'[21]

The leader writer of the *Sydney Morning Herald* seemed more in tune with the situation than Malaya Command. The paper commented on 2 February under the headline 'SINGAPORE'S FINAL STAND', 'The withdrawal of the Empire forces across Johore Straits into the island of Singapore brings to an end a campaign which, despite the heroism of the forces engaged, will always be a depressing chapter in British military history because of inadequacies of preparation and, in some respects, of performance.' The leader writer added presciently, 'As for the future, only a rash man would venture a definite opinion. In spite of the disheartening conditions under which they have had to fight, the Imperial troops have entered Singapore Island in good spirit and determined to do what is humanly possible to beat off the Japanese until the promised help arrives. But the critical nature of their position is obvious. Singapore was not originally designed to withstand determined assault from the landward side, and only time will show whether the island can be successfully defended as a fortress.'

Tony Ferrier was promoted to commander of C Company when his commanding officer, Major Charles Wood, was wounded by shrapnel. It was his responsibility to fire the SOS signal by Very pistol which would bring down artillery fire on the beaches. 'The signal was red Very light, green, red, and no other officer in my company could actually give that signal,' he says. 'I realised that if it was going to be effective it had to be fired jolly quickly. It was no good trying to wake me up for me then to give the signal – by that time the Japanese would have landed. So I did my best to be down with a forward post on the beach so I could see straight away if there was an attack.

'We didn't want to bring those guns down opening a tremendous barrage of fire unless it was the real thing. For several nights I sat in a slit trench at a forward post with the Very pistol in my hand on my knee and at times would find myself nodding off. Nevertheless, one was right there on the spot and if there had been any sound one would have regained consciousness in a split second. One was very, very tired. We were working at night and I was on sentry-go to be able to give this signal and one had various administrative tasks to do by day so one was very short of sleep.

'We heard these big naval 15-inch guns which had been put in gun emplacements to protect Singapore harbour from naval attack firing at the Japanese at their positions in Johore. They had turned them around and they were firing them into the jungle. But they mainly had armour-piercing shells to sink battleships and, of course, when they fired into the jungle the force of the explosion was in the ground and they just made an enormous hole and caused minimal harm to Japanese targets. Some of them fired straight over our heads and it sounded like an express train going about 20 yards above your head.'

Admiral Spooner and his wife Megan had not joined the mass exodus of naval personnel from the island. On 4 February they entertained General Sir Lewis Heath and his pregnant wife to dinner. Later, Meg Spooner wrote in her diary, 'General Heath has a strong, honest and not unclever face. His left arm is withered. He thinks there are too many generals here.' To reduce the number, Heath suggested that he should be evacuated to India, as III Indian Corps was no longer required in Singapore. Percival, however, refused to grant permission on the grounds that it would make a bad impression on the Indian Army.[22]

He wrote, 'I cannot help feeling that the presence of Lady Heath in Malaya and the knowledge that she was shortly to give birth to a child may have had a profound effect upon him. Certainly during the fighting on

Singapore Island it distracted his attentions, to a greater or lesser degree, from the conduct of the operations.'

So Heath had stayed and become part of the débâcle. 'It was decided that the enemy would not have sufficient craft to cross [the straits] in large numbers,' he says. 'We had not taken into consideration the thoroughness with which he had carried out all his planning.'[23] Heath did not elaborate on who had made this mistake, but it was plain to all commanders (and to the GOC in his Dispatch) that Malaya Command's intelligence service had been second-rate throughout the campaign, and it appears to have been at fault again. Percival had watched the Japanese leapfrog down the west coast in boats ever since the fall of Penang. Japanese trucks and pack animals had also hauled armoured barges and collapsible craft from the landing sites at Kota Bahru and further north at Singora and Patani down the entire length of the peninsula. Yet British Intelligence and air surveillance had noted none of this southward movement. As Heath put it in his Changi lecture, the enemy 'had produced sufficient landing craft to bring across one division and one brigade – 18 battalions – in one night!'.

The coastline of the Western Area was made up of tidal mud flats and mangrove swamps intersected by streams and inlets, a defender's nightmare. As Percival had ordered, the troops were placed in clusters. Those in the soggy ground on the foreshore closest to the water could see little through the mangroves, although their view improved considerably as the days passed and Japanese artillery removed many of the overhanging branches. Others were stationed on tidal islands which were cut off for hours at a time; still others were in dinghies and small craft bobbing in shallow water. Inland, the troops hid in plantations of young rubber trees and on scrub-covered hills, which provided a better view of the straits. In the centre of the position was a seawall, an ideal landing stage for Japanese guns and tanks. From there Lim Chu Kang Road led four miles south through Ama Keng village to Tengah airfield.[24]

The 22nd and 27th Brigades had been allocated a frontage totalling 11 miles, but the portions given to each brigade were disproportionate. The two brigades were also separated by the Kranji River, which widened as it meandered down to the sea to form an estuary 1,200 yards wide at the seafront. From east to west, the 27th Brigade's three battalions – the 2/30th, the heavily reconstituted 2/29th, including no fewer than 500 reinforcements, and the 2/26th, in that order – covered an area of 4,000 yards between the Causeway and the Kranji River, supported by two batteries of the 2/10th Field Artillery Regiment. Russell Savage says, 'It was upsetting to discover there were no prepared positions and that it was more chaotic on Singapore Island than it had been up-country. We had to dig our own gun-pits among the virgin scrub, mangroves and *kampongs* at Kranji. It took a bit of the smile off our faces. Our first thought was, "Where are the maps?" There seemed to be none available; there had been no thought that we would end up on Singapore Island.'[25]

Lieutenant Bob Goodwin headed into Singapore to borrow some maps from the Survey Department in the Cathay Building. 'As I got in the lift, a British officer got in with me,' he says. 'There were three or four Malays or Chinese and I saw with amazement the scorn with which he strode past them. They were dirt under his feet. I was only 20 and that was the first time I had ever experienced that sort of colonial attitude. It surprised me enormously. I remember that almost more clearly than anything else.'

The maps clearly showed the problems facing the Australians. The three battalions of the 22nd Brigade – the 2/20th, the 2/18th and the battered 2/19th, in that order – stretched from the Kranji River to the Berih River, a distance of 16,000 yards, with the 2/15th Field Regiment providing artillery support. At the back of the 22nd's position, a narrow neck of land extended for 3,000 yards to the headwaters of both rivers. As Percival saw it, the problem was whether to allow the enemy to land unopposed if he attacked the 22nd's area and to stop him on this narrow strip, or to hold forward positions near the coast with a view to attacking the enemy when he was most vulnerable while crossing the straits. Having considered his options, Percival ordered Brigadier Taylor to occupy the forward positions and oppose the landings in accordance with the general policy of Malaya Command, which was to spread the vast majority of combat troops around the island's 70-mile circumference, with a small reserve to meet emergencies.

The 2/20th Battalion, with an attached company of Dalforce Chinese volunteers, was sited on the right on a front of 8,000 yards between the Kranji River and Sarimbun Island. The 2/18th Battalion was in the centre on a front of 4,000 yards between Sarimbun Island and Murai Point. The 2/19th Battalion, which had absorbed 370 reinforcements since its losses at Muar, was on the left on a front of 4,000 yards between Murai Point and the Berih River. One company of the newly arrived 2/4th Machine Gun Battalion was distributed among the battalions, while 30 field guns covered the landing sites.

The biggest blow to the 2/19th was that it had lost Lieutenant-Colonel Anderson VC, who had been struck down with a serious illness. The men wanted his second-in-command Major Tom Vincent to replace him but, on

General Bennett's orders, Major Andrew Robertson was promoted from the 2/20th Battalion. Robertson did not know the area and he did not know the men in the battalion – two major drawbacks on the eve of a big battle. The 2/20th Battalion consisted of 750 men, including 80 untrained reinforcements, and its front of 8,000 yards was twice as long as the frontage allotted to all three of the 27th Brigade's battalions put together.

John Wyett says Percival's placement of the Australian forces 'offended all the rules of an effective tactical disposition. For such an abrasive temperament as that of Gordon Bennett, it was strangely out of character for him to accept this arrangement without vigorous protest. It was a recipe for disaster but his mind was elsewhere.'[26] Had Bennett insisted, Percival could easily have extended the Northern Area's boundary slightly to the west to include the Causeway sector, thus enabling the 27th Brigade to act as reserve for the 22nd Brigade and give some badly needed depth and cohesion to the Western Area's defences.

But Percival was convinced that the attack was coming on the north-east shore, and Bennett had made no protest. It would also have been logical for Bennett to transfer the 2/29th Battalion to help Taylor cover the longer frontage, but that would have increased the importance of his role at the expense of Maxwell. The old rivalry between the two commanders had not been forgotten – the two men were barely on speaking terms – and Bennett allowed the glaring anomaly to stand.

He later wrote, '1,900 untrained Australian troops arrived in Malaya in January 1942, a few weeks before the fall of Singapore. Some of them had never fired a rifle. Some of them were recruited in Martin Place, Sydney, on the Friday and put on a boat for Malaya the following week. Reinforcements for the 8th Division had been sent to the Middle East. There were no trained reinforcements left for the 8th Division in Australia.'[27]

Jim Thyer, Bennett's Chief of Staff, commented that the great majority of the 2/29th's reinforcements had arrived in Singapore as late as 24 January. 'A large proportion had not qualified at a small-arms course, nor been taught bayonet fighting. Some reinforcements to all battalions had never seen a Bren gun and none of them had handled a sub-machine gun or an anti-tank rifle. Worse still was the fact that there were some who had never handled a rifle.'[28] The 2/18th had received 90 new troops to replace its losses. John McGrory says, 'A lot of them didn't know how to load a rifle. It's a very sore point.' It is difficult to resist the thought that sending a man who had never fired a rifle into one of the most dangerous locations of the entire Malayan Campaign was little short of murder.

The horrendous task that Percival had set the Australians became evident when officers were taken to the foreshore to be shown the positions that their companies were to occupy. As Captain Frank Gaven of the 2/20th looked at A Company's position on the edge of a mangrove swamp, a wave of desperation swept over him. 'I realised that forward defence in this situation was an impossible task,' he says. 'There were no defences or fortifications and no field of view of an enemy approach. It was a situation that would not offer the troops any glimmer of hope.'[29]

Nevertheless, on 1 February the three battalions of the 22nd Brigade moved into their positions and started preparing their own defences. Most of the work had to be done at night owing to bombing, strafing and shelling during the day. The small amount of barbed wire made available for waterfront positions was soon used up, and when the 2/20th's Quartermaster Captain Alex Betteridge took trucks to the huge Nee Soon Ordnance Base, where hundreds of tons of barbed wire were stored, he was told it was reserved for other sectors.[30] 'It was an absolute shambles – we had no defences,' Frank Baker of the 2/20th Mortar Platoon remembers. 'I was told this was all done in the interests of the civilian population – Percival didn't want them to be alarmed by making elaborate preparations, so to save them from being alarmed they gave us no barbed wire, although they had miles of it in the stores.'[31]

The battlefront had in fact been cleared of civilians, mostly small farmers and their families who had added their pathetic bundles to the caravanserai of homeless refugees swarming into Singapore City from *kampongs* and farms all along the north shore. To the very end, Malaya Command at Fort Canning, known to the Australian troops as 'Confusion Castle', continued to function as though it were a field day at Aldershot. It informed 8th Division headquarters that leave arrangements for troops would begin on 15 February, while there were instructions on how to deal with the laundering of soiled uniforms. After the invasion had started, one battalion was informed that their practice session on the grenade range had been cancelled.

Brigadier Taylor was informed that the 2/15th Field Regiment would be supporting the 22nd Brigade, even though they had spent the previous 11 months working so closely with the 2/10th Regiment that every battalion officer knew every artillery officer by name. Taylor appealed to Brigadier Boots Callaghan to leave the artillery as it had been on the mainland, but Callaghan refused, and when Taylor appealed to Bennett he was knocked back.

Bob Goodwin, however, provides a sound reason for the switch. 'The 2/10th was the last regiment with heavy vehicles to cross the Causeway,' he says. 'We came on to the island just ahead of the Argylls, and all the other units had already deployed their vehicles around the perimeter, so there wasn't a great deal of room for our guns. There was a feeling we had been let down when we were put with the 27th Brigade, but it was probably a sensible thing to do. It was logical that we would support the brigade immediately to the west of the Causeway.'

On 2 February Bennett visited the 2/20th Battalion and saw for himself the weakness of the Australian positions. He later wrote in his diary, 'The men are cheerful but the posts are lonely. The gaps between the posts are wide. The position is extremely weak.'[32] He could clearly see Japanese moving around on the other side of the straits. When Private Vic Saville asked him what he was going to do about the Japanese, he replied, 'We will blow them off tomorrow.' The Australian gunners waited eagerly for the order to come through, but Boots Callaghan refused to give it.

Percival had agreed to Pulford's request to withdraw the bulk of his Air Force to Sumatra after Japanese gunners found the range of Tengah, Seletar and Sembawang airfields. Within 36 hours, all three had been abandoned and the handful of Hurricanes remaining on Singapore had flown south to Kallang. Yamashita then ordered his gunners to destroy the huge oil-storage tanks at the Naval Base and the Shell petroleum tanks at Kranji, for fear that the British might release the fuel on the incoming tide and turn the straits into a raging inferno. Before long, a great pall of black smoke soared skywards from the ruptured tanks and filthy soot rained down on troops all along the north shore. 'They looked more like miners than troops,' Percival noted.

General Bennett visited the 2/18th and 2/19th Battalions and found their front thickly covered with timber, mostly rubber, with thick mangrove growing right down to the water's edge. 'The posts, which are many hundreds of yards apart, have a field of fire of only 200 yards. The gaps are patrolled regularly. I am beginning to worry about the extreme weakness.' But he made no protest, nor did he chase up vitally needed building materials for his men. He returned to his headquarters and did not go forward again.

The first Chinese volunteers of Dalforce left 101 Special Training School for the front on 5 February, to a rousing send-off from their comrades. Speeches were made, honours handed out and heads wrapped in bandannas in the manner of Chinese soldiers of old. As the group headed north, they sang a song: *'Arise, arise, those who do not want to be slaves. Build a new Great Wall with your flesh and blood.'*[33]

The Chinese troops were assured that they would soon be armed with modern pistols, rifles, tommy-guns and plenty of ammunition. A special consignment of these weapons was travelling in the holds of the SS *Empress of Asia*. She was due in Keppel Harbour that very day.

CHAPTER 18

Death of an Empress

FIFTEEN-YEAR-OLD Len Butler was the youngest seaman among *Empress of Asia*'s crew of 416. 'My action station was on the bridge,' he says. 'I was the captain's messenger.' Len had been born in Manchester on 20 August 1926, and in 1941, when he was still only 14, he had exaggerated his age to 16 to enlist in the Merchant Navy. 'I was at a convent school in Oxford and my family had friends who were in junior management with the Canadian Pacific company,'[1] he says. 'My father got an interview for me with Canadian Pacific in London and as I was tall for my age they accepted me. I went through the Blitz in London and, after training at Banstead, Surrey, was sent to Liverpool to join *Empress of Asia*. She was due for the knacker's yard but we were losing so many ships that she was still in service. I didn't realise the Merchant Navy was such a suicide job; the casualty rate was horrendous.'[2]

Launched in 1912, *Empress of Asia* had been built as a three-funnelled coal-burning liner for Canadian Pacific by Fairfield Shipbuilding & Engineering of Glasgow. She made her maiden voyage, Liverpool–Cape Town–Hong Kong, and from there entered Canadian Pacific's trans-Pacific service between Yokohama and Vancouver. She had made more than 300 voyages on that run and was well known to the Japanese. 'She came across to England from Vancouver, which was her home base, and half the crew were Canadian,' Len says. 'She was refitted as a troopship in Liverpool, painted battleship-grey, and on 12 November 1941 we headed for South Africa and thence to India in a massive convoy with troops who were to be reinforcements for the Eighth Army in the Libyan Desert. When we got to Durban, we discovered that the Japanese had attacked Pearl Harbor and the whole thing changed.'

'The *Asia*', as she was known to her crew under Captain A. B. Smith, discharged her soldiers at Bombay and then picked up 2,235 members of the 18th British Division who were bound for Singapore. All that remained of the division in India were the 18th Division Reconnaissance Battalion

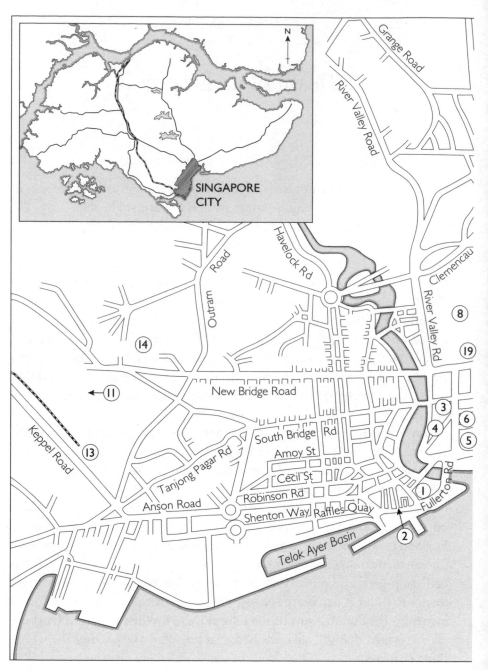

Singapore City at the time of the Japanese invasion

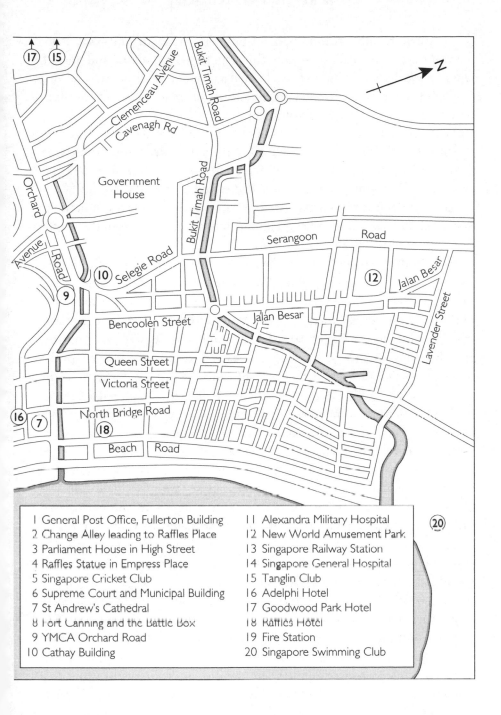

1 General Post Office, Fullerton Building
2 Change Alley leading to Raffles Place
3 Parliament House in High Street
4 Raffles Statue in Empress Place
5 Singapore Cricket Club
6 Supreme Court and Municipal Building
7 St Andrew's Cathedral
8 Fort Canning and the Battle Box
9 YMCA Orchard Road
10 Cathay Building

11 Alexandra Military Hospital
12 New World Amusement Park
13 Singapore Railway Station
14 Singapore General Hospital
15 Tanglin Club
16 Adelphi Hotel
17 Goodwood Park Hotel
18 Raffles Hotel
19 Fire Station
20 Singapore Swimming Club

(5th Loyals), the 9th Northumberland Fusiliers, the 125th Anti-Tank Regiment, the 251st Field Park Company, the 197th Field Ambulance and the 18th Division Workshops. The *Asia* also loaded a number of desperately needed tanks and anti-tank guns, and large quantities of small arms and ammunition destined for the Chinese volunteers.

With Lieutenant-Colonel J. Dean of the 125th Anti-Tank Regiment detailed as Officer Commanding Troops, the ship sailed from Bombay on 23 January 1942 in company with SS *Felix Roussel*, a Dutch steamer SS *Plancius* and SS *Devonshire*. The Japanese had sealed off the Malacca Straits, so the convoy was forced to make a detour through the Sunda Strait between Sumatra and Java and then negotiate the Banka Straits between the southeast coast of Sumatra and Banka Island.

Shortly after leaving Bombay, the *Asia*'s convoy joined up with a bigger convoy of eight ships sailing along that route to Batavia. At the approaches to Batavia, these ships broke away from the *Asia* but *City of Canterbury* remained with her, so there were now five ships making for Singapore together through the Banka Straits. 'The Banka Straits were very narrow and the ships had to go through line astern, or single file,' Len Butler remembers. 'The *Asia* was the biggest ship and she just happened to be the last ship. We were only a few miles from Singapore and we were in the minefields with no room to manoeuvre. My position was to stand on the wings of the bridge and wait for messages to come through.'

At 11 a.m. on 4 February the *Asia* was travelling at 12½ knots in a single line, led by the heavy cruiser HMS *Exeter*, when a large V formation of 18 two-engine Japanese bombers flew overhead at 5,000 feet. The *Asia* was armed with one 3-inch anti-aircraft gun, a 6-inch anti-submarine and surface raider weapon, six Oerlikons of approximately .55 calibre and eight Hotchkiss machine guns. To this firepower was added 14 Bren guns from the anti-tank gunners, 10 from the reconnaissance corps and two, with 100-round containers, from the divisional workshops. The fiddley deck atop the ship was bristling with armaments, and all guns opened fire as the Japanese planes began their approaches.

One bomber unloaded its bombs in the direction of the *Asia*; all missed their target, although there were five near misses. Captain Smith says, 'The bombs exploded on striking the water, sending up columns of water to a height of about 20 feet which descended on the deck. Two of our lifeboats were pierced by bomb splinters and some splinters were found round the decks. Otherwise, no damage was sustained, although the ship was badly shaken. All the ships had opened fire, including our escorts HMS *Exeter*,

First-aid helpers carry a Singapore bombing victim to safety, February 1942.

Bombed-out ruins smouldered throughout Singapore.

Survivor Len Butler prepares to lay a wreath at the spot where the *Empress of Asia* sank in February 1942.

Empress of Asia ablaze after being hit by Japanese bombs ... she carried reinforcements and vital small arms for Chinese Volunteers.

Firemen tackle burning buildings and machinery after the bombing of the Naval Yards.

Smoke forms a dense cloud over Singapore's skyline.

Wounded soldiers evacuate a bombed hospital ward, Singapore City, February 1942.

General Yamashita, with his staff during the Malayan Campaign. His Chief of Staff, General Sosaku Suzuki, is on his left.

Surrender: The Flag Party heads for Bukit Timah on 15 February 1942 (from left): Major Wild, Brigadier Newbigging, Brigadier Torrance and General Percival.

General Yamashita faces General Percival across the table at the Ford Motor Factory during the surrender discussions.

Many civilian cars were pushed into Singapore Harbour to deny them to the enemy.

British troops surrender to the Japanese after disarming themselves, Singapore City, 16 February 1942.

BELOW Victorious Japanese troops march past the Hong Kong & Shanghai Bank, Singapore, 16 February 1942.

Crowded Selarang Barracks, photographed by Australian POW George Aspinall during the notorious Barracks Square Incident, September 1942.

This rare picture of Changi POW Camp was taken shortly after the surrender on 15 February 1942. The camera was buried and the film developed by one of Frank Davies's Chinese friends. From left, standing, back row: Don Moffat, Frank Davies, Doug Bennett and Staff Sergeant MacLennand. Front row: Bridgeland, Ben Smith and Jack Hutchinson.

Major Ivan Lyon spies on Singapore Harbour from an island hideout during the successful Jaywick raid, September 1943.

Squadron Leader Arthur Scarf, VC.

Colonel Charles Anderson, VC.

RIGHT Commonwealth war graves at Kranji Cemetery, May 2004.

HMS *Danae*, HMAS *Yarra*, HMS *Sutlej* and two destroyers.' None of the planes had been brought down.[3]

That afternoon two of the faster ships, *Plancius* and *Devonshire*, parted company with the convoy in order to reach Singapore first thing in the morning. The remaining three ships – *Empress of Asia*, *City of Canterbury* and *Felix Roussel* – were due in later that day.

The morning of 5 February dawned fine and clear, with smooth seas and a light breeze. Singapore was just visible on the horizon as a black smudge from the pall of smoke hanging over it. The little convoy steered an easterly course in single line, led by the cruiser *Danae*. As the *Asia* approached Sultan Shoal at 10.45 a.m. at a reduced speed of six knots prior to taking on her pilots, a large V formation of 24 Japanese bombers flew over at high altitude and disappeared into the clouds. Fifteen minutes later, at 11.00 a.m., the planes returned singly, or in twos and threes, and attacked the convoy from all directions at both high and low altitudes.

'All the ships of the convoy and the escorts opened fire at once and bombs started falling all around us,' Captain Smith says. 'We, as the largest ship with three funnels and well known to the Japanese owing to our peacetime voyages to that country, seemed to bear the brunt of it. Terrific concussion shook the ship and standing on the bridge it was difficult to know what were near misses and what were direct hits.'

Felix Roussel received a direct hit from an incendiary bomb which caused a fire, but miraculously a second direct hit landed in a water tank which burst its sides and extinguished the flames. She was able to continue towards Singapore. Then it was the *Asia*'s turn. Blazing fire from the guns on the fiddley deck forced the first wave of bombers to veer away and drop their loads wide of the ship, while a second wave also passed overhead without scoring a hit. Then at 11.05 a.m. a lone plane suddenly appeared directly overhead, and the men saw it drop a bomb – which landed on the *Asia* with a sickening thud on the starboard side near the forward funnel.

The bomb passed over the bridge, smashed through the roof of the Officers' Lounge and penetrated to the dining saloon on B deck. Fourteen officers who had gathered in the lounge were engulfed in searing flames which scorched their hair and eyebrows, while tin hats, water-bottles and haversacks were sucked from their bodies by the blast. The men stumbled through thick black fumes to the boat deck to gulp fresh air into their lungs. One officer of the 125th Anti-Tank Regiment was killed and two were seriously injured.[4]

Thick clouds of smoke started pouring from the bomb crater. Fire parties, under the direction of the Chief Officer, tackled the blaze, which had taken hold in dry woodwork, but although the pumps were working at full pressure they were unable to obtain any water from the fire hydrants. The firefighters had to make do with fire extinguishers and fire buckets.

Less than an hour after the first strike, four other bombs found their mark on the *Asia*. 'I was on the bridge and could see the bombs coming down,' Len Butler recalls. 'There was nowhere to run; you just had to hope they weren't going to hit you. Five bombs had penetrated deep into the ship and blown up the water system, so we had no water pressure to put the fires out. There was no communication with the rear of the ship because all that had gone as well. All the steam pipes were broken and they were encased in asbestos which was flying all over the place.'

Captain Smith had ordered troops to take cover below deck when the attack started. Down in the mess halls, the men sat at their tables well below the waterline, singing and joking. There were no signs of panic. At 11.25 a.m. the Chief Officer reported that the fires below decks were out of control. Captain Smith told Colonel Dean to assemble all troops at their muster stations on A deck. The men came up from below in orderly fashion to find that the *Asia* had been virtually cut in two, with the midships section of A deck obscured by smoke and flames.

At 11.30 a.m. the engineers reported that the engine room and stokehold were filling with smoke and they could not remain below. The accommodation above was on fire, and pieces of burning material were dropping into the machinery. Captain Smith gave the order for the stokehold to be evacuated. 'Some of the soldiers saw the stokers coming up and thought they were deserting their post,' Len Butler says. 'But they were coughing their lungs up because the smoke from the fires, and bits of the asbestos were going down into the stokehold through the vents. They couldn't breathe, so they were coming up. They weren't deserting their post – they were doing it to save their lives. The stokers were given a bad reputation for that and it wasn't true at all. They were a rough, tough lot – we'd had trouble with them in Durban for drunkenness and fighting – but they weren't deserters.'

The *Asia* was now 11 miles from Singapore and, realising she would not make it, Captain Smith decided to swing her round and anchor close to the Sultan Shoal lighthouse. The lower bridge, chartroom and officers' accommodation were ablaze and the heat drove him on to the flying bridge, where Colonel Dean joined him, but soon even this position would have to be abandoned.

Len Butler remembers, 'The *Asia* was well and truly on fire, and I received a message from the Captain to go to the rear of the ship and give the officer in command of the troops there the order to abandon ship. But before he did that, I was to ask him would he allocate eight men to throw the 6-inch shells over the side before they caught fire? Otherwise, they would have blown the stern of the ship off and also damaged HMAS *Yarra*, an Australian sloop which had stuck her nose under the *Asia's* stern, allowing loads of troops to jump on to her foredeck to get away from the flames. I hadn't had any orders to abandon ship at that time. My job was to get back to the bridge and I couldn't get back to the bridge because the whole of the midships section was completely on fire.'

Back on the flying bridge, Captain Smith's position had become untenable. As escape down the ladders was impossible, he instructed all bridge personnel and gunners who had collected there to slide down a rope to the foredeck. Some jumped or fell and broke their legs; the Chief Officer broke both ankles. Meanwhile, the Captain threw a steel box containing confidential documents over the side of the ship before following the others down the rope.

It was then midday and the ship had gradually swung round to a position slightly east of the lighthouse. The entire midships section from bridge to after funnel was ablaze, while the two ends of the ship were packed with troops and crew. Japanese planes circled overhead, but they did not attempt to hamper rescue operations and soon disappeared. The deck was almost too hot to stand on when, with the help of the men, the Captain lowered first one anchor and then the other. Colonel Dean, standing on a bollard, shouted orders for ropes to be lowered and rafts slung over the side to ferry the men to the lighthouse. At the aft of the ship, *Yarra*, captained by Lieutenant-Commander Wilfred Harrington RAN, had moved away to a safe distance after rescuing well over 1,000 troops and crew.

The *Asia's* hospital was cut off below decks by the fire; the medical officer in charge evacuated his patients by pushing them through portholes into the sea. Len Butler says, 'We tried to lower a lifeboat full of wounded men, and the flames were going across our heads and singeing our hair. One of the rope hawsers caught fire and snapped before the lifeboat was in the water. One half of it was still attached to the ship and it was spinning around and tossing the wounded into the sea. Some of them were already burned and scalded, so they had no chance.'

One group of gunners actually jumped from their position on the fiddley deck into the sea. All men forward had to climb down a 60-foot rope into the water, where they were joined by those already in the sea who could not board rafts or rescue craft from the escort vessels. Burning pieces of wreckage fell among the bobbing heads, and exploding small-arms ammunition added to the danger. Exhausted men clambered on to Sultan Shoal, some without shirts, some without shorts and the majority without footwear.[5] Everything in the holds, including the precious tanks and anti-tank guns and small arms and ammunition, was lost. *Empress of Asia* later sank, although her three funnels remained above the water.

'During the attack we had no protection from our own fighters,' Captain Smith says. 'There was not one British plane overhead but I learned later that this deplorable lack of air support was probably due to the fact that at the same time as the attack on the ships, the Japanese were bombing the aerodrome at Singapore and our planes were kept fully occupied in that area. There was no gunfire from the island itself during the attack but our escorts put up a splendid show. Everyone behaved very well indeed. There was no panic, the troops were splendid and everyone did their job.'

Len Butler had gone over the side and swum to Sultan Shoal lighthouse. 'It was covered with so many wounded and survivors that you could hardly stand up,' he remembers. 'In the distance, I could see two heads floating. If you're a swimmer, you can tell whether people can swim or not by the way they lie in the water. I realised these two couldn't swim, so I swam out to them. When I reached them, I found that they were both officers in lifebelts and one of them had a pair of South African brown veldt shoes hanging around his neck. They'd probably cost him a week's wages.

'The currents were very fierce and they took hold of us. Some distance away, I could see about seven heads bobbing up and down, so I told these two officers to hang on to one another and I'd drag them towards the others. We'd been in the water for three hours by then and there were a lot of sharks in that area. We joined the other seven, none of whom could swim. They had lifebelts and were hanging on to some burned-out oars. I told the two officers to grab hold of one of the oars and to paddle their feet up and down as though they were on bicycles to keep the sharks away.

'The sea was like a sheet of glass and there wasn't a ship in sight. The estuary crocodiles of Sumatra grow to 15 feet long and they go out to sea and I was worried we'd encounter one of them. Eventually, this little tugboat came over the horizon and we all started waving and they saw us. It was five o'clock by then, about six hours since the ship had been hit. The tugboat took us to Singapore.'

As they neared Keppel Harbour in the vanishing twilight, an astonishing sight greeted the survivors. Flames from the conflagration along the quayside tinged the tropical night with a blood-red hue, while overhead the pall created by burning oil from the storage tanks on the north shore had been driven seawards where it had merged over the city with clouds of smoke pouring from burning buildings. The docks themselves were in chaos after another bombing raid. Smoke and flames belched from the godowns, and firefighters struggled vainly to quell the infernos. Bodies were trapped in the wreckage of bombed buildings and ambulances fought their way through the traffic to take the latest casualties to hospital.

The sailors were put into a field and sorted into different groups: 'artillerymen to the left, medics to the right and merchant-navy men over here'. There were 135 crew members out of 416 in this batch; the remainder, including Captain Smith, some of his officers and 127 firemen, had landed elsewhere on the island. Butler had stripped off his clothes in the water and was dressed only in a vest. He was given a pair of army trousers. The men were put into lorries and taken to Bidadari camp, which had been vacated by the 5th Norfolks when they moved forward. The only two fatalities in the *Empress of Asia* were a Canadian crewman and a lieutenant in the 125th Anti-Tank Regiment, but many hundreds of men suffered from burns and wounds.

Len Butler and his crewmates were just settling down for the night when a British officer dashed in, revolver drawn, and ordered them out of bed. 'We were issued with a rifle and bayonet and put into the trenches,' Butler says. 'We had just come out of the sea that same night. The island was under martial law and we were semi-fit, I suppose. He had no idea who we were – we were just a bunch of blokes in his camp. We didn't say anything, so he ordered a man into the trench every five yards. As we jumped in, we discovered it was three-quarters filled with water. We were the second line of trenches; the ones in front were manned by an Australian battalion from Sydney. We stayed there all night.'

At 11 a.m. on 6 February Yamashita summoned his senior commanders to his headquarters in Kluang to receive final orders for the attack on Singapore. This would begin at 10 p.m. Tokyo time (8.30 p.m. in Singapore) on 8 February. Units of the 5th and 18th Divisions would go in first with the objective of capturing Tengah airfield, 14 miles from Singapore City in the western half of the island, and the adjacent village of Bukit Panjang. In the second phase, the Imperial Guards would attack the Causeway sector and take Mandai village, then swing eastwards to Nee Soon village to isolate British forces in and around the Naval Base. The next target would be occupation of the high ground at Bukit Timah, to be followed by seizure of the

Seletar, Peirce and MacRitchie reservoirs. With the pipeline across the Causeway broken, Yamashita calculated that Percival would have no alternative but to surrender if he lost control of his water supply.

Nishimura viewed Yamashita's plan to relegate the Imperial Guards to the second phase of the operation as a grave insult. After the meeting, Yamashita consulted his Chief of Staff, General Sosaku Suzuki, a friend of Nishimura, and asked him to settle the problem with the Imperial Guards; however, Suzuki's attempt at peacemaking was rebuffed. The incident merely deepened Yamashita's loathing of the Guards' commander. Late that afternoon he moved his headquarters to the Sultan of Johore's palace at Bukit Serene. From the grand five-storey Moorish tower, he had a bird's eye view of virtually every key target in the northern sector of Singapore Island. He was just a mile from the Australian front line across the water, but he ordered his artillery to intensify its fire on the north-eastern front towards Changi, as part of a plan to deceive Percival into believing that his main attack was coming in that direction.

The Australian gunners could see enemy officers moving about behind the glass panels in the Sultan's tower but were refused permission to fire at them. Bob Goodwin says, 'We were forbidden to fire at the tower despite the fact that the Japanese were directing their fire on us from it. They also had observation from men in a hot-air balloon, but it was out of range of our guns, and our Air Force consisted of seven Hurricanes.' Bennett's explanation to his staff was that the Japanese Command would simply move to another location if the tower was fired on. The real reason was that he had promised Sir Ibrahim that he would not damage his palace.

Lance-Corporal Frank Davies was a gun fitter with the Royal Ordnance Corps. 'We repaired some of the Australians' 25-pounders, gave them new firing pins and breech blocks,' he says. 'The gunners then fired a few shots at some Japs in a gap between the buildings in Johore Bahru.' Russell Savage confirms, 'We tried a few shots to hit trucks at Johore Bahru but then we got strict orders that we were not allowed to shoot at the observation tower because reparations would have to be paid after the war. Some of the Australian officers disobeyed that order and took a few unauthorised pot shots, one of which knocked a hole right through one administrative building.'

Bennett's attention was diverted from the seafront to the makeshift medical arrangements that his Chief Medical Officer had been forced to make after evacuating his two field hospitals to the island. Following a visit to the 2/10th Australian General Hospital at Manor House, Bennett decided to take over several additional houses in the neighbourhood. The AIF casualty clearing station had already moved into the Swiss Rifle Club, a two-storeyed alpine chalet where 40 RAF personnel were living. 'This caused congestion which was unpopular among those who had been living in comparative comfort for so long,' he says.[6] 'My attempt to obtain additional homes for the 2/10th AGH was obstructed by the civilian occupants. They lodged their objection with the Colonial Secretary [Hugh Fraser] who seemed sympathetic towards them.'

The following day while Bennett was visiting his second hospital – the 2/13th AGH at St Patrick's School at Katong on the south coast – Japanese gunfire landed 15 shells on Manor House, killing one patient and wounding others. The nurses were cool and courageous throughout the shelling, neglecting their own safety to protect their patients. 'These nurses are the nearest things to angels I can imagine,' Bennett says. 'They never quarrel among themselves. They devote themselves wholeheartedly to their heavy task, frequently working continuously for over 24 hours to deal with a rush of casualties. They never complain and always have a smile and a kindly word for our wounded and sick men.'

Bennett interrupted Percival at Fort Canning to demand occupancy of the homes. Percival sent a staff officer to investigate and then agreed to sign a requisition order. 'I regretted my impatience afterwards as General Percival is always so well disposed to me and the AIF,' Bennett says. 'He has always endeavoured to comply with our wants.'

In fact, Percival's concentration was focused on enemy activity opposite the Naval Base, which seemed to confirm his belief that the main Japanese attack would fall on the eastern shore of the island. The Imperial Guards Division had been busy driving empty lorries backwards and forwards between Johore Bahru and dummy camps opposite Ubin Island, the granite outcrop opposite the 54th Brigade's area, to give the impression of a large military build-up. A force of 400 Guards then allowed themselves to be seen boarding noisy motor boats in which they proceeded to occupy the island. The attack was a feint and Percival, who desperately wanted to believe that the invasion would take place in that sector, was completely fooled. Early on 8 February, he informed Wavell at his headquarters in Lembang, 'Present indications show main enemy strength north of Ubin Island.'

Meanwhile, Len Butler and other survivors of *Empress of Asia* had been in the trenches for two days when an officer from the Malayan Medical Corps arrived at Bidadari camp looking for volunteers. 'He pulled us out of the trenches, sat us in a circle and gave us a speech to say the hospitals were heaving with wounded and they had no orderlies to give them water or to change their bandages,' Butler says. 'I'd never done dressings on a badly wounded man, and the only dead body I'd seen was my grandmother in the front parlour. They said the situation was quite desperate and wanted us to sign up to be part of the Malayan Medical Service. Every one of us signed up for a dollar a day, which was 2s. 4d. in those days. My group was put into lorries and taken down to Singapore General Hospital.'

In the early hours of 8 February, two Australian patrols, one from the 2/20th and one from the 2/19th, returned from Johore after a 24-hour reconnaissance in enemy territory, to report that there were Japanese gun emplacements every 50 yards as far as the eye could see going back into the rubber inland from the Perepat, Malayu and Skudai rivers. Each gun was dug into a pit and camouflaged. There were few boats or troops to be seen, but large kitchens had been constructed to feed an army. The report did not alarm Brigadier Taylor. He says, 'The patrols which came back on the night of the 7/8th had spent 24 hours behind the Japanese lines and pinpointed their headquarters, vehicle parks and other details. They did not, however, find any means by which the Japanese might cross the straits.'[7]

Taylor failed to appreciate that the Japanese troops had gone to fetch their boats and were carrying them to suitable points on the Johore waterways. Gordon Bennett says he received the patrol reports from Taylor during the morning and 'ordered the artillery to concentrate fire on the enemy'. Taylor, however, says there was no fire from the Australian guns, and Bennett's Chief of Staff, Colonel Jim Thyer, says it did not 'enter anybody's head to order harassing fire'. Furthermore, Bennett says that Percival was 'pleased with the work of these patrols' when he paid a visit to divisional headquarters later that day.[8] According to General Kirby, Bennett did not know the contents of the patrol report when Percival arrived at midday, and it was not until 3.30 p.m. that a copy reached Malaya Command, where it was disregarded as being of no particular significance.[9]

Percival persisted in his belief that the eastern shore was the prime Japanese target long after enemy gunners started hammering the fronts of the 22nd Australian and 44th Indian Brigades with a merciless barrage. It had started at dawn on 8 February and, apart from two brief intervals, lasted for 15 hours. Lieutenant-Colonel Varley of the 2/18th Battalion, a veteran of the World War I trenches, says, 'During my four years' service 1914–1918 I never experienced such concentrated shell fire over such a period.'[10] The troops were scattered over so vast an area of undulating ground interspersed with mangrove swamps and eight-foot high *belukar* (or secondary jungle) that casualties were light, but nevertheless they began to mount up.

There was a 40-minute lull at 12.50 p.m. when the Japanese gunners stopped, presumably for lunch. On the 22nd Brigade front, carrying parties from B Echelon dashed forward with hot boxes containing thick stew, bread and jam, two pastry turnovers and two bananas per man. The soldiers had time to eat their lunch in peace before the Japanese gunners resumed heavy artillery fire at 1.30 p.m.

Telephone communications had been repeatedly cut during the day, and signal linesmen were fighting a losing battle to repair them. The forward companies had been issued with reconditioned radios but were forbidden to use them – a senseless order considering that the Japanese knew exactly where the Australian units were dug in. The men could see Japanese pilots circling overhead in reconnaissance planes. They also knew from footprints in the mud that Japanese swimmers had crept ashore and, posing as Malays or Chinese, had spent hours pinpointing Australian and Indian positions before swimming back to Johore.

Showery rain during the morning had turned into a deluge which reduced visibility to a few yards. Ian Morrison made his way through a mangrove swamp to visit Dalforce, which was located to the right of the 2/20th on the Straits of Johore. Following the loss of *Empress of Asia*, the Chinese had been armed with a motley collection of weapons, including sporting rifles and shotguns, and had been issued with only seven rounds of ammunition per man. Nevertheless, they impressed Morrison with their cheerfulness and fortitude under fire. 'It was pouring with rain and while we were talking to the Chinese it suddenly began to lighten and thunder,' he says. 'The uproar was enough as it was without the heavens also taking part in it.'[11]

The rain continued until nightfall, leaving soldiers all over the front soaking wet, cold and miserable in slit trenches filled with rainwater. Colonel Varley had stationed three of the 2/18th's companies forward, with one in reserve. Each company had an extra platoon comprised of pioneers, anti-aircraft and administrative staff. The 30th Battery of the 2/15th Field Regiment was to provide artillery support on a given signal, and two anti-tank guns had been placed on the coast to fire over open sights at enemy landing craft.

The Australian battalions were so widely dispersed and visibility through the broken terrain so poor that there was no chance of platoons, let alone companies, making visual contact with one another. The 2/19th's Official History says, 'Even if we had been able to hear a voice from another section post or Platoon HQ or Company HQ over a telephone line, it would have helped no end, but the long periods of being completely cut off were proving a nightmare.'[12]

Then Colonel Robertson, concerned about the damage caused by the Japanese shell fire, decided to change the position of battalion headquarters. Despite the 'heated and vehement' opposition of his staff officers, he selected low-lying ground overlooked on three sides, with a river at its back. At 6.30 p.m. the men had to make their way to this location in the dark and then dig new positions. Colonel Anderson later wrote, 'I am quite certain a profound difference would have taken place had Robertson not changed the battalion position. It was most carefully chosen and the only position at all favourable and astride the most likely route of advance open to the enemy; [it was] very sad.'[13]

After a lull at sunset, the Japanese bombardment continued with increased intensity, with more guns than ever being employed. Field guns each received 1,000 rounds and heavy batteries 500 rounds. The Official Historian says no order was given that evening for artillery fire to be brought down on the probable enemy forming-up areas by either Malaya Command or Western Area Headquarters. They seemed to believe that the Japanese bombardment was the first of several days of softening up and that the enemy would probably switch the gunfire back to the Causeway and north-east shore the following day.[14]

The Japanese were in high spirits. Over the past 55 days, they had advanced an average of 12 miles a day, fought two battles and repaired at least four bridges to reach the southern tip of the Malay peninsula. Their casualty figures were comparatively light, with 1,793 dead and 2,772 wounded. Under Yamashita's timetable, the Japanese should have completed the crossing of the straits by midday on 7 February, which would have given them four days to conquer Singapore Island in time for *Kigensetsu* on 11 February. However, they were running a day late in their preparations and Yamashita, overruling the complaints of his General Staff, granted divisional commanders an extra 24 hours to bring their collapsible boats overland along jungle paths to join armour-plated barges and motor launches which had quietly slipped into secret harbours on the Skudai, Malayu and Perepat rivers. The Japanese avoided embarkation points marked on British maps and had constructed new jetties in unlikely locations.

Finally at sunset on 8 February the vast armada of small boats had been assembled and the boarding of the 5th and 18th Divisions began.[15] But the tide was going out, and some of the embarkation points had been fixed too far into the water to prevent the boats from going aground. Soldiers slipped in the mud and floundered in the water as they tried to climb into their landing craft. Some boats drifted away, others capsized; guns and equipment were lost. Nevertheless, at 8.30 p.m. the first flight of 150 boats reached the wide mouth of the Skudai River and fanned out in the Straits of Johore. It would take them just six minutes to cross Churchill's 'splendid moat'.

CHAPTER 19

North Shore Nightmare

HALF AN HOUR EARLIER John McGrory and Cliff Olsen, two young privates in C Company 2/18th Battalion, were under heavy bombardment on Singapore's western shore and thinking things couldn't get any worse. Shells were landing around them at the rate of one every five seconds. 'It was real 1918 stuff,' Olsen says. All the two Australians could see in the dark were the vague outlines of rubber trees and a wall of undergrowth. 'My battalion was covering a frontage of three miles,' McGrory says. 'All I had was a .303 rifle, but some fellows had tommy-guns or Lewis guns, and four Vickers machine guns had been spaced through the companies close to the shore.'

Cliff Olsen was a Lewis gunner. He and his number two were stationed 400 yards from the shoreline in the same section as McGrory, but the men were spread out so thinly that it was impossible to keep in touch. 'We were 50 yards from anybody else,' Olsen recalls. 'Our company was in front of the mortars and it was our job to protect the guns. The trouble was, it was so dark we couldn't see anything.'[1]

Sergeant Mervyn Blyth of the Mortar Platoon was in an observation post on a hill adjacent to the platoon's four mortars. 'I was with Private Joe Forsyth and we had had time to dig a slit trench, but the shelling was so severe that our communications were shot to pieces,' he says. 'They really gave us heaps. My rifle and our wireless were both destroyed and we had no telephone. One shell landed so close that I could put my hand into the shell hole. It was a real bloody shambles – nothing went right.'[2]

At 8.15 p.m. the enemy bombardment increased in intensity from heavy to drumfire when all 168 Japanese guns opened up simultaneously. Almost the whole of the north-west shoreline was saturated with shell fire; in one sector, shells were falling at the rate of 100 per minute. Australians in the forward posts could actually see the muzzle flashes of some of the Japanese guns on the high ground opposite. Private Paul Gemmell of D Company 2/18th says, 'Don Company received the heaviest shelling since the Somme, according to the record books. There weren't any trenches in my area – we didn't have any entrenching tools. Most of that time I was crouching in a drain on a rubber estate.'[3]

After 15 minutes, the barrage lifted from the seafront and crept back towards the rear areas, where headquarters, the regimental aid posts and the artillery were located. For the first time that night, the men were able to listen for the sound of approaching craft. Drenched to the bone and isolated in their dugouts or sheltering behind hastily erected breastworks, they strained for the tell-tale sound of engines. The moon had yet to rise, but flashes of firelight from the burning fuel tanks at Kranji illuminated the skeletal branches of the shell-blasted trees along the waterfront, casting patches of light on the dark waters.

The Japanese had allocated 16 battalions, with five more in reserve, to attack the three Australian battalions of the 22nd Brigade. Yamashita's intention was that the attack be concentrated on just two of the battalions, the 2/18th and the 2/20th. The 5th and 18th Divisions had each been given 150 craft – 50 barges and 100 collapsible boats – capable of shifting a total of 4,000 men across the straits at any one time. The defenders numbered fewer than 3,000, with no adequate reserves to back them up and an open road to Singapore behind them. It was the most one-sided contest of the campaign.

B Company of the 2/19th Battalion broke radio silence to report to battalion headquarters that tiny dots could be discerned against the backdrop of the far shore and that the murmur of distant engines could be heard. Then the dots grew larger and gradually became recognisable as barges and other landing craft, some of which were being rowed by softly dipped oars, some driven by engines, some in tow, a few faster ones heading for pre-selected weak points. B Company counted 50 craft heading towards their position.

In the middle of the 2/20th's section, Captain Rod Richardson's D Company was even closer to the craft heading their way from the Skudai and Malayu rivers. As the engine sounds grew louder, Colin Nicol fired a burst from his Bren gun as a signal that the invasion had begun. The Japanese had been spotted when they were about halfway across the strait and Lieutenant M. E. Wankey, platoon commander of the 2/4th Machine Gun Battalion, ordered his four gunners to hold fire until the barges were within 30 to 50 yards of the foreshore.[4]

'Sergeant Jim O'Rourke and three or four men of the Mortar Platoon were in an observation post at the water's edge,' recalls Frank Baker, a 21-year-old member of the platoon. 'When one of the men became ill, they sent him back and I was told to go forward to take his place. It was rather a leery journey through the shelling but I got to the slit trench and stayed there.' The position was at the end of Lim Chu Kang Road, which had been designated by Yamashita one of the main targets for his 5th Division.

'One of the Vickers machine gunners near us on the water's edge had his arm just about blown off by shrapnel and I went down to help him,' Baker says. 'I had had some medical experience with the 10th Australian General Hospital before transferring to the 2/20th, but his sleeve was just a bag of mincemeat and I couldn't do anything for him. I lay down beside him and tried to keep still because the guns were still firing at us. Then the observation balloon above the straits sent over two flares, one red and one orange, which lit up the whole area. As they came over, the wounded man moved and the Japanese fired at us with a Bofors gun on low trajectory. This was as their troops were coming across under cover of darkness. I didn't feel any fear, I didn't have any worries. I was so busy staying alive that everything passed me by, including the bullets.'[5]

In the leading craft, Japanese troops fired into the shore positions with small arms, while mortars set at a fixed elevation provided a curtain of spray, which gradually crept forward as the boats approached the Australian section posts until the bombs were exploding among them. It was at that moment that the Vickers machine guns opened fire 'in a steady rhythmic beat, solid and continuous, the crackling small arms non-stop, the mortars adding to the fire bursts'.[6]

The machine gunners were credited with sinking several of the leading craft and capsizing others. Machine-gun bullets struck sparks off armour-plating, while steel-helmeted Japanese soldiers were sprayed with fire in the water. The first wave was repelled from this position and the landing craft probed for a gap in the line further west.[7]

Many of the searchlights had been blasted out of existence, while others remained inactive because the order to switch them on was never given. Percival says in his Dispatch that this disadvantage 'was countered to some extent by the illumination provided by burning ammunition barges'. Such light was sporadic, however, and in those frantic first few minutes of the Japanese invasion the Australians had to rely on flares fired from Very pistols. In the absence of any other form of communication the flares were intended to bring down artillery fire on enemy landing craft, but they also provided the main source of light.

The 2/15th Field Regiment had spent all week registering their zones of fire and could pinpoint any section of coast. Yet the seconds ticked by and there appeared to be no response from the guns. Desperately, the men of the

2/19th used their radios to call in mortar fire from the battalion's 3-inch mortars. Accurate rapid fire hit several landing craft but there were too many of them for the oncoming rush to be prevented.[8]

The first Japanese troops swarmed ashore at 8.45 p.m., and over the next 60 minutes the whole of the front between the Buloh River and the right-hand company of the 2/19th Battalion was under attack. As the first and second flights of barges reached the 2/19th's section posts they were blasted by heavy fire, but they kept coming and figures could be seen jumping ashore. The Vickers guns cut many of the invaders to ribbons, but still the craft kept coming and Japanese troops managed to close on the 2/19th's section posts and weapon pits. The men in these positions held their own for about 15 minutes but were soon overrun. The Japanese then began to vanish inland under cover of the scrub, trees and darkness.[9]

The fire from the 2/19th had forced many of the barges to swing into the mouth of the Murai River on the left of the 2/18th's position, thus creating a gap between the two battalions. Over the next hour, two full-scale attacks were launched against the 2/18th, one on the right against Captain John-stone's A Company and the other on the left against Captain Okey's C Company. Armed with a tommy-gun on the water's edge, Arthur Cobcroft was the battalion's first man in action, while the four Vickers machine guns of the 2/4th in that section then opened fire. 'They did a magnificent job,' says one of the men. 'They kept firing, and firing, and firing, until they were just blotted out – the whole six or seven of them on the guns.'[10]

Having overrun the forward positions, the enemy dashed past the troops situated at the inland positions. 'All I could see was bush and shrubs and Japs,' John McGrory of C Company says. 'They came towards me in the dark, with bits of trees and shrubs tucked into their webbing for camou-flage. They had burst through the company in front of us – just swamped them with numbers. We tried to stop them but they kept on coming. We were shooting madly and still they were coming.'

Cliff Olsen remembers, 'You could hear them heading towards us – they were singing out and all this sort of nonsense – but we were horribly spread out and it was pitch black and they were very hard to see. They walked through us half the time.'

The boat carrying machine gunner Ochi Harumi of the 5th Division hit the foreshore at Buloh River between Dalforce and A Company of the 2/20th Battalion. Japanese soldiers leaped ashore and tackled the defenders with cries of 'Fix bayonets! Attack!' Harumi says the killing on the shore was frenzied, with the Japanese darting at the enemy 'like rabid dogs' and goring anyone in their path with the bayonet.[11] Some craft attempted to enter the mouth of the river but were driven off. Infantryman Maseo Maeda says Japanese casualties were high: 'I was among the first troops who landed. Only one-third of us made it through.'[12]

One of the 2/20th's sections comprised Lieutenant Bill Reid's Pioneers and a group of Bandsmen whose normal function in action was to act as stretcher-bearers for the wounded. Tonight, they were armed with Lewis guns of World War I vintage and while they poured fire into the approaching craft, Reid hurled grenades into their midst. Screams could be heard; some Japanese jumped overboard and tried to swim ashore. Reid grabbed a Lewis gun and fired into the barges, but the muzzle flash gave him away and he was shot dead.

Frank Baker says, 'I had a .303 rifle and we had a few tommy-guns but the Japs all seemed to be armed with automatic weapons. The shocking thing was that in our briefings we had been told their armaments were inferior to ours and their grenades were just toys. In fact, they were well ahead of us.'

Back at brigade headquarters east of Tengah airfield, Brigadier Taylor tried to make sense of the scrambled bits of information reaching him from the front. With telephone communications cut and his signals staff still observing radio silence, Taylor received the first coherent report of the Japanese attack when Captain Arthur Ewart of the 2/20th arrived from the front on his motor bike at 9 p.m. Taylor learned that the Japanese had streamed ashore in their thousands and that it would take a concerted counterattack to dislodge them. As he had no reserve with which to make such an attack, Taylor ordered Ewart to return to battalion headquarters and instruct the CO, Colonel Charles F. Assheton, to form a perimeter and, if hard pressed, to fall back on 2/18th headquarters near Ama Keng village. This was the key point between the headwaters of the Kranji and Berih Rivers on the route to Tengah airfield.

Meanwhile, frantic signallers used their Lucas lamps to flash a prearranged message to the guns at the rear – 'Landings CDF', 'Landings CDF' – but still there was no noticeable reply from the artillery.[13] It was then 9.45 p.m. Lieutenant Holloway, the senior artillery forward observation officer, was in despair. He kept saying, 'We train and practise for years and now we get nothing.' It seemed incredible that the sounds of battle could not be heard several miles inland where the guns were sited, but the noise was lost in the hail of exploding Japanese shells.[14]

The Official Australian Historian's version says the batteries of the 2/15th

Field Regiment *had* opened fire but had no chance of keeping up with the calls that started flooding in. One request through a liaison officer had been to 'bring down fire everywhere'.[15] The gunners themselves say that they did nothing else but fire after the first Very lights went up, expending 4,824 rounds before dawn.[16]

Armed with a tommy-gun, Paul Gemmell of the 2/18th was with his company at the mid-point of the Lim Chu Kang Road. 'My battalion took the full force of the landing along with the 2/20th,' he says. 'We went up to meet the Japanese but they were already behind us. It was absolutely chaotic.'

Merv Blyth and Joe Forsyth had crossed a creek and made their way back to the mortar section 'but by this time the Japs had well and truly landed on our frontage', he says. 'To cap it all, the cartridges that trip the mortars off had got wet in the rain and many of them didn't work. We got a few shells away but by that time the Japanese were passing through us and we had to get out.'

Lieutenant John Fuller, the platoon commander, ordered his men to fall back to battalion headquarters near Ama Keng village. Heavy losses were sustained in the withdrawal. 'One section of mortars was on a little island in the middle of a swamp and they had to get back across the water,' Blyth says. 'They lost quite a few men. A large number of our fellows were still behind the lines; it was two days before my brother got through.'

The anti-tank gunners at the water's edge on Lim Chu Kang Road sank three craft and damaged others before their gun was put out of action. One of the gunners then rolled grenades down under the embankment on top of the Japanese who had swum ashore. The Vickers gunners in the 2/18th's position had fired 10,000 rounds per gun when Lieutenant Wankey ordered the guns to be destroyed and, arming the men with rifles and bayonets, set off as a fighting patrol. He was badly wounded in the next engagement and was evacuated to company headquarters.

General Bennett had retired for the night at his bungalow near Bukit Timah village and did not realise that anything was amiss until 11 p.m. when he was awoken by the noise of the encroaching bombardment. 'Very perturbed', he got out of bed and rang Major Cecil Dawkins, the duty officer at his headquarters on the Hillview Estate on Jurong Road north-west of Bukit Timah village. Dawkins had no idea what was happening on the beachfront but contacted 22nd Brigade headquarters, who told him that all telephone lines to forward posts had been cut by shell fire. 'As Dawkins did not seem to be worried even after contact with the brigade, I thought my concern over the unusual shelling was needless,' Bennett says. 'So I returned to my couch again.'[17]

However, the AIF commander could not sleep; he got up, dressed and summoned his Kent-born aide-de-camp, Lieutenant Gordon Walker, to drive him to the 8th Division operations room. Reports were trickling in that the 18th and 20th Battalions had been in action against Japanese forces. At 11.30 he received a phone call from Taylor informing him that the Japanese had landed on the west coast and had achieved considerable inland penetration. Taylor estimated the enemy's strength at six battalions and pointed out that he had no reserve with which to launch a counter-attack.[18]

Meanwhile, Yamashita watched the invasion from the Sultan's tower. He had no communication with his front-line units, and it was impossible to judge the progress of the battle from the disjointed bursts of gunfire and firelight that emanated from Singapore Island. But his anxiety lifted at midnight when a red star-shell burst over the straits in front of the palace. This was the signal confirming that the 5th Division was firmly established on Singapore soil. It was followed a few moments later by a white star-shell which indicated that the 18th Division had also gained a bridgehead on the island.

The battle was going better than Yamashita had dared to hope. 'By midnight, it was obvious that the Japs were getting ashore through the undefended sectors between the companies, and were pressing on our flanks,' Captain Richardson says.[19] Between 1 a.m. and 3 a.m. the commanders of all three Australian battalions ordered their forward troops to withdraw to battalion perimeters in accordance with Taylor's orders. This difficult manoeuvre had to be conducted in darkness over broken country while many units were engaged at close quarters with the enemy.

Three companies of the 2/20th Battalion were concentrated in the Namazie Estate two miles north of Ama Keng village but the fourth company, which had received no orders, remained in its forward position. The 2/18th Battalion was also closely engaged with the enemy and only about half of their number reached their perimeter at Ama Keng. Three companies of the 2/19th Battalion fought their way back, while A Company remained in position at Choa Chu Kang to the east of Tengah airfield. The withdrawals had disrupted the whole brigade area, but the fact that two companies were still in their original positions gives the lie to post-war suggestions that the Australians had broken and fled from the battlefield.[20]

Shell fire had set Ama Keng village ablaze and it acted as a beacon for the enemy on their way to Tengah airfield. Captain Richardson says, 'At the Tengah fighter strip, contact was made with Battalion Headquarters and some artillery fire was brought down at last on the waterfront. The Australians could hear the Japanese screaming as it fell among them. For the previous three hours I had been asking for artillery but to no avail.'

Several members of Dalforce had reached the south-west section of the perimeter and taken shelter in a hut. But the sight of Asians bearing arms aroused the suspicions of a 2/20th platoon who had no idea that Chinese were fighting with the 22nd Brigade. Brian Flanagan, the company marksmen, armed himself with a Bren gun and crept through the *lalang* to within 20 feet of the hut. He saw an Asian dressed in a sarong and holding a gun by the muzzle, with the butt on the ground.

Sergeant MacDougal called on the man to drop his rifle; when he failed to respond to the order three times Flanagan was ordered to shoot him. The man dropped to the floor of the hut with the first burst, and MacDougal ordered the hut to be sprayed with fire.

An officer ran up to the Australians and in a Scottish accent demanded, 'Why the bloody hell are you shooting there – they are my men!' Putting a khaki handkerchief over his torch, the officer walked over to the first Chinese. Then he said, 'You've shot my leader!'

Brian Flanagan then discovered that the man was a Chinese irregular fighting with Dalforce. 'It made me sick in the stomach to think we were killing our own men,' he says.[21]

Flanagan made amends when his section spotted a group of Japanese 200 yards ahead in the long grass. Bobby Addison fired a few shots with his Bren gun – but then it jammed. The Japanese yelled out, 'Don't shoot, Aussie – Punjabi coming through ... Don't shoot, Aussie – Punjabi coming through your lines!' This time there was no doubt about the identity of the enemy, and Flanagan instructed his men to 'shoot straight and shoot often'. Several members of the Japanese group were killed or wounded, and the firing continued until mortar fire was brought in against the Australians.[22]

Yamashita had walked down to the Straits of Johore in front of the palace to take a closer look at the 5th Division's boats which were shuttling men from the Skudai River to Singapore. By 4 a.m. he felt confident that the invasion was proceeding according to plan and, having ordered his air force to attack the Australian positions at first light, he went to bed.

Japanese sources say that 13,000 troops were landed on the north-west shore during the night and a further 10,000 soon after dawn. The defenders were so heavily outnumbered that defeat was inevitable. 'The enemy landing craft in the first flight were in many cases sunk or beaten off by the Forward Defended Localities and the machine guns,' Percival says, 'but they were quickly followed by others and the enemy succeeded in landing at many points. Very heavy and, in many areas, fierce hand-to-hand fighting developed. Some of the machine guns continued fighting until their ammunition was practically exhausted. Unfortunately, it appears that the SOS calls for artillery support were not answered until some time after the attack started. This was due partly to the inadequacy of Very light signals in that close country, partly to the severing of cable communications by the enemy's bombardment and partly to a failure to make full use of wireless telegraph. When the artillery fire did come down, however, it was maintained, within the limits of the resources available, at a high level throughout the night and must have done considerable damage.'

Meanwhile, Frank Baker had managed to extricate himself from the forward position on the seafront and had moved back with two mortars to battalion headquarters. 'Dawn had just broken,' he says. 'We got our orders to fire and we kept firing until we ran out of ammo – we fired about 300 bombs.' At 9 a.m. Colonel Assheton ordered his men to move south and link up with the 2/18th at Ama Keng, but when they arrived at 7.30 a.m. they found the village occupied by the enemy. The remnants of 2/18th had been attacked shortly after dawn and, after fierce fighting in which the gunners of the 2/10th Field Regiment distinguished themselves, had been forced to withdraw to Tengah airfield.

Colonel Assheton went forward with three Bren gunners to attack the enemy. 'He stood up to encourage the troops as much as possible,' Baker remembers. 'He was in clear view with his map cases hanging from him and directed the troops individually. C Company were in a bit of a mess after being attacked but they were getting stuck in and he was urging them on. Shortly afterwards, he was shot. I saw him lying there with his map cases on top of him.'

The Japanese attacked the 2/20th again, but the Bren gunners held them off long enough to give the men a chance to withdraw towards Bukit Panjang village to the east of Tengah airfield. The battalion was split up into isolated parties, however, some of which crossed the Kranji River and reached brigade headquarters at its new position at Bulim, west of Bukit Panjong. 'I crossed the airfield and got lost, crossed a river with all my gear on and nearly drowned and then was fished out,' Frank Baker says. 'I was trying to find my way back to my battalion when I came across a British

Army mess parade. One fellow looked at me and asked what had happened. I was covered in mud and oil. I said we'd been fighting the Japanese all night. He said, "Are they on the island?" That's how bad communications were.'

Further south, the remnants of the 2/19th Battalion had found themselves surrounded and, in breaking out, suffered heavy losses. Only scattered parties eventually reached Tengah airfield, at around 10 a.m. It was the same for the 2/18th. 'The Japanese were passing us as we were heading back to battalion headquarters,' Merv Blyth recalls. 'We didn't stay there very long before we were pulled back to the airfield. Then we were split up. It was a terrible night.' Cliff Olsen says, 'We were rushed from here to there and put in front of the mortar guns, and then there was a mob of them coming down the road on bicycles, so we raced up to the road to get clear.'

Paul Gemmell opened fire with his tommy-gun as D Company got to a creek on the way back to Tengah airfield and encountered 'huge numbers' of enemy troops. 'We formed a rough perimeter in the hedgerows around the airport but it didn't last five minutes,' he says. 'There were thousands of them and we were just a company. But the battalion held together pretty well.'

Since midnight, men from all three battalions had become detached from their units during the savage fighting or had lost their bearings in the rugged terrain. Some were collected and taken back to the General Base Depot, where they were refitted and reorganised; others made their way into Singapore City in search of food and rest at the Anzac Club, which was the only collection point for stragglers at that time. Many in this latter category were young reinforcements who had just experienced their first taste of warfare and were shellshocked, confused and frightened. Bob Goodwin says, 'Many of our troops were young reinforcements – kids of 16, 17 or 18 who had never held a rifle in their hands and suddenly found they were in the front line with 16 Japanese battalions coming across. They did a wonderful job in the circumstances. They were in the dark with shells landing everywhere and many of them had no idea of even how to handle their rifle.'

'The action of these men must be judged in relation to the existing conditions,' Percival says. 'They were not long-service soldiers and discipline was not deep-rooted. They had volunteered for service and had been sent to Malaya to defend the Naval Base. The Naval Base was no longer of any use but Australia, their homeland, was being threatened. Many of them belonged to units which, after sustaining heavy casualties on the mainland, had been reorganised but had had no time to regain their full fighting efficiency. They had fought well throughout a long night against heavy odds and were exhausted. This is the true picture and should be judged on its merits.'

Bennett had had a sleepless night. He had ordered the 2/29th Battalion to move from the 27th Brigade into the Tengah area and come under Taylor's command with a view to counterattacking the Japanese in the morning. But the battalion was widely dispersed and did not reach Tengah until 6 a.m. Bennett ordered Taylor to use the 2/29th to recapture Ama Keng village as soon as possible. The enemy, however, had been strongly re-inforced and launched an attack on the airfield around Taylor's right flank. He was forced to cancel his instruction for the 2/29th to attack, and go on the defensive.

Paul Gemmell says, 'The whole thing was a foul-up from start to finish. General Percival had been advised that the Japanese would land on the west coast, so he sent all his troops to the east. We felt we could have held them and then pushed them off the island with reinforcements, but the mentality was such that there was no way it was going to happen. We felt betrayed.'

Asked after the war whether he thought there had been any chance of holding the Western Area, Brigadier Taylor replied, 'In my mind, none.'[23] John Wyett says, 'We put up a jolly good show when you analyse it. Our little force suffered more casualties in battle than anyone else and it wasn't a bad effort.'

CHAPTER 20

Battle for Singapore

WORD OF THE BATTLE for Singapore – the battle that had been lost in the sweltering jungles and dripping rubber plantations of Johore but still had to be fought out to the last drop of blood on the island itself – hit Singapore City at 8.25 a.m. on the morning of 9 February, when Ian Fitchett, the official Australian war correspondent, burst into the press room in the Cathay Building with the news that the Japanese had landed on the north-west shore during the night. Five minutes later, in the Malaya Broadcasting studio upstairs, Rohan Rivett, who had received a brief communiqué from Malaya Command, broke the sensational news to the island's startled population. Offensive action, the public were assured, was being taken to 'mop up' the enemy, as though the Japanese were some sort of stain on the island's pristine beaches. Singaporeans noted grimly that the same 'mopping up' phrase had been used when the enemy had first landed at Kota Bahru.[1]

Two hours later, Fitchett, Rivett, Ian Morrison and Harry Stokes of the BBC presented themselves at Gordon Bennett's headquarters on Jurong Road. The area had just been carpet-bombed and there were huge craters in the road north of Bukit Timah Hill. 'We could see many Japanese dive-bombers operating over the Straits of Johore and over the western half of the island,' Morrison says. 'Shells were falling on the outskirts of Singapore City.'[2]

Realising it was too late for platitudes, Bennett came straight to the point. There was no possibility of preventing the Japanese from reinforcing their bridgehead, he said, or from extending it each night along the northern shore of the island. After a titanic struggle with the official censor, journalists were permitted to file reports to their newspapers telling of severe enemy shelling of the Australians' forward positions, of the tremendous crescendo of gunfire after darkness had fallen, of the many craft being seen crossing the straits, of the desperate fighting on the shore and of a successful withdrawal by the Australian troops to a stronger line further inland which was now being defended.

Percival had spent the night in his office next to the Operations Room at Sime Road, its wooden walls covered with maps and charts, its nicotine-stained desks piled high with the detritus of the previous month's shattering reverses. In the small hours, he had informed the Governor of the invasion and had then spoken to Gordon Bennett about reinforcements. When he had finally turned in, his sleep had been disturbed by the constant hubbub of whirring fans, clattering typewriters, the urgent shrill of telephones, the raising of voices desperately trying to maintain contact down failing connections and, in the distance, the ominous thudding of the artillery.

After receiving reports from all brigades in the morning, Percival still seemed reluctant to believe that no attack was likely to develop against the Northern Area. Leaving all of his formations there intact, he ordered the 12th Indian Brigade from the Command Reserve to move to the Bukit Panjang area at the junction of Woodlands and Choa Chu Kang roads and come under Bennett's command. This brigade now consisted of the 2nd Argyll and Sutherland Highlanders – 460 strong with the addition of 210 Royal Marines from *Prince of Wales* and *Repulse* and now known as the Plymouth Argylls[3] – and the 400-strong 4/19th Hyderabads. Considering the magnitude of threat developing on the west coast, it was a miserly response: fewer than a thousand men to help the Australians halt the Japanese advance, while the bulk of the British Army awaited Percival's phantom army on the north shore.

The GOC's mind, however, was on other matters. He cabled Wavell, 'Enemy landed in force on west coast last night and has penetrated about five miles. Situation is undoubtedly serious in view of the very extended coastline which we have to watch. Have made plan for concentrating forces to cover Singapore [City] if this becomes necessary.' At a time when he should have been devoting all his energies to dealing with the danger in the west, Percival was planning a last-ditch stand. If the Japanese broke through, his forces would hold a tight arc embracing Kallang airfield, MacRitchie and Peirce reservoirs and the food, fuel and munitions dumps and depots in Bukit Timah area.

All through the daylight hours of 9 February, the one remaining squadron of Hurricane fighters harried the enemy on the west coast, inflicting damage on Japanese planes supporting the invasion, but also suffering losses themselves. Tengah airfield fell into Japanese hands in the afternoon, giving Yamashita his first objective on the island. Colonel Tsuji noted that he found fresh bread and soup on the mess tables, and other signs of a hasty retreat.[4] The loss of Tengah left Kallang as the only serviceable air base on the island, but it had fared no better than the others. The airport hotel and the control tower had been reduced to a mass of blasted concrete and twisted girders, while the cratered runways were littered with piles of junk which had once been Buffalo and Hudson aircraft. Percival gave his consent for Pulford to withdraw the last of the Hurricanes to Sumatra. From then on, no British aircraft were seen in the skies over Singapore. Percival, however, absolved the Air Force of all blame. 'They did their willing best,' he says, 'and it was no fault of theirs that it was a poor best.'[5]

The pressure had become too much for Conway Pulford, whose staff had laboured impossibly long hours for eight weeks alongside Malaya Command in the long wooden hut, trying to keep his embattled force in the air. The Air Force commander had finally cracked. 'I was shocked at his appearance,' cipher clerk Muriel Reilly says. 'He was obviously in a state of great nervous tension – almost mental it appeared to me – and he kept walking up and down the room, muttering to himself and thumping tables and chairs as he passed, and every now and then stopping in front of me and saying, "This is a dreadful business – this is a dreadful state of affairs – the whole show is damnable – utterly damnable. An Air Force with no planes and no aerodromes – what the hell are we to do? What can we do?"'[6]

There was little Percival could do to comfort his friend. He had already suggested that Pulford evacuate the island, but Pulford had declined to go; he would, he said, stick it out with Percival to the bitter end. Most of that day was spent organising the transfer of Malaya Command's operational headquarters from Sime Road to Fort Canning, where some of Percival's staff would occupy the air-conditioned, bomb-proof concrete bunker known as the Battle Box.

Lieutenant Alan Lewis of the 1st Cambridgeshires had been summoned to Fort Canning to become a junior staff officer. 'The first blow was to lose my platoon, which I had trained with for 18 months,' he says, 'but my commanding officer, Colonel 'Chips' Carpenter, had decided I should join the battalion's first-line reinforcement platoon and then I was made GSO3. I thought it was ridiculous but it may well have saved my life because the casualties with the first-line reinforcements were quite heavy. I was given some rather spartan accommodation at Fort Canning and reported for duty. I was completely out of my depth and felt rather useless. I had to visit various units and once I took a message to Government House on behalf of the Commander – all sorts of bloody stupid things.

'We were at the receiving end of fairly horrifying news as one day followed another – and there weren't very many days. The atmosphere was one of increasing depression. I saw a little bit of Percival. He had moved out of Fort Canning but that didn't stop him coming back. He was tall and thin and had the misfortune to be rather notably chinless, which unfortunately led to people ascribing to him a certain chinlessness in character. He wasn't like that – there was no lack of guts. The most disappointing feature was that there was no suggestion of dynamism.'[7]

Captain Smith, the *Empress of Asia*'s master, was in Singapore City on 9 February sorting out passage home for members of his crew who had not joined the Malayan Medical Service. 'Business in the city carried on much as usual, the population appearing confident that the situation was well in hand and that the enemy would be driven off without difficulty,' he says. 'The city itself was rather badly bombed but not the central business portion and Raffles was still intact. Fire stations were still functioning. The wharves had suffered severely but the buildings along the waterfront were not touched. There was not a great deal of shipping in Keppel Harbour. Apparently there was no labour to discharge cargo, most of the discharging being done by troops.'

At 1.30 p.m. the commander of the 12th Brigade, Brigadier Archie Paris, reported to Brigadier Taylor's headquarters at Bulim. Paris's father, Major-General Sir Archibald Paris, had commanded the Royal Naval Division at Gallipoli and the two men got along well. Taylor explained that their best chance of containing the Japanese was to occupy the Kranji–Jurong Line, which had been partly reconnoitred by John Wyett and two other AIF officers a few days earlier. He asked Paris to take up a defensive position at the northern end of the line, while the 22nd Brigade plus the 2/29th Battalion occupied the southern end.

Owing to broken telephone lines, there had been no contact between Taylor and Bennett for several hours, and at 2.30 p.m. Bennett's staff quite independently suggested to him that it might be advisable to withdraw the 22nd Brigade and the 44th Indian Brigade, which was still holding the south-west sector of the coast, into the Jurong Line before dark. Bennett refused to order such a move; he still wanted Taylor to counterattack the Japanese at Ama Keng and drive them back to the beaches. When communications were restored, Taylor informed Bennett of his decisions and was told that he had acted without orders, that what he had done was quite wrong and that all he could think of was withdrawing. Taylor was under great strain; the conversation with his old adversary moved him a step closer to breaking point.

Later that afternoon, Percival visited Bennett at his headquarters and alerted him to the fact that the enemy's thrust represented a serious threat to Malaya Command's depots and dumps along Bukit Timah Road, especially the large Kranji ammunition magazine and the vital food and petrol dumps east of Bukit Timah village and in the racecourse area. He impressed upon Bennett the great importance of safeguarding these areas and, as though realising the gravity of the situation himself, ordered the 6/15th Brigade from the Northern Area to move there as soon as possible. He also sanctioned Taylor's decisions regarding the Jurong Line and ordered the 44th Indian Brigade to fall back as previously suggested.

At that stage, Bennett knew nothing of Percival's plan for a last-ditch stand. It was disclosed verbally to Heath and Keith Simmons that evening and issued to Bennett and other senior commanders shortly after midnight as a 'Secret and Personal' instruction. 'It was issued,' Percival says, 'in order that responsible senior officers might know my intentions in case the situation developed too rapidly for further orders to be issued.' In different circumstances, such foresight would have been admirable, but bitter experience during the campaign should have warned him that any precipitate order was likely to be misunderstood. 'Secret and Personal' to Percival meant that the order was for the commander's eyes only – but it did not mean that to Gordon Bennett or to some of the other commanders, who promptly showed it to their unit commanders.

News of the Japanese landings in 22nd Brigade's area had reached Brigadier Maxwell of the 27th Brigade in the early hours of the 9th. As had been his practice throughout the campaign, he had placed his headquarters well away from his troops, this time at the Singapore Dairy Farm. This was located on a grassy hillside six miles south of the Causeway, halfway across the island, but it was handy to Maxwell's commanding officer at Bukit Timah village. The Brigadier's most pressing concern on the morning of the 9th was that the loss of the 2/29th Battalion had opened up a gap on his left flank. The 2/30th Battalion still occupied its position immediately west of the Causeway, while the 2/26th Battalion was located in swampland between the 2/30th and the Kranji River. Both battalions, however, were vulnerable to an attack from the west if the Japanese crossed the Kranji. At 11 a.m., Maxwell sought permission to withdraw the 2/26th along Woodlands Road and turn his left flank to face north-west. He was told to leave his dispositions as they were, but was permitted to form a composite company by taking a platoon from each battalion and, with the addition of D Company of the 2/26th, to plug the gap with this force.

The brigade had already seen a major change earlier that day. The 2/26th's commander, Lieutenant-Colonel A. H. 'Sapper' Boyes, had handed over command to Lieutenant-Colonel R. F. Oakes of the 22nd Brigade after Maxwell had assigned Boyes to the AIF's General Base Depot with the nebulous brief 'to co-ordinate rear defences'. The truth was that Boyes, despite the battalion's credible performance on the mainland and his popularity with his men, did not see eye to eye with Maxwell. 'This changeover at such a critical time of the campaign was to have a noticeable effect on activities during the next few days,' the battalion's history says.[8]

In the afternoon, V. G. Bowden informed the Australian Government that the Japanese final assault was expected in two days' time and he saw no hope that the island could be held. 'It appears significant that 11 February is the greatest Japanese patriotic festival of the year, namely anniversary of accession of their first Emperor Jimmu,' Bowden cabled, 'and it can be taken as certain that they will make a supreme effort to achieve capture of Singapore on this date.' The Far East War Council had held its last meeting that morning, and Bowden informed Canberra that he intended to escape from Singapore on a cargo steamer the following day.[9]

His plans were scuppered by his bosses in Canberra, who replied, 'We appreciate your difficulties but think you should stick to your post. Otherwise we shall be deprived of independent information and effect on morale would be bad.' It was signed 'Very best wishes'.[10] A second cable advised Bowden that he and his staff should 'insist on full diplomatic immunities, privileges and courtesies if worst comes' – that is, if they fell into Japanese hands.[11]

At 1.30 p.m. Colonel Oakes, Black Jack Galleghan of the 2/30th and two intelligence officers were summoned to Maxwell's headquarters. The Brigadier was still obsessed about the western threat to his flank, although no such threat had developed. He warned Oakes that, in order to close the gap between the 27th and 12th Brigades, both battalions might have to be withdrawn from the Causeway to a position further south along Woodlands Road. This withdrawal, if authorised, would begin after the oil tanks at Woodlands had been destroyed later that night. Furthermore, it would be Oakes's responsibility to co-ordinate the movement of both battalions.[12]

Oakes returned to his battalion at about 5.30 p.m., unaware that Galleghan, who had suffered a recurrence of a World War I injury which affected his hearing, had reluctantly gone to hospital on Maxwell's orders and that his second-in-command, Major G. E. Ramsay, had taken over the 2/30th Battalion. Both battalions, therefore, had lost their commanding officers on the eve of what would be the most important battle in their short, violent histories.

During the day the enemy's artillery barrage had concentrated on the Causeway sector, a sure sign that an attack was imminent. Many of the basic shore defences at Kranji village had been blasted to pieces, and an observation post in a pineapple factory was destroyed. This did not cause Maxwell any undue concern; his eyes were firmly focused on the huge Japanese build-up in the west, the force of which, he was sure, would be unleashed against him at any moment.

At 7.30 p.m. a battalion of the 4th Guards Regiment attacked the 2/26th Battalion in landing craft launched from the mouth of the Skudai River. Large numbers of boats were knocked out by heavy fire, and many Japanese troops became stranded on tidal flats or lost in the swamps when they hit the shore. All telephone communications to the forward positions had been cut, and the Australians were again bedevilled by the same absence of searchlights and lack of artillery fire as the 22nd Brigade had experienced the previous night.

The 2/10th battery supporting the 2/26th had been ordered to move after dark to the Mandai Road area south of Kranji because of the supposed threat to the brigade's left flank. The gunners were still taking up their new position when the Japanese attacked, and artillery fire had to be brought down from the 2/30th's area. The machine gunners on the 2/26th's front were also slow to engage the enemy, having missed the flare that was to be their signal to open fire. The 2/26th's mortars, however, fired on troops landing at Kranji pier and caused severe casualties. Nevertheless, the Guards succeeded in getting a foothold west of the Causeway and were soon fighting hand to hand with the forward platoons.

Soon after 9 p.m. a beach light was switched on, and a Japanese officer was seen at the head of the Causeway shouting and gesticulating as though commanding troops prior to an assault from that direction. The 2/30th's B Company under Captain John Duffy realised this was an attempt to distract attention from a large number of troops who had gathered further along the shore and were preparing to cross the straits in barges. 'Several well-placed shells deprived him of any further interest in activities,' the battalion's War Diary says, 'while the main weight of shell fire fell on the troops he had been striving to cover.'

Malaya Command's switch from Sime Road to Fort Canning had given Bill Drower an opportunity to seek a transfer from the Intelligence Corps to one of the artillery units. 'I told Brigadier Torrance I was a trained artillery officer and could he find me a regiment? Next day, he said there had been a casualty in the 135th Field Regiment, otherwise known as the Hertfordshire Yeomanry. He said the commander was a Colonel Philip Toosey and he thought I would fit in. I dropped rank to a lieutenant and joined the 135th just as the Japs were crossing the Causeway. We were situated on the east coast just south of the Naval Base and opened fire with our 25-pounders. We shelled the Causeway in support of the 27th Brigade. I was lucky – I had an accounts clerk from Glasgow who worked out my ranges far better than I could ever have done.'

By midnight, the 2/26th's three forward companies had sustained serious casualties and had fallen back 300 yards to the neck of the Kranji peninsula, where they fought off all attempts to dislodge them. When communications between Maxwell and Oakes were restored, Maxwell learned that the 2/26th had been forced off the beaches. He informed Oakes that his withdrawal plan had been approved and that he was to co-ordinate the move with the 2/30th as soon as the oil-storage tanks had been destroyed.

Plans for their demolition went awry when the truck bringing explosives and detonators to the shore was destroyed by shell fire. The leader of the demolition party, Captain Arthur Watchorn, opened the valves on some of the tanks and allowed thousands of gallons of petrol to gush into the drains and creeks which were already flowing with blazing fuel from other ruptured tanks. Watchorn then walked four miles to replace the explosives and on his return at 2 a.m. informed Oakes that the demolition would be completed by 4 a.m. Oakes was uncertain that he could hold the enemy for that long and ordered both battalions to withdraw to their new positions at 4 a.m. The Causeway was thus abandoned and the road to Singapore left wide open.

Watchorn coolly blew up the remaining tanks within earshot of the enemy, sending another huge wave of burning petrol surging into the river system and out into the straits. Bill Drower was transfixed by the conflagration. 'I was absolutely fascinated and horrified by the blazing fuel roaring up into the sky,' he says. 'A number of Japanese soldiers were caught in the flames and burned alive.'

A short time earlier General Yamashita had landed on Singapore Island. He came ashore on the seawall at the Lim Chu Kang Road. It was a moving moment for him, made all the sweeter by the sight of trussed Australian prisoners lying at his feet. The Japanese commander set up his headquarters in a tent on a rubber plantation a short distance north of Tengah airfield.

As dawn was breaking, a panic-stricken Guards officer dashed in with the news that a major catastrophe had befallen his regiment. The front-line troops had been enveloped in fire on the water and had been annihilated.[13] Nishimura, the informant said, wanted to cancel the attack on the Causeway sector and land his troops behind the 5th Division further west. Yamashita's suspicions were aroused. He did not trust the Guards commander, and the Causeway was vital to his plans. If he could gain access to Woodlands Road, he could attack the vital strategic strongpoint at Bukit Timah from both the north and the west. He sent an officer to investigate the extent of the damage. This officer returned to report that not only were the Guards still intact but all opposition on the beaches had mysteriously melted away. Yamashita snapped, 'The Guards can do as they please in this battle.'

At the end of the night's fighting, the 2/30th and 2/26th Battalions had pulled back to their new positions north and south of Bukit Mandai on Woodlands Road. Maxwell's withdrawal had exposed a vital hill over-looking the Causeway and uncovered the left flank of the 11th Indian Division. It had also enabled the enemy to consolidate his landing unopposed. Black Jack Galleghan said later that the front held by his battalion had been 'the strength', and that once that had been conceded 'you gave the whole show away' because the Causeway had not been adequately demolished and could be reopened.[14]

After the war, Maxwell admitted that his headquarters had been too far back for him to exercise proper control over the battlefield. He defended his conduct by adding that Bennett was in agreement that he should stay in close touch with divisional headquarters, and that Bennett had also told him he was making a great mistake by giving orders and then going forward to see that they were carried out. But Maxwell acknowledged that his delegation of authority to Colonel Oakes over the withdrawal from the Causeway 'was again an error of judgement'.[15]

Bennett, however, was unaware of the events taking place in the Causeway sector. He had moved his headquarters from Bukit Timah to a large villa at Holland Road and was out of touch with the situation. At 3.10 a.m. on the 10th, his headquarters informed Fort Canning that all was quiet at the Causeway, when in reality fighting had been taking place for more than five hours. Percival did not know until 5 a.m. that the enemy had succeeded in landing at Kranji and it was 5.10 before he heard that the 27th Brigade had retreated. 'I suppose I did it because I am a doctor in civil life,' Maxwell said, 'and did not know enough about soldiering.' It was a curious fact that a general who abhorred the 'retreat complex' had promoted a man suffering from precisely that condition – so much so that he had earlier called on Percival at Fort Canning and told him he did not think Singapore was worth a further loss of life. The astonished GOC had heard him out and then shown him the door. Having had similar conversations with Maxwell, Bennett knew that his protégé had given up the fight, but he did not replace him because to do so would have meant admitting he had made a mistake.

General Billy Key, commanding the 11th Indian Division, was amazed to discover at first light that his left flank was completely exposed. He telephoned Western Area asking for the immediate reoccupation of the Causeway area, but was told that there were insufficient troops to mount a counterattack. Key then ordered the 8th Brigade, the new divisional reserve, to move west and reoccupy the high ground south of the Causeway. This was done by 10 a.m. 'If Maxwell was a British officer, I would place him under arrest,' he told his GSO1 Colonel Harrison.[16]

On the western front, Bennett had ordered Brigadier Taylor to hold Bulim till 6 a.m. on the 10th and then move into the central sector of the Jurong Line between the 12th and 44th Brigades. The 6/15th Brigade would also have taken its place in the Line by then. At 7.30 a.m., however, the Japanese launched a strong attack against the 12th Brigade at the northern end of the line, and the fighting later spread southwards. The defenders were forced back to positions covering Bukit Panjang village to the east and further south to a position astride Jurong Road covering Bukit Timah village. A wide gap had been opened up between the left of the 12th Brigade and the right of the 6/15th Brigade.

At 9 a.m. a new crisis arose when Brigadier Taylor received a copy of Western Area's orders – based on Percival's 'Secret and Personal' instructions to Bennett – with regard to the possible perimeter around Singapore City. He took these orders to mean that the brigade should occupy its new positions at once. All units under his command, except those already engaged in fighting on the Jurong Line, were ordered to occupy a line immediately west of Reformatory Road (today's Clementi Road) south of Bukit Timah village. Bennett was furious when he learned of Taylor's blunder, but allowed the orders to stand.

The 2/18th Battalion and the remnants of the 2/19th and 2/20th Battalions duly took up their new positions, where they were joined by X Battalion, a scratch force of 200 men under the command of Colonel 'Sapper' Boyes, former commander of the 2/26th Battalion. Its members were young rookies from the Base Depot, men from disbanded administrative units, detainees facing courts martial and others who had become separated from their units. Bob Goodwin saw them go into action. 'On one of my trips between the town and the front line I saw a long single file of men going over the ambulating hills,' he says. 'This was X Battalion, going forward to their doom.'

The domino effect that would topple the Jurong Line was set in motion later that morning, after General Paris had sent out patrols that failed to make contact with 27th Australian Brigade on his right. He realised that this probably meant the Japanese had a clear run from Kranji to Bukit Timah. On his own initiative, he withdrew his brigade from the Jurong Line to defend the road junction at Bukit Panjang village. This move uncovered the right flank of more southerly units, which were then obliged to change position. The line collapsed completely when Brigadier Ballantine, commander of the 44th Indian Brigade on the extreme left, reacted to his 'secret' orders in much the same way as Brigadier Taylor. Within the course of a few hours, Percival's best chance of stopping the Japanese was in tatters. It was as big a catastrophe as the loss of the Jitra Line in Malaya, and it had been self-inflicted.

'It was all very confusing on the Jurong Line,' Jim Dixon of 19th Battery 2/10th Field Regiment says. 'We were told the Japs were advancing and we were to abandon the guns and make a hasty retreat. We left the guns and got away but our gun sergeant said to me, "We haven't got the firing pin." I was sent back to get it so the Japs couldn't use our guns. When I returned, the sergeant said, "We'll make a stand here." I said, "What with?" I had a firing pin and he had a revolver.'

General Wavell had no means of knowing that his arch-enemy was on Singapore Island when he flew in from Java on his final trip to the besieged island early on the 10th. He found Percival 'composed, very tired and presenting a controlled stoicism in the face of the harsh realities of his situation'. At 11 a.m., he and Percival arrived at Gordon Bennett's headquarters at Holland Road, sweeping up the wide, curving drive in Wavell's shiny black limousine with the Union Flag flying from its bonnet. The driver parked among a collection of staff cars in full view of passing Japanese aircraft.

Fifteen minutes later, dive-bombers swooped low over the horizon, and a stick of bombs straddled the house, causing severe damage. John Wyett found the switchboard operator lying dead, still wearing his headphones. In the conference room, the top brass had flung themselves to the floor as the bombs exploded. All except Gordon Bennett, that is. 'He was standing there with a supercilious grin on his face watching Wavell, Percival and Heath and their senior staff members struggling to get to their feet,' Wyett says. 'They were covered in plaster and their uniforms and hair were white with the dust.'[17]

Bennett had little information about Taylor's dispositions, and the only thing he knew about Maxwell's withdrawal was that he had not sanctioned it. He had no intention of going forward to find out what was happening. 'Gordon Bennett was not quite so confident as he had been up-country,' Percival noted. 'He had always been very certain that his Australians would never let the Japanese through and the penetration of his defences had upset him.'[18]

The shiny black limo headed up Thomson Road in search of answers, skirting the reservoirs and passing through the strategic village of Nee Soon to Heath's III Corps and General Key's 11th Indian Division on the north shore. To minimise the damage caused by the huge gap in the Causeway sector, Percival ordered Maxwell's brigade to come under the command of 11th Division, and instructed them to move forward into Mandai village to protect the vital road leading through Nee Soon to the north-east defensive positions. At Wavell's urging, Percival also ordered Heath to dispatch three infantry battalions to rendezvous east of the racecourse near Bukit Timah village to beef up defences in the Western Area. This force, commanded by Lieutenant-Colonel L. C. Thomas of the Machine Gun Battalion, was named Tom Force.

At 2.30 p.m., Wavell and Percival stopped off at Holland Road again to inform Bennett of these decisions. Wavell then learned to his consternation that the Jurong Line had collapsed owing to a misreading of Percival's orders. He reprimanded Percival and demanded that the Line be recaptured. As he left Bennett's headquarters, Wavell shook hands with two Australian staff officers, Captain Adrian Curlewis and Captain Harry Jessup. 'Well, goodbye gentlemen,' he said, 'and God bless you.' The men knew then that Singapore was doomed.

Back inside the villa, Bennett made two stabbing marks with a pencil on a small-scale map and ordered that X Battalion should counterattack the enemy from one mark to the other. Brigadier Taylor chose this moment to arrive at divisional headquarters but was unable to dissuade Bennett from issuing the order, which went out at 4.05 p.m. 'It looked like murder,' he said. Percival, however, had arrived back at his headquarters, where he planned a much grander, three-stage offensive involving most of the 22nd Division's units. He then returned to Holland Road with this plan and

Bennett sent out new orders – but he did not cancel X Battalion's forward movement.

At nightfall, the shiny back limo was parked outside Flagstaff House, where Wavell took delivery of a telegram from Churchill. 'There must at this stage be no thought of saving the troops or sparing the population,' the Prime Minister cabled. 'The battle must be fought to the bitter end at all costs. Commanders and senior officers should die with their troops. The honour of the British Empire and of the British Army is at stake.'

After reading the telegram, Wavell drafted an order of the day in pencil on the back of a naval message form and handed it to Percival. 'It is certain that our troops in Singapore Island heavily outnumber any Japanese who have crossed the Straits,' Wavell had written, closely following Churchill's wording. 'We must destroy them. Our whole fighting reputation is at stake and the honour of the British Empire. The Americans have held out in the Bataan Peninsula against far heavier odds, the Russians are turning back the picked strength of the Germans. The Chinese with an almost complete lack of modern equipment have held the Japanese for four and a half years. It will be disgraceful if we yield our boasted fortress of Singapore to inferior enemy forces.

'There must be no thought of sparing the troops or civil population and no mercy must be shown to weakness in any shape or form. Commanders and senior officers must lead their troops and if necessary die with them. There must be no question or thought of surrender. Every unit must fight it out to the end and in close contact with the enemy. Please see that the above is brought to the notice of senior officers and by them to the troops. I look to you and your men to fight to the end to prove that the fighting spirit that won our Empire still exists to enable us to defend it.'

Having issued the order, Wavell felt honour bound to share the fate of the garrison, but his responsibilities for Burma, India and the Dutch East Indies were too pressing for him to make a heroic but foolhardy gesture in Singapore. After visiting the Governor, he headed for the harbour to board his Catalina for Java, knowing that Singapore was lost and that many men, women and children would needlessly die for the sake of someone else's 'honour'.

Meanwhile, Colonel Boyes was leading X Battalion towards its forming-up place in timbered country on the outskirts of Bukit Timah village. Most of the men were armed with rifles; a few had Bren guns or tommy-guns and there were a couple of mortars. Others, however, had only hand grenades or ammunition, or were carrying a *changkul*, the Malayan hoe. Dressed in an

odd array of clothing including overalls and plimsolls, the men had difficulty keeping together in the dark.[19]

The Japanese had succeeded in concentrating three infantry regiments
of the 5th Division, supported by tanks, around Tengah airfield and three
regiments of the 18th Division on the Jurong Road. Yamashita ordered these
forces to push forward overnight to capture the heights of Bukit Timah at
dawn. He could not deliver Singapore to his Emperor on *Kigensetsu* but he
could fly the Japanese flag from the highest point on the island in his
honour. The 5th Division was ordered to advance east along Choa Chu
Kang Road towards the junction at Bukit Panjang village, while the 18th
Division headed along Jurong Road to Bukit Timah village.

At the harbour, there was a delay in the arrival of a motor boat to take
Wavell out to his Catalina. He stepped out of the shiny black limo to see
what was happening, but the driver had parked too close to the edge of the
seawall and the Supreme Commander, on his blind side, failed to see the
danger. He plunged over the wall and crashed on to the rocks and barbed-
wire entanglement below, badly injuring his back.

Back in Bandung, Wavell was admitted to hospital. He was in great pain
when he cabled Churchill, 'Battle for Singapore is not going well. Japanese
with their usual infiltration tactics are getting on much more rapidly than
they should in the west of island. I ordered Percival to stage counterattack
with all troops possible on that front. Morale of some troops is not good and
none is as high as I should like to see. The chief troubles are lack of sufficient
training in some of reinforcing troops and an inferiority complex which bold
and skilful Japanese tactics and their command of the air have caused. Everything possible is being done to produce more offensive spirit and optimistic
outlook. But I cannot pretend that these efforts have been entirely successful
up to date. I have given the most categorical orders that there is to be no
thought of surrender and that all troops are to continue fighting to the end.'

Advancing along the Jurong Road at 3 a.m., forward patrols of the
Japanese 18th Division came across X Battalion, which had bivouacked in its
forming-up position to await the dawn. After setting fire to a small petrol
dump with tracer bullets, the Japanese fell upon the Australians in the firelight. Many of the men were asleep and were bayoneted where they lay. Two-
thirds of X Battalion, including Colonel Boyes, were wiped out in the
petroleum-soaked scrub. The Japanese then attacked two other units of the
22nd Brigade which had been sent in support of X Battalion. Bennett
blamed the catastrophe on Taylor, for having misunderstood his orders and
withdrawn prematurely.

Shortly after nightfall on the Choa Chu Kang Road, the 5th Division had attacked the 4/19th Hyderabads, forcing them back through the 2/29th Battalion on the outskirts of Bukit Panjang village. The Australians were holding the enemy when the familiar sounds of motorised armour reached them and a column of tanks loomed out of the darkness. The Australians disabled the first three tanks but there were more than 40 others queuing up behind them; the troops were driven off the road into the hills east of the village. At the junction, the column swung right into Upper Bukit Timah Road and headed for Bukit Timah village.

The Plymouth Argylls, meanwhile, had thrown up two makeshift barricades consisting of trucks and a few anti-tank mines south of Bukit Panjang village. As they had done so often in the campaign, hardened veterans among the Scots braced themselves for the onslaught. The leading tank was stopped by a hail of gunfire – but others crashed through the roadblocks and charged towards Bukit Timah. The Argylls' last surviving Lanchester armoured car, *Stirling Castle*, engaged the tanks but was knocked out by shell fire and its commander, Sergeant Harry Nuttall, wounded.[20]

While the defenders sought cover in some rubber trees, Major Angus MacDonald, the brigade major, sped down the road ahead of the tanks. Passing the Ford Motor Factory, he set up a third roadblock at the entrance to Bukit Timah village, which was blazing fiercely. Following closely behind, the leading tank opened fire just as MacDonald drove the last vehicle into position. Despite the presence of two anti-tank guns, the enemy had gathered such momentum that there was no stopping them. Around midnight, triumphant Japanese troops marched in to seize their prize.

Twelve Argylls who tried to break out of the village were captured, tied up with barbed wire and, in the grasslands near the Dairy Farm, bayoneted and then shot. One of the men, Private Hugh Anderson, was bayoneted six times but still lived. He was rescued by local Chinese who treated his wounds.

After visiting Taylor's headquarters that night, Major Charles Moses had set off at 2 a.m. for divisional headquarters in a car with a batman at the wheel. Later, he wrote in his diary, 'Start off as quietly as possible down lane, then speed up in Jurong Road and rush for village. Yells from side in foreign tongue – I know they're Japs but hope they're Indians. Right in front of us are dark solid objects across road. Have to stop. Put on brakes – brake lights show up Japs to right of road standing, sitting, lying – scores of them. Car stops. See objects are two tanks astride road. Tommy-gun opens up from 10–15 feet away to right. Rattle into radiator. "Come on" to batman. Open my door and shoot out and back up street. Everyone shooting. Then hear many heavy crashes – tank guns smash into my car. Four shells. Then I hear my army boots clatter on road and I'm flying over the 200 yards to the last house on the left. Then across the small stream and scramble up bank at other side and rush up hill into *lalang* and sit down to take stock …'

Moses hitched a lift in a Bren-gun carrier to Malaya Command Headquarters and informed General Percival about the presence of the tanks. 'What do you think we should do?' the GOC asked. Moses then went to Bennett's new headquarters at Tanglin Barracks, where he had breakfast, a bath and a shave. His diary continues, 'See Gordon Walker in Ops Room. He asks what I think is going to happen. I said there could be only one result: capitulation – and that I for one would not be taken prisoner as I intended to make a break for it when the time came. [Walker] said, "Wouldn't it be marvellous if we could arrange to get the General away?" I said I'd do all I could and perhaps manage to get a boat. He said he would speak to the General and tell him of our conversation. A little later he said that the General was in favour of making an attempt if he found himself free to do so.'[21]

On the morning of the 11th, Percival sent Wavell's 'no surrender' order to Heath, Bennett and Keith Simmons, instructing that 'the gist' of it should be conveyed to all ranks. He added cover note of his own: 'In some units the troops have not shown the fighting spirit which is to be expected of men of the British Empire. It will be a lasting disgrace if we are defeated by an army of clever gangsters many times our inferior in numbers. The spirit of aggression and determination to stick it out must be inculcated in all ranks. There must be no further withdrawals without orders. There are too many fighting men moving about in back areas. Every available man who is not doing other essential work must be used to stop the invader.'

Most commanders and senior officers refused to pass Wavell's order on to their units. Colonel Alf Derham read it, put it back in its envelope, tore it into small pieces and threw it into a waste-paper basket. 'My medical units had not run away from anything,' he says.[22]

Russell Savage and his battery from the 2/10th were moving about with the infantry from one position to another under heavy shelling. 'I thought there was still hope,' he says. 'You become so tired that all you want to do is sleep. After four or five days, we were brought back to a bivouac and could finally rest, but word came down that we had to get up and have a bath. Almost at gunpoint, we were forced to clean up and have a shave. No doubt about it, it put a lot of life back in us. The change in morale was almost unbelievable. A lot of the 2/18th fellows were covered in oil that had got up the creeks. They had also been in bayonet fighting. I didn't realise how much blood the winner of a bayonet fight gets over him.'

At Singapore General Hospital, the volunteer orderlies from the *Empress of Asia* had been split up and dispersed to various wards. Len Butler found himself working with an 18-year-old Ceylonese nurse who was in charge of two wards. 'There were hundreds of patients,' he says. 'The badly wounded were on the beds, the not-so-badly wounded were under the beds; they were in the passageways, the toilets, the kitchens. Civilians and military patients were all mixed up: there would be a soldier next to a Chinese woman. There was no running water. The only water we had was in demijohns and that was needed for operations. The wounded were perspiring and needed water continually and we didn't have it. Some were screaming in agony. The stench was unbelievable from gangrene and dead bodies that had been lying there for two or three days in temperatures of 100 degrees.

'Firstly, we had to get rid of these from the wards, so another chap and I lifted them out into the passageway. Then the nurse said we needed to go round and do some dressings. I was given a kidney bowl and we started off. We came to one chap in a corner. It was quite dark and I could something glowing. The nurse said, "We'll start with this one." I bent down and there was a white heaving mass on this man's face. I wondered what the hell it was. She said, "Put the kidney bowl underneath." When I did that, I realised it was a heaving mass of maggots and they were eating his face. A piece of shrapnel had hit him in the cheek and shattered the whole of his jaw and flies had got in. He wasn't murmuring. She picked these maggots out and put some ointment on the wound and covered it with a bit of gauze; that's all she could do for him. Then we went the next one. He had gangrene and she cut all the dead flesh off his wound. We came across people who were dying and we could no nothing for them.

'Then we were asked to take the dead bodies to the morgue, which was situated down a corridor and had a lift-up door like a garage. We put a Chinese woman on the stretcher and went to the door. There was a flood of liquid like a foul-smelling cloud coming from underneath it. I lifted the door up and there was a pile of bodies six feet high, all on top of one another. The top ones were crushing the ones underneath and the body fluids were seeping under the door. There was a little Chinese boy about two years old just inside the door with his guts hanging out and a smile on his face. We got hold of this lady by the arms and legs, tossed her on the pile and went back for the next one.'[23]

Meanwhile, Yamashita, assessing the capture of Bukit Timah, thought of a clever plan to impress his Emperor. That morning, a Japanese plane dropped a red-and-white tube containing a letter addressed to the British commander. Percival reported to Wavell, 'Have received letter from Commander of Japanese Army asking for surrender of fortress. Letter was dropped by air. Have no means of dropping message so do NOT propose to make reply which would of course in any case be negative.'

Percival's prospects were grim. Following the loss of Bukit Timah, there was nothing to prevent enemy troops from moving east and seizing the reservoirs and cutting off Singapore's water supply. General Heath had realised the danger and ordered a new formation called Massy Force, under Brigadier Tim Massy-Beresford, to protect MacRitchie Reservoir and the Woodleigh pumping station one mile south-west of Payah Lebar village. That evening, a new defensive line had been established from the reservoir in the east to the racecourse in the west. From there, the 2nd Battalion of the Gordon Highlanders, summoned from the Changi area, the 22nd Australian Brigade and the 44th Indian Brigade formed an arc facing west along Reformatory Road. The Japanese attacked the centre of this position all afternoon, but the Australians, revitalised by large numbers of stragglers who had been returned to their units, held their line under heavy artillery and air bombardment.[24]

General Heath had also decided there was no longer any point in defending the Naval Base and ordered the final demolitions to be put in hand. The power station, cranes and workshops were destroyed and the remaining fuel tanks holed or fired. However, there wasn't time to destroy everything; some machinery and stores were left intact. By 6 p.m. on the 11th, all personnel had been evacuated.[25]

Major Harry Schulman's company was the last to leave the base. 'It was being raided by everybody,' he says. 'I could have built the *Queen Mary*, victualled the *Queen Mary* and fuelled the *Queen Mary* from the stores, but all that was going to be left to the Japanese. All I did was empty "Nelson's Blood" – the naval rum. We opened the big casks to let it out. My company was rearguard again when we pulled back towards Singapore City.'[26]

CHAPTER 21

The Lost Angels

LIEUTENANT JAMES RICHARDSON of British Intelligence was busy burning sensitive documents in the abandoned hut at Sime Road on 10 February when he heard that his wife Doris, a secretary at Fort Canning, had been ordered to leave the colony. The couple, who had been married for three years, were inseparable, but although Doris wanted to stay behind, Richardson managed to persuade her to take this opportunity to go. The order was not accompanied by a berth on a ship, however, and inquiries at the P&O office revealed that no passages were available.

Grabbing a few possessions, the Richardsons dashed down to the battered, smouldering docks, where the Chief Officer of MS *Empire Star*, J. L. Dawson, told them that passages in his ship were obtainable from the Sea Transport Officer. The *Empire Star* was a 17,000-ton freighter of the Blue Star Line built in Belfast in 1935. She had survived the evacuations of British and Australian troops from Greece and Crete in 1941, and had arrived in Singapore on 27 January 1942 with a cargo of trucks, weapons and a large number of late Christmas presents.[1]

James Richardson organised passages for Doris and her friend Grace Harral and the following day saw them safely on board ship, in the company of more than 2,000 RAF personnel, British, Australian and Indian nurses, and women and children. One of the RAF contingent was Jimmy Thompson, a friend of the Richardsons. 'I took Jimmy down to the ship and said last farewells to Doris and Grace,' Richardson says. 'It was hellish parting like this, but I was glad that they at least have the chance of going away to safety. I did not feel at all brave about coming back here to the city under bombardment. Thus was our married life together sundered abruptly with no certainty when or if it would be resumed.'

Many loving relationships had been torn asunder but there were still thousands of vulnerable women and children on the island, many of them refugees from the mainland with no means of support. One of Ivan Simson's first actions on becoming Director-General of Civil Defence had been to ask Sir Shenton Thomas to order all *bouches inutiles* – useless mouths – to leave Singapore immediately. Thomas refused. Anybody could leave voluntarily, he said, irrespective of race or creed. He would not order European women and children to go because that would amount to discrimination.[2]

Churchill had raised the question of reducing the number of useless mouths on 19 December and again on 2 February, yet evacuation remained voluntary to the end. European women and children could travel free on warrants from the Government, but this fact was not publicised for fear that it would be seen as discriminatory. As a result, many people were left to fend for themselves. Six elderly European ladies were found sheltering from gunfire in a house in Gilstead Road on the northern edge of Singapore City. 'I call it disgraceful,' one cried. 'Here am I, stranded without a taxi, and the Japs only five miles away.'

As martial law had been proclaimed, Wavell or Percival could have ordered European civilians out of the colony on the simple military expedient that they would be in the way and would consume valuable food and water. But they did not do so. Many Chinese were desperate to go because they feared they were on Japanese hit lists for helping the British or for contributing to Chiang Kai-shek's war chest, but they were refused exit visas by the Chinese Secretariat. Shenton Thomas refused to intervene on their behalf and a great deal of bad feeling was generated. At the same time, Thomas was insistent that Commonwealth countries should open their doors to Chinese and Indian families for the duration of the war.

Australia had enforced a strict 'White Australia' policy since Federation in 1901, and its Government decided that it would admit only a token handful of Asians with sufficient funds on arrival to tide them over for two years. Thomas fired off a blistering cable to Prime Minister Curtin. 'I am afraid that I must let you know that the decision to admit only 50 Chinese and 50 Eurasians in the first instance has caused acute bitterness and uneasiness here,' he said. 'Two Representatives of the Chinese Government, one of whom is Representative at the Allied War Council, have spoken of it in the strongest terms and so have local Chinese leaders who are giving us every assistance in civil defence and to whom I have promised and intend to give my full support. I ask most earnestly for early and favourable reply to my request to be allowed to send you up to 5,000 people of Chinese or Eurasian extraction at my discretion.'[3] This request was considered by the Australian War Cabinet and referred to the Advisory War Council, which accepted Thomas's recommendations.

With the Governor's permission, the staff of the Singapore Harbour Board, including the Raffles dance champions Richard and Dorothy Lowery, made their way to the harbour on the night of 11 February. 'They escaped at the last minute and my mother lost her first child as a result,' says Peter Lowery. The harbour personnel reached Batavia in an old Penang ferry, and the Lowerys later made it to Melbourne without further mishap. However, Ivan Simson had not been warned by Thomas or the board's chairman that the Harbour Board officials were departing, and Chinese labourers reporting for duty at the docks the following day found that they had no one to work for.[4]

Early on the 12th Bowden cabled Canberra, 'All merchant shipping under British naval control has already left Singapore and naval and other offices for dealing with it including Harbour Board have been closed. Except as a fortress and battlefield Singapore has ceased to function.'[5]

Back on board the *Empire Star*, there was some doubt that the ship would sail at all. Chief Officer Dawson said, 'During one period I was called to the gangway because of panic at the shore end of the gangway and on investigation found that a large number of Australian troops were panicking to get on board. I went to the gangway and told the troops that there was no need to panic and that this ship was reserved for RAF personnel, women and children. Eventually, these Australian troops quietened down and we were able to proceed with the work of getting our own people on board. During the day I noticed that Australian troops were climbing up the mooring ropes on board to the afterdeck and by any other means they could find.'[6]

The *Empire Star* had been scheduled to sail on the afternoon of the 11th, but a heavy bombing raid on the harbour delayed her departure. 'I watched it from ashore, little knowing that one of the targets was the *Empire Star*,' Richardson says. On board, Doris and Grace were packed into one of the lower holds with other women and children for safety during the bombing. The ship, however, was badly damaged and one of its two Burmeister & Wain engines was disabled. Twenty-four people, mostly crew and service personnel, were killed.

By this time it was too dark for the master, Captain Selwyn Capon, to sail through the harbour's minefields, and the ship did not weigh anchor until first light on the 12th. By 9 a.m., she was receiving the attentions of more Japanese bombers. Passengers reported that explosions around the ship's bows were so enormous that she seemed to jump out of the water, but even with one engine out of action she caught up with a convoy escorted by HMS *Durban*.

The passengers included 63 Australian nurses, two of whom, Sister Margaret Anderson and Sister Veronica Torney, were on deck when a Japanese fighter strafed the ship. Several soldiers had been wounded in the earlier attack and the nurses threw themselves over the soldiers' bodies to protect them from the bullets.[7] Down below in the holds, passengers suffered terribly from the reverberation of exploding bombs, one girl having both eardrums ruptured. The *Empire Star* suffered three direct hits in which 13 men were killed and 37 others badly wounded. One of only two merchant ships that had left Singapore on the 12th to have survived the crossing, she limped into Tanjong Priok, the port of Batavia. The 135 AIF soldiers on board were disarmed and marched ashore, where they were turned over to an army guard. After being held in a civilian prison for a few days, they were released without charge.[8]

Shortly after dawn on the 12th, the Imperial Guards attacked the 8th Indian Brigade one mile west of Nee Soon village in the Northern Area. Under intense pressure, the 1/8th Punjab Battalion, which had been re-formed almost entirely with untrained reinforcements, began to disinte-grate. Russell Savage found himself being shelled with the remnants of this battalion. 'I was in a slit trench with a young British officer who was such a pukka sahib you would have thought he should be taking Bible lessons at school,' he remembers. 'He said, "I must get my chaps together and attack those Japanese in that scrub over there." I said, "You'll get killed if you do." He said, "My father led such-and-such a charge in the last war and my grandfather was in the Crimean War. The least I can do is get these Punjabis out of the trenches."

'The last I saw of him he was waving a .45 revolver around his head and charging across the paddock with his Punjabis. I thought it was far safer to keep my head down. Why did he do it? Family? Empire? Extraordinary!' The Punjabis were rescued when General Key threw the 2/9th Gurkhas and the 499th Field Battery from 28th Brigade into the battle. The Indian troops reoccupied their position and the situation was restored. The fate of the young officer is unknown.

At 9 a.m., the enemy attacked with tanks down Bukit Timah Road and almost reached the Chinese High School before being stopped. Percival toured the front and decided there was a very real danger that enemy tanks would break through all the way into Singapore City. After consulting Heath, he decided the time had come to implement his plan for a last-ditch stand. Orders were dispatched that a 28-mile-wide perimeter was to be established around Singapore City during the night of 12–13 February. The plan involved the withdrawal of all troops from the beach defences on the north shore and also from the Changi area, with the consequent loss of the Changi guns.

Percival instructed Heath to use the 11th Indian Division and the remainder of the 18th British Division to cover the reservoirs and to link up with General Keith Simmons's forces in the Southern Area. Percival then called on Shenton Thomas to inform him of the steps he had taken. The Governor arranged for the greater part of the stock of currency notes held by the Treasury to be burned. Considering the difficulties Percival had experienced in paying labourers to fortify military positions or clear up bomb damage or bury the dead, this seemed like a lunatic waste of money.

Throughout the day, the 22nd Brigade held its salient west of Holland Road despite furious attempts by the enemy to break through into the city. Much of the fighting was at close range; the Australians gave no quarter until late afternoon when the enemy made a deep penetration south of the position. The brigade was withdrawn under cover of darkness to Holland village. Percival says, 'It had fought a gallant action for 48 hours and done much to hold up the enemy's advance in this area.'

A total of 1,200 casualties had been admitted to the 13th AGH in St Patrick's School at Katong, and more wounded were flooding in. The hospital had sustained bomb damage to its kitchen and one of the wards, and space was so tight that some of the new admissions had to sleep outside in the grounds. Colonel D. C. Pigdon, the hospital's commander, complained, 'Why in the name of heaven Australia hasn't sent up hospital-ships to evacuate the casualties is beyond me. Many will die as a result.'

One of the surgeons, Colonel Thomas Hamilton, waved goodbye to the remaining nurses who were leaving Singapore that day in HMS *Vyner Brooke*. None of them had wanted to go. 'Smiling wistfully, they fluttered tiny handkerchiefs to us from the open doors of the ambulances, as orderlies and doctors lined the drive to cheer them on their way,' he says. The youngest was Sister Shirley Gardam of Tasmania, who was taking a letter from Hamilton to his wife. From the hospital lawn that night, he watched the *Vyner Brooke*, an ugly little coastal freighter, sail out of the harbour against the backdrop of a vivid scarlet sunset.[9]

The *Vyner Brooke*'s captain was 'Tubby' Borton of the Sarawak Steamship Company. Among his 300 passengers were 65 Australian nurses, including Matron Olive Paschke of the 2/10th AGM and Matron Irene Drummond of the 2/13th AGM. On entering Banka Straits, Captain Borton sought shelter from roving Japanese bombers. Riding at anchor in the lee of little Banka Island by day and travelling by night, he managed to give Japanese warships and aircraft the slip until at 2 p.m. on 14 February his ship was spotted by six Japanese planes. In an attempt to dodge the bombs, Tubby Borton zigzagged his ship but the *Vyner Brooke* was slow and clumsy and she was hit several times. One bomb destroyed the bridge and another wrecked the lower deck, where many of the passengers were hiding. A third bomb went straight down the funnel and blew a hole in the engine room. Then the planes dropped height and machine-gunned the people on the decks. Borton gave orders to abandon ship; in just over 20 minutes the *Vyner Brooke* sank.

Sister Vivian Bullwinkel, a 26-year-old blue-eyed blonde from South Australia, describes the events of that day in her diary: 'Beautiful sunny morning, calm sea, and anchored [near] very pretty island. Peacefulness disturbed as planes flew over and machine-gunned boat, all took to lower deck as prearranged, but raid all over and much discussion on planes sinking us and enemy aircraft. Took up anchor and steamed along. 2 p.m. air-raid siren. All down to lower deck and flatten down. Six planes attacking once more, bombs hit, second, third time, third bomb below the waterline. Whistle for all on deck to take to lifeboats.'[10]

Captain Borton was in the water for 18 hours before swimming ashore at Muntok Lighthouse. Vivian and 21 other nurses and a large group of men, women, and children landed at Radji Beach on Banka Island. One of the survivors was Matron Drummond, who had been wounded in the air raid but had been helped into a lifeboat. The survivors were joined the next day by 20 British soldiers from another stricken vessel.[11] Without food, clothing or medicine, the group elected to surrender, and while a naval officer went off to the town of Muntok on the north of Banka Island, civilian women and children set off for a nearby village in search of sustenance. The nurses and soldiers stayed with the stretcher cases on the beach. On 16 February the naval officer returned with a Japanese patrol consisting of an officer and 10 men. The officer ordered those who could walk, including Chief Officer W. S. Sedgeman and Second Engineer J. J. Miller, to march around a small headland, where they were bayoneted. The wounded were then bayoneted on the beach, although one English private crawled unseen into the undergrowth after being stabbed through the chest.

The 22 nurses, including the wounded Matron Drummond, were ordered to walk into the sea. It was around midday and the water was warm and tranquil, the palm-fringed setting idyllic. Matron Drummond, supported between two nurses, said, 'Chin up, girls, I'm proud of you and I love you all.' When the water reached waist height, the Japanese opened fire with a machine gun, raking them back and forth from behind. All of the nurses were killed except Vivian Bullwinkel, who was shot above the left hip. The bullet knocked her over and she floated for some time before raising her head. 'All my colleagues had been swept away and there were no Japs on the beach,' she says.[12] After passing out again, she came to on the beach. 'I was so cold that my only thought was to find some warm spot to die. I dragged myself up to the edge of the jungle and lay in the sun where I must have slept for hours. When I woke the sun was almost setting. I spent the night huddled under some bamboo only a few yards from my dead colleagues, too dazed and shocked for anything to register.'[13]

The following morning Vivian had just enough strength to find fresh water in a spring close to the beach, which kept her alive for the next 48 hours. On the third day, she went down to the lifeboat, looking for food, and heard a voice call out, 'Where have you been, nurse?' Private Kinsley, already wounded by shrapnel, had been bayoneted in the chest but the blade had missed his heart. Vivian dressed his wounds and helped him into the jungle.

Over the next 10 days she made daily trips to the village to obtain food. Kinsley told her he came from Yorkshire and had a wife called Elsie. When the pair were sufficiently recovered, they decided to walk to Muntok to give themselves up. Kinsley had removed a shirt from one of the dead men which covered his chest wound; Vivian slung a water-bottle around her neck and carried it on her hip. On the way to Muntok, they were picked up by a Japanese naval officer in a car. He gave them a banana and took them to Naval Headquarters, where they were questioned; they said that they had survived a shipwreck and had stumbled ashore. The Japanese, finding nothing suspicious about their story (and not noticing their wounds), sent them to a prison camp. Vivian found herself among 31 other nurses from the *Vyner Brooke* who had landed on other parts of the island. Matron Paschke and several of her friends, she learned, were missing, believed drowned.[14]

In hushed tones, Vivian related the details of the massacre to a few of the women and swore them to secrecy. She knew she would be executed if the Japanese discovered she had survived. Private Kinsley, the only other witness, was admitted to the crude hospital inside the prison; he died a few days later.[15]

Meanwhile, the feud between Gordon Bennett and Brigadier Taylor which had poisoned the air since the beginning of the Malayan Campaign reached its unseemly climax on the morning of 12 February. Harold Taylor, at the point of physical collapse, asked Arthur Varley to assume command of the brigade while he got some sleep. 'I realised that I would have to get a few hours' rest in a quiet spot,' Taylor says. 'My brain refused to work and I was afraid that if I carried on without rest the brigade would suffer.'[16]

When Bennett heard what had happened, he confirmed Varley's appointment as commander of the 22nd Brigade – permanently. Taylor was shunted off to hospital and then given the task of organising the Australian section of the final perimeter. After the war, Bennett wrote, 'I have never forgiven myself for not sending him home when I originally decided to do so. That was my greatest mistake.'

That night, Charles Moses filled a water-bottle with 30-year-old brandy and packed a haversack in preparation for his escape bid with the two Gordons. He included two boxes of cigars ('for Gen. and self'), a camera, socks, a writing pad, milk powder, Glucose D tablets, raisins, biscuits, Dettol, bandages, a felt hat with a cut-down brim, a sarong and a bottle of potassium permanganate ('for dyeing ourselves if necessary'). 'My load weighed the best part of 50lb,' he scribbled in his diary, 'but I was determined to carry it as long as I could.'

Moses, who had celebrated his 42nd birthday on 21 January, had every reason to want to return to Australia. He had emigrated there from England in 1922 after graduating from Sandhurst and serving in Ireland during the Troubles. Following a spell as a farmer and car salesman, he had taken to radio journalism, and by 1935 had worked his way up to become general manager of the Australian Broadcasting Commission. If he could get back to Sydney, a glittering career (and a mandatory knighthood) awaited him.

CHAPTER 22

Black Friday

As BOMBS AND SHELLS crashed around his house in St Michael's Road, Serangoon, Zacharia Pattara gathered his wife and five young daughters in the dining room. 'We sheltered under the dining-room table for several days while the house was badly bombed and shelled,' Terpie Pattara says. 'We were getting shells from both sides – from the Japanese and the British.'

Terpie had been engaged to Benny Szynkiewicz for several months but the young couple had not been able to set a date for their wedding. Benny was torn between returning home to Poland to fight the Germans and staying in Singapore. When the Pacific War broke out, he joined the Volunteer Force and had been fighting the Japanese with an armoured-car unit. 'We'd decided that we would have a hurried wedding ceremony on one of his days off but things didn't turn out,' Terpie says. 'When it became too dangerous for us to stay in our house any longer, Father packed us all into the car and told the chauffeur to drive us to town. It was Friday 13 February and Japanese planes were swooping down and trying to shoot us. The chauffeur kept saying, "*Takut! Takut! Takut!* – I'm afraid, I'm afraid, I'm afraid."[1]

The Pattara family reached the city centre, where scenes of appalling devastation greeted them. At midday, a heavy and accurate air raid had obliterated a large number of shop-houses in Orchard Road. One stick of bombs had fallen on a petrol station, which had exploded in flames, hurling two cars into the air. An officer who witnessed the sight says, 'Buildings on both sides of the road went up in smoke. Soldiers and civilians suddenly appeared staggering through clouds of debris; some got on the road, others stumbled and dropped in their tracks, others shrieked as they ran for safety. We pulled up near a building which had collapsed onto the road – it looked like a caved-in slaughterhouse. Blood splashed what was left of the lower rooms; chunks of human being – men, women and children – littered the place. Everywhere bits of steaming flesh, smouldering rags, clouds of dust – and the shriek and groan of those who still survived.'[2]

The Pattaras' store in High Street had been bombed and burned out and all of Zacharia's stock destroyed. In tears, the family made their way to Capitol Building, where a friend had a flat. Capitol Building was between the Convent of the Holy Infant Jesus and St Andrew's Cathedral – well within Percival's perimeter, but it was clear to Zacharia and his wife that they would not be safe for long. The couple made an agonising decision to split up: Anthoula would take the twins, Ino and Clio, and the middle daughter, Thetie, and board a ship for Australia; Terpie, however, would not leave the colony without her fiancé, so Zacharia decided to remain with her. The youngest girl, Thalia, elected to stay behind with her father.

While Terpie and Thalia dashed across Stamford Road to the convent, Zacharia headed for Keppel Harbour to see his wife and three of his daughters off. 'A lot of refugees were crowded into the convent but we were allowed to stay,' Terpie says. 'We were bombed shortly afterwards – I was taking a shower when it happened and I was slightly hurt.'

That morning, Admiral Spooner had decided that 13 ships and smaller seagoing craft in Keppel Harbour should set sail for Java on the night of 13–14 February. He estimated there would be room for 3,000 evacuees – the last opportunity for organised parties to get away from the island. Ivan Simson was allotted 300 places, and ordered his deputy Bisseker to go. He gave his passes to young technical civilians who would be useful in continuing the war elsewhere, as well as to older men, women and children. Spooner himself and Air Vice-Marshal Pulford were due to depart in a fast Fairmiles motor launch. Percival bade his old friend goodbye. For two military men, it was an emotional moment. Pulford wished him well, then remarked, 'I suppose you and I will be held responsible for this but God knows we did our best with what little we had been given.'[3]

Before dawn that morning, Yamashita had moved his headquarters to the Ford Motor Factory on Bukit Timah Road. His intelligence officers reported that the British, Australians, Indians and local forces were digging in on a tight arc around Singapore City. Yamashita believed that Percival was preparing for a protracted campaign of street fighting and was probably awaiting reinforcements. The Japanese commander knew he had neither the men nor the ammunition to sustain his own army through a prolonged siege. He alerted the Japanese Navy and Air Force to search all sea approaches to Singapore for a British expeditionary convoy. The order reached a large Japanese naval fleet which had assembled at the head of the Banka Straits for an attack on Palembang. It was stationed directly in the path of Spooner's little ships.

Yamashita had completed his plans for a two-pronged assault on the city. The 18th Division would drive along the south coast to capture the Alexandra Barracks, while the Imperial Guards enveloped the MacRitchie Reservoir and crashed through Braddell Road from the north. Throughout Black Friday, Japanese aircraft and artillery hammered the city in preparation for the final assault. Most of Percival's field artillery was now sited in open spaces in the city, making the built-up areas around them legitimate military targets.

Singapore's very fabric was being torn apart. Hospitals were inundated with wounded soldiers and civilians. Precious water gushed from broken mains which Simson's labour force had no chance of mending, since it was impossible to reach many of the breakages because of the enemy bombardment. Nor could he turn off the water to stop it running to waste because cost-conscious water engineers in the past had installed so few stopcocks.

Admiral Spooner's final order was for the destruction of the huge fuel-storage depot on Bukum Island south of the harbour. These stocks comprised naval fuel, lubricating oil and the Asiatic Petroleum Company's petrol reserves. When the tanks exploded into flames that afternoon, it sounded like a volcanic eruption.

At the General Hospital, Len Butler says, 'We were getting to the end of our tether. We'd had no sleep for quite a while and very little food or water. The incessant shelling and bombing slowly wore you down and we knew we had to go back to the wards to face the people in there, knowing we had nothing to give them. They were so brave. I clearly remember a Gurkha sitting on a bed surrounded by black ash. He had been guarding a petrol dump which had been bombed, and a whole sheet of petroleum had gone over him and burned him from head to toe. His eyelashes were burned, he had two little holes where his nostrils had been, he had no hair and the whole of his face was cracked and burned. It was just black ash. I cannot imagine how anyone could possibly have survived those burns. He was so incredibly brave.'

At 2 p.m., Percival met his senior commanders in the Battle Box at the request of General Heath. The Indian Army veteran, whose pregnant wife was still in the colony, was tense from stress and lack of sleep. He proposed that the garrison should surrender to prevent further loss of life and was supported by Gordon Bennett. Brigadier C. H. Stringer, commander of the medical service, had recommended to Percival as early as the 11th that only an immediate surrender could prevent an outbreak of malaria and hygiene-related diseases, while other commanders had expressed grave concern about the horrendous number of civilian casualties.

Percival then astonished the group by proposing that far from surrendering they should take the fight to the enemy. 'I indicated that I hoped to organise a counterattack shortly to relieve the pressure on the defences,' he says. Heath told him, 'You have already tried one counterattack and it was a complete failure. You have no fresh troops available for a counterattack. I do not think a counterattack has the least chance of success.'

All formation commanders agreed with Heath, who again urged Percival to surrender. Percival replied, 'There are other things to consider. I have my honour to consider and there is also the question of what posterity will think of us if we surrender this large Army and valuable fortress.'

'You need not bother about your honour,' Heath snapped. 'You lost that a long time ago up in the north.'

Percival insisted that the troops must fight on but made one concession: he agreed to cable Wavell seeking 'greater discretionary powers' in deciding when resistance should stop. Wavell's reply, however, was unrelenting: 'You must continue to inflict maximum damage on enemy for as long as possible by house-to-house fighting if necessary. Your action in tying down enemy and inflicting casualties may have vital influence in other theatres. Fully appreciate your situation but continued action essential.'

Bennett's belief that the battle for Singapore was lost was confirmed on his way back to his new headquarters at Tanglin Barracks, when his car was stopped in a street where a bombed building had fallen on an air-raid shelter. A group of Chinese, Malays, Europeans and Australian soldiers were frantically digging to reach the people in the shelter. A Chinese boy, scratched and bleeding, was dragged from the debris and immediately turned to help in the rescue work. 'My sister is under there,' he said. The rescuers dug furiously among the fallen masonry, one Chinese man doing twice as much as the others. 'At last the top of the shelter was uncovered,' Bennett wrote. 'Beneath was a crushed mass of old men, women, young and old, and young children, some still living – the rest dead. The little Oriental never stopped with his work, his sallow face showing the strain of anguish. His wife and four children were there. Gradually he unearthed them – dead. This was going on hour after hour, day after day; the same stolidity and steadfastness among the civilians was evident in every quarter of the city.'4

Government House had become uninhabitable. Sir Shenton and Lady Thomas were driven to the Singapore Club on the top floor of Fullerton Building, where two rooms had been reserved for their use. Thomas had issued a statement which eclipsed all previous efforts for fatuity: 'We are all in the hands of God from whom we can get comfort in our anxieties and strength to play the man and help one another in all the ordeals which are to come.'

Zacharia Pattara set off from Capitol Building in his chauffeur-driven car with Anthoula and three of his daughters. It was only a short distance around the Padang and across Anderson Bridge to Collyer Quay, but the traffic had swollen tremendously as word had spread about the 'last chance' convoy leaving that night. Long lines of motor vehicles carrying hundreds of desperate people became entangled with other convoys taking the wounded to hospital, or troops to the front line, or moving stores from one area to another.

Sirens blared and gunfire exploded overhead. Most shops and business premises were boarded up, while the bars and brothels had finally ceased trading. Burned-out cars and buses littered the gutters; refugees clutching large bundles or pushing handcarts sought shelter from the Japanese bombardment. The remains of a Zero fighter stood in one of the parks, placed there in the early days of the war to show that the Japanese were not invincible.

Zacharia's car crawled over the Singapore River, where a barge blazed in the oily slew, past Fullerton Building and on to Collyer Quay. The merchant looked seaward and his heart sank. The huge mushroom of smoke from the north shore had blended with an immense new conflagration which had flared up among the massive fuel reserves on Bukum Island. Everywhere he looked, scenes from Dante's *Inferno* were enacted in the firelight. Abandoned vehicles were manhandled into the water to clear a path to the wharves. There was a menacing drone overhead and a stick of bombs ignited like fireworks among the ships further along at Raffles Quay.

At Clifford Pier, Zacharia and his family joined a queue which snaked through the dockyard gates to a desk, where a shipping clerk was methodically ticking off passengers' names in a ledger. Beyond the desk, the gangway led invitingly to the deck of the ship. Suddenly, the air-raid sirens sounded and the crowd surged forward. Anthoula and the girls were swept away on the human tide. The last he would ever see of his wife and daughters was their curly black heads disappearing into the smoky gloom. Zacharia fought his way to the road and headed back to his friend's flat. 'They could not take any of their suitcases on board the ship,' Terpie Pattara says. 'They were left on the quayside and looted.'

The Japanese were only a mile to the west of the harbour on Pasir Panjong Ridge after their main offensive had swung down to the coast and descended upon the men of the 1st Malay Brigade. The Malays fought magnificently but had suffered heavy losses. Alan Ryall's anti-aircraft gunners were equipped with rifles and sent in as reinforcements. 'The Japanese were coming towards us from the north and they hammered us with mortars,' he says. 'We were armed with Lee Enfield .303 rifles and, after taking a beating, we were told to come off the ridge.

'A Malay officer gathered us together. I had lost my rifle up on the ridge and he gave me a weapon and said, "Here, use this." When I saw the Japanese coming towards us, I fired it from my shoulder and was thrown about 50 yards backwards. I learned later it was an anti-tank rifle. We were pushed down to Keppel Harbour, where it was pretty hopeless; there wasn't an awful lot that could be done. I had a small platoon of five men – all Welsh lads – and they had had no training whatsoever, in either anti-aircraft guns or small arms. They had been sent to our battery with the idea that they would be trained in Iraq, but we didn't go there and they didn't get any training.'[5]

On the northern front, the 53rd Brigade had withdrawn under heavy Japanese pressure along Thomson Road. By the evening, they had taken up their allotted position north of Braddell Road. The 18th Division now had all three of its brigades in line, with the 53rd on the right, the 55th in the centre and the 54th on the left. 'On the way south we were attacked by air two or three times and we were mortared at one crossroads,' Tony Ferrier says, 'but my company was in a Chinese graveyard with good fields of fire. A funeral was being held when we made contact with the Japanese. The Chinese had come to bury one of their people and it seemed rather incongruous to see this funeral wending its way between the opposing armies.

'We dug trenches and that night the Japanese started attacking. We were in action against them continuously, sometimes in hand-to-hand fighting. We could see them on various hillocks in this enormous graveyard. They tried intimidating tactics by screaming out, or they tried to imitate us by saying they were friends and they were advancing. They made a tremendous noise. I had two forward platoons on little hills and on one ghastly occasion they got in among one of the sections in the night and bayoneted some of the men. The screams and cries of anguish were really quite terrible. On another occasion, I was watching out from my command post when I suddenly saw a Japanese officer and about a dozen men crawling up behind one of the forward positions. Fortunately, our machine-gun battalion, the Northumberland Fusiliers, were with us and we had a section of machine guns. It was a very good target and in a very short time we had put paid to that attack.'

Early on the morning of the 14th, Percival was told that well over half the city's water was running to waste through broken pipes. It was estimated that the water supply would last for 48 hours at the outside – and that it might only last for 24 hours. Percival reported this to the Governor at the Singapore Club and said that he intended to go on fighting 'as I did not consider that the water situation, though undoubtedly serious, had yet rendered the further defence of Singapore impossible'.

It was agreed that Thomas would inform the Colonial Office about the situation, while Percival would report to Wavell. The Governor's cable said, 'GOC informs me that Singapore City now closely invested. There are now one million people within radius of three miles. Water supplies very badly damaged and unlikely to last more than 24 hours. Many dead in streets and burial impossible. We are faced with total deprivation of water which must result in pestilence. I have felt that it is my duty to bring this to notice of GOC.'

Percival told Wavell, 'We are fighting on but all troops except those on islands are now on Singapore perimeter and dependent with civil population upon one water supply. Both petrol and food supplies are also short owing to most of our dumps being outside the town area. Morale of Asiatic civil population is low under bombing and shelling from which they have NO protection. Will continue to comply with your intention but feel must represent situation as it exists today.' In his reply, the Supreme Commander said, 'In all places where sufficiency of water exists for troops they must go on fighting.' In a later telegram, he added, 'Your gallant stand is serving purpose and must be continued to limit of endurance.'

The enemy's main thrust that morning had again been directed against the western front of the Southern Area, where the Loyal Regiment and the Malay Regiment distinguished themselves. But British forces had been driven back by sheer weight of numbers, and the Alexandra Military Hospital had fallen into enemy hands. At 1 p.m., hospital staff on the upstairs veranda saw Japanese troops in green uniforms and steel helmets approaching along Ayer Rajah Road. The hospital, built to accommodate 550 patients, had admitted another 350 on camp stretchers and was packed with 900 sick and wounded soldiers. Water was in such short supply that each man had been rationed to one pint a day – not nearly enough to prevent dehydration. With the toilets out of action, excrement had to be carried out of the wards in buckets, and piles of soiled bed linen and blood-stained clothing lay everywhere.

At 1.40 p.m., the first group of Japanese soldiers entered the hospital. A lieutenant from reception dashed to the entrance with a white flag to indicate that the hospital had surrendered. He was bayoneted to death. More Japanese then entered the premises and started to kill patients and staff on the ground floor. Orderlies pointed to their Red Cross brassards and shouted 'Hospital!' but to no avail. One hundred Japanese soldiers, wearing twigs and branches attached to their combat gear, stormed through the building, killing patients and stopping only to loot watches and any other items of value from the bodies.

In the operating theatre, five of the staff were bayoneted to death, as was a patient who was under anaesthetic on the operating table. Captain Smiley received a thrust in the breast, which was deflected away from his heart by a metal cigarette case in his pocket. He blocked the next thrust with his arm and took the blow in his groin. The next two thrusts injured his right arm and hand. Smiley fell against Private Sutton and both men pretended to be dead.

The Japanese left the room and after lying still for 15 minutes Smiley saw the hospital's commanding officer, Lieutenant-Colonel J. W. Craven, coming along the corridor from his upstairs office. It had taken him half an hour to make his way through the ravaged wards to the operating theatre. Some 50 dead and many more wounded were strewn throughout the hospital. Meanwhile, 200 patients and staff from other wards had been herded together outside the hospital and had their hands tied behind their backs. Some of the patients could only hobble, some had only one arm, some were in plaster and others were grievously ill.

This large group was marched out of the hospital grounds at bayonet point, along the railway tracks and through a tunnel under the embankment to Ayer Rajah Road. Anyone who fell down was bayoneted and left for dead. The rest were then packed into three small rooms in a building a quarter of a mile from the hospital. The doors were barricaded and the windows nailed shut. There was no ventilation; during the night many men died from suffocation and all suffered agonies of thirst.

Back at the hospital, staff had managed to evacuate many of the survivors. Harry Hesp, then a 17-year-old member of the catering staff in the *Empress of Asia*, says, 'I was at the Tan Tok Seng Hospital, and the Alexandra Military Hospital was the one up the road. The Japanese came in and bayoneted and killed everybody they could find. I saw some of the bodies. The wounded came into the hospital where I was working. I had to strip one man of his gear but he was holding two grenades and he wouldn't let go of them for all the tea in China. One was for the Japanese when they came and one was for himself.'[6]

Meanwhile, Admiral Spooner's little armada had come to grief soon after leaving Keppel Harbour. 'I regret to have to report that the flotilla of small ships and other light craft which left Singapore on the night of 13–14 February encountered a Japanese naval force in the approaches to the Banka Straits,' Percival says. 'It was attacked by light naval craft and by aircraft. Many ships and other craft were sunk or disabled and there was considerable loss of life. Others were wounded or were forced ashore and were subsequently captured.'

Terpie Pattara's mother and sisters were among those who were torpedoed and thrown into the sea. 'My mother, Clio and Thetie managed to land on Banka Island,' Terpie Pattara says. 'Ino had been wounded and had been helped by a sailor in the sea and landed on the other side of the island. My mother went across the island to find her, but meanwhile Clio, Thetie and the others were picked up by a passing Australian ship, which was subsequently torpedoed, and all perished. My mother found Ino and they were finally rescued and made their way to India.'

The casualties included the motor launch in which Spooner and Pulford were travelling. Their boat had been driven ashore on a malarial island in the Banka Straits by a Japanese destroyer. The party of 53 men was marooned for two months during which time Spooner and Pulford both died of starvation and exhaustion – but not before they had accused Shenton Thomas of exercising a malign influence on the whole of the Malayan Campaign. Their most serious accusation was that he had protested vehemently about fighter aircraft being withdrawn from Singapore to defend Force Z.[7]

Percival says, 'I wish here to pay a special tribute to the loyalty of Air Vice-Marshal Pulford. Though at liberty to leave Singapore at any time on or after 5 February he preferred, from a sense of duty and of personal friendship to myself, to remain there until 13 February and would have remained longer had I wished him to do so. This gallant officer's self-sacrifice cost him his life.'

V. G. Bowden's final cable had been received in Canberra. 'Our work completed,' it said. 'We will telegraph from another place at present unknown.'[8] The message had been transmitted on a small handset located at the point where the cable entered the water. In the early hours of 15 February, Bowden and two colleagues – A. N. Wootton, the Commercial Secretary, and J. P. Quinn, the Political Secretary – knowing that capitulation was imminent, left Singapore in the motor launch *Mary Rose*. At the entrance to the Banka Straits, a searchlight was shone on the boat and two

Japanese patrol vessels threatened to open fire. In the absence of a white flag, the party hoisted a pair of underpants to indicate surrender.

The men were taken to Muntok Harbour, where Bowden was involved in an altercation with a Japanese guard about the removal of an item from his baggage. The party was then marched to a hall which was being used as a reception centre for hundreds of captives. Bowden knew the Japanese mentality from his years as trade commissioner in Shanghai and, although aged 52 and white-haired, was not prepared to tolerate their bullying. He attempted to make known his diplomatic status, as he had been instructed to do by his Government, but was punched and threatened with a bayonet. The guard then sought to remove his gold wrist-watch.

The situation had now become tense, and Bowden was motioned to leave the hall with two guards. Throwing back his shoulders, the tall Australian marched out of the hall at bayonet point. Half an hour later two shots were heard. It was later learned that V. G. had been forced to dig his own grave and was then executed.[9]

CHAPTER 23

Surrender

LANCE-CORPORAL FRANK DAVIES's earliest childhood memories are of the mean streets of Salford, Lancashire, with mills at one end and docks at the other. 'The place was always covered in a cloud of muck and smoke and mire from the rubber works and other industries,' he says. 'The house we lived in was two up and two down and we had one gas light in the front room, a cold-water tap in the kitchen – or the scullery as we called it – and an outside toilet. Our Saturday-night entertainment was going down Trafford Road along the docks into Cross Lane. They used to call it the "Barbary Coast" and we'd wander up and down looking at these foreign seamen drinking and fighting. It was a tough upbringing, but it was the Depression and you had to learn how to look after yourself.'

Davies, a 20-year-old engineer, had been working for Metropolitan Vickers Electrical Company in Manchester when war broke out. 'We were exempt from military service but a few of us joined the Territorials so that we would be called up,' he says. 'I was a bit of a rebel and I had visions of becoming Errol Flynn. I didn't expect to end up in Singapore. During the siege, I was put into the British Battalion. There were Navy lads who had lost their ships, RAF blokes and our kind of bloke. They herded us together and tried to make soldiers of us. I had a revolver strapped to my leg from working on the gun sites and they gave me a rifle.'

The battalion counterattacked the enemy on the Jurong Road but they came under heavy fire when Brigadier Coates, commander of the 15th Brigade, ordered them to withdraw across Sleepy Valley, heading for the 22nd Brigade's lines at Reformatory Road, and suffered severe casualties. The brigade had been reduced from 1,500 men to just 400. 'We were shuffled from one place to another and at one point I ducked into one of the abandoned houses and picked up a magazine,' Davies remembers. 'It was a copy of *Picture Post*. I was thumbing through it and came across pictures of what the Japs had done in Nanking and Manchuria. They had people strung up and were using them for bayonet practice; others were in trenches they had dug and were about to be bayoneted. I thought, "God love us – what are we facing here?" When I could get to sleep, I had nightmares about it.'

On the morning of 15 February, a Japanese officer opened the door of one of the rooms containing prisoners from the Alexandra Hospital. 'We are taking you behind the lines,' he said. 'You will get water on the way.' The men were led two at a time through a courtyard and out of sight behind a lavatory block. The prisoners left behind heard screams and saw a Japanese soldier wiping blood off his bayonet. One hundred men were killed in this cold-blooded, premeditated manner. Suddenly, a shell struck the building and blew open some of the doors and windows. A number of men made a dash for freedom. Most were shot down, but eight managed to reach the brush surrounding a storm-water drain and disappear. The 90-odd patients and staff still in captivity were never seen again.

For the butchers of Nanking, the Alexandra Hospital massacre – both the frenzied killing on 14 February and the cold-blooded, premeditated murders on the 15th – was all in a day's work. The motive was to show Percival that an utterly mindless and totally ruthless force would be unleashed upon the citizens of Singapore if he persisted in ignoring Yamashita's demand to surrender. Colonel Tsuji was only 300 yards away from the hospital when the massacre was carried out and was most probably the brains behind it. Yamashita certainly knew about the killings after the event, but whether he had approved them in advance is unknown.

Subsequent claims that the Japanese had been fired on by Indian soldiers and were searching the hospital for the offenders are demonstrably false.[1] 'The Japanese Army ... was dangerous because it was liable to be swayed by terrible spasms of inane and savage barbarism.'[2]

General Percival had slept in the Battle Box on Saturday night, slightly cheered by Wavell's cable asserting that his gallant stand was serving a useful purpose. These few words of encouragement, Percival later wrote, had had 'a wonderful effect'. He had taken a love letter from his wife Betty with him to Singapore and he may have reread it. 'Thank you, darling, for your love, our lovely children and the happy years we have had together,' she had written. 'I commit you to God's care, sure that He will do what is best for you.'

Percival rose early on Sunday morning and took Holy Communion in his office from Chaplain George McNeill. Then he read the latest reports, which were all gloomy: Ivan Simson reported that the water supply would run out in 24 hours, the Japanese had renewed their attack in the south-west and were in danger of capturing the remaining depots at Alexandra Barracks, and the 18th Division was under pressure on all its fronts.

Shortly after 8 a.m. Percival received a cable from the Supreme Commander: 'So long as you are in position to inflict losses and damage to enemy and your troops are physically capable of doing so must fight on. Time gained and damage to enemy are of vital important at this crisis. When you are fully satisfied that this is no longer possible I give you discretion to cease resistance. Before doing so all arms and equipment and transport of value to enemy must of course be rendered useless. Also just before final cessation of fighting opportunity should be given to any determined bodies of men or individuals to try and effect escape by any means possible. They must be armed. Inform me of intentions. Whatever happens I thank you and all troops for your gallant efforts of last few days.'

The breakthrough had come shortly after 4 a.m. that morning. Wavell had been woken up in Bandung and handed a telegram from Churchill. The fiery, uncompromising rhetoric of earlier days had been replaced by a calmer, more reasonable tone: 'You are of course sole judge of moment when no further results can be gained in Singapore and should instruct Percival accordingly. CIGS concurs.'

At 9.30 a.m. Percival's commanders negotiated the narrow, subterranean corridors of the Battle Box to the inner chamber. The reports were now even more depressing. During the night, enemy infantry had infiltrated in all sectors of the 18th Division front and had also succeeded in getting a footing on the Mount Pleasant Ridge. Percival then told the meeting that there was enough food and small-arms ammunition for a few more days but mortar, field and anti-aircraft artillery ammunition was running out, the only petrol was that in the tanks of vehicles, and the water situation was now critical. He then invited his commanders to speak.

Heath went first. 'In my opinion there is only one possible course to adopt,' he said, 'and that is to do what you ought to have done two days ago, namely to surrender immediately.'

Bennett agreed.

'The Commander-in-Chief's orders are that we should continue the struggle at all costs and without consideration to what may happen to the civil population,' Percival persisted. 'It is our duty to continue fighting as long as we can.'

Heath interrupted, 'How can General Wavell command this battle from Java?'

Percival ignored the remark and said that in his opinion there were two possible courses of action: a counterattack to recapture the food depots at Bukit Timah, or surrender. Heath, Bennett and Keith Simmons all agreed that a counterattack was out of the question, and Percival therefore agreed to surrender. 'I could see no immediate solution for the critical water situation and decided to capitulate,' he says. 'The other members of the conference concurred unanimously with this decision.' Percival said he would request a cease-fire at 4 p.m., but stressed that resistance should continue until agreement had been reached with the Japanese. The meeting then adjourned and the commanders walked out into the sunlight.

Major Cyril Wild, a Japanese-speaking member of the Indian Army, had been asked to attend the conference in case an interpreter was required to write a letter to the Japanese. 'The decision to ask for terms was taken without a dissentient voice,' he says. 'Some minutes later when details of the surrender were being discussed Major-General Gordon Bennett remarked, "How about a combined counterattack to recapture Bukit Timah?" This remark came so late, and was by then so irrelevant, that I formed the impression at the time that it was not made as a serious contribution to the discussion but as something to quote afterwards. It was received in silence and the discussion proceeded.'[3]

Frank Davies could see Fort Canning through the windows of the United Engineers building in River Valley Road. 'This was going to be our last stand: we wanted to die with some kind of glory,' he says. 'We carried as much weaponry as possible down into the cellar and some barmy officer turned up and gave us a rousing speech. He told us to use all our ammunition "and then fix your bayonets and take as many of them with you as you can". He then disappeared and we found out later he was heading for the docks hoping to get away. All it did was put the bloody wind up us. The Japanese had occupied the surrounding houses and we could hear the shouts and screams of the poor locals copping it and it wasn't a pleasant experience.'

Two miles west of River Valley Road, past the Botanic Gardens, Paul Gemmell was with the 2/18th Battalion in the AIF perimeter on Holland Road. 'In the afternoon of the 15th we shot up a 12-man Japanese patrol,' he says. 'They came up on push-bikes to try to get through into Holland Road and didn't take any precautions. We were all half asleep in the hot sun – we hadn't slept for six days – but fortunately I was [more] awake and saw them and the hillside blazed with fire. They were all killed.'

The front line ran straight through the Botanic Gardens, where shell fire had ripped apart many of the trees, shrubs and flowers that were the pride and joy of the assistant director, Professor John Corner. The 36-year-old Yorkshireman had been tending plants there since 1929 and had been instrumental in the creation of the colony's abundant nature reserves. Despite a crippling stammer, he had become a forceful advocate for the storehouse of irreplaceable botanical specimens that had been collected in the gardens over the previous century. At that time, there were about 400,000 specimens in the gardens' herbarium. It was clear to Corner that Singapore was lost, and that something must be done to save them.

North of the gardens late that morning, an open roadster bearing Cyril Wild, Brigadier T. K. Newbigging and Hugh Fraser, the Colonial Secretary, drove north up Bukit Timah Road as far as a mined roadblock of Dannert wire across Bukit Timah and Dunearn roads at the Adam Road crossing. This was the front line. Taking a Union Flag and a white flag from the car, the group walked 600 yards into Japanese territory. They were stopped by a Japanese patrol, who removed their pistols.

Wild explained that the flag party had come to see General Yamashita; they were taken to a small villa 100 yards west of the road. After an hour, Colonel Ichiji Sugita arrived with another officer, and Brigadier Newbigging handed over a letter from Percival. Sugita then handed Newbigging a typewritten letter with a one-page appendix. The letter requested that Percival meet Yamashita at Bukit Timah. A space had been left blank for the time; Newbigging inserted '4 p.m.'. The letter further stated that prior to this meeting the British forces must comply with the orders given in the appendix. Wild drew Newbigging's attention to a clause stating that British forces must lay down their arms and remain in their positions. He pointed out that there was no reciprocal undertaking by the Japanese that they would also cease fire and stand fast. Newbigging told Wild to raise this point with Sugita.

Sugita: 'There is no such undertaking by us in this document.'

Wild: 'That is why we were raising this point. Will you give us such an undertaking?'

Sugita: 'No. The document does not say so.'

Wild: 'How can Lieutenant-General Percival order his forces to lay down their arms if the Japanese Army does not agree not to continue its advance against our unarmed troops?'

Sugita: 'You are not the negotiator.'

Wild reported failure to Newbigging, who said, 'Leave it. It's getting late and we must get back.'

Sugita then handed over a very large Japanese flag with the order that it be displayed from the top of the Cathay Building as a signal to the Japanese that General Percival had accepted the conditions and was on his way to meet the Japanese commander. Sugita said that this would enable them to cease fire along Bukit Timah Road.

Wild: 'We cannot display it for more than 10 minutes.'

Sugita: 'On the contrary, you must leave it there permanently.'

Wild: 'If we do, our troops in the city will not know why it is there. They will shoot at it, or tear it down and you will be angry afterwards.'

Sugita: 'Very well, take it down after 10 minutes.'

The flag party returned to the British lines and, despite a burst of pistol fire delivered at a somewhat unsporting range by a provost corporal of the 18th Division who thought they were spies, made it safely to Fort Canning. A few minutes earlier, at 3.02 p.m., Percival had informed Wavell, 'Owing to losses from enemy action water petrol food and ammunition practically finished. Unable therefore continue the fight any longer. All ranks have done their best and grateful for your help.'

Newbigging, Fraser and Wild assembled in Percival's office. 'The windows looked out in the direction from which the enemy's batteries were firing,' Wild says. 'Some of their shells were bursting on the glacis of the fort below. I particularly admired the cool way in which General Percival continued to sit at his desk when the concussion from a stick of bombs brought down some of the ceiling boards and raised a cloud of dust in the room.'

Newbigging ordered Wild to go over to the Cathay Building to display the Japanese flag. It was already past 3.30 p.m. At that hour, Tony Ferrier had been summoned with other company commanders to battalion headquarters, where Colonel Eric Prattley informed them that Percival had surrendered and that they would have to stop fighting at 4 p.m. He said that if the Japanese came over to their positions they were stand there without any weapons and offer no resistance. Ferrier went back to C Company and, choked with emotion, informed them of what had happened. 'I put out sentries just in case the Japanese suddenly came in and attacked us, but I told them they couldn't fire,' he says. 'We just had to say we were British troops and hold our hands up. The only answer was to lie down and go to sleep, to be awoken immediately if any Japanese appeared.'

Meanwhile, Cyril Wild had draped the Japanese flag over the parapet of the Cathay Building on the side facing Bukit Timah, giving orders that it was not to be left there longer than 10 minutes. He then checked with General Heath, whose headquarters were in the building, and discovered that no orders had been received concerning the time of the cease-fire. When Wild returned to Fort Canning shortly after 4 p.m. he found General

Percival seated at his desk, with Brigadier Torrance, his Chief of Staff, and Brigadier Newbigging standing beside it.

Wild informed Newbigging about the lack of orders, but Newbigging ignored him and remained silent. Wild then said it could be disastrous if the Japanese took advantage of a unilateral cease-fire. He addressed this remark to Percival, who had stood up behind his desk, his head bowed. Percival made no reply. After a time, he said, 'We ought to go.' The three senior officers walked out of the room and down to two waiting cars. 'I had no choice but to follow them,' Wild says. 'I had become inured during the past week to seeing General Percival's painful inability to make any reply whatever when points of operational importance were referred to him, particularly by my corps commander [Heath].'

It was well after 4 p.m. when the two cars swung into Bukit Timah Road and stopped at the front line. Again, the party had to proceed on foot until they were met by the Japanese. They were then driven to Yamashita's headquarters at the Ford Motor Factory, where a conference table had been set up in the works canteen. Percival and Yamashita viewed each other across the table while Japanese camera crews, photographers and journalists jostled for position. Six Japanese officers sat on one side of the table, the four British men on the other. The parley was conducted through interpreters.

Yamashita: 'Have you seen our terms, which were handed over to the peace envoy?'

Percival: 'Yes.'

Yamashita: 'Further details are given in an annexed sheet. [*The appendix was placed within Percival's reach.*] I want everything carried out in accordance with this.'

Percival (*after glancing through the contents of the appendix*): 'There are disturbances in Singapore City. As there are non-combatants in the city, I should like to keep 1,000 men under arms.'

Yamashita: 'The Japanese Army will be stationed there, and will maintain order. So you need have no worry on that score.'

Percival: 'The British Army is familiar with the situation in Singapore. I should like to keep 1,000 armed men.'

Yamashita: 'The Japanese Army will look after that; you need not concern yourself with it.'

Percival: 'Looting is taking place inside the city. And there are non-combatants.'

Yamashita: 'Non-combatants will be protected by the spirit of *bushido*. So everything will be all right.'

Percival: 'If there is a vacuum, there will be chaos in the city and looting. Outbreaks of looting and rioting are undesirable, whether from the Japanese or the British point of view. For the purpose of maintaining order, it is desirable that 1,000 men should be permitted to retain their arms.'

Yamashita: 'As the Japanese Army is continuing its assault on the city, an attack is likely to go forward tonight.'

Percival: 'I should like to ask you to postpone any night attack.'

Yamashita: 'The attack will go forward if we cannot come to an agreement.'

Percival: 'I would like you to postpone it. [*Yamashita repeated what he had just said.*] Because of the rioting in Singapore, I would like 1,000 men left with their arms.'

Yamashita (*turning to Colonel Iheya*): 'What time is the night attack scheduled for?'

Ikeya: 'Eight o'clock.'

Percival: 'If there is a night attack, then you put me in a difficult situation.'

Yamashita: 'Does the British Army intend to surrender or not?'

Percival (*after a pause*): 'I wish to have a cease-fire.'

Yamashita: 'The time for the night attack is drawing near. Is the British Army going to surrender or not? Answer [*Yamashita spoke the next words in English*] "Yes" or "No".'

Percival: 'Yes. But I would like the retention of 1,000 armed men sanctioned.'

Yamashita: 'Very well.'

Yamashita asked Percival at what time he would be prepared to cease hostilities, and Percival nominated 10 p.m. (11.30 p.m. Tokyo time). Yamashita, however, said that he would prefer 8.30 p.m. (10 p.m. Tokyo time), and that if Percival insisted on the later hour he and Sir Shenton Thomas would have to be held as hostages. Percival then agreed to 8.30 p.m.

Yamashita openly expressed his relief that the earlier hour had been accepted. He said, 'I can now tell you frankly that my assault on Singapore was timed to begin at midnight [Tokyo time – 10.30 Singapore time] tonight. If you had declined to cease fighting until 23.30 p.m. [Tokyo time] I should have had only 30 minutes in which to stop the advance and might not have been able to halt it everywhere. As it is, I shall have time to order my forces to stand fast.'

Percival signed the only copy of the instrument of surrender, which the Japanese retained, and the two generals shook hands.

After Percival and Torrance had returned to Singapore, Wild remained for some time at Bukit Timah with Newbigging. He stole a quick glance at a Japanese staff officer's map of Singapore Island. From the blue pencil marks, it appeared that the spearhead of the attack would have thrust east of the Bukit Timah Road, across the golf course and Mount Pleasant. The 18th Division, defending this sector, had a total front of about 17,000 yards and many of the troops were exhausted. The Japanese had medium tanks and 6-inch guns available in that area. 'Few acquainted with the situation can doubt that had the attack gone in that night, it would have broken clean through to the sea, splitting the garrison in two,' Wild says. 'The half-million citizens of Singapore would then have shared the fate of those of Nanking and Hangchow. As it was, Yamashita never allowed these three divisions to enter the city after the capitulation.'

While Percival headed for the Singapore Club, where he informed Shenton Thomas over a fortifying *stengah* that he was no longer Governor of the Straits Settlements, Frank Davies and his comrades were preparing to die in their cellar in River Valley Road. 'The Japanese were shelling and bombing us, but we held on until word came around that when we saw the flag come down at Fort Canning, that was it – it was the end.'

At the General Hospital, the staff feared a repeat of the Alexandra Hospital massacre when Japanese snipers opened fire in the hospital grounds. 'We knew something was going to happen because there was no way we could carry on,' Len Butler says. 'There were bodies in the grounds but we couldn't reach them because of the shelling and sniping. We were concentred in the lecture hall, a building in the hospital grounds. We'd closed the door and about eight o'clock on Sunday night there was a thumping on the door. It was opened, and in walked a Japanese officer with four scruffy soldiers with rifles and fixed bayonets. He marched in, had a good look around, never said a word, about-turned and marched out again. He left a guard on the door overnight and we wondered what was going to happen to us.'

Bill Drower ended up in a school in Serangoon Road with the 135th Field Regiment. 'I felt very lonely,' he says. 'I expected Japs at any moment but none of them turned up. We were told that there had been a surrender and we mustn't touch our guns. Philip Toosey, who struck me as a very competent chap, ordered the guns to be blown, so we blew our guns up. There were bits of metal flying everywhere – it was much more dangerous than being under fire. I then organised an escape party. We'd been told the order was that no one was to escape and I thought that was bloody nonsense. It was against regulations – we all had a *duty* to escape. I got this party together and we were going to grab a boat, but it got to Toosey's ears and he said, "You're under close arrest." I wasn't allowed to move, and I surrendered along with everybody else.'

Chapter 24

Bennett's Breakout

WHILE GORDON BENNETT had been attending the final conference at Fort Canning that morning, Dr Rowley Richards, the 2/15th's Regimental Medical Officer, had driven in his truck to divisional headquarters at Tanglin Barracks to consult with the division's senior medical officer Colonel Alf Derham. 'Just after I arrived, Bennett screamed up in his staff car and got out,' Dr Richards says. 'His staff were with him and he announced the termination of hostilities. Then he went off and left us. I returned to my unit and waited until the CO, Colonel Wright, had been officially notified of the cease-fire before passing any comment.'[1]

The flag party was still on its way to Bukit Timah when Bennett announced that General Percival had called an armistice. He ordered all ranks to stand fast within unit areas and to ensure that 'the spirit of the cease-fire is not destroyed by foolish action'. All arms were to be unloaded under strict supervision. Two days' rations would be issued and all water-bottles should be filled. The AIF's guns fell silent – but there was no corresponding let-up in incoming mortar fire, shelling or bombing. 'Those vultures circle round and round over us without a break,' Charles Moses wrote, 'a stick of bombs, then machine-gunning, swooping and soaring like birds of prey.'

Bennett had hoped to make his getaway in the Sultan of Johore's motor yacht, but the British Navy had commandeered it and he was now forced to make other arrangements. His new escape plan was to head north across the straits and make for Malacca, where he hoped to find a boat to take him to Burma. At 1 p.m. he asked Moses and Walker to accompany him on an inspection of the AIF perimeter, with the objective of finding a weak point in the Japanese lines that they could slip through at the appropriate time. Russell Savage was with the 2/26th Battalion at a forward observation pit in Farrer Road. He remembers, 'For the past 48 hours, they had been bringing down chaps from the Army Service Corps who had never been out of a vehicle in their whole army life – nice, soft, fat blokes were being brought down in 20s and 30s to form platoons for the 2/26th. It was a tragedy to see these fellows in the front line.'²

The Japanese were situated on a ridge just 400 yards away; Bennett and his co-conspirators looked for a safe place from which to spy on them. They went into the home of a Commander Cole, 'whose property was just as he left it. Apparently he hadn't had time to collect a single item – photos, sword, gold-braided uniforms, all were there and some delightful furniture'. The intruders had tea with a young captain from the 2/26th in the Commander's dining room, with doilies, fine china and biscuits with butter and jam. 'We enjoyed it immensely,' Moses says. 'It was a bit different from the scrap meals we'd swallowed standing up in the storeroom at Tanglin Barracks.'

On the way back to headquarters, the merry trio popped in on the Gordon Highlanders and took sherry with one of the company commanders. Toasts were drunk and hands shaken. 'The AIF and the Scottish regiments always get on well,' Moses noted. On returning to his headquarters, Bennett learned that Percival was meeting the Japanese near Bukit Timah. After destroying most of his private papers and eating a last meal, he handed over command of the AIF to Brigadier Boots Callaghan as soon as news came through that the instrument of surrender had been signed.

Callaghan was weak from an attack of malaria. 'I went to his shelter and told him of my resolve, asking him to let the Japanese think I had escaped some days earlier,' Bennett says. 'I found him seated in a room, badly lighted by a kerosene lamp. He seemed dazed. He was an old friend and a very good soldier. Our farewell was short but full of deep feeling.'

Bennett, Moses and Walker made their way to the waterfront at the Arab Street pier. Walker, a strong swimmer, stripped off, dived in and swam 100 yards to secure one of the sampans bobbing at anchor offshore. Bennett and Moses jumped into the boat and the three were about to depart when they were hailed by eight armed men. These turned out to be European planters, lawyers and civil servants who had been serving in the Malay Volunteers and wanted to escape.

One of the men, Bombadier H. R. Oppenheim, an Ipoh accountant, wrote in his diary, 'There was complete chaos on the sampan. The General screams like a young girl and curses Gordon Walker who is standing up in the nude for being so, saying that it would be scandalous if the Japs saw him like that. He was like that because he had swum out to collect the sampan.'³ Luckily, a Chinese junk loomed out of the mist, and its opium-smoking skipper agreed, for a few hundred dollars, to take the party to Sumatra.

Little progress was made on the 16th as the junk meandered through the chain of islands close to Singapore. 'Everyone argued about the route to be taken,' Oppenheim says. 'Bennett completely useless, first crying and then imploring Moses or Walker to do something. Eventually we crash into some fishing stakes and anchor for the night.' By the morning of 17 February, however, Gordon Bennett was safely away from Singapore and heading towards a controversial freedom.

Percival had been informed about Bennett's unauthorised departure at 7 a.m. on the 16th. 'He just went off the handle,' Jim Thyer says. Half an hour later, a message arrived at Tanglin Barracks from the GOC, confirming Callaghan's appointment as head of the AIF and promoting him to major-general.

Stanley Prout had been put in a police station on the south coast with other civilians, under Japanese guard, but he escaped. 'He was near the coast and as we had lived in Katong all those years he knew that area well,' says his daughter Maisie Duncan. 'He also knew the waters around Singapore and where the mines had been laid. People were on the beaches still trying to escape in boats even after the surrender. My father got on a yacht but only because they needed a sailor to take them across to Sumatra. Dad happened to be the lucky one. They passed Gordon Bennett and his two officers while at sea – he said they were dressed as Malays and had blackened their hair. They had come up close to Dad's yacht and he had got a good look at them. When Dad reached Sumatra, he drew lots for a place on a ship to Perth, where our stepmother and her children had gone before the trouble started. Dad got a berth on the ship and was safe in Perth when we thought he was in a concentration camp.'

The only good thing about 15 February was that many thousands of dog-tired soldiers and civilians got a first good night's sleep. 'I crawled into my truck and went to sleep,' Dr Richards says. 'We hadn't had any real sleep for six weeks. Next day, it was just like waking up with a dreadful hangover and, in fact, I likened the next week or two to one long hangover.'

Tony Ferrier woke up after eight hours' sleep to find members of the Japanese Guards Division in his position. 'They were big men, minimum height around six feet,' he remembers, 'and were in uniform but they were not wearing boots, just black, soft-soled shoes which had the ends cut away so you could see their toes. Their uniforms were very scruffy: some wore puttees, some of the officers wore leggings, different-coloured shirts – they looked a pretty scruffy army. Some were shaved, some unshaven; it was not a very impressive sight. A Japanese captain came over and wanted to know whether we had any food. We had plenty of food at that time. We gave them some tins of pineapple and they started tucking into it. They tried to be reasonably chatty – there was no sign of any offensive action on their part towards us. They asked in broken English how long had we been in Singapore and where had we been fighting. I spoke the bare minimum because I didn't feel very kindly disposed towards them. We were marshalled together and the next day we were told we were going to march up to Changi. One truck was allowed for kit; otherwise we took what we could carry.'

Frank Davies saw Japanese soldiers crawling out of the monsoon drains in River Valley Road: 'We didn't know they were so close. We knew we had been shot at and things were flying around, but we didn't know there were so many of them so near to us. They looked a right ugly bloody lot. They were real front-line troops with grass in their hair. They surrounded us and started pushing us around, pinching any valuables such as rings and even glasses. They were pinching specs off blokes who could hardly see. You daren't argue. We just stood there like 'nanas and threw all our weapons down.'

Russell Savage was angry, then philosophical about the sudden collapse. 'We thought Singapore would be another Tobruk,' he said. 'We didn't realise that we didn't control the water supply and that Percival had no option at the end.'

The Reverend Ray Rossiter, then a 19-year-old signaller in the 18th Division, says, 'We had only been in action for a fortnight. We were at Bukit Timah racecourse when we landed, then we moved to a rubber plantation at Payah Lebar. I was on flying-picket duty when a convoy started moving out and somebody said to me, "You'd better jump on the running-board – the Japanese are a mile up the road." I suppose I deserted my post by moving without orders, but I wasn't going to stay behind to find out. I jumped on the running-board of the last vehicle, and ended up at divisional headquarters in a large house at Chancery Lane on the outskirts of the city.

'I was a wireless operator in a dugout in the grounds of the big house; we had wireless silence for security reasons during the whole of the siege. We weren't allowed to transmit but we could listen in to the Japs screaming at us. We were marshalled together and handed in our arms and waited for orders from the Japanese.'

Winston Churchill rose wearily to his feet after Question Time in the House of Commons. 'This extremely grave event was not unexpected and its possibility was comprised within the scope of the argument I submitted to the House on the occasion of the vote of confidence three weeks ago,' he said. 'The House has, of course, many opportunities of discussing this and other aspects of the war situation. I am sure it would be a great mistake to try to discuss it today in the short time available. I have no information to give to the House other than that contained in the public press, nor would it be prudent to speculate in detail upon the various evil consequences which will follow from the fall of Singapore. Moreover, it would ill become the dignity of the Government and the House, and would render poor service to the Alliance of which we are a part, if we were drawn into agitated or excited recriminations at a time when all our minds are oppressed with a sense of tragedy and with the sorrow of so lamentable a misfortune.'[4]

After the war, Churchill was more candid about the fallibility of Fortress Singapore. 'I ought to have known,' he confessed. 'My advisers ought to have known and I ought to have been told and I ought to have asked. The reason I had not asked about this matter, amid the thousands of questions I put, was that the possibility of Singapore having no landward defences no more entered into my mind than that of a battleship being launched without a bottom.'[5]

There was no shortage of high-ranking candidates to blame for the catastrophe. General Kirby says in his own book, *Singapore: The Chain of Disaster*, 'One can sum up by saying that those responsible for the conduct of the land campaign in Malaya committed every conceivable blunder.'[6] Wavell, Percival, Heath and Bennett had all made serious errors of judgement regarding the enemy and the best ways of dealing with him. From the beginning Wavell, as he later admitted, had underestimated the Japanese soldier just as he had overrated Percival's chances of beating him. The Supreme Commander had also made the fatal mistake of placing his faith on short acquaintance in Gordon Bennett, who had been an embarrassing failure in the campaign, and of interfering with the command structure and dispositions during the vital Battle of Johore.

On reaching Australia, Bennett was snubbed by the country's top brass and never again commanded troops in battle.[7] Nevertheless, he was vocal in his criticisms of the higher direction of the Malayan Campaign, declaring that the British leadership relied far too heavily on the 'old school tie'. He singled out the 'low morale of Indian troops' as the prime cause of Britain's defeat, and noted the 'poor quality of the 18th Division'. He was on safe ground. Many Indian troops, young and untrained, had been reluctant to lay down their lives for the Empire. It was not surprising that, as subjects of an occupied country, many later joined Chandra Bose's pro-Japanese Indian National Army. The 18th Division had been trained to fight a desert war and had arrived in Singapore in sand-coloured uniforms, weak-kneed and unfit after three months at sea. Moreover, they had been deprived of much of their equipment, from anti-aircraft guns and vehicles to small arms and ammunition, all of which had gone to the Middle East.

In a letter to Sir Lewis Heath after the war, General Percival wrote, 'From what I have since heard I believe that Gordon Bennett painted a very false picture, both to you and to me, of the situation on his front and the state of his troops. He was a very vain and self-centred man and I believe now, though I admit I did not fully realise it at the time, that from the time he left Segamat he had but one object in mind. You can guess what I mean. I believe that, if the Australians had been properly led, they would have risen to the occasion even at the eleventh hour.'

To discredit Gordon Bennett in the eyes of the Chiefs of Staff, who had received his appraisal in March 1942, Wavell commissioned a report from Major H. P. Thomas of the Indian Army. Thomas, who had been in charge of the reinforcement camp in Singapore, formed his impressions after interviewing 50 British officers and civilians who had reached Ceylon and India from Singapore. The report's Appendix B contained inflammatory criticism which Wavell allowed to stand because 'it represents accurately much current opinion'. In Appendix B, Thomas wrote, 'The name of Sir Shenton Thomas will go down in history as the most abused Englishman and the Malayan Civil Service will be named as one of the most incompetent institutions which has ever existed. Among civilians generally the failure of the Air Force receives more unfavourable comment than the inability of the Army to hold the Japanese on the mainland.

'For the fall of Singapore itself, the Australians are held responsible, while their presence in the town in disproportionately large numbers during the last days, coupled with the escape of large numbers on ships and in boats, has aroused great indignation.

'All criticism is mingled with bitterness and disillusionment.

'Most civilians resent what they regard as gross and calculated deception on the part of Sir Shenton Thomas in that he repeated, both in public announcements and privately, assurances that there was no need to think of evacuation as Singapore would not fall.'

With regard to the AIF, Thomas says elsewhere in his report that it had started the campaign in 'a refreshingly offensive spirit at a period when this was sorely needed', but the Australians had been very severely handled in a series of actions near the west coast, notably at Parit Sulong and Batu Pahat and Muar. 'Thereafter a rapid decline must have set in, because signs of a break in morale were noticeable even before the Japanese landing in their sector [of Singapore Island]. Large numbers of AIF stragglers were seen in the town: many undoubtedly took the opportunity to desert in boats to Sumatra. Finally, the events of the night of 8th/9th February seem to have destroyed almost completely their discipline and morale.'

Thomas concludes, 'Though it must be admitted that the behaviour of the Australians in the final phase was a very bad example particularly to Indian troops, it is only fair to remember that they had been really heavily punished by shell fire on the night of the 8th/9th and were in fact the only troops in the whole campaign to come under heavy shell fire; secondly, a rumour got about that they were to be evacuated, and, lastly, they were near home and that home was under imminent threat of invasion.

'While these are not justifications for desertion and indiscipline, they do explain that glancing over the shoulder.'[8]

Much of the contents of Thomas's report was rumour and hearsay. There were sweeping generalisations – how many troops, for example, were a 'disproportionately large number'? – and many of the allegations were impossible to substantiate. Nevertheless, it was true that many Australian troops did not believe that their government would abandon them to the Japanese and expected to be evacuated in the manner of Dunkirk and Crete. Their anger at finding themselves involved in another Gallipoli-style débâcle – a purely *English* débâcle – was a key factor in the breakdown of discipline in the latter days of the campaign.

The Australians had borne the brunt of the Japanese attack and suffered heavy losses. Many of the stragglers seen wandering in Singapore City were looking for the collection point at the Anzac Club and were later returned to their units, where they continued to fight. The history of 2/18th Infantry Battalion AIF says, 'In the nine days of its total fighting history the 2/18 lost 225 men killed and more than 400 wounded out of 1,323 officers and other ranks.' It added that these losses were the *lowest* sustained in the 22nd Brigade AIF in the Malayan Campaign.[9]

Wavell's contribution to Thomas's report was to write a cover note to General Alan Brooke, dated New Delhi, 1 June, 1942, in which he says, 'I forward herewith a summary of statements on operations in Malaya and Singapore, collated from the evidence at present available. The officer who drew up this summary interviewed many persons, military and civil, who had been in Malaya and had knowledge of what occurred. The compiler had been in command of the mixed Reinforcement Camp in Singapore and had himself much knowledge of events and of currents of feeling. I have read, I think, all the principal reports which compose the evidence, and a good many others, and I consider this summary fair and accurate.' But he concluded, 'I would remind you of what I know you will bear in mind, that these statements available are mainly those of comparatively junior officers with a limited view; and that the great majority of senior officers whose preparations, planning and conduct of the operations are criticised have not had the opportunity of explaining their actions.'

Russell Savage says, 'We heard stories about deserters in Singapore and like a loyal Australian I assumed they couldn't be Australian, but having had occasion to go through the outskirts of Singapore [I saw] there were hundreds of deserters of all sorts, including Australians. You couldn't blame them. I later got to know one of them and he had been in the Army for three weeks. They say give an Australian a rifle and a bayonet and he's as good as anybody, but he's not until he's trained.'

Five days after the capitulation, Wavell wrote to his confidante Joan Bright, 'We have lost the battle here by a month or six weeks I think – the additional time that we should have gained at least in Malaya and Singapore and the time by which we should have built up in these islands an air force capable of holding and hitting back. I have a hunch the Jap is stretched to the utmost in the air but he is using his forces boldly and well and has been too quick for us.

'I went four times to Singapore and Malaya in a month but could never stop the rot; the front always seemed to be crumbling under my hand. I am still wondering if I might have found the answer somehow. I won't tell you more of the sad story here. You will have seen something of it in the official records and cables and can judge for yourself how my failure came about. I feel I ought to have pulled it off but the dice were rather heavily loaded and the little yellow man threw them with considerable cunning. I hate making excuses. I was given a job and have fallen down on it; whether it was "on" or not others can decide, I feel myself that it might have been but I think it wanted a bigger man than I have ever pretended to be. So that's that. We shall win the war all right in the end.'[10]

Tony Ferrier felt that his regiment had been placed in an impossible position and that the outcome had been inevitable. 'We were not fighting fit when we disembarked and we were in action 48 hours later,' he says. 'We felt we had been dropped in it. We were very conscious of the fact that there had been minimal support from the Navy and the Air Force – through no fault of their own. At that stage of the war, I suppose we weren't any worse off than other British armies but nevertheless we knew we had had a pretty raw deal. We reckoned we had been rather let down.'

Harry Schulman described Churchill's dilemma as 'a hell of a political muddle. He had to send the 18th Division to stop the Australians withdrawing from the Middle East. All the Spitfires were fighting the Battle of Britain and the Hurricanes were going to Russia. He had to supply Stalin because if the Germans had captured Russia, Britain was doomed. We were doomed anyhow but with bad management we fell much too quickly. We should have held on another two or three months but we were trained for desert warfare. My men were from Norfolk farms and they had never seen jungle or a swamp. I was always told if my company was in any trouble all I had to do was press a button and ask for an artillery barrage.'

Russell Savage thought the British commanders had a lot to answer for. 'I never had much regard for them, from Wavell down, for letting the Singapore thing develop the way it did,' he says. 'If they knew they couldn't hold it, they should not have been sending in troops up to the last day. I personally don't blame Churchill. If he could dominate the military leaders, it showed weakness on their part. They should have kept the troops up-country and fought. I know it was hard being outflanked, but when you think of what happened afterwards we would have been a damn sight better off taking a few more Japanese with us and delaying them for another month or so. It could have been done – but we were expendable, weren't we?'

Yamashita blamed Britain's defeat on the racial prejudice of senior British generals which had encouraged them to underestimate Japanese military capabilities. Percival, he said, was 'good on paper but timid and hesitant in making command decisions'. Yamashita had bluffed the British general at every turn of the Malayan Campaign. He had deliberately restricted his 25th Army to three divisions instead of the five he had been offered, because he knew he could not supply 100,000 troops along his long and tenuous lines of communication from Bangkok to Singapore. Yet Percival believed he was facing at least five Japanese divisions and had deployed his troops in a thin line around Singapore Island, with almost no reserves to mount a counterattack once the Japanese had made their initial landing. Even when the Japanese showed their hand and pounced on the 22nd Brigade on the west coast, he had been slow to react, believing that a bigger attack might be launched to the east. There was no second attack because Yamashita had no other troops except the Imperial Guard, who came over the Causeway close to his 5th and 18th Divisions and attacked the 27th Brigade.

As to the artillery duels, Yamashita ordered his artillery to pound away as though they had plenty of ammunition. In fact, when the guns fell silent, the Japanese guns had just 100 rounds apiece and could have continued firing for only a few more hours. Had Percival mounted a counterattack, as he had wished, he might have turned the whole campaign around.

In his diary, now at the Imperial War Museum, Yamashita records how he adopted a hectoring manner to disguise his own operational difficulties at his meeting with Percival. 'I was supposed to have spoken to Percival rather abruptly,' he said. 'If I did, it was because I now realised that the British Army had about 100,000 men against my three divisions of 30,000 men. They also had many more bullets and other munitions than I had. I was afraid in my heart that they would discover that our forces were much less than theirs. I am afraid that in my anxiety I emphasised the "Yes" or "No" in English too much ... The interpreter also emphasised the words very loudly when he repeated them to the British commander. This, however, did end the matter quickly and Percival agreed to my demand for unconditional surrender.'

One of the Australian commanders, Lieutenant-Colonel (Sir) Frederick 'Black Jack' Galleghan, turned on his superiors. 'I don't think the higher command showed itself able to command the confidence of the forces,' he says. 'In saying that, I include my own General. I am not impugning to him lack of courage but had even our own Brigadier come up to my headquarters and shown himself it would have made a big difference. I never saw a Malaya Command staff officer during the whole of the war in Malaya. Had they come forward it would have engendered confidence.'[11]

Churchill, on the other hand, says, 'Of course, the reason [for the fall of Singapore] was that the people we sent out were an inferior troop of military and naval men.'[12] Wavell's Chief of Staff Sir Henry Pownall pulled no punches. He admitted the British had been 'outgeneralled, outwitted and outfought'.[13] And he added, 'We just hoped it wouldn't happen and it did.'

The psychologist Dr Norman Dixon examines Percival's failure as a military commander in *On the Psychology of Military Incompetence*. He writes that Percival had a weak ego and feelings of dependency and that he was driven by the fear of failure. He suggests that if Percival had erected defences in Malaya or Singapore it could have meant admitting to himself the danger in which he stood. His refusal to do so was the behaviour of someone who tried to avoid the unpleasant consequences of failure by not really trying.

Part Four

The Occupation

CHAPTER 25

Road to Perdition

THE MORNING FOLLOWING the surrender – Monday, 16 February – a blood-red sun leaped up behind the curtain of acrid black smoke from blazing fuel-storage tanks and smouldering city buildings. The pall covered the city and filled the lungs of everybody who ventured outdoors. The stench of death hung in the rank, sultry air and the signs of defeat were everywhere.

It did not take long for the citizens of Singapore to discover what life would be like under the Rising Sun. Waking up in the unnatural silence, 11-year-old Mel Bruce peered through the front windows of his house in Simon Road. Three Japanese soldiers were smoking cigarettes on the front porch. Mel dashed into his parents' bedroom to warn them. Moments later, the Japanese walked in.

'One of the soldiers chased after our amah Sai Mui, who had rushed to the servants' quarters at the back, screaming,' Mel says. 'The other two came into the bedroom, where Dad was lying in bed, with Mum and us kids cowering around her. We were all absolutely terrified. One of the soldiers pointed his rifle at Mum and us, indicating that we should back away from Dad. He cocked his rifle, which made Mum scream out and move towards the bed.

'Somehow she managed to explain that Dad had an injured leg. Dad showed him the leg and the soldier lifted his rifle away. Then he caught sight of Dad's Waltham half-hunter watch on the dresser and picked it up for a closer look. He looked at Mum and Dad as if to say, "I want this," and they nodded. He put it in his pocket. His companion spied Dad's silver cigarette case and lighter and took them for himself.'

The two Japanese soldiers then searched the rest of the house for further loot, while the terrified family stayed in the bedroom. The third soldier attacked Sai Mui in the servants' quarters. 'We later learned that poor Sai Mui had been raped,' Mel says. 'Mum tried to console her but, of course, we children had no idea what he had done to her. After they left, Dad began to breathe more easily and I heard him say to Mum, "The buggers even took my cigarettes, sod 'em.'"

That morning, Shenton Thomas left the Singapore Club and met the Japanese at Fort Canning, where he was informed that European civilians would be interned at Changi Jail but firemen, doctors, nurses, postal staff and other essential workers would remain at liberty to prevent a breakdown in civil administration.[1] Thomas agreed to broadcast this news to the people of Singapore. The broadcast was made from the Malayan Broadcasting studios in the Cathay Building, with an English-speaking officer standing beside the Governor to ensure he stuck to the script. The existing administrative and economic systems were to continue, he said, and all personnel would retain their present positions for the time being. Public utility services, such as water and electricity supply, would be restored as quickly as possible. Wireless communication and broadcasting were prohibited. There was to be no communication with the outside world.

One of the first Europeans to seek exemption from internment was Professor Corner of the Botanic Gardens. Corner had the Governor's ear, having advised him on the vice-regal gardens. Many of the specimens in the Botanic Gardens' herbarium would be looted or vandalised unless action was taken, he stammered. Someone had to protect them and no one was more qualified for the task than him. Thomas agreed – in fact, he had been thinking along similar lines himself. He wrote a pencilled note to the Japanese authorities in which he requested that they preserve the scientific collections, libraries and matters of historic interest at Raffles Museum and Library, the Botanic Gardens, Raffles College and the King Edward VII College of Medicine.

'He handed me the note and, with a twinkle in his eye, charged me to deliver it,' the Professor says.[2] Corner took the note to the Municipal Building, where he made an impassioned speech to Toyoda, the Japanese Consul-General, who was in the process of taking over from the British administration. After reading the note, Toyoda granted Corner the right to remain free on parole to look after the gardens. Professor Hidezo Tanakadate would be arriving from Saigon shortly to take charge of Singapore's scientific affairs, he said, and Corner could work with him. As he walked around the Padang to report back to the Governor, Corner was astonished to discover that his life-long stammer had disappeared.

James MacIntosh, a post-office accountant from Inverness, and his wife Maimie had moved into Fullerton Building after fleeing their home in Kuala Lumpur. Maimie had left Singapore with three other post-office wives in *Mata Hari* on 12 February and, unknown to James, had been captured by the Japanese when their ship was stopped off Banka Island. Following the Governor's broadcast, MacIntosh was retained at Fullerton Building with three colleagues to keep the mail moving. Scrounging around for items to furnish their makeshift dormitory on the fourth floor, the men found an Overseas Four radio receiver. 'Had I then known how the Japs dealt with people found using radio receivers, I might well have hesitated,' MacIntosh says. 'One of their favourite tricks was to destroy the eardrum and so cause deafness.'[3]

Lieutenant James Richardson woke up on 16 February in the Cathay Building, which had been the base for British Intelligence. He scribbled in his diary, 'A magnificent sunrise but there is no elation in me. Unconditional surrender! Jap troops in lorries. Our envoys have gone out to meet Japs at 0700 and some details were arranged. One is almost dazed by the suddenness of this capitulation. How triumphant the Japs must have felt as they entered "impregnable Singapore". Oh, that the positions had been reversed!'[4]

The Japanese instructed Allied soldiers to hand over their weapons and march into captivity. British and Australian soldiers and white officers of the Indian Army would head for Changi Barracks on the eastern extremity of the island, while Indian soldiers would go into a camp in Farrer Park for further dispersal. But first the Japanese staged a victory parade through the streets of Singapore, ending up with a rally in honour of the Emperor at the Padang. Civilians of all nationalities were ordered to line the streets.

The only Japanese permitted into the city after the cease-fire on Sunday night had been members of the Kempeitai, the Japanese Military Police, with auxiliary Hojo Kempei drawn from the Japanese 5th Division. Yamashita had kept the bulk of his victorious army outside the city to avoid trouble. But at 2 p.m. on Monday thousands of Japanese troops marched into the city for a victory parade.[5] 'We counted 165 tanks passing Bras Basah Road going to the Padang for the big victory demonstration,' Brother Vincent later remembered. 'We saw the tanks passing in front of St Joseph's and the Japanese soldiers marching on either side. It was very impressive.'

The shock troops who made the first landing in Singapore – many of them Koreans and Formosans – marched in front of the tanks; then came military lorries and many more infantrymen, with officers' cars carrying Japanese generals and colonels interspersed through their ranks. Soldiers waved Japanese flags and yelled, '*Banzai, banzai, banzai*' – 'Long live the Emperor!' The crowd remained largely silent, not knowing what to expect.

Some Malays and Indians waved little Japanese flags. Allied soldiers, marshalled three deep along the route, bowed their heads.

Captain Denis Russell-Roberts had made his way to Robinson's in Raffles Place after the surrender and had fallen asleep on a large comfortable sofa in the furniture department. He was surprised to be woken by a woman offering him a cup of tea. She explained she was Mrs Hutchings, wife of the store's manager; she had seen no reason to leave the elegant establishment – which was still packed with consumer goods.

Mrs Hutchings led Russell-Roberts into the ladies' hairdressing department for a wash – in eau-de-Cologne, in the absence of running water. Downstairs, he found fruit, vegetables and mineral water in a refrigerator, while a search unearthed illicit bottles of whisky and gin. He slipped past a Japanese sentry into Kelly & Walsh's bookshop in Raffles Place, where he purloined a 1,200-page Somerset Maugham anthology, a good long read for the few months he expected to be in captivity. Out on the street again, he joined a passing column of soldiers led by four files of brigadiers and full colonels, all heavily laden with attaché cases and personal possessions.

As the column swept past Raffles Hotel, a group of English women appeared at the upstairs windows. The women made Churchill's 'V for Victory' sign to the men, who burst into a rousing rendition of 'There'll Always Be an England'. They were still singing as they passed Brother Vincent at St Joseph's. 'They were all walking in step and they were singing something that would break your heart,' he says. 'They were singing, "There'll always be an England and England shall be free."'[6]

Gunner Vince Broe, Lieutenant Joe Staples and Lieutenant Bob Goodwin of the 2/10th Field Regiment had slept on the grassy slopes outside Tanglin Barracks. An inspection of the storerooms revealed an Aladdin's cave of goodies. 'There are top hats and tennis rackets, golf-clubs and gold braid, ceremonial swords, cigars and *crème de menthe*,' Vince Broe wrote in his diary. 'We silently toast the day and pledge to stick together. What the hell is it all about?'[7]

The men were ordered to sort, stack and count all arms and ammunition (except illegal lead revolver bullets which were buried) prior to marching the 14 miles to Changi. Rumours that they would be searched by the Japanese caused Broe and his friends to bury valuables, letters and photographs for fear these irreplaceable items would be confiscated. 'We'll dig 'em up when Archie Wavell comes – a couple of months at the outside,' Joe Staples said. Russell Savage took a pair of pliers to some silver jewellery he had collected to send home as Christmas presents. 'I still had it because the war had intervened,' he says. 'I destroyed it and threw it away. I came to regret it afterwards – it would have been very handy for bartering.'

The first Japanese had come into the barracks and the Australians watched in amusement as one tried to ride off on a Norton motor bike. The owner had foreseen such an eventuality and placed a spoonful of sugar in the petrol tank. One of the Diggers seized a bayonet from another Japanese and used it to open a tin of marmalade jam, then calmly handed it back. Such acts were bravado to hide anger, frustration and heartbreak. Fourteen miles from Singapore to Changi (or more for many units further west) was an unendurable marathon to exhausted and dispirited men heavily burdened with all the gear that they could carry – and with the heaviest burden of all, shame, surrounding them like a dense cloud.

Lieutenant-Colonel Alfred 'Flicker' Knights, commanding officer of the 4th Battalion, Royal Norfolk Regiment, found himself passing through his former battalion headquarters at the village of Teck Hock. 'An old Chinese man came up to me and handed me two pairs of khaki shorts,' Knights says. 'He said he recognised me and would I return the shorts to two of my men who had left them with him to wash before the battalion left the area. The old man refused payment. He considered that what money remained in my possession would be more essential for my needs than for his.'[8]

Japanese propagandists were having a field day. Captain Frank Robinson, a Londoner, noted in his diary, 'Motion picture cameras busy throughout town – population sheepish and many "Rising Suns" in evidence – all pretty humiliating. Arrived at Changi about 1700 hours.'[9]

John Wyett intended to walk to Changi with Colonel Wilfrid 'Billy' Kent Hughes – who had represented Australia in athletics at the 1920 Olympic Games. Kent Hughes's rank meant that he could have taken one of the cars, but he said, 'Damn that – I'm going to march out with the men.' Then the new commanding officer, Major-General Callaghan, stepped in: 'You're coming with me, Wyett – I need a staff officer with me.'

Wyett found himself in the General's car – in which, as they edged through that long column of tired, straggling troops, they were cursed by some of their own men who had to step aside to let the vehicle pass. 'When we got out to Changi, we found out where the headquarters was going to be and we pushed the old General out and drove off,' Wyett says. 'I went up and down the ragged column and was able to help the others quite a lot. I'd managed to bring with me a Thermos of hot Ovaltine and I gave a small mugful of that to some of the faltering chaps – helped them along a bit. Then I came across Billy – he wasn't quite the athlete he used to be and he was just about dropping. I said, "Come on, Billy, and pushed him into the car." He didn't want to come, even then.'[10] The journey stopped at Selarang Barracks, which had been allotted to the AIF. Wyett helped the troops to find their quarters and collapsed into bed at 4 a.m.

James Richardson managed to get a lift in a car from Fort Canning to Changi where he found quarters in a house overlooking the sea, at 7 Fairy Point Road. Bomb blast had brought down the asbestos ceiling and the accommodation was cramped with 40 officers and 30 other ranks all sleeping there. But Richardson's spirits revived after a swim in the sea and he found the tranquillity 'a welcome rest after the noise and strain of battle'. The men in Richardson's mess received two small meals a day, with coffee at midday. By scrounging, they acquired two cases of tinned stew, one case of tobacco and 2½ cases of milk. 'For the while, all worries and cares are over. Everyone relaxed – even the General Staff,' he noted.

Dr Rowley Richards drove from Tanglin Barracks in his truck loaded with medical supplies. 'We'd received instructions that we were allowed to take only three vehicles, including the water truck,' he says. 'We watched the Brits go past in trucks laden with cane chairs and lots of other stuff for the officers' mess, so my CO Colonel Wright agreed that we should take two extra trucks full of food and medical supplies. When we got to Changi, a couple of shiny-arsed brigade majors from divisional headquarters ticked him off in front of the troops for bringing the extra vehicles. They said they'd call around in the morning to collect all the stuff from us. I was furious.

'We had got to Birdwood Camp at Changi at two o'clock in the morning. The place had been bombed and there was a lot of damage. Our second-in-command got a team together and built a false wall in one of the huts and stacked all our food and medical stuff in the cavity behind it. When these blokes arrived the next day, we gave them a few supplies but nearly all of it was hidden behind the wall.'[11]

It was nearly midnight when Vince Broe and his mates flopped down under the rugby posts in Birdwood Barracks Square. At 34, Broe was a good ten years older than his comrades and at the time of enlistment had given his occupations as clerk, draftsman and musician. 'He could play Reveille on a piece of water pipe,' says Bob Goodwin, who was 20 years old and known to Broe as 'the boy Lieutenant'.

The next day 20 gunners were assigned a bare atap hut which they furnished with a table, a couple of stools and a calendar depicting an Oriental pin-up. It was Ash Wednesday – 'a fine way to start Lent,' Joe

Staples said. 'I'll go without roast turkey.' But there was no food – their carefully packed ration trucks had been forbidden at the last minute. 'The officers have a veranda studded with easy chairs overlooking the sports oval but they have no more real necessities than we have and their dollars are just as useless as ours,' Broe wrote.

The black market, however, was born that first day, with tins of fish changing hands for $5. Someone started the Australian gambling game of two-up on the grass outside the hut; it soon overflowed on to the parade ground as more players joined in. The pots got bigger and bigger until by nightfall $1,000 was in the kitty every time. Revolvers, compasses, binoculars, cameras and other 'hot stuff' emerged from secret hiding places followed by diamond rings, pens and watches as men tried to win their money back.

Broe and his mates dropped out of the game and went for a walk around the Changi environs. They passed one of Changi's big 15-inch guns, its muzzle blown to pieces. The whole area had been bombed and shelled. Selarang Barracks, where the Gordon Highlanders had been based, was now 'five grim, blackened, three-storeyed reminders of the glory that was Changi, with the ruined officers' mess and married men's barracks to further stress the tragedy'. Things brightened up a little when they walked through the coconut groves to Changi Beach and went for a swim. 'It was very pleasant in the limpid, shallow bay and on the way back the prospects of the evening meal are enhanced as a few coconuts, guavas and green papaws are gathered. What a picture Changi must have looked in the days of its pre-war serenity. The palm-lined avenues between the officers' bungalows, the playing fields and the swimming pool mollify the severity of the parade ground, blending the red-tiled roof and the trim green lawns into a peaceful panorama.'

Many of the buildings had been damaged by bomb blast, and corpses, offal and rotting garbage made the camp a breeding ground for flies, mosquitoes and rats. Outbreaks of diarrhoea and dysentery began within a fortnight; scores of men were rushed to hospital where 18 soon died. Malaria and dengue fever, both spread by mosquitoes, became facts of life. Urgent preventive measures were required: hundreds of men were put to work in shifts, digging latrines to a depth of 14 feet and boreholes to 12 feet. Fly-proof wooden 'thunderboxes' were built over the latrines, and thereafter admissions to hospital steadily declined.

Once the camp had been cleaned up, most of the health problems related to the shortage of food. James Richardson says the men were living on about half-scale army rations which they had carried from the city. When the Japanese took over the provisioning of their 'guests' (the official euphemism for prisoners of war) they put them on an Asian rice diet – but one devoid of ingredients that would have made it palatable and healthful. Rations consisted of polished white rice, much of it the sweepings off godown floors. Not only was the quality of rice sub-standard but the amount provided per man per day was considerably less than a Malay would have consumed. The results were catastrophic. British and Australian cooks had no idea of how to cook rice in quantity and produced a frightful sloppy sludge, rather like billboard paste.

But there was a windfall when a 100-strong party went to collect seawater in which to boil the rice. Separated from the open bay by a narrow sand spit was a large pond, in which several large fish could be seen describing flashing silver arcs. Vince Broe describes the scene: '"You beaut," someone exclaims; "how would he go in the pan?" The idea becomes general as another and yet another loud plop disturbs the mirror-like surface of our lake. The cavalcade halts and the mouths water. The place is literally teeming with fish (ranging from five to 50 pounds, according to the fishing experience of the hungry amateurs). A dozen or so of us take direct action. Flinging ourselves into four feet of water (including one of mud) and with linked arms forming a cordon across one corner, we begin to close in. Fish? Fish to burn. We're standing on 'em; they're squeezing through our legs; one lad collects a 10-pound trout fair in the right eye and goes down. Other groups follow our example with similar success, as startled fish churn the water into muddy foam.

'"Let's get organised," says Joe as we simultaneously spot a wire-netting fence around a hut. Willing hands make light work, and inside five minutes, with everyone shouting orders, a solid wall of wire netting and naked men right across the pool is slowly but relentlessly advancing upon the "enemy". The gap is steadily lessened as the agitated water begins to seethe – many of the leaping escapees being caught behind by joyful wicket-keepers, equipped with bamboo baskets.

'With 20 yards to go, more recruits are needed as the almost solid wall of slippery fish realises that the game is up. Another 10 minutes and the catch is ours. Hundreds of beautiful fish (averaging five to six pounds) are safely stacked in baskets and dozens more are hidden under towels, shirts, and discarded trousers. Well into the night, forbidden fires flickered in remote corners where those who voted against the pooling (and others) fried their ill-gotten gains in Brylcreem, dubbin, Vaseline, mosquito repellent or any other grease available.'

James Richardson and his companions tackled the cooking problem when they moved to a new headquarters mess in a house at 1 Temple Hill. Richardson, Johnnie Service, Wally Pollock, Peter Leicester (ex-Burma Oil Company) and Peter Golder (ex-Hong Kong Police Force) took over the kitchen and showed the cooks how to prepare rice. 'I have seldom seen a group of Europeans so pleasantly surprised to be served an edible portion at dinner that evening, although it was only rice slightly garnished by stew,' Richardson says. 'Golder, who was a really tough copper, took the opportunity to scout around the cookhouse and – surprise! surprise! – discovered that the cooks had been withholding disproportionate amounts of the limited stew for their own gourmandising. Whatever he threatened to do to them was evidently dire enough to discourage this practice.'

The Changi areas were relatively spacious and there was access to swimming beaches – but after a few days the Japanese decided that there was too much freedom of movement and brought in coils of barbed wire for the POWs to wire themselves in. It was a grim irony: the wire that had been so badly needed for the defence of the north shore of the island but had never been issued was now to be used to fence them in.

'At last we're totally surrounded by barbed wire and I feel much safer,' Vince Broe noted. 'A guard of bearded Sikhs is stationed at each gate, armed with .303 rifles.' There were six principal areas: the AIF, 18th Division, 11th Division, Southern Area, Temple Hill, and the Hospital Area at Roberts Barracks. Fraternisation was still possible. A 'ferry service' was established in which a flag party was permitted to pass through checkpoints at certain times, provided they all saluted the Sikh sentry. POWs could attach themselves to the flag party if they wanted to visit another section. 'We did not feel caged,' Richardson says. 'On the whole, we were a reasonably good-tempered group. Sure, there were flashes of temper but seldom anything really serious.'

On Sunday 22 February, Vince Broe and Joe Staples heard 'sinister bursts of machine-gun fire' as they walked along the main Changi road – sinister because the fighting had stopped, so who was shooting and at whom? The gunfire had come from the beach and the Australians were trying to guess what might have happened when a truck approached. As it sped past, Broe noted that it was full of Japanese soldiers who were 'grinning deliriously'.

Meanwhile, General Wavell was informed by the Combined Chiefs of Staff that Java, the last link in the Malay Barrier, should be defended to the last man. 'The Chief' himself was instructed to withdraw his headquarters from the island. Not wishing to be made the scapegoat for another fiasco, he argued that the ABDA Command should be not withdrawn but dissolved altogether and all Allied forces in the Dutch East Indies placed under the control of the Dutch. This suggestion was accepted; many of Wavell's headquarters staff just had time to pack their bags and scramble aboard the liner *Orcades* before she sailed for Australia.

Thus Beryl Stevenson found herself jobless and cut off when the joint command ceased to exist. Beryl says, 'It was what I'd call a "quick quit" by the British at Lembang. Wavell was there, walking along the outside verandas with his aide, Sandy Reid Scott. Wavell had lost an eye in the First World War and he'd chosen an aide who'd lost an eye in the Second World War. He took a rather jocular view of this; they walked along with their two blind eyes in the middle so that they had a good eye on either side. Then Wavell was gone and the place was empty. A Scottish major was left to do the handover to the Japanese. Can you imagine anything quite so British? He came to the window of my office, putting a cheerful air on it, to say goodbye and wish us well. What happened to him God alone knows. The attitude of the British was quite out of this world – leaving an officer behind to hand over to the Japanese!'[12]

CHAPTER 26

Sook Ching (Purification by Elimination)

THE DAY AFTER HEARING the mysterious machine-gun fire, Vince Broe and Joe Staples were in a work party of 100 POWs who were ordered to go to Changi Beach for 'an emergency job'. 'Off we march to the beach again, quietly singing, laughing, chattering as the sunlight dances on the distant water through the waving palms,' Broe wrote. 'Beyond a ridge the beach bursts into view; it's low tide, and – oh God! The laughter freezes on our lips.'[1]

Everyone's gaze turned to the sunlit sea, calm and serene off the spit. Bobbing in the gentle swell at the water's edge were the bodies of human beings. They seemed to be everywhere – more than 100 bodies, already swollen and hideous in death, bundled together in groups, with hands tied behind their backs. Every eye slowly turned towards the Japanese guards. 'You bloody murdering swine!'

The Japanese started grinning. They handed out shovels from the back of a truck and told the men to dig graves. Joe Staples's face was white and his blue eyes blazed. 'This isn't warfare,' he said, 'it's downright bloody murder.' The true significance of the machine-gunning some of them had heard the previous day hit the men like a blow in the stomach.

Splitting the work party into five groups, a Japanese officer ordered, 'Twenty men, four shovel, 20 men, four shovel,' and the digging began. When four men had dug down a certain distance, the officer roared, 'Changee, changee,' and another four men took over the work until five graves 10 feet deep had been excavated in the loose sand.

'Try as we would, we could not prevent our eyes from wandering towards the beach, wondering what those bodies were and what devilry was behind their deaths,' another member of the work party, Sergeant Reg Mahoney, wrote after the war. 'Then came the gruesome job of dragging the corpses to the grave. To make this worse, their hands had been tied together.'

As the Australians had expected, the victims were Chinese, mostly wearing the coarse blue clothes of the Volunteers. They could not tell whether some were young men or women. There were bullet holes in different parts of the bodies. Clearly they had been brought to the beach, tied together and marched into the sea, whereupon a burst of machine-gun fire had ripped into their backs.

Once the graves had been dug, the men went about their macabre task, while the Japanese soldiers sucked on bottles of McEwan's Red Label beer. At first, they tried to make the burial as decent as possible by placing the bodies straight, but the Japanese sentries ordered them to hurry up. One man was dragging a body from the water's edge when he started to shout, 'Jesus, this one is still alive!' He was joined by others who examined the body and confirmed that there were unmistakable signs of life. A Japanese guard rushed to the scene, kicked the body, and then made signs for it to be held under the water. He wanted the Australians to drown the wounded Chinese.

The men stood their ground, refusing to obey. The Japanese swung his rifle forward and made it clear he would bayonet the nearest man unless his order was carried out. Slowly, the men moved to the sickly task. They were forced to mete out similar treatment to other bodies in which life was suspected. By the time the grave had been filled, the body count ran to about 120. As they trudged back to camp, there was 'not much to say', but every Australian made the same resolution to himself: 'The Japanese must pay for this.'

That the Japanese military had perpetrated the atrocity on Changi Beach was self-evident. But was it an isolated incident? How many other Chinese had been killed? And who was responsible? They did not have to wait long for the chief suspect to arrive in person. On 25 February the whole camp was turned out to line the Changi streets for a Japanese victory parade in which General Yamashita — nicknamed 'the Tiger of Malaya' by an ecstatic Japanese press — was the star performer. 'Another red-letter day — Victory parade by Jap CIC General Yamashita,' James Richardson wrote. 'All the troops lined the road as the Japanese drove by.'

Vince Broe thought the POW troops looked fine, 'showing no sign of repression as six deep we line the circuitous route of the triumphant way. Cars full of fat, slit-eyed generals and wrinkled, donkey-faced admirals sail through a battery of strong silence.'

The High Command in Tokyo ordered Yamashita to prepare his army to leave Singapore as soon as possible. When the fighting had stopped in Singapore, the 25th Army consisted of the 5th Division (13,000 men), the 18th Division (10,000), the Imperial Guards Division (9,000) and ancillary troops (3,000). Yamashita decided to send the Imperial Guards to Sumatra in early March to drive out the Dutch and seize the oilfields. Some of the 5th Division would move across the Causeway within a week to garrison the Malay peninsula, while the rest of that division would sail as reinforcements to the Philippines, where fierce resistance was still being encountered on the Bataan peninsula. The 18th Division would also be split up, with some men going to fight the British in Burma and others to occupy the Andaman and Nicobar islands. The Army's strength throughout Malaya and Singapore would be reduced to a single brigade.

To enable these moves to take place, Yamashita's first priority was to restore law and order in Singapore City. He had already delegated control of the city to the Kempeitai, who dealt severely with looters, anybody with 'bended delusions' and anybody who resisted the New Order. But there was urgent work to do: all Chinese who had taken up arms against the Japanese must be ruthlessly purged. Punishment was one motive, but also Yamashita knew that he had to neutralise resistance to Japanese rule to pave the way for the 25th Army's redeployment.

While the Japanese were celebrating their victory on 16 February, Yamashita put a secret plan into action to eliminate Chinese resistance. He ordered his four commanders, Nishimura, Matsui, Mutaguchi and Kawamura, to initiate Operation Clean-up to wipe out all Dalforce volunteers who had survived the battle and all other Chinese who had taken up arms against the Imperial Japanese Army. It was Yamashita who gave the order, but the detailed plans were worked out by Lieutenant-Colonel Masanobu Tsuji, the High Command's Chief of Planning and Operations. And the devil was in the detail. For, without reference to Yamashita, Tsuji wanted to eliminate all anti-Japanese elements in Malaya, not only Volunteers but all contributors to the China Relief Fund, all Chinese officials and servants who had worked for the British, anyone who had joined anti-Japanese organisations, and young men of military age capable of bearing arms.[2]

Tsuji handed this macabre task to Lieutenant-Colonel Masayuki Oishi, commander of No. 2 Field Kempeitai Group, with the help of hundreds of Hojo Kempei. These were mostly young soldiers from the countryside of western Japan, ill-educated and brutalised by battle.[3] Under Operation Clean-up or *Sook Ching* – 'Purification by Elimination' – Singapore City was divided into zones, and on 17 February the entire Chinese community was ordered to congregate at assembly points in those zones within the next five days. They were told to bring their own food and water as none would be provided. There were to be no exemptions: the old and the sick were expected to turn up or face unpleasant consequences. Anyone who had not reported by midday on 21 February would be severely punished.

The main assembly points were: (1) Jalan Besar Road between Maud and Syed Alwi roads, with overspills into Victoria School and Jalan Besar Stadium; (2) an area near the junction of Clemenceau Avenue at the eastern end of River Valley Road; (3) an area adjacent to the Tanjong Pagar Police Station; (4) a rubber factory near the junction of Geylang and Kallang roads; and (5) an open area off the Payah Lebar Road.

At the time of the surrender Elizabeth Choy and her family – her father, stepmother, three sisters, elder brother and his pregnant wife, and younger brother – were sheltering in a relative's home in Outram Road, having been bombed out of their house in Mackenzie Road. 'The next day we peeped,' she says. 'We saw all the Japanese soldiers marching. Oh, we felt as if that was the end of the world.'

The family reported to Tanjong Pagar Police Station to be registered but were redirected to the centre in Jalan Besar, which was closer to the family home in Mackenzie Road. The street was packed with thousands of Chinese men, women and children. Hundreds of families sat at the side of the road, huddled in doorways or lined up in lanes running off the main thoroughfare. The Japanese had enclosed the area with coils of barbed wire, dividing the street into pens in which Chinese citizens stood waiting their turn to be screened for possible anti-Japanese traits. Members of the Kempeitai, aided by interpreters and informers, scoured mimeographed lists of names in search of known suspects, while scowling armed guards patrolled the barricades.[4]

Elizabeth's name was not on the wanted list, but she was questioned to see whether she was a Communist. She was fortunate: at other checkpoints people who spoke English or had worked for the British were purged, but she, despite being a teacher in an English school and so in the high-risk category, was allowed to return to her family in one of the wired-off pens. The following day old people, women and children were allowed to leave the Jalan Besar registration centre; Elizabeth's older brother was also told he could go. 'We had to go through a passage [of barbed wire],' Elizabeth says, 'and as each one passed they gave us a stamp to say we had been present.' The word 'Examined' in Chinese was stamped either on a piece of one-inch-square paper or on one of the hands and had to be presented on demand at every roadblock or sentry point thereafter.

Elizabeth's father was walking away with his younger son, aged 18, when a Kempeitai soldier told him, 'You go – but leave your son behind.'

'Daddy, what's going to happen to me?' the boy asked, suddenly terrified. 'Why can't I come with you?'

But the soldier insisted, 'You just stay behind.'

The family returned to their wrecked house in Mackenzie Road and waited for the young boy to return. Day after day they waited in vain; the old man pined for his son. After two weeks, going insane with worry he pleaded with Elizabeth to find her brother. She went to Japanese police stations and other buildings to enquire about the boy. It was 'just like going into a lion's den'. At every turn, she was shooed away, sometimes with a slap on the face. On her journey she encountered mothers, wives and sisters, all of whom were looking for lost menfolk, the ones who had not come home.[5]

The experience of Elizabeth Choy's family was repeated in Chinatown, in *kampongs* across Singapore Island and throughout the length and breadth of Malaya. The Kempeitai and their henchmen struck without warning and often without rhyme or reason. One man would be spared while his neighbour was taken away and never seen again. Informers were active at all assembly points, their heads hooded. As the miserable columns of humanity shuffled past to be registered, a nod was all that was required for somebody to be tapped with a stick wielded by one of the Kempeitai and then have to step aside. His hands were bound and he was taken away.

Mamoru Shinozaki, a Japanese diplomat, witnessed the Kempeitai performing their grisly duties: 'The victims were told to write their names. Some wrote in Chinese, some in English. A knowledge of English at once classified them as pro-British and dangerous. Those with tattoo marks were classified as members of secret societies. Those who failed to apologise at once to the young Kempei for not being able to write their names in Chinese, or for having tattoo marks, were detained and later slaughtered.'[6]

Francis Chan, a pupil in Elizabeth Choy's class at St Andrew's, was another witness: 'I was 12 years old and every male over 12 was ordered to report for registration,' he says. 'My mother said I should not go – I looked younger and would probably get away with it. But I went with my brother who was 16 and my father. I was the only one who came home.'[7]

Cheng Kwan Yu, a civil servant, had gone to the assembly point on Jalan Besar. At three o'clock in the afternoon of the fifth day – 21 February – a Formosan shouted to the crowd that all former government employees and clerks in European firms should identify themselves. As a civil servant in the War Tax office, Cheng stepped forward, as did many others. These men were told to form groups of four and were then marched in the direction of

Victoria School in Kitchener Road. About half had gone through the school gates when a Japanese officer ordered the rest to halt and squat down on the pavement. Two hours later, they were told to get up and enter the school grounds, where their hands were tied behind their backs with rope. Then they were ordered to board a fleet of 20 trucks which had chugged into the compound. Cheng estimated that there were about 20 men in each truck, making a total of 400.

The trucks set off in a convoy, heading east. No one spoke – there was nothing to say – but as the grey concrete guard tower of Changi Jail came into sight, one of the men remarked that it looked as though they were going to prison. The trucks passed the jail, however, turned to the right and continued on to the sands near Changi Beach.

The men were told to get down, and were then tied into groups with lengths of thin telephone cable. 'We were next told to move off towards the beach,' Cheng says. 'I saw a pillbox erected on the seawall of a demolished bungalow and in the slit of the pillbox one or more machine guns. When the lot of us were all on the beach, about 400 of us, the machine-gunning started. I was at the end of my drove. As my companions were hit, they fell down and pulled down the rest of us. As I fell, I was hit in the face.'

The machine-gunning stopped, and Japanese soldiers moved amid the carnage, bayoneting anyone who was still alive. Cheng shut his eyes. He had been hit on the nose and his face was covered in blood. He felt a soldier step on his body to bayonet his neighbour who had shown signs of life, but he did not touch Cheng.

Cheng kept his eyes closed until he heard the trucks drive off. It was already night and in the moonlight he saw a lump of coral a few inches away and wriggled towards it, pulling against the bodies to which he was tied. He rubbed his wire bonds against the coral until they snapped, then sawed through the rope and freed his hands. He crawled out of the sea and staggered on to the beach.

For two days, Cheng hid in the undergrowth, bathed the wound on his nose and drank from storm-water drains. He finally encountered a group of British soldiers sitting under a tree near Changi Jail. The soldiers gave him a biscuit and examined his wound. An officer scribbled a note on a piece of paper and told him to give it to the first ambulance that came along the main road. The officer gave Cheng a raincoat to sit on while he was waiting. The ambulance took Cheng to an Indian Army field hospital. 'There my wound was dressed,' he says, 'and I went home.'[8]

Chan Cheng Yean, a Malaccan Chinese, was one of 90 members of the

373

Straits Settlements Volunteer Force who was rounded up after the surrender. They were taken by lorry to some waste ground at Bedok, where three trenches had been dug. Chan's group were pushed into the first trench and ordered to stand close together. When the Japanese gunners opened fire, Chan was in the second row of the first trench. He was shot in the knee and when a dead man fell past him, he collapsed on top of him and a third man covered him up. 'I controlled my breath,' he says. 'I did not make any movement.'

The Japanese fired another 10 rounds to make sure everybody in the first trench was dead before moving on to the next group. Chan estimates it took them 20 minutes to shoot all the Volunteers. Then, when he heard footsteps moving away, he slowly extricated himself from the mass of arms and legs. He was the only one still living. He hid in a large drain and washed the blood off his wounded knee. Then he threw away his army shirt, trousers and boots and, dressed in singlet and short pants, struggled to a couple of huts where an old Chinese man gave him some clothes and $2. A Chinese nurse extracted the bullet from his knee.

With amazing bravado, Chan then lined up with other Chinese in a school at Chai Chee to be registered as a civilian. The school had been turned into a registration centre, with many Chinese waiting to be interrogated. When his turn came, Chan bowed politely to the Japanese soldier and, in answer to questions, passed himself off as an itinerant ice-cream seller. He was given a pass to pin to his coat. Thus attired, Chan made his way by foot, train and bicycle to the safety of his home in Malacca.[9]

British POWs rescued four more Chinese victims of the *Sook Ching* from the long *lalang* near Changi Beach, all of them Volunteers who had made the mistake of admitting their military service to the Japanese at the Jalan Besar registration centre. These men were smuggled into British hospitals inside the Changi camp and secretly treated. All are thought to have recovered from their wounds.

It was clear to the British High Command that an atrocity was taking place. General Percival and his commanders had no way of knowing the extent of the disaster that had befallen the Chinese population, but it was decided to raise objections at a meeting with Colonel Ichiji Sugita, the 25th Army's intelligence chief who was visiting Changi to discuss the running of the camp.

The British representatives were Brigadier Newbigging and Major Cyril Wild – both of whom exactly a week earlier had faced Sugita across the table in the Ford Motor Company's canteen at Bukit Timah. Far from being cowed by the surrender, Newbigging now rebuked Sugita over the killings 'just outside the wire of the Changi Prisoner of War camp'. Sugita's moustache bristled. To be addressed by a captive officer was one thing but to be challenged over official Japanese military policy was intolerable. 'These Chinese were bad men,' he stormed. 'That is why we shot them. Have you anything else to ask?'

Newbigging calmly said, 'Yes, I have got something to ask. I ask that you should not shoot any more Chinese and that you should not ask our men to assist you by burying them.'

Arrogantly, Sugita snapped, 'We shall shoot them whenever we want to if we find bad men.'

'Bad men' had been identified in a directive issued by the High Command on 18 February as: (1) members of volunteer forces; (2) Communists; (3) looters; (4) anyone bearing arms; and (5) anyone obstructing the Japanese operation or threatening law and order.

Yamashita had given verbal orders that the Kempeitai should have three days to 'mop up' hard-core Communists who might join bands of anti-Japanese guerrillas on the mainland or the stay-behind parties organised by the British. But the High Command directive that put Operation Clean-up into action did not bear Yamashita's signature. It had been drafted by Lieutenant-Colonel Tsuji and it named him as the officer in charge of the operation. The *Sook Ching* was Tsuji's plan to subjugate and punish the Straits Chinese; he had been working on it ever since being appointed chief planning officer to drive the British from South East Asia 15 months earlier. And he pursued it ruthlessly, deceiving Yamashita about his methods and their outcome.[10]

Tsuji knew that Yamashita's three-day time limit would not give him nearly enough time to carry out his mission, and it was secretly extended to two weeks. Military cordons were thrown around Chinese residential areas to prevent Chinese males aged between 12 and 50 from escaping. They were then 'disposed of' at suitable sites around the island. It was not a military 'mopping-up' procedure but a wholesale massacre. At its end, thousands of Chinese were executed in cold blood. The Japanese admitted to responsibility for 6,000 deaths. The figure most commonly quoted by the Chinese community was 40,000. However, another source told the author that 100,000 Chinese had perished in the *Sook Ching*. Considering that *sook chings* were carried out at Penang, Johore, Malacca and other parts of the mainland, as well as in downtown Singapore and at other centres on Singapore Island, the figure seems quite credible.[11]

By 3 March the number of 'anti-Japanese' Chinese to have been detained had reached 70,699, and it was reported that control of 'anti-Japanese Chinese and anti-Axis persons on Syonan' was making good progress.[12] Top of Tsuki's hit list was Tan Kah Kee, head of the China Relief Fund. But Tan and his family had been spirited away from Singapore by British Intelligence and never fell into Japanese clutches.

Vince Broe's diary reports that the killing was still going on in March, when he helped to bury more Chinese bodies: 'There are only ten bodies – tied in bundles of five, and we silently bury the mangled remains in a few feet of sand.'

CHAPTER 27

Life under Dai Nippon

MAJOR CHANGES HAD swept through every level of civil life. Singapore was renamed Syonan (Bright Southern Light) and the clocks were put forward 90 minutes to correspond with Tokyo time.[1] Yamashita established his headquarters at Raffles College, but everything else associated with the great colonist was removed. Thomas Woolner's bronze statue disappeared from its plinth outside the Victoria Theatre with orders that it must be destroyed (in fact it was stashed it away in the storeroom at Singapore Museum for safekeeping).

Raffles Hotel was renamed Syonan Ryokan (Bright Southern Hotel) and became a bordello for the exclusive use of high-ranking officers. In place of the colonial *tuan besar* drinking his *stengah*, Japanese warriors disported themselves in loincloths, drinking bottles of Tiger beer and twirling samurai swords. 'Comfort girls' – sex slaves imported from Korea or beautiful Chinese girls abducted off the streets of Singapore – pleasured Nippon's conquering heroes. Robinson's was taken over by Matsuzakaya, and John Little's by Diamaru. Telecommunications were handed over to the Nippon Denkitsushin Kaisha.

European civilians in Singapore City were ordered to parade on the Padang on 17 February, bringing sufficient clothing for ten days but no rations and few belongings. The sick were told that they could stay at home but had to be registered, while civilians working in essential services such as fire-fighting and medical care were to remain at their posts. European residents living outside the city area would be dealt with at a later date.[2]

One of the civilians was 17-year-old Bernie Clifton. 'My sister June had got away to Australia on one of the last boats, but I was on the Padang with my mother and father,' he says. 'The women were taken away in lorries to Katong, and that left all the European men such as planters, government workers, engineers, municipal workers. There were so many of us the Japanese were quite surprised; they'd only been expecting a few. We heard later that on top of the Cricket Club there was a lovely big machine gun waiting to say, "Cheerio, boys." But there were too many for them – our numbers saved us.'[3]

At Katong, the women took up lodgings at Karikal Mahal, the former mansion of a wealthy Indian known as the Cattle King of Malaya. His palatial homestead was in a filthy, dilapidated state, as were the five identical houses in its grounds for his wives, but these buildings provided shelter for the internees for the next two weeks. Shenton Thomas noted in his diary, 'This day all British troops marched to Changi. Some women to Sultan of Trengganu's house and the Roxy Cinema, some civilian men to Karikal and Hoo Chiat Police Station, and Indians to Farrer Park.'

Yamashita permitted Governor Thomas to remain at the Singapore Club until early March when he was ordered into internment with other European men who had hitherto been exempt. In his white drill suit, the Governor strode across Anderson Bridge to the Padang to join his fellow internees. One of them, Ted Fozard, says, 'They paraded us, of all places, on my favourite bowling green. They kept us – including the Governor – standing in the blazing sun for five hours before a Japanese officer, standing on a box, interrogated us. Next day we walked six miles to our first internment camp.'[4]

Brother Vincent was at the camp at Katong when Shenton Thomas arrived. He was allowed 24 hours to recover before the order was given for the men to move to Changi Jail. Brother Vincent packed his small suitcase and at 9 a.m. marched off, with the Governor leading the way along East Coast Road. The streets were almost deserted, although local people had been ordered to come and witness the Governor's 'humiliation' at the head of the column of white prisoners. 'The population, however sympathetic they might have felt deep down, were dead scared of the Japanese,' Vincent says. 'We could see they had been terrorised.'

No water was provided *en route*; when the column was allowed to rest at the corner of East Coast and Bedok roads, the men rushed into shops to buy beverages – but were forced back on to the street at bayonet point. 'The Japanese guards stopped us from getting water,' Vincent says. 'They were afraid we would pass a message.'

Around 2 p.m. the high watchtower of Changi Jail loomed into view and the ragged column, thirsty and exhausted but with Shenton Thomas still doggedly at its head, reached the road leading up to the grim grey prison walls. Instead of marching straight in, however, the internees had to wait outside in the heat for several hours before being admitted and given water. Brother Vincent says, 'Never were prisoners so eager to enter a prison!'

There were four blocks in Changi Jail. The women would be assigned to A Block when they arrived, while the men were placed in B, C and D blocks. Brother Vincent and 17 others, including priests, the Director of Education Dr Lionel Harman and a couple of police officers, were given a storeroom. Each man was allotted a space three feet by six feet. Next door were a dozen members of the Salvation Army. Initially, there were 2,400 internees in the prison, although the number later rose to 4,500 when others were brought in from Malaya.

A week later, European women and children covered the seven miles on foot from Katong to Changi. As they reached the prison, nearly 400 female voices burst into song. Inside the walls, the men heard the singing and a great cheer went up. Then the sound of male voices joined in, and the whole jail echoed to the words 'There'll always be an England and England shall be free.'

Len Butler, who was 15, says, 'It was a grim, horrible place. There was a ground floor, first floor, second floor and third floor. They put the younger ones on the top floors and I was sent to B3 Cell 11. There were lifts but they didn't work; you had to climb the metal stairs. Things were chaotic until they got the water and electricity working. We sailors were put in with the civilians but we didn't consider ourselves internees. We'd come from the battlegrounds of Europe, we'd been in the Atlantic convoys, we'd been bombed through the Banka Straits and we'd been in the trenches so we didn't classify ourselves as civilians.'

Former Royal Marine Herbert Bruce was seized at his house in Simon Road, after going, as ordered, to register his family, when the Japanese had discovered he was Scottish. He was driven to Changi Jail in a truck with other European residents who had been living in the northern suburbs. 'We had no idea where he was being taken and thought we would never see each other again,' his son Mel says. A few days later a Japanese officer informed Gwen Bruce that all the bungalows in Simon Road had been requisitioned and she would have to find alternative accommodation for her family. They moved into their grandmother's house in Glasgow Road.

The family were ordered to wear badges showing a red star and bearing the words 'Enemy Alien' in Japanese script. 'We were not allowed out after six o'clock in the evening,' Mel says. 'If you were out on the street after that time and you had this red badge on you were shot on sight. There was still no news of Dad's whereabouts, but rumour had it that all felons had been set free and that the internees had been imprisoned in Changi Jail.'

The family's stocks of tinned food soon ran out, but tapioca and rice were plentiful and Gwen bought more tinned goods on the black market. The two elder Bruce boys, Syd and Mel, were put to work by the Japanese, checking ponds for malarial mosquitoes.

'My mother had problems getting milk for my youngest brother Errol, who was only two years old,' says Barbara Glanville. 'Syd and Mel had befriended a Japanese officer and he brought a whole case of condensed milk to our house for the baby. The Japanese were very fond of children. This man said to my mother that he was a professor at Tokyo University and he wanted to take me back to Tokyo and educate me and, when I was old enough, marry me. My mother pointed to a picture of my father hanging on the wall and said, "You see that picture? She is my only daughter and if I lose her my life won't be worth living." He was quite content with that explanation and remained friendly towards us.'

Meanwhile, Yamashita ordered Chinese throughout Malaya to hand over a $50 million 'gift of atonement' for the 'crime' of having supported Chiang Kai-shek. Leaders of the Chinese community were harangued by Yamashita and his staff and threatened with torture or death if they refused to pay up. They were forced to form a Japanese-sponsored Overseas Chinese Association (OCA). At the association's first meeting, a Japanese official named Takasei hammered on the table, shouting, 'You are my enemies, you know? You have been carrying out subversive activities against Japan the last few years. Now you know our strength, don't you? Your activities have deprived the Japanese of any standing here in recent years. You have helped the wicked to do greater evil. Now we have got you. We have a chance to have injustice done to us avenged. Or we shall have to kill you all.'[5]

The atrocities and extortion in the first month of the occupation destroyed any chance the Japanese might have had of establishing good relations with the Straits Chinese. From that time on, the Kempeitai were universally loathed, while personal contact with ordinary Japanese soldiers engendered for the most part feelings of revulsion and contempt. 'Yes, they beat us by their lust,' N. I. Low says. 'Individual soldiers roamed into our houses. They good-humouredly turned over photograph albums. Woe unto us if we had pictures of pretty girls! They would demand a peep at the originals, and as likely as not cut up rough if we failed to produce them.'[6]

When Elizabeth Choy, her mother and sister-in-law Maureen returned to their house in Mackenzie Road, they found it had been looted. There had been 500 guests at Elizabeth and Maureen's double wedding; all of their wedding presents had been stolen. The women were tidying up the mess when several Japanese soldiers walked in through a hole in the bombed wall. One of them dragged Maureen to an upstairs bedroom and locked the door, with the intention of raping her.

Maureen was six months pregnant with her first child; Elizabeth could hear her crying out, 'Save my child!' Elizabeth grabbed a mattress off the floor, dashed up the stairs and banged on the door, shouting, 'Open, open, open.' The soldier opened the door and, shamed at having been caught in the act, ran down the stairs. The other soldiers quickly followed him out – Yamashita's wrath towards looters and rapists was well known among the rank and file of the Japanese Army. 'I got there just in time,' Elizabeth says. 'God was merciful.'

Food was scarce, prices were going up and there was a desperate need to earn a living. Elizabeth and her husband Choy Khun Heng sought permission to set up a canteen selling groceries at the former Miyako Mental Hospital, which now housed patients from the General Hospital. The Choys' request was granted, and their canteen was soon being patronised by doctors, nurses and patients. One of the regular visitors was Bishop Wilson, who had been granted parole to tend to the spiritual needs of his flock. Two clergymen, the Reverend Sorby Adams, principal of St Andrew's School (and Elizabeth Choy's boss), and John Hayter, the youngest of the Anglican clergy, had been allowed to join him.

The Bruce family learned that Herbert was alive when they received a visit from Adams and Hayter at their grandmother's house. They had seen him during one of their visits to Changi Jail, they said, and he was in good health. Gwen burst into tears when she heard the news. The two clergymen, however, then informed the family that the Japanese were interning all 'enemy aliens' and they would soon be joining their father in Changi.

John Hayter's pastoral duties took him all over Singapore City, and he witnessed many of the bizarre and sometimes barbaric rituals of the occupying force. He saw a large crowd gathered on the pavement in Stamford Road, where a severed head had been displayed on a wooden platform. Eight Malays had been arrested and executed for attempted theft and their heads placed outside the Municipal Building, the Post Office, on Kallang Bridge and at other sites as a warning.

Olga and Maisie Prout saw the head in Stamford Road when the boarders returned to Singapore. The Victoria Street convent reopened in April in accordance with the Japanese school system. 'Two bombs had exploded in the first boarders' dormitory and we would have been killed if we had still been there,' Maisie says. 'Two female refugees had been killed and a number of others wounded in that raid.'

Olga was put into the commercial class, where she learned shorthand and typing. She says, 'Everybody had to learn Japanese but I refused. I said, "My father is English and I am not going to learn Japanese." I was a bit older than the other children. When a Japanese came in, we would all have to bow, and I wouldn't bow. I just stood there looking at this fellow. He pointed his finger at me and said to the nun, "Send her out to learn how to bow." The nun told me, "If you're not going to submit, you'd better leave the class or you'll get into more trouble." Mother Superior got me a private pupil, a Dane from the Danish Embassy who wanted to learn shorthand and typing. I spent my time teaching the Dane and keeping out of the way of the Japanese.'

Others were not so fortunate. Most people who refused to bow to the Japanese had their faces slapped or were beaten into submission. Face-slapping became one of the hallmarks of the New Order; ill-treatment and malnutrition everyday facts of life. As had happened in Manchuria, Japanese colonists and carpetbaggers flooded into occupied Singapore to take advantage of every opportunity for exploitation, from seizing established businesses to running gambling, drug-dealing and prostitution rings. The new *tuan besar*s were black-market racketeers, gaming tycoons and brothel-keepers, while the new *memsahib*s were their wives and mistresses, often prostitutes and procurers.[7] The much-vaunted Co-prosperity Sphere materialised as nothing more than a gigantic confidence trick on a defeated people.

Chapter 28

Changi's Secrets

Changi Jail, erected as a municipal prison for 600 inmates, was modelled on New York State's infamous Sing Sing Prison. By the end of the first week in March, civilian internees numbered 2,000 men, mainly Britons above military age, and 400 women and children, half of whom were British. Prison walls 18 feet high separated the men and women.

Within days of incarceration, a 'secret service' had been set up to circulate information and intelligence between the internees and the prisoners of war at Changi POW camp. The risks were extremely high. Possessing a short-wave radio set in captivity was a capital offence under Japanese law – but several went into operation almost immediately, giving internees and troops daily news bulletins from the BBC. The radios were built out of components smuggled into the camps with the help of friendly Chinese. All manner of disguises were employed to hide the receivers. Walter Stevenson, an elderly internee, built a radio into a wooden stool which he was permitted to carry around with him.

In the Australian officers' quarters at Selarang Barracks, the radio was secreted in the hollowed-out head of a broom which was left in full view of Japanese searchers. It was such an imaginative device that Japanese soldiers picked up the broom several times and never realised that wires had been poked down two woodworm holes to connect a set to batteries. To listen to the radio, an officer poked a hollow tube down a slightly larger hole to pick up the words from a small speaker. The listener repeated these words to a shorthand writer sitting beside him. At the end of each broadcast, the shorthand writer read out the news from his notes to a group of six runners who disseminated it to various sections of the camp. The system was rated a tremendous help in maintaining the morale of the troops.[1]

Norman Coulson, the city's chief water engineer, who was free on parole, contacted Leslie Hoffman who had a short-wave radio set at his home that could pick up British broadcasts in India. These broadcasts contained hours of morale-boosting personal messages from wives, relatives and friends to the people in Changi Jail. Hoffman transcribed the messages on rice paper and delivered them to a Chinese plumber, who then placed them inside water pipes which Coulson took back to Changi whenever he serviced the prison water supply.

The internal administration of the men's prison was run by a five-man central committee, which co-ordinated the operation of the increasing number of hidden short-wave receivers. The identities of the committee and the radio operators and messengers were known to only a few people, and even inside the organisation many did not know the names of their colleagues. The network worked with astonishing efficiency for many months.

James MacIntosh, the post-office worker, was interned at Changi Jail in December 1942 when the Japanese had learned how to operate the postal system for themselves. He was amazed at the efficiency of the internees' secret service. 'The illegal activities went beyond the mere reception and dissemination of general news of the war and of its effect on the people of Singapore,' he says. 'Almost the first interest of the internees was to obtain news of friends and relations. A records section was set up in the camp at Changi and by devious means contact was established with other internment and prisoner of war camps. This led to a still more dangerous activity, the collection and dissemination to other camps of information of military value – the movement of Japanese troops and units, the building of airfields, the sailing of ships.'

The committee realised that the Japanese had no intention of providing drugs and medicines or additional foods without which the children, the elderly and the sick were at serious risk. However, Japanese officers at Changi could be bribed to buy such items on behalf of the committee. Initially, funds from the internees' own pockets were loaned to the general camp fund to make these purchases, but this money soon ran out, whereupon a message was smuggled out to Bishop Wilson asking him to help. Wilson's only access to money was the church's collection plate, so he borrowed £25,000, or $200,000, in the name of the Anglican Church, repayable after the war, from Hans Schweizer, a Swiss neutral who worked for a firm called Diethelms.

The money was paid in $10,000 instalments, but Schweizer had attracted the attention of the Kempeitai and it was unsafe for Wilson to visit his house to pick it up. They worked out a simple system whereby Schweizer left the money inside a particular book at a second-hand bookshop in Bras Basah Road. Soon after Schweizer had left the shop, Wilson would show up and retrieve the money. It would then be smuggled piecemeal into the camp, either in Coulson's water pipes or in one of the jail's two ambulances. These were driven by British soldiers and were used to ferry patients from Changi Jail to the Miyako Hospital, where they were allowed to visit the Choys' canteen. There, they could pass messages or pick up the Bishop's money. 'It was all very innocent – no politics, nothing military,' Elizabeth Choy says.

John Hayter acted as courier to distribute the clandestine mail further afield. Fifty small handwritten notes at a time would be smuggled from Changi Jail into the Miyako Hospital, where Hayter would pick them up and take them to the Bukit Timah Rifle Range camp, where they would be handed over to the POWs for distribution on the POW network. Bishop Wilson also delivered letters to several camps by car after visiting patients at the Miyako.

Meanwhile, the Japanese endeavoured to interrogate officers, in search of information on a bewildering range of subjects. 'The Japanese demanded one man from every unit in Changi to go for interrogation,' Major Harry Schulman remembers. 'I was sent from Changi to Changi Jail for interrogation. They wanted to know what was happening in England and why I had joined up and what I knew about the Japanese and why I disliked them. You had to have your wits about you – you were put into a cell with a Japanese who spoke good English, with an armed guard behind you. It lasted for half an hour. It was a lot of intelligence kerfuffle all brought together.'

General Percival was asked to supply 'radio announcers' and 'technicians for repairing AA guns'. When he refused to co-operate, he was shut in a cell at the jail without food for four days. General Heath was assaulted and imprisoned for declining to 'discuss the defences of India'. He was punched in the face and dragged off to a flooded cellar at Fort Canning, where he was left in the dark for 48 hours. 'The Nips are trying to get information out of us concerning our guns,' Lieutenant C. Baume noted. 'General Heath has been through a certain amount of the 3rd degree in an attempt to get valuable information out of him but needless to say he did not speak. We are determined to do likewise; in fact, we have already been ordered to fill in forms on how to fire our guns. A typical reply is that of the 5th Field: 'Open the breech. Put the shells in. Close the breech. Fire.'[2]

Most of the guards at Changi were Sikhs who, detesting British rule of their homeland, had defected to the Japanese in the belief that they would carry out their promise to liberate the peoples of Asia. The Sikhs were very conscious of their position and insisted on being saluted by POWs or bowed to by internees at all times. On 19 April several Sikh guards drove past a party of 15 POWs who failed to salute them. The Sikhs stopped their car and paraded the POWs in front of them. The men were harangued and slapped, then dismissed. James Richardson, who watched the scene, wrote in his diary, 'Bad show! Nasty incident.'

Most of the Sikhs belonged to two regiments that had deserted to the enemy early in the campaign. According to John Wyett, they were despised not only by the POWs but also by the Japanese. 'This was effectively demonstrated one day when one of our troops went to the edge of our perimeter where a Sikh had mounted a machine gun,' Wyett says. 'He beckoned to the Sikh who, used to obeying orders, left the machine gun and walked over to the Aussie who swung a billet of wood that he was holding behind his back, and struck the Sikh a blow on the head which flattened him unconscious on the ground. A Jap soldier had another machine gun mounted nearby and we expected him to fire. Instead he burst into laughter and danced about clapping his hands in glee. It was our first lesson in how unpredictable their reactions were.'[3]

Alan Lewis spent several months down on the docks repairing damage caused by the Japanese bombing. 'The Japanese didn't treat us any worse than they treated their own people,' he says. 'There was a warehouse near us and there must have been something in it that needed to be guarded. One of the sentries dozed off and an officer came around the corner and saw him. He beat him insensible. He was still lying there the next morning. What they did to their own people when they transgressed was almost unbelievable. I have the greatest respect for the Japanese as a fighting force but no time whatever for the character they manifested. Basically, I think they are a good race. When the militarists took over they harnessed that extraordinary devotion which the Japanese had towards their Emperor to their own evil ends.'

On 29 April, because it was Hirohito's birthday, pineapple cubes were handed out to the POWs as a special treat. That day, James Richardson learned from some newly arrived prisoners that ships evacuating nursing sisters from Singapore had been bombed off Sumatra. 'Many sisters lost. Bloody shame. All small craft which left Singapore after 12. 2. 42 captured or sunk. Hope *Empire Star* reached Australia safely. Damnable not knowing where Doris and Grace are.' Richardson celebrated his own birthday – his 28th – on 30 May with a bowl of rice and *belacan*, fermented shrimp paste. Richardson admitted that it was an acquired taste but added, 'It has a very high protein content and is an excellent food additive. I love it.'

All the prisoners rapidly became aware of the effect of a rice diet on their metabolism. With scant roughage in their food, constipation was wide-spread. But there was an unexpected side-effect: the high water content of cooked rice stimulated kidney function and, without warning, the men urinated copiously. Harry Schulman says, 'We changed from a European diet to no diet at all – I was constipated for three weeks.' Lectures were given to advise the troops on preventive measures. They were told that polished white rice had lost its brown skin containing vitamin B complex and that without adequate vitamin-rich additives they would develop avitaminosis in its various forms. Their metabolism would adjust to the new conditions but not to the deficiencies of a diet consisting of rice, a few vegetables and a little meat.

Within the next two months, beriberi (vitamin B deficiency) had appeared in the camp. According to entries in Richardson's diary, on 21 April there were 36 cases; on 2 May, 156 (with nine deaths); and by 11 May, 290 cases. Many of the men became partially paralysed in the legs. Scrotal dermatitis (one form of avitaminosis) was rife. This was a particularly distressing complaint in which the skin on the genitalia became inflamed, began to peel off and itched abominably. Popular names were 'rice balls', 'pink pills' or 'Dr Williamson's disease', referring to a popular British medicament, Dr Williamson's Pink Pills for Pale Persons (i.e. anaemics). Doctors prescribed small amounts of vitamin B-rich Marmite for the treatment of scrotal dermatitis. One patient showed no signs of recovery until it was explained to him that he should eat the Marmite, rather than paint it on the affected area.

The other affliction caused by vitamin B1 deficiency was 'happy feet', a gnawing, burning sensation in the soles of the feet which forced men to hobble up and down all night seeking relief from the discomfort. This condition was also treated with Marmite.[4] The men learned to grind rice into flour and bake rice bread in clay ovens. With a little money they were able to purchase a few extras from the new camp canteen and, now and then, from a rather nebulous black market. It was the occasional duck egg or piece of fruit that prevented many of them from dying of starvation.

The food situation improved considerably for many thousands of POWs when the Japanese called for working parties to perform duties at the docks and elsewhere on Singapore Island. Japan had signed but not ratified the Geneva Convention of 1929, which stipulated that prisoners from the ranks could be compelled to work but officers were exempt; work could not be excessively heavy, dangerous or directly concerned with the war.

Within days of the surrender, the Japanese had put POWs to work at camps outside Changi, notably at the Great World and New World amusement parks, Bukit Timah and the old Malaya Command Headquarters at Sime Road. Thousands of troops volunteered for the working parties because they offered the chance of more food, now the primary obsession of every POW. The working-party volunteers received four ounces of meat a day in addition to Changi rations, and there was always the chance of scrounging foodstuffs and other essential items from the godowns lining the wharves at Keppel Harbour.

'Life in the garrison area was rough at the start because food was short, but I left Changi when I was detailed to go down to Singapore in a work party and never went back,' Ray Rossiter says. 'We loaded and unloaded ships at Keppel Harbour. You always knew when you went on board a ship that it had been in Singapore before because the galley was locked up. We went in and out of the godowns and one could do a bit of looting now and again – sugar, mostly, and a bit of tinned stuff. The Japs couldn't read the labels so they didn't know what was in it.'[5]

At the Great World off River Valley Road, eight officers and 276 other ranks from the Australian 2/19th and 2/20th Battalions were quartered in Chinese cinemas, just inside the main gates, and in the main dance hall – where many of the men had danced with the local taxi girls. The men built false bottoms into their water-bottles and secreted small items, such as tins of gramophone needles – a valuable commodity for trade – in the cavities, while still being able to pour out some water if they were searched. Indian boots, longer than Australian boots, were found in one godown and promptly used for smuggling a bicycle chain in each boot.

The policy on food was to eat as much as possible on the job, then carry a substantial amount back to camp, where a roaring black market was in operation. Gramophone needles and bicycle chains were bought by the Chinese for cash which the men used to buy tobacco or used in two-up games with POWs from other camps, who would slip into the Great World at night. Men sent money, food and tobacco back to their mates at Changi with those returning through illness.

Joe Staples was one of the first to volunteer for the working parties and joined a similar set-up at New World. Vince Broe recorded his return to Changi a few days later on 31 March: 'Movement in the Barracks Square attracts my attention; a newly arrived truck is disgorging men and gear as I hasten to the scene. There's no illusion, it is Joe! I shout a welcome from the outskirts of the crowd, my excited heart pounding.

'Good old Joe! A touch of dysentery following three joyful days on the wharves put him off the payroll, and after a restful spell of "no duty" he is back with a crowd of sick. Tobacco, cigarettes, food, news and money! Joe has the lot, and substituting bread rolls with fish or strawberry jam for the monotonous midday rice, we're envied by many.

'He tells tales of daring and mischief under the very noses of the Japs, describing his New World quarters as first-class, with radio, electric light, running water, plenty of money and every variety of food. Joe's generosity knows no bounds: hungry-eyed strangers don't need to ask for a smoke and throughout the afternoon he scatters largesse by the tinful! It appears that a broken case of tobacco was secreted under a pile of debris and, risking the Japs' casual search, his gang finished each day's work with tins strapped and tied to every portion of their anatomy!'

The forlorn figure of General Percival could be seen 'sitting, head in hands, outside the married quarter he now shared with seven brigadiers, a colonel, his ADC, cook sergeant and batman. He discussed his personal feelings with few, spent hours walking around the extensive compound, ruminating on the reverse and what might have been.' One of the brigadiers was Ivan Stimson.[6]

On 8 July, Yamashita sent Shenton Thomas 150 bottles of beer, two bottles of Crabbies Ginger Wine, 30 tins of butter and 30 cheeses. Thomas wrote a brief note acknowledging the gift and assuring Yamashita of his 'high consideration'. The following week, however, Thomas learned that he and all senior officers, full colonels and above, were to be moved to Korea, Formosa or Japan. General Percival appointed Lieutenant-Colonel E. B. Holmes of the Manchester Regiment to command British and Australian troops in Changi, while General Callaghan appointed Lieutenant-Colonel Galleghan to command the AIF and act as Holmes's deputy.

'Black Jack' Galleghan quickly established his authority, touring the camp and ticking off in round terms anyone found guilty of laxity in discipline or behaviour. 'He was a good soldier,' says Wyett. 'I wouldn't want to have seen him promoted beyond the colonelcy he had – he wasn't good enough for that. He was very good as one of the middle-ranking officers. He was a very strict disciplinarian and one of the best things that could have happened to our mob. He pulled them all together.'[7]

Galleghan and Holmes had been in charge for only a few weeks when a major crisis developed after the Japanese demanded that everyone in Changi sign a document declaring that they would not attempt to escape. The document read, 'I the undersigned do hereby declare on my honour that I will not, under any circumstances, attempt to escape.'

The new Japanese commander General Shimpei Fukuye was so confident that the POWs would sign that a large quantity of documents had been
distributed throughout the camp. But with three exceptions, everyone
refused to sign. Fukuye was furious at this rank insubordination and the
following day, 2 September 1942, he ordered all prisoners in Changi, except
the three who had agreed to sign, to congregate in Selarang Barracks. What
ensued was to become known as the Barrack Square Incident.

Selarang Barracks, built to accommodate 800 men, consisted of a
barrack square or parade ground surrounded on three sides by three-storey
buildings, with a number of smaller houses for officers and married couples
spread out in spacious grounds. Fifteen thousand men were now crammed
into a parade ground of about 140 yards by 230 yards and in the
surrounding buildings. Dysentery broke out and quickly spread. George
Aspinall, who photographed the crowded square with a hidden camera,
says, 'The first and most urgent problem we had to face up to was the lack
of toilet facilities. Each barracks building had about four to six toilets,
which were flushed from small cisterns on the roofs. But the Japanese cut
the water off, and these toilets couldn't be used. The Japanese only allowed
one water tap to be used, and people used to line up in the early hours of
the morning and that queue would go on all day. You were allowed one
bottle of water per man per day, just one quart for your drinking, washing,
and everything else. Not that there was much washing done under the
circumstances.'[8]

When there was no sign of the POWs' backing down, General Fukuye
ordered E. B. Holmes and 'Black Jack' Galleghan to attend the execution of
two Australians, Breavington and Gale, and two English soldiers, Waters
and Fletcher, who had escaped but been captured.

Breavington, the older man, appealed to the Japanese to spare Gale. He
said that he had ordered Gale to escape and that Gale had merely obeyed
orders; this appeal was refused. As the Sikh firing party knelt before the
doomed men, Holmes and Galleghan saluted; the men returned the salute.
Breavington walked to the others and shook hands with them. A Japanese
lieutenant then came forward with a handkerchief and offered it to Breavington, who waved it aside with a smile; the offer was refused by all the men.
Breavington then called to one of the padres present and asked for a New
Testament, from which he read a short passage. Thereupon the order was
given by the Japanese to fire. The Sikhs were poor shots, however, and the
men writhed in agony on the ground before being shot several times more.[9]

With a major epidemic threatening, the Barrack Square Incident ended when the Japanese ordered the POWs to sign the no-escape document – which was thereby rendered invalid in Allied eyes. On 5 September the Japanese allowed the prisoners to move back to their former areas. Galleghan told the Australian troops in an address at 6.30 p.m. on 4 September, 'What I am mainly concerned about is that I have seen by your move here a spirit of co-operation, of unity and above all of brotherliness which makes any commander proud. I have seen in this barrack square the extension of that spirit to the other British troops that are here. And I have always deplored that there has been any question of separating us Australians from our brothers by race. We are British, just as much part of the British Army as the cockney who came out here to go into the Gordon Highlanders. I say that we are British.'

'He handled the situation very well indeed,' Wyett says. 'There was a small group of officers around him and we managed to help him over some of these hurdles but he did a really good job, no question about it. There are very few people who could have done as well.'[10]

The Japanese were paranoid about spies operating within their midst – and with good cause. British and Australian officers had established a sophisticated system of surveillance and were passing valuable information to the Allied forces in India, although the exact method of transmission was known to only a handful of people. The most reliable sources of information were the work parties, whose labouring jobs around the wharves and docks gave them ample opportunity to monitor Japanese shipping and spot any naval build-up. The men passed the information to a go-between who relayed it to senior officers.

The information was sent to India via the only possible means: a clandestine radio transmitter. 'We were fairly well informed on the events of the war in our region and knew about most of the setbacks the Japanese had received, especially those inflicted by the Americans in the Battle of Midway and by our combined forces in the Java Sea,' Wyett says. 'Working parties in Singapore were bringing back information of increased activity in shipping and troop movements and I longed for the opportunity to convey such information back to Australia.'[11]

The opportunity to build his own transmitter arose when Wyett met Corporal S. K. Elliman, a West Australian engineer and 'a bit of a wizard at this kind of thing'. Elliman was a radio ham who had constructed his own transmitters in civilian life. Working in total secrecy with a few smuggled components, he assembled a transmitter capable of sending signals as far as listening posts in India – 'a risky undertaking if ever there were one, but risks had to be taken and were accepted'.

The risk in this case, however, was so high that Wyett was not prepared to store or operate the transmitter inside the camp itself. If it were to be found inside the boundary, the Japanese could inflict the death penalty on dozens of POWs. One night Wyett slipped outside the wire and investigated the housing of Changi Battery's 15-inch naval guns, which had been wrecked by the Royal Navy before the surrender. 'We hid the transmitter in the labyrinth under the big guns where they kept all the bags of cordite and the shells,' Wyett says.

The labyrinth was a network of concrete tunnels and storage rooms beneath the gun emplacements. When Wyett and Elliman climbed down into it, they discovered that as well as wrecking the guns, the Navy had flooded the tunnels and storage rooms. Wyett waded into the water and found that it came up to his chin; any Japanese who wanted to search the tunnels would probably have had to swim.

Deep inside one of the pitch-black tunnels the two Australians groped around with the aid of a lighted candle and found a steel plate bolted to the wall, concealing a space just big enough to hold their transmitter. Wyett was now ready. He knew that members of the Indian Army monitored a certain frequency at a prearranged time every Wednesday night in the hope of making contact with rogue operators such as Wyett.

Over several months, Wyett transmitted messages of varying lengths – some quite detailed when a work party brought back news of sufficient importance – while standing up to his neck in dirty water, with Elliman, similarly discomforted, providing light from a guttering candle. Wyett, who had spent some time at Quetta Staff College, in India, signed himself 'Quetta John' in the hope that his name would be recognised without giving away his identity to Japanese monitors. But although his transmissions got through to India, Wyett never received any replies from his colleagues. 'The messages were carefully coded – but the Japanese were soon searching for the wireless,' Wyett says. 'A Japanese officer woke up to the fact that there was something going on and that's when he grabbed me – on the last day of the year.'

Wyett and other members of AIF headquarters were preparing to hold a little celebratory New Year's Eve dinner, prepared from food that had carefully been put aside. He was chatting to Major Phil Head, the AIF's senior legal officer, when six armed Kempeitai dashed in. Two of them pinned Wyett's arms to his sides, while the rest searched the room, leaving the other Australian officers to watch in bewilderment.

Wyett was nonplussed when he realised that the Japanese knew exactly who to arrest and what to look for. His next message for India was sitting on his packing-case desk prior to transmission later that night. It contained sensational information provided by Adrian Curlewis, who was in charge of a work party on Singapore docks. He had noticed that a number of moored Japanese freighters had white bamboo blinds rolled up and fastened to their sides. Guns and ammunition were being loaded on to the ships, and Japanese troops were going on board in large numbers. One of the blinds accidentally unrolled and was hastily rolled up again – but not before Curlewis had seen a huge red cross painted on the white background. He realised that the freighters were troopships disguised as hospital ships and clearly part of a convoy that was preparing to sail for Java and possibly Australia.

While several Kempeitai searched Wyett's trunk, his two guards released their grip on their prisoner to get a better look. Wyett took the opportunity to stroll over to his desk and pick up a sheaf of papers, which he handed to Phil Head, saying quietly, 'Get rid of the top one.' The two guards rushed up and grabbed Wyett again while others snatched the bundle of papers, but not before Head had quietly crumpled the dangerous scrap of paper into the palm of his hand. The rest of the papers referred to routine matters of camp administration; the Japanese tossed them aside after a quick glance. Then they hustled Wyett downstairs and placed him between two guards on the back seat of a waiting car. The corporal in charge of the arrest operation sat in the front next to the driver.

Wyett recalls that as the unmarked car reached the camp gate, the Japanese sentry ordered it to stop. The corporal leaned out of the window and, with a leer on his face, uttered the single word 'Kempeitai'. The effect on the sentry was startling; all his swagger collapsed, his body jerked and he began to shake. The corporal chuckled as the car gathered speed on its way to the YMCA torture centre at 1 Orchard Road.[12]

Rob Scott, head of the Information Bureau, had escaped from Singapore but had been captured in Sumatra. He was brought back to Singapore in handcuffs and kept in solitary confinement for eight and a half months, in a cell with no light or running water. Each day he was roughly questioned for 14 hours at the YMCA. He was still there when John Wyett was hauled upstairs and tied to a chair in the centre of a brightly lit room. Under the Japanese criminal-justice system, a prisoner had to confess to a crime before he or she could be charged with it. Therefore, the interrogator was permitted to use any amount of force, intimidation or coercion to extract a confession.

A Japanese officer shouted at Wyett in English, saying that he was a spy, and when he made no reply two guards started punching him in the face and head. Wyett still refused to utter a sound, so the officer unfastened his thick leather belt and began thrashing him. The blows were so severe that the chair toppled over and Wyett hit the floor head first. This was only the start of the beating. The officer inflicted deep head wounds with the brass buckle of his belt, and when even that failed to elicit any response from Wyett, he unsheathed his sword and struck him with the flat of the blade on many parts of his body. Wyett says the softening-up process had the opposite effect on him. 'I was determined that I wasn't going to let them beat me,' he says. 'It was almost crazy determination that got me through.'13

Wyett was spared further punishment that night after the most savage blow of all had struck him on the neck, knocking him backwards across the room. He woke up hours later on the concrete floor of a cell. The cell was 12 feet square; in one corner there was a lavatory and a tap. Twenty Chinese, Tamil, Sikh and Malay prisoners were seated with their backs to the wall, their hands folded. They were allowed neither to move nor to speak, and were watched around the clock by a sentry who would punish any infractions with a severe beating. At night, the prisoners were permitted to lie on the floor. They were fed mainly on rice, which had been cooked to a sticky consistency so that it could be moulded into a ball the size of a cannonball.

Wyett observed all of this between visits to the 'treatment room' for further interrogation. As well as beatings, he was given electric shocks to different parts of his body. He was told he had been plotting against the interests of His Imperial Majesty the Emperor of Japan of whom he was now a subject. He was charged with communicating with the enemy by radio, with attempting to escape and with plotting to steal the property of the Emperor. The latter charges related to Wyett's friendship with Flight Lieutenant Jack Macalister, a Royal Australian Air Force officer with whom Wyett had discussed the possibility of seizing a Hudson and flying it to Australia. Macalister was also in custody but had not yet been tortured. The two men had been betrayed by an Indonesian soldier in the Dutch Army who often lounged around the Australian sector. Wyett caught a glimpse of him at the YMCA when he was being taken back to his cell and realised that he was a Japanese spy.

'The Japanese were under a lot of pressure to find out what was happening and I wasn't going to let those little sods get the better of me,' Wyett says. 'But it was obvious they knew a great deal, so after some more electric shock treatment I made a "little confession". They jumped up out of their chairs and danced around the room, and then they gave me a cup of tea. I'd been careful all along not to take Mac into my confidence about the wireless and a few other things. I thought if I kept him in the dark he wouldn't be able to tell them anything. So I told the Nips I would order Mac to cease any resistance and tell them all he knew. That put him on a neutral basis – it took away any suspicion from him and he wasn't beaten. It all stopped. I was quite surprised, but it was a tense time. Mac and I were marched over to the Supreme Court, where we were sentenced to be beheaded – but that was commuted to 20 years in Outram Road Jail.'

Meanwhile, Lorraine Stumm had returned to Brisbane as an accredited war correspondent for the *Daily Mirror*. She cabled stories from General Douglas MacArthur's headquarters on the fight-back against the Japanese, and interviewed film stars John Wayne and Gary Cooper when they paid visits to the Queensland capital. Lorraine spent a great deal of time in the communications room at GHQ in a city insurance building, where one of her acquaintances was Beryl Stevenson – now secretary to the dynamic General George C. Kenney, creator of the US 5th Air Force.

Lorraine was travelling through Brisbane in a tram one afternoon when she was hailed from the pavement by Commander Donald Davidson, a British naval officer whom she had known in Singapore. He was with Major Ivan Lyon of the Gordon Highlanders, who had escaped from Singapore Island to India in a small boat with seven other men. With Davidson as his second-in-command, he was training commandos at a camp in north Queensland for a secret mission.

Lyon's wife Gabrielle and one-year-old son Clive had disappeared in June 1942 on a voyage from Perth to join him in India. Their ship, the *Nankin*, had been intercepted by a German raider and they were presumed to have been taken prisoner, but their whereabouts were unknown. That night, Lorraine Stumm and her sister Margot joined Lyon and Donaldson for dinner at Lennons Hotel. Over fillet steaks and a bottle of Veuve Cliquot, Lyon told Lorraine he had given Gabrielle a little diamond brooch in the shape of three bears. 'You'll see, she'll come out of prison camp wearing it,' he said. 'I'm sure they won't get it from her.'[14]

CHAPTER 29

Children in Captivity

AFTER THE CLERGYMEN'S VISIT to their grandmother's home, the five little Bruce children packed their bags and waited for the Japanese to cart them off to Changi Jail. One morning in May 1942, a Japanese army lorry swung past the flame-of-the-forest trees at the entrance and made its way up the long driveway, past the rows of orchids, to the front door. Two Japanese soldiers climbed down; one of them produced a list of names, which he showed to Gwen Bruce and her mother. 'Our names were on the list, and they gestured that we were to collect our belongings and board the truck,' Mel Bruce says. 'Gran stood there with tears streaming down her face, waving goodbye.'[1]

The truck called at a number of other homes to collect similar batches of dispirited women and children, and all these hundreds of 'enemy aliens' were deposited in a field in the Tampenis Road area. A Japanese officer then told them in English that there would be no further transport and they would have to walk to Changi. 'The thought of marching all that way in the afternoon heat was very daunting to us all, but march we did,' Mel says. 'Somebody started singing "Pack up Your Troubles" and before long, the whole column was singing along. The older boys among us carried the younger ones on our shoulders, and some even tied their belongings to either end of long poles.'

It took almost seven hours for the ragged column to arrive at the assembly point outside the jail, where they were permitted to sit on the grass in front of the massive stone walls. Then the families were split up, with women and young children being marched through the gates and down a long corridor to the women's wing of the prison, while the men and older boys went into the main courtyard, where they were met by the British representative who notified them of their cell blocks. Syd and Mel were directed to cell number 2 in H Block, where they were greeted by their father. 'He hugged us both and for a while he was quite overcome with emotion,' Mel says. 'Then he asked us about Mum and the rest of the family.

He seemed to heave a sigh of relief, knowing that we were all safe and sound.'

Meanwhile, Terpie Pattara, who had been on parole at the Victoria Street convent, also lost her freedom after contacting her fiancé. She says, 'I was at mass in the Church of the Good Shepherd one morning and a friend tapped my shoulder and said, "Benny is in the Portuguese church." It was only a few yards away. I dashed across and saw him there for a few minutes. We had a chance to talk outside the church. They had brought Catholic prisoners to mass there and allowed them to have breakfast with their friends – that was in the early days but then they got tougher. I saw Benny once more when we were going to the Carmelite convent and I caught a fleeting glimpse of him going past in a lorry.

'Some kind soul managed to pass letters between us but there were a lot of fifth columnists around and we were watched all the time. One day the Mother Superior, Mother St James, called me in and said, "You're in trouble – your name is on the list to be beheaded." I'd been reported by someone. I was on the list to be beheaded because I had contacted my fiancé. Thalia and I were taken in about six o'clock one morning. They just marched into the room with a Sikh with a fixed bayonet and took us to Changi Jail. I was in Changi with Thalia and my father.'[2]

The two Bruce brothers lived in a cell that housed 16 men and boys, mainly fathers and sons. The cell was in two halves, with four suspended cots in each half and folding camp-beds in the middle. 'The rest of us had to sleep on hessian mats on the concrete floor,' Mel says. 'There were no luxuries like blankets or pillows.' The boys began to learn prison routine. They took their meals in the shower block under the supervision of two Franciscan monks, Brother Flattery and Brother Ryan.

Breakfast consisted of rice porridge, a slice of bread with margarine and a mug of tea. Once a week, there was a hard-boiled egg. Lunch was boiled or fried rice, with a selection of fried or curried fish, or – a great delicacy – a spicy pork sausage called *lapchong*. Pudding was stewed prunes or rice pudding with brown sugar. On Tuesdays and Thursdays they were given a banana in lieu of the pudding. The evening meal consisted of rice, baked potatoes and boiled tapioca root rolled in grated coconut with brown sugar.

From 10 a.m. until 1 p.m., the boys attended school lessons with teachers who had been interned, while older boys and men were put to work on cleaning duties inside the prison – including the Japanese guardhouse – or sent in work parties outside the prison. The boys were permitted to see their mother once a month. Barbara Glanville says, 'We were allowed to meet in what they called the Rose Garden – there wasn't a rose in it, but it was called the Rose Garden. This was how we kept in touch with my two brothers and got news of my father.'

Bernie Clifton says that Changi was 'a very severe, very strict place. I didn't see my mother for many months, and I don't think my father ever saw her until the very end. It was a great shame – it really broke him. As a young son, I was allowed to go and see her and he would say, "Well, what did she say?" I would have forgotten, which didn't please him much at all.'[3]

Len Butler was still 15 years old until August 1942, but he was six feet tall 'and I did the same work as everybody else. I could hold my own. I'd learned in the Merchant Navy that if you let someone bully you, that was it – they'd step on you. I'd had many a beating but had learned how to fight. We went out on work parties clearing the jungle, building Changi airport, draining the swamps, making roads. If you didn't work, you didn't get any food. If you were sick, you didn't get any food. Even if you were slightly ill, you went out to work to be on the work roster so you got a food ration which you then shared with sick people.

'The prison had become so overcrowded that prisoners were sleeping in corridors and on landings. My cell was 12 feet long by 7 feet wide and they put three prisoners into each of these cells, then four. Between each floor there was a wire mesh to stop suicides, and it was so crowded that people were living on the mesh on every floor.'[4]

The children witnessed distressing scenes which they never forgot. 'A lot of people were taken away and tortured,' Barbara Glanville says. 'Mrs Mulvanney was Swiss and she shouldn't have been in the camp because the Swiss were neutral, but she had worked for the British so she was interned. She had a little matchbox radio and she used to give information whenever she could get it. She would say, "Take heart – the British are coming." Someone hoping to get extra rations – nobody knows who – split on her and they took her away and tortured her. When she came back, she was absolutely mad.

'They had to put her in a padded cell because she used to bang her head. Every time the moon came out she would sing "Rule Britannia" as loud as she could through the grille. At two o'clock one night a Japanese sentry came to the cell door and banged on the grille with his rifle and told her to shut up. She put her hands through the grille and clung to him by his neck. He dropped the rifle. He was short and she was a very tall Swiss lady and his feet were dangling in the air. The other guards had to come and prise her hands apart. She was so strong that she nearly strangled him.'[5]

Len Butler thought the Korean guards were worse than the Japanese. 'They were a bloody shower – really cruel,' he says. 'If they created great pain, they would laugh – they would think it was great fun.'

As Christmas approached, the children's spirits rose when they heard they would receive Red Cross parcels. 'A large consignment arrived at the prison and the news spread like wildfire,' Mel Bruce says. 'We had high expectations of some extra luxuries at last. The allocation of parcels was one case between four people, so we received four cases in our cell. When we placed the contents in the centre of the cell, we discovered that all items such as tins of coffee, fruit, milk, bars of chocolate, cigarettes and matches – in fact, even the tins of Christmas cake – had already been removed by the Japanese. It was a terrible blow.'

Daphne Davidson, a civil servant at the Colonial Secretariat, had been four months pregnant when Singapore fell. 'My mother didn't escape in one of the last boats – many of which were bombed anyway,' her daughter Jennifer Martin says. 'She actually stayed at her post, burning documents in a big incinerator at the back of the office. She was still there when the Japanese walked in.'[6]

Mrs Davidson was permitted to spend the last few days of her confinement at the Kandang Kerbau Hospital at 100 Bukit Timah Road, where her daughter Jennifer was born on 31 July 1942. Chinese friends sent in an amah, who looked after the baby and scrounged nice things for her to eat from the kitchen. Daphne took the baby back to Changi when she was two weeks old. Her two sisters, Diane and Isobel, had also been interned and Diane had a one-year-old daughter, Genevieve. 'It was very hot in Changi, so they built a dormitory shed in the courtyard for mothers with children,' Jennifer says. 'I can remember the high grey walls – but as I didn't have any other memories they represented security to me.'

Genevieve Evans has no memories at all of her incarceration. 'I was eight months old when I went in and I was suffering from shellshock,' she says. 'Our house was under the guns of Fort Canning and the noise affected me very badly. I was four and a half when I came out, but I just blotted the whole thing out. I know I was there with my mother, two aunts and a cousin. My father, Frederick Logan, was a member of the Gordon Highlanders. The Japanese gave him a terrible time – he was tortured and he caught tuberculosis. He was sent up to Thailand. He worked on the Death Railway.'[7]

CHAPTER 30

An Up-country Retreat

I N A P R I L 1942, prisoners in Changi POW camp were offered a once-in-a-lifetime trip to a new resort, where there would be an abundance of food in a healthy climate. The party would travel to this promised land by ship. Any health problems they had suffered in Changi would soon disappear and they would not be required to work. It sounded too good to be true – and so it proved. In reality, the men were to be used as slave labour to build a strategic 258-mile railway between Nong Pladuk in Thailand and Thanbyuzayat in Burma to transport the Japanese Army to the battlefront for its attack on India.[1]

Russell Savage was one of 3,000 British and Australian troops who assembled at the docks in Keppel Harbour on 15 May as members of A Force, the first contingent to avail themselves of the Japanese 'offer'. The force consisted of a headquarters staff and three battalions of around 1,000 men each. In overall command was Brigadier Arthur Varley.

'We had as our CO Colonel Charles Anderson VC, and he had as interpreter Captain Bill Drower,' Savage says. 'When I first saw these two on the wharves, I thought, "My God, what have we got here?" Charles Anderson had thick glasses, looked like a schoolmarm and seemed indecisive. Bill Drower was a soft-looking Englishman, six feet three inches tall, with an upper-crust voice. But I don't think we could have had two more formidable men looking after us. They were absolutely outstanding.'[2]

Bill Drower was pleased about his assignment. 'I'd realised that I wasn't cut out to be a regimental officer, and Brigadier Torrance told me I'd become a captain again if I did this interpreting job,' he says. 'A Force was predominantly Australians and I was instantly impressed with Charles Anderson. We got on terrifically well. The thinking was done by Anderson, not Varley. We used to call him "Bwana Charlie".'[3]

The Australians had had little contact with their Japanese captors at Changi, but there at the wharves they soon learned a lesson, as they waited to board two tramp steamers. 'One of our chaps was smoking, and a Jap came over and hit him over the head and told him not to smoke,' Savage says. 'That was supposed to be the final warning. A bit later, another chap lit up and the Jap came over and belted him within an inch of his life with his rifle butt and boots. This was the first time we had seen what these blokes were capable of doing. That sort of set us back a bit.'

Russell Savage and hundreds of other members of A Force were crammed into the steel holds of one of the ships, *Toyohashi Maru*. His baggage consisted of a prismatic compass, a pair of boots, a change of clothes, water-sterilising tablets, a field dressing and a tin of meat. The *Toyohashi Maru* set sail, and when Savage's compass showed that they were heading north towards Burma he thought they might be part of an exchange of prisoners of war.

'The hold was so cramped that the chaps couldn't lie down at night, and we had dysentery on board,' Bill Drower says. 'I was busier than at any other time. I was dog-tired. I got up and Anderson said, "Bill, take a rest." I flumped on to the hot glass cowling over the engine room and was so exhausted I fell asleep there despite the heat.'

Charles Anderson's 800 men were put ashore at Tavoy, Lower Burma, where they went to work repairing an airfield. There was no sign of any holiday resort or prisoner exchange, so eight members of the 2/4th Anti-Tank Regiment took off into the jungle in the hope of reaching India. The Japanese at the camp were Imperial Guards, who caught up with the escapees after a few days. All of them were executed.

After completing the airport work, A Force was transhipped to Moulmein, where they were ordered to set up camp in the centre of town as an object lesson to the Burmese in how the Japanese had subjugated the white man. Bill Drower remembers, 'I was sitting there when I felt a tap on the shoulder and a Burmese said, "We very sorry." The next day we marched off and we were pelted with dozens of little cakes, blocks of palm sugar and cigars. The Japanese were furious. The Burmese were all saying sorry.'

A Force was marched to Thanbyuzayat, the first staging camp for the construction of the railway. There they were handed over to a squad of impressed Korean guards, who hated the Japanese but knew there were informers within their ranks. Forbidden to speak their own language on duty, they took their frustration and hostility out on the prisoners. Dr Rowley Richards was beaten by both Japanese and Korean guards on a number of occasions for defending patients who were too sick to work; he lost bits of his front teeth. 'Medically, it was very difficult,' he says. 'I left Singapore with a pannier full of medical supplies, but it was looted on the way and I arrived at Thanbyuzayat with very little. The Japs gave us virtually nothing.'[4]

Security within A Force was tight. 'Charles Anderson restricted everything to a little circle of people,' Bill Drower says. 'We had some Dutch with us and we didn't trust them – they were careless. Arthur Watchorn had built a miniature radio in a water-bottle to listen to the news, so Charles had to be very careful that no one let on that they knew any war news such as the Battle of Midway. They knew that if I was going to be grilled by the Kempeitai the less I knew the better, so I didn't know about the radio.'

The commanders didn't always see eye to eye. 'Charles Anderson did a wonderful job from the point of view of maintaining morale,' Dr Richards said. 'I was also involved with another CO named John Williams from Williams Force, which had joined us from Sumatra. He was the absolute opposite to Anderson. Anderson was "Softly, softly, catchee monkey, let's educate the Japs," whereas Williams would clash with them at the drop of a hat.'

This created difficulties for Bill Drower who, as interpreter, often found himself in the middle of arguments between POWs and the guards. One such confrontation almost cost Drower his life. It began when a British officer refused to fill a bucket of water for a Japanese medical orderly; Drower was called in to interpret during the subsequent inquiry into why a prisoner had refused to obey a Japanese order. 'I said something regarding this miserable little Japanese fellow's bad behaviour towards officers,' Bill Drower says. 'I said he ought to be aware there was an international treaty that stopped that sort of thing. I reckoned that the guards had heard that things were going badly for the Japanese and I thought they'd probably think, "Well, yes, we'll have to be a bit careful." I was taking a chance.

'The orderly was the boyfriend of a Japanese sergeant who was a fanatical so-and-so. I'd said the wrong thing to the wrong bloke. The sergeant reported me to Captain Noguchi, the camp commandant, for making a statement against the Emperor. Noguchi summoned me up and things went on from there. He bashed me over the head [with a sword stick] and I crashed on to his table. I broke his table, I'm glad to say – I get some satisfaction from that. He threw me into a very small, one-man dugout. I was wearing flip-flops made out of a rubber tyre and I woke up to find my feet were being tickled by a rat. It wasn't very pleasant. Fortunately, I'm fond of music and I used to sing refrains I'd learned at Clifton. I was frightened that my boots would be found – I'd hidden my signet ring in them and the Japanese would have taken that to mean I was planning to escape. It would have gone hard on whoever was looking after my boots – they would have been punished as an accomplice. Fortunately, the boots weren't discovered.

'Colonel Toosey arranged to keep me alive by instructing one of his chaps to secrete vitamins in the rice ball I was allowed to have twice a day. Had it not been for that I would not have survived blackwater fever – which I had got very badly. I was in solitary confinement for 77 days. I was delirious when they pulled me out. At that point, I was in a ramshackle hut on the boards. The doctor reckoned a few more days and I would have had my toes up. Captain Lacey from the 6th Norfolks gave blood for a transfusion. I'd lost a great deal of weight and my blood was well down. I was very lucky. Philip Toosey was responsible for demanding again and again to know what had happened to me and what I had done wrong. I'm very grateful to him. In my mind, he's a quite splendid chap. I'm very proud to have known him.'5

Meanwhile, the rate of attrition through death and disease among those building the Thailand–Burma railway had caused a manpower crisis back in Changi. 'We were getting a little short of other ranks, so it was decided that 300 officers would go up to Thailand,' Harry Schulman says. 'We got there and after about a week they called on the officers for work parties to go on to the railway. The officers said no, we won't work. The Geneva Convention says that officers do not do work beneficial to the enemy. We were put into a square and were surrounded by the Japanese Army while we argued with the hierarchy. They said you will work, we said no. They brought in more troops. We said we will do camp chores which would release more men. They said no, you will work. We said no, we will not work. I heard the triggers being pulled and the first volley of shots went over our heads. We said yes, we will work. The Wampo Viaduct was the first big job we worked on, a magnificent engineering feat.

'I was sent into the jungle to cut the trees – I had been trained as a forester. We were in a teak forest and there was a lot of hardwood there. We had no proper tools, only hand tools, and teak is a hell of a thing to cut. So we cut down soft trees to fill our quota – when they used them in the rail construction you could hear the bugs boring in. Then a Japanese officer who knew something about trees came down and there was hell to pay. There were good Japanese, there were bad Japanese. They employed Koreans to guard us, with Japanese NCOs. Japan had conquered Korea and a lot of these Koreans had had their mothers and fathers killed by the Japanese, so the Japanese NCOs worked them up to hate us. The Japanese Army was ruled by terror. It was terror discipline.'6

Frank Davies worked all the way from Thailand to Burma after being told he was going to a 'nice camp'. When his contingent got to Singapore Railway Station, they were herded into metal rail trucks. 'There were blokes with dysentery and we were huddled in this truck with nothing to lie on for five days,' he says. 'Our first camp was Ban Pong. It was a foot under water and the latrines had overflowed with faeces and maggots. As time went on, the camps got worse.

'I survived through pure luck. A lot of my mates were big tough lads and they were going first. A medic put it down to the fact that if you came from a rough area like Salford and were brought up in the gutters, you had a better immune system. Some of the lads who came from the country couldn't cope with the diseases. In the camps, we'd eat anything. Some blokes were a bit fussy. As kids we'd been up to our elbows down grids looking for pennies. You'd be thick with all this muck and you'd wipe it off as best you could. We picked up a few germs but it was good for your immune system.

'I'd started work at 14, getting up at 6.30 to start at 7.30, 40 hours a week flogging you to death. I was an errand boy at first – a brew lad they used to call it – and I was a skinny little bloke at that age, but you were expected to carry heavy items all over the firm, going up and down metal stairs. Nobody said, "Can you manage it?" or, "Are you strong enough?" You just had to get on with it. The hard work on the railway didn't cause any problems, that part of it. And I wasn't fussy about what I ate. Blokes would spend ages picking the weevils out and having not much left. I used to say, "Bugger it – shut your eyes and eat the stuff." '

Harry Schulman's family believed he was dead. 'After the Battle for Singapore, a soldier was debriefed in Ceylon or India and he said he had seen me shot and killed in the Batu Pahat area,' he says. 'I was reported missing believed dead to my family. My brother was working in Downing Street at the Ministry of Economic Warfare and in 1944 somebody tapped him on the shoulder and handed him a memo. It said, "We've been listening in to the Vatican Radio and your brother's name came out alive 200 miles up the Burma Railway."

'I'm not a Roman Catholic and there had been no Red Cross in that very remote camp. What had happened was that a French woman in Bangkok had sent food into the camp with a servant and asked him to get a list of names. This list was sent out to Vichy France in a diplomatic bag and was passed on to the Vatican.'

After the railway had been completed – at a cost of 200,000 European and Asian lives – Russell Savage and some of the survivors of A Force were returned to Singapore via Bangkok and Saigon. They were marched to the POW camp at River Valley Road. 'We were a pretty sorry looking lot, filthy, smelly and emaciated,' he says. 'Who should be there but the Gurkhas. They all stood to attention and saluted us as we came in. The Gurkhas had refused to work so the Japs had pulled out their fingernails and chopped off their toes, but they wouldn't break their promise to serve the King. It was quite a shock for them to see the state we were in after working for the Japanese. It really upset them.'

The Japanese put the Australians to work building a graving dock on one of the islands off Singapore. 'They took us over on landing barges by day and night to dig out clay in a huge pit. The clay was taken out of the hole in skips pulled along little railway lines by a winch. We quickly learned that it was possible to adjust the pins on the links between these skips so that when they reached a certain angle they would come out. It was a sight for sore eyes to see 15 or 20 of these laden skips racing back down the slope and overturning. Of course, we blamed the Japanese winch driver. The Japanese would be screaming and leaping about, which we enjoyed no end.

'As we weren't making much progress, the Japanese brought out a lot of food and fruit, put it on a platform and lowered it halfway down into the pit. We were told that the work team who achieved the required output would get this food. The word went around that the work team who won would also get something from the rest of us. The rate of work was so inadequate that no one won the food.'

As the men were returning to Keppel Harbour late one afternoon, they saw a German U-boat at a dock. 'No one in our party could speak German, but we made our feelings known with taunts,' Savage says. 'Then an amazing thing happened: the U-boat skipper called his crew to attention on deck and had them salute us as we passed.'

CHAPTER 31

The Double Tenth

IN THE SUMMER OF 1943 a branch of the Kempeitai under Lieutenant Haruzo Sumida was charged with finding the culprits of acts of sabotage in Singapore City, mainly the cutting of telephone lines and the burning down of warehouses. Lieutenant Sumida, both vicious and ambitious, surmised that he would gain great favour among his superiors if he could prove that these crimes against the Emperor had been organised by European internees in Changi Jail.

With commendable efficiency, the jail's 'secret service' picked up the gist of Sumida's intentions. It had succeeded in tapping the telephone line between the camp and the city and knew that something sinister was afoot. Careful preparations were being made for a raid on the camp somewhere around Christmastime to catch the ringleaders of an anti-Japanese conspiracy. Sumida's chief suspect was Rob Scott, who had been released by the Kempeitai and sent to Changi Jail – and had indeed concerned himself with the running of the camp.[1]

Neither Scott nor anyone else in Changi, however, had anything to do with any of the attacks that had already been perpetrated or with the one that would turn the jail upside down on 10 October – the Double Tenth. On 28 September, Scott received a message from one of his contacts in the city, saying that early the previous morning six Japanese ships had been blown up in Singapore Harbour. It was sensational news: the first spectacular act of sabotage since the Japanese had captured the island. The loss of shipping in such an important place was an enormous blow to Japanese prestige.

Scott and his fellow internees supposed that the saboteurs must have been Chinese guerrillas who had slipped across the straits from their base in Malaya. Sumida, however, believed that Scott and his associates had planned the whole thing from Changi Jail. He had high hopes of solving the mystery of the sunken ships and ending the general anti-Japanese conspiracy at the same time. At his subsequent trial for war crimes, he said, 'I felt that the state of peace and order and this serious incident were related and that a thorough measure must be taken to prevent the recurrence of such serious incidents.'

The raid had nothing to do with guerrillas or fifth columnists. It had been carried out by Ivan Lyon and a group of Anglo-Australian commandos who had sailed from Western Australia to Singapore in an old Japanese fishing boat, the *Krait*, named after a particularly vicious Malayan snake. The attack on Singapore Harbour had been codenamed Operation Jaywick (after a popular lavatory deodoriser). Once within striking distance of Singapore Harbour, the commandos had taken to folboats – folding canoes – and paddled up to the docks under the cover of night. They had attached limpet mines to the sides of six Japanese ships, including several oil tankers, and then slipped away. They were paddling to their rendezvous with the *Krait* at Pompong, an island 80 miles distant from Singapore, when the limpet mines exploded, shattering the morning calm.

According to Colonel Jack Finlay's report to Australian Military Intelligence, with a copy to the War Office, the raiders inflicted losses on the enemy totalling 46,000 tons of shipping. 'A number of captured Jap documents and radio broadcasts show that this attack had a very considerable effect on the harbour defence precautions throughout the South China Seas, and even as far as Manila,' Finlay wrote. 'A general warning was issued against potential strikes of this nature, and all harbour defences specially guarded. The correct method of attack was never appreciated, and was regarded by the Jap authorities as due to local Chinese guerrilla activities from within Singapore itself.'[2]

Len Butler says, 'The Japs had no idea who had blown up their ships. They couldn't conceive that anybody could travel that far through their lines of defence and have the audacity to attack their shipping. They thought it was an internal job done through Changi Jail with Chinese guerrillas.'

One of the captured Japanese documents confirms Sumida's mistaken beliefs about the raid: 'Singapore shipping espionage is carried out by natives under European instructions. An enemy espionage affair developed early in the morning of 27 September 1943 at Singapore and was commanded by Europeans hiding in the neighbourhood of Pulai in Johore. It was carried out by Malayan criminals through a Malayan village chief, and the party was composed of ten or more persons, all of whom are Malayans. As a result of the raid, six ships of 2,000–5,000 tons (three tankers among them) were sunk by bombs due to a clever plan.'

On the day before the Double Tenth, internees were ordered to parade in the open at nine o'clock in the morning. No explanation was given. When the parade had assembled, the camp commandant came out with a large number of Kempeitai and troops, who closed all the exits. The names of a few men were called out for immediate arrest. Scott's name was top of the list.

Len Butler remembers, 'The Kempeitai went through every single cell in Changi looking for radios. If they found a piece of wire or an earphone or anything they thought could be connected to radio, or a lot of money, they would drag the prisoner out and give him a going-over. If they didn't get a satisfactory answer, they would take him down to Kempeitai headquarters. He might not come back – and a lot of them didn't.'

James MacIntosh had paraded with the rest of the internees and was wondering what the emergency was all about when his name was suddenly called out. MacIntosh ran a course for amateur radio hams among the inmates and imagined this was the reason. He was right – he was a prime suspect. 'My kitbag was searched and questioning began,' he says. 'Where was the apparatus I used when teaching? I had none and said so. They told me to come with them and, grabbing a khaki jacket, I did so. Together with some others, we were bundled into an open truck and taken to the Kempeitai substation at the junction of Smith Street and Newbridge Road. I remained there for nearly six months.'[3]

Mel Bruce remembers the Double Tenth very clearly. 'The whole of the men's wing in the prison was turned out into the main exercise yard and made to stand in rows in the boiling heat all day, while the Kempeitai did a thorough search of the entire prison,' he says. 'During this time many prisoners, including youngsters, fainted and fell to the ground, but the guards insisted that they should remain where they had fallen, We were not allowed to assist anyone. By late evening, we were allowed to return to our cells.'

Several more arrests had been made, mostly of people who had been involved in monitoring news broadcasts and running a secret information service throughout the jail. The whole jail had been searched, and various diaries containing bits of war news unearthed. The most incriminating evidence that radios were operating inside the jail was discovered in the cell of a committee man who had kept notes of a BBC news broadcast. The Japanese had also found a tin box containing $210,000 in the cell of the camp treasurer, a British banker. It was the combination of radio and money that excited Sumida; clearly he had uncovered a nest of subversion and sabotage.

That was just the beginning of the Double Tenth. The reign of terror lasted for months. Suspects were hauled from their homes and places of work – or, in the case of internees, their prison cells – and taken to the Kempeitai interrogation chambers, where they were subjected to torture and starvation to make them confess to acts of sabotage and treason. As none of the suspects had even heard of Operation Jaywick, let alone been part of it, any confessions they made were meaningless. Lieutenant Sumida was mystified. Despite great suffering, not one of his victims had told him anything about the raid itself, how it had been organised or where the explosives had been obtained.

Bernie Clifton says, 'The most important man I met in camp was Adrian Clark, number one in the judiciary. The Japanese Gestapo killed him off. He couldn't survive the torture. One of the survivors was Jimmy Milne. He worked for Malayan Motors and because of that they put him in charge of the transport, and we had a couple of lorries going around Singapore looking for food. He was one of the drivers and the Kempeitai thought he was too familiar with the locals. They nabbed him and took him to the YMCA. That was a very bad do but he survived.

'He told me he only survived because his so-called contact was also brought in but had died under torture. This meant they couldn't get any more information, so they let him go back into camp. Only a very few managed to get away with their lives. We had one fellow executed, John Long. He used to work with Jimmy Milne on the lorries. We had two lorries and Milne was in one and Long was in the other. He was taken by the Kempeitai and beheaded. He was the only one executed; the others died of torture.'

The introduction to the record of the Double Tenth war-crimes trial describes the reign of terror: 'To the cosmopolitan city of Singapore the "Double Tenth" case was no small affair. It was a huge and ever-growing spider's web which caught now Europeans, now Asiatics, now Eurasians, within its coils. From the Bishop of Singapore himself to the humblest coolie, none could be sure that the next knock would not arouse his house-hold from its early-morning sleep to provide another victim for the torturers of the Kempeitai. For it was by such melodramatic methods that the Japanese Military Police achieved the dread in which they were univer-sally held in the occupied territories.

'The darkness of night, the sudden swoop, the atmosphere of terror were their agents to impose submissiveness upon a reluctant people. But, as the terror grew, so the popularity of the Japanese diminished and the popula-tion of Singapore grew less submissive. It was a vicious spiral descending into ever greater depths of horror. Thus the case of the "Double Tenth" was in effect the story of the occupation of Singapore, of an alien enemy in the midst of a hostile people, of fear on one side breeding fear on the other.'

Elizabeth Choy and her husband were running their canteen at the Tan Tock Seng Hospital, after all the patients and doctors had been moved there from the Miyako Hospital. Things had changed. The internees' ambulance was no longer allowed to call there and the only customers were nurses. The Choys' information and exchange service had come to a halt, but an informant had told the Kempeitai that the Choys had been involved in smuggling money into Changi Jail. A carload of Japanese called at the canteen and arrested Choy Khun Heng.

After several days, Elizabeth went to the YMCA to inquire about her husband. He had no change of clothes, she said, and no blanket, and she was worried that he would be sick. The Japanese denied all knowledge of him – but three weeks later they called at the hospital and offered to take her to see him. Elizabeth gathered up a small blanket and drove to the YMCA with the Japanese. Once she was inside, her handbag and jewellery were taken away and she was thrown into a filthy concrete cell packed with Chinese and Changi Jail prisoners. There was no sign of Khun Heng. The prisoners were forbidden to speak to one another – although one of the internees, John Dunlop, secretly taught them to communicate in sign language.

The cell measured 10 feet by 12 feet and the prisoners were forced to squat on a wooden platform built over a concrete floor. It was bare apart from a filthy lavatory in one corner; water was obtained from a tap used to flush the toilet. There was a foot-square opening in one wall through which food was passed to the prisoners. The cell was infested with bugs and, despite the discomfort, on the command of sleep, the prisoners would lie down beside one another and sleep like sardines while a bright light blazed all night.

'Almost every day I was taken for interrogation,' Elizabeth says. 'When they interrogated you, they would beat you, they would torture you, they would do all kinds of things to you. It was terrible.' In common with the other prisoners, Elizabeth's only food was a cup of rice with a little bit of meat or vegetable three times a day. The only beverage was a brown liquid identified as tea, which was poured into a filthy communal mug from a putrid bucket.[4]

After nine months in captivity, Elizabeth had lost half her body weight. The people were terribly depressed, she says, especially Mr Tan whose son she had taught at St Andrew's School. She spoke to him in sign language and learned that the Japanese had threatened to kill his wife and children. He was so grief-stricken he was going insane.

Elizabeth asked a sentry whether he would provide her with a stone so that she could scrub away some of the filth. He did so, and she cleaned the lavatory and its filthy, bacteria-infested surrounds. She then used her blanket to block the lavatory so she could wash in the bowl. Everyone else then borrowed her blanket for the same purpose. Teeth were cleaned with a finger. There was no soap, no comb, no change of clothes. But 'the greatest torture of all was not knowing what had happened to my family,' she says.

At Elizabeth's first interrogation session, the Japanese told her that some ships had been sunk in the harbour and they wanted to know the location of a large amount of money. They mentioned a British bank manager. 'Where did he keep the bank money?'

'I don't know.'

'But you are a friend of the British man and surely he must have told you. You must know.'

'It was rumoured that days before the surrender they burnt all the banknotes.'

'No, no – they have hidden it somewhere.'

'I don't know.'

'Oh, you won't tell the truth. All right, we are going to kill you. Maybe tomorrow morning, we will take you to Johore and there you will be executed. But if you tell us, we will let you go and your husband also.'

'I don't know.'

'What do you know about the ships? You must tell us the truth otherwise we will kill you.'

'We don't know anything.'

'Then we are going to execute you.'

'Well, if you have to execute me for telling the truth, I can't help it. Go ahead.'

Seven days after the Double Tenth, Bishop Wilson was called to the guardroom at Changi Jail. He put on a thin black cassock and walked with John Hayter to the front yard, where the guardroom was situated. Hayter saw his friend being driven away. Bishop Wilson was taken to the YMCA, where his cassock was removed and, dressed only in shorts and shirt, he was placed in the cell next to Elizabeth Choy. He was severely beaten for three days before the Japanese accepted that he was not one of the ringleaders in their phantom conspiracy.[5]

Meanwhile, the Kempeitai forced Elizabeth to kneel on some angled bars of wood on the floor. They stripped her topless and tied her to the wood so she could not go either forwards or backwards. Then they applied electric shocks to her. They brought in her husband. 'He was kneeling there watching me being tortured,' she says. 'They said, "Now, both of you confess. We'll let you go. If not, we'll execute you."' Tears were streaming down Elizabeth's face; her nose was running. She said goodbye to her husband. Then she collapsed. She has no memory of what happened next.

Because everybody in Elizabeth's cell became constipated, the Japanese decided that they must exercise in time to counting in Japanese: *Ich, ni, san, si, we, ou, hach, uck* – one, two, three, four, five, six, seven, eight. They could hear Bishop Wilson in the next cell, chanting, '*Ich, ni, san, si* . . . ' and then he would say, 'Lift up your hearts, be of good cheer.' 'That cheered us up a lot,' Elizabeth says. 'Then he would go back to the Japanese [for more torture].'

John Dunlop told Elizabeth in sign language about his travels through Europe, especially to Lake Como in Italy.

'I'll never be able to see these places,' Elizabeth signed back. 'I'm going to die.'

'Don't worry,' Dunlop said. 'You will be great and everybody will read about you in the papers.' She told him not to be silly. 'You just mark my words,' he replied.

Then she was hauled away for more questioning: 'Who had sunk the ships? What had happened to the banknotes? Who was anti-Japanese?' All night long the interrogations went on . . . the beatings, the howling, the cries of agony. Sometimes a victim would be so badly injured that he would be carried down to the cells and left to die in a passageway, while Elizabeth and the others could only watch.

One night Elizabeth saw Rob Scott. He was badly disfigured from beatings and water torture. He had been kept awake for an entire week, forbidden even to lie down or to relax. For the first four days he was on half-rations; then he was given no food at all. When not being questioned, he had to squat, Japanese-fashion, in front of the sentry, who could see at a glance everything inside his cell. Scott later wrote that during questioning he was usually forced to kneel on a rack, sometimes tied by a wrist to a window, with his arm fully extended. Japanese sentries doubled his legs under him and jumped on the soles of his feet until the open wounds exposed the ligaments and bones. He was flogged repeatedly. He would be called out of his cell at about 11 p.m. – 'my interrogator preferred working at night' – and put on a rack for a couple of hours in silence, then questioned for 20 minutes and beaten up for an hour. At last it would be over, and by 2.30 a.m. Scott would be sent back to his cell. Then would come the worst torture of all. Tottering with fatigue and pain, he would be called out again only half an hour later to go through the entire procedure once more.[6] At the end of one session he was told he had been sentenced to death and compelled to write a farewell letter to his wife.

Meanwhile, Elizabeth had fallen into the hands of the most dreaded torturer, a man named Mona. He talked and joked with Elizabeth, then all of a sudden gave her a terrible whack across the face. 'I glared at him and after that I refused to answer his questions,' she says.

At a later time, an officer told her, 'You'd better tell me the truth. We know the whole story.'

Elizabeth said, 'Yes, we sent food in to help the people who are interned. We sent medicine in. We sent money in.'

'Because you are anti-Japanese?'

'No.'

'You are pro-British?'

'No. Everything we did was to help people.'

Elizabeth was kept in the YMCA for 193 days and nights while the Kempeitai meticulously followed up every point in her story, cross-examining people she said she had helped. After a huge dossier of interviews had been compiled, the Japanese concluded that she was telling the truth. One of them said to her, 'We have been told that you are very kind, very ready to help people.'

She replied, 'I told you – I'm not anti-Japanese, not pro-British. I'm just wanting to help those in need, never mind what race.'

The officer nodded. 'We asked everybody. Everybody agreed [that you helped them]. So we'll let you go.'

It was not a trick. Elizabeth was freed. Khun Heng, however, was sentenced to 12 years in Outram Road Jail. People shunned Elizabeth when she came out, too terrified to speak to her.

Two of the women at the YMCA were Freddy Bloom, an American journalist, and Dr Cecily Williams. For a large part of their time there, one of their cellmates was Norman Coulson, the water engineer, whom the Japanese believed to have been a ringleader in the sabotage plot. Day after day for several weeks Coulson was flogged with such severity that, in Freddy's words, 'his back and legs were as raw as liver in a butcher's shop'.

Norman Coulson died soon afterwards, and James MacIntosh was moved into the cell. On 24 March 1944, Freddy, who was seriously ill with beriberi, asked him whether he thought they would get out alive. He replied that he thought they would.

'Next morning,' he says, 'our names were called out: Bloom, Williams, Mashintosh (they always called me that) and so on – five of us. We were taken to a room close by and told that we were being sent back to Changi. We were warned most categorically that we must not speak of our incarceration under penalty of being brought back for good.'[8]

Late one afternoon, a badly beaten Walter Stevenson walked into B Yard at Changi Jail with eight Japanese soldiers and took them to a point in a low bank, where he removed some turf resting on a wooden board to reveal a cavity holding his wooden stool. He had built a radio set into the stool.

Thirteen Europeans died in the Kempeitai cells during the Double Tenth inquisition. Walter Stevenson was one of them. The suffering spread to the entire civilian population of Changi Jail. Rations were cut – even for children. Games, concerts, plays, lectures and school lessons were forbidden for months. It was the lowest point of the occupation.

Then one day in 1944 Len Butler saw with his own eyes evidence that the Japanese were losing the war. 'My cell was high up and at the end of the block there was a big window,' he says. 'I could jump up and grasp the bars and look out over the Straits of Johore. I saw the Japanese fleet come in badly battered. They had been clobbered, and that was very nearly the end of their navy.

'Then some time later when we were clearing some underbrush with a Korean guard who had become very friendly for some reason, the air-raid sirens went off and we heard the sound of throbbing engines. I looked up and saw three echelons of massive planes – they were Flying Fortresses, but I didn't know that at the time. They were in lines of three about a mile behind each other, and they bombed the Naval Base.'[9]

The battle for Singapore had gone full circle.

CHAPTER 32

Liberation

As THEIR EMPIRE CRUMBLED, the Japanese in May 1944 moved all internees to Sime Road and, in order to exercise greater control over the prisoners of war, imprisoned them in Changi Jail. Sime Road, the former nerve centre of Malaya Command, consisted of 150 long wooden huts surrounded by a high wire fence.

'Sime Road was worse than Changi,' Len Butler says. 'There was a lot of disease and death, and food was very scarce. We were eating leaves, snails, snakes – anything we could get hold of. We were absolutely desperate. The rice we got was full of weevils and maggots. You would put the maggots around [the edge of] the leaf you were eating from and there would be more maggots than pieces of rice. Our bodies were at the end of the line – even mine, as an 18-year-old. I hadn't eaten meat or fresh bread for years – I'd been eating filthy food. I'd had malaria 22 times and I was passing tape-worms.'[1]

In the women's camp, the huts were sited on the hillside in two rows. 'We walked from Changi Jail to Sime Road camp,' Barbara Glanville says. 'My two elder brothers, being over 12, were put into the men's camp and had to do manual labour. My mother, my two younger brothers and I had a space measured out – six feet by six feet for the four of us in one hut. We were treated very badly.

'There was another family, the Harris family. Their three girls stole some chillies from the vegetable garden. The Japanese got hold of their father and made him kneel on really hard gravel in the boiling-hot midday sun and beat him with a truncheon. Every time the girls screamed they beat the father more until he collapsed. They were a cruel lot, the Koreans and the Japanese.'

Maureen Gower was eight years old when she was interned in Changi with seven members of her family. 'One lady took a sick child to the toilet and because she wasn't in line we all got punished,' she says. 'We had to stand out in the burning sun all day with no food. There were big barrels

415

with a lot of sloppy stuff for breakfast and they put it under the hut and we couldn't touch it. We had to stand there, children, old people, everybody. We had three roll-calls every day and whenever something went wrong, everybody got punished.[2]

'If you didn't bow to them, they'd smack you or kick you. Japanese soldiers used to be drunk and they would run through the camp and frighten everybody. We didn't know what they were going to do. They'd grab hold of you ... but the really bad things you block out. There was a punishment hut right at the top. It was called the Green House. If anything went wrong you were sent up there for punishment. Towards the end, they were saying we had to dig trenches because they were going to kill us all. It was hard for the children.'

But Singapore's three-and-a-half-year agony was almost over. On 6 August 1945, a B-29 Superfortress, the *Enola Gay*, piloted by Colonel Paul Tibbets, dropped an atomic bomb on Hiroshima. When Japan refused to surrender, a second bomb, on 9 August, obliterated Nagasaki. At noon on 15 August, Hirohito announced in a radio broadcast that the enemy had begun to employ a 'new and most cruel bomb, the power of which to do damage is incalculable, taking the toll of many innocent lives'. For this reason, he had ordered the Japanese Government to capitulate.

The war was over.

General Seishiro Itagaki, Commander-in-Chief of the Seventh Area Army which had taken over control of Singapore, suppressed the news of Japan's surrender for four days to give his troops time to cover up their atrocities. Lieutenant-Colonel Ivan Lyon had been killed while making another attempt to destroy ships in Singapore Harbour in the ill-fated Operation Rimau expedition of October 1944. Ten of his comrades had been beheaded at Bukit Timah just five weeks before Japan's surrender; documents relating to their executions and to those of seven American airmen were burned. In the case of the Americans, the cover-up went obscenely further. These prisoners had been executed at the Naval Base and their bodies buried at an airfield. On the day of surrender, their executioners drove to the airport, dug up the airmen's bodies, brought them back to camp and cremated them on a big fire in the barrack square. The ashes were then thrown into the sea.[3]

The Allies' Supreme Commander, General Douglas MacArthur, had ordered that no landings could be made in any of the occupied territories, including Singapore, until the surrender document had been signed in Tokyo on 2 September. The British force for the reoccupation of Singapore

– Operation Zipper – was already steaming through the Straits of Malacca at full speed when the order was received on 19 August and had to slow down and bide its time, giving the Japanese another two weeks to destroy evidence, falsify reports and murder witnesses.

There was a very real risk that the Japanese would carry out an order from their High Command to exterminate all 300,000 prisoners of war throughout South East Asia. Charles Peall of the Burma Star Association provided this author with a translation of a Japanese order for the 'extreme measures' to be taken for the 'ultimate disposition' of POWs: 'Whether they are destroyed individually or in groups, or however it is done, with mass bombing, poisonous smoke, poisons, drowning, decapitation, or what, dispose of them as the situation dictates. In any case it is the aim to annihilate them all and not to leave any traces.'[4] To prevent the mass murder of internees and POWs, Mountbatten ordered British paratroopers to land in Singapore, Thailand, Burma and elsewhere to protect the camps, all of which had been pinpointed by aerial surveillance. They were to move in at the first sign that the Japanese were slaughtering their captives.

Len Butler had heard rumours on 15 August from the Korean guards about a 'big bomb'. 'We didn't know what a big bomb was – the biggest bomb I knew about was the 1,000-pounder that the Germans had dropped on London in the Blitz,' he says. 'I'd never heard of an atomic bomb. All of a sudden, there were six soldiers dressed in a uniform I'd never seen marching through the camp with the Japanese commandant to the hospital. They were British paratroopers. I'd never seen their red berets before, or their guns – Sten guns, I found out later.

'They didn't speak to anybody. They walked to the hospital and had a look around and spoke to the doctors. They were ascertaining our needs. Next day, three or four planes flew over the camp and dropped medical supplies and food. There were also leaflets saying that we were to stay in the camp, and that the Japanese had been ordered to patrol the outer rim of our camp for our own safety, because there was a lot of trouble in Singapore. The Chinese were getting even with the Indians who had backed the Japanese and co-operated with them against the Chinese. They were taking their revenge – and our troops turned a blind eye in many cases.'

At first light on 2 September, British navy minesweepers cleared a channel through the Japanese minefields and the brave little *Kedah*, pride of the Straits Steamship Company fleet, led the British navy convoy into Singapore Harbour. Surgeon Lieutenant Bill Horsfall was one of first doctors to reach Changi with the Royal Navy after his ship berthed at

Loyang, just a mile from the camp. 'We had wanted to relieve Singapore earlier, but General MacArthur refused to let us make a landing,' he says. 'The soldiers in Changi had unfairly nicknamed Mountbatten "Linger Longer Louie" – and when he got to Changi, he stood on a soapbox and explained why he had lingered longer.

'We were the first ship to arrive with a bakery, and our cook baked bread until we ran out of flour. I looked down from the ship at a row of Australians standing on the wharf waiting for the loaves. They were just skin and bones.'[5]

Barbara Glanville was 13½ years old when she was liberated by British soldiers. 'We woke up one morning and there were no guards at the gate,' she says. 'Everybody was curious, but we didn't dare venture to the men's section. Then we saw the British army lorries coming in. They brought rations and opened up all the warehouses. The Red Cross had been sending parcels into the camps and the Japanese had been storing them in the warehouses. Tons of Red Cross parcels were now released into the camp. We had butter for the first time in three and a half years. Nobody had a can-opener, so we rubbed it on the rough stones to wear the lid out to get to the butter. The children were eating butter like it was ice cream and we all got sick.'

Len Butler and three Australians left Sime Road and made their way down to Keppel Harbour. 'We bumped into a petty officer from the Royal Navy who was plying liberty between an aircraft carrier out in the roads and Singapore Harbour,' he says. 'He looked at us and said, "God, where did you come from?" We said, "We're Japanese ex-prisoners. Have you got any food?" He said, 'We've got plenty on board – if you'd like to jump into that boat I'll take you out to the carrier and make sure you get whatever you want."

'We jumped in the boat very rapidly and went out to this massive aircraft carrier and we climbed on board. He took us down to the bakery and the smell of fresh baked bread was wonderful. They gave us bread and cheese to start with and – oh boy! – that made us ill. We reacted to the cheese; we weren't used to it. They gave us sacks of loaves and tinned milk and vitamin tablets to take back to the camp hospital and away we went. We took it up to the hospital and made sure that the sick got a slice of bread each. We had to stay in the camp until ships were available to take us back to the UK. I came back on a Dutch ship, the *Nieuw Holland*.

'We were escorted out of Singapore Harbour by the French battleship *Richelieu*, and as we were going out through the minefield she ran into a mine which blew the bow off her. We carried on to Colombo. As we were going into the harbour, the American fleet was on one side and the British, Portuguese and French fleet was on the other side. Every sailor was paraded on deck of both fleets, and as our little ship sailed through the centre of these two massive fleets they gave us three cheers which rippled across the water. My stomach had never churned so much in my life. They knew we were ex-prisoners. I weighed 116 pounds and was coughing blood. If the war had gone on another six months, there wouldn't have been many of us left. I got back to the UK in November 1945. I'd been away exactly four years.'

Jennifer Martin and her mother were taken from Sime Road in a British army truck and placed in Raffles Hotel. 'It wasn't very posh at the time,' she says. 'There were dormitories with camp-beds and they were using the building as a resettlement camp. People filled in forms and were reunited if they could find the rest of their family. We were very lucky. My father had survived the Death Railway and we were on the first boat back to the UK with my cousin Genevieve and my Aunt Diane. I was three and she was four.'[6]

Zacharia Pattara did not survive. 'The surrender was on 15 August and he died in May,' Terpie Pattara says. 'I had malaria and beriberi and was on the verge of death. Thalia and I were taken out by the first hospital ship to India to be reunited with my mother. I found out later that my fiancé Benny was on the death march in Borneo.'[7]

Olga and Maisie Prout were reunited with their father when he came back from Australia to Singapore to look for them. 'Bishop Devals was one of the first people Dad enquired about,' Maisie remembers. 'He discovered that he had been sent to Bahau, a new settlement on the mainland, to cultivate crops. He was bitten by a poisonous spider. They amputated his leg but he died of blood poisoning. Dad was genuinely sorry to hear of his passing. "We were such good friends," he said.'[8]

Wing Commander Harley Stumm, having survived 70 sorties against the Japanese over Singapore and a crash-landing in Java, was killed when his Mosquito fighter-bomber broke up during a training exercise over India on 13 May 1944. His wife Lorraine and three-year-old daughter Sheridan had joined him just six weeks earlier.

Ivan Lyon's wife Gabrielle and son Clive had spent the war in a concentration camp in Japan; they were repatriated to Australia. Clive Lyon has no memory of his mother wearing a little diamond brooch in the shape of three bears.

Lieutenant Alan Lewis was evacuated in one of the first ships home. 'I'd had malaria, dysentery, pellagra and beriberi and I was one of the fortunate ones who survived diphtheria,' he says. 'I'd been apart from my wife Marjorie for four years and it took us months to put our marriage back together.'

James MacIntosh learned that his wife Maimie, who had been held prisoner in Sumatra, had been flown to hospital in Singapore. He was shown into the ward where she was lying in bed. MacIntosh checked every bed and failed to recognise her. 'Then I came back more slowly, and there she was,' he says. 'But she looked terribly ill, a shadow of her former self. I took my darling in my arms. I could hardly speak.'

On 12 September at a ceremony at the Municipal Building, Admiral Mountbatten accepted the surrender of all the Japanese forces in South East Asia. Outside in the quadrangle the Union Flag was run up the flagpole. It was the same flag that Percival had surrendered to Yamashita three and a half years earlier. Tomoyuki Yamashita (1885–1946) was hanged in Manila as a Class A war criminal. His last act was to write a poem:

> *The world I knew is now a shameful place.*
> *There will never come a better time*
> *For me to die.*[9]

General Nishimura of the Imperial Guards went to the scaffold for the slaughter of Australian and Indian prisoners at Parit Sulong – although doubts were later raised about his culpability. Colonel Tsuji, however, got off scot-free from orchestrating the *Sook Ching* massacres and served for many years as a member of the Japanese parliament. The Kempeitai threw away their uniforms and tried to mingle with ordinary Japanese soldiers, but many were recognised and hanged or imprisoned for their crimes. Lieutenant-Colonel Sumida, described by the prosecutor as 'the cunning brain under whose direction the instruments of torture performed their evil task', was one of those sentenced to death.

Elizabeth Choy was awarded the OBE for her bravery and travelled to London, where she was presented to King George VI and Queen Elizabeth at Buckingham Palace in the company of Sir Shenton and Lady Thomas. She stayed in London for four years, getting to know the young Princess Elizabeth, teaching at a London County primary school and, with her fine deportment and high cheekbones, accepting assignments as a model.

Returning to Singapore, Elizabeth adopted three daughters and taught at St Andrew's Junior School. She went to England again in 1953 to attend the Coronation of Queen Elizabeth II – who has remained a firm friend for 60 years. She finally retired in 1974, and two years later she and her husband

Choy Khun Heng visited England together. In 2005, Elizabeth Choy Su-Moi, now widowed, celebrated her 95th birthday.

After months in solitary confinement at Outram Road Jail, John Wyett had been returned to Changi in 1944, emaciated and on the brink of death. 'The Kempeitai were covering their tracks,' he says. 'They wanted me to die at Changi rather than on the floor of my prison cell.' However, Wyett recovered his health after months of patient nursing, and remained an inspiration to his former POW comrades for 60 years, until his death, in his beloved Tasmania, in December 2004 at the age of 96. The military and civilian commandants of Outram Road Jail, Majors Shuzo Kobayashi and Koshiro Mikizawa, were both hanged for multiple war crimes, as was the wretched General Itagaki, who had sought to cover up evidence of Japanese atrocities in Singapore.

Bill Drower regained his strength at the Chulalongkorn Hospital, Bangkok, where he had the honour of being nursed by a Three Umbrella princess of the Thai Royal Family. He was then repatriated to join his parents in Baghdad. He was demobbed in March 1946, and his post-war career took him to Washington as a lobbyist on Capitol Hill and later to the University of California at Berkeley. Returning to England in the 1990s, Bill settled for the quieter pastures of Somerset County Council. His would-be murderer, the Japanese camp commandant Noguchi, was hanged as a war criminal in Singapore.

After the heat and disease of the tropics, Russell Savage's final agony lay in being transported to Japan to work as a slave labourer in the country's frozen north. *En route* to Japan, he was one of only 241 prisoners out of 1,319 to survive the sinking of the unmarked POW ship *Rakuyo Maru* by an American submarine off the China coast on 12 September 1944. When peace was declared, Russell was evacuated to his home town of Brisbane and, after a period of convalescence, returned to his father's accountancy business, Cooper Brothers Savage Co. In 1947, he married Patricia Wright with whom he had six children. He was one of the driving forces in the merger that created the accounting firm Coopers & Lybrand.

Asked by a visiting Japanese diplomat whether he had ever visited Japan, Russell replied, 'Oh yes. I spent nearly a year there in 1944–45.'

'You were a member of a delegation?'

'Oh no, I was a guest of the Emperor.'

'You mean you stayed in the Palace?'

'No, I was a prisoner of war.'

'Ah – how you must hate us.'

Hirohito, in whose name the Pacific War had been waged, and whose divine status had been invoked to justify the inhuman treatment of the nations he enslaved, renounced his divinity and posed for photographs beside General MacArthur, the new Mikado. The vanity of this 'modest, gentle' man had been responsible for the deaths of 20 million Asian people, including more than three million of his own subjects and 60,000 Westerners, but instead of being hanged as a war criminal with the blood of millions on his hands, he was portrayed as a mere tool in the hands of the militarists. The Tokyo War Crimes trials arraigned 25 senior Japanese commanders and politicians. Just seven, including Tojo, were hanged.

The YMCA building at 1 Orchard Road was demolished in the early 1980s and, some 20 years later, Changi Jail was pulled down.

The new Japanese Prime Minister, Shigeru Yoshida, Bill Drower's former employer at the Japanese Embassy in London, described World War II as 'the Great Miscalculation'.

'Their greatest miscalculation,' Russell Savage says, 'was bombing Pearl Harbor.'

Afterword

It was a bittersweet moment. Arthur Percival had been evacuated from his prisoner-of-war camp in Manchuria to witness the formal capitulation of Japan's forces in the Philippines, commanded by his old adversary Tomoyuki Yamashita. The Tiger of Malaya's victories had failed to bring him the desired reconciliation with his Emperor and, after a period of banishment as a commander in, ironically, Manchuria, he had been sent to Manila with the hopeless task of resisting the American invasion. At the surrender ceremony, Yamashita momentarily registered his amazement at seeing the tall, erect figure of Percival, even gaunter than when they had first met, but then his countenance resumed its inscrutably passive stare and he watched proceedings without any sign of emotion.

Percival retired from the Army in 1946. He worked for the British Red Cross and served as life president of the Far East Prisoners of War Association. Many former POWs crowded into St Martin-in-the-Fields for a memorial service following his death on 31 January 1966. The address was given by the Bishop of Birmingham – his old friend Leonard Wilson, formerly Bishop of Singapore.

With hindsight, it is relatively simple to list the reasons for the defeat that sounded the death knell for British rule in South East Asia. Every commander from Churchill and the Chiefs of Staff to Wavell, Brooke-Popham, Pownall, Percival, Heath and Bennett underestimated the capabilities of the enemy. On the first day of war, Percival failed to force Brooke-Popham to abandon Matador and to occupy the vital Ledge position – but if the failure was Percival's, the main culprit was Brooke-Popham. From Jitra onwards, Percival's intelligence was inferior, and his dispositions frequently incorrect. He failed to fortify Singapore's northern shore and to recognise the threat from the west coast even after the Japanese had landed there in force.

In mitigation, it must be said that too many of his troops were either inadequately trained or too green to be of much use; he had no tanks and

423

too few anti-tank and anti-aircraft guns, and he was tragically short of aircraft. Moreover, after the sinking of the *Prince of Wales* and *Repulse*, he received negligible support from the Navy. Percival was also badly let down by Gordon Bennett, who compounded his lack of military skill by abandoning his troops – an unforgivable crime in Percival's eyes. Bennett claimed he had escaped in order to reveal the best methods of combating the Japanese in jungle warfare (a feat he had singularly failed to accomplish in the Battle of Johore), but Ian Stewart had already been evacuated on Wavell's orders for precisely that purpose, and Bennett's observations were of little value. Officially, he was a deserter.

In terms of blood, British and Commonwealth battle casualties during the 70-day campaign numbered 7,500 men killed and 11,000 wounded, compared with Japanese losses of 3,507 killed and 6,150 wounded. Among the British battalions, the highest toll was suffered by the Argyll and Sutherland Highlanders, who lost 244 men killed and missing presumed dead, and 150 wounded. The 2/19th Battalion AIF lost 335 men killed and 197 wounded – in fact, the Australians, who comprised 14 per cent of British and Commonwealth forces, incurred 73 per cent of Allied deaths in battle.

The biggest per capita loss, however, was suffered by Dalforce, the valiant band of 2,000 Chinese irregulars who faced the crack Japanese front-line troops with a pathetic array of inadequate weapons and who were virtually wiped out.

In the southern spring of 1945, Dr Rowley Richards arrived back in Sydney in an aircraft carrier with 1,000 other Australian POWs, many of whom had survived the privations of the Death Railway. 'Gordon Bennett came down to the ship to welcome us,' he says, 'and launched into a tirade about what a hard time they'd given him when he got back. That was the type of bloke he was. Most of the fellows just walked away from the parade.'[1]

After returning to England, Sir Lewis Heath drafted a letter to Percival in which he held the GOC and Brooke-Popham responsible 'for the hole in which the poor 11th Indian Division was to find itself enmeshed in the first days of hostilities'. He continued, 'Hitherto, loyalty to you and the decision to avoid unpleasant disclosures has constrained me from ventilating the errors which led up to the severe and unnecessary mauling which the 11th Div. received in the opening days of the campaign. I refer in particular to the appalling failure to come to a timely decision as to the cancellation of Matador and secondly your failure to place reliance on Murray-Lyon when he sent his first report to be permitted to withdraw to Gurun. The battle of Jitra and the operation at the Ledge would have been a very different story had your orders to cancel Matador been received early on 8 December.' The draft is undated; it is not known whether the letter was ever sent.[2]

Percival's task as commander of a disorganised and demoralised army had been impossible from the start and he had borne it – and his subsequent captivity – with a stoicism that could be seen as heroic. 'When things go wrong the public are naturally inclined to blame the man on the spot,' the scapegoat of Singapore wrote in his memoirs. 'Why was this not done and why was that not done? The answer generally is that the man on the spot was not a free agent.'[3] Indeed, Percival was a victim of the very system he strove to uphold.

Notes

CHAPTER 1: **Blood on the Sun**

1 Timothy Hall, *The Fall of Singapore*, Methuen Australia, 1983; Sheila Allen, *Diary of a Changi Girl*, Kangaroo Press, NSW, 1994.
2 A. V. Toze Papers, Imperial War Museum.
3 Alfred Duff Cooper, *Old Men Forget*, Rupert Hart Davis, London, 1954.
4 Ian Morrison, *Malayan Postscript*, Faber & Faber, London, 1943.
5 Joseph Conrad, *Youth: A Narrative*, William Blackwood, London, 1902.
6 Lorraine Stumm, *I Saw Too Much: A woman correspondent at war*, The Write-on Group, New South Wales, 2000.
7 Caroline Moorhead, *Martha Gellhorn: A Life*, Chatto & Windus, London, 2003.
8 Ronald Lewin, *The Chief: Field Marshal Lord Wavell*, Hutchinson, London, 1980.
9 Most accounts give the date of the opening of the Naval Base as 15 February 1938 and comment on the uncanny coincidence that Singapore should fall on that day in 1942. *The Times* supplement published at the time of the opening says it took place on 14 February.
10 Malcolm H. Murfett, 'The Singapore Strategy at Sixty', published in *Sixty Years On*, Eastern Universities Press, Singapore, 2002.
11 Major-General S. Woodburn Kirby, *The War Against Japan, Volume 1: The Loss of Singapore*, HMSO, London, 1957.
12 Winston S. Churchill, *The Second World War*, Pimlico, 2002.
13 Prime Minister's Personal Minute, D4/2, 'Most Secret', 19 January 1942: Churchill Papers, 20/67.
14 Ivan Simson, *Singapore: Too Little, Too Late*, Leo Cooper, London, 1970.
15 J. A. Richardson Papers, Imperial War Museum.
16 Author's interview with Len Butler.
17 Raymond Callahan, *The Worst Disaster: The Fall of Singapore*, University of Delaware Press, Newark, 1980.
18 Author's interview with Maisie Duncan (née Prout).
19 *Singapore: Too Little, Too Late*.
20 A. V. Toze diary, March 1942–October 1945, IWM 90/34/1A.
21 Interview with Brother Vincent, 28 February 1996, Oral History Centre, National Archives of Singapore, 468/30.

22 Author's interview with Russell Savage.

23 Interview with Elizabeth Choy, 23 August 1985, Oral History Centre, National Archives of Singapore, A597/05.

24 *stengah* – literally a half: a half-peg of whisky diluted with water or soda.

25 H. Gordon Bennett, *Why Singapore Fell*, Angus & Robertson, Sydney, 1944.

26 Leslie Froggatt, *Nothing Lasts for Ever: Singapore Swan Song – and After*, unpublished memoir, Melbourne, 1945, Froggatt Papers; quoted with kind permission of his son Sir Leslie Froggatt.

CHAPTER 2: **Good Times**

1 J. A. Richardson Papers, Imperial War Museum.

2 *Straits Times*, 4 September 1939.

3 Letter from D. A. Murdoch of the Eastern Extension Telegraph Company to the Australian Department of Commerce, Canberra, 26 October 1939; National Archives of Australia.

4 J. G. Farrell, *The Singapore Grip*, Weidenfeld & Nicolson, London, 1978.

5 E. M. Glover, *In Seventy Days: The Story of the Japanese Campaign in British Malaya*, Frederick Muller, London, 1949.

6 James Neidpath, *The Singapore Naval Base and the Defence of Britain's Eastern Empire* 1919–1941, Clarendon Press, Oxford, 1981.

7 Raffles's health was failing and in 1823 he returned to England, where he died three years later of a brain tumour.

8 Straits Steamship Company website.

9 Author's interview with Olga Page (née Prout).

10 Helmut Newton, *Autobiography*, Duckworth, London, 2003.

11 H. M. Tomlinson, *Malay Waters*, Hodder & Stoughton, London, 1950.

12 *Nothing Lasts for Ever*.

13 Peter Elphick, *Far Eastern File*, Hodder & Stoughton, London, 1997.

14 Lieutenant-Colonel Thomas Hamilton, *Soldier Surgeon in Malaya*, Angus & Robertson, Sydney, 1967.

15 Lieutenant-General A. E. Percival, General Officer Commanding Malaya, Dispatch: 'Operations of Malaya Command from 08.12.1941 to 15.02.1942', published in the *London Gazette*, 26 February 1948.

16 Quoted in Percival's Dispatch.

17 *Singapore: Too Little, Too Late*.

18 Peter Thompson and Robert Macklin, *Kill the Tiger*, Hodder Australia, Sydney, 2002.

19 ibid.

20 Clifford Kinvig, *Scapegoat: General Percival and the Fall of Singapore*, Brassey's, London, 1996.

21 WO106/2431; 'New Proposals for the Defence of Malaya', October/November 1938, National Archives.

22 William McElwee and Michael Roffe, *Argyll and Sutherland Highlanders*, Osprey, Oxford, 1972. As a result of the sweeping Cardwell reforms of the British Army, the 91st Argyllshire Highlanders and the 93rd Sutherland Highlanders were merged in 1881. The 91st became the 1st Battalion and the 93rd the 2nd Battalion.

CHAPTER 3: **Bad Times**

1 Author's interview with Kenneth McLeod.
2 Brigadier David Wilson, *The Sum of Things*, Spellmount, Staplehurst, Kent, 2001.
3 Author's interview with Major-General David Thomson (retired).
4 David Twiston Davies, *The Daily Telegraph Book of Military Obituaries*, Grub Street, London, 2003.
5 *The Sum of Things*.
6 ibid.
7 C. A. Vlieland, unpublished memoir, Liddell Hart Centre, King's College, London.
8 ibid.
9 *London Gazette*, 1 January 1915. In 1945, Sir John Babington changed his name to Sir John Tremayne.
10 Vlieland's unpublished memoir.
11 *The War Against Japan*.
12 Vlieland's unpublished memoir.
13 The Reverend Sorby Adams.
14 The main supply route to Nationalist forces in China was along the Burma Road which traversed the 712 miles between Lashio in northern Burma and Kunming, capital of China's Yunnan Province. After the fall of France, Britain agreed to close this road for three months in an attempt to appease Japan. She also agreed to pull her garrisons out of Beijing, Tientsin and Shanghai. It was conceded in the War Cabinet at the time that Britain could fight only one war at a time.
15 COS 195 (40) 1, Cab. 79/5, Cabinet Office Records, National Archives.
16 Brooke-Popham to General Ismay, 5 December 1940, V/1/3 Brooke-Popham Papers, Liddell Hart Centre, King's College, London.
17 Vlieland's unpublished memoir.
18 Peter Elphick, *The Pregnable Fortress*, Hodder & Stoughton, London, 1995.
19 Cab. 79/8; quoted in Peter Lowe, *Great Britain and the Origins of the Pacific War*, Clarendon Press, Oxford, 1977.
20 Heath Lecture on the Malayan Campaign in the officers' mess of the Argyll and Sutherland Highlanders, Changi Prisoner of War camp, 21 June 1942.
21 *The War Against Japan*.
22 Captain J. W. McClelland and others quoted in *Old Friends, New Enemies*, (Arthur J. Marder, Clarendon Press, Oxford, 1981). By permission of Oxford University Press.
23 David Day, *The Politics of War*, HarperCollins, Sydney, 2003; War Cabinet Minutes, 14 February 1941, CRS A2673, Vol. 5 Minute 802, NAA.

24 Christopher Thorne, *The Issue of War*, Hamish Hamilton, London, 1985.

25 Laurence Rees, *Horror in the East*, BBC, London, 2001.

26 Brooke-Popham to Ismay, 28 February 1941, V/1/7 Brooke-Popham Papers; quoted in *Great Britain and the Origins of the Pacific War*.

27 David French and Brian Holden Reid (eds), *The British General Staff 1890–1939*, Frank Cass, London, 2002.

28 Report WO 106/5684, National Archives.

29 Major-General I. S. O. Playfair.

30 Letter from Colonel Grimsdale to General Ismay, 8 March 1942, Ismay Archive IV/Gri, la-7/2d. Liddell Hart Centre, King's College, London.

31 Author's interview with John Wyett.

32 Author's interview with Russell Savage.

33 Russell Savage, *A Guest of the Emperor*, Boolarong Press, Brisbane, 1995.

34 Author's interview with Beryl Stevenson Daley, quoted in *The Battle of Brisbane* (Peter Thompson and Robert Macklin, ABC Books, 2000).

35 Squadron Leader W. J. Harper, 'Secret Report on No. 21 and No. 453 RAAF Squadrons, AIR 20/5578', National Archives.

36 Paul Gibbs Pancheri, a member of the SSVF, quoted in *Moon over Malaya* (Jonathan Moffatt and Audrey Holmes McCormick, Tempus, Stroud, Gloucestershire, 2002).

CHAPTER 4: **Asian Sphinx**

1 Author's interview with Bill Drower.

2 'A riddle wrapped in a mystery inside an enigma' was Churchill's description of Russia in a broadcast on 1 October 1939. He could well have applied the same metaphor to Japan.

3 Herbert Bix, *Hirohito and the Making of Modern Japan*, HarperCollins, New York, 2000.

4 'Our Japanese Visitor', *The Times*, 7 May 1921.

5 Peter Thompson and Robert Macklin, *The Man Who Died Twice*, Allen & Unwin, Sydney, 2004.

6 Peter Calvocoressi, Guy Wint and John Pritchard, *Total War: The Causes and Courses of the Second World War*, Penguin, London, 1972.

7 *The Man Who Died Twice*.

8 *The War Against Japan*.

9 *The Man Who Died Twice*.

10 The Imperial Conference was a four-yearly meeting of ministers from the Empire and Great Britain.

11 The Anglo-Japanese Alliance was due for renewal in 1921, and the British Government wanted the approval of the imperial prime ministers. However, the Canadian Prime Minister, Arthur Meighen, knew that renewal would upset the United States and he urged a new treaty that would include all the Pacific powers.

His proposal was violently attacked by the Australian Prime Minister, Billy Hughes, who called the imperialist Meighen 'the American ambassador'. The attack convinced the British that Meighen was right, and the treaty was not renewed. Instead, a conference of the Pacific powers was arranged in Washington, DC, for December 1921. Although Meighen had been responsible for the change in British policy, the United States almost forgot to invite Canada to the Washington Conference.

12 Statement in the House of Representatives by the Rt Hon. W. M. Hughes, 30 September 1921. Parliamentary Papers No. 146, pp. 10–11.

13 The *Katori* is described in naval lists as both a battleship and a battle-cruiser, although it is officially listed as a pre-Dreadnaught battleship.

14 The Kwantung Army had been created in 1905 to guard Japan's Kwantung leasehold on the Liaotung peninsula of southern Manchuria.

15 Lord Russell of Liverpool, *The Knights of Bushido*, Cassell, London, 1958, pp. 39–47.

16 Timothy Brook (ed.), *Documents on the Rape of Nanking*.

17 *Hirohito and the Making of Modern Japan*.

18 *Horror in the East*.

19 *Total War*.

20 Report by A. G. Hard, Commercial Secretary, Australian Legation, Tokyo, after a visit to Manchukuo in May/June 1941. National Archives of Australia.

21 Australian Station Intelligence to Department of Naval Intelligence (DNI), 1 February 1938, FO 371/22192.

22 The 00 markings represented the last two digits of the year in which the plane went into full production: 2600 in the Japanese calendar (AD 1940). The fighter was known to the Japanese as 'Zeke'.

23 Douglas Gillison, *Royal Australian Air Force 1939–1942*, Australian War Memorial, Canberra, 1957.

24 Richard Overy with Andrew Wheatcroft, *The Road to War*, Penguin, London, 1999.

25 Zhukov's blitzkrieg in the Battle of Khalkin-Gol pre-dated the Nazi blitzkreig on Poland by 33 days.

26 Raymond Lamont-Brown, *Kempeitai: Japan's Dreaded Military Police*, Sutton, Stroud, 1998.

27 *The Road to War*.

28 Quoted in *Old Friends, New Enemies*.

29 F. W. Ikle, *German-Japanese Relations, 1936–1940*, Bookman, New York, 1956.

30 Judith Stowe, *Siam Becomes Thailand*, Hurst, London, 1991.

31 US Ambassador Grant to Cordell Hull, quoted in *From Versailles to Pearl Harbor: The Origins of the Second World War in Europe and Asia* (Margaret Lamb and Nicholas Tarling, Palgrave, New York, 2001).

32 Elizabeth-Anne Wheal and Stephen Pope, *The Macmillan Dictionary of the Second World War*, Macmillan, London, 1989; *Total War*.

CHAPTER 5: **Quiet Commander**

1   Arthur Percival, *The War in Malaya*, London, Eyre & Spottiswoode, 1949.

2   A. C. Alford, 'Japan and the United States of America', *Army Quarterly*, 1924.

3   Report by Major Wards, 15 December 1937, WO 106/5684, National Archives.

4   Sir John Smyth, *Percival and the Tragedy of Singapore*, Macdonald, London, 1971; *Scapegoat*.

5   Percival's two main biographers were Major-General Clifford Kinvig, author of *Scapegoat*, and Brigadier Sir John Smyth, author of *Percival and the Tragedy of Singapore*.

6   Arthur Percival, 'Guerrilla Warfare – Ireland 1920–21' (two lectures, lecture 1), p. 18, Percival Papers, IWM.

7   Tim Pat Coogan, *Michael Collins: A Biography*, Hutchinson, London, 1990; Frank Thornton Memoir, Irish Bureau of Military History. Coogan says in his Endnotes that this was attested by witnesses at the time. The subsequent account of the tortures was based on a sworn affidavit by Hales, quoted by Kathleen Keyes McDonnell in *There Is a Bridge at Bandon*, Mercier Press, 1971. James Mackay (*Michael Collins: A Life*, Mainstream, Edinburgh, 1996) says that 'One of the worst offenders was Major A. E. Percival of the Essex Regiment whose role as a torturer of suspected Shinners has been well documented.' Mackay quotes Coogan's as his only source for this statement.

8   *Scapegoat*; *Four Corners*, ABC Television, 11 March 2002.

9   Tom Barry, *Guerilla Days in Ireland*, Anvil, Dublin, 1949.

10 Michael Collins was assassinated by the IRA for signing this treaty agreeing to a divided Ireland. The assassination squad was led by Tom Hales.

11 *Scapegoat*.

12 Clifford Kinvig, 'Scapegoat: General Percival and the Fall of Singapore', published in *Sixty Years On*.

13 Interview with General Gordon Bennett by General Kirby and Lionel Wigmore, 30 January 1953, AWM 73.

14 *Singapore: Too Little, Too Late*.

15 ibid.

16 Lieutenant-Colonel F. Spencer Chapman, *The Jungle Is Neutral*, Times Books International, Singapore, 1997; General Percival later wrote, 'As regards plans for the "stay-behind" parties, Col. Spencer Chapman may be surprised to learn that the leader of his organisation exercised such extreme secrecy that neither I nor any of my staff knew what he was planning until at least two months after his arrival in the country. Of course, it should all have been part of the military plan, but at that time these activities were not under any of the Service Ministries. So far as I know, the organisation was under the Ministry of Economic Warfare and was sponsored by GHQ Far East. In these circumstances, we of Malaya Command can hardly be accused of lack of willingness to co-operate. Col. Spencer Chapman may also be interested to learn that I had myself, before going to Malaya, organised similar "stay-behind" parties in another theatre of war, and that I also,

like him, have the honour of wearing a decoration awarded for leadership in guerrilla operations.' (Letter, *Daily Telegraph*, London, 14 February 1949.) Percival was referring to his OBE for counter-insurgency measures against the IRA.

17 Chin Peng, as told to Ian Ward and Norma Miraflor, *Chin Peng: My Side of History*, Media Masters, Singapore, 2003.

18 FO371/28134; F7487/246/40; Cable No. 472; 30 July 1941; NA.

19 *The Pregnable Fortress.*

20 *Scapegoat.*

21 Brooke-Popham to Ismay, 3 July 1941, V/1/14 Brooke-Popham Papers.

22 Margaret Shennan, *Out in the Midday Sun: The British in Malaya 1880–1960*, John Murray, London, 2003.

23 Author's interview with Sir Leslie Froggatt. Sir Leslie returned to Shell after the war and in 1969 was appointed Chairman and Chief Executive of the Shell Group of Companies in Australia. He relinquished this appointment in November 1980 and remained on the Shell board as a non-executive director until 1987.

24 *Old Men Forget.*

25 Angela Lambert, *Unquiet Souls*, Harper & Row, New York, 1984; talk by John Julius Norwich, son of Duff and Diana Cooper, Royal Geographical Society, 14 June 2004.

26 John Julius Norwich.

27 John Charmley, *Duff Cooper: The Authorised Biography*, Weidenfeld & Nicolson, London 1986; letter from Duff Cooper to Loelia, Duchess of Westminster.

28 Advisory War Council Minute, 533 Melbourne, 16 October 1941.

29 Letter, 28 October 1941, V/2/16, Brooke-Popham Papers, King's College, London.

30 Cadogan diary, 5 November 1941, ACAD 1/10, Cadogan Papers, CC.

31 ABCD – American, British, Chinese and Dutch. Cablegram Winch 1 London, Winston Churchill, to John Curtin, 26 October 1941.

32 *Scapegoat.*

33 Cablegram 102 London, S. M. Bruce to John Curtin, 19 November 1941; *The Politics of Power*; Minute D300/1, Churchill to Ismay, 24 November 1941, PREM 3/52/4, National Archives.

34 Cable, Churchill to Duff Cooper, 26 November, 1941, 'The Prime Minister's Personal Telegrams 1941', VI/I Ismay Papers, King's College, London.

35 *Scapegoat; The Politics of War.*

36 *Duff Cooper.*

37 AWM PR 00683, Captain H. E. Jessup Papers, folder 2, Jessup to his wife, 20 September 1941; *Old Men Forget.*

38 Author's interview with Maisie Duncan (née Prout).

39 Author's interview with Olga Page (née Prout).

40 *Old Friends, New Enemies.*

41 *Kill the Tiger.*

42 Raymond Lamont-Brown, *Kempeitai: Japan's Dreaded Military Police*, Sutton Publishing, Stroud, 1998.

43 *The Road to War.*

Chapter 6: **Angry Australian**

1 Author's interview with John Wyett.
2 Members of the Unit Association, *The Grim Glory of the 2/19th Battalion AIF*, Australian War Memorial, Canberra, 1975.
3 A. B. Lodge, *The Fall of General Gordon Bennett*, Allen & Unwin, Sydney, 1986.
4 *The Grim Glory of the 2/19th Battalion AIF*.
5 ibid.
6 Lionel Wigmore, *The Japanese Thrust: Official Australian War History*, Australian War Memorial, Canberra, 1957.
7 James Burfitt, *Against All Odds: The History of the 2/18th Battalion 8th Division AIF*, 2/18th Battalion, French's Forest, NSW, 1991.
8 Percival's Dispatch.

Chapter 7: **Slippery Sultan**

1 *Out in the Midday Sun: The British in Malaya 1880–1960*.
2 *The Man Who Died Twice*; Cyril Pearl, *Morrison of Peking*, Angus & Robertson, Sydney, 1967.
3 National Archives WO106/2579C.
4 *Why Singapore Fell*.
5 Author's interview with Dr Bob Goodwin.
6 Author's interview with General Thomson.
7 *I Saw Too Much*.
8 Leslie Hoffman later became editor of the *Straits Times* and was made a Tan Sri, a Knight of Singapore. The author had the honour of meeting him in Melbourne.
9 Author's interview with Sheridan Stumm.
10 *Why Singapore Fell*.
11 *Old Friends, New Enemies*.
12 Field Marshal Lord Alanbrooke, *War Diaries 1939–1945*, edited by Alex Danchev and Daniel Todman, Weidenfeld & Nicolson, London, 2001.
13 *Old Friends, New Enemies*.
14 *Old Friends, New Enemies*.
15 Interview with Richard Smith, IWM 008663/04.
16 *Old Men Forget*.

Chapter 8: **Matador Farce**

1 Air Vice-Marshal Sir Paul Maltby, 'Report on Air Operations during the Campaigns in Malaya and Netherlands East Indies', *London Gazette*, 20 February 1948; Major-General S. Woodburn Kirby, *Singapore: The Chain of Disaster*, Cassell, London, 1971.
2 The 14th, 15th, 16th and 25th Armies were each the equivalent of a British corps.

3 'Order of Battle of the Japanese Army', US Military Intelligence Service, Washington DC, December 1942.

4 *Scapegoat.*

5 *Singapore: The Chain of Disaster.*

6 James Leasor, *Singapore: The Battle That Changed the World*, Hodder & Stoughton, London, 1968.

7 *Percival and the Singapore Disaster.*

8 Lord Halifax, Washington, to Foreign Office, 1 December 1941, FI 3001/86/23, FO 371/27913, National Archives.

9 *The War Against Japan.*

10 Ted Morgan, *FDR: A Biography*, Grafton Books, London, 1986. Frank Knox was not referring to Yamamoto's Pearl Harbor Striking Force which had not been detected.

11 Cordell Hull and Andrew Henry Thomas Berding, *The Memoirs of Cordell Hull*. The President's message did not reach Hirohito until after the attack on Pearl Harbor. The Emperor regarded the note delivered to Cordell Hull by Nomura and Kurusu following the attack as his reply.

12 Circular cablegram M426 London, Lord Cranborne to John Curtin and others, 5 December 1941.

13 Parliamentary Debates: House of Commons Official Report, Fifth Series, Vol. 376, HMSO, London, 1941.

14 *Old Friends, New Enemies.*

15 Noel Barber, *Sinister Twilight*, Collins, London, 1968.

16 *Old Friends, New Enemies*; Brian Montgomery, *Shenton of Singapore: Governor and Prisoner of War*, Leo Cooper, London, 1984. James McClelland, born in 1907, retired as Captain in 1957. He gave this account to authors Arthur Marder and Brian Montgomery.

17 *Shenton of Singapore.*

18 Arthur Marder puts the number of Japanese planes that bombed Singapore at 31. In *Shenton of Singapore*, the figure of 17 planes is cited by Flight Lieutenant Harry Grumbar, Filter Officer in the Radar Filter Room near Kallang airport. The Official Historian says the raid involved 17 Japanese naval bombers. It is probable that the Japanese planes arrived in more than one group over different parts of the island.

19 *Sinister Twilight; Old Men Forget; The War Against Japan.* General Kirby says in the Official History and in *The Chain of Disaster* that 'the staff of the headquarters of the ARP organisation were sleeping peacefully in their own beds and the headquarters was unmanned'. However, Flight Lieutenant Grumbar says, in *Shenton of Singapore*, 'I also telephoned ARP Headquarters, which *was* manned, on my direct line; but I was told that they were powerless to sound the air-raid sirens because their Chief Warden was at the late-night cinema and only he had the keys that controlled the Alarm switch.' Despite this, numerous witnesses, including Ian Morrison and Brother Vincent, recalled hearing air-raid sirens at the start of the raid. Maisie Duncan and Olga Page say there were no sirens until after it had finished. Terpie Pattara agrees. Duff Cooper put the order as: bombs, guns, sirens.

20 Maltby's 'Report on Air Operations during the Campaigns in Malaya and Netherlands East Indies', *London Gazette*, 20 February 1948. After the Official History appeared in 1957, Sir Shenton Thomas published a rebuttal of both Maltby's and Kirby's criticisms of the ARP performance on the night of 8 December 1941. The Governor claimed to have telephoned the Harbour Board and ARP from Government House after receiving a phone call from Pulford at 4 a.m. These calls, Thomas claims, were made before the Japanese planes appeared over Singapore at 4.15 a.m. As Arthur Marder established from an eyewitness source, quoted in *Old Friends, New Enemies*, Thomas was at the Naval Base at the time of the raid, so he could not have been at Government House from 4 a.m. onwards unless Marder's source was mistaken. Thomas also wrote in his rebuttal, 'I put it to Maltby that it was not "conceivable that on the night in question the C in C Far East, the C in C China Station, the GOC, the AOC and myself should all have gone happily to bed with every light on the island blazing if any one of us had thought that a raid was even remotely possible. Of course it isn't: it just doesn't make sense." He did not answer.' (Quoted in Louis Allen, pp. 221–22.) According to Marder's version, none of these officers went to bed until some time after the air raid, so the Governor's case collapses.

21 Author's interview with Terpie Pattara.

22 Barbara Walsh Schreck, Jan Bell and Graham Bell, *Forty Good Men: The Story of the Tanglin Club*, Tanglin Club, Singapore, 1991.

23 Brooke-Popham says in his 1948 Dispatch, 'The observation system worked satisfactorily and 30 minutes' warning of the approach of Japanese aircraft was received at my headquarters. For some reason that I never ascertained, the Headquarters of the ARP organisation had not been manned and it was only a few minutes before bombs were dropping on Singapore that contact was made by Fighter Group Headquarters and the sirens sounded giving warning for blackout. In my opinion, the absence of blackout had but little effect, since there was a bright full moon, and the coastline and most of Singapore must have shown up very clearly.' He added that all naval, army and air force establishments had been blacked out.

24 Patrick Bishop, *Fighter Boys*, HarperCollins, London, 2003.

25 Parliamentary Debates: House of Commons Official Report, Fifth Series, Vol. 376, HMSO, London, 1941.

26 Brian Bond (ed.), *Chief of Staff: The Diaries of Lieutenant General Sir Henry Pownall*, Leo Cooper, London, 1973–74. Pownall had been on the Cabinet Secretariat in the mid-1930s when it was decided to cut back on the Naval Base and other Far East defence requirements.

27 *Singapore: The Chain of Disaster*. The extent of the confusion surrounding Operation Matador was reflected in Sir Archibald Wavell's report in June 1942 which states, ' It was understood that no move across the frontier was to take place unless ordered by Malaya Command, *who in their turn had to await instructions from London*. The final orders, cancelling the advance on Singora and directing that the Jitra position be occupied, were received at 11 Division HQ on

the afternoon of 8th December. Obviously a surprise move of this description, allowing for only a narrow margin of error in time, *should not have been subject to the risk of delay between Singapore and London.*' Wavell appears to have been in ignorance of the Chiefs of Staff's signal to the Commanders-in-Chief on 5 December. General Heath also mistakenly believed that Brooke-Popham had to await a decision from London before activating Matador. *'It had to be referred home,'* Heath says in his Changi lecture. 'It was unfortunate that a decision was not made at once in Singapore.' (Author's italics.)

28 *Old Friends, New Enemies.*

Chapter 9: First Blood

1 The 8th Indian Infantry Brigade consisted of 3/17th Dogra Regiment, 2/10th Baluchistan Regiment and the 1/13th Frontier Force Regiment.
2 Heath Lecture.
3 Colonel Masanobu Tsuji, *The Japanese Version*, published in the UK as *Japan's Greatest Victory, Britain's Worst Defeat*, Spellmount, Staplehurst, Kent, 1997.
4 Interview with Oscar Diamond, *Four Corners*, ABC Television, 11 March 2002.
5 *Royal Australian Air Force 1939–1942.*
6 Percival's Dispatch.
7 *Royal Australian Air Force 1939–1942.*
8 *Percival and the Tragedy of Malaya.*
9 Heath Lecture.
10 ibid.
11 *The Japanese Version.*
12 *The War Against Japan.*
13 *Daily Mail*, 22 July 1946.
14 Sallie Scarf recorded her version of events in an affidavit to her friend Mrs Pat Boxall to correct several contested facts about her husband's death. The affidavit was passed on to Pat's daughter, Sallie Hammond, Sallie Scarf's goddaughter. Sallie Scarf, who remarried to become Sallie Gunn, died in April 1985.
15 Maltby's 'Report'.
16 Cablegram M52 Singapore, V. G. Bowden to Dr H. V. Evatt, 14 December 1941.
17 *Duff Cooper.*
18 Duff Cooper's diary, 11 December 1941.
19 House of Lords Debates, 8 January 1942.
20 *The War Against Japan.*
21 *Scapegoat.*

Chapter 10: Battleship Disaster

1 *Old Friends, New Enemies.*
2 Vice-Admiral Sir Geoffrey Layton, Dispatch: 'Loss of HM Ships *Prince of Wales* and *Repulse*, 17.12.1941', published in the *London Gazette*, 26 February 1948.

3 Interview with John Gaynor, IWM 008246/07.
4 Tsuji claimed in *The Japanese Version* that one of the British destroyers 'blew up and sank' during the action off Kuantan. This is not correct.
5 Author's interview with Alexander Pimson. The cruiser HMS *Exeter* arrived in Singapore on 10 December 1941. She was sunk in the Battle of the Sunda Strait in March 1942.
6 Winston S. Churchill, *The Grand Alliance*, Cassell, London, 1949; Phillips Papers, quoted in *Old Friends, New Enemies*.
7 Letter, 30 January 1942, Phillips Papers, quoted in *Old Friends, New Enemies*, p. 497.
8 Parliamentary Debates: House of Commons Official Report, Fifth Series, Vol. 376, HMSO, London, 1941.
9 *Old Friends, New Enemies*.
10 Arthur Grenfell, *Main Fleet to Singapore*, Macmillan, 1952.
11 *Old Friends, New Enemies*.
12 Letter from Sir Shenton Thomas to Sir Folliott Sandford, Parliamentary Under-Secretary at the Air Ministry, April 1954. Hilary St George Saunders Papers, 69/64/I, IWM.
13 *I Saw Too Much*.

CHAPTER 11: **Retreat from Jitra**

1 Peter Chamberlain and Chris Ellis, *Tanks of the World 1915–1945*, Cassell, London, 1972; George Forty, *Japanese Army Handbook 1939–1945*, Sutton Publishing, London, 1999; S. L. Mayer (ed.), *The Japanese War Machine*, Bison Books, Greenwich, USA, 1976; David Miller, *Tanks of the World*, MBI, St Paul, Minnesota, 2003.
2 Heath Lecture.
3 Stanley L. Falk, *Seventy Days to Singapore: The Malayan Campaign, 1941–1942*, Robert Hale, London, 1974.
4 *The Japanese Thrust*.
5 ibid.
6 *Seventy Days to Singapore*.
7 K. D. Bhargava and N. V. Sastri, *Campaigns in South-east Asia 1941–42*, Combined Inter-Services Historical Section, 1960.
8 Heath Lecture.
9 *The War Against Japan*.
10 A. M. L. Harrison, *11th Indian Division in Malaya*, unpublished.
11 Prime Minister's Personal Telegram, T.996, 'Lanca', No. 53, 'Personal and Secret', 14 December 1941: Churchill Papers, 20/46.
12 Prime Minister's Personal Telegram, T.996, 'Grey' No. 8, 15 December 1941: Churchill Papers, 20/50.

CHAPTER 12: **Disgrace at Penang**

1 *The Japanese Version.*

2 Brooke-Popham's Dispatch.

3 *Royal Australian Air Force 1939–1942.* Tim Vigors survived the war and became a noted bloodstock breeder. He also founded his own aviation company.

4 E. M. Glover, *In 70 Days: The Story of the Japanese Campaign in Malaya,* Frederick Muller, London, 1949.

5 Sir George Maxwell, *The Civil Defence of Malaya*, Hutchinson, London, 1948.

6 *The Japanese Thrust*; Bryan C. Cooper, *Decade of Change*, Graham Brash, Singapore, 2001.

7 *Shenton of Singapore*; *Decade of Change.* Shenton Thomas's diary entry appears to contradict his instruction to Leslie Forbes that European males should be forced to remain. His role throughout the evacuation crisis was ambivalent. While he preached a paternalistic form of racial equality, his motive appears to have been to keep up a semblance of 'business as usual' in northern Malaya. There were numerous complaints that the Governor had failed to recognise the realities of war and react accordingly. (Author's italics.)

8 *The Civil Defence of Malaya.*

9 *Decade of Change.*

10 Heath Lecture.

11 *Decade of Change.*

12 *The War Against Japan.*

13 *Sinister Twilight.*

14 Tsuji claimed in *The Japanese Version* that Penang had fallen to the Japanese on 15 December and that British troops returning to the island from the Battle of Jitra had been greeted by a Japanese flag flying from the wharf. This is one of Tsuji's more glaring distortions.

15 CO967/77, Duff Cooper to Winston Churchill, 18 December 1941, National Archives.

16 *The Worst Disaster: The Fall of Singapore.*

17 *The Japanese Thrust.*

18 Also rendered as Boyes anti-tank rifle.

19 *Moon over Malaya.*

20 *History of the Argyll and Sutherland Highlanders.*

21 Percival's Dispatch.

22 Alanbrooke's *War Diaries.*

23 *I Saw Too Much.*

24 Author's italics.

25 Author's interview with Kenny McLeod.

26 *Singapore 1941–42.*

27 Cablegram 73 Singapore, V. G. Bowden to H.V. Evatt, 23 December 1941.

28 Harrison, unpublished MS.

CHAPTER 13: **Defeat at Slim River**

1 *Chief of Staff: The Diaries of Lieutenant General Sir Henry Pownall*, Vol. 2.
2 ibid.
3 *Singapore: Too Little, Too Late.*
4 ibid.
5 Percival's biographer Sir John Smyth says Rose Force was named after Angus Rose, the liaison officer from the Argylls. The Australians dispute this. The Rose Force War Diary for Tuesday, 23 December 1941: '...to be known as Rose Force, the name being chosen following the line of the Tulip Force already formed from the AIF and had no connection with Major Rose of Malaya Command' (AWM PR 01013). The coincidence, however, seems too striking, so perhaps both explanations are true.
6 *The Jungle Is Neutral.* The paragraph listing the British Army's impedimenta appeared in the first edition of the book but was cut from later editions. Freddie Spencer Chapman, disguised as a Tamil, later led one operational party behind enemy lines and created mayhem. Over the ensuing months, his team were credited with wrecking seven trains, blowing up 15 bridges, destroying 40 motor vehicles and killing hundreds of Japanese troops. He spent much of the war training Chinese Communist guerrillas at a series of secret jungle bases. For a time he worked with the young Communist leader Chin Peng.
7 Harrison, unpublished MS.
8 *Why Singapore Fell.* As the Battle of Kampar was only just beginning on 31 December, Bennett's prescience would seem astonishing were it not for the fact that many entries in his so-called diary appear to have been written after the event. In fact, both the 6/15th and 28th Brigades withstood frontal attacks with distinction at Kampar.
9 Alanbrooke's *War Diaries.*
10 M. Casey, *Tides and Eddies*, London, 1966.
11 *The Grand Alliance.*
12 Letter from John Curtin in Canberra to his wife Elsie in Perth, 5 January 1941. Quoted in article by Curtin's biographer Lloyd Ross, *Sunday Australian*, 9 January 1972.
13 Quoted in *The Japanese Thrust.*
14 *The War Against Japan.*
15 Cab. 106/156, Stewart, 'Comment'.
16 Author's interview with General Thomson.

CHAPTER 14: **Enter the Chief**

1 *The Japanese Thrust.*
2 *The Grand Alliance.*
3 The triplets remark was made to John Wyett and other officers (see below). The quadruplets reference was made to Sir John Dill (*Wavell: Supreme Commander*).

4 John Connell, *Wavell: Scholar and Soldier,* Collins, London, 1964; letter from Wavell to Liddell Hart, 1935.

5 'Grey' No. 156, 'Winch' No. 13, Prime Minister's Personal Telegram, T.1078, 29 December 1941: Churchill Papers, 20/47.

6 AA:A981, WAR 54, R. G. Casey, Minister to the United States, to Department of External Affairs.

7 Cable, Curtin to Churchill, 1 January 1942, DAFP, Vol. 5, Doc. 247.

8 Cable, Churchill to Curtin, 3 January 1942, DAFP, Vol. 5, Doc. 254.

9 Lord Moran, *Winston Churchill: The Struggle for Survival*, Constable, London, 1966.

10 Robert O'Neill, *Churchill: Japan and British Security in the Pacific*, Oxford University Press, 1993.

11 CO967/78 National Archives.

12 *Old Men Forget.*

13 ibid.

14 John Julius Norwich.

15 *The War in Malaya.*

16 *Shenton of Singapore.*

17 Philip Ziegler, *Diana Cooper*, Collins, London, 1981.

18 *The Chief.*

19 British Minister of State Walter Edward Guinness, 1st Baron Moyne (1880–1944), was murdered by two members of the pro-Israeli Stern Gang on 6 November 1944 in Wavell's former house in Cairo.

20 *The Japanese Thrust.*

21 *The Grand Alliance.*

22 Major General Sir John Kennedy, *The Business of War*, London, 1957.

23 Joan Bright Astley, *The Inner Circle: A View of War at the Top*, Hutchinson, London, 1971.

24 ibid.

25 *Wavell: Soldier and Scholar.*

26 ibid.

27 *Four Corners*, ABC Television.

28 Author's interview with John Wyett.

29 Wavell to Chiefs of Staff, 9 January 1942; *Wavell: Scholar and Soldier.*

30 Cablegram Johcu 16 Canberra, John Curtin to Winston Churchill in the United States, 11 January 1942.

31 *Malayan Postscript.*

32 *Staff Wallah.*

33 *The Fall of General Gordon Bennett.*

34 Cablegram Winch 7 Washington, Winston Churchill in the United States to John Curtin, 12 January 1942.

35 John Wyett says, '[Bennett] always consulted his horoscope before making important decisions.' *Staff Wallah* and interview with author.

Chapter 15: **Battle of Johore**

1 Author's interview with Major Tony Ferrier.
2 Imperial War Museum interview with Major Tony Ferrier.
3 Whitelocke, Cliff, *Gunners in the Jungle*, 2/15th Field Regiment, Royal Australian Artillery, AIF, 1983.
4 A. W. Penfold, W. C. Bayliss and K. E. Crispin, *Galleghan's Greyhounds*, 2/30th Battalion Association, Sydney, 1949.
5 *Gunners in the Jungle.*
6 David Horner, *The Gunners: A History of Australian Artillery*, Allen & Unwin, 1995.
7 Kenneth Harrison, *The Road to Hiroshima*, Rigby, London, 1966.
8 ibid.
9 *Why Singapore Fell.*
10 *Getting On With It*, 2/30th Battalion AIF Association, Sydney, 1996.
11 *Why Singapore Fell.*
12 *The Second World War.*
13 'Grey' No. 341, Prime Minister's Personal Telegram, T.62/2, 14.011942: Churchill Papers, 20/88.
14 Russell Braddon, *The Naked Island*, Werner Laurie, London, 1951.
15 *Why Singapore Fell.*
16 *Percival and the Tragedy of Singapore.*
17 Interview with Ray Broadbent by Lionel Wigmore, AWM 73; interview with Sir Frederick Galleghan by General Kirby and Lionel Wigmore, 22 January 1953, AWM 73.
18 *The Road to Hiroshima.*
19 ibid.
20 Gunner Colin Fikemeyer, *It Happened to Us*, 4th Anti-Tank Regiment AIF, Melbourne, 1994.
21 *The Naked Island.*
22 Forbes Wallace, *Wartime Interlude of a Temporary Soldier*, Thorndike & Dawson Ltd, Norwich, 1980.
23 Other sources put the number of destroyed tanks at nine.
24 *Staff Wallah.*
25 Goodman diary, IWM 86/67/1.
26 *The Naked Island.*
27 Brigadier J. H. Thyer, Foreword to *The Grim Glory.*
28 *The Naked Island.*
29 *The War Against Japan; The Naked Island.*
30 *The Naked Island.*
31 *Royal Australian Air Force 1939–1942.*
32 *The Naked Island.*
33 Percival Papers, IWM, P42, Percival, 30 November 1953.
34 ibid.

35 Prime Minister's Personal Telegram T.82/2, 'Personal and Secret', dispatched 4.30 a.m., 20 December 1942: Churchill Papers 20/68.
36 Cablegram Winch 10 London, Winston Churchill to John Curtin, 4.20 a.m., 19 January 1942.
37 Wavell's source was mistaken. The majority of the guns could also fire landwards.
38 *The Grand Alliance.*
39 Cablegram 69 (extract) Singapore, V. G. Bowden to Department of External Affairs, 23 January 1942.
40 Cablegram Johcu 21 Canberra, 23 January 1942.

CHAPTER 16: Over the Causeway

1 *The War Against Japan; The Japanese Thrust.*
2 Author's interview with Major Harry Schulman.
3 *The Japanese Thrust.*
4 Clive Lyon. Despite their heroism and self-sacrifice, neither Mark, nor Welch, nor Duckworth received any decoration or even a Mention in Dispatches.
5 *Wartime Interlude of a Temporary Soldier.*
6 *Bloody Shambles; The War Against Japan; The Japanese Thrust; Singapore 1941–42*
7 ibid.
8 Author's interview with Bob Goodwin.
9 Bob Goodwin, *Mates and Memories: Reflections on the 2/10th Field Regiment,* Boolarong Press, 1995.
10 *The Pregnable Fortress.*
11 Parliamentary Debates: House of Commons Official Report, Fifth Series, Vol. 377, HMSO, London, 1942.
12 Interview with Lieutenant-Colonel Charles Moses by General Kirby and Lionel Wigmore, 29 January 1953, AWM 73.
13 Interview with Brigadier W. A. Trott by Kirby and Wigmore, 19 January 1953, AWM 73.
14 Interview with General Gordon Bennett by Kirby and Wigmore, 30 January 1953, AWM 73.
15 *Malaya Postscript.*
16 *The Japanese Thrust;* Gordon Bennett interview; Denis Russell-Roberts, *Spotlight on Singapore,* Tandem, London, 1965.
17 *Spotlight on Singapore.*
18 Author's interview with Fred Ryall.
19 Cablegram 98 Singapore, V. G. Bowden to Department of External Affairs, 31 January 1942.

CHAPTER 17: Phoney Fortress

1 *Sinister Twilight.*
2 *Spotlight on Singapore.*

3 Author's interview with Sheridan Stumm.

4 Leslie Froggatt's unpublished memoir, Melbourne, 1945, Froggatt Papers; quoted with kind permission of his son Sir Leslie Froggatt.

5 *Singapore: Too Little, Too Late*. Bisseker was never reimbursed for this expenditure.

6 *The War Against Japan*.

7 Rohan Rivett, *Behind Bamboo*, Angus & Robertson, Sydney, 1946.

8 Churchill reporting on a Boer War battle, February 1900.

9 When the Japanese captured Singapore, Lim Bo Seng escaped to India and joined Force 136. He was captured after infiltrating Japanese-occupied Malaya in 1944, but despite severe torture refused to reveal any information about the resistance movement. Lim died in captivity and became a martyr to the cause of Singapore. A memorial to him stands now beside the Singapore River.

10 Ivan Lyon was awarded the MBE for his rescue work in the Malayan Campaign.

11 *Singapore 1941–42*.

12 *Malayan Postscript*.

13 Gordon Bennett interview.

14 *The Hinge of Fate*.

15 *The War Against Japan*.

16 General A. P. Wavell, Commander-in-Chief, India Command, formerly Supreme Commander South West Pacific, 'Operations in Malaya and Singapore 15.01.1942 to 25.02.1942'; report drawn up by Major H. P. Thomas, 30 May1942; submitted to Combined Chiefs of Staff, 1 June 1942. This report was suppressed until 1992. Percival claimed in his 1948 Dispatch that he had said the Japanese would attack on the north-west coast and he repeated this claim in his book, *The War in Malaya*. However, the Official Historian General S. Woodburn Kirby says in his book, *Singapore: The Chain of Disaster*, which clarified many of the points in his official *War Against Japan*, 'In a letter to the author written after the war, General Percival affirms that the statement in his book, *The War in Malaya*, to the effect that he expected the Japanese attack to be made in the north-west, was incorrect and based on hindsight.' *Singapore: The Chain of Disaster*.

17 *The Hinge of Fate*.

18 Author's interview with Major Tony Ferrier.

19 It seems strange that Percival did not mention this fact to Ivan Simson during their lengthy and heated discussion three days later.

20 *Singapore: Too Little, Too Late*.

21 *Malayan Postscript*.

22 *The Pregnable Fortress*.

23 Heath Lecture.

24 Don Wall, *Singapore and Beyond: The story of the men of the 2/20 Battalion*, W. Mantach, East Hills, NSW, 1985.

25 Author's interview with Russell Savage.

26 *Staff Wallah*.

27 *Daily Mail*, London, 15 November 1957.
28 *The Japanese Thrust.*
29 *Singapore and Beyond.*
30 Much of this wire was later used to fence the men into Changi POW camp, while the rest was loaded into Japanese ships for use elsewhere.
31 Author's interview with Frank Baker.
32 *Why Singapore Fell.*
33 *Malayan Postscript.*

CHAPTER 18: **Death of an Empress**

1 Canadian Pacific Steamships Ltd.
2 Author's interview with Len Butler.
3 Captain A. B. Smith's report on the sinking of the *Empress of Asia*, courtesy of Len Butler.
4 From an account of the sinking of the *Empress of Asia* compiled for the 125th Anti-Tank Regiment Relatives' Association, 1946.
5 ibid.
6 In fact, there was plenty of room for everybody in the club's 47 lush acres and, according to Lieutenant-Colonel Thomas Hamilton, the airmen in residence left for Batavia after two days; *Soldier Surgeon in Malaya.*
7 Interview with Brigadier Harold Taylor by Kirby and Wigmore, AWM 73.
8 *Why Singapore Fell*; *Singapore and Beyond.*
9 *Singapore: The Chain of Disaster*; *The War Against Japan.*
10 *The Japanese Thrust.*
11 *Malayan Postscript.*
12 *The Grim Glory.*
13 ibid.
14 *The War Against Japan.*
15 Henry P. Frei, *The Island Battle: Japanese Soldiers Remember the Conquest of Singapore*, Eastern United Press, 2002; O. Harumi, *Maree senki* (Malaya War Diary), Tokyo, 1973.

CHAPTER 19: **North Shore Nightmare**

1 Author's interviews with Cliff Olsen and John McGrory.
2 Author's interview with Mervyn Blyth.
3 Author's interview with Paul Gemmell.
4 *Singapore and Beyond.*
5 Author's interview with Frank Baker.
6 *The Grim Glory.*
7 *Singapore and Beyond.*
8 *The Grim Glory.*

9   The Official History says that the Japanese attack started about 10.30 p.m. when landing craft were seen approaching the north-west coast (*The War Against Japan*). However, Australian battalion sources place the time of the first wave at 8.45 p.m. or later, depending on location.

10   *Against All Odds.*

11   *Maree senki*, quoted in *Sixty Years On.*

12   *Four Corners*, ABC Television.

13   CDF – Close Defensive Fire.

14   *The Grim Glory.*

15   *The Japanese Thrust.*

16   *Gunners in the Jungle; Against All Odds.*

17   *Why Singapore Fell.*

18   *The Japanese Thrust.*

19   *Singapore and Beyond.*

20   *The War Against Japan.*

21   *Singapore and Beyond.*

22   ibid.

23   Interview with Brigadier Taylor, AWM.

Chapter 20: Battle for Singapore

1   *Malayan Postscript; Behind Bamboo.*

2   *Malayan Postscript.*

3   After the Plymouth Argyle Football Club.

4   *The Japanese Version.*

5   *The War in Malaya.*

6   'Mrs Muriel Reilly's Diary of Her Experiences in Singapore and of Her Escape to Australia, March 1942', British Association of Malaya Papers, Royal Commonwealth Society Records, Cambridge University Library; quoted in Margaret Sheenan's *Out in the Midday Sun.*

7   Author's interview with Alan Lewis.

8   Lieutenant-Colonel Ron Magarry, *The Battalion Story*, 2/26th Infantry Battalion Association, Brisbane, 1994.

9   V. G. Bowden, Singapore, to Department of External Affairs, 9 February 1942.

10   Department of External Affairs, Canberra, to V. G. Bowden, 10 February 1942.

11   Department of External Affairs, Canberra, to V. G. Bowden, 11 February 1942.

12   *The War Against Japan.*

13   *The Japanese Version.*

14   Galleghan interview, AWM 73.

15   Interview with Brigadier Duncan Maxwell by Kirby and Wigmore, 26 January 1953. AWM 73.

16   Interview with Colonel A. M. L. Harrison by Kirby, 19 November 1952.

17   *Staff Wallah.*

18 *The War in Malaya.*
19 *Singapore and Beyond.*
20 *Moon Over Malaya.*
21 Charles Moses diary, AWM 52.
22 Letter from A. P. Derham to Thomas Hamilton; quoted in *Soldier Surgeon in Malaya.*
23 A total of 187 bodies in the morgue were later buried in the hospital's front lawn by Indian soldiers. After the war they were disinterred and given a decent burial at Kranji War Cemetery.
24 As well as at the Anzac Club, three new straggler posts had been set up at Newton Circus, the Orchard Road–Grange Road crossroads and the River Valley Road–Tiong Bharu Road crossroads.
25 *The War Against Japan.*
26 Author's interview with Harry Schulman.

CHAPTER 21: **The Lost Angels**

1 The *Empire Star* was sunk by a German submarine north of the Azores on 23 October 1942. Twenty crew, including Captain Capon, six gunners and six passengers were lost.
2 *Singapore: Too Little, Too Late.*
3 Department of External Affairs, Canberra, to V. G. Bowden, 15 January 1942; Sir Shenton Thomas, Singapore, to Commonwealth Government, 23 January 1942.
4 *Singapore: Too Little, Too Late.*
5 V. G. Bowden, Singapore, to Department of External Affairs, 12 February 1942.
6 ADM 267/138, Mr J. L. Dawson, chief officer, MV *Empire Star.*
7 For their bravery, Margaret Anderson was awarded the George Medal and Veronica Torney received the MBE.
8 HMS *Durban* Secret Report No. 0180/615, paragraphs 39 and 40, 21 February 1942, to the Commodore Commanding China Force.
9 Lieutenant-Colonel Thomas Hamilton, *Surgeon Soldier in Malaya*, Angus & Robertson, Sydney, 1957.
10 Vivian Bullwinkel's 1942 diary, AWM.
11 Hank Nelson, *Prisoners of War: Australians Under Nippon*, ABC Books, Sydney, 1985.
12 *Prisoners of War: Australians Under Nippon.*
13 *The Japanese Thrust.*
14 Betty Jeffrey, *White Coolies*, Angus & Robertson, Sydney, 1954.
15 Vivian Bullwinkel spent three and half years in captivity and was one of just 24 of the 65 nurses who had been in the *Vyner Brooke* to survive the war. She gave evidence to the Tokyo Tribunal of the deaths of prisoners in Japanese hands. Vivian married in 1977 and returned to Banka Island in 1993 to unveil a shrine to the nurses. The Japanese officer who had ordered the massacre committed suicide

and a camp commandant was sentenced to 15 years' imprisonment. Vivian Bullwinkel died in July 2000.

16 *The Japanese Thrust.*

CHAPTER 22: **Black Friday**

1 Author's interview with Terpie Pattara.
2 D. H. James, *The Rise and Fall of the Japanese Empire*, 1951.
3 *The War in Malaya.*
4 *Why Singapore Fell.*
5 Author's interview with Alan Ryall.
6 Author's interview with Harry Hesp.
7 Commander R. A. W. Pool, one of 12 survivors on the island, reported Spooner and Pulford's conversations in letters to author Arthur Marder in 1976 and 1978.
8 V. G. Bowden, Singapore, to Department of External Affairs, 14 February 1942.
9 *The Japanese Thrust.* Wootton and Quinn were interned in Sumatra for the duration of the war and reported on V. G. Bowden's fate on their release.

CHAPTER 23: **Surrender**

1 Wigmore says the Japanese troops were advancing along Ayer Rajah Road 'in pursuit of some detached Indian troops who fell back into the hospital still firing' (*The Japanese Thrust*). Kirby says the Japanese entered the hospital 'on the excuse that the hospital had been used as an artillery position' (*The War Against Japan*). Neither version has been substantiated.
2 *Total War*; *Kempeitai.*
3 Major Cyril Wild, 'Note on the Capitulation of Singapore', New Delhi, 30 November 1945. Heath Papers, IWM.

CHAPTER 24: **Bennett's Breakout**

1 Author's interview with Dr Rowley Richards.
2 Author's interview with Russell Savage.
3 H. R. Oppenheim, *Diary of an Escape from Singapore*, British Association of Malaya Papers, Royal Commonwealth Records, Cambridge University Library.
4 Parliamentary Debates: House of Commons Official Report, Fifth Series, Vol. 377, HMSO, London, 1942, p. 1,674.
5 *The Second World War*, p. 520. Note: Churchill wrote these words in 1948.
6 *Singapore: The Chain of Disaster.*
7 Mr Justice Ligertwood, who held a Royal Commission into Bennett's escape in 1945, found that 'In relinquishing his command and leaving Singapore General Bennett did not have the permission of any competent authority. There was, in

fact, no competent authority who could give him such permission. General Percival could not do so because he had signed the capitulation under which he had agreed that General Bennett as one of the troops under his command would be surrendered. Even the Australian Government could not have given him such permission because it was within the competence of General Percival to agree that General Bennett as one of such troops would be surrendered, and the capitulation bound the Australian Government as much as it did General Percival. At the time General Bennett left Singapore he was not a prisoner of war in the sense of being a soldier who was under a duty to escape. He was in the position of a soldier whose commanding officer had agreed to surrender him and to submit him to directions which would make him a prisoner of war. Having regard to the terms of the capitulation I think that it was General Bennett's duty to have remained in command of the AIF until the surrender was complete. Having regard to the terms of the capitulation I find that General Bennett was not justified in relinquishing his command and leaving Singapore. (*The Japanese Thrust.*)

8 PREM 3/168/3 PRO. General A. P. Wavell, Commander-in-Chief, India Command, formerly Supreme Commander South West Pacific, 'Operations in Malaya and Singapore 15.01.1942 to 25.02.1942'; report drawn up by Major H. P. Thomas, 30 May1942; submitted to Combined Chiefs of Staff, 1 June 1942.
9 *Against All Odds.*
10 Joan Bright Astley correspondence, Imperial War Museum.
11 Interview with Brigadier Sir Frederick 'Black Jack' Galleghan by General Kirby and Lionel Wigmore, 22 January 1953.
12 Churchill Papers, Churchill College, Cambridge.
13 *Chief of Staff: The Diaries of Lieutenant General Sir Henry Pownall,* Vol. 2, p. 92.

CHAPTER 25: Road to Perdition

1 *Shenton of Singapore.*
2 ibid.
3 James MacIntosh, *Life Is Eternal,* New Horizon, Bognor Regis, 1983.
4 J. A. Richardson diary, Imperial War Museum 87/58/1.
5 John Coast, *Railway of Death,* Commodore Press, London, 1946.
6 Interview with Brother Vincent, 24 August 1984, Oral History Centre, National Archives of Singapore, A468/30.
7 'The PoW Diary of Gunner Vince Broe, 2/10th Field Regiment 8th Division AIF'; unpublished; quoted with kind permission of his son John Broe.
8 Imperial War Museum.
9 Captain Frank Robinson's diary, Imperial War Museum.
10 Author's interview with John Wyett; *Staff Wallah.*
11 Author's interview with Dr Rowley Richards.
12 Author's interview with Beryl Stevenson Daley.

Chapter 26: *Sook Ching*

1 Vince Broe's unpublished diary; interview with Reg Mahoney on Australians at War website.
2 Ian Ward, *The Killer They Called a God*, Media Masters, Singapore, 1992.
3 Mamoru Shinozaki, *Syonan – My Story*, Times Books International, Singapore, 1982.
4 *The Killer They Called a God*.
5 Elizabeth Choy interview, Oral History Centre A000597/05
6 *Syonan – My Story*
7 Author's interview with Francis Chan. Mr Chan later studied law at Cambridge and became a superintendent in Singapore Special Branch.
8 Low Ngiong Ing, *When Singapore Was Syonan-to*, Times Editions, Singapore, 1973.
9 Chan Cheng Yean interview, Oral History Centre A000248/10.
10 *The Killer They Called a God*.
11 ibid.
12 Domei News Agency report, 3 March 1942, in Office of Strategic Services (OSS), State Department, USA, 'Programs of Japan in Malaya (Intercepts of shortwave broadcasts from Radio Tokyo and affiliated stations from February 1942 to June 1945)'; quoted in Cheah Boon Kheng, *Red Star Over Malaya*, Singapore University Press, Singapore, 1983.

Chapter 27: Life under Dai Nippon

1 Maisie Duncan in conversation with the author: 'Syonan and Shonan are interchangeable as Japanese names for Singapore. The Hepburn system of Romanisation (Shonan) is the most frequently used nowadays. The other form in Romaji spelling (Syonan) was used during the Japanese occupation and is seen in documents of that era. Syonan-to was the Japanese name for Singapore Island.' The *Straits Times* became the *Shonan Times,* and there was another broadsheet newspaper named the *Syonan Sinbun*, often rendered as *Syonan Simbun*.
2 Mary Turnbull, *Dateline Singapore*, Singapore Press Holdings, Singapore, 1995.
3 Author's interview with Bernard Clifton.
4 Kenneth Attiwill, *The Singapore Story*, Frederick Muller, London, 1959.
5 *When Singapore Was Syonan-to*.
6 ibid.
7 Kee Onn Chin, *Malaya Upside Down*, Jitts & Co., Singapore, 1946.

Chapter 28: Changi's Secrets

1 *Staff Wallah*.
2 R. P. W. Havers, *Reassessing the Prisoner of War Experience*, RoutledgeCurzon, London, 2003; Lieutenant C. Baume diary entry for 15 March 1942, IWM.
3 *Staff Wallah*.

4 *Mates and Memories.*
5 Author's interview with Ray Rossiter.
6 *Scapegoat*; *Singapore: Too Little, Too Late.*
7 Author's interview with John Wyett.
8 *Hindsight*, ABC Radio, Australia 2001.
9 General Slim avenged the men's murder three years later in 1945 by ordering the Japanese commander to be executed on the same spot.
10 Author's interview with John Wyett.
11 ibid.
12 *Staff Wallah.*
13 Author's interview with John Wyett.
14 *I Saw Too Much.*

CHAPTER 29: **Children in Captivity**

1 Author's interview with Mel Bruce.
2 Author's interview with Terpie Pattara.
3 Author's interview with Bernie Clifton.
4 Author's interview with Len Butler.
5 Author's interview with Barbara Glanville.
6 Author's interview with Jennifer Martin.
7 Author's interview with Genevieve Evans.

CHAPTER 30: **An Up-Country Retreat**

1 *Mates and Memories.*
2 Author's interview with Russell Savage.
3 Author's interview with Bill Drower.
4 Author's interview with Dr Rowley Richards.
5 Author's interview with Bill Drower.
6 Author's interview with Harry Schulman.

CHAPTER 31: **The Double Tenth**

1 *Life Is Eternal.*
2 *Kill the Tiger.*
3 *Life Is Eternal.*
4 Elizabeth Choy Interview, Oral History Centre A000597/05.
5 John Hayter, *Priest in Prison: Four Years of Life in Japanese-occupied Singapore*, Graham Brash, Singapore, 1989, p. 160.
6 *Sinister Twilight.* Reprinted by permission of HarperCollins Publishers Ltd © Noel Barber 1968.
7 *Sinister Twilight.*
8 *Life Is Eternal.*
9 Author's interview with Len Butler.

Chapter 32: Liberation

1 Author's interview with Len Butler.
2 Author's interview with Maureen Gower.
3 *Kill the Tiger.*
4 The original of this order is in the United States National Archives, Washington DC.
5 Author's interview with Dr Bill Horsfall.
6 Author's interview with Jennifer Martin.
7 Author's interview with Terpie Pattara.
8 Author's interview with Maisie Duncan (née Prout).
9 *The Killer They Called a God.*

Afterword

1 Author's interview with Dr Rowley Richards.
2 Heath Papers, IWM.
3 *The War in Malaya.*

Select Bibliography

Alanbrooke, Field Marshal Viscount, *War Diaries 1939–1945*, edited by Alex Danchev and Daniel Todman, Weidenfeld & Nicolson, London, 2001.

Allen, Louis, *Singapore 1941–1942*, Davis-Poynter, London, 1977.

Astley, Joan Bright, *The Inner Circle: A View of War at the Top*, Hutchinson, London, 1971.

Attiwill, Kenneth, *The Singapore Story*, Frederick Muller, London, 1959.

Barber, Noel, *Sinister Twilight: The Fall and Rise Again of Singapore*, Collins, London, 1968.

Bayly, Christopher, and Tim Harper, *Forgotten Armies*, Allen Lane, London, 2004.

Bennett, Lieutenant-General H. Gordon, *Why Singapore Fell*, Angus & Robertson, Sydney, 1944.

Bhargava, K. D., and N. V. Sastri, *Campaigns in South-east Asia, 1941–42*, Calcutta: Combined Inter-Services Historical Section, India & Pakistan, 1960 (part of the series entitled 'Official History of the Indian Armed Forces in the Second World War, 1939–45').

Bishop, Patrick, *Fighter Boys,* HarperCollins, London, 2003.

Bix, Herbert, *Hirohito and the Making of Modern Japan*, HarperCollins, New York, 2000.

Bond, Brian (ed.), *Chief of Staff: The Diaries of Lieutenant General Sir Henry Pownall*, Volume 2, Leo Cooper, London, 1973–74.

Braddon, Russell, *The Naked Island*, Werner Laurie, London, 1951.

Burfitt, James, *Against All Odds: The History of the 2/18th Battalion 8th Division AIF*, 2/18th Battalion, French's Forest, NSW, 1991.

Callahan, Raymond, *The Worst Disaster: The Fall of Singapore*, University of Delaware Press, Newark, 1980.

Calvocoressi, Peter, Guy Wint and John Pritchard, *Total War: The Causes and Courses of the Second World War*, Penguin, London, 1972.

Chamberlain, Peter, and Chris Ellis, *Tanks of the World 1915–1945*, Cassell, London, 1972.

Chapman, Lieutenant-Colonel F. Spencer, *The Jungle Is Neutral*, Chatto & Windus, London, 1949.

Charmley, John, *Duff Cooper: The Authorised Biography*, Weidenfeld & Nicolson, London, 1986.

Cheah Boon Kheng, *Red Star Over Malaya*, Singapore University Press, Singapore, 1983.

Chin, Kee Onn, *Malaya Upside Down*, Jitts & Co., Singapore, 1946.

Chin Peng, as told to Ian Ward and Norma Miraflor, *Chin Peng: My Side of History*, Media Masters, Singapore, 2003.

Churchill, Winston S., *The Second World War* (abridged edition), Penguin, London, 1959; *Volume III: The Grand Alliance*, Cassell, London, 1949; *Volume IV: The Hinge of Fate*, Cassell, London, 1951.

Conrad, Joseph, *Youth: A Narrative*, William Blackwood, London, 1902.

Coogan, Tim Pat, *Michael Collins: A Biography*, Hutchinson, London, 1990.

Cooper Sir Alfred, Duff, *Old Men Forget*, Rupert Hart Davis, London, 1954.

Cooper, Bryan C., *Decade of Change*, Graham Brash, Singapore, 2001.

Cruickshank, Charles, *SOE in the Far East*, Oxford University Press, 1983.

Davies, David Twiston, *The Daily Telegraph Book of Military Obituaries*, Grub Street, London, 2003.

Day, David, *The Politics of War*, HarperCollins, Sydney, 2003.

Elphick, Peter, *The Pregnable Fortress*, Hodder & Stoughton, London, 1995.

Elphick, Peter, *Far Eastern File*, Hodder & Stoughton, London, 1997.

Falk, Stanley L., *Seventy Days to Singapore: The Malayan Campaign, 1941–1942*, Robert Hale, London, 1974.

Farrell, Brian, and Sandy Hunter (eds), *Sixty Years On: The Fall of Singapore Revisited*, Eastern Universities Press, Singapore, 2002.

Farrell, Brian P., *The Defence and Fall of Singapore 1940–1942*, Tempus, Stroud, Gloucestershire, 2005.

Farrell, J. G., *The Singapore Grip*, Weidenfeld & Nicolson, London, 1978.

Flower, Jane, 'Captors and Captives on the Burma–Thailand Railway', in *Prisoners of War and Their Captors on the Burma–Thailand Railway*, B. Moore and K. Federowich (eds), Berg, Oxford, 1996.

Forty, George, *Japanese Army Handbook 1939–1945*, Sutton Publishing, London, 1999.

French, David, and Brian Holden Reid (eds), *The British General Staff 1890–1939*, Frank Cass, London, 2002.

Gill, G. Herman, *Royal Australian Navy 1939–1942*, Australian War Memorial, Canberra, 1957.

Gillison, Douglas, *Royal Australian Air Force 1939–1942*, Australian War Memorial, Canberra, 1957.

Glover, E. M., *In Seventy Days: The Story of the Japanese Campaign in British Malaya*, Frederick Muller, London, 1949.

Goodwin, Bob, *Mates and Memories: Reflections on the 2/10th Field Regiment*, Boolarong Press, Brisbane, 1995.

Gough, Richard, *SOE Singapore, 1941–42*, W. Kimber, London, 1985.

Grey, Jeffrey, *A Military History of Australia*, Cambridge University Press, 1995.

Hall, Timothy, *The Fall of Singapore*, Methuen Australia, Sydney, 1983.

Hamilton, Lieutenant-Colonel Thomas, *Soldier Surgeon in Malaya*, Angus & Robertson, Sydney, 1967.

Harrison, Kenneth, *The Road to Hiroshima*, Rigby, London, 1966 (originally published as *The Brave Japanese*).

Havers, R. P. W., *Reassessing the Japanese Prisoner of War Experience*, RoutledgeCurzon, London, 2003.

Hayter, John, *Priest in Prison: Four Years of Life in Japanese-occupied Singapore*, Graham Brash, Singapore, 1989.

Hogg, Ian V., *British and American Artillery of World War II*, Arms and Armour Press, London.

Horner, David, *The Gunners: A History of Australian Artillery*, Allen & Unwin, Sydney, 1995.

House of Commons, *Hansard: The Parliamentary Debates*, HMSO, London.

Howarth, Patrick, *Undercover: The Men and Women of the SOE*, Phoenix Press, London, 1980.

Hull, Cordell, and Andrew Henry Thomas Berding, *The Memoirs of Cordell Hull*, Macmillan, New York, 1948.

Jeffrey, Barbara, *White Coolies*, Angus & Robertson, Sydney, 1953.

Kirby, Major-General S. Woodburn, et al., *The War Against Japan, Volume 1: The Loss of Singapore*, HMSO, London, 1957.

Kirby, Major-General S. Woodburn, *Singapore: The Chain of Disaster*, Cassell, London, 1971.

Kinvig, Clifford, *Scapegoat: General Percival and the Fall of Singapore*, Brassey's, London, 1996.

Kratoska, Paul H., *The Japanese Occupation of Malaya*, Allen & Unwin, Sydney, 1998.

Lamb, Margaret, and Nicholas Tarling, *From Versailles to Pearl Harbor: The Origins of the Second World War in Europe and Asia*, Palgrave, New York, 2001.

Lamont-Brown, Raymond, *Kempeitai: Japan's Dreaded Military Police*, Sutton, Stroud, 1998.

Lambert, Angela, *Unquiet Souls*, Harper & Row, New York, 1984.

Lee, Kuan Yew, *The Singapore Story*, Times Books International, Singapore, 1998.

Leasor, James, *Singapore: The Battle That Changed the World*, Hodder & Stoughton, London, 1968.

Lewin, Ronald, *The Chief: Field Marshal Lord Wavell*, Hutchinson, London, 1980.

Lodge, A. B., *The Fall of General Gordon Bennett*, Allen & Unwin, Sydney, 1986.

Long, Gavin, *The Six Years* War, Australian War Memorial, Canberra, 1973.

Low Ngiong Ing, *When Singapore Was Syonan-to*, Times Editions, Singapore, 1973.

Lowe, Peter, *Great Britain and the Origins of the Pacific War*, Clarendon Press, Oxford, 1977.

McElwee, William, and Michael Roffe, *The Argyll and Sutherland Highlanders*, Osprey, Oxford, 1972.

MacIntosh, James, *Life Is Eternal*, New Horizon, Bognor Regis, 1983.

Magarry, Lieutenant-Colonel Ron, *The Battalion Story*, 2/26th Infantry Battalion Association, Brisbane, 1994.

Manning, Paul, *Hirohito: The War Years*, Bantam, New York, 1989.

Marder, Arthur J., *Old Friends, New Enemies*, Clarendon Press, Oxford, 1981.

Maxwell, Sir George, *The Civil Defence of Malaya*, Hutchinson, London, 1948.

Mayer, S.L. (ed.), *The Japanese War Machine*, Bison Books, Greenwich, USA, 1976.

Meacham, Jon, *Franklin and Winston*, Random House, New York, 2003.

Members of the 2/30th Battalion AIF, *Getting On With It*, 2/30th Battalion AIF Association Research Project, Sydney, 1991.

Members of the Unit Association, *The Grim Glory of the 2/19th Battalion AIF*, Australian War Memorial, Canberra, 1975.

Miller, David, *Tanks of the World*, MBI, St Paul, Minnesota, 2003.

Moffat, Jonathan, and Audrey Holmes McCormick, *Moon over Malaya*, Tempus, Stroud, Gloucestershire, 2002.

Montgomery, Brian, *Shenton of Singapore: Governor and Prisoner of War*, Times Books International, Singapore, 1984.

Moore, Michael, *Battalion at War: Singapore 1942*, Gliddon Books, Norwich, 1988.

Moorhead, Caroline, *Martha Gellhorn: A Life*, Chatto & Windus, London, 2003.

Morgan, Ted, *FDR: A Biography*, Grafton Books, London, 1986.

Morrison, Ian, *Malayan Postscript*, Faber & Faber, London, 1942.

Neidpath, James, *The Singapore Naval Base and the Defence of Britain's Eastern Empire 1919–1941*, Clarendon Press, Oxford, 1981.

Nelson, David, *The Story of Changi Singapore*, Changi Publication Co., 1974.

Nelson, Hank, *Prisoners of War: Australians Under Nippon*, ABC Books, Sydney, 1985.

Newton, Helmut, *Autobiography*, Duckworth, London 2003.

Overy, Richard, with Andrew Wheatcroft, *The Road to War*, Penguin, London, 1999.

Owen, Frank, *The Fall of Singapore*, Michael Joseph, London, 1960.

Penfold, A. W., W. C. Bayliss and K. E. Crispin, *Galleghan's Greyhounds*, 2/30th Battalion Association, Sydney, 1949.

Percival, Arthur, *The War in Malaya*, Eyre & Spottiswoode, London, 1949.

Poole, Philippa, *Of Love and War: The letters and diaries of Captain Adrian Curlewis and his family 1939–1945*, Lansdowne Press, Sydney, 1982,

Rees, Laurence, *Horror in the East*, BBC, London, 2000.

Rivett, Rohan, *Behind Bamboo*, Angus & Robertson, Sydney, 1946.

Ritchie, John (gen. ed.), *Australian Dictionary of Biography, Volume 13: 1940–1980*, Melbourne University Press.

Robertson, John, and John McCarthy, *Australian War Strategy 1939–1945*, University of Queensland Press, Brisbane, 1985.

Russell of Liverpool, Lord, *The Knights of Bushido*, Cassell, London, 1958.

Russell-Roberts, Denis, *Spotlight on Singapore*, Tandem, London, 1965.

Savage, Russell, *A Guest of the Emperor*, Boolarong Press, Brisbane, 1995.

Schom, Alan, *The Eagle and the Rising Sun*, W. W. Norton, New York, 2004.

Sheenan, Margaret, *Out in the Midday Sun: The British in Malaya 1880–1960*, John Murray, London, 2003.

Shores, Christopher, and Brian Cull with Yasuho Izawa, *Bloody Shambles, Volume 2: The Complete Account of the Air War in the Far East, from the Defence of Sumatra to the fall of Burma*, Grub Street, London, 1993.

Simson, Ivan, *Singapore: Too Little, Too Late*, Leo Cooper, London, 1970.

Smith, Michael, *The Emperor's Codes*, Bantam, London 2000.

Smyth, Sir John, VC, *Percival and the Tragedy of Singapore*, Macdonald, London, 1971.

Starns, Penny, *Nurses At War: Women on the Frontline*, Sutton Publishing, Gloucestershire, 2000.

Stumm, Lorraine, *I Saw Too Much: A woman correspondent at war*, The Write-on Group, New South Wales, 2000.

Swain, Bruce T., *Australian Armed Forces at War 1939–45*, Allen & Unwin, 2001.

Thompson, Peter, and Robert Macklin, *The Battle of Brisbane*, ABC Books, Sydney, 2000.

Thompson, Peter, and Robert Macklin, *Kill the Tiger*, Hodder Australia, Sydney, 2002.

Thompson, Peter, and Robert Macklin, *The Man Who Died Twice*, Allen & Unwin, Sydney, 2004.

Thorne, Christopher, *The Issue of War*, Hamish Hamilton, London, 1985.

Tomlinson, H. M., *Malay Waters*, Hodder & Stoughton, London, 1950.

Tsuji, Colonel Masanobu, *The Japanese Version*, published in the UK as *Japan's Greatest Victory, Britain's Worst Defeat*, Spellmount, Staplehurst, Kent, 1997.

Turnbull, Mary, *Dateline Singapore: 150 Years of the Straits Times*, Times Editions, Singapore, 1995.

Wall, Don, *Singapore and Beyond: The story of the men of the 2/20 Battalion*, W. Mantach, East Hills, NSW, 1985.

Ward, Ian, *The Killer They Called a God*, Media Masters, Singapore, 1992.

Ward, Ian, *Snaring the Other Tiger*, Media Masters, Singapore, 1996.

Warren, Alan, *Singapore 1942: Britain's Greatest Defeat*, Hambledon and London, London 2002.

Wheal, Elizabeth-Anne, and Stephen Pope, *The Macmillan Dictionary of the Second World War*, Macmillan, London, 1989.

Whitelocke, Cliff, *Gunners in the Jungle*, 2/15th Field Regiment, Royal Australian Artillery, AIF, Sydney, 1983.

Wigmore, Lionel: *The Japanese Thrust: Official Australian War History*, Australian War Memorial, Canberra, 1957.

Wilson, Brigadier David, *The Sum of Things*, Spellmount, Staplehurst, Kent, 2001.

Wyett, John, *Staff Wallah: At the Fall of Singapore*, Allen & Unwin, Sydney, 1996.

Yoshida, Shigeru, *Japan's Decisive Century 1867–1967*, Frederick A. Praeger, London, 1967.

Zhou Mei, *Elizabeth Choy: More than a War Heroine*, Landmark Books, Singapore, 1995.

Other published sources

Air Chief Marshal Sir Robert Brooke-Popham, Commander-in-Chief Far East, *Operations in the Far East from 01.10.1940 to 27.12.1941*, published in the *London Gazette*, 22.01.1948.

Vice-Admiral Sir Geoffrey Layton, Commander-in-Chief Eastern Fleet, *Loss of HM Ships Prince of Wales and Repulse*, 17.12.1941, published in the *London Gazette*, 26.02.1948.

Air Vice-Marshal Sir Paul Maltby, Assistant Air Officer Commanding Far East Command, Royal Air Force, *Report on the Air Operations During the Campaigns in Malaya and Netherlands East Indies* from 08.12.1941 to 12.04.1942.

Lieutenant-General A. E. Percival, General Officer Commanding Malaya, *Operations of Malaya Command from 08.12.1941 to 15.02.1942*, published in the *London Gazette*, 26.02.1948.

Military Intelligence Service, *Order of Battle of the Japanese Army*, Washington, December 1942.

General A. P. Wavell, Commander-in-Chief, India Command, formerly Supreme Commander South West Pacific, *Operations in Malaya and Singapore* 15.01.1942 to 25.02.1942; report drawn up by Major H. P. Thomas 30.05.1942; submitted to Combined Chiefs of Staff 01.06.1942; released 1992.

Unpublished sources

Broe, Vince, 'The PoW Diary of Gunner Vince Broe, 2/10th Field Regiment 8th Division AIF'; quoted with kind permission of his son John Broe.

Galleghan, Lieutenant-Colonel (Sir) Frederick 'Black Jack', 'Address to Australian troops, Selarang Barracks, 04.09.1942', AWM.

Page, Olga, 'Magic Memories – Life under the Japanese Occupation of Malaya'.

Index